Seven Decades of
DEEP PURPLE

DEEP

Seven Decades of DEEP PURPLE

AN UNOFFICIAL HISTORY

MARTIN POPOFF

SCHIFFER PUBLISHING

4880 Lower Valley Road • Atglen, PA 19310

Other Schiffer books by Martin Popoff

The Art of Metal: Five Decades of Heavy Metal Album Covers, Posters, T-shirts, and More
978-0-7643-6597-3

Dio: The Unholy Scriptures; The Complete Unofficial Chronicle of Ronnie James Dio's Solo Canon
978-0-7643-6940-7

Hallowed by Their Name: The Unofficial Iron Maiden Bible
978-0-7643-6816-5

Library of Congress Control Number: 2025930115

Designed by Zach Kline
Cover design by Danielle Farmer
Type set in Contempora Sans heading font/text font Adobe Caslon Pro

ISBN: 978-0-7643-6991-9
Ebook: 978-1-5073-0600-0
Printed in China
10 9 8 7 6 5 4 3 2 1

Published by Schiffer Publishing, Ltd.
4880 Lower Valley Road
Atglen, PA 19310
Phone: (610) 593-1777; Fax: (610) 593-2002
Email: Info@schifferbooks.com
Web: www.schifferbooks.com

CONTENTS

Introduction

It's an innocuous enough question: Who's your favorite band?

I get asked it all the time; I've done podcasts about it and myriad various YouTube shows about it. Even if the answer varies from year to year, it's always a boring answer. I won't go through the spin cycle of the five bands I'm inclined to name-check on any given day or year, but I'll give the yappy part of the answer, the justification for the boring answer, and it's this. Given how there's actually lots of bands ever, it had better be one that's been with me since at least my midteens, which begins about 1977 for me. It also better be a band that has given me happy pills, time to time or regularly, across many decades of their output.

But Deep Purple chucks in a bonus that most of those five choices don't have, and that's the fact that the 1990s and 2000s of this band are stronger than the 1990s and 2000s of all my other picks, with ZZ Top being a close second. My favorite part of this book explains how the band managed that. It's the walk that Ian and Roger did in Portugal. It's such a key concept contributing to the majesty of Purple that I kinda covered it twice in the book, both in the *Purpendicular* and *Abandon* chapters.

Essentially, Ian explains that he decided he was going to write like a grown-up, that his lyrics were going to reflect what he was pondering right there at that age he was dealing with on any given record cycle. Now, if it wasn't for Steve Morse essentially doing the same thing on the guitar, it might not have been enough. But it most definitely was, to the point where, pound for pound, a pile of the records beginning with *Purpendicular* right up to the first Simon McBride album, *=1*, any one of those could serve plausibly as my favorite Deep Purple album of all time.

Because of that, because of getting to grow as old as dirt with these guys (from a distance, but close enough—I've sure gotten enough interviews with them), this book, the longest I've ever done, was an absolute soul-replenishing joy to write.

Let me give you a little glimpse into the methodology of this monster tome. Thankfully, I had a core book to work from, or two, actually, because Deep Purple was about the sixth band I ever did a one-band book on. An early-days book called *Gettin' Tighter* was done in 2008, with a *Perfect Strangers*–onward book called *A Castle Full of Rascals* done the following year. Both were trade paperbacks though, and man, I was not happy with the writing now, looking back. There was a whole lot of "What the hell is he talking about?" going on, as over and over again I went for these long, complicated sentences that went over the edge of sensemaking regularly and embarrassingly.

The happy results of a meeting backstage at Massey Hall, Toronto, Ontario. *Martin Popoff archive*

But the bones were there, notably all the interview footage I had going back to my first chats with Roger Glover and Ian Gillan, which were in the region of my first 25 interviews ever, from the 2,000 to 2,200 I've logged as of today. But the end of the second book tapped out with *Rapture of the Deep*, allowing for a really satisfying last portion of writing here; namely, bringing the story up to date, culminating in seeing Simon McBride with the band just a few weeks ago as I tap out this introduction. That constituted the second-to-last big job, with the last being the curating and placing of all the photography amassed to support the story, which represents a fine bonus to this gargantuan project as far as I'm concerned.

A point of process I'd like to make. I'm aware that we have some early chapters on live albums, but then later ones don't get the same attention. This reflects what has happened with Deep Purple and most heritage acts and indeed the music business in general, where live albums have just become more plentiful and therefore less significant as time goes on, not to mention the blurring of the lines between live albums on CD and their DVD counterparts.

Before we get on to the book proper, please allow me to indulge myself in my favorite Deep Purple memory. It goes back to elementary school. This would have had to have been either grade 6 or 7. We had to break into groups and come up with a musical number for assembly. A few of us took it as an opportunity to walk girls home just as it was getting dark after postclass practice on this thing we had to do, so like 4:00, 4:30. So what we did is this sort of courtly European renaissance dance thing to a song in French I can still hear in my head. The ploy worked a charm in the romance department, making those connections walking home in the fall with one or another of my dance partners.

Come time to do the assembly in the Glenmerry School gym, and we do our little geometric, bowing square dance thing, shuffling off to sit down in the perimeter to polite applause.

But then next up, my cool friends, led by my partner in crime in terms of being an insane hard rock music freak like me, Forrest Toop, leap to center court, dressed as bandits, and start running around with toy machine guns, shooting at all the kids sitting cross-legged around the rim of the gym. Playing not full blast (I know, that's the cliché, isn't it?—no one *ever* plays music full blast) is Deep Purple's "Burn." The effect was electrifying. Everybody's whooping and yelping and clapping. To hear that riff in the gym, those drums, that crazy classical-music/heavy metal solo, David and Glenn singing, that was pure heavy metal magic. What I learned that day is that is there's more to life than girls. There's Deep Purple.

MARTIN POPOFF

martinp@inforamp.net | martinpopoff.com

Chapter 1

Early Years

"Screaming Lord introduced me to showmanship."

Makes for an untidy history, but life's messy, isn't it?

Yes indeed, Deep Purple have this dodgy psychedelic past that few talk about, and in which even fewer see merit. Messiness stalks Deep Purple throughout their, ahem, organic career, the most demoralizing bit being the eight-year layover from 1976 to 1984, as well as the multitude of lineup changes over nearly six decades. But even the first days of the mess are messed up even further by a weird classical album just before a bomb goes off called *In Rock*.

So, let's look at these murky beginnings, shall we? Except as a qualifier, I'd like to dive right in and skip the majority of the childhood stuff, because we have a lot of ground to cover, and you might have noticed already that this is a hefty book.

The germ of the band begins with a couple of chaps by the names of Tony Edwards (heir to a textiles business, but more interested in pop music) and Searchers drummer Chris Curtis, the latter hatching this psychedelic scheme to create Roundabout, a musical roundabout, whatever that was. A natural to join the project was twenty-seven-year-old Jonathan Douglas Lord, whom Curtis was then sharing a flat with along with a number of other rockers. Lord was formerly of the Art Woods (a.k.a. the Artwoods, named for Art Wood, Ron's bother!), as well as a session man, one who had cut his teeth playing all manner of jazz, blues, and R&B during his seven-year tenure in London, after moving to the big city to seek his fortune, first in acting, from his hometown of Leicester.

Given his age, Lord was starting to feel like he was spinning his wheels, although offers both from the Animals and Them were proffered to the obviously talented keyboardist. With Art wanting to hang up the Art Woods anyway, Jon figured this was the time for him to get excited about music again, having, he admits, stagnated or at least stalled. By this point he was demoralizingly part of the Garden, backing band to the Flower Pot Men, more of a psych cash-in ruse than an actual band.

“Jerry Lee Lewis” is Jon’s quick answer, when asked by Sam Dunn what first got him interested in rock ’n’ roll. “Elvis too, maybe, but to me Elvis wasn’t rock ’n’ roll. Elvis was this kind of deep, dark, strange voice that I wasn’t quite sure whether I liked or not. But then I heard Jerry Lee do ‘Whole Lotta Shakin’,’ and my world flipped. That was an absolutely seminal day when I first heard that. He was raw and it was untrained. I could tell—because by this time I was a reasonably well-trained pianist—that what he was doing on the piano was nothing to do with what I had been taught to do, and by God I wanted to sound like that. But I couldn’t make the piano in the front room sound like Jerry Lee’s piano in the recording, because I didn’t know at the time [about] echo chambers and all that kind of thing. But there was a kind of animal edge to it that I found tremendously exciting.”

Singles by the Art Woods, a pre–Deep Purple band for Jon Lord

“And then, also, Little Richard for the same reasons,” continues Lord. “On the one hand, it took the simplest of forms and this astounding voice, this raw emotion in the voice. And the feeling, even before I knew he was talking about something a bit rude. I’m sure ‘Tutti Frutti’ means something else, but I’m not sure. And ‘Long Tall Sally,’ I pictured this woman . . . remember, I was a teenager, and I had dreams. I think there was a raw, animal, untrammeled, untextured, untutored feel to me, and that to me, as a very textured, tutored young man who’d been poring over Beethoven and Bach and the like for years, this was massively exciting. But what happened to me—and I have to say this, which is why God granted me great luck here—is that when I heard that and it spun my head around, I didn’t lose the love of the stuff that I’d been working on for all these years. I just conflated the two, and it just became music to me. And that’s really, I suppose, identified my life for me ever since. It’s defined it.”

Asked by Sam if that raw emotion was something he wanted to infuse into Deep Purple, Lord figures that “it was something that I had been fighting to get into my playing from the first time I became a professional musician with the Art Woods and started casting around and finding ways to identify myself different from everybody else I heard. So, I could say—like Gillan says in one of his lyrics—we danced and sang and stood on a mountaintop. And that’s where you yell from when you’re a young musician. You stand on the mountaintop and say, ‘This is me.’”

On the subject of whether it was important that a band like Purple was populated by large personalities, Jon says, “I don’t know if it’s important; I just think it’s endemic.

It's part of it. It's a kind of thing that your audience expects you to be. It's like, okay pal, if you're going to stand up on that stage and turn me on musically, then I want you to be someone different. I don't want to find out that you go backstage and have a cup of tea and a digestive biscuit. Which actually, surprisingly, a lot of musicians do. You didn't know that, did you? I expect the film stars, for example, that I like, or the actors I go to watch in the theater, I expect them to be larger than life because that's what they are when they're performing to me. An actor always looks larger onscreen and on the stage than he does when you meet him around backstage afterwards.

"And people have said that to me over the years. 'My God, I thought you were nine foot tall.' It's because we inflate people to that when we watch them doing what they do best, and the better they do it, the larger than life they seem to be. So, it doesn't surprise me that people expect musicians, rock musicians, to be all as mad as hatters."

Other early influences on Jon were the likes of Jimmy Smith and Jimmy McGriff.

"Jimmy Smith, first of all, is pretty much responsible for me being a Hammond organ player. I almost cringe with embarrassment to say it, but the first time I heard that organ intro on 'Walk on the Wild Side,' Jimmy Smith's version, I had to ask someone, What is that? What instrument is that? Says, 'Hammond organ.' Wow, I've got to have one. I want it now. Where do I get one? 'Well, you can have one, but they're £4,000.' Ah, okay. That's the first difficult step.

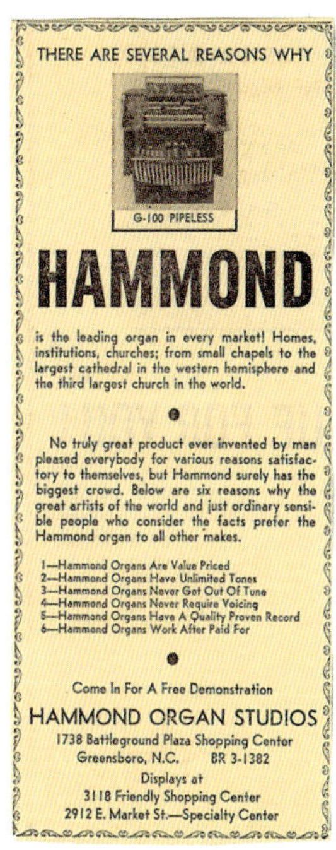

Hammond organ ads from 1954.
Martin Popoff archive

"But Jimmy Smith is almost single-handedly responsible for me playing the Hammond. Then, when you're aware of something, you start to hear it all around you. And I started to hear it in blues records. Some of the Muddy Waters records, I suddenly realized there's a Hammond in the background, and some of the big bands too. McGriff, I heard later, and he was a much-freer, less structured, less brilliant, I have to say, player than Jimmy Smith. But Smith always had that Hammond sound that I always wanted, and you can't have it because it's his, and there's no point trying to copy it. So, you try to bend it a little and make it your own. McGriff taught me about big fistfuls of chords and how to make them sound funky.

"And then the rest, really, was just me forcing myself into battling with Ritchie Blackmore and trying to find a sound that would compete with him and support him. I was kind of the rhythm guitar role, as well as being the lead keyboard sound; I had to support him rhythmically, so I had to find a way of playing that, a way of making the Hammond respond to that need. So that was huge fun. But the two Jimmies that you mentioned, hugely important to me because they taught me what a Hammond organ could do."

In any event, Tony Edwards indicated to Jon that he might think about getting together a new pop band to participate in the then-thriving British psychedelic scene, one a little tighter around pure organ-swirled psych than the disparate folk- and country-influenced "West Coast music" psychedelia happening, sensibly, in America, specifically San Francisco. A telegram from Curtis sent to Ritchie Blackmore—or about three hundred of them, according to Ritchie—in November 1967, introduced the Man in Black to the concept of this new group Edwards was devising. Blackmore had set up shop in Hamburg. He whisked himself over to England to assess the idea, then went back to Hamburg before returning home for good to make this new band a reality.

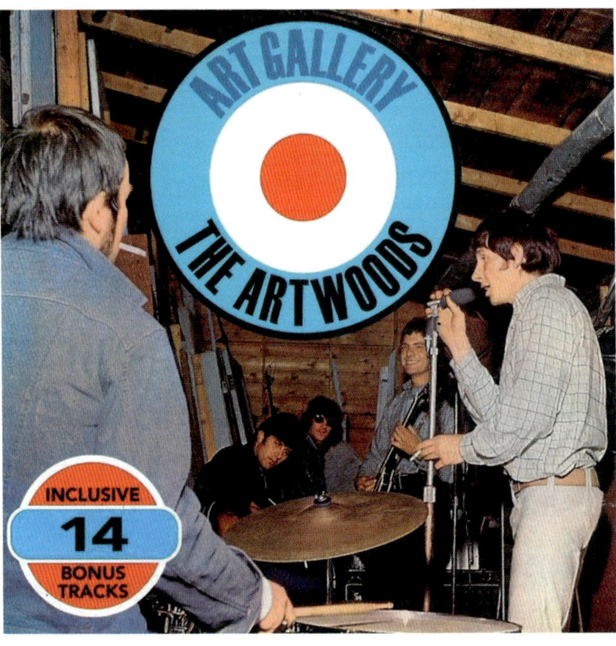

An Art Woods EP from 1965, plus the front cover (shown in German reissue format, 1995) and label from the band's only album, on Decca, 1966

Richard Hugh Blackmore at this point was twenty-two years old, but already he had been a sort of John Paul Jones / Jimmy Page / Jimi Hendrix / Ronnie James Dio figure, having jumped into the music business as a mere slip of a teenager, working with Screaming Lord Sutch and his Savages already back in 1962. Sutch was a mercurial showman known for arriving onstage in a coffin, with Ritchie getting his first taste of what would be a lifetime predilection for mischief and the macabre. Next came Mike Dee and the Jaywalkers, the Outlaws, and session work for fabled producer Joe Meek, followed by additional inconsequential bands and then the relocation to Hamburg, where Ritchie said he did little for thirteen or fourteen months, other than meeting his wife, practicing guitar four or five hours a day, and occasionally sitting in with bands making the circuit.

"Basically, I started when I was eleven," says Ritchie, charting the course of his development toward becoming an icon of the guitar. "I don't really have a musical background from my parents, but my father was a kind of mathematician, and he helped me with the notes in a purely mathematical way. I would show him some music and ask, 'Why is this like this?,' and he would work it out without knowing why, which I couldn't do at that age. And that's what I've been doing since I was eleven. Also when I was eleven, I took classical lessons for a year. I thought I had to start playing on the right foot and the right hand, and I felt I had to learn properly. So, I took lessons for a year, and then I went my own way after that. You lose your identity unless you do it yourself. You've got to get off on the right footing, but after that you have to carry on with your own identity, which for me came later. I suppose my style originated from not being able to pick things up very easily. I used to play my own solos rather than copy other people's. The first six months were difficult, and then it became very easy; then after about three years, it became very difficult again."

One of many compilations over the years that culls Ritchie's pre-Purple session work. This one is on Castle Music from 2005.

It was about five years before Ritchie would get his first electric guitar. "The acoustic I was using was a Spanish guitar that had about four hundred pickups and knobs and switches. And then I bought a Hofner, which was a very thin guitar. It was a great guitar; I wish I could find it today. It didn't have any f-holes; it was a solid body. And then I bought a Gibson ES-335 when I was about sixteen, and I stayed with that one until I was twenty-one or twenty-two, something like that. And then I heard Hendrix's sound, which hit me in the stomach, and I went for that. With the Gibson you really lose that identity—everybody sounds the same, I think, unless you're listening to one of the top-notch guys.

"I played in a skiffle group, and there were about twenty guitarists involved and none of them could play," continues Blackmore. "We were playing Lonnie Donegan stuff, 'Rock Island Line' and things like that. But first I started playing off what you call a dog box. It's a piece of string attached to a broom handle which goes through a tea chest and gives you certain notes. And any one of the notes will do, as long as it goes boom. Then I progressed to the washboard with thimbles and things."

Instrumental was an apprenticeship with Big Jim Sullivan. "He was teaching me when I was about twelve. My brother's girlfriend knew him, and he would come

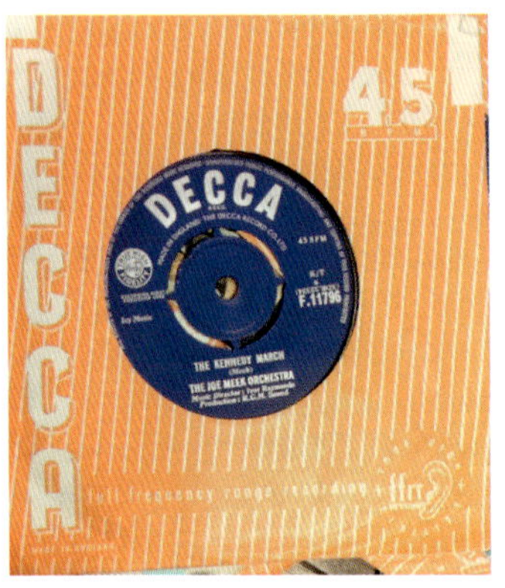

A single by the Joe Meek Orchestra pairing "The Kennedy March" with "The Theme of Freedom," 1963

over to the house; of course, after I heard him play, I idolized him. I would always be around his house trying to learn different things. He was good because I could see how far I had to go to try to keep up. At first, I thought, 'Oh, no; I'll never make it if this is just the guy around the corner.' But luckily not everybody was like him. It just so happened he lived around the corner, and it was like having a genius around, and you think everyone else is the same way. He was teaching me classical—Bach, and things like that—and he was teaching me to read better than I was. He said to me once, 'Whatever type of music you're going to play, you must stick to it; don't be a jack-of-all-trades.' So, I decided rock 'n' roll was the thing. Which is ironic. He didn't practice what he preached. He plays country and western, classical, just everything, and very well. But of course, people don't know him for anything. And so, I started to play rock 'n' roll because I was excited by it."

Next for Ritchie was his stint with the Outlaws, "which was a band that used to do a lot of sessions. Chas Hodges was on bass—he used to be with Heads, Hands & Feet. We stayed together for about two years and did a lot of sessions. That was a very good band; it was instrumental, and we didn't have a singer. I learned a lot from sessions; I did about four a day when I was seventeen or eighteen. It was the same time Jimmy Page was doing sessions. If they wanted a rock 'n' roll player, they'd get Pagey or myself, because they had a lot of people who could read, but they didn't have too many people who could feel heavy-rock music. All these readers didn't want to know about playing rock, whereas Jimmy and I didn't read too well, but we could just feel the sessions.

Ritchie was on this Heinz single, pairing "Movin' In" with "I'm Not a Bad Guy," issued on June 10, 1966.

"Screaming Lord introduced me to showmanship," continues Ritchie, who would indeed soon become a legendary loose cannon of chaotic choreography. "Before that I used to play in the wings, and when I met him, he pulled me out front and demanded I jump around and act stupid. My first impression of him was that I thought he was mad. In those days, nobody had that kind of long hair; God knows how long it was. And he had his own act. But yeah, he pulled me on the stage, and I was slightly electrocuted, because he was touching the mic and me. After that, I thought, if he can get away with it, I can do that, because I could see how well he was going down and how much money he was earning. I thought, I can run around the stage and act like a maniac. Maybe I'll get paid for it too. But he had an amazing band: Ricky Benson, who later went with Georgie Fame, and Carl Little, who the Stones wanted, and he turned them down—he's been kicking himself ever since. And pianist Nicky Hopkins used to come along now and then, because we all lived around the same area."

For his last gig before the big one, in April 1967, Ritchie would rejoin Neil Christian and the Crusaders for about six weeks in Hamburg. Up into what would become Purple, on December 8, 1967, Ritchie catches the Flower Pot Men at a show in Dunstable, getting to see Jon Lord and Nick Simper in action. Before the month is through, Ritchie and Jon commence work on song ideas, while in the background, Tony Edwards was forming what would become, later in 1968, HEC Enterprises Ltd., a business alliance with Brighton salesman Ron Hire and financier and ad executive John Coletta.

It was Coletta who decided to put the band together, so far consisting of Lord, Blackmore, bassist Nick Simper—Buddy Britten, New Pirates, the Flower Pot Men—and, as suggested by Blackmore, drummer Bobby Woodman, who'd played with Vince Taylor's Playboys and Johnny Halliday. Coletta then sent the guys into a farmhouse in Hertfordshire, in February 1968, to start shaping their sound. This place, Deeves Hall, was reputedly haunted, a happenstance that Blackmore, ever the joker, played to the fullest. It seems that a number of small test holes had been drilled, looking for dry rot. These turned out to be great for stringing black thread through or having cups slide along the top of an upright piano, occasionally to smash to the floor. Séances were also to be thrust upon visiting rock 'n' rollers.

A single by The Flower Pot Men, circa 1966

So, was Deeves Hall haunted? "Well, I think it was," says Nick Simper, bassist for the now-almost-configured Deep Purple. "When we moved in there, we took it over from a young lady who had been living there quite a while, and she thought it was haunted. And I think one of the farmers who used to keep his tractor in one of the barns on the land told Jon Lord one day that a woman had died there and was supposed to haunt the place. We didn't take it too seriously.

"And then one day a guy turned up to retrieve some items of furniture that had belonged to him, and we had never met this guy before. And he said, 'Have you seen the ghost yet?' 'What ghost?!' 'You haven't seen him yet?' A lot of funny things used to happen there. It's hard to pin it down. You thought you saw things. You definitely heard things. I mean, footsteps going over the ceiling, which was very odd because the floorboards had been pulled up in the loft, you know, in the attic, because guys were testing for dry rot and had picked up all the floorboards. But you still used to hear footsteps at night. How can there be footsteps when there are no floorboards? It was very, very strange. Yeah, there would be knocking sounds, windows banging, and all sorts of strange stuff. But we spent so much of the time playing gags that it kind of defused it, really. I mean, me and Ritchie used to have things tied up with bits of cotton, and we had rocking chairs that rocked on their own, smoke bombs, and all kinds of things to spook people [laughs]. As a sort of antidote to the real stuff going on. But yeah, there was definitely something there."

By this point, Chris Curtis was out of the picture, basically because he was wildly unrealistic about the band's prospects. First off, recalls Ritchie, Curtis pronounced that he himself would be drumming, then singing, then playing lead guitar, with Ritchie providing support. He'd also charitably offered to be the band's bassist. Plus, Cream was going to back them up. Very little Curtis said had anything to do with reality, and he was finally jettisoned. A few months later he would surface, suggesting that he produce the band's album, only to shuffle off once Ritchie refused to play if Curtis were involved.

"I didn't know him personally," begins Simper, asked about Curtis. "He was a drummer in a band called the Searchers, who were enormous. When the Beatles happened, they weren't far behind in the popularity stakes. For a while they were as big as the Beatles. They had a string of hit records; they were a Liverpool group like the Beatles, and Chris Curtis was the main spokesman, and he kind of came across as the main personality. So, when he left, he was quite a well-known figure, you know?

"So, when he met the guys who were basically funding Deep Purple, they were quite impressed to meet someone of his status. And when he said he wanted to form a new band, they said, 'Well, we've got some money to invest in a venture like that,' and unfortunately his ideas were so outlandish and over the top that everybody involved wanted to give him a wide berth. And he involved Jon Lord, who I think he met at a party, and Ritchie Blackmore came over from Germany, where he was living to check the scene out, and he just had some very strange ideas.

"I think the main idea was that it was going to be a band of different people. People would drop off and drop in, quite a loose kind of outfit, with no particular members at any one time [laughs]. It was kind of a strange idea, and then when the businessmen realized that nobody wanted to be involved with Chris Curtis, they dropped him and went with the rest of us. He was a good drummer, did his job; he could sing a little bit and had a lot of hits. So, at the time he had a lot of clout in the business. But then in the end he squandered it all and eventually dropped out, basically from being an eccentric."

To fill Deep Purple's singer slot, Dave Curtiss of Dave Curtiss and the Tremors was mooted, as was Rod Stewart, Spooky Tooth's Mike Harrison, and one Mick Angus, whose contribution to the tale turned out to be the hiring of drummer Ian Paice.

Recalls Curtiss, "I was in Paris working for Michael Pomareff at the time, when Bobby Clark-Woodman rang me up and said this band was getting together and could I come over. I think manager John Coletta might've called too. So, I did, and I met Jon Lord and Ritchie Blackmore, sitting on a bed, going through ideas for about a week or ten days. And nothing really occurred, so I said, 'I've got this gig in Paris,' and I just went. And six months later they had a #1 in the US, and I thought, Oh shit! Maybe I shouldn't have left!"

There was no real playing done at that time. "Not really. I just sat with Ritchie and gave him my ideas, some of which he absorbed! [laughs]. I hadn't met him or Jon before, but Bobby and I were a good unit, and I would've been a really good bass player for them, but Jon asked if I was as good as some big star like Jack Bruce or someone, and I said I didn't compare myself to anyone, which is obviously not what he wanted to hear! I should have given him some bullshit and said I was as good as him!"

The job went to Nick Simper, with respect to corralling all the front-man hopefuls and bringing them to the band's practice space, given that he was the only one with a car. As Simper told Dmitry Epstein, the band could have wound up with future Warhorse singer Ashley Holt. "Rod Freeman suggested that we listen to Ashley, who was also in the Ronnie Smith Band. Unfortunately, we were all extremely fatigued by the audition process, being besieged by more vocalists than we ever imagined would show up and, sadly, not giving them the attention they deserved. Ashley elected to audition with soul material, which was not what we wanted to hear, although we did not really know then what we were looking for. The result was that Ashley never really got a fair hearing. Later on, once I heard what he was capable of, it dawned on me that we had passed up one of the greatest voices in the business, and certainly, in my opinion, far better than any of the various vocalists who fronted Deep Purple. In all my years in the business, I have yet to hear anyone who can match Ashley's awesome range and power."

Another suggestion, who didn't actually get as far as jamming with the band, was Episode Six's Ian Gillan. Eventually, Mick Angus felt he had secured the job, but at the last minute a chap by the name of Rod Evans, singer with Ian Paice's Slough-based band the Maze (and before that, Horizons and MI5), swooped in and nicked the gig. It was Mick who had brought Paice around, suggesting that Ian was better than Bobby Woodman. Essentially, it had been a twofer maneuver that wound up leaving Angus in the lurch. Ironically, the next time Deep Purple would do any hiring, we would also see a pairing arrive to save the day.

"One night Jon Lord asked me to come to the pub for a pint," recalls Woodman, telling the tale of his ignominious exit. "And I said, 'Jon, you know I don't drink beer.' He said, 'I fancy a drink, and I don't want to go by myself,' and he practically forced me to go to the pub. I noticed a new drum kit by the front door as we were leaving, and asked myself, 'What are they doing here?' About an hour later, we came back, and I saw the whole band playing with a new drummer, Ian Paice. I've got nothing against Ian; he's a great drummer. But the managers called me in for a meeting. They told me that they didn't need my style of drumming: 'We've got another drummer, so anytime you like, please get your things and move out.' I said, 'I just got rid of my flat to live here.' And they answered, 'Of course, take as long as you need to find another place.' I said, 'I wouldn't stay in this fucking house another fucking minute! And I've got no money, either.' So, they offered me 20 quid. I said, 'You must be fucking joking!' So, they made it 40 quid. Jon Lord admitted in a Deep Purple TV documentary a few years ago that he treated me like shit. It doesn't trouble me anymore. If I met them now, I'd shake their hands and be very nice to them. I have a successful career in France now as part of the rock 'n' roll revival."

"He just wasn't on our wavelength," adds Simper. "I think he was expecting to be doing 'Shakin' All Over' rockabilly. Every time we showed him some music, he just shook his head and said, 'This is circus music.' So, Rod brought Ian Paice down from the Maze, and we all thought he was great. Ritchie said, 'He's a good drummer, that kid.' They snuck him in and put him on Bobby's kit, which I thought was a bit naughty. Bobby smelled a rat, so they called the management, who told him he was out, in front of the whole band. I can remember he said, 'I don't think that's very nice.' Then he looked at Ritchie and said, 'This is your doing, isn't it?' So, I said, 'Bobby, this was a group decision.' Two days later, he packed his bags. But he's a good bloke, and I see him from time to time."

Actually, Ritchie Blackmore had seen Ian Paice play in Hamburg, and there they voiced vague sentiments about working together some day. Paice at the time was nineteen and had played with Georgie and the Rave Ons, who became the Shindigs and then the aforementioned MI5, which morphed into the Maze, which worked mostly over on the continent, hatching three singles and an EP.

Recalls Paice, "I had met Jon before at the Marquee in London. A band I was in was the support act to a band he was in. The band I was playing with, called the MI5, had been doing a three-month gig in Milan, Italy. We found we could pick up three weeks at the Star Club in Hamburg on our way back. That's what we did. It was at that time that Ritchie was living there, and we just sort of bumped into each other. In those days, it was very much a musician's place. Everyone who was good but hadn't really gotten any success would go over to Germany because they could make more money. For three weeks it was sort of 'Hi, how are you?' with Ritchie. We went back to England and carried on working. About nine months after that, Purple was being formed. The singer in my band auditioned for the job, and Ritchie said, 'Do you still have the drummer with you?' He said yes, and that's when I came along to the gig."

Remembering Hamburg, Ian explains that "you worked hard. You were building up your physical power to actually play, while at the same time, completely crucifying yourself by being silly because it was very hard to be normal there. Midweek at the Star Club, you'd start at 6:00 in the evening and finish at 4:00 in the morning. There would be three bands up. You'd play an hour, take two hours off, play an hour, take two hours off. So, you'd play four hours a night. On the weekends there would be four bands on, and you'd still play four hours, but you'd start at 4:30 in the afternoon and play until 8:00 the next morning, by which time you were so wired that you couldn't go straight to sleep. So, you'd go down to a little beer house, and before you knew it, it would be time to go back onstage. After three days you wouldn't be feeling too well [*sic*]. I found that the first three days I was there, I hadn't gone to bed, and I was in a real state because it seemed like we were always at the club ready to go and play another set. You had to say, 'Okay, I must go home to bed now.' As an eighteen-year-old, of course, you didn't care about it too much, but eventually you realize you are standing up shaking and you don't know why. But once you got into the swing of it and learned how to pick up a half hours' sleep here and forty minutes' sleep there, you'd end up with a lot of physical power, especially for a drummer, where the more you play, the stronger you become.

"My father used to be a musician and used to play a lot of big-band stuff around the house," adds Ian, asked about first finding his footing as a drummer. "Then I saw a couple of Krupa movies, and I thought the guy just looked so flashy that I thought it might be something I'd like to do. It was really the visual side rather than the music side that I went for first. When I was fifteen, they sort of got fed up with my taking biscuit tins to use as drums, so they bought me a red sparkle kit, which cost about $50 brand new. It sort of went from there. After about six months, I joined a little rock 'n' roll band, which I stayed with until I was about seventeen. Then I turned professional, which didn't mean I earned any more money; rather, I just didn't have a daytime job. From that band, which worked extensively throughout Britain and Europe, I ended up at the Star Club in Hamburg in '67, which is where I met Ritchie. The rest became history."

"I have a brother who is ten years older, and so when I was little, his records were in the house," explains Ian, speaking with Sam Dunn. "It was Elvis Presley, Little Richard, Jerry Lee Lewis, all the fantastic stuff that came out in the '50s. Those records, you could sit on them and break them, which I invariably did, which really pissed him off. There were two sorts of music going on in the house. There was my father's music, which was all big-band swing music and the classic vocalists of the

'30s and '40s, and my brother's music. The more aggressive style of rock 'n' roll was more appealing, even though the beauty of what went before with the '30s and '40s captured my imagination as well. So that's where it started, with my brother's music being around me. And that magic is still there. I could still put a Little Richard record on now, and it hits me the same way. The emotion, the power, the musicality, the swing of it. It never goes away. That may go out of style but that never goes away."

Asked by Sam to elaborate on the magic of Little Richard, Paice says, "He made it violent; he really made it violent. And it came at a time when the musicians around him had no idea what they were really doing. And the same thing applied when we started doing what we did in the late '60s into the '70s. We didn't really know what we were doing. The music changed direction. When rock 'n' roll started in the '60s, you had guys who were used to playing bebop swing. So, half of them were playing bebop swing, and the other half are doing what Little Richard would do, which is straight eighths boogie piano. And theoretically the two things shouldn't work, but they worked so well. You listen to it now and half the band's doing that, and the other half is doing that—why is it working? But it does. It was a glorious moment in time when nobody really knew what was going on. But what came out of it was something only human beings can create, that wonderful thing called art. Even if it's got a little tiny 'a,' it's art because it's totally unique.

"It's almost physical," continues Ian. "You don't actually have to know too much about music. You don't have to delve too deeply into it. All you know is [that] when it's right, for some reason your foot starts going up and down and your head starts shaking, and you feel good, and you don't know why. And that's great. And what came before that, in certain instances, had to do the same thing. Witticism, beauty, incredible musicianship was far more important before that. Rock 'n' roll was earthy, and good rock 'n' roll is still earthy, even with the way we embellish it with technology and clever stuff nowadays. The good stuff still hits you in a primal place."

On Jerry Lee Lewis, Ian proclaims, "He was the first bad boy, wasn't he? He was the first guy that did things you shouldn't do, onstage and offstage. I'm sure jazzers did things they shouldn't do, but he was the first one you can think of that actually got big press by being controversial in everything he did. Some things intentionally. You could say they were part of the hype of show biz, and some things personally where you look back and say that's mysterious. I mean, Beethoven was a bad boy. He was a bad guy in the classical situation. Mozart was a bad guy. Maybe we like bad guys a little bit.

"I've got to be honest; I was never really a rebel," chuckles Ian. "I look back at it now and for me it happened so quick, and I was so young, I was just having a party. I got my first drum kit when I was fifteen years old. When I was nineteen, I was in Deep Purple. So, my whole learning curve and growth from being rank amateur to being able to play happened in four years. I was working all the time. I didn't have time to be political. I didn't really take much notice. All I knew was my life was turning from a little party into a big party every day, and that's all I had time for. Other guys in the band were much more cognizant of what was going on around them, but they were older than me. When you're eighteen or nineteen and the world is suddenly given to you, you don't have a lot of time for much else."

And where exactly does Elvis Presley figure in Ian's formative years? "For me it's not so important as a lot of the other guys you talk to, because I was that bit younger. When I joined Purple, everybody in the band was in their twenties. I was still a teenager. And the only real connection I had with early Elvis—which, to me, is the only stuff worth talking about—is my brother's music. As I was getting into rock 'n' roll music, I was listening to the next generation of it, and Elvis—obviously massively important—wasn't something I took a lot of notice of. I liked the songs, but it could have been anybody singing them to me. I go back to your Little Richards and Fats Dominos and Chuck Berrys. That was important, maybe because it wasn't white, it wasn't cleaned up. By the standards of everybody else, Elvis's music was dirty; if you put it to what most white artists were doing then, it was dirty. But again, from what was going on with the Black guys, it was squeaky clean."

The way you received music in Britain at the time also affected Paice's apprenticeship years.

"When I was a young teenager, TV was so limited with what it could play, when it was on, when it wasn't on. Radio stations were totally controlled by the BBC, what it would or wouldn't play, how many hours a week they'd give to this new kids' music. It was hard to get hold of. It was hard to find stuff that you wanted to watch and listen to.

"So, what was the newest thing you could get was to go and see a live band. It was to go and see some other kids doing what you wanted to do. So it was all about live music. You'd wait for Saturday to come around so you could go and see some village band and just feel the power that you couldn't get from radio, and you never saw on television. By the standards of today, those bands were incredibly quiet. When you listened to them back in those days, they seemed devastatingly loud. It was in your face and it was three-dimensional, and it just took you away. The bass drum hit you in the gut in a way you've never felt it before. It's hard to try to get that impression over to kids who have known it all the time. They've got stereo systems that are bigger than this room, so they can actually duplicate what a live show sounds like. You couldn't do that back then. You had a record player with a speaker this big, and that was it.

"So live music was it. And as I was growing up, and to the point that I was playing in a local band, it was still it. When I turned professional at seventeen and became part of that, it was still something kids wanted to do, and it was so important. Records were a way of reminding yourself of the live show. It was all about live music, and the way it can hit your emotions in a way, that when you take something home, no matter what your memories are, it's not the same.

"I don't know if this generation now actually gets it. I'm not talking about the kids and the fans who go to see live shows. And when I say live shows, I mean live, not pretaped mobile Broadway shows, which most of them are. When they go and see a bunch of musicians having fun, creating something unique for them in that moment in time, there's nothing like it. And it's the same when I was a kid going to see some village band. If I go and see Aerosmith doing what they do onstage, I go, 'That's great.' And that's it; there's nothing else. Nothing competes.

"Britain was pretty much like now, just about bankrupt," reflects Paice, echoing what so many rockers of his vintage have said about the rockscrabble existence they had as kids. "We had food rationing into the early '50s. Two world wars took away all our power, financially. We were wiped out, so Britain was a pretty austere place. The generation that came out postwar felt like they had to do something and change something. Lots of things changed socially, but music decided it was going to make a change as well. I don't think it's anything conscious, but we had all this stuff filtering over from the States. All this great young music, this new generation of music. And we harnessed it to what was real for us. We had these records coming out played by really good session musicians. You get a bunch of fourteen-, fifteen-year-old kids striving madly to find what that damn third chord was. But it was accessible. The feeling at the time was somebody had to change something, and if all you could do was play a guitar or smack a drum, then you'd change that. But it's not a conscious thing; it has to be this way. It can't be what it was before, because that's changed, that's finished, done. We can't do it anyway; it's too difficult. You did what you really felt you had to do and wanted to do."

Of course, Deep Purple weren't about to remake 1950s rock. Those early albums were very much influenced by the state of music as it flourished in the mid-1960s, just previous to the band's trio of records by the "Mk. I" version of the band—the "Mk." designation was a later conceit to demarcate the various Purple lineups over the years.

"Beatles are really important," says Ian. "Not for the prettier tunes, but every now and then they came up with something really disturbing. You take something off the *Revolver* album called 'Tomorrow Never Knows.' That's a very disturbing track. Rhythmically it's quite nasty, and the whole sound of it is like going through another dimension. Very strange. So that's important. All of a sudden you weren't thinking in terms of three-minute pop singles.

"Hendrix of course is massively important. Not so much onstage, because onstage he could be hit or miss. I saw a few shows and usually they weren't great, but the records, those first three albums, changed it. Jeff Beck changed the way electric guitars were played too. Very important. And we had offshoots that were really different, like Jethro Tull. Totally unique. But that's what happened, and people were not confined to say we have to do it that way. It was 'We'll do it that way.' A guy with a flute. You can't have a flute in a rock 'n' roll band! Well, of course you can. You can have a guy with an accordion if you want; it doesn't make a difference. If you're saying something, it's fine, which is the only way you can do it. If you play flute, you can't play guitar, probably, so you've got to do it with a flute. The diversification was great, but it was all under the umbrella of rock 'n' roll. Jethro Tull, some of their tracks were just so off-the-wall that you couldn't have imagined them being created ten years before. And if they had, nobody would have played it, because everything was jukeboxes. Three minutes, finished, get another nickel in the slot. So, it had changed.

"I remember the first time I ever saw Jethro Tull. It was in a little club, a drinking club in London called the Cromwellian; it's on Cromwell Road in the west end. There were about eight people in there, because most of the guys who went in there were from the east end of London, with great big suits with bulges here, and there was a rock 'n' roll band in the bar downstairs. Maybe eight people there. And there was this weird guy with a long coat who stood on one leg playing the flute. Nobody took a bit of notice. And about a year later, everybody knew who they were. But I remembered the guy with the flute."

In any event, with the hiring on of Paicey, Deep Purple Mk. I was now born, with lead singer candidate Mick Angus now signing on as a roadie. For a brief spell, the band still operated under the moniker Roundabout. Concrete God, Orpheus, Fire, and even Sugarlump were alternate monikers briefly considered, with the eventual choice deriving from the schlocky easy-listening hit "Deep Purple," which Ritchie said was his granny's favorite song.

"We thought about Roundabout," recalls Nick, "with the idea being that members would come and go. But in the end, Ritchie suggested Deep Purple. At first, we thought it was a bit girly—we were rock 'n' roll—but we went with it. I remember telling a reporter on the boat to Denmark, where we did a short tour—because both the Art Woods and the Flower Pot Men had been big there—that we were going to be called Deep Purple. Our doubts were dispelled the first time we saw it up in massive lights on the Sunset strip in Hollywood!"

Now, whether it was remembering Chris Curtis's idea about heavying up songs such as "If I Were a Carpenter" or Rod Evans's similar suggestion for a bolder version of "Help!" by the Beatles, that became somewhat the plan, articulated more so by Jon Lord's admiration for Vanilla Fudge, a New York combo who vamped and extended and made very dramatic the hits of the day, their trademark being a heavy emphasis on Hammond organ.

"Oh, without a doubt," says Fudge drummer and vocalist Carmine Appice, asked if he thinks they were an influence on Purple. "I mean, we know as a fact, if you ever read a book about Ritchie Blackmore, he paints Vanilla Fudge as a total inspiration for the band. If you listen to the first album, you can hear them redoing other people's songs with the Fudge arrangements, you know? And one of the songs that's on our *Rock and Roll* record, 'Good Good Lovin',' is sort of like a blueprint for a lot of the Deep Purple sound that came in the early '70s, where it was really heavy, with the keyboard playing the riff in the bottom of the organ, which makes it sound really heavy. If you listen to that song, it sounds very Deep Purpleish, with the sound that made them really big in the '70s. So, if our band would have stayed together, we probably would have fit in that realm of where Deep Purple was."

Vanilla Fudge's debut album, Atco 1967

Speaking further on the history of the sound that Deep Purple would take to the bank, Carmine adds that "the Hammond thing probably came from the Rascals originally, from New York. But being a New York band, in those days, most bands had a B3 in it, a heavy James Brown and Jimmy Smith influence, I would think. But the heaviness came from the fact that the amplifiers were becoming popular; manufacturers were just starting to make big amplifiers. And on my part, the heaviness came from the fact that there were no microphones, no PA systems, so you just had to play as loud and hard as you can. In my case, I went out and bought a big bass drum at the pawn shop for five dollars, and I re-covered it with my red sparkle, and what that did is that it made the whole drum sound heavier, from the bottom. And I had to turn my sticks around and hit with the butt ends in order to equal the volume that was coming out of the rest of the guys. Before you know it, I created this heavy-rock-drumming thing out of necessity [laughs]."

Simper figures that Deep Purple were simply looking for "something different to what had gone before. It was kind of a peculiar time, because pop bands still dominated, and there was kind of a sea change. For me, I mean, the band in England that did it for me, which changed everything, was the Graham Bond Organization. Graham was a bit into black magic and stuff. But the actual Graham Bond Organization, I mean, the music was just so far out, and I think it would be termed sort of heavy rock now, which it wasn't at the time. But the band itself, with Jack Bruce and Ginger Baker, kind of changed the way everybody thought. It was just a different tack, and I was really getting into that stuff.

"And then along came Vanilla Fudge, which sort of compounded it, really [laughs]. Wow, these guys are playing so far out and so different, the way they attack their instruments, the way they play, the volume and everything else about it. It was so different, and I think whoever came into contact with that realized that it was something very new. So, when we got together with Purple, when the guys got together, we knew we didn't want to do what had been done before, and we all kind of vaguely had liked Graham Bond and the Fudge as our, how would you say it . . . we didn't exactly want to copy that, but they kind of inspired us. So, when Purple first started, we got billed a few times in America as the English Vanilla Fudge, which we weren't really trying to be. We weren't trying to do the amazing vocal harmonies that they had, because we couldn't sing that good. But they were an influence, without a doubt.

An ad for Vanilla Fudge's second album, *The Beat Goes On*, issued in February 1968

"But we really didn't have time to think about trying something special," continues Nick. "What we knew was that we wanted to do something that was different. We had all been on a bit of a treadmill, backing different people, sidemen to people, where you collect your wages for doing the job you're paid for. Jon Lord came up to me one day when we were working with a band called the Flower Pot Men, who were an enormously big outfit at the time, and he said, 'Would you give all this up, all the money, to do your own thing?' And I said, 'Yes, you bet your life I would!' [laughs]. We went from sort of, well, we were earning hilarious money for the time, and we went to about 10 percent of that to start Deep Purple, but it was worth it. There comes a time in your life where you think, well, if you don't do it, you'll be kicking yourself forever. So, when someone offers you an opportunity, if there isn't much finance in it, at least if it didn't come off, you could say, well, at least we gave it a shot. Someone else picked up the tab, and we had a damn good go, and that was half the battle, that all we had to worry about was the music and someone else was picking up the bills [laughs]."

In deference to the Fudge sound, a whopping £7,000 was spent by Edwards and Coletta on setting Lord up with his own turbojet setup of a Hammond honker, and the effects of that decision started to reverberate around the world.

Contrary to legend, Lord plays a C3, not a B3. "Yes, that's correct, I play a C3. The B3s are sturdier; they can handle more abuse onstage and can be carted around more easily. I kinda stuck with the C3 because it was the one that I first started playing."

With respect to his preference for the Hammond sound, Lord figures, "There's a certain warm attack and a 'living' quality that doesn't exist on other organs. I think it's due to the fact that the tones are mechanically generated. You can buy a little Korg, and it sounds incredibly like a Hammond, but you can't play it like a Hammond. It's not a beast under your fingers. It's just a dinky little thing that goes, 'Hi, I'm sounding like a Hammond.' Just imagine me—I'm a big guy, over 6 feet tall and more than 200 pounds—standing behind one of those little things and shaking it back and forth. It would not look right. The Hammond is a classic instrument. If you want that sound, there's really no other way to get it. It's difficult to explain, but it's like a piano—you gotta play it. The Hammond is having a bit of a comeback, but I'm surprised that even more people aren't playing it. It's an adaptable and very versatile instrument. I can play 'Highway Star' and then crank it down and play in a jazz trio. It's a fabulous instrument. I apologize to it every night for kicking it around.

"It was a few years before the first Purple album," recalls Jon, asked about acquiring his very first Hammond. "I got my hands on an L-100, which looks like an upright piano. It's a simple Hammond, but it's still got the 'click' sound. I got my first C3 on February 12, 1968—I'm much better at remembering dates than describing technical stuff—during the time of Deep Purple's first rehearsals. It didn't have Leslie speakers; it had a big reverb cabinet. Great things, but they don't travel. It died in 1973. Then I bought the one I have now from Christine McVie. In the early '70s we were touring constantly, and Fleetwood Mac played with us constantly. They did about four tours with us. Christine needed money, and at the end of one tour she decided to sell it. It had two Leslies, it was in perfect condition, and it was about sixteen years old then. I can't remember exactly what I paid her for it. I know it wasn't much, probably about $15,000. Of course, they were still being made in those days. I've had that one ever since."

With respect to his trademark "manhandling" of the beast, Jon says, "I don't know how I discovered it. Because of the bulk of the thing, it looks like it's gonna tip over. But there's a balance point. Just under the keyboard, there's a natural groove. Funnily enough, I arrived at throwing the Hammond around before Purple. One day I went to see a band called the Nice and saw Keith Emerson doing it, and he was also playing some classical licks in his music. We were both separate, and we never even met until about the time he joined ELP. We arrive at the use of classical licks and abusing our instruments quite independently. It must've been something in the water in England at the time.

In further deference to the Fudge, even Ian Paice gets in on the accolades cast that band's way. Asked to expand upon his influences, Paice explains that "after Krupa, I got into rock and the music of my generation. There was a British band

MANAGEMENT • HEC ENTERPRISES LIMITED • 17 NEWMAN STREET • LONDON W1 • TELEPHONE 01·580 1022

DEEP PURPLE

Deep Purple Mk. I is born. *Left to right*: Ritchie Blackmore, Rod Evans, Ian Paice, Jon Lord, and Nick Simper. *Pericle Formenti archive*

called the Hollies, and their drummer, Bobby Elliot, just had a sound that was different from everybody else. Everybody else had a very woody, woolly, mucky sound where you couldn't actually pick out anything. He had a clean sound that just cut through. He played patterns and put interesting fills into a middle eight or into a chorus. He was actually thinking about the song he was playing. I tried to pattern myself after what he was doing. In about '66 or '67, Vanilla Fudge happened with Carmine, and I don't think there's any good rock player who Carmine hasn't influenced to some degree. John Bonham was greatly influenced by Carmine, although he never actually admitted it. I certainly am, and people like Cozy Powell are."

And Carmine's particular strengths would be? "Not to think in straight fours. Carmine thinks in accents and pushes. He just looked at it a different way. Over here in England and Europe, we weren't looking at things that way. He was looking at sound as well. By that time, we were getting very hung up with studio drum sounds, which were all very flat and small and not very interesting. He was the first one to really get away from that and get back to the way a drum kit used to sound

in the '50s, when it was really just a couple bad mics and the room and the drum sound. I'm still trying to achieve the drum sound that I hear in my drum room at home and get that on record. I still haven't done it. I put on a little cassette machine, play, and the drums are monsters—big and nasty. When I get into the studio and try to do the same thing, it's just too clinical. But I keep on trying. Carmine has come the closest to what I think is the perfect sound."

Chapter 2

Shades of Deep Purple

"For which he got a huge percentage"

Front cover of the US issue. *Pericle Formenti archive*

Deep Purple's first album, *Shades of Deep Purple*, was recorded at Pye Studios in London over the course of a day and a half (May 11 and 12) utilizing a four-track board, absolutely bare bones for a record of such historical importance. Producer Derek Lawrence had picked up a few unconventional ideas from Joe Meek, who also had a connection to Blackmore, as well as through shared experiences with the Outlaws.

Nick Simper is emphatic about Derek Lawrence being an early key man with respect to the band's career. "Let's put it this way: without Derek, we wouldn't have got the deals we got, because Derek had contacts, the contacts with the publishers who already had a deal in the can with Bill Cosby's organization, Tetragrammaton, and without that, we may never have broken through. We had already promised another record producer in England that he had got the deal for the band, and this is before Ian Paice was in. We had Bobby Woodman on drums, and this was before we had a singer. A guy came along, and he heard me, Ritchie, Jon, and Bobby just playing some instrumental stuff, and the guy was so excited, he wanted to sign us, and this was with the Decca record label, and the management agreed to it.

"But then Derek showed up with this amazing offer, and they couldn't really turn it down. And he did say, 'You don't have to make me the producer, but I'd appreciate it.' And we said of course you'd be the producer. And Derek had a pretty good track record. He worked with a lot of people we knew. When it came down to the studio, I think we felt that Derek's strength, really, was as a liaison between the band and the desk, you know?

"And you probably know how different it was in those days. You would be in the studio, and it was separate from the engineer, and you relied mainly on what you heard coming over the intercom thing, you know, through the headphones [laughs]. It was a different way of recording. Derek was like the go-between. And he would say, 'Well, you can do a better one than that.' And we wouldn't even bother to come out of the studio to have a listen. We would say, 'Okay, Derek,' and we would go at it again. I think he was kind of learning on the job. We used to watch Derek when we went into the control room, and he was always watching carefully what the engineer did, and he would sort of mimic something he did with the faders or the controls on the module, and you knew that he just picked that up off the engineer. But at the same time, he was an integral part of it, and it worked nicely.

"There was no reason for anybody not to include Derek in it," figures Nick. "He got it done in the end, but he was a good kind of catalyst for us. The only real problem was that he took it upon himself to mix a few tracks when we weren't there, and they weren't really what we want to hear. It's the usual situation when time is of the essence. We were out doing a gig somewhere in London, and Derek meanwhile is mixing our tracks, and the management assumed that Derek knew what was best for us. Later on, we said, well, actually, this isn't how we wanted it to sound. So that's probably where a bit of conflict came. And as Deep Purple got more successful, Derek felt that a lot of the success was due to him, and he kind of wanted to assert himself, you know? It was a good team—it worked. That's all I can say. I can't say that Derek was the greatest producer, but it was a good team, and it worked okay. There was no reason to get rid of him, but I guess that's what they wanted to do."

"The producer, God bless him!" adds Ian Paice. "Derek Lawrence, basically, his job was to keep everybody smiling. And he used to do that by bringing in a bottle of scotch and then putting his feet up, reading his paper, and if we broke down, he'd just come in and tell us we needed to do that again. For which he got a huge percentage. Quite honestly, he didn't actually contribute anything to the music or the sound. He was a coordinator more than anything else. He had the deal with the record company in America to find an English band. And he had known Ritchie for years and years and years back with Joe Meek's studio and all those sorts of guys. And as we were the newest thing that wasn't signed up to anybody, it just sort of fell into place. But as I say, sound and musical input were not his strongpoints."

In later years, Lawrence was back producing, and with bands similar in many ways to Deep Purple, specifically Angel and Legs Diamond. Mickie Jones, bassist for Angel, bluntly says that Lawrence "was soused most of the time" when working with them, figuring coproducer Big Jim Sullivan was of more use. Michael Prince, keyboardist for Legs Diamond, voices other complaints.

"Deep Purple was one of our favorite bands, and we put out a call to several people, and he was one of the people who said, 'Sure, I'll do it.' And I don't really want to say anything bad about him, but by the time we worked with him, I would say he was in the middle stages of his career. There were a lot of things we wanted to try on the first album that he didn't want to let us do, because he had already done them before. It was one of those things. I was talking to Roger [Romeo, guitars] about this the other day; we'd have an idea like 'Well, we want this echo on the vocal' or something like that, and he would go, 'No, no, I did that on the blah blah album in 1970 something.' And I was thinking, why didn't we come back with 'Well, this is our first album; we want to do this'?

"But we're thinking, well, he's done a bunch of albums, and we haven't done anything, so I guess he's right. And then I thought, we can't make that mistake anymore. If you've got an idea, you've got to run with it. Also, it was funny because when he came down to pick out the songs for our album, we literally had probably thirty songs ready to go. So, we start playing songs and he'd go, 'Yeah, like that one, like that one.' He basically picked the first ten songs. We said, 'Well, we've got a lot more.' 'Nope, no, that's it. Great songs. I don't want to hear any more.' And you just felt like he was trying to get his money and get out of there as fast as possible. Looking back, we should've hit him over the head with a big hammer. But it was our first chance, our first time, so you try to play along and make everybody happy."

US ad for *Shades of Deep Purple*. *Pericle Formenti archive*

Shades of Deep Purple was issued in America on July 17, 1968, with its lead single, "Hush" (backed with "One More Rainy Day," also from the album), emerging a month earlier in the UK on Parlophone. The album's imprint in the US was called Tetragrammaton—this deal was brokered for them by Lawrence, who also helped in the UK negotiations. Shockingly, Deep Purple found themselves with a #4-charting hit single on their hands, with the funky, Hammond-laced Joe South cover selling over 600,000 copies in America. Canada sent the song to #2, and Italy #16. Apparently, the small advance the new US imprint was offering (Purple were signed to Parlophone/EMI back home) barely covered everything HEC had poured into the band for new Marshalls, not to mention Lord's weighty end of the deal as well as the band's idyllic rented house, Deeves Hall.

With regard to "Hush," there was a whack of Cream influence upon the song, as well as modern enough psych components, not to mention a pile of rhythm and a memorable chorus. It seems that Ritchie had picked up on the Billy Joe Royal version of the song and not the original country western issue, with his gleaming new band infusing the thing with percolating, quaking keyboards and the odd guitar lick strafing the proceedings, not without a considerable amount of fuzz.

A couple of "Hush" picture sleeve singles, along with the US non-picture-sleeve single on Tetragrammaton. *Pericle Formenti archive*

"It was my idea to do 'Hush,'" recalls Ritchie, "a song by Joe South. I heard it in Hamburg, Germany. So, I mentioned it to the band, and we did it. The whole thing was done in two takes. We did the whole album in forty-eight hours. I liked the guitar solo, especially the feedback. That was done with my Gibson ES-335, which I don't have anymore because my ex-wife stole it. I used that right up to the *In Rock* album, on 'Child in Time' and 'Flight of the Rat.' The reason I changed to a Stratocaster was because the sound had an edge to it that I really liked. But it was much harder to get used to. When you're playing a humbucking pickup, you've got that fat sound, and it's quite forgiving. But when you play with Fender pickups, they are so thin and mean and edgy and hard. And every note counts; you can't fake a note."

Elsewhere on side 1 of the original vinyl, the guys took on "I'm So Glad" by Skip James, also covered by Evans and Paice in the Maze, not to mention Cream two years earlier. The song was prefaced by "Prelude: Happiness," which found the band in proggy instrumental terrain led down the garden path by a verbose Jon Lord on keyboards, positioning his playing over military snare from Paice. Soon Ritchie joins in, and you can almost picture the band woodshedding ideas that would blossom during their 1970s heyday. It's an unremarkable version, but one dimension stands out, and that is the manic, propulsive drumming of Ian Paice, who evokes images of Keith Moon and the idea of playing the riff on the drums, or, if not the riff, mimicking disparate bits of keyboard and guitar lines and jumping into fills both at early and seemingly inappropriate times. We mustn't forget that *Shades of Deep Purple* is a record from the middle of 1968. To be sure, this hastily assembled band is playing what is squarely 1960s music, but there's an explosiveness to the individual performances upon what are essentially weak song ideas.

Speaking with Sam Dunn on the band's more adjacent influences, Ian Paice is quick to credit Cream, again, famed for their version of "I'm So Glad." "Very important. When Cream came out, I was still very much a kid. And I didn't think much of Ginger's playing. I thought, eh, that's a bit slow, a bit ploddy. And I listen now, and I realize how perfect everything he played was. And some of it is very subtle. It's not very in-your-face, obvious stuff. Rhythmically the way he plays . . . the lines he plays complement everything that's working on top of him. So yeah, Cream, incredibly important."

"Mandrake Root" (for about five minutes, Ritchie had a band called that) was a poor man's "Purple Haze," although there's an amusing lick of doomy heavy metal to portent future glories. The song is credited to Blackmore and Evans, but somewhat like Zeppelin and their lifting habit, Rod Evans likens the song to "Lost Soul" by Bill Parkinson, who, like Ritchie, was a Screaming Lord Sutch acolyte.

Purple's cover of "Help!" by the Beatles goes the opposite direction of their Vanilla Fudge blueprint, or at least it left out the two bands' shared heavying-up vibe. But everything else Fudged was included, such as the involved introductory section, the dozy psych vibe, the progressive all-new passages, the occasional roar of everybody on ten, and the gleeful deconstruction of the song. Like I say, the heaviness was skipped over, which arose, one surmises, from the decision to play it at half speed to the original, the idea coming from a combination of Lord's interpretation and a spontaneous idea from Evans to sing it as a ballad.

"Hey Joe" gets somewhat Fudged as well, this time the band adding a pomped-up "Bolero"-like musical intro (actually based on "The Miller's Dance," a piece from a ballet score by Manuel de Falla) and then turning in a fairly conventional if keyboard-heavy rendition of the Jimi Hendrix version of the Billy Roberts classic. Late in the sequence, the "Bolero" bit returns, and then the band gets fairly up and caterwauling for an echoey and fluid Blackmore blow. Lord would eventually dismiss these long passages the band cooked up in their early days as extraneous and aimless.

Indeed, Jon Lord is relentless on this elaborate rendition, really defining the band's sound at this juncture. Remarked Ian Paice on his bandmate, "You can probably put two hands up and find ten really great guitarists. You try to do that with organ players. I'm not talking about piano players, but people who can drive a Hammond organ and make it sound like it's not in a church. If you need it in a church, it's there, but the ability to make it growl and know how you set the different draw bars, where you set the speaker, all those things, that's when it needs to be violent. It really is the most glorious keyboard sound still. Nothing compares to it. It's mechanical, it's organic, it's not artificial. You can hear one of the latest techno Hammonds, all electronic. Sounds exactly the same when you play on an old mechanical Hammond. But you put it in a band and the modern one tends to disappear, where[as] the old one, with its plywood generating the sound, still cuts through and still has the rasp and that full, wonderful throaty sound. It's still the best keyboard there is, but you've got to have the right guy doing it, and who knows what he has to get out of it.

Two eight-track tape versions of *Shades of Deep Purple*. *Pericle Formenti archive*

"I just know that one guy knows how to make it sound like a rock 'n' roll Hammond and one guy doesn't," continues Paice. "But if I liken it to drums, which is easier for me, you can put two guys on the same drum kit. Take aside the way they play, one will create a sound which is full, majestic, deafening sometimes. Another guy on there on the same drum kit will sound absolutely weedy and puny. Not because he's hitting them any less; he's just not hitting them the same way. That's down to the personality of the guy doing it and that intangible talent of knowing how to hit it to get that sound. The drum has to sound like that, and the only way I can make it sound like that is to hit it like this. And if you don't know what that sound is, you're never going to find out how to hit it. Bonham had that ability. He knew how to hit his drums correctly to create that glorious sound. You put somebody else on John's kit, and it probably wouldn't have sounded anything like it. But it's the same instrument, so it's down to the guy. That's what makes it happen."

"Love Help Me" was one of five originals on the record, credited to Ritchie and Rod. It's a fairly brisk bit of psychedelic rock, made slightly heavy like the Who, even if Rod Evans's laconic vocals hold it back, a problem on the majority of the album. To his credit, Evans was not put in the best of circumstances. Because accommodations for the band near the studio were hard to come by on short notice, he'd spent the night in the equipment van! A highlight of this one is an aggressive and sophisticated yet brief series of breaks over which Ritchie adds a few distorted squawks.

"One More Rainy Day" is a laid-back, West Coast psych-type thing, credited to Jon and Rod, with prominent bass guitar throughout, and an opening bit of thunder lifted from a BBC sound effects record. "One More Rainy Day" was cut on the Monday morning, with three songs being laid down on the Sunday and the rest on the first day, the Saturday. The balance of Monday found Lawrence mixing the album, with the band polished enough to get most of the tracks down on the first try, having rehearsed at length as well as having knocked off a small Danish tour. Album opener "And the Address" is a driving, dated instrumental that is so egregiously underwritten enough that it could have done us a favor and sprouted some vocals.

Oddly, the best original of this period, "Shadows," which was recorded at a Trident Studios demo session in the spring of '68 with Lawrence (along with "Help!," "Hush," and "Love Help Me"), was left off the album. Its fey chorus notwithstanding, this was at least a fledgling and stomping riff rocker, the added bonus being a wah-wah solo from Ritchie.

Over in America, Tetragrammaton spent some serious money to push "Hush," their preference for a first single, although the band had proposed their indulgent version of "Help!" The single was even afforded a picture sleeve, and the label's all-around efforts—working only their second release ever—helped push *Shades of Deep Purple* to a #24 placement on the charts, when neither the single nor the album would chart at all back home in the UK, where the album didn't emerge until September 1968.

From the label shoot for the debut album

The success of Deep Purple Mk. I was beginning to be felt as far away as . . . Kansas? "Big influence on us," says Kansas guitarist Rich Williams. "Back in the late '60s, all of us were playing Deep Purple material in various cover bands. Ritchie Blackmore . . . there are a lot of great guitar players, but there aren't that many that have their own voice. It's 'Right, Jeff Beck—that's Jeff Beck!' You hear a phrase, and you know it's him. Joe Walsh has that. He starts playing, and it's Joe Walsh. They have their own signature. B.B. King has that. I think that is the rarest, hardest thing for a guitar player to find, beyond his chops. It's that unique voice. And Ritchie Blackmore had that too. So even that Mk. I version, they were a big influence because they were outside the box. They were a butt-kicking rock band, but with that big grinding organ sound, they were somewhat like Steppenwolf even. But their material had all these preludes and very interesting musical passages that were one of a kind."

All told, the first Deep Purple album turned out to be a fine example of British psychedelic rock, but with a distinct flavor, both proto-progressive rock and somewhat heavy-handed. Adding to the building of a unique persona for the band was the fact that they liked their covers, but then they also liked blowing them up and putting them back together. Still, this was squarely psychedelia and, as a result, quick to date badly, with the negative effect enhanced by the nondescript singing of Rod Evans.

Back in the UK, Purple was seen as a bit too flashy, with the favorable American response causing jealousies. As a result, touring for *Shades of Deep Purple* was minimal—amusingly, the band's first gig was at a pub supported by Sweet, then called the Sweetshop.

"When 'Hush' started breaking the charts in America," recalls Sweet bassist Steve Priest, "they decided to do some warm-up gigs in England. And one of them was the Red Lion in Warrington, and they actually supported us. And that was when we first met them. I had seen Paice and the singer in another band, before I joined Sweet, or before Sweet was formed. I went, 'I've seen these two before.' And you know, it was a put-together band. So, like the crème de la crème. We were blown away by how professional they were, at that particular gig. It went down like a dollar for crap, because it was all skinheads, and they didn't know what music was. But just the professionality of it all, it really gave us a boost. And then we kept sort of bumping into them here and there, at different gigs, for a long time.

"They wore makeup, which I thought was strange," continues Priest. "I mean, not Kiss or anything, but stage makeup, and they had their hair poofed up. It was actually old-fashioned in some ways, but it did inspire us to do more of a show rather than just go on and play. They had their own style, and they were

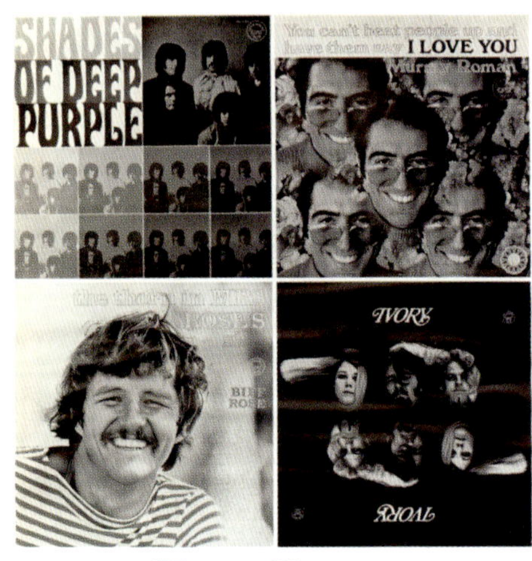

Multiple-album US ad from July 1968. *Martin Popoff archive*

all brilliant. Roger Glover, of course, wasn't in the band at the first gig. Ian Gillan and Roger Glover were a songwriting team, and I think Purple decided that they needed a songwriting team, and the singer wasn't that good, I'm afraid. And Nicky Simper, the bass player, liked his ale, if you like. So, when they heard about Roger Glover and Ian Gillan, his songwriting partner—and of course Gillan has a great voice—they chucked them out and got them in the band. I don't know; the whole band took on a different sound completely."

"Yeah, we did," affirms Simper as to Priest's comment about the makeup. "Not over the top. Maybe a little bit of what you would call slap. Everybody put kind of a bit of toner on their face, so they didn't look too pale. It was no big deal. Everybody in show business did that, whether you were a comedian going on in a club or whether you were a band. And if you went on TV, you always had to do that anyway. In the old black-and-white days, you would have been made up. But no, the only real makeup we had was that we all dyed our hair black [laughs]. Sweet adopted that themselves [laughs], apart from Brian Connolly."

Further on the skinheads comment, Steve clarifies that the Red Lion show "was when reggae was huge. We were doing stuff like 'Eight Miles High' and 'Sunshine of Your Love,' and they wanted all this reggae stuff, and they were all wearing the big boots. They didn't want to hear us namby-pambies; they just want to hear reggae [laughs]. That was a hard, tough beginning, I tell you, for all of us. It was different in different parts of the country. The south of England was totally reggae, and I remember at the time, I didn't realize, Mr. Naïve here, that the kids were taking heroin and stuff. I never thought I would see that happen in England. As I said, Mr. Naïve [laughs]. But Purple were great. Ritchie . . . just his stage presence, his style, which is *his* style. He just looked like a professional, totally in command of what he was doing."

Another label promo shot of the Mk. I band. *Pericle Formenti archive*

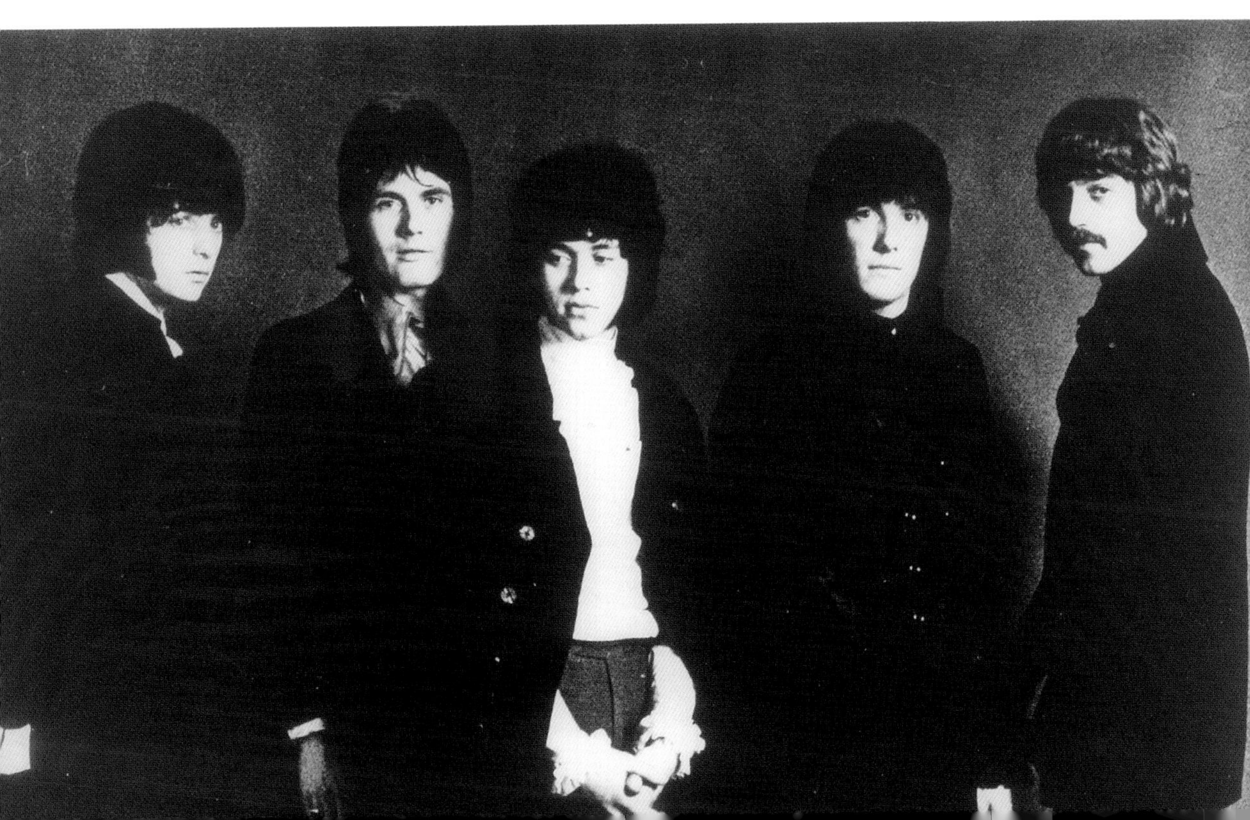

"Oh yeah, Ritchie was already a good mover," agrees Simper. "He was taught to be a good mover when he was with Screaming Lord Sutch. And the same thing went with me. You know, I was with Screaming Lord Sutch, and we used to do sort of similar antics, and we kind of discussed this when we first started. Ritchie and I used to stand in a room with some mirrors up, and we used to work these things out in unison. It usually involved kind of gyrating the guitar around and trembling your knees. It seemed a bit old hat at the time, but ZZ Top are still doing it now [laughs]. I was watching the other night this new DVD they've got out, and they're doing this stuff in 'Waitin' for the Bus' and I thought, oh, that's what Ritchie and I were doing in Deep Purple, to try to impress the crowd. We always thought that moving was particularly important to the guitarists, and it goes back to the Screaming Lord Sutch days. And I mean, when we used to do it, sometimes it was to the detriment to the music, because we dropped so many bad notes because we were trying to be cool with the movements [laughs]. So you had to compromise a little bit and make sure you played the right notes.

"Oh yeah, right from the beginning," answers Nick, on whether Ritchie was already smashing guitars. "He had a guitar especially to break, but he couldn't break it. He bought this old Telecaster in Jim Marshall's shop; he used to fly it around and drag it along the front of the stage and make noises with it, and he set out to try to destroy it, because it wasn't a very good one and he wasn't worried about it. And the funny thing was that he couldn't break it.

"And I remember, I think it was only about the second Deep Purple gig ever, after we came back from Denmark. We were playing in this ballroom down on the coast, and there was a big pipe that ran across the stage, tied to the ceiling, and he threw the guitar at it like a javelin, and it kind of wedged between this pipe and the ceiling, hovering there like an arrow. He couldn't break it, and in the end the thing was so chipped and busted and smashed, he still couldn't break it. But yeah, he was always doing that stuff. He always played a Gibson 335, which was his pride and joy for years, and once or twice he used to hold it up by the tremolo arm and would kind of go to throw the guitar away but hang on to the arm, and the arm would bend. And a couple of times the screws came out and the guitar hit the deck, and he was hanging on to the tremolo bar and the strings. So, I think he realized pretty quickly that that guitar wasn't going to stand it. He turned to solids then and started bashing those about. Yeah, he always did those kinds of things."

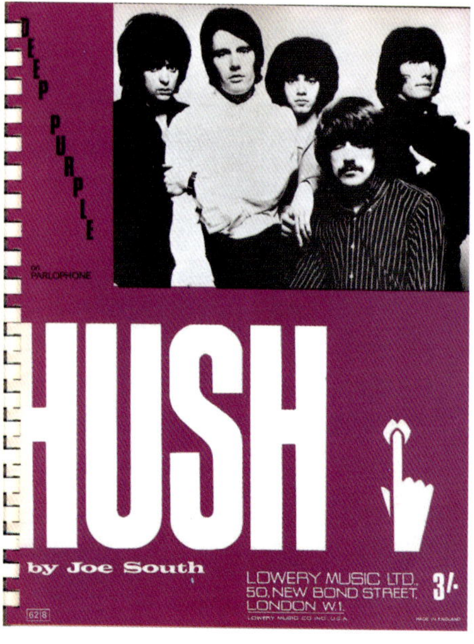

"Hush" sheet music. *Pericle Formenti archive*

In tandem, concert sound was getting much more powerful as well. "We have to thank the Who for that," says Ian. "The Who were the first band who took onstage power to a different level. As a kid I was lucky enough to see them in a big dance hall about 20 miles from here, and I think I was maybe sixteen at the time. It was devastating. With many rock 'n' roll bands, you could raise your voice and talk. When the Who came on with these first Marshall stacks anybody had ever seen, whoa, you were just pinned back by the sheer power of it. Physical air moving. And it was shocking and dazzling and fantastic.

"And of course that started the revolution. Once you'd heard a loud band, the next band had to be just as loud or louder. It didn't become like a conscious thing to be louder; instead, everybody started using bigger amps. Subsequently you were playing bigger places. I remember my first band; we had more gear than some of the headliners we played with or supported. Oftentimes the headliner would ask us if they could borrow our PA, because we had more PA than they did. So, when we finished, nobody could hear them. It became that once the criteria had been set; everybody else had to move up to it. Now, of course, things aren't as loud today as they used to be. We have limits that you're not allowed to break because they switch the current off. But the stuff we use now is more clever. It gives the impression of power without the volume. But if you go back to the mid-'70s, when it was just brute force and ignorance with cabinets this big, that was loud and probably quite damaging to everybody within a mile of it."

Japanese issue LP. *Pericle Formenti archive*

Regarding Paice in a live setting, "He was a good drummer," notes Nick. "He was very, very nervous when he first got with us, because he was like eighteen years old, and he knew that we had all played with some of the best drummers in the business. But he made his mark straightaway. And we all kind of likened him to a pal of ours called Johnny Mitchell, you know, Mitch Mitchell with Jimi Hendrix, who we had known for years. He had that sort of style, very fast, very busy, very exciting, and he didn't drop any bad notes. I used to criticize him in the early days because he sped up a bit, but there aren't many drummers that don't, you know? You get a bit excited and all that; that's what drummers do [laughs]. No, I thought we had pretty good rapport. I occasionally listen to the first album we recorded, and I thought we did okay. He used to say to me that I was the best bass player he ever worked with, but that was a long, long time ago. He's probably changed his opinion since. But I think as a rhythm section we carried on okay."

The late UK launch of *Shades of Deep Purple* turned out to be a nonevent, and, as if to underscore the enthusiasm of Tetragrammaton versus staid EMI, the band's storied UK label used nothing more than the band shot on the cover, while its sprightly US counterpart took the photo and made somewhat of a psychedelic rock pastiche of it. The stage had been set for the operation of the Purple machine to be somewhat of a botch back home, while stateside, the joint would be jumping.

Chapter 3

The Book of Taliesyn

"All I know is the guy's name was John Lord."

For their second record, Deep Purple would show wild growth yet still remain in a psychedelic rock box, even if they were now the eccentric, aggressive, dramatic, crazy uncles locked in that box, a band worth talking about and most definitely seeing live, given Ritchie's predilection for destruction, noise, and a certain intrigue through the oxymoronic clash of the words "brooding" and "showmanship."

The Book of Taliesyn was named for the entertainment director, or bard, in the court of King Arthur of Camelot, the figure responsible for dialing in the moods or vibes within the court. Or so it says on the back of the record jacket, the leafy prose going on to say that the enclosed seven tracks represent seven "feelings" of Taliesyn, creating a book (in sound). But we are cautioned not to consider this an end in itself, but a "link in the chain of musical progression which is evolving as Deep Purple."

As discussed, *Shades of Deep Purple* saw delayed release back in the UK versus its launch in America. There it was on the racks, September 1968, just as the band was getting set to hit America for an eight-week tour in October. But at the warp speed at which things happened back then (just ask Grand Funk or Kiss), in anticipation of this booked-in-advance tour, Tetragrammaton figured that even though the first album had been out only three months in advance of the planned US landing, wouldn't it be nice to have a second record set to sell? Ergo, Deep Purple found themselves back in the studio in August 1968, a month before their first album would see belated issue on home turf.

The setting this time would be De Lane Lea in London, and even though the pressure to create would be immense, there were the Purps showing a year or two's growth in a handful of months. The band was still signed to EMI in the UK, but they were off the Beatles-related Parlophone imprint and onto the new and hip Harvest, created in June 1969 for the label's more cutting-edge artists, the new wave, so to speak. The album would arrive wrapped in a truly psychedelic gatefold, with the front cover featuring an elaborate illustration by John Vernon Lord, not to be confused with you know who.

Nick Simper, February 1, 1969, Gladsaxe TeenClub, Gladsaxe, Denmark. © *Jørgen Angel*

"I didn't know the guy," comments Simper. "All I know is the guy's name was John Lord. I don't know where he came from. We didn't really question it too deeply at the time. Our Jon Lord had come up with this vague idea about the Book of Taliesyn, and we said, 'Yeah, sounds fine with us,' because we didn't have any better ideas. But he obviously gave the guy his take on that name. It was involved with the court of King Arthur, and when you give something like that to an artist and he's got a bit of a creative streak, the sky's the limit, isn't it?"

To clarify, the UK issue of *The Book of Taliesyn* would coincide with the invention of Harvest, in June 1969. Yet again, the US issue would be much earlier, in October 1968, to correspond to the US campaign. Deep Purple's first show on American soil would be October 18, 1968, supporting Cream at the Inglewood Forum in Los Angeles.

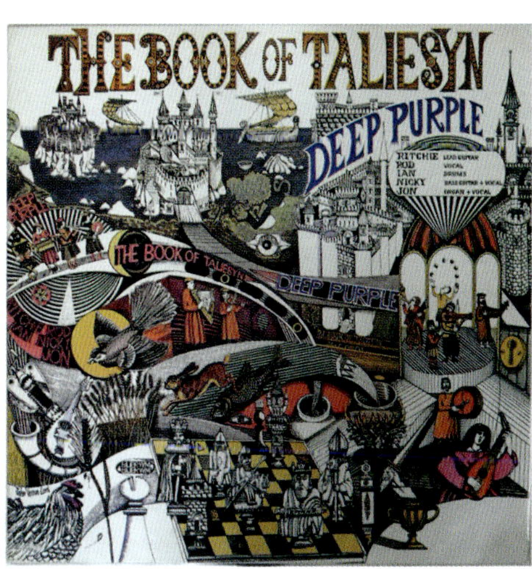

The striking cover art for the second Deep Purple album

Once one was inside the surreal wrapper, the band offered three covers and four originals, with the hit single being a driving but still relatively light-in-the-loafers cover of Neil Diamond's "Kentucky Woman," which, backed with "Hard Road" in America (this was "Wring That Neck" renamed), rose to #38 on the Billboard charts. There's an inventive, loopy solo on this one from Ritchie, indicative of that mind space where he's looking at the blues and wrinkling his nose, creating a near parody of a form for which he had little patience. It's hard to get past the clapping and tambourine on this one though. The arrangement represents a throwback to bands we know and love churlishly—the Kinks, the Stones, the Who, Golden Earring, and Status Quo—trying to cook up hits in their prepsychedelic or just barely psychedelic days. Even though "Kentucky Woman" was a Jon Lord suggestion, Nick Simper helped heat it up by suggesting the band do it in the style of Mitch Ryder and his Detroit Wheels.

Ike and Tina Turner's "River Deep, Mountain High" gets the Vanilla Fudge red carpet, with Purple creating a haunting, harrowing instrumental intro that goes everywhere and then nowhere fast—included is an indulgent nod to *2001: A Space Odyssey* via Richard Strauss's "Also Sprach Zarathustra."

The Beatles' "We Can Work It Out" gets a similar mash-up between classical music and the future of metal tacked onto the front of it, titled "Exposition." The Beatles cover is kind of frustrating, with the band adding a few untuneful jazzy chords to it and then drowning it in tambourine and a stodgy rhythm. "Exposition" was a Jon Lord item based on Tchaikovsky's "Fantasy Overture to Romeo & Juliet." Salvageable from the dog's breakfast of a song is Jon Lord's solo late in the sequence, during a sort of chugging proto–*In Rock* section.

With respect to originals, "Wring That Neck" was an instrumental with proto–Mk. II licks. The title refers to the act of playing guitar or bass aggressively, something the band used to say from time to time. Again, you can hear classical butting heads

Jon Lord, February 1, 1969, Gladsaxe TeenClub, Gladsaxe, Denmark. © *Jørgen Angel*

with blues and boogie structures, not to mention the jazz that the guys held at least in their peripheral vision. The track is credited to everybody but Evans, but it is largely the work of Blackmore and Simper, with Blackmore having nicked some of its gist from a violin piece he'd once heard.

Jon Lord remembers "Wring That Neck" as a track where he had to mimic Blackmore. "Absolutely. This way of playing came early on, when I tried to play exactly what Ritchie was playing. That really caused me some problems, but they were great ones to solve. Ritchie came up with the main riff. It's much harder on the piano, because the guitarist can do hammer-ons. There's a lot of stuff on things of his which I have to copy, especially on the faster stuff."

"I think I probably brought more blues-playing experience to the band than anybody else," reflected Jon, speaking with Sam Dunn. "And that's for the simple reason that I'd been four years in quite a good British R&B band in the mid-'60s, and the lead singer of that band, Art Wood. Ronnie Wood's older brother—oldest brother—was a mine of information about blues music, and I only had to ask him a question about where did that song come from blah blah blah, and he would read me chapter and verse. And I think what drew me in to blues music, to listening to it and trying to play it, was that it's the simplest form and yet it's the deepest emotion. And if you put a simple form and a deep emotion hand in hand, they can take an audience anywhere you want to go. And I think that's maybe at the root of my belief about all kinds of music. It's a deep, dark, wide, all-encompassing emotion, and some blues music can really make you feel the pain. I think that's what drew me in. If I ever felt that I could twist an organ phrase into twisting someone's heart, then that would be cool.

"And then rock 'n' roll, if you like, the '60s rock 'n' roll, almost famously now came out of a melting pot which was blues, country music, and maybe a little jazz from some of the players who were using improvisation in it. And there was also country blues and city blues. City blues was harder, more angst involved, more angular, and I think the same thing happened in rock 'n' roll.

Ian Paice was glad to bring in his love of jazz stylings, evident in this song as well. "Before my brother's stuff started appearing on the turntable, my father's stuff was always there," Ian told Sam Dunn. "That was Tommy Dorsey, Glenn Miller, Sinatra, Ella Fitzgerald, Count Basie, and Duke Ellington. All this stuff was playing all the time when I was a kid on the floor playing with toys. Now I may not have been taking conscious note of what was going on, but those sounds were going in. And when I started wanting to play drums—before I had drums, I just had a pair of my mother's wooden knitting needles—I'd sit on the sofa and play along to the music, and the only music that was playing was my father's music.

"We got one hour a week of rock 'n' roll from the BBC. That was it. So, the only time you had music was my father's music from the records. So, I'd play along, and if the music's going, that's what you had to do. So, you started playing, and those influences, I still find, they're there today. I was going to say it's impossible to get rid of, but I don't want to get rid of them. I love them. And when I play rock 'n' roll, if I do it a bit differently, it's because those jazz/swing feels are underneath. Even if it's a straight eighths thing. Even "Smoke on the Water," I hear other people do covers of it and it just sits like a lump of lead. It has to swing. You don't have to play the notes. You have to think the swing. Then it works. But if you don't do that, it's just ugh, what a dirge.

A shockingly youthful Ian Paice, sans spectacles, February 1, 1969, Gladsaxe TeenClub, Gladsaxe, Denmark. © *Jørgen Angel*

"As I said, Gene Krupa was the first drummer I took notice of. Before I wanted to be a drummer, I definitely wanted to look like him. I thought he was a great-looking guy, and he made these wonderful old Hollywood movies that made him look even better. I thought he was mesmeric. I understood why he was doing what he was doing. That's when I had the knitting needles, and when the movies came on, I'd try to flap along with him. So, he was the guy who triggered it.

"Then once I started playing and had a kit, you couldn't not know about Buddy Rich. Nobody like him before, nobody like him since. Best drummer in the world? Probably. One of those guys that if he imagined it, he could do it. You didn't have to like everything he did, but you would always be astounded by everything he did. And when you're a kid, that in itself is a driving force to become better. To try to get somewhere near what this master did. He wasn't great at everything. When he used to try to play straight eights, he used to have his band play a rock, big-band thing. Lame. It's not what he did. You stuck that bounce in again, and he turned into a different creature. You try to get him playing Blood, Sweat & Tears stuff, nearly any kid off the block could outplay him because he was trying to do stuff that didn't fit. He didn't know what it was. But in his own vehicle he was just a master.

"I think by the time we started doing it, jazz had gone through its rebellion, and it had become the accepted orthodox norm. So, to me, the really great jazz came out earlier. Again, when it was being created by very young people who maybe weren't as adept as they were later in life, but they had the fire and imagination and this love of what they were doing. Before the reality of it turning into your business and becoming more serious. So, when you listen to some of this stuff from the '20s and '30s and into the '40s, it has the fire for its generation that rock 'n' roll had for ours. And when you go twenty years further on, maybe it's become a little cleaner, a little more grown-up, and it's traded some of the fire for musical quality. Maybe a generation

A couple of US magazine ads for *The Book of Taliesyn*. *Pericle Formenti archive*

was getting bored with jazz in the same way that a generation got bored with rock 'n' roll when punk started. Maybe rock 'n' roll was getting a bit too clever and a bit too remote, and a bunch of kids in a garage said, hey, we can do better with that, and started making a god-awful racket which made them really happy."

Says Blackmore on the band's incorporation of classical-music characteristics, also evident in "Wring That Neck," "There was another band out at the time called the Nice, Keith Emerson's band, and they were doing similar stuff to what we were doing—they were doing classical music rocked up. I suppose the music I'm doing now with Blackmore's Night is not so different from the music I was doing then. It's just that we're not doing it with such a loud guitar; it's mostly acoustic. But the progressions are very similar, and the arrangements are similar to what we would have done back in those days. But I've always been impressed with the classics. They have a sense of drama, a sense of depth that rock 'n' roll doesn't have for me so much."

The other originals on *The Book of Taliesyn* were the album's strongest tracks, even if opener "Listen, Learn, Read On" was a little deconstructed and not in the least bit modern for 1968. Conversely "The Shield" and "Anthem," both recorded in the first sessions for the album in early August, were a bit more universal. "The Shield" was a dark and unsettling semiballad, but sophisticated with interesting dual

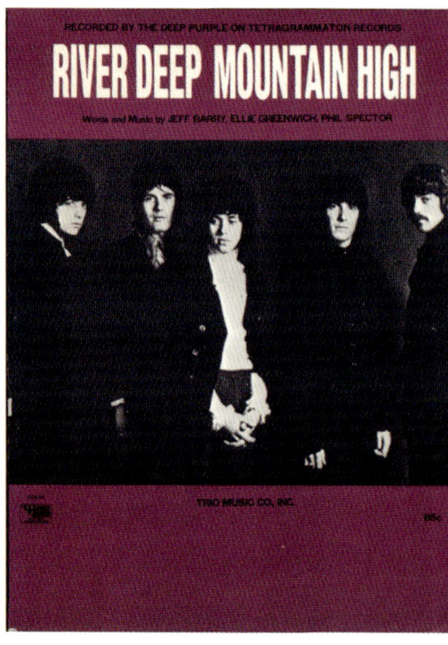

US ad promoting "Kentucky Woman" and two versions of the sheet music for "River Deep, Mountain High." *Pericle Formenti archive*

leads between Jon and Ritchie and some wacky percussive work at the end. Doors-like perhaps, this was the most accomplished track by the band to date. "Anthem" was even more so a ballad, quite funereal and melancholy for the verses, but a little sunny and psych come chorus time. Look for both the temperamental mellotron, pipe organ, and a full-on string arrangement from Jon. Ritchie soloing with the strings as backing is quite delightful, evoking images of Brian May.

Veering dangerously into the terrain of a pop chart band, Purple saw three singles launched from this record, in a number of variants. As noted, "Kentucky Woman" was backed with "Hard Road" in the US and "Wring That Neck" in the

The elusive Rod Evans, February 1, 1969, Gladsaxe TeenClub, Gladsaxe, Denmark. © *Jørgen Angel*

UK, which, as discussed, was the same song. "River Deep, Mountain High" saw US issue, backed with "Listen, Learn, Read On," reaching #53 in the charts. Finally, non-LP hard rocker "Emmaretta" was issued with "Wring That Neck" as its B side in the UK, but "Bird Has Flown" (from the third album) as its B side stateside—the tune failed to chart in either territory.

Purple was supposed to have been over to the States and touring with Cream for twenty dates beginning on October 4, 1968, but didn't get over until the fifteenth, in time to play two dates in Los Angeles. Word was out that all this "Clapton Is God" stuff was a bit exaggerated, and Ritchie would quip as much whenever asked. Right off the bat, Cream was either noncommunicative or hostile, and after a couple of more gigs, Purple were kicked off the tour, with fans widely acknowledging that Blackmore handily cleaned up with the overrated "slow hand."

Nick remembers this well. "I think when it came to going over and doing the live stuff, don't get me wrong, I'm not saying we were the greatest live act ever, but we did manage to nick the honors of a few other people who were basically much better than us. That's true; we supported the Cream when we first went over to America, and by the third show they had us kicked off because we were going down too well. Now I'm no Jack Bruce, and I don't think Ian Paice was any Ginger Baker at that time. As far as Eric Clapton is concerned, I mean, Ritchie Blackmore was light-years ahead of him as a guitarist, so that helped us to no end. But a lot of people were kind enough to say, 'We saw you guys last night with the Cream, and you just blew those guys off the stands.' And I thought, well, we must be doing something right, because you can't knock the success that they've got and how good they are. And most of the people are paying to see them; they aren't paying to see us.

"But in the end, we managed to do something right and took some of the honors. And it became very good for us when we went to New York, because we did three nights at the Fillmore East, and we were on with the Fogerty guys, Creedence Clearwater Revival, and they were just about the hottest thing going, and a lot of people during their act were shouting out for Deep Purple [laughs]. It's kind of quite gratifying that people thought we weren't just as good, but they thought we were better. So, we did some gigs that touched a chord with some people.

"We headlined a lot of gigs," continues Simper, "but the bigger ones, we were usually supporting somebody else. But like I say, we worked with most of the big acts of the day, and we held our own with those guys. By the end of the first American tour, we had sort of chart success more or less all over the world, except for England. England was the one that eluded us. It's always been a different territory entirely. There are some great bands in England, but the general music following is quite fickle. You're only as good as your last hit record. Difficult to gain a reputation on your ability alone. You needed to be sold, really. You needed press guys and things like that, and we didn't have that in position. We had people in England who were supposed to be working with us while we were traveling around Europe and America, and to be quite blunt, they weren't doing the job that they were being paid for. We were creating quite a buzz where we were press worthy, and the people who were supposed to be working for us just wouldn't do their job.

"And also record companies; they didn't do it either. 'Hush' was being asked for and they couldn't get it to the shops. And the main reason was that everything was dropped in favor of Beatles records. The Beatles put out a new single and nobody else got a look in. That got shipped to the shops and everyone else was forgotten about, and we were a victim of that. So consequently, it was so much harder back home."

Remembering other bands that Mk. I Purple shared stages with, Simper figures, "The one that I thought would be enormous and wasn't but should've been was called It's a Beautiful Day, which was one of Bill Graham's bands. We were on the bill with them, and they supported us three or four times, just a lovely bunch of people, and they were terrific, with this amazing violinist leading them. They were just so ahead of their time that if they were out there today, it would be an enormous hit. But it didn't happen for them.

Concert ad from the *Los Angeles Free Press*, October 18, 1968, for a show at the Forum in Inglewood, California. *Pericle Formenti archive*

"And there was another group called the Flock, also with an electric violinist [Jerry Goodman]. And I remember when we played in Minnesota, in St. Paul, I remember that particularly because Led Zeppelin were there as well, and they were in one town and we were in the other, and everybody was wondering who was going to pull the biggest crowd. Luckily, we did, because we had the chart hit at the time.

"But then we had just this amazing band supporting us. They just frightened us to death. And I went up to one of the guys and said, 'I love the band; what are you called?' And he said, 'Santana' [laughs], and they were supporting us! Another one . . . I helped form a band many years ago called the Gods. I never went on the road with them, but we had Mick Taylor, who went to the Stones. He was touring with John Mayall in America, and we were touring with them, and we renewed our friendship, and he said, 'You gotta come and see this band at the Whisky a Go Go. They play for pretty much nothing, and they're really good.' And this band was called the Chicago Transit Authority, and a year later they became Chicago.

"We used to hang out at this club in New York, Steve Paul's Scene Club, and there was this band with a fantastic guitarist in there, had kind of a miniature Fender, put it straight into a Fender amp and just blew everybody away. And one night Jimi Hendrix walked in, and this guy really showed him the way. And he said to Ritchie Blackmore, 'Boy, this guy's going to be big one day,' and his name was Johnny Winter. And about a year later he was selling out as well. We saw all these things happening. Quite amazing."

All told, there had been many parallels between the band's second album and their first. Both albums relied heavily on covers, with the odd original not moving things forward. The only remarkable dimension to the Deep Purple experience circa the two records from 1968 would have been the somewhat illogical and surprising proto-progressive-rock approach to parts. Again, as with the Vanilla Fudge, what on paper would be a simple song would be festooned with solos and sounds and sound excursions that found Purple gleefully pushing back against pop norms. And as discussed, these parts would benefit from the considerable classical, jazz, blues, and rock acumen of their composers. Indeed, as much as the Moody Blues and the

Fillmore East program. *Pericle Formenti archive*

DEEP PURPLE

Deep Purple received attention in America with the success of their first single, "Hush," several months ago. The group just released a second album, "The Book of Taliesyn," to coincide with their first tour in the United States.

Deep Purple is: Rod Evans, vocals; Jon Lord, organ and vocal harmony; Ritchie Blackmore, lead guitar; Nicky Semper, bass and Ian Price, drums. All have been musicians since childhood and are embarking on their first major group effort. Evans and Lord are the composers of the group's original material, although Deep Purple also tries to treat standard songs in a unique way.

Rod Evans, hiding the Man in Black, February 1, 1969, Gladsaxe TeenClub, Gladsaxe, Denmark. © *Jørgen Angel*

Nice deserve credit for inventing progressive rock pre-1970, *Shades of Deep Purple* and *The Book of Taliesyn* represent the case for Deep Purple being part of that conversation as well.

As for what was happening at the business end, a staggered (and action-packed) release schedule between the US and UK singles and 45s takes place with both

Label promo shot, Mk. I. *Pericle Formenti archive*

records. Curiously, the band does better in the US, perhaps fueled by the early-days enthusiasm of Tetragrammaton Records, newly established and not finding much success with anybody but Deep Purple on their imprint.

Chapter 4

Deep Purple

"Let's just bleed these guys for every cent until they're finished."

Deep Purple reconvened in January 1969, still trying to figure out how to break the UK market. All these novelty covers were doing nothing back home, and the guys were truly getting restless to write more songs of their own. In tandem, February saw the release of Led Zeppelin's first album, with that band holding much in common with Deep Purple, most notably the fact that both bands were populated by sort of storied session musicians having a go at their own thing, along with the fact that both operated in a sort of "underground music" or "progressive blues" space.

But Led Zeppelin's first record sparked a rock 'n' roll revolution. Psychedelic rock had now grown tired and tattered, and a new, explosive, frantic sound was on the horizon, as suggested by Zeppelin's self-titled from early 1969 and an even more impactful second album from later in the year.

Deep Purple, on the other hand, turned in a third album that was as woefully behind the times as the first two: pop, baroque, psychedelic, indulgent and not particularly advanced of sound, given that it was also the third Deep Purple album produced, unimpressively by Derek Lawrence. What's more, the album went by the confusing title of *Deep Purple*.

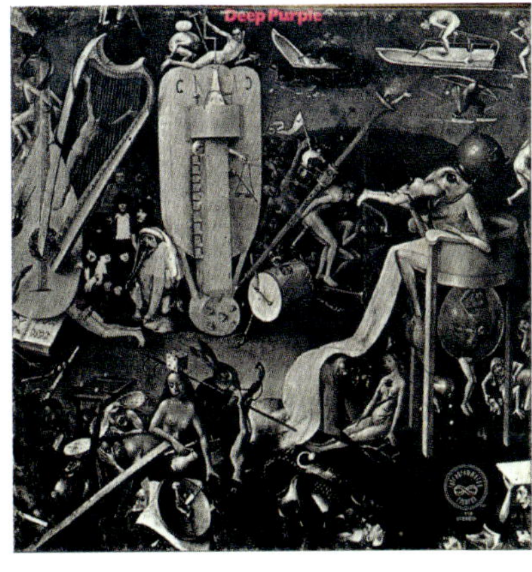

Deep Purple front cover. *Pericle Formenti archive*

Fortunately, the termination of this nonsense was forecast even before the album was to be issued. Ritchie, Ian, and Jon had essentially formed an opinion and subsequent alliance around the fact that Rod and Nicky had to go if the band were to achieve wilder dreams with wilder music. Touring of the States had taken place with communication between the two camps at a miserable minimum, while the third album had been launched by Tetragrammaton in the US in June 1969 to the sound of crickets—*Deep Purple* would turn out to be a stiff.

In accordance with the pattern that had been set, *The Book of Taliesyn* was just seeing issue in the UK, with *Deep Purple* not getting issued back home until September 1969. Gigs in the UK were paying around £100, with upward of $3,000 being proffered in the US. Indeed, the UK was still not getting it, with the band being relegated to the clubs, while talk of the band jumping on tours with the likes of the Rolling Stones being more the norm stateside.

But it's not hard to see why the writing was on the wall for this particular collection of guys. *Deep Purple* was a hard album to love, right from the ghoulish Hieronymous Bosch cover art down through the suicide-inducing music.

Opener "Chasing Shadows" was a malevolent, sort of tribal thing, like "Hush" but without the fun chorus. Paice identifies this one's rhythm as "basically a double-paradiddle between two tom-toms. If you play that notation, it gives you an amazing thundering rhythm. It's just a rudiment, but if you don't know that rudiment, you'll never come out with that configuration of notes, because it's not an obvious thing to do."

Moving on, "Blind," credited to Jon alone, is equally dour of melody, truly baroque, written like hard rock but played and arranged lightly. "Lalena," a Donovan cover, was even mellower and just as morose, like the Doors meets easy listening, say, Three Dog Night on downers. "Fault Line," a short instrumental, was nearly an early form of doom metal but, alas, despondently dated, like anything Mk. I Deep Purple ever tried.

"The Painter" picked up the pace but was yet another jammy, out-of-touch psych rock song, underscored in its has-been status by its bluesy chord progression. This one had been showcased earlier on the UK's *Top Gear* show as "Hey Bop a Re Bop." "Why Didn't Rosemary?" was inspired by Roman Polanski's classic and disturbing 1968 horror movie *Rosemary's Baby*, which single-handedly did more for the rise of swingin' '60s occultism over any other film, even if *The Exorcist* freaked more people out four years later. As for what Deep Purple does with the idea and the inspiration, incongruously, "Why Didn't Rosemary?" is little more than a hard Chicken Shack blues.

"Bird Has Flown," second to last on the album, is the first piece, really, that one could say points to the provocative and fresh hard rock sounds we'd start experiencing in 1970, immediately with the first Black Sabbath album but also on records by Uriah Heep and Deep Purple themselves. "Bird has Flown" and sure, grudgingly, "Why Didn't Rosemary?," reimagined and performed and recorded with a different mindset, could have made it as Deep Purple Mk. II songs, most pertinently because the former finds the band crossing over into the realm of doom made famous by Black Sabbath, slight Jimi Hendrix influence notwithstanding.

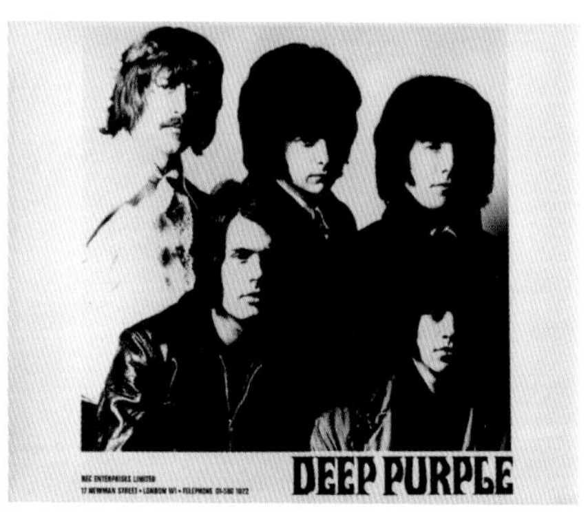

Mk. I promo photo. *Pericle Formenti archive*

Deep Purple closes out with "April," which is what one might kindly call an epic, featuring long instrumental passages and even strings and woodwind. Parts of it are fully classical, with Jon Lord getting his say and way for a long and involved midsection before the band jumps in for a typically uneventful psych-rock closing third of the track's twelve-minute girth. "I was born in that month," quips Ritchie. "It was just a little throwaway tune I had. I brought it to Jon, and he worked out the classical thing in the middle of it. I haven't heard it in twenty-five years. It was pretty adventurous for this time, especially given that we did it in the key of A flat."

All told, one comes out the other end of *Deep Purple* as if beaten up during a bad acid trip. Even though it's late 1969, the guys have us trapped in a druggy den of iniquity, the trio of Mk. I records as soundtrack but also Steppenwolf and Iron Butterfly, not to mention the Yardbirds, Cream, and the Doors. It was all too much for anybody to take, and, perhaps mercifully, the band's previously quite amenable and fully capable US label found themselves going bankrupt, unable to get records pressed on time, struggling to help the band pay for hotel rooms and the like on the road.

Nick Simper looks back at the three albums Deep Purple stamped out with such inhuman speed, with the haste and the pressure that produced them, in fact, becoming the defining factor in his assessment of the canon.

"Totally different vibe to each of them. When we made the first album, the band had only been together for a couple of months, and it was very, very new. We had gone out on a tour on the strength of my old band, the Flower Pot Men, which Jon Lord was also with, and the band that he was with before, the Art Woods, featuring Ron Wood's brother, Art. So, we went to Denmark, where we were quite well known, and did that tour. It was just a case of cobbling enough songs to get away with it. So, we had a mixture of covers that we all fancied doing, and we had a couple of hybrids that we sort of concocted together, with original material, and the very second we came back to English soil, the studio was booked and we were in. We were told that we had the studio for a total of eighteen hours. That's what it worked out at—eighteen hours to record basically what we had been playing live in Denmark.

"So the complexion of the first album was everything kind of one take, more or less, a few overdubs obviously, done on a four-track machine, which didn't give you a lot of choice. It was recorded almost live in the studio. It was such a rush job, although I don't know why there was so much pressure on us. But we were young, and we just did as we were told. And I think that's the reason why songs like 'Hush' sounded kind of live and exciting, because it was almost live, as opposed to the second album, where we demanded and got a bit more time.

"For *The Book of Taliesyn*, we had an eight-track machine, and I think towards the end of that we actually had a sixteen-track machine, so it's a little bit more relaxed. But the same pressure was on us to deliver, and there wasn't much time to come up with new material. So, pressure-wise,

Gig ad, October 24, 1969.
Pericle Formenti archive

it wasn't quite as bad, but we managed to sit down and actually construct some stuff, which we were pleased with.

"And when it came to the third album, there again there was a lot of pressure because we had absolutely no time ever to write material. The management was just working us to death, getting every buck we could make until we kind of fizzled out. That's the way the business was done in those days. There wasn't any sort of long-term thought on it. Let's just bleed these guys for every cent until they're finished, you know, burned out. Of course, when they said, "Go in the studio and do the third album," we didn't have any material. But we managed to cobble some stuff together, and because we had actually been together for over a year and a half and we had done a hell of a lot of touring—toured America twice, been all over Europe—I think the direction was really starting to come together. We really started to change.

"There was a lot of pressure from Jon Lord to do this kind of semiclassical stuff, which Ritchie Blackmore always thought was a little . . . well, we didn't actually rebel against it until the third album. But we weren't as keen on it as Jon was, because he was dominating the band. And gradually it came around to the guitar being a little bit more dominant. We were getting somewhere by the third album, so each one is vastly different. But for me, the first one was the magic because it was new and exciting and the pressure was on, getting into it, and we delivered. And it was a big album. I'm not saying it was a great album, but it was certainly big in terms of sales worldwide, and it still makes my hair stand on end when I listen to it."

I asked Nick if Ritchie had been grousing about songwriting credits at that point, something that would famously become a point of irritation toward the end of his tenure in 1974.

"Well, I don't think Ritchie had ever really written anything in his life when we had gotten together," recalls Simper. "And none of us were songwriters. We discovered, like a lot of bands, if we got together and put in our five bobs' worth, we could come up with some reasonable things. The problems really came when we had 'Hush.' Because Rod Evans and Jon Lord were responsible for the B side, they found themselves with a nice fat check, and that was when Ritchie suddenly realized the value of songwriting, in terms of finance, and he got a bit annoyed and started demanding more credit. Particularly with Rod Evans, because Ritchie didn't place any value on the ability to write lyrics. And my idea was the opposite; I think lyrics are everything, and Rod Evans, whether you like his voice or not, I think his lyrics are outstanding, better than anybody else who'd ever been in front of Purple. His lyrics were good; he had quite a gift for it. And Ritchie started grousing . . . yeah, he started grousing. It was unfortunate, because by the third album, certain people were hiding themselves away creating stuff in secret, purely because they didn't want anybody to share in the finances [laughs]. It's all very sad—very greedy and very sad."

Contrary to what's been said by the guys in Rod's post-Purple band, Captain Beyond, Nick didn't seem to notice any confidence problems in Evans.

"I don't know. I only knew him as . . . the last time I saw him, he had just gotten Captain Beyond going, and as far as I was concerned, he was a fairly easygoing guy. We used to gag each other all the time, and he could always take a joke. We didn't, of course, criticize him too much, because we all thought at the time that he was a pretty special guy. I still think he's pretty special. When he came along, he delivered the goods, and he was very, very different, and he was quite a breath of fresh air. He had original ideas and came up with some great lyrics, and we never really had cause to criticize. You know, maybe if he was doing a take, we'd say, 'You can do that better, Rod' or 'There are a few flat notes there.' But I never, ever saw him complain. So, this is something new. But maybe those guys were winding him up; I don't know. Maybe he got supersensitive. I really don't know because I never saw him again."

So yes, besides vocals, Rod was valued as a lyricist in Purple. Few paid attention, frankly, but if you read what is said in those songs, one quickly comes to the conclusion that there was a lot of substance there, compared to what else was being floated in the late 1960s.

"Yeah, definitely. We got Rod Evans to do it because he was so damn good at it. But nobody was any kind of a gifted songwriter. Ian Paice, as far as the music went, contributed nothing at all. He just played his drums. You couldn't really expect much more from a drummer unless he played an instrument as well. But we had gotten together, and everybody put in their two pence worth. I used to come up with things and we would kick them about, and Jon Lord said one day, 'What should we do about credits?' And we kind of all agreed that whoever came up with the original idea would get the credit as a writer. If anybody put in anything majorly to change it, then they would get a credit as well. It was very unsatisfactory, actually, because at the risk of sounding like I'm knocking dear old Jon, he always managed to slip in a few chords to make sure he got a writer's credit [laughs]."

"But quite often it was down to group efforts. And it wasn't very satisfactory when the money started coming in, because most of us realized that we weren't getting an even crack at it. And, of course, it really showed when Roger Glover and Ian Gillan came into the band, and they were a sort of songwriting team in their own right. And from what I understand, I mean, I wasn't there, but what I've gathered from people around and road crew and people I knew well, those two guys had all the ideas, and very, very quickly the policy was changed that any song recorded was a joint effort. And I think if they hadn't changed the policy, *Deep Purple in Rock* would mainly have been credited to Gillan and Glover [laughs]. So, it would have put the other guys in the same position as sometimes myself or Rod Evans. It was a very unfair setup. You know, at the time you don't worry about these things so much, because it was all kind of new."

Cassette copy of *Deep Purple*. *Pericle Formenti archive*

Nick makes it abundantly clear why, despite obvious problems around writer's credit and even the quality of the rushed records the band was making, the band did great business in the United States and were much less successful at home.

"Yes, there's no question, in the States it was because Tetragrammaton had bought so much advertising time. As far as the records go, when your record is being played every five minutes on KHJ, people are going to take notice, aren't they? It was really pushed; there was no doubt about it. It was properly launched. They wanted a band to launch Tetragrammaton, and they wanted it to be an English band, and we kind of got in on the tail end of that period when everything that's English was gold, with the Beatles and Freddie and the Dreamers and Dave Clark Five. Everybody that was English went over to America, mainly, purely, because they were English, and I think we just caught the tail end of that. So, there was a bit of interest in us because we were English.

"I thought the band was up to it; I think it was good enough. But there is no doubt that it was the commercial sale of the album by Tetragrammaton—the Campbell, Silver, Cosby Corporation—that did it for us. You know, we were only together six weeks in the final lineup, and we were starting to make waves in the Top 100. That's not down to building a reputation as a group, because we were brand new.

"And that's what we came to expect from the Americans," continues Nick. "The whole thing was geared up to promote us big time. For example, when we came back and I started Warhorse, I tried to take a leaf out of the Americans' books and book the band to do personal things in record stores, you know, talk to the folks, sign autographs, sell albums. And when I got there, the record company didn't have any albums. You've got all these people, and you couldn't sell any records because there was no product there. And it wasn't like that in America. Every town we went to promoting *Shades of* or *Book of Taliesyn*, there was a stack of albums 6 to 8 feet high—more albums than you could shake a stick at. And always, always coordinated with the local radio. There were always appearances at the local station before the gig; you know, you meet the jock, he's playing the record all the time, you have a chat. Everything was organized so well. Canada as well. It was just good organization. And we never knew anything like this in England and Europe."

Finally, I asked Nick if he ever met Bill Cosby.

"Yeah, yeah, met Bill Cosby quite a few times. Very cool, very laid back; he was all right. Maybe he was a little bit distant because he was head of the company. Yeah, what we saw of him was fine."

Rod Evans and Nick Simper were out of the band by June 1969, even before *Deep Purple* had been issued in the UK. Nick was particularly bitter about his sacking (Rod had met a rich girl from America, so his eyes were on different prizes) and indeed ended up suing the band, receiving a lump sum buyout, which he later regretted taking, given the future fortunes of the band.

And even though Ritchie, Ian, and Jon would carry on, Ritchie was none too pleased with Lord sticking his classical nose into things, grumbling that it was getting in the way of the harder rock. As discussed, Blackmore was already voicing his dissatisfaction with doing most of the writing and then having to share credit, whereas when Jon wrote something, he more or less was taking sole credit. This particular sore point around writing credits would cause strife in Purple's ranks anytime Ritchie would be involved, forever on upward, indeed until all the way up until his final exit from the fold in 1993.

Chapter 5

Concerto for Group and Orchestra

"A difficult area, and not one you should treat lightly"

We talked about messy, right? Well, the much-lauded Deep Purple Mk. II started on a terrifically messy note, with vocalist Ian Gillan and bassist Roger Glover joining the band to record . . . a classical album.

Drummer Mick Underwood, passed on, sadly, in 2024 due to dementia, figures in the tale of the lineup change. Mick had played with Ritchie as a teenager and later on drummed for Gillan, Ian's underrated, prolific, manic-panic heavy metal concern of the late 1970s and early 1980s. And most importantly to the task at hand, Mick was the drummer for Episode Six in the late 1960s, which also included in its ranks Ian Gillan and Roger Glover.

Mick begins by giving a sense of who Episode Six were, how he had joined, and, for archival interest's sake, I've left in a bit of detail about how he almost ended up joining Led Zeppelin!

"I had met Gloria Bristow, who managed the band; I knew her, for about a year. I knew she managed the band, and Episode Six had done a lot of radio stuff and sessions and all that, for BBC recordings. Their mainstay at that point was as a vocal outfit; they were great singers. Ian was in there, Roger was in there, another guy was singing, and that was all going good. And I had been doing something with the singer. We did a thing in central London which was filmed, and I was talking then to . . . I bumped into Peter Grant. I suppose you would know him. And all I knew from the times I was working with Ritchie (Mick had played with Ritchie Blackmore in the Outlaws—this is the early 1960s), with Gene Vincent, Peter was the road manager, and I thought he was a great bloke. I really got on very well with Peter. And I met him at this thing, and he was there with Terry Reid. He was also filming this thing, and Peter said, 'Mickey, look, Jimmy Page is putting the Yardbirds back together. Because, you know, we're looking for some people. Would you be interested?' And I said, 'Well, I might be, Peter; it could be good.' It was purely the New Yardbirds. They were the Yardbirds then, and the Yardbirds were a little bit 'a few years ago,'

Roger Glover, Club Six, Copenhagen, Denmark, September 7, 1969. © *Jørgen Angel*

then, at the time. And he said, 'Okay, give me a ring, Mickey. Give me a ring, give me a ring.' 'That might be good.'

"So anyway, just about on the same night, I got a phone call from . . . I think it was Gloria. And then Ian phoned me up, and I didn't know Ian at all. And he said, 'We'd really like you to play with us in Episode Six,' blah blah blah. And Episode Six were quite a happening band at that time. They weren't selling huge records, but they were busy; they were doing recording sessions and stuff, and radio sessions. And I gave it a thought, and I thought, well, the Yardbirds, it was a little bit . . . it was only going off to Scandinavia to fulfill some dates, you know? And I actually passed on it. And I called Peter back, and I said, 'Sorry Peter, I can't do it.' And he said that's fine. You know, there were no offers of jobs; it would've been a case of what worked out. And well, you know the history after that [laughs]. And good luck—I loved Bonham. He was fabulous, loved his playing. I don't feel bitter and twisted about that, because it wasn't meant to be, you know? So that's a little story. And that's how I came to join Episode Six. They were pretty much a vocal band. I think they needed, particularly at that time, a little bit more weight in the rhythm section, if you like. Which is what I tried to achieve with them. I probably screwed them up, I don't know [laughs]."

Asked for a profile of the soon-to-be-new Purple members, Mick remarks that "I always got on fantastic with Ian. In those days, he was a very, very good friend. And Roger also; fabulous guy, lovely bloke. Ian's voice was absolutely amazing. The band were fun to play with. It was pretty much a covers band. You know, that's what they were doing, mainly covers, a few little originals, bits and pieces, but nothing to write home about particularly. But the band was a working band. You know, went to work, did three or four gigs a week plus radio sessions, all sorts of stuff. At one point, they were probably one of the most forecasted bands for a short period there, and they were just great guys. And Ian lived fairly locally to me, so we would go have a drink and socialize. His girlfriend and my then girlfriend, we would all go out together.

Episode Six's cover of the Beatles' "Here There and Everywhere," backed with "Mighty Morris Ten," written by Roger Glover. *Pericle Formenti archive*

"Episode Six went on for . . . I don't know how long I was with them—a year, eighteen months or so—and stuff was coming out. The Zeppelin album was out, Deep Purple were out. But that was the early band, with Nicky. Now, I personally really do like hard, heavy-rock music. I wouldn't say heavy metal because I don't know much about that. It's really hard rock that I like. And Ian did too, and we could see the end of Episode Six coming. It was beginning to not be current; shall we say that? You could see the writing on the wall there, and Ian and I were talking, because we both talked about putting another band together that would be more in the area that we were looking at, yeah? Much harder. And that was being mooted.

"So, the writing was on the wall for Episode Six, to be honest with you, and that's about the time when Ritchie Blackmore phoned me up and asked if I knew a singer. Purple was doing fairly well. They weren't massive; they were doing well in the States, and they weren't doing that well in the UK. But they were doing a lot in

America, and they wanted to change their singer. I mean, as I say, Ian was a good friend, and we had nothing planned to do as such; we were just mulling it over. And I just thought, jeez, this has got to be a good move for him. So, I got them to come and see him. So, they did, as you know, and gave him an offer he couldn't refuse.

"The slightly sad part of it is that they actually changed their bass player as well. Nicky was not in the band anymore, and Roger was taken into the band, which has always gutted me a little bit. Not that Roger got the gig, but that Nicky lost it, if you know what I mean. Because that was never mentioned to me. All I knew is that they wanted a singer. Which obviously screwed Episode Six up. But it was going to happen anyway."

I asked Mick why Ritchie thought Deep Purple needed a new singer.

"I don't know. You would have to ask Ritchie that one," laughs Mick. "I think that one of the things that came to light when they were actually dealing with Roger in the initial stages—I'm surmising here; I might be miles off—but I think because Purple . . . they didn't really have that big a direction at that time. You've listened to those first three albums, right? Well, I personally don't hear much direction in that. There's a bit of this, a bit of that, a bit of the other. Whereas Ian and Roger did have some very strong writing going on between them. They didn't use it with Episode Six because the band wasn't of that ilk, you know? And I guess that might have come into play. 'Well, these two write together; that's what we need.' That's my opinion—I might be absolutely wrong there, mate."

Responding to whether he had seen evidence of Ian as hard rocker in the Episode Six days, Mick figures, "Ian has always had that voice, to do what he does there. And Roger is a fine bass player, and he was an extremely fine player then. Like everything else, sometimes you need a catalyst to put these things together. And the chemistry obviously became right, because *In Rock* came out and it was a stunning album, wasn't it? Absolutely stunning. Against, say, what was going on before with Deep Purple. It suddenly became the foundation of what they became. But the hard rock . . . no, I never saw any evidence of that. That came out when they were working with Ian Paice and Jon Lord and Ritchie. It took a little while. It didn't happen overnight, although it was quite quick.

Gig ads for January 17, 1970, and April 18, 1970. *Martin Popoff archive*

"I played with Ritchie roundabout when I was fourteen, when we were kids," adds Mick, asked for an impression of the "Man in Black" early on. "I had very few guitarists to compare him with, because nobody much could play in those days. When I saw him play, I was blown away; he could actually do it. And we were playing in a little local band, little bits of gigs in Newcastle and things like that, and he played great. He was always a slightly complex character, shall we say. I mean, I got on great with him, super. He was a little bit nervous about standing up in front of a crowd, and he never wanted his mom and dad to see him play and things like that. In those days. That eventually changed, as you know. No, I've got nothing bad to say about Ritchie at all. But I couldn't say how good he was, really. I didn't know much about the instrument myself to see that coming. I had been playing my drums for about nine months [laughs]. We were all sort of beginners. Ritchie probably less of a beginner than I was, as he had been playing two or three years, but I'd not been playing long. All I knew is that he sounded loads better than anyone I ever knew before. Later we worked in the Outlaws together, and that used to have its moments of slight lunacy."

And Mick's thoughts on Nick?

"The most down-to-earth guy you could ever wish to meet. Very, very down-to-earth guy. I've got nothing bad to say about him. Super bass player, one of the smoothest I've ever heard. Super to play with, absolutely great bass player. He doesn't talk about Purple, really, to be honest. I think he's like, well, that was then, that's it. I don't think he's particularly bitter. To be honest with you, he hasn't confided with me on anything. He's never ever taken me to task on it, which he might've done, because of the way the cookie crumbled, you know? But he realizes that that was not my doing, that part of it. That came as the sort of aftermath of it, which is really sad."

"It was kind of a funny old time," says Simper, recalling his exit. "It was all getting a bit fractured. You know, we were being worked to death, no doubt about it. Like I said before, nobody thought that maybe these guys could have a long-term future. Can you imagine making three albums in the first year? People don't even make three singles in a year. I don't know what other people did, but looking back on it, it was a bit silly. And I think the demand came from Tetragrammaton, and unfortunately, the guy who financed us, our managers, they were as green as grass. They didn't have the first clue about showbiz and rock 'n' roll, anything about it. One guy came from a family business in textiles, another guy was from an advertising agency, and they didn't know anything at all about rock 'n' roll. And we did try to advise them. Because all of us guys have been around a little bit, and we had had a little bit of success, so we tried to advise them on what we thought was best, and they didn't listen. They went their own way. And to be quite frank, they didn't do the best job, because they didn't listen to us.

"And Tetragrammaton was just pulling strings: 'We need an album; we need an album!' And it got really, really silly. We did this ten-minute track of 'River Deep, Mountain High,' and Tetragrammaton demanded that it be turned into a single, and nobody asked us. And one day the management came up to us and said, 'Your next single is "River Deep, Mountain High."' And we said, 'Well, how can you do that? It's ten minutes long.' And they said, 'Well, it's been edited down to three minutes.' 'That's impossible; it can't be done.' And they just said, 'Well it had been done, and it was in the charts!' Of course, when I heard it, it was so bad, it was embarrassing. You can almost see the edit in the vinyl. It was that gruesome. And this, to me, this was real desperation. This was Tetragrammaton going down the pan, because none of their other acts had sold a dime, you know? It was all founded on Deep Purple, and they weren't cutting it with their other acts, and they were signing people left, right, and center and they just couldn't hack it, and everything was based on us. And things were getting tight, and the management was heading for a big fall. It was kind of desperate stakes, and our management went along with it, which was bad.

"And I think Rod began to lose interest," continues Simper. "I don't really know, but it seems he had lost a bit of interest, and he was about to marry this American girl whose parents were quite rich, well-to-do anyway, and I think he felt that this would open the door for him. He started mixing with people in the acting fraternity, and he fancied that maybe he could get into movies and build his outlook that way, and it showed in his performance. Because it didn't seem to be bothering him too much. And we all kind of mentioned this; everybody kind of said, 'Rod, it doesn't seem like he's really bothered.'

"And I had already offered the gig before to this guy Ian Gillan, because I knew him before, and he turned it down—this is before we even started the band. He resurfaced again because he was working with Micky Underwood, who knew Ritchie Blackmore. And to cut a long story short, we were doing some recording, and Ian was going to be taken into the studio in the afternoon to learn the stuff, and I was told that we couldn't have the studio that afternoon, so I was to see the guys again in the evening. Unfortunately for me, he brought his pal Roger Glover along for the ride, and he picked up my bass in the studio and spent the afternoon with the other guys, with Ian Gillan. And very quickly, I think, Jon Lord and Ritchie Blackmore realized that this was a potential good position for them to control the whole show, and to get guys in who could write the stuff, create the music, and help it move along, you know? And at the same time control the whole thing, because it was becoming blatantly obvious that they wanted to dominate the band.

"And it was sad, really, because it was so good. And Ian Paice just went along with it and said, 'I don't want to get involved in the politics, I just want to play me drums, so don't even bother with me.' This is what I've been told, and I have no reason to disbelieve it. And Ritchie . . . it's not easy with a guy like that. And it wasn't always like that! I knew him when I was about fifteen years old, and he seemed like a regular guy, good for a laugh. And it didn't change until money was being made. And that seems to change a lot of guys, especially the guys in Deep Purple [laughs]."

"But the outcome was that when I was about to leave for the studio that evening, I got a phone call saying that the recorders had quit and had broken down and we couldn't record. So, I had a night off and they started off the Mk. II that very night. And to put it bluntly, they shit on us, you know? That's the way it is. I think Rod was quite relieved, actually. He planned to leave, so he wasn't bothered at all. I can't say that I wasn't bothered, because I had sunk everything into Deep Purple, and the guys, I not only admired them as musicians, but I loved them as friends. It was unforgivable, really, and I haven't spoken to them since. It was a long time ago. It's not really important to me now. I've played with people who were as good and even a lot better since."

Simper in fact quickly formed the well-regarded Warhorse, whose two Vertigo albums, *Warhorse* and *Red Sea*, are now storied rock collectibles. Later on, Simper played with Fandango, Flying Fox, and Quatermass II and now gigs locally with a band called the Good Ol' Boys.

"I am very lucky to have worked with some great bands, but people naturally remember me for Deep Purple because they were the biggest success commercially," reflects Nick, speaking with Dmitry Epstein on the subject of Warhorse. "No, I do not find that offensive; in fact I think it's a bonus in a musical career to be remembered at all! But Warhorse, the combination of personalities and original ideas was a huge antidote to the Deep Purple experience, and for me a far more rewarding time. Of course, success is only measured by record sales, but I will always think of Warhorse as the better band."

We also learn that Rick Wakeman nearly became a member of Warhorse. "I was introduced to Rick Wakeman in 1968 by ex-Flintstones member and Joe Meek artist Rod Freeman, at his West London home, where the two of them were attempting to write new material. 'Ritchie' Wakeman, as he called himself then, was working with Rod in the Ronnie Smith Band at the Top Rank ballroom in Reading. Post-Purple, I did several BBC radio sessions with rock singer James Royal, which featured Rick on keyboards, and it was obvious that he had considerable talent. We got on pretty well, and Rick said that he would like to be involved if ever I formed a new outfit. He jumped at the chance to join Warhorse, but he seemed very uneasy adapting to hard rock and, at that time, lacked the necessary commitment needed to launch a new band. There were no regrets when we parted company. Then, when Rick's career was peaking with Yes, he expressed interest in producing a third Warhorse album, helping with several demo recordings. However, his solo career left him with little time, and the plans were shelved. The success of his solo venture led to him recruiting Ashley Holt and Barney James, resulting in the collapse of Warhorse in 1974."

For his part, Evans ended up in minor supergroup Captain Beyond, appearing on the first two of that band's three albums, the hard rocking, self-titled semiclassic from 1972 and the proggier *Sufficiently Breathless* the following year. "Rod Evans was a nice bloke," sums up Ian Paice, on the changing of the guard, "but his voice was limited when Purple tried more intensive rock 'n' roll. And Nick . . . unfortunately Nick was stuck in the late '50s and early '60s!" When Deep Purple were inducted into the Rock & Roll Hall of Fame in 2016, Nick would be the only member left off the ticket from the Mk. I, Mk. II, and Mk. III incarnations of the band.

"I started in a blues group," says Ian Gillan, Deep Purple's brand-new vocalist, offering a detailed background as to his place in the world of rock 'n' roll, and eventually the celebrated Mk. II version of the band at hand.

"We were doing some weird stuff. There was a great deal of difference between what music was available to us as kids and what was available to Americans. I have spoken to a lot of people in the American music business, and they had no idea that music like the Black rhythm and blues even existed, because they never listened to the Black music stations. The young Elvis was the first white guy to get this feeling. We were getting records from labels like Blue Note, Pye International, Chess, and of course, in the early days, Stax and Atlantic. In particular it was Chess and Pye International. We were getting turned on to Sonny Boy Williamson, Memphis Slim, and Howlin' Wolf. We were going, 'Jeez, this is fucking great. It's just two or three chords. We can do this!' All you had to be was a rank amateur with attitude and a guitar with preferably three to four strings on it, and you could do it. We had no inhibitions, and we had no idea what they were singing about, but the words were so great that we sang them with passion. There was that lovely rhythm. You could get into a shuffle beat or a great backbeat. It was simple for drummers and simple for bass players. We moved on from skiffle.

"Another thing that no one in the States was getting into that was huge in the English underground were the prison songs and the field laments. It was the pre-blues music. It was early turn-of-the-[twentieth-]century southern music. We were getting inspired because they had such magical lyrics. Folk music is what it is, and everything that we have done has evolved from folk music or classical music. We had jazz. We had all these different genres that were in our minds.

"We were lucky because we had all of this in our minds, and we knew Jim Marshall as well," continues Gillan. "He gave us some incredible equipment to make music with. He lived just down the road. Jim is an old friend of mine. I remember when he just had a little store. His friend designed this little thing because the Fender amps were not giving out the power that people wanted. It really was amazing how it all happened. We were looking for things. There were a lot of pro bands in Liverpool and in West London and Birmingham. They were hotbed areas. There were jazz clubs, blues clubs, and rock clubs. The festivals were beginning to happen. There was a great deal of excitement. The Rolling Stones were doing a Saturday night residency at the Castle Hotel in Richmond. Our band took over when they had 'Come On' as their first hit. We got the same £20 that they got. The Yardbirds and the Who were coming out. I remember sitting next to Alison and Christine Wise. Allison got married to John Entwistle, who went to the same school. All these things were happening in the same area.

"We watched bands get this natural style because of a powerful personality they had in the band or because they had a leaning into a particular type of music. Then surf music came out, and we were all thrilled about that. There were a lot of great harmonies. There was a lot of work in England and in Germany as well. We were doing five shows a night and eight shows on Saturday. We would get paid four marks, which is about a pound a day, which is about two and a half dollars a day. You would get a bed to sleep on and a sausage in the morning. You would get free beer during the show. You learned your trade and you paid your dues. You never got it quite right, because there was always some guy in the band who owned the van or had a telephone. He was in the band by rite of passage. He enabled the band to exist because his father had some money and was able to sign the purchase forms for equipment. He would be a musical weak link, so you never got it quite right. That happened everywhere until you progressed, and people were plucked from this band and that band.

"So, when Purple started, they had big hits with 'Hush' in America, but they didn't want to be that kind of a band. They wanted to do something more within themselves in terms of writing. I got recommended, and there was a vacancy for a bass player as well. Roger and I were in the same band. It was a struggle getting him to leave because of loyalty. He thought if we both left the band, then it would fold. Having said that, it was past its day anyway. We both joined, and we brought not only a singer and a bass player to Deep Purple, but we brought a songwriting team. That is when it all changed. I remember looking at Roger when we did our first rehearsal, and I told him, 'This is it. This is what we have been working for all these years.' The sound came upon us quite accidentally. The identity of the band was just putting together two units, the three founding members of Deep Purple and Roger and myself. We just locked together as two units. It was a very significant time."

Fortunately, says Ian, "I was a fan of the band before I joined, so my favorite lineup was the one with Rod Evans and Nick Simper. Those albums are absolutely fantastic. I played them to death before I got the gig. And then, obviously, the first incarnation when I joined was extremely special, because of the innovations that came in at that time. The camaraderie was brilliant."

Ritchie Blackmore, Club Six, Copenhagen, Denmark, September 7, 1969. © *Jørgen Angel*

So, a new era of Deep Purple begins, and one wonders if the original three were now figuring that they were also playing with better people. Yes, there were Ian and Roger, but beyond that, of all things, they were about to record an album with a classical orchestra! And what did the staid upper crust of the Royal Philharmonic Orchestra think of the idea? This was indeed an audacious clash of two cultures, even if thirty years later, collaborations between heavy metal and classical musicians would become quite commonplace.

The curious proposed meeting of the minds contains within it at least a kernel of logic. After all, the first three Deep Purple albums featured Jon Lord more than anybody, and Jon Lord knew and loved classical music. Second in command, Ritchie Blackmore, would turn out to be a modern-day Mozart himself, although at his early juncture, he was still a passenger.

Asked by Sam Dunn about his admiration for Johann Sebastian Bach, Jon indicates that "Bach proved, perhaps more than anything else, that although music has a mathematical quality—of course it's a system by which we reproduce sound—but he proved that those mathematics could also be emotional and that you could forget the mathematics and discover the emotion. This giant intellect of his was at the service not of science or of a system or a scheme, but as a service of the human heart. So that's a lesson for any musician right there. You can practice and practice and practice on the guitar or keyboards or whatever until you're blue in the face and fleet of finger, but if you don't play from the heart, then you might as well stand out in the street and whistle tunelessly; it will have the same effect."

On the incorporation of Bach into the music of Deep Purple, Lord explains that "it's a thing called a sequence. It's a system of chords with rising or falling sequences, which is repeated either in the same key or the next key up or the next key down, whatever. That sort of effect, I think it's something for the listener to hang on to. And if you like, that's something also for a performing musician to hold on to. A guy who's writing rock music or whatever to hold on to. It's the basic premise of something attractive repeated. I'm not saying Bach invented the hit chorus, the zing in the middle of a song, but the same kind of rule applies. I learned about him as a young pianist and discovered the ripeness of it, how it felt under your fingers to be going where he was taking me, and I guess other musicians have followed the same path and discovered the same things that I discovered. I don't quote him laboriously at every opportunity, but as a nascent performing musician, as a young kid just learning my chops, it was interesting to see what JSB's chops were, to see if they had any relevance to what I was doing.

"It's wonderful to be good at what you do," reflects Jon, when Sam brings up the proud legacy of "virtuosity" in Deep Purple's music. "There's an enormous pleasure knowing that whatever someone puts in front of you, or whatever idea you might come up with, that with the right amount of application and the right amount of belief in yourself, you can do it. That in itself is a good feeling. But technique and virtuosity are only ever a servant; it's not a master. In my opinion, and I hope in most people's. But it's fun to show it off. For example, when Ritchie and I were first learning about each other as musicians and playing with each other, it was fun to invent patterns and scales and runs that were difficult to play, and then work out how we could play them together and be pleased that we could play them fast. It's a law of diminishing returns. It doesn't get you anywhere but to a point of personal enjoyment.

"But I think for Ritchie, the speed of playing—when he was a young man, I'm speaking of now—I think that was an end in itself for him. I think he just wanted to be the fastest guitarist on the planet. When he was doing sessions for Joe Meek way back in the day, he was booked occasionally because 'Oh yeah, let's get Ritchie because he's the guy who can play really fast solos.' And some of these heroes from the American music scene in the late '50s and early '60s were guys who had real technique. I came out of a more improvisational school of music. It was the rhythm-and-blues kind of thing, after my classical training. And one of the things you're trained to be as a young classical pianist is to be able to play that very difficult music, which is often very fast. So, the technique was there, and it seemed a shame to let it lie on the shelf. And of course you're young. You're full of spit and vinegar and you want to show off. I think part of the improvisational way of playing music is a preening, especially when you're younger. As you get older, you play more in the service of the emotional content rather than the intellectual content. But it's all part of being young, to stand onstage and be proud and strut your stuff."

And then there's Richard Wagner, Germany's first heavy metal maker.

"I suppose there's a parallel," figures Jon. "Wagner's thing was music drama. He invented this synthesis of word and music where music flagged up emotions as well as the words. You had these motifs where a little bit of music would tell the audience that so-and-so was about to come onstage or that he was feeling such and such an emotion. I mean that's Wagner in a nutshell. But again, it's a huge subject. I suppose there's a kind of a pomp about Wagner which you could say is mirrored in '70s rock. Rock did start to get larger than life. When I first started playing what could arguably be defined as rock music, it was on a small stage not much bigger than a chair at the back of a pub. Not much pomp there. But then ten, twelve years later, you've got lasers, and light shows and stages 20 feet high and 100 feet across and so on."

Not all keyboardists could fill a stage like that, but Jon Lord could, by virtue of his choice of weapon.

"I think one of the things I really liked about the Hammond organ is, one, its adaptability. I managed to adapt what was initially a church instrument, which was then adapted by jazz musicians and blues musicians, and I managed to kind of shoehorn it into a hard rock band, which took some doing, I might tell you. Especially when you're up against someone like Blackmore. So, I loved that all-encompassing roar the Hammond could make, especially with a couple of Leslies tacked onto one side and a 200-watt Marshall cabinet. I could make a heck of a noise.

"But I'm not sure rock bands were leafing through the works of Richard Wagner looking for reference points. But Wagner was trying to push the bounds of orchestral music and opera further and further, and his imagination was thankfully up to the task of taking it further and further. Maybe in the late '60s and early '70s, rock bands were looking for that outer perimeter to see what else we could get into the genre, to feed our own imaginations. In the end I think any rock band worth its salt, and any rock band that survives, is a band that understands it has to feed the fantasies as well as the musical desires of its audience. So maybe that was part of it too. Maybe somewhere in the ether, Wagner and Hendrix touched hands.

"One of the great English composers," avows Jon, asked by Dunn to comment on Gustav Holst. "Even with a name like Gustav Holst, he was born in Yorkshire. Yeah, an amazing mind, and again, one of the first English composers to use a really mighty orchestra. Huge orchestral use in *The Planets* suite, for example. Which although it's a very hackneyed piece now, it's played at least four times a day around the world, I should think. But if you go back and look at what he did and look at the score and see what he was doing just prior to the First World War, you see an amazing mind at work there. He's an influence on me as a writer and as a musician. I don't think he was ever an influence on Deep Purple. We might have used a couple of his tunes by mistake."

As for Edward Elgar, "He affected me as a composer—and I discovered him quite late, actually—but I don't see that he would have influenced my playing in Purple. I think I was more . . . the kind of classical music that I was fired up about in the late '60s was Rimsky-Korsakov and Tchaikovsky, with all the kind of bombastic elements. I tried to shoehorn some of that in there until we discovered what we actually were, which was a rock band, which we discovered with *Deep Purple in Rock*. From then on, really, the only time I used classical music was in improvisation, or I might have borrowed a chord sequence here and there. But in those first three albums, that's when I was kind of fired up by trying to incorporate that. I think what it was . . . I don't think I was trying to teach anybody anything. I wasn't trying to be didactic about it. I think what I was saying was 'You've got to listen to this! It's a fantastic bit of music. See how it fits in here?' Maybe it was mistakenly or overenthusiastically, but it was all done genuinely from the heart, like a kid might show you his collection of beetles he's collected or worms or seashells. 'Look at this one!' It was that sort of element, almost like a collector."

If classical music became part of Purple in any way whatsoever, it was because of a fan-based thing. I was a fan of classical music and still am. It's meat and drink to me as much as anything else. And I think it was only a question of saying, 'What can we use here? How can I get this emotion across?' The further we progressed down the line, the less we used it. But going back to talking about sequences, like a sequence that Bach might have used, 'Highway Star' and 'Burn' are two examples of Ritchie and myself using almost baroque-style sequences to support a keyboard or guitar solo. I think maybe it was always in the back of the mind. If I'm ever going to be an evangelist, it's going to be on this one point: it's all music. I'm not a great fan of labels, although you've got obvious labels. Of course, classical music would have wanted a better label. But it's immensely different to rock music by its very nature. It would be a dull world if it wasn't different. But the larger umbrella that I would prefer to use is that it's all music, and you dip in where you want. It's Forrest Gump's box of chocolate. You can go wherever you want. And to me, where I'm sitting in my life, pretty much every chocolate I've ever taken out of that box has tasted good, so I'm all right with that."

Sam points out that there's a secondary parallel between classical and heavy metal, and that's the wild lifestyles some of these guys lived centuries ago.

"I don't see why you wouldn't look at them that way. Being a musician anyway, especially in a gentler age, must have been more on the edge than it's ever been in our age. The sort of classic portrait of the starving artist in the garrote, subsisting on bits of wine and bread that these pals bring around, and then carousing in the evening in the pub and then going back and writing a symphony and all that kind of stuff; it's cliché, but clichés are such because they're generally true. It's difficult enough being a musician, whether it's writing symphonies or being in a rock band,

Concerto for Group and Orchestra front and back covers. *Pericle Formenti archive*

so I imagine the template works equally well in either. I know a few orchestral musicians now, and they're just as mad as my lot. Just as crazy.

But before we see any semblance of classical music being applied to Deep Purple's form of kerranging hard rock, there's an actual classical-music album to deal with. *Concerto for Group and Orchestra*—like many classical albums, it's impossible to agree on the one true title of the damn thing—is credited to Deep Purple in big purple print, along with "The Royal Philharmonic Orchestra" in pink, in a slightly smaller point size. Then there's a line break, with "Conducted by Malcolm Arnold" in orange, with a point size that matches the orchestra designation. A bunch of smaller black-ink text muddies the waters further. Then you can forget trying to name the pieces of music that comprise the record, fully one hour of it, crammed onto a single piece of vinyl.

Explains Jon, "The whole performance—the band, the orchestra, the conducting—was of a very high standard, and it's great to see it vindicated all these years later [Lord was speaking on the occasion of its 1999 reissue]. I've never been a great fan of using the orchestra as a giant backing group for a rock band. We did a little bit of that in 1999, when we played the *Concerto* again—we did three or four Purple numbers with the London Symphonic Orchestra—but I'm generally not into doing that. When I wrote the 'Concerto' in 1969, it was a genuine attempt to write something for two opposing forces, to try to see if there was any way they had some kind of common ground. It was a terrifying experience because it was something that had never been done before, and looking back on it now, we must have been out of our minds to think that it would happen [laughs]. But because the band and most of the orchestra played it for what it was—an honest and emotional piece—we got away with it. If the *Concerto* proved anything, it proved that it's a difficult area, and not one you should treat lightly."

The idea had been with Jon for four or five years, back to the days of the Art Woods, when their plans to work with the New Jazz Orchestra were scuttled by Decca. Also, the climate seemed right, with the Nice in operation and with Barclay James Harvest rumored to be working on something similar.

Lord didn't even know he could pull the thing off, figuring he would need nine months to write it. A fire was lit under him when management informed him that the Royal Albert Hall had been booked months in advance for the historic event. Noted classical composer Malcolm Arnold was along to help with much of the structure of the thing, with Jon Lord later describing him as the cornerstone of the project, and essentially the crucial interface between him and the orchestra.

Asked by *Modern Drummer* in 1984 whether his lack of technical training had helped or hindered his progress as a drummer, Ian Paice offers some anecdotes about the orchestral experience. "There are certain things I would like to have done with formalized arranged music, but I have always found that very difficult because I don't read a note. There are certain things that become very difficult unless you know

DEEPER PURPLE

Deep Purple, once memorable for a gaggle of Top 40 hits, last summer embarked on a bold musical experiment with Malcolm Arnold's Royal Philharmonic Orchestra in London's Royal Albert Hall. For the occasion, Deep Purple organist Jon Lord composed a <u>Suite for Group and Orchestra</u>, which resulted in a couple of hours of intriguing music, uniting the more exciting ingredients of rock and the classics.

Fortunate are we to have a splendid stereo recording of this wildly-acclaimed event, now available at better record shops everywhere under the enticing title "Deep Purple and the Royal Philharmonic Orchestra." This live recording of a new and Deeper Purple, not to mention the Royal Phil, will amaze and delight the discerning.

Deep Purple deepens on Warner Bros. albums and tapes, where they belong.

Ad for the *Concerto* album, December 1969. *Martin Popoff archive*

how to throw every rudiment in the book in. Yet, on the other hand, I have never had any preconceived ideas about what anything should be, which gives me a lot more freedom than people who maybe know a little too much for their own good.

"When we did the stuff in Purple with the orchestras, you should have seen my score. Everybody had a proper score with notes, treble clefs, and staffs, except me. For the first movement it said, 'Hang around for about six minutes, wait for three big bangs, and come in with first rock 'n' roll rhythm.' That was good enough for me. The fiddle section the first time through were saying, 'Is this guy for real? Is he joking?' But the funny thing was, on the first two run-throughs, I got it right and they got it wrong. It only needs one note to be in the wrong place and the whole section goes, whereas I know exactly where my piece of music is. I wrote it for myself. It was quite something to see their faces.

"It was a lot of hard work for basically a very short time. We maybe did orchestral work three or four times—two different pieces—and I'm talking three or four weeks of heavy work. There are easier ways to enjoy yourself. I'm glad I did it so I can say I did it, but I wouldn't want to do it again, nor would I wish it on anyone else. Orchestras don't play in time. We play on the downbeat, and they play on the upbeat. There's a fraction-of-a-second difference, and they're always late. There's nothing you can do about it, and there's nothing they can do about it. It's just the way things are."

With respect to the audacity to attempt the project in the first place, Paice noted that "in those days, it was a lot easier to be lots of different things. Now, you're either a rock band, or a blues band or pop band. You can't say, 'We do this and this.' People won't take it. They put you into a little niche and bag, and if you say, 'But we can do this as well,' they're really not too interested. Back then, the whole thing was to break down the barriers, knock all walls down, and say, 'Look, we can do anything we want.'"

"I have no idea what to say about that," adds Ritchie, washing his hands of the experience. "I never play it. I didn't even listen to the live record. It was something of a novelty. Trying to play with twenty-five violinists sitting next to you was not the greatest fun. I had my small Vox amplifier, and they were basically holding their ears and saying, 'Too loud!' So here I am trying to play to an audience, and I've got these violinists sticking their fingers in their ears. I felt like, 'Oh, yeah! Great! I'm feeling on top of the world here. Boy, this really inspires me to let go.' I didn't like it. I like proper classical, purist classical. That album was just a compromise; the orchestra was never playing at its best, and the band was certainly out of its depth. I like chamber music, basically, medieval music, more so than big orchestrations."

Ringleader Jon Lord helpfully provided, within the original gatefold sleeve to the album, a detailed blueprint of the musical event. "The realization that an ambition was about to become a reality was for me both incredibly exciting and terrifying. I had long had the idea of writing a 'Concerto for Group and Orchestra' but probably would not have done it at this time had I not the confidence I had in Ritchie, Ian, Roger, and Ian. Many further thanks are due to Anthony Edwards and John Coletta, who, among a thousand other things, booked the Albert Hall. Merely to say thank you to Malcolm Arnold for what he did misses the mark by a million miles. But having no better words, 'Thank you, Malcolm.' And 'Thank you' to Judith, who was very patient.

"Finally, a few observations on the critical reaction to the *Concerto*," continues Jon and his liner notes. "This was mixed but, happily, quite heavily biased in the direction of favorable. I am sure that critics are generally sincere in what they do. I am sure that critics are a necessary, if slightly archaic, appendage to the music business. What puzzles me is that an evening which was intended to be and, in fact (as witnessed by a very large and glorious audience), turned out to be FUN should be treated by some of the critics with such long-faced seriousness. Still, to those of you who enjoyed

European Harvest record labels for the *Concerto* album

it, God bless you, and to those of you who didn't—God bless you too! It is still only a beginning. Jon Lord."

The critical reaction that Lord was referring to was in fact a review of the original show, which occurred on September 24, 1969 (a week earlier, Blackmore had married—for the second time!). So, in effect, this was all discussed in the press long before the album came out in America in December of the same year (and two months later, Tetragrammaton would be bankrupt). For the performance, the "Concerto" was debuted as a new piece of music, following another debut, Malcolm Arnold's Symphony No. 6, which was played by the orchestra alone. Deep Purple also played a short conventional set, offering 'Hush,' 'Wring That Neck,' and the previously unreleased 'Child in Time.' Ritchie struck up a bit of characteristic mischief when, in what might be viewed as a protest against the rigid structure of classical music, he went way over time with his planned ninety-second solo in the 'First Movement,' which practically gave Arnold a heart attack as he frantically tried to hold the whole house of cards to center.

True to predicted human nature, the classical guys were quite disdainful of the whole exercise, with particular clashes occurring with respect to the percussion section and its dominance by this long-haired hippie in glasses called Ian Paice. As well, disputes arose as to how, or if, the band's volume could or should be tamed. Arnold turned out to be more open-minded than his peons (one female cellist rose to her feet and denounced having to play with a "second-rate Beatles") and indeed had to rein them in from time to time as their attitude showed and glowered. The show itself went infinitely better than the rehearsal, though, with the large collective encouraged into an encore presentation of the 'Third Movement' over again, while Lord positively glowed with pride at seeing the seemingly impossible resoundingly achieved—and perhaps more importantly, over and done with.

Most fans were indeed completely untaken by the subsequent recorded document of the event and viewed it politely as a valiant experiment. The record's issue did, however, garner the band some much-needed buzz as well as secure their reputation as something a bit flash. Curiously, much of the album is orchestra alone and then Deep Purple alone, with one quite raucous extended jam by the guys being a highlight. Paicey gets a drum solo, and Ian gets to warble along for a bit in the 'Second Movement' (his lyrics were written the day of the dress rehearsal with Malcolm Arnold, over wine and lunch at an Italian restaurant). At the end of it, one is left with a crooked grin, coming to the conclusion that for now, the two musical lobes of hard rock and classical were still a case of oil and water splattering the page and stage.

Leading into the record, we'd already heard the newly staffed Deep Purple. The first conventional foray for the guys had been a reworking of a Greenaway/Cook composition called "Hallelujah (I Am the Preacher)," which found the new band still sounding like the old band. In fact, Ian was appalled at the results, considering it Episode Six all over again and "shite." Backed with "April Part 1," the single was issued on July 25, 1969, and failed to chart on either side of the pond, despite its overt purpose; namely, the desperate search for a hit, especially back home. Completely uneventful, the song is yet another morose and dumpy psychedelic rocker structured like a noisy Jimi Hendrix ballad. Amusingly, Gillan does rattle off a couple of his yelps, but it is Paice who gets minor showcase status, marbling in fills like Keith Moon while Ritchie lackadaisically twangs the blues.

Two white-label promotional issues of the "Hallelujah" single

Playing live and rehearsing for the first album together was broken up by preparations for the classical gig. Lord in particular was preoccupied and away from the band, causing collective grumbling. Also, mercifully, in advance of the classical album, rehearsals attended by the whole band along with the orchestra were kept to a handful. Back to the assembly of the new lineup, progress had been tentative there as well. Initially, Ian Gillan wasn't sure he would take the offer of joining the band. Previously, Ritchie had jumped onstage with Episode Six, and Ian was not impressed. As well, the next day after their jam, the rest of the guys weren't completely sure they wanted him anyway. On the bass side of the equation, Roger Glover was put on three months' probation and, months later, would still have to bow to Jon Lord's pronouncements on how things should be. And back to Ian: up into November 1969, Lord had congratulated some support band's lead singer—one David Coverdale—asking for his phone number just in case things with Ian didn't work out.

Plus, fingers were being pointed at Jon Lord himself. With there already being tension over doing the *Concerto* album in the first place (mainly between Ritchie and Jon), now the project was viewed by insiders and watchers as a ruse intended to further Lord's career, with the keyboardist in fact having been asked to do more work of the type. Jon was also touted in the press as the leader of the band, and worse, the key writer, where, in the context of rock 'n' roll, he wasn't much of a writer at all.

The idea was floated to take the *Concerto* experience stateside, and at home, fans started showing up at shows wondering where the orchestra was. One promoter was said to have helpfully hired a brass band, given that he couldn't locate a full-blown orchestra. With Lord seemingly ready to quit, he in turn reaffirmed his commitment to the band, with the agreement that classical commissions could be pursued if they didn't interfere with Purple rocking out from now on. As it turns out, the "Concerto" indeed wouldn't be played again until thirty years later, when a fan reconstructed the long-lost score to the piece and presented it to Lord. This modern-era show was captured on CD and DVD and issued in 2000. In addition, the original album saw rerelease three years later, expanded to include more of Purple's performance, although not Arnold's Symphony No. 6. In other words, Deep Purple would indeed now concentrate on rocking out and rocking out hard, with the balance of power shifting from Jon to the Man in Black.

Dal repertorio "underground" del complesso

deep purple

1 - ANTHEM *(Il vento della notte)*
2 - APRIL
3 - BLIND *(Riflessi)*
4 - WRING THAT NECK
5 - EXPOSITION
6 - PAINTER *(Colori)*

B. FELDMAN & CO. Ltd. - London

EDIZIONI MUSICALI

FRANCIS - DAY - Milano

Sheet music, featuring old songs with new picture. *Pericle Formenti archive*

Chapter 6

In Rock

"If it's not dramatic or exciting, then it doesn't have a place on this album."

The year is 1970, and heavy metal is about to be invented, or invented proper, or at least formalized, notably across four very convincing full-length albums.

But initially, Deep Purple's groundbreaking *In Rock* album—one of the abovementioned fearsome foursome—would be tied up in knots, subject to Deep Purple finding themselves losing their US record label. With Tetragrammaton going under, it came to pass that Warner Bros. would buy out the band's back catalog for $40,000, not, fortunately for the band, offset as any sort of advance against royalties.

And if the diversion of the classical album wasn't enough of an additional spanner in the works, in the meantime Ian Gillan found himself singing the role of Jesus on the soundtrack album to the hit musical *Jesus Christ Superstar*, a gig that came about when manager Tony Edwards had sent Tim Rice and Andrew Lloyd Webber a recording of Ian howling his way through "Child in Time." For his part, Gillan would have preferred to have done the role onstage, but Purple's schedule was just too tight. Instead, Ian knocked off his songs in a matter of hours, and the album went on to sell eight million copies, a boon for Gillan given that Edwards had negotiated for him royalties instead of a flat rate.

What's more, Ritchie Blackmore found himself in one of those supergroup jam situations, recording the *Green Bullfrog* sessions for Decca with Big Jim Sullivan, Ian Paice, Tony Ashton, Chas Hodges, and Matthew Fisher, among others. They were credited under silly pseudonyms, the music was unsurprising and casual old-time rock 'n' roll, and not much notice was made of it.

Recalls Ritchie, "That was me, Albert Lee, and Jim Sullivan. Ian Paice and Roger Glover were on it, and whoever else was around at the time. Tony Ashton was on it, I think. It was awful, disgusting. It was done in a day, and nobody knew what we were doing. I was embarrassed; I never heard that LP actually. I was there with my stack, Albert was there with his little amp and Telecaster, and Jim was doing his fingerpick stuff."

Green Bullfrog was recorded back in the spring of 1970 but didn't emerge until March 19, 1971. Essentially a pile of blues covers, the record was commandeered by Deep Purple Mk. I producer Derek Lawerence. Engineering was Martin Birch, soon to figure prominently in the Deep Purple story.

All the while, playing live simply to keep the band afloat would interfere with the recording of the new Deep Purple album, which would be spread over many months, with the band ultimately recording the tracks at three separate studios. Incidentally, the first live show by the Mk. II lineup would take place on July 10, 1969, at the Speakeasy, and there was Ian, right off the bat, playing his ubiquitous congas! Then there was the stress of the "Concerto" rehearsals, the concert and the subsequent album release, not to mention the ensuing confusion in the press and within the fan base about whether Deep Purple had gone classical. Still, there was an excitement in the air as a clutch of bold new songs slowly started to take shape.

What was also taking shape was a sound; namely, a grinding and more expansive and powerful Hammond and guitar fusion than the one Mk. I had been toying and tinkering with. As discussed, the foundation for how Ritchie and Jon Lord would interact goes back to Vanilla Fudge. Here's Ritchie offering his homage to that source, adding, as well, a few choice words on the band's brash new competition in these specific stakes, Uriah Heep.

"Our biggest influences in the band were Vanilla Fudge meets Mountain—two American bands from Long Island. Paicey used to love the Vanilla Fudge drummer, and we loved the sound that Mountain got. So that was a big influence to us. And of course, Zeppelin had just done their heavy-rock stuff in '69, so we were aware of that sound. But what I said to Jon Lord was 'Look, Jon, the trouble with what we're doing is that we're showcasing our musical abilities, but we don't have a direction here. One minute we're playing with orchestras and then we're playing a rock song and then we're playing a ballad.' And I said, 'I think we have to make a whole record of hard rock songs.' Because I wanted to get that out of my system, at the time.

Ostseehalle, Kiel, Germany, May 28, 1970. © *Friedrich Magnussen (1914–87), CC BY-SA 3.0 DE, Wikimedia Commons*

"And he said, 'Yeah, great.' So, we did that; we were very pleased with the way it came out. And of course, it did very well, especially in England. In Europe, it was like #1 for like a year. Everything was so natural. You would go into the studio, play it; everything would work. You know, after three hours you were nearly finished, each song. Whereas sometimes, it's like pulling teeth, going into the studio. We would take two weeks over one track and have all sorts of problems and go through that period of thinking it's just not a good idea. So, everything just worked naturally with *In Rock*, and I love that. We just went into the studio, and every song worked out the way it should have worked. And that's how Deep Purple *In Rock* worked. It was very easy to make."

Paice concurs, almost to the letter. "Not so much the English bands. Fudge was very important to those first couple of albums, when we were into the big, arranged stuff. But Mountain was on the scene then, and we thought they were great. So that sort of crept in. Hendrix was still really important to us, even though the heyday had gone, and it started drifting down. Cream was very important. These bands have the ability to play and then go somewhere else. Okay, that's the verse; let's do something else for five minutes. Sooner or later, we'll get back to the verse again. So, the bands that actually played were always in our consciousness."

"Uriah Heep were coming up at the same time, and they had a good vocalist going," continues Ritchie, "but I think there was a bit of copying going on there, to be quite honest. Because they were like about a year behind us. And I know them quite well. Yeah, there was. It was a bit kind of disconcerting, when I'd meet them. David Byron would say, 'Hey, we're catching you guys up!' Everything revolved around catching you guys up. And there would be periods when I would hear certain little throwaway things I would do onstage. I used to do this Bach's piece, just as a novelty thing, and then suddenly Mick Box would be playing it the next time I saw him. So, there was some copying going on there. I'm not having a go at them, but you know when somebody is listening to you and copying you. It's not just coincidence. They were a very good band, and I love stuff like 'Lady in Black' and 'Gypsy,' some of my favorite songs."

"I always found that difficult to take seriously," says Heep keyboardist Ken Hensley, with respect to those sorts of accusations. "The only comparison between Deep Purple and us is that we emerged about the same time and there were five people in the band. They had no vocal harmonies. They didn't structure their songs anywhere near like we did, and that's not to say one was any better or worse than the other, but I found it was a little blinkered for that comparison to be made. I loved it when we went out and toured with them, because then people could clearly see the difference. I mean, both acts are valued in their own way and in their own sense. Both bands contributed something important. But the differences were much more obvious when we played together live.

"I'll tell you what I think it was," opines Ken, looking way back, to the birth of hard rock and Heep's place in it. "There was a convergence of stars and influences taking place in the late '60s. You had the blues, which drifted over from the early '60s, and that got really big. You had early rock 'n' roll in the form of Elvis Presley, Bill Haley and the Comets. That was typical rock 'n' roll, but it was rhythmic, and the lyrics didn't matter too much. Then emerging from that you had Dylan, the Beatles, and then the Who. So, if you look at the music that came around in the late '60s in the form of Zeppelin, Sabbath, Deep Purple, and Uriah Heep, it was a convergence of all those stars which manifested themselves in just straight-ahead, high-energy rock 'n' roll.

"And then somebody gave it the name 'heavy metal,' and I never understood that and probably never will. But that is what it was to me, more of a convergence of musical styles. The gap was there; the space was there. It was a good time to be going off in some new direction. I could flash back to early Stones and bands like the Pretty Things, who really were very rebellious in terms of their volume and style and reckless abandon. So, I think we just refined that a little bit."

Hensley confirms that everybody was well aware of each other. "Oh yeah! We used to play a lot of European festivals together, and we all hung out together. Those were some of the funnest times I can recall, playing these big old open-air festivals in Germany, which is really where European heavy metal was born, because it was so much more readily encouraged and accepted there first over anywhere else. Deep Purple and Uriah Heep used to rehearse in the same building. We used to just keep turning the volume up to see who was loudest. And we always won [laughs]."

Adds Uriah Heep guitarist Mick Box, underscoring the Hensley line, "Well, the one major difference between Deep Purple and Uriah Heep is that we've got five vocalists, and they've got one. Harmony is one of the major essences of us being different from them, really. Because we were the first band to use harmony in a really hard way. Back in the '60s it was used really soft, very Beach Boys, if you like. And we tended to treat it almost as another instrument. So that was a major difference. Yeah, we did rehearse in the early days in a place called Hanwell, a community center in Acton. There were two big rooms there, and one was for Uriah Heep and one was for Deep Purple, as it were [laughs]. It was a hell of a racket, but exciting times. So, harmony has always been the big difference."

Mick, like the Purple guys, understands all too well the albatross that is the Hammond.

"Yes, it was very expensive, and, don't forget, the Hammond organ is like taking a big wardrobe around full of clothes. It's just a very heavy, lumpy piece of equipment. But the best thing about the Hammond organ is that you've got all the dynamics that we have in our music. It can be romantic, very soft, very quiet, or it can be very aggressive; it has all of those qualities, pretty much the same as a guitar, really. And when we started out, really, we went into the studio as a four-piece, and when we heard what was coming back, we decided we would embellish it with keyboards.

"At the time, I was a very, very big Vanilla Fudge fan, and with their Hammond organ and distorted guitars and the volume, we thought, yes, that would be fantastic. So, we started putting some keyboards onto the music we already recorded, and that suddenly became the template of what Uriah Heep was going to be about, an exciting part of what we do.

"There was a real creative spirit in the '70s. When you would get your record deal, you would sign for five or six albums, and the canvas was wide open. That's why you had so much experimentation. Deep Purple weren't so much an influence but a contemporary. Like I say, we used to rehearse in the same space, this big community hall in Acton, which was just split into two sections. Our sound was just down to the lineup at the time. We would just jam and get off on the vibe of all of us learning at the same time, to be honest. It was the joy of playing and respecting each other's abilities. We just played hard progressive rock. The term 'heavy metal' was invented way after all these bands—Deep Purple, Sabbath, Heep—were successful. Heavy metal was just a journalistic pigeon hole."

Last word on the subject goes to Roger Glover, who, when asked if there was any copying going on by Heep, says, "In a word, yes [laughs]. I remember the first time I ever saw Uriah Heep was on television, and we'd come back from a gig somewhere, and it was at a flat we had in Fulham—Jon Lord and I and Ian Paice.

Ritchie Blackmore, KB Hallen, Copenhagen, Denmark, November 14, 1970. © *Jørgen Angel*

I think we had arrived back late at night, and it was one of those late-night rock shows. There was a band on, and we sort of looked at it, and Jon went over to the TV, turned it up, and we listened to it for a bit, and Jon went back over, turned it down, and said, 'I don't fuckin' believe it. They just ripped us off! They're doing all our tricks, all our trademark bits and pieces, the silly guitar bit, the organ.' And that's how I first saw Uriah Heep. In fact, their nickname used to be You're All Sheep.

"However, credit where credit is due, they are a band that has survived. And any band that survives, really, is due a pat on the back. They did carve their own career out of it. I mean, I think they were uncomfortably similar to us at times. But that's a serious form of flattery, if you like. And they have carved their own thing out, and we became friends and in fact we worked with them since. I saw Mick Box a couple of months ago at a European festival. They're a nice bunch of guys, and they're survivors. So, I don't hold any grudges. But in answer to your question, that's how we felt at the time."

One additional curio with respect to influence: back in the day, Arthur Brown and his lone hit "Fire" from his lone album *The Crazy World of Arthur Brown*, at the top of his fame, had famously claimed Deep Purple to be "an extension of the Crazy World sound." Ian Gillan, according to Brown, somewhat agreed. "I think Alice Cooper has admitted a certain influence there, and yes, the people in Deep Purple too, from my vocal style. And from what I've read in reviews and things, the Pink Floyd stage show was influenced by us as well. So yes, it's been there. There's been a reasonable amount of influence. But yes, Ian Gillan, with his high screams, has said as much, which was nice of him."

The tracking of what was to become *In Rock* was done at high volume and with no typical producer in sight. The production credit would go to the band, with the all-important engineers listed as Andy Knight (the first sessions, at IBC Studio A, Portland Square, London), Martin Birch (De Lane Lea, "Flight of the Rat" and "Hard Lovin' Man"; Martin had engineered for the Mk. I version of the band), and Philip McDonald (Abbey Road, which were the last sessions).

For cover art, the guys went with a painting that depicted the band's faces on Mount Rushmore. It was a bold idea,

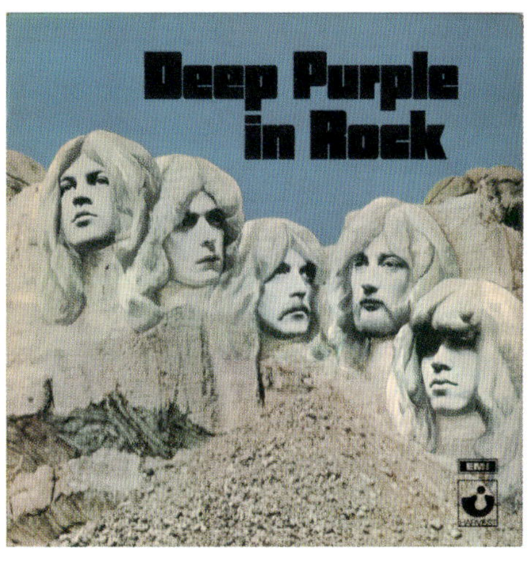

Cover art and side 1 record label of original UK issue of *In Rock*

but frankly a little boring in the end, given the dull colors and not particularly imaginative application of text.

"Great idea, terrible execution," says Paice. "You can see the joins. It's a failing we've actually done many times throughout our career, and that's not having somebody follow through on the smallest details to make sure they're done properly. And it always happens when you leave somebody else to do it; they generally knacker it up. With the cover, you know that if one of us had taken a real close interest in the proofs, we'd have said, 'No, you've got to take those lines out; you've got to airbrush those out.'"

The inner gatefold was even worse, not that Deep Purple's use of this particular piece of real estate ever turned out all that impressive. But at least we were offered the lyrics, as well as quite insightful and sage-like quips commenting on each song. We've all seen them, but they are worth a reminder, the full tab reading "Speed King / Just a few roots, replanted"; "Bloodsucker / A particularly nasty sort of fellow, there are lots of us"; "Child in Time / The story of a loser—it could be you"; "Flight of the Rat / Just to remind you there are other ways of turning on"; "Into the Fire / Out of the frying pan . . ."; "Living Wreck / It takes all sorts—support your local groupie"; and "Hard Lovin' Man / For Martin Birch—catalyst."

That last one is telling. Birch would become a big part of getting Purple onto tape, and then years facilitating the same magic for the likes of Rainbow, Whitesnake, Black Sabbath, Blue Öyster Cult, and Iron Maiden.

"Martin was great; he was like one of the guys," says Gillan. "We could relate to him; he wasn't from another era. He didn't try to boss anyone around, and he always tried to really achieve what we wanted. It makes you realize how simple it all is, really. That's all there is to it. When we called him a catalyst, I think that was very true. He was. He was a good friend to everyone, we all loved him, and he was as near to my ideal of what a producer would be today: someone who has total empathy with the band. Someone who doesn't try to impose a producer's will or direction on things, except when it's needed. Just picking the stones out of our path, really, a guiding hand. I don't think any of us really knew anything other than that we were totally sick to death of the studio experiences we had before. We didn't want to be like that, so we decided we were going to produce it ourselves. But the bloody chaos of everybody leaning over the death desk . . . 'I can't hear this; I can't hear that,' and fucking Blackmore saying, 'Who the fuck do you think you are? Tom Jones?' when I said I can't hear the vocals. He basically didn't want to hear the vocals, except just as sort of noise in the background."

Adds Paice, "Martin was a great engineer. For his time, he was streets ahead of practically anybody in England. I think with Martin, eventually you ended up with Martin's sound rather than your own. But initially it was such a good sound, you didn't mind."

Joe Bouchard of Blue Öyster Cult says much the same, that band having made two of their greatest albums with Birch, right in that era where he worked with Black Sabbath and not long from setting up shop with Iron Maiden, exclusively.

"The first time I saw Deep Purple, we were in Chicago, and we had a day off," begins Joe, with his first impressions of Purple. "We went to the Deep Purple show at some amphitheater out of town, and it was pure pandemonium. We were just blown away. They started out with 'Highway Star.' They had the red cop lights going, and there was smoke. The place went absolutely nuts. And we played with them after that at a stadium in Florida, and ZZ Top was also on the bill.

"And then every once in a while, I would run into Roger Glover in the studio. I think it was probably Kingdom Sound when we were making our records with Martin. And Martin Birch was good friends with Ritchie Blackmore, so we were invited to Ritchie Blackmore's house in Huntington Bay, Long Island. And he was the nicest guy! When he was on tour, he was like a tyrant [laughs], but when you went to his house, it was like, whoa, hey, the nicest, sweetest guy. He had no studio in the house. I think he had like one guitar, and he just didn't do any music at home. It was very nice, kind of plain, a Long Island house, very classy. Huntington Bay is a very classy part of Long Island, right on the water; everybody there has a boat. I think it was a Tudor, and he had a little pub off the living room. One end of the living room was made out to be a pub. So, it was a very nice visit.

"Unfortunately, when he started Rainbow, and we were out with Blue Öyster Cult, we had a little run-in, and it was not good. We were playing in Denver, and Rainbow were playing and they were just way over time, and our manager, Steve Schenck, pulled the plug [laughs]. He pulled the plug on them, and that was the end of their set, and we never saw Rainbow again after that. You don't want to have to do those kinds of things, but you're talking . . . it's a big city, it's a very expensive room, we're already going to go over time and pay all these extra charges—and for what? You know, we don't mind giving somebody extra time if they're doing really well, but it was just way over that. Like way over time. So, it was kind of bad.

"But yes, the reason we got Martin to do *Fire of Unknown Origin* and *Cultösaurus Erectus* was because of *Machine Head*. Martin Birch was great to work with, really kind of laid back as a producer. But he would tell us that he had the same style when he was working with Deep Purple. He didn't try to get in the way of the music. He let it happen. Those records have a lot of spontaneity, and he would fix the things that had to be fixed up, but there are still a lot of flaws in those Deep Purple records. But it adds to the fun, and obviously they are huge hits all over the world. His style was good because he knew just where everything was. You could have a big complicated twenty-four-track setup, and he just knew exactly what he was looking for. I mean, since he recorded this stuff from inception, he knew exactly how he wanted to mix it, and if there was a problem, he would sort of lay back and wait until we solved the problem. Then he would jump in and say, 'Ah, that's it!' because we were searching for this thing. So that was his approach, and I imagine he would have had the same approach with Deep Purple. That they would really work something out and then he would say, 'That's it! Let's tape it now before we lose it!'"

"Martin was one of my best friends," adds Ronnie James Dio, who worked with Birch within Rainbow as well as Black Sabbath. "Martin came to the Sabbath situation because I called him. Tony asked me if Martin might be interested in doing it. I called Martin and said, 'I'm just joining Black Sabbath; are you interested? Would you like to do this?' And he went no. Because I'm sure, like a lot of people, he thought that there was a time when Sabbath was incredibly successful, and he remembered them more from a nonmusical attitude. After all, he had been doing Purple all these years, and you're talking some pretty stiff musicians—by stiff, I mean really great people. And I think, like everyone else, he thought, 'Oh, I don't know about this. I don't want to get into that can of worms.' I reassured him that 'you're going to love it, and you're going to love the songs that we're doing. You've always loved me. You know I wouldn't do anything that wasn't great.'

"So, he went okay, and he loved them right away, and they just adored Martin too. Just a brilliant, brilliant guy. Again, he was able to capture all the sounds that we needed because he was a great engineer, the best engineer I ever worked with. As far as that goes, I thought it was just an easy process, because he had a wonderful sense of humor, and everybody appreciated that sense of humor, and he gave them his expertise, something that they'd never had before. Had Martin not retired and been a fisherman or a golfer or whatever he may be now, we would always want to use Martin again. But Martin wasn't available when we did the reunion album, *Dehumanizer*, because he had really dropped out of the field by that point. And Mack was Martin Birch's assistant engineer, at Musicland in Munich, where we did that album, and where I had done a lot of the Rainbow material. So, I knew Mack from that. I love Mack's great sense of humor, great ears, technically brilliant. Martin was different. I can't tell you that one is better than the other because I'm biased, because Martin has been my friend for such a long time, and truthfully, having been a producer myself, I learned so much from him. And he will always be the best producer for me."

Promo photo of the Mk. II lineup. *Pericle Formenti archive*

Back to Purple and Martin's coming-out party, if you will: the first session for *In Rock* produced "Living Wreck" and, more importantly, explosive album opener "Speed King."

"Speed King" is immense in the annals of heavy metal because one could cogently argue that the song single-handedly invented the modern era of the genre, usurping anything we heard on the first Black Sabbath album. Uncompromisingly riffy and based nowhere on the blues, "Speed King" is a complex and fully visionary heavy metal barnstormer that quickly builds upon songs such as "The Wizard," "N.I.B.," and "Black Sabbath." It's a throughline that takes us from *Black Sabbath*'s release date of February 13, 1970, through to *In Rock* hitting the shops on June 5, 1970. Like I say, Uriah Heep also deserves some credit—and also this very month, in 1970—and then so does *Paranoid*, later in the year.

"That was originally called 'Kneel and Pray,'" notes Gillan, "which had another meaning altogether. But no, there was no talk or realization of inventing heavy metal as it were. We wanted to write our own songs. I think Jon, Ritchie, and Ian . . . that's why they wanted to change the lineup of the band from the one that did 'Hush,' 'Kentucky Woman,' etc. They wanted to be writing their own stuff. So that's why they brought Roger and me in, because we were already a kind of songwriting team. And so it just happened, really, pure luck.

"If you listen to Jethro Tull, you'll see that they're very obviously based in folk music. If you listen to Free, you see they're very obviously based in soul music. And if you listen to Zeppelin, it's blues, as you've said. With Purple it's kind of weird, because Jon grew up in the Royal College of Music, so his background's in orchestral music and jazz. Ian Paice grew up in the Buddy Rich school of music, so big band and swing—stuff like that was the major influence in his life. Roger Glover was into Lonnie Donegan and every form of ethnic music you could imagine, folk music basically. And of course, when Dylan came along, that was Roger's idol. And Ritchie and I were pretty much pop, rock, sort of country, and then delving into the blues and jazz.

"So, we had a fairly diverse set of influences, and so when the band came together, just an expression, it was enthusiastic and loud [laughs]. I don't know, I've always just been lucky, I think, standing in the middle of these guys. They're just great musicians; that's what it is. I've never, ever imagined . . . we never even had any ambitions to have our photographs taken. There was never any ambition to be stars or anything like that. We just wanted to play music; you know?"

But *In Rock* is really the start of something, a real blip on the radar screen.

"It is; you're right. With the benefit of hindsight, it looks to be a pretty significant record. And I think there are things like that, because I've listened to almost everything that came out of Seattle, and I can trace it almost directly to Tony Iommi, in my opinion."

Ian also recalls that "Speed King" was the first thing the band had written together—instigated from a Roger Glover riff—and that it was such an impressive blast of aggressive music that he almost started speaking in rock 'n' roll tongues at the challenge of keeping up with what Ritchie was doing. Hence the memorable nearly stream-of-consciousness intro where Gillan essentially riffs about his rock 'n' roll upbringing.

And what was a speed king? Not what you'd think, says Ian. "'Speed King' was about fast singing, believe it or not. Everybody thought it was about speed, drugs, whatever. But it was about fast music. A bit of a literal one there—took everyone by surprise." Ritchie loved the track as well. It fulfilled his desire to kick off the album with something fast like "Fire" by Jimi Hendrix, and also to respond to Led Zeppelin, who were living large off *Led Zeppelin II* by this point, introduced to the world in October 1969. That album also contributes to this new form of music, as does the first album and even *III*, through basically a trio of songs, all on the first side.

Press shot, *left to right*: Ian Gillan, Jon Lord, Roger Glover. *Pericle Formenti Archive*

As a point of trivia, the original UK version of "Speed King" starts with a caterwaul of a wind-up, framed by Ritchie on very electrocuted whammy over a mess of distorted recorded sounds of the underground, followed by Jon with a churchy and, at one point, comical organ solo. The US version of the song begins with a simple snare whack, and we're straight into the glorious business of announcing to the world a virtually new kind of music. The demo version of the song is slower and more relaxed, with Jon playing piano rather than organ—necessarily, the solo section is radically different from the official. This can be heard on *The Deep Purple Singles A's and B's* compilation from 1978.

We've seen Ian Gillan somewhat flummoxed with this proposal that Deep Purple invented heavy metal. But what's amusing is that you get much the same confusion from the Black Sabbath or Judas Priest guys with respect to this concept or debate. Deep Purple's powerhouse of percussion can offer only similar vague points of recognition.

"When we started, there was no such thing," reflects Paice, on whether one would call Deep Purple a heavy metal band. "What happened was bands like Purple, Sabbath, and Zeppelin, and Cream and Hendrix, had a facet of their music which was hard and aggressive—but it was one facet. What happened in the next generation of bands, they took that one thing and they made it their everything. And so that to me is what metal is. It's part of something we spawned. But we had other things that we did. What metal bands did is that they just took that one idea, and they just concentrated it. So no, we don't feel we have any connection with metal music. It's so far mutated from whatever spark bands from our generation started with. It has nothing to do with us whatsoever.

"Again, I'll go back. What happened then was the only thing that could happen. It couldn't have been anything else, because it wasn't a conscious decision to make that album. With the personnel change, when you change two people in a five-piece band, that's a hell of a lot of . . . that's a big percentage swing. And what you have is a totally different chemical balance, a totally different emotional balance. With two totally different quantities in the band, whatever they do will affect you, and whatever you do changes what the next guy feels. And just the way the music came together, the way the songs were written, Ian's and Roger's take on what it was going to be lyrically; everything changed in an instant. It wasn't a conscious decision. It was something we wanted to do before, but we couldn't.

"Because Rod, God bless him, didn't have the voice that could do that. He also didn't have the songwriting skills to create some of those things. But we didn't sit

Ian Paice promo photo. *Pericle Formenti archive*

down and say, 'Okay, we're going to make a record that's going to be like this.' What happened was, as soon as we got together and started rehearsing, the music started coming out that way. Again, most things are not conscious creations; they just have to be that way. You have no choice in it."

Sure, there's Ian and Roger joining, but how does that have such a pronounced effect on the biggest change in the band; namely, this torrent of doomy heavy metal riffs previously heard only sporadically and pretty much never this modern and devoid of the blues? Surely, out of everybody, it's Ritchie who has transformed the most.

"Well, yeah," begins Paice, "but I think all the ideas that Ritchie wanted to use but really couldn't with Rod and Nick, when Ian came into the band, all of a sudden, he had a different vocal range to work with, and a different power and intensity vocally to back it up, to use. And Ian's voice, when he decides to make it shattering, is exactly that. So, you can make it as hard as you want or you can make it as high as you want—you can do what you want with it. So it opens up a vista in front of you. You're not stuck in this narrow lane of what is possible for a limited-range voice.

"And Roger Glover's bass playing . . . Roger doesn't know how good he is; he never has done. But he is a superb player, and he generally knows exactly what to do without thinking about it. So that was refreshing as well. Nick was a great bass player, but there was a lot of baggage from before, a lot of late '50s, early '60s stuff which he couldn't let go of. And I'm not saying . . . there's a lot of great stuff from that period, I love a lot of it, but you have to keep looking at how you improve. You have to keep taking more things on, while still holding true to your own beliefs about it. But you can't keep playing 1958 forever."

In conversation with Sam Dunn, Paice elaborates on this shift from the old to the new, at this point talking us through how we get to this place from the classical album.

"*In Rock* was the direction. That was the main street we were driving down. The *Concerto* was a side road, and it was something Jon really wanted to try to do. As usual, within the band, we said we'll try to help you do it. But it was always a dead end, as far as the band would go. Look, a rock band can play with an orchestra and play a piece of music which may be deemed to be semiclassical, and yes it does work to a point. And that point is that four rock 'n' roll guys would totally outstrip, volumewise, a ninety-piece orchestra. So, there's a compromise on both sides. I remember we made the record, and we couldn't hear one thing the orchestra played. We just had to trust that we were somewhere in the same bar of each other, because we didn't know.

"And when we did it twenty-five years later, when we could hear the orchestra, and you think that should make it easier, it doesn't. Because then you lost the freedom you had as a kid, when you didn't even know the orchestra existed. So everything is a compromise when you do that. It's interesting as an exercise, and I'm glad I did it because I can say yes, I played with orchestras. I've been a virtuoso player with an orchestra. But it's hard work and it's not something I'm actually . . . it's not my focal point in music. But Jon wanted to do it, and Jon was in the band, and we did it. And we had a good time doing it."

"That's the received wisdom, but it's not actually the case," corrects Jon Lord, asked by Sam if the heaviness of *In Rock* was in reaction to the *Concerto* album. "In fact, if you look at the recording of the *Concerto for Group and Orchestra*, on the same concert we played 'Child in Time.' So we'd already written 'Child in Time' that summer, and it had been performed live elsewhere up and down the country. We were already embarking on *In Rock* as a recording project when we started working on the *Concerto*.

"So no, it wasn't a reaction. What it was, however, was a reaction to the slight preciousness of the first three albums. Of the feeling that we had something really rather good and interesting, but it wasn't gelling right. It wasn't making the right noise somehow. And fortunately—unfortunately for Nick Simper and Rod Evans—we came to the conclusion that it was their fault. It wasn't their fault, but they were not the two right guys to help Paice, Blackmore, and myself quite realize where we wanted to go, or to realize that we were on a certain journey that they weren't helping us out with. It's a difficult subject, that, because it involves two guys who were great friends at the time and had done a lot of hard work trying to make Purple the band it became.

"But Gillan and Glover took their places with honor and took it onwards. But really the *Concerto* is a byway for the band, not for me. For me it became a massively important moment in my life. But for the band it was like, hey, we can do this. Now let's get back to what the band is really all about, which is *In Rock*."

As for the new record's relentless riffing and power chording, Jon says, "Again, we were responding to an inner compulsion, and the inner compulsion was driven by an exterior world, something around us that was driving us towards the way . . . I wanted the organ to get louder and fiercer and harder. I wanted the contrast. I'll go back to 'Child in Time.' That's why I love 'Child in Time,' because we start about as quiet as Purple ever got, and we get about as loud as Purple ever got, in one small song, a journey. There was a feeling that barriers had to be pushed, had to be moved outwards. I think I was just responding to—to use a ten-dollar word here—I was responding to the zeitgeist of the time. That was what pushed the band towards, well, this journey that we'd actually begun without realizing where we were going. But when we got to Deep Purple *In Rock*, everybody in the band knew exactly where we were going. We couldn't have named the place we were going to, but we knew what we were going to be doing when we got there. If that makes any sort of sense at all, then good luck."

For his part as to why *In Rock* ended up so heavy—and, for the record, it has six squarely heavy metal numbers on it, and only one not so heavy song, "Child in Time"—Ian Paice reiterates that "it was the first album we created when Ian and Roger joined the band, so the songwriting immediately changed. What we'd acquired was we had an amazing voice, but we acquired another riff master. Ritchie writes great riffs, but so does Roger. They're bass riffs, but the mixing of the two together came up with four or five ideas which were very solid. And with this different sound on top, this amazingly powerful voice on top and these riffs everywhere, it couldn't help but be heavy.

"We were playing all the time, and we'd record a track between two live dates, so everybody was what you might call match fit. You didn't have to say we've been off the road for three months writing songs, and now we're going to make a record. You could do it, but maybe you wouldn't play the same way as if you'd been touring for four weeks and had a day off and went straight in. You play better when you're doing it all the time. If you had three months off writing music, you don't play badly, but maybe you don't play the same way. I think *In Rock* captured a lot of that live ability, which, off the road for a few weeks, maybe you lose that 1 percent, which makes a difference."

Asked by Sam the extent to which there was a desire for the record to be this heavy, Ian says, "Again, it's not conscious. You find yourself in a set of parameters that says the only way this will work is if I do this. If they're coming up with this song and I play it like I'm in a lounge trio, it's going to sound like crap. But if I do it this way, it's going to sound right. So, you're led to the only logical conclusion you can have per piece of music. And as the band develops, the direction becomes more focused, and you find that the music has to be played this way. It's enjoyable, but you're sort of funneled into this only logical conclusion.

Paice then underscores the fact that Roger is "a great constructor of riffs. To this day, when we're messing around in the dressing room before we go onstage, he'll still be finding riffs, finding little things to do. As that's his driving force, when I say he plays simply, I don't mean that as a put-down. He leaves lots of room, and the more room he leaves, the more I can do. When Glenn Hughes was in the band, Glenn's a fabulous bass player but he's much busier. His whole attitude was much different. And as a rhythm section, you've only got 100 percent. Roger plays 30 and gives me 70 to play around with. But a bass player who plays 50 or 60, I've only got 40 or 50 to play around with. So, the way Roger plays allows me to do more things, which, over the course of all these years, has allowed more people to take notice of me. So, Roger, in that respect, is really kind, the way he plays for me. But when he plays, he plays exactly what you need him to play, and he doesn't play any more. You've got it down exactly right."

"Roger was incredibly enthusiastic," seconds Jon. "Still is. He's a total music enthusiast. He was also a good lyric writer, and he and Ian Gillan had written songs together, so that was a big plus too. But Roger, I think he'd started as a guitarist. So, he'd moved to bass, and I think it had perhaps been more a necessity than a need. So, he played a bit more like a guitarist. Nick Simper played quite—and again, I hope he doesn't take this as a criticism, because it's not—but he played quite a '60s-style bass, sort of pop bandish. Roger had much more of an eight-to-the-bar feel. And Roger was very good at little riffs. 'Speed King' is a riff of Roger's, not of Ritchie's. I think that's what Roger brought, and this massive enthusiasm, this almost puppy dog enthusiasm at first. We can do this, we can do that, we can do anything."

On the subject of the centrality of the riff in heavy music, Paice begins by laying out a contrast. "I think if you have a solo songwriter in an outfit who comes along with a finished song, chord sequence, basically you're playing somebody else's music. It doesn't make it bad; you're just playing somebody else's music. When you're creating pieces of music between the five of you, sometimes it has to start with something that is immediate and memorable. Good riffs are immediately memorable, and they tend to come from guitarists and bass players. It's the nature of the instrument they play. Most great rock 'n' roll tunes are riff driven. They just are. What comes afterwards is not important. What started it was the riff. And the riff may become hidden inside the melody, but it was a riff that started it. 'Lucille' is a riff. The rest of it becomes great, but without the riff it's nothing. 'Smoke on the Water' without the riff is nothing. 'Crossroads' without the riff is nothing."

Adds Jon, on the concept of riffing, "Ian Paice discovered a way to make the bass drum and the bass shake hands with more force, and also with these sometimes quite complicated riffs that Ritchie was coming up with. I think Roger was easing them out into slightly more usable ways. He has a very good sensibility about where a song should go. He sees the arc of a song quite soon, and because of the way we were writing most of the material, which was based on improvisation, it needed a song architect to be around, and that was Roger a lot of the time. Plus, also, like I said before, he could pay eight to the bar very well indeed.

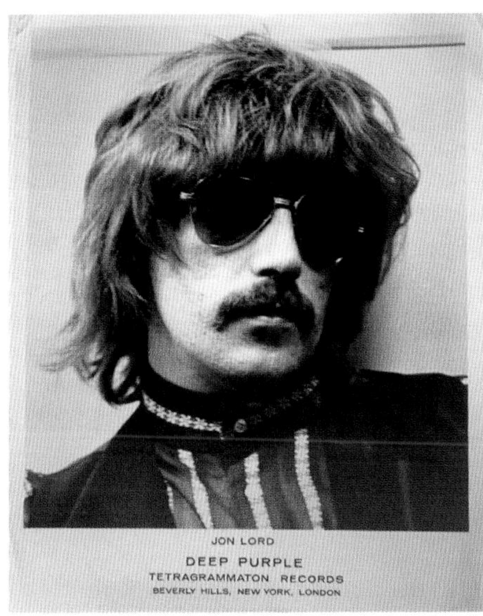

A couple of Jon Lord promo shots. *Pericle Formenti archive*

As for the importance of the riff, "The guitar was becoming more and more important, much to the chagrin of people like me who were trying to elevate the importance of the Hammond organ. It's rock 'n' roll. The guitar is the symbol of rock 'n' roll, and it's the sound of rock 'n' roll. Again, it's that animal ferocity that it's capable of, and that's exemplified by a great riff. The exception that proves the rule sometimes . . . if you listen to the riff of 'Smoke on the Water,' for example, which is often said to be one of the most famous guitar riffs ever, it actually achieves its strength by the confluence of the guitar and the organ being played in fourths. When the organ comes in on that riff, you know it's there. So, I'm pleading my case a bit there. But generally, I think what exemplifies hard rock is a great guitar riff. It's a way of leading you in; it draws you instantly. A great riff and a killer chorus, and you've got it made."

"I can only give you what I feel about it," reflects Ian, asked about how Ritchie Blackmore had changed. "Ritchie may turn around and say that's not right. I think Hendrix is very influential for broadening Ritchie's horizons. I think if you ask him now, he'd still say Beck was probably the best player around then, and he's probably the best player around now. There were a couple guys like that who thought outside the box, and I think Ritchie sat down with a guitar for a couple months and went, 'I can change.'

"If you go back to what Ritchie used to play pre-Purple, it's pretty standard; it's well played, but standard British lead guitar rock. The word 'reinvent' is used all the time now, but I think he probably did reinvent himself once Hendrix had happened and Clapton. Ritchie has a talent you cannot teach. When he can write riffs, he hears a sequence of notes in a certain way that other people didn't hear. Why wasn't 'Smoke on the Water' written fifty years before? It's so bloody simple, but nobody did it. So he has this genius inside him. I still believe if he wants to use it that way, he could still do it again."

Adds Jon on the Man in Black, "It seemed to me that Ritchie had this sound in his mind that he was always after, and he came close. If you imagine a 30-foot cello being played at 1,000 watts of volume, it might be what he had inside his mind somehow. That round and yet fierce sound that he got, as he got more towards his Rainbow days, I think, is where he finally found the sound he wanted. But it needed volume to make it happen, and it needed control of feedback, which he became very expert at. And he was a great showman, of course, as well. Quite as Little Bo Peep offstage, but onstage, capable of a kind of animal excitement. And I think he wanted more all the time. His famous phrase was 'Can we have everything louder than everything else?' And until you think about it, you go, sure, and then you go, uh, what does that actually mean? He was a great believer in the power of volume."

Comparing the early-days contribution of Led Zeppelin, Black Sabbath, and Deep Purple, Ian avows that "each of those bands is totally different. They have a different focal point, and the musical ability within each of the bands is a little bit better than the other guys around them, and the ability to translate that talent onto vinyl is the difference. So yes, nobody can go back and see Purple in 1969 and feel the emotion of it, but you can hear a pretty close facsimile of what it must have been like with these records, because the records captured the humanity. They captured the mistakes, they captured the genius, they captured the aura.

"Not just our records, but Zeppelin and Sabbath. You can see the smoke in the studio, you can hear the atmosphere, you can see the air. You just don't get it with new records. It's just not there. It's cleaned up to the point of, yes, you have a perfect product, but is it as good? I don't think so. Because at the end of the day, people are watching a human being, they're learning about me, I'm telling them stuff, and there's a connection there on that level. Music has to have that. If you take that away, it's just a product. It's just another thing. And if you don't have any connection with the people who created it, and you don't feel that we're living, breathing entities that helped make this happen, because it's so technically perfect, you don't get the connection. And when people hear these old records, they are a little bit better. That connection is exactly the same for the person hearing it now as the person hearing it forty years ago.

"I remember when my kids were small and early in their teens—my son especially. He'd be in watching MTV. He was about thirteen, and he started looking at albums and CDs. 'Who's this?' 'That's Jimi Hendrix.' 'Who's he?' I said, 'Well, go play it.' 'Yeah, that's great. Got any more?' 'Try Zeppelin, try this, try that.' He fell in love with those records. He said they just sound different. As a kid he couldn't analyze it; he just said they sound different. And they do sound different. And that connection between human beings is what makes them sound different."

Circling back around to the heaviness of *In Rock*, heavier than the first Black Sabbath album, in fact, Ian says that "there were lots of bands playing hard, loud rock music. The difference is how well you did it. You can get hit with the emotion of being someplace on a night where you see something you think is really impressive. And the next day maybe it wasn't so impressive. But when it was really good, it was still impressive. And those records—Zeppelin stuff, Purple stuff, Cream, Hendrix—they captured the ability and the uniqueness of those musicians. And that's what still flies out of the speakers to you. That's immediate, and it doesn't go away. Even if the people go away, that doesn't go away."

1970 concert ads. *Martin Popoff archive*

Back to the *In Rock* album: the second track, "Bloodsucker," was just as noggin' knockin' as the first, and actually more intensely heavy metal, given chords closer to what Tony Iommi might have conjured. Point blank, "Bloodsucker" demonstrated Ritchie's ability to be the best at this new music, top tier. The riff is smart and complicated and, again, without precedent, given that metal before this—proto-metal, as we like to call it—had come from loud psych, loud blues, and loud garage rock, end of story. Logistically, "Bloodsucker" would be the last track recorded for the album, at Abbey Road, up into April 1970, which perhaps accounts for its status as arguably the least 1960s-sounding song on the album. At the lyric end, Gillan and Glover examine the idea of one's early, soured relationships building character, or at least destroying one's innocence, teaching us that the stakes are raised in adulthood and that things are now no longer so carefree. It's hard to tell who the cad is, though, with the most plausible conclusion being that crap happening will make rogues out of any and all parties, given the opportunity for any one of us to be roguish.

"I like that song a lot," says Paice. "I thought that was not so much typical of us. It was one of those tunes which showed the way to a lot of other bands of a certain style of really hard, nasty playing. An unsung little gem, that one. It just became part of the *In Rock* album, but it's really a great song."

Side 1 of *In Rock* ended with "Child in Time," which is both long, at 10:17, and a ballad of sorts, maybe even a proto–power ballad. To be sure, the song rocks out dervish style as it wears on, and Gillan gets to work out extensively the high end of his range, but frankly, even its loud bits are oldish, and not on a creative par with the rest of the album. As a trivia note, Blackmore wields a Gibson on this track as opposed to his standard, harsher Fender Stratocaster. The song was well routined, having been played live already. It was recorded at IBC in November 1969, having been one of the early songs invented at the band's Hanwell rehearsal space.

"'Child in Time' was a nick," says Gillan. "We nicked it from a group called It's a Beautiful Day, who had a song called 'Bombay Calling.' We played that and slowed it down. It was very fast, and it was with a violin. So, we were just impressed with that, and we got into the rehearsal room one day and it just evolved out of a jam, really."

Gillan has also recalled at various times that it was Jon Lord who started playing something similar to "Bombay Calling," with Ian improvising some sentiments about the Cold War and the fragile nature of life amid it. Later, he took pleasure in the fact that folks on the other side of the Berlin Wall ended up hearing the tune and finding commonality in its warnings. There's also a closing chord that intentionally pays homage to "A Day in the Life" by the Beatles.

"That record was sort of a response to the one we did with the orchestra," remembers Ritchie, referring first to *In Rock* as a whole. "I wanted to do a loud, hard rock record. And I was thinking, 'This record better make it,' because I was afraid that if it didn't, we were going to be stuck playing with orchestras for the rest of our lives. 'Child in Time' is a great song. Ian Gillan was probably the only guy who could sing that. It was done in three stages. That's him at his best. Nobody else would have attempted that, going up in octaves. I think the guitar solo is relatively average. I did it in two or three takes. Back then, whenever it came to guitar solos, I was given about fifteen minutes. In those days that was enough for the guitar player. Paicey would be there tapping his foot, looking at his watch, going, 'How much longer?' And I'd be like, 'I've just got my sound together.' And he'd go, 'You going to be much longer?' Sometimes onstage I would play it much faster than the record. I'd like it really fast, and Paicey would like it really fast. The only problem was coming into that part at the end of the guitar solo that the band would do in unison. You can only play that so fast—unless you start tapping, which I don't do, out of principle. It's just an A-minor arpeggio, but it's all downstrokes. You try to play that really fast after you've had ten scotches! That's hard to do."

Further to the It's a Beautiful Day story, that band, in turn, sent up Purple's "Wring That Neck" for a track on their subsequent *Marrying Maiden* album called "Don and Dewey." Years later, in 1976, the Ian Gillan Band would call their debut album *Child in Time*, including a 7:23 version of the song on the record. Deep Purple Mk. II played the song live regularly, immortalizing it on the *Made in Japan* live album; however, its appearance in the set list diminished over the decades.

Side 2 opener "Flight of the Rat" is perhaps the most tuneful, most melodic, and most strictly chordal of the hard rockers on the album. It indeed feels like flight, briskly gliding along to creamy chords by Blackmore. Gillan explains that it's an attempt to articulate his transformation (partly through meditation) from the old, pessimistic, dark Ian Gillan to the progressively more enlightened and certainly excited and enthusiastic version of the man making such wonderful and invigorating music. It's a poetic and motion-filled lyric, perfect for the mystical times but not grave and occultish, more like playful, amused with its own wordplay, one example of that being the idea of a rat used as a metaphor for a drug habit.

Says Ian about the lyrics for the album, and, in the telling, offering a different version of the "Flight of the Rat" story than the one above: "Well, we combined. Roger and I joined together as a songwriting team and as well as bassist and vocalist. I can't remember much about it; we were so drunk. 'Flight of the Rat' just came out as . . . there's an orchestral piece called 'Flight of the Bumblebee,' so we were talking about some sort of psychedelic experience that somebody had told us about, and thought that they might have experienced the 'Flight of the Rat' as opposed to the bumblebee. So, I addled on and wrote some stuff about it."

"Flight of the Rat" is a favorite of Ritchie's but, alas, didn't make the live set due to Ian Paice's disdain for the drum part.

"I have one pet theory of why it's such a hard album," muses Roger, after taking heed of how many brisk rockers were on the album, "Flight of the Rat" being one of the more straight-ahead examples. "Although I think a lot of it has to do with the chemistry of the band. When I first met them, they used to rehearse in this big old gymnasium called Hanwell Community Centre, big, echoey, horrible sound, and I had never jammed before. I was in bands that you learn the songs and then you play those songs. So that was a revelation to me. They seemed to want to play their instruments; I was impressed with the way Jon and Paicey played their instruments to the full. Loud, turned up, they didn't care what anybody else thought. That was a good impression.

DEEP PURPLE

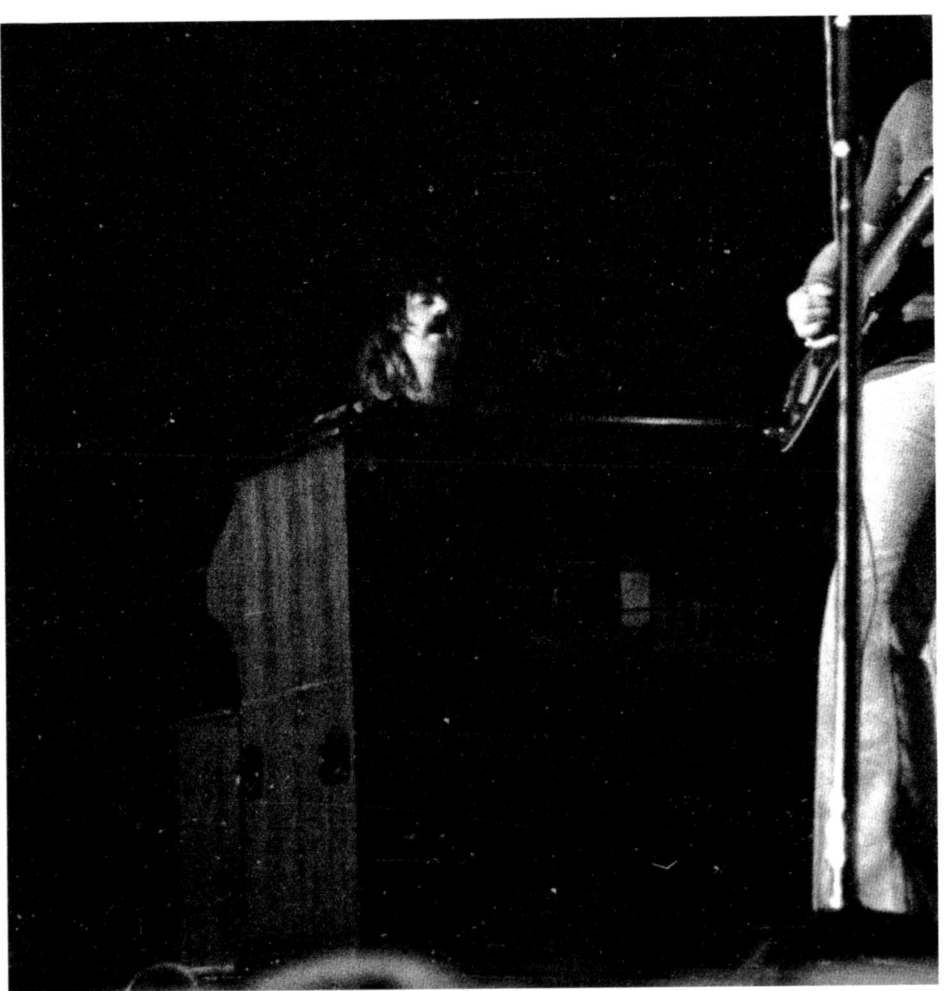

December 1, 1970, Niedersachsenhalle, Hannover, Germany, December 1, 1970. © *W. W. Thaler–H. Weber, Hildesheim, CC BY-SA 3.0, Wikimedia Commons*

"But the main reason, I think, is that when I first joined the band, the manager said to me that one of the first things you'll be doing is a concert at the Albert Hall with an orchestra. Jon Lord's written this thing, which is a concerto, and meanwhile we started doing gigs. The first gig was at the Speakeasy in London, playing mostly Mk. I material, and meanwhile in one of our first rehearsals we had already written 'Speed King,' although it wasn't called 'Speed King' at the time, and 'Child in Time.' 'Speed King' was actually called 'Kneel and Pray,' and there are several bootlegs of it with it called 'Kneel and Pray.' And I suppose we were evolving into quite a hard sound, which even in the beginning wasn't exactly soft.

"But I think the eighth gig we ever played was the *Concerto*," continues Glover. "And immediately it brought us to the attention of the media. We were in every newspaper—rock band and orchestra! But it was never meant to be that serious. And it had the effect of catapulting Jon Lord to the forefront of the band, to the point where he was being called the leader and the main composer, which got right up Ritchie's nose, and Ian Gillan's nose, specifically those two. And the rest of us, really, because Jon wasn't the leader. We were pretty much a democratic band; even though we were new, everybody pretty much had their say.

"This led to a great deal of resentment, especially when we turned up to gigs and the promoter would say, 'Where's the orchestra?' And we realized that we were being misrepresented. People thought of Deep Purple as some sort of artsy, pseudoclassical thing. And we weren't—we were a rock 'n' roll band. And yes, you are correct when you say we were no longer based in psychedelia and not really based in blues, but there was this classical influence. And what would happen in the studio is that there was this resentment, which built up, so we had a determination to put, once and for all, our stamp on what we were, which was a rock band, and not a classical, pseudo-artsy progressive band. Very simple straightforward rock. And it became hard rock, because heavy metal wasn't even a term that was around at the time. I remember it that way, anyway. I remember we were rock, but we were harder than that, so hard rock became our epithet. And I think that's the reason that the album is the way it is. I remember Ritchie saying at one time, 'If it's not dramatic or exciting, then it doesn't have a place on this album.' And those were pretty good words to live by."

In general, Roger was thrilled with the fact that all the ideas he was turning in for *In Rock* (including a stockpile from the Episode Six days) were both enthusiastically received for vigorous tryouts and then, in the testing, played brilliantly and deemed suitable for the record. Paice noticed the enthusiasm as well, which resulted in strong material that, in his opinion, was always purposeful, whether that be lyrically or as a showcase for the guys as musicians. As well, Paice was glad to shed the stigma of having hits as some sort of cover band, while Ritchie was relieved to finally put the classical experiment to rest.

German concert poster. *Pericle Formenti archive*

"'Into the Fire' was another thing about drugs," says Ian, with respect to the second track on side 2. This one's main dimension is its pushing of the instrumentation into the red, resulting in the album's most distorted and almost erroneous-sounding presentation. Jon Lord uses a Leslie speaker instead of a Marshall on this one, but everybody, in turn, sounds cooked and boiling and bubbly amid Lord's extreme textures.

It was a racket, to be sure, and that's the first thing that comes to mind when Ian Gillan recalls the *In Rock* sessions. "It was just yelling. There was a racket going on, and I just yelled, and that's all it was to me. It was just great fun just opening up and doing what came naturally, being very derivative in the early days, certainly not having anywhere near mastered the art of writing.

"But it was honest; it was naive. Looking back over the years, it's very clear to me that the best stuff is the stuff that comes out naturally. The stuff that requires more than a minute or two's thought is always the shit that sounds contrived at the end of the day. Beautiful, craftsmanlike songs that mean nothing are nothing to do with the spirit of originality, what the band was about.

"And we didn't want to get airplay," continues Ian. "We sneered at the idea. We wanted to make a conscious difference between rock music and pop music. And there is a difference to it. People have been confused over the years. People think that rock is just something that's louder than pop music, but it's not really that. Rock music is people saying exactly what they want to say. And it doesn't necessarily have to be loud or proud. It can be sad, and it can be tender and sensitive. But everyone's got their own idea of what rock music is. I grew up with Buddy Holly and the Everly Brothers as well as Little Richard and Chuck Berry. And Elvis used to sing some nice songs as well.

"But talking about Purple more specifically than the general thing, I didn't think about it at all at the time, but with the benefit of hindsight, it may come somewhere near to the truth. And one is, first of all, everyone could perform. There was a good, balanced chemistry, a suitable amount of eccentricity, and a suitable amount of common sense, I suppose. Drunkenness and sobriety mixed together in the right proportions."

"Into the Fire" certainly captures that loose vibe, with Gillan going full caveman with his celebrated "Into the fire!" screams.

As Ian Paice explained to Sam Dunn, "Ian was brought in exactly because he had this voice. God bless him, Rod Evans before that had a really nice voice but he was a balladeer. He was happier when he was singing nice gentle songs, and he didn't have the range to go up. Which, when you're going to try to create this overall sound . . . rock 'n' roll is so much about the sound, as well as what you may be singing about. Every voice is unique, but there's this sound that makes it right, and the songs are then slotted to this sound.

"And especially if the singer is one of the writers. Then he'll be writing top lines where he knows he's most effective. So, the whole thing is this inevitability. It has to be this way. You don't have a choice in it. You get some people saying, 'Why did you make the album like that?' Because we couldn't make it any other way. Whether it's *Fireball* or *Machine Head*, it couldn't have been any other way. If we had have done it any other way, it wouldn't be."

"Ian was a more heavy and aggressive person than Rod Evans," seconds Jon Lord. "Ian had quite a forceful—still has—personality. One that doesn't brook any interference with what his beliefs are, which I think was, in the end, the cause of the difficulty between him and Blackmore—they were both that kind of person. An immovable force and irretrievable position. So, he had this attitude. He had that astounding ability to hit that top A, the one you hear in 'Child in Time,' that meant his voice was enormously elastic and usable. He had a massive facility with words. He was very good with odd, quirky ways of looking at lyric writing. From Gillan, you never got your regular rock lyrics. Who else wrote a rock song about a casino burning down? Not many people have done that. So, we had this kind of slightly difficult-to-control element moved into the band in the form of Ian Gillan. But what it added to the band, to the mix, was invaluable."

And Gillan had to be a powerhouse to compete with the advancements in amplification going on.

Deep Purple share the stage with Paul Rodgers and Free, March 13, 1970, in Blackpool.

"Yes," agrees Lord. "What Ian Gillan had, or found himself in, or what he walked into . . . he was discovering himself, and his arrival helped us to discover ourselves. But what he walked into was the arrival of the belief and the knowledge that the guitarist was going to be playing louder. The keyboard player found a way to make the Hammond organ growl and turn into some sort of beast. It wasn't this polite piece of furniture anymore. And our drummer, in the same way Keith Moon was unbelievably exciting because he had no barriers, Paice was that plus technique. Keith was learning to swim while he was drowning. Paice had this astonishing technique that he arrived at, and he was able to flail about and push the emotion of what the band was doing.

"And what we saw was what by then we were calling hard rock. Gillan was able to match that, decibel for decibel, because he had this immense, strong voice. He's a strong man, a big guy. Handsome dude—I hated him for that. But he wasn't just a handsome dude; he was a big, strong man, not afraid of a confrontation. And he brought that to the mix. Immense ferocity sometimes in his singing. You listen to the anger in a song like 'Living Wreck,' where he's really annoyed that he's been fooled by this errant groupie that the song is all about.

"Gillan is a massively important part of the story of early hard rock because I think he grasped the essence of what hard rock was about before a lot of singers did. His peers were not doing that. Robert Plant was doing it in a very much different way. He was still one foot firmly in the blues. I think Ian Gillan was much more firmly in rock 'n' roll, and perhaps even soul music. He was a big fan of Cliff Bennett and the Rebel Rousers, that sort of West London soul, and I think Gillan was the first hard rock singer to understand what it meant to be a hard rock singer."

As alluded to by Jon, "Living Wreck," third track on side 2, is a humorous tale of a groupie turning out a little rougher than first conceived. Ian raises his histrionic game and Jon flash-floods the song with nightmarish washes. Recalls Paice on Mr. Lord's contribution to the maelstrom that is Deep Purple in its prime, "Jon was never really, for most of the pieces of music, Jon was never one of the guys who conceived riffs or rhythms, because that's not what he did. I mean, rock 'n' roll is pretty much a guitar-dominated form of music. So, guitarists tend to bring in more ideas; that's just the way it is. In the same way that drummers are the boss of the rhythm department, so they tend to come up with different feels and different rhythm patterns. But Jon's genius was, when somebody had an idea, he'd say, 'Well, that sounds great, but what if we did this to it?' And then he'd put a whole different chord inversion there, and what was good suddenly became magnificent. So, Jon's musical knowledge was where his strengths really were. When the idea was there, he would take it somewhere else."

As Dunn indicates, given Paicey along with the power of the C3, Ian had to compete or be crushed.

"Very much so," says Jon. "And luckily, he could compete because we gave him quite a lot of time off, because we had these long improvisation passages when we played live. Once he was famously missing at the end of a long improvisation passage and was found under the grand piano at the side of the stage with a certain pliant young woman who thought she was improving his life in some way, I think, and probably was. And he had to be pulled back into center stage to resume the end of the song. Oh, to be a lead singer, eh?"

As for Paice himself, who plays in the pocket and groovy on this butt shaker of a song, "I don't even try to analyze it. You know why? I've always thought, if I know too much about it, that might screw it up by trying to do something different. People say I have a different way of playing, a different style of playing rock 'n' roll, than a lot of other players. Well, then that's good enough for me, and I never really query it. When you have something that people treated as slightly individual, it's a very fragile thing. And you ask most people who have that . . . let's call it a gift. If they know what they're doing, they'll tell you they haven't got a clue. They'll tell you it's the only way they can do it. And if you start trying to break things down, you might say, well, if I don't do that anymore, and if I played this, making it a little bit better, and then all of a sudden you're not yourself anymore. You start losing the magic. Or you take the chance of losing the magic."

Asked how Glover dovetails with himself to form a rhythm section, Paice says that "as I explained earlier, the less notes the bass player plays, the more notes I can play. The more notes the bass player plays, the less I can play, because that starts to get cluttered. You start getting in each other's way. Roger leaves holes for me to do things. I did a couple of gigs with McCartney about five years ago, and Paul is sort of like Roger. He leaves holes, and that's so great to play with. Because you can put things inside the holes, or you can leave it empty. But it's amazing, the creative process when you have an empty page. And a hole is exactly that; you can leave it empty, or you can fill it in. But when everything is filled in, it's a little more difficult to pick out what's important."

"Living Wreck" benefited, in Paice's opinion, by having been cut at those first sessions, at IBC. "My favorite drum sound came out of there, and that was on 'Living Wreck.' It's a bonky little snare drum sound, but it's really live and metallic and hard and nasty. I like that studio lot. It was like somebody's huge living room; there was a fireplace in the corner and all sorts of things! Yeah, it was two stories high, wasn't it? They knocked a floor out. 'Living Wreck' was nice in its simplicity, and the actual rolling feel of it was good."

In Rock closes with another imposing and important hallmark of original metal. "Hard Lovin' Man" is widely considered the first heavy metal "galloper." Sure, Led Zeppelin's "Communication Breakdown" is framed on what is perhaps the first punky staccato machine gun riff, and then "Whole Lotta Love" refines this idea, while simultaneously adding complication as well as a nod toward gallop. But "Hard Lovin' Man" goes full gallop, while also raising the stakes on rapidity and rigidity. In this respect, it's the first proto-thrash song, where palm muting, the muting of the strings with the palm to shorten the notes, is paramount.

Elsewhere, and a million miles away from thrash, Jon Lord does some crazy atonal horror movie stuff, while Ritchie gets to add his own flamboyant noise—he's somewhat proto-Slayer in this respect. But again, the beauty of this one is its raging neometal riff—not proto-metal, because Deep Purple is now inventing heavy metal in real time.

The song is in fact Roger Glover's favorite on the album, due to its mixture of eccentric writing, its aggression and bravado, and its chaotic, dissonant soloing. As it turns out, Ritchie's incendiary demonstration of noise was pointedly designed to annoy someone who was not a rock 'n' roll engineer on the session, with Gillan wholeheartedly in agreement that there were far too many suit-and-tie types in the industry, that a housecleaning was in order.

Says Lord, "'Hard Lovin' Man,' where the guitar is doing this galloping kind of rhythm, I play a solo that goes just about anywhere, but in the chord that Ritchie's playing. You want to do whatever you can to slightly pervert that rather jolly German beer-barrel rock you might end up doing. I'm very proud of 'Hard Lovin' Man.' The solo on 'Lazy,' from *Made in Japan*, was also really inspired. I was off somewhere quite special."

"Hard Lovin' Man" is in fact Jon Lord's first solo excursion of real distinction, or at least the first that is widely remembered and celebrated, to this day, perhaps second only to what he does in "Highway Star." But of course, in heavy metal or in neo–heavy metal, the guitarist was king, not to mention the lead singer.

"It's always been the singer," concedes Jon, with a sigh. "In rock 'n' roll, the pivotal position, the point the audience was drawn to in the band was the singer. It was Billy J. Kramer and the Dakotas, Gerry and the Pacemakers, and so on. When we get into hard rock and the end of the '60s, then suddenly there's this eminence grise on the other side of the stage who starts to become even more and more apparent. You start to get the great guitarists coming out, because of the element of improvisational skill and songwriting that is coming from the guitarist. And therein lies the cause of many a battle.

"But we might have hit on an idea there. Maybe that's what hard rock was, was more performance-based rock 'n' roll. It's less about the singer standing up and singing a song and more about four or five guys examining their abilities onstage and examining a song in a way that was less about the singer and more about the sound that we were getting towards. And that sound was the sound of rebellion; it was the sound of the underground, in a way. Purple was a very underground band, until we started to get a hit single. What?! A hit single? But it was quite an underground experience."

As for his chosen weapon, the instrument that created the celebrated grinding Deep Purple keyboard, which we first hear, significantly, on *In Rock*, Jon explains that "the only difference between a B3 and a C3 Hammond is the B3 has legs. It's a spinet model. It has four rather shapely legs. I don't want to sound too interested in its legs, but that's what it does. Whereas the C3 is encased, and therefore for carrying around it was easier to split a C3's top from its bottom and was easier to carry around. A B3 would have to be pretty difficult to carry around, and it looked a little poncy, whereas the C3 was this great cabinet. It's got lots of wood. And when you lifted it up and dropped it on the stage, it made a very satisfying clunk, which pleased me greatly. I used to mistreat the poor beast rather terribly in the early days. I loved the mass of it, and I loved the feeling that I was somehow having to be in charge of it. If I just turned it on and tinkered with it, it would make a very wussy noise. So, turn it up, control it, make it growl. I loved climbing all over a Hammond organ. It was great."

Why it's sensible as a weapon to be used in defense of heavy rock, Jon says, first off, that "it has an enormous amount of low sounds. You pull out the lower draw bars and get a good lower note there and then start improvising on the top manual. The resulting growl and the sounds beating against each other is very satisfying. What I discovered in '69 is that if I took that effect, took it away from a Leslie and put it through a 200-watt Marshall amp and a big speaker box, then I had a beast. Then I had an almost uncontrollable beast, and here, now finally, I had something that could compete with Ritchie, you see? So, this was hugely important to me. Not because it was a battle, [which] he didn't enjoy being part of, and likewise me, but I wanted to emancipate the organ from being something that just sat in the background and colored the sound. I wanted it to create that hard sound.

"The first time I really became aware of what I could do with a Hammond on record was when I heard it joining in with the riffs on 'Living Wreck' and 'Speed King,' and then the organ solo in 'Hard Lovin' Man,' which was the first time I let myself loose in the studio to see exactly what I could make that beast do. That's when I discovered hard rock Hammond; it was the liberating of it from the Leslie speaker. I later found a way, of course, to bring the Leslie speaker back in by taking the amplifier out and replacing that with a Marshall amplifier. So, then the Leslie became a beast. So, I had beasts all around me, and I was a happy camper."

The result is what we call overdrive. It's an abstract term, or at least it can be used in the abstract, and there's also a gray scale to it. Additionally, it can apply equally to what Jon and Ritchie are doing.

"Yeah, and there's the point at which musicians became aware that they could overdrive the overdrive. And equipment manufacturers were responding to the need to be heard in bigger venues, of course. It wasn't just in the backroom of a pub anymore. Stadium rock, or at least arena rock, had started to be a regular thing. If you've ever watched the Beatles at Shea Stadium, bless them, I mean, nobody could have heard them anyway, because the girls were screaming. But there wasn't a lot of equipment onstage there. So, I think one side fed the other. The need to play in bigger places fed the need for equipment manufacturers to make that stuff possible, and then musicians started using the volume to a massive extent. Because raw volume, at the service of fast, exciting music, that's a heck of a combination. Almost unstoppable."

To reiterate, "Hard Lovin' Man" was firmly modern metal in 1970, and really, quite impressively, for all of the 1970s, pertinently and critically with no blues in sight.

"Blackmore is very self-contained," agrees Lord. "He practices as much as any musician I've ever met. But he's sometimes quite dismissive of other ideas. He has some sort of tunnel vision when it comes to playing. You have to understand, though, that a lot of the big guitarists of, say, the past twenty years came from a blues tradition. Ritchie never went the blues route at all. The only musician who ever heavily influenced him and had anything to do with blues at all was Jimi Hendrix, and that's a very different way of looking at the blues. Ritchie came from British rock of the early '60s, without that R&B influence that crept in later on."

And speaking of Hendrix, well, the ax legend figures into one of Lord's fondest tour memories of all time. "I'll never forget the time I jammed with Jimi Hendrix at Steve Paul's Scene club. It must've been around 1970. Whenever we were in New York, we either went to Max's Kansas City, a club on Bleecker Street called Nobody's, or the Scene club. The Scene had the most beautiful women who loved to go to bed with rock musicians. That was innocent days, when the most you could get was a dose.

"I had met Jimi several times in London, and I was good friends with his manager, Chas Chandler. I was at the Scene one night, and Jimi comes over to me and says, 'You're playing. There's an organ onstage, man.' I don't know what he was on, but I asked him if he had thirty dollars' worth [laughs]. Jimi was a gentleman, and he was very soft spoken. I told him I'd love to jam, and we did. Steve Stills was on bass, Buddy Miles on drums, Jimi on guitar, Dave Mason on sax, and me on organ. We played for about three hours, and it was fantastic. We did it again the next two nights. After the first night, Steve Paul told us that if we'd come down the next night, the drinks would be on him. I was there at 7:30 in the evening. I especially remember trying to get a solo in edgewise. There'd be so much guitar, guitar, guitar. Suddenly there'd be more guitar, guitar, guitar. That's Jimi for you."

Muses Lord, with respect to his own influences, "I've been told this over the years, and it's constantly surprising and flattering, because I don't really know what I do that differently. To try to examine it in one way, I was a pianist until sometime in the '60s. I didn't really have an epiphany or anything. I didn't have a vision on the road to Damascus. But I was dissatisfied with what was coming out when I played. I didn't want to sound like Georgie Fame or Zoot Money, and I didn't want to sound like a rock version of Jimmy Smith, although he was an immense influence on me. I was thinking of ways around this, and I started to bring in a bit of classical music.

"And I discovered that if you leaned on the keyboard and played with the draw bars, interesting things happened. I always put the draw bars roughly the same way. And the pedal is very underused. People don't seem to be aware of how important it is. It's not a volume pedal; it's an expression pedal. Really, it's the only way you have of controlling expression on an organ.

"Another thing is, from '68 onwards, I spent two or three years really working with Ritchie to find the best way to make our sounds work together. He and I started the band, and what we very much wanted was this synthesis of organ and guitar—a gorgon [laughs]. And as we've discussed, I arrived there roughly about the time of *In Rock*; that's when I began to feel that I was learning how to integrate into what Ritchie does. I like to think that you often can't tell which of us is playing what. Interestingly enough, it's become almost second nature now when we're rehearsing or writing. I've got a sort of hand-to-hand style, kind of rocking from one hand to the other, which I can almost describe as Stevie Wonder's Clavinet technique. It just seemed to have arisen from attempting to make the effect as amorphous as possible, to make this gorgon. That's what Ritchie and I were searching for in those early years."

Asked whether he goes so far as to notate parts for Ritchie and himself, Jon says, "Sometimes. He doesn't write notation—no reason why he should. He'll say, 'What's this? Can you write this down so I don't forget it?' I'll notate it, and sometimes I'll find myself having to teach it back to him [laughs]. I can score pretty quickly; it doesn't take me more than a couple of minutes. I often write down little bits and pieces that Ritchie plays without him even knowing, because I know he'll forget them."

Recalls Ritchie with respect to "Hard Lovin' Man," "One of the engineers who originally worked on that album was this stuffy bloke who didn't like rock 'n' roll music. While I was recording the solo on that song, I got this urge and started rubbing the guitar up and down the doorway of the control room to get all that wild guitar noise. So, this bloke looks at me, and he's got this expression on his face as if I'd lost my mind.

"Another time, we were listening to a playback, and I went, 'I can't quite hear the guitar.' And this guy's going, 'Guitar? It's deafening; it's absolutely deafening! I can't take it; it's too loud.' And I'm going, 'You know, I can't hear it. I really can't hear it.' And this guy's going, 'You can't hear the guitar? It's fucking deafening, man. What's wrong with you?' And then Martin goes, 'Oh, wait a minute,' and he pushes the fader, and the guitar had been completely off. So, the guy went, 'Oops!' He had me thinking it was me, that I had lost my senses or something."

Paice has a laugh recalling the mixing session for *In Rock*. "Yeah, I remember hundreds of hands, all over the board. Everybody was looking after their own. I knew that if I had a drum fill that I wanted everybody to listen to, then the faders went up. If there was a bit that I didn't play too well, the faders came down. And so, there was this great jiggling. You could see the engineer start to tear his hair out as all the meters were going into the red and coming down again!"

And there you had it—*In Rock* rocked out in a blaze of glory, indeed, with only half of its longest song slowing down for anything resembling quiet moments. The mathematical truth was that this was hands down the heaviest record of 1970, with only *Paranoid* from Black Sabbath coming close. Uriah Heep's *. . . Very 'Eavy . . . Very 'Umble* debut was arguably in the same weight division, but definitely at the lesser end (save for "Gypsy"), while's Sabbath's self-titled debut sounded stodgy and pot-smoked in comparison to any of those three.

And not only was *In Rock* the heaviest, it was the smartest and most complicated, the most action-packed. Sure, *Paranoid* was a monumental achievement, emotionally more leaden and harrowing, given Geezer's blunt words of doom versus Ian's stories of broads as well as more-mature topics manhandled through the lens of solid poetic wordplay. But on the musical tip, *Paranoid* was no more than *In Rock*'s inebriated younger brother, a bit thick, on downers and wine and always getting in trouble at school.

And what should we make of Led Zeppelin?

Well, by the end of 1970, their three albums combined couldn't cough up as much flash rockin' musicianly music as was found right here on one Deep Purple record, stacked track upon track. Add to the mix the band's smash-hit fourth album from 1971 and compare it to *Fireball*, and maybe we have a fight on our hands. Add in the crumbling mountain music of the majestic *Master of Reality*, and both Purple and Percy find themselves in need of a cold compress for the head and a bit of quiet time in a dark room.

"No, each band was different," explains Lord. "Zeppelin cornered the sex symbol angle, with Robert Plant being so damn good looking, and they had more of a blues-based side than us. We were more of a heavy-rock band. Robert still calls us, with his tongue firmly in his cheek, Deep Sabbath. Although there was no rivalry between us, we were a bit [envious] of their initial success. If Purple would have stayed together, we might have achieved the same mid-'70s status that they did. They embraced the arena rock 'n' roll show with open arms, whereas we didn't embrace it quite so completely. We were a touch weary of arenas because we had spent so much time in the 4,000-seaters, and we were ever so comfortable in those halls. That was the kind of hall in which *Made in Japan* was made."

Gillan's Uncle Ivor didn't think much of *In Rock*.

In a rare interview of Gillan conducted by Roger Glover, Ian explains. "I had an acetate, and I took it and played it on my radiogram at home. And my Uncle Ivor was in the room, who was a musician and an artist, a painter. Wonderful man. Photographer, painter, and musician. And he ran from the room screaming, holding his hands over his ears. I felt vaguely let down, because I wanted to impress him. Then a couple of buddies came 'round, and I suddenly realized that he couldn't focus on it. To me it was . . . I loved it. I've never been proud of music, I don't think. For me, music is instant. It's all gone now; I don't really think much about it at all. I don't think I've ever played Deep Purple *In Rock* since that day. I've heard it, obviously, accidentally, or when I got to people's houses. I mean, I don't even know if I've got a copy. I must have it somewhere.

"I think if it had been a year or two earlier or a year later, nothing would have happened," conjectures Gillan. "Nothing significant anyway. We would just have been part of a movement, or something like that. But because it happened exactly at the right time, and because of *Concerto* and because of various other elements, I think it was successful. I don't know. Chaos theory; I'm a great believer in that. It was probably successful because of a butterfly in the Andes. I think another reason it was successful was because it had a brilliant cover. I think a lot of the visuals . . . there were some good photos of the band. There's much more to it than music.

People are concerned with image, and if you don't express yourself by staring straight into the camera and letting people know exactly what you're thinking, either by the clothes you're wearing or the attitude you have, you're gonna present a confused image. So, it had a great cover, and there was lots of attendant publicity for other things at the time."

With *In Rock* set for release in June 1970, oddly the band's UK label Harvest found themselves pining for a song to issue as a single. They asked the band to give them something new and not originating from the album, given that *In Rock* distinctly lacked single material. "Black Night" was cooked up quickly in the Newton Arms, a pub close to the studio. Blackmore carted over an acoustic guitar and began toying

US white-label promo issue of "Black Night." *Pericle Formenti archive*

with a James Burton riff idea he lifted from Ricky Nelson's 1962 version of "Summertime," written by George Gershwin. The galloping tempo was said to be stolen from Canned Heat's "On the Road Again"—mostly Ian Paice's doing—and the words from an Arthur Alexander song that Episode Six had covered.

"The end result, knocked into shape in three hours and considered a wrap by about four in the morning, was curiously similar to a situation and song and sound experienced by upcountry rivals Black Sabbath. An extra single-intentioned song on some issues of that band's debut album was a Crow cover called "Evil Woman." Similar to "Black Night," it's a simple tune with a slow-trot heavy metal doom riff set to a headbanging version of swing. Deep Purple wasn't sure that this was the song to hand over to Harvest, suggesting that it could be a good B side. But managers John Coletta and Tony Edwards disagreed. In any event, the ruse worked better for Deep Purple than it did for Ozzy and crew, with "Black Night" vaulting to #2 in the UK charts, remaining the band's biggest single back home to date, although achieving only #66 stateside. In truth, "Black Night" was duking it out not with "Evil Woman," but with Black Sabbath's quicker and more direct song called "Paranoid." In the end, both songs established their respective makers as potential

Led Zeppelin usurpers, especially given the confused reaction from fans and critics to Zeppelin's mostly acoustic *III* album.

Despite "Black Night" not being included on *In Rock*, the buzz about the Purples created by the single helped vault the album to #4 on the UK charts, where it hung around for an astonishing sixty-eight weeks.

Canadian guitar legend Pat Travers, who covered "Black Night" on his all-covers album *P.T. Power Trio 2* in 2006, lets it be known that Blackmore's importance to the history of guitar cannot be overstated.

"I'm a huge Deep Purple fan from Deep Purple *In Rock* and *Machine Head*. Well, I liked Deep Purple, I think, right from the beginning. Especially Ian Paice, the drummer—he's just incredible. It doesn't matter what recording they're doing; he always gets the best drum sound and greatest drum performance. And I love the keyboards. And Ritchie . . . my twelve-year-old son has now started to play guitar, and I'm trying to steer him into listening to different people, and he likes to play fast. And I tell him to listen to Ritchie Blackmore, because he plays fast but he also plays bluesy. He knows when not to play. It's okay to be able to play fast, but sometimes you've got to learn how to play slow, and expressive. And Ritchie, when we did a tour with Ritchie and Rainbow, a coheadlining tour, Ritchie was . . . I guess he's bipolar or something [laughs]. Because he can be super nice, and we had a lot of fun and he's playful and mischievous and we got on really well. But other nights he would just be a jerk to everybody. It's just the way he was. I don't think he's like that anymore. I think he's more comfortable with himself."

Of note, there was another "extra" from the *In Rock* era, and that's the slamming and rhythmic "Cry Free," a fully formed original that could have stood shoulder to shoulder with anything on the album. This one was tracked near the end of the album's sessions and took more than thirty takes to get right. Its production is huge and snarling, like most of the album itself, with instruments bleeding and blending into each other all over the place but a bit treble challenged. "Jam Stew" is another one, but of less importance, being a fairly structured enough instrumental, but instrumental all the same, tracked during the November 1969 session that yielded "Into the Fire."

In closing, indicative at my frustration that the guys in the band continue to fail to see the historical significance of *In Rock* as a key cornerstone in the invention of heavy metal, I circled back with Roger on the subject in 2013 and with Ian Paice on the subject in 2020.

"I think when Ian Gillan and I first joined the band, they had been to America, and 'Hush' went very high in the charts," recalls Roger. "They'd done a couple of tours, and they were full of stories about America. We had never toured America as Episode Six. They were full of stories, certainly about the women, the music, the bands, the clothes, the experiences they had—they were full of stories. Vanilla Fudge and the Flock and It's a Beautiful Day, they got mentioned.

"But in the meantime, Jon had written this concerto, which we did. I think it was our sixth gig with the band, Ian and I. It was really right into the deep end; pardon the pun. And there was a feeling in the band that I think Ritchie wasn't that into it. He felt like we were a rock band, and this was kind of toying with artsy-fartsy stuff a bit too much. But he gave Jon the okay—go ahead, we'll do it. We did it, and the reaction it got was that Jon Lord got hailed as the maestro of the band, the leader of the band, the main composer of the band, and that further kind of got right up the noses of Ritchie and Ian Gillan, in particular, and to a certain extent all of us.

"So, there was a desire, really, to be a rock band, in the face of this diversity. Looking back on it now, had we not done that concerto, Deep Purple *In Rock* wouldn't have been as hard as it turned out to be. There's a real determination to say who we were. I remember turning up doing several gigs, and promoters would be there, and they'd go, 'Where's the orchestra?' So, the identity of the band was a bit mixed, going into *In Rock*."

But one supposes that Jon Lord was a more substantial part of the band in the beginning.

"Yeah, actually, I read an interview of Jon's just a while ago, and he was saying that in the early days of the band, he was more of a musician and a writer. He had more of the experience. Ritchie was the rocker, but he had more breadth to his composing talents. So, I think yeah, it was more keyboard oriented."

Finally, I wondered if Roger was able to realize now what a strange and groundbreaking album *In Rock* was in the middle of 1970.

"I don't think of it as strange, as somehow . . . I love the album. Probably, it's where we found ourselves. So, obviously, it's one of my top albums. And it's where the stage shows that we were doing came together. Because we recorded it in between gigs, in whatever studio at the time was free. It was recorded in IBC, in Abbey Road, and finally in De Lane Lea Kingsway. And what was happening live was that the band was really exploding, yet we were in the studio trying to make a sedate record. And I think on that album, the shows were coming into the studio. The live performances came into the studio. And I think that's what defines Purple. Because Purple is essentially a live band, and making records is a byproduct. That was the key point—the experience of playing live came into the studio. Because it really was vicious. And dutifully recorded by Martin Birch."

When I asked Ian the same thing, how the band suddenly found themselves making a kind of music that didn't exist before (not to exaggerate the premise), he focuses not on the classical album but the Mk. I edition of the band. But there's a lining up with Roger with respect to the knock-on effect of playing live.

"How that came about," explains Paice, "is that by the time we had done the third record, with Rod Evans and Nick Simper, there was an unconscious movement, definitely from Ritchie and I and somewhat John, where the music was actually getting harder. Because we were playing live so often and we were getting better at it, the ideas were becoming slightly more aggressive, and we needed a different sound at the top. Rod Evans's voice was lovely, but he wasn't what I would call a rock 'n' roll voice—it really wasn't.

"So, when that change came and we got Ian and Roger in, not only did we get that voice, we got a couple of songwriters in, and the shift was sort of inevitable. The amalgamation of those five musical influences, and the way that the musical dynamic was shifting, we had to make a statement and said, okay, this changes naturally, but let's make sure everybody realizes this is a big shift from the first Deep Purple. I wouldn't say it was a conscious thought, but there was a deliberate effort to make a record we thought reflected that. When you look back on it now, we were just making the record we thought was right. To show that there was a difference between Deep Purple Mk. I and the existing Purple of that time. A lot of it had to do with Ian and Roger coming into the band and giving a new possibility to ideas that just wouldn't have worked with Rod's voice, and therefore those ideas would probably never have been brought to the table. *In Rock* was very, very hard. And then when we heard Mountain's first record, we went back and said, 'We've got to do some work' [laughs]."

Chapter 7

Fireball

"I think I probably had a few drinks when I wrote that."

Immortalized in a mountain of stone and now forming a five-headed comet shooting across the universe . . . who do Deep Purple think they are? Similar audacity would play itself out in the musical proposals from the band, with *Fireball* being this band's *Led Zeppelin III* of a sort, a stepping out into outlandishness when simply another of the same would have paid huge dividends.

It is of no matter, because *Fireball*, on the strength of a swaggering metal shuffle song called "Strange Kind of Woman" and its #8 placement on the UK charts, would become the first of the band's three #1-charting albums back home, with the record rising to #32 stateside as well. Of note, "Strange Kind of Woman" would emerge in February 1971, fully eight months before the album would be released. This wasn't a gap scheduled by design. The writing and recording of *Fireball* saw delays due to schedules and arguments within the band, now that Mk. II's honeymoon period had emphatically passed.

Recorded over the course of a nine-month period ending in June 1971, the album would be issued the following month in North America, but not until September back home. Fans and critics were up in arms over the album's wild oscillations between light and shade, given that *In Rock* stuck blasting caps in the mountain and basically didn't stop making noise until the quarry had crumbled. *Fireball* was also the first difficult album to make for the band, adhering to Roger Glover's famous theory that Deep Purple seem to make a great album without much effort, followed by a not-so-great album with difficulty, followed by another classic album enjoyably. But *Fireball* marked the beginning of the feuding between Ritchie and Ian, with Ritchie grousing that Ian was drinking too much and not being serious about his voice, while Ian decried Blackmore's grumpiness and prima donna qualities.

It eventually became the case that basically anything could set Ritchie off, whether it was getting a good guitar sound in rehearsal or in the studio or at soundcheck, or if creature comforts weren't to his liking at a live venue. "We didn't have any cancellations," recalls Gillan, "except lots of tours just didn't get booked because he didn't want to go anywhere, except for Germany and America and the UK. So, we would never go to any of the countries we visit now. But he didn't cancel anything once they were in. But he did used to walk offstage as soon as he got miffed about something. And nobody knew what it was about. But, you know, all things return, don't they? People tend not to talk about him anymore. He's kind of faded away."

Ian has admitted over the years to drinking heavily, so Ritchie's not in the wrong there, and even adopting a measure of LSD, or lead singer disease—attitude, basically, or entitlement—which, oddly enough, he was contracting directly from his guitarist. Because Ian's growing crankiness was in fact exacerbated by Ritchie's petulance in the live environment, which included refusing to do encores and, on one occasion, playing a pub gig plugged in from the dressing room, because the venue, Eel Pie Island, had experienced a bit of a flood.

In turn, Ritchie found himself frustrated at having no time to write, making it up on the road or right there in the studio, renting outposts and fiddling around with séances while waiting for inspiration, or getting a chance to fashion some riffs when someone was ill, and the Deep Purple machine had to necessarily slow down. Blackmore himself fell victim to appendicitis, and Ian (up into October 1971) had contracted hepatitis, while Roger laid claim to a variety of stomach maladies as well as "exhaustion."

Meanwhile, Jon Lord was plagued by recurring back pain that originated from his days of hauling his own gear in the Art Woods. When Ian got hepatitis, prompting the cancellation of a US tour after just three shows, Ritchie got together with Ian Paice and Thin Lizzy's Phil Lynott to try to put together a power trio with the working title of Babyface. Nothing came of it other than a few jams, which Blackmore denigrated as too close to what Hendrix was doing. Phil had once said the band worked up a good five songs, but the only one anyone can recall now is a cover of Johnny Winter's "Dying to Live."

"I knew Ritchie was looking for something outside of Purple just to fill time in," recalls Ian Paice. "And I said, 'Well, probably nothing serious, but Lynott's got a great, great stage presence, he's got this Hendrixy way of talk-singing, and he looked really weird: a big, tall, Black Irishmen!' And Ritchie was sold immediately. So, we went into the studio and did it, but Phil was so young and inexperienced that when you analyzed what he was doing, it wasn't that good. He couldn't really play bass very well, and it took him a long time to learn to sing songs he hadn't written, so it didn't really follow through. We knew that one day he was gonna be great, but not yet. Lovely man, yeah. It's a shame he was a dummy to himself."

Adds Lord, "I remember the rest of us saying, 'What?! What are they doing?!' [laughs]. It was the weirdest thing, though, to see this big, tall, thin, Black Irishman come up and go, 'How th'devil are yah? Good t'see yah!' Ah, he's sadly missed."

Ritchie also looked wayward toward Paul Rodgers, whom he fancied as a great British blues singer and a possible project partner. And amusingly, when Roger's situation got so bad as to have Chas Hodges replace him during encores of "Lucille," Ritchie quipped that if his condition proved fatal, perhaps the band could cremate Glover onstage—quite an improvement over trying to smash up a guitar, which, frankly, always looks a bit ridiculous.

Further in the diversion department, Roger and Ian Paice ensconced themselves in Atlanta recording the first album by Elf, whose lead singer was one Ronnie James

Dio. Roger would go on to become a well-regarded producer for such bands as Nazareth for three of their biggest albums in 1973 and 1974, and then Judas Priest in 1977, tracking the classic *Sin After Sin*.

Back to the mother ship, *Fireball* would be recorded in and around what would be considered Deep Purple's first British tour proper, with Heads, Hands & Feet and other bands as support, from January through March. Heads, Hands & Feet included in its lineup the aforementioned Glover stand-in Chas Hodges, as well as Albert Lee, who is considered a bit of the guitar inspiration for a *Fireball* track called "Anyone's Daughter." Ritchie's antics were well known and regularly executed by this time, with the man prone to knocking amps over or, worse, lighting them on fire, along with whacking his guitar onto the stage and playing it with his feet, busting in hotel room doors with fire extinguishers and axes, and augmenting his regularly occurring séances with additional occult-suggestive trickery. To lighten the mood, Roger would be cast out of the band's new limousine naked. At one point, he was tied up in a Marshall case and left on the Severn Bridge, which links England to Wales.

Japanese-issue *Fireball* poster. *Pericle Formenti archive*

In any event, once *Fireball* had become painfully and distractedly birthed, its opening title track scorched away concerns over band fatigue. "Fireball" was so heavy and fast that it would be sensible to view it as stronger stuff than most of the songs on *In Rock*. The track is widely discussed as the world's first "speed metal" song.

Now, speed metal is a term from the early 1980s, quickly supplanted by the idea of "thrash," which arguably begins with Metallica's *Kill 'Em All* album from the summer of 1983. But it's not untoward to call "Fireball" speed metal, even by the definition applied to bands from the early 1980s, such as Raven and Exciter. Basically, it's superfast and flanked by a wall of guitars, and there's extremity at all corners, including at the microphone.

Ian Paice's opening drum signature is legion. Set off by the whoosh of the studio's air- conditioning unit being fired up, Ian then turns in a pioneering double-bass pattern that one might argue helps invent the idea of the "blastbeat," although it's a fleeting thought, given that Paice rarely would play double bass for the remainder of his career. Its use on "Fireball" was a spontaneous decision, in fact. Keith Moon's kit was still hanging around the studio from a previous session, so Ian, feeling he needed to add some oomph, simply borrowed it for the track.

"Right; we had the riff," begins Paice, explaining to Sam Dunn what happened. "The song was sort of semiwritten when we went to the studio. So, I knew what the pattern was of the riff, and I tried to match the notes with one bass drum, trying to get the bass drum going. I could just about get the speed, but I couldn't get the power—it wouldn't come.

"And the night before in the same studio, the Who had been recording, and Keith Moon's kit was still there. The roadies didn't take it away. So, I just thought, well, I'll borrow one of Keith's bass drums and I'll stick it where my high hat would be. Because I can't play two bass drums. To this day, I can't play them. That's just making a big noise. I realized with the way the riff was with the song, if I could just get this really solid and then put some slightly more interesting touches on top of it, it would really work well as an intro.

"So, what we did, if you listen to the music, the bass drum on my left is mine and the bass drum on my right is Keith's. Of course they sound identical. We didn't have double-kick pedals in those days. If you wanted two bass drums, you had to have two bass drums. You couldn't have one with a double kick. So, when we did do it onstage, we had to drag another bass drum on, and we had to have a certain point in the show which gave us time to do that. So, the whole thing got quite complex.

"But it's one of those things that, as a drummer, anybody out there would know what I played was not difficult, and that's not the point. What I played for that piece of music was absolutely perfect, which makes it a great piece of music. Which is the name of the game. As a setup for that piece of music, you couldn't beat it. I've got to be honest, the influences from that came from Corky Laing with Mountain. Because they did a couple tracks where he was starting off with double kickers. It wasn't quite that complex. I thought, our song was faster, and I still need to put my clever chops on the top, but the two kicks with that riff will make it work. Influences come from everywhere. The first Mountain album was incredible. We were so impressed when that came out. Again, that was a really seminal hard rock record. You listen to that now and it really is aggressive and powerful. Leslie's voice and the songs and the recording technique—fantastic. So again, a good influence there."

As for its now-ubiquitous use in heavy metal music, Ian says that "it's a very easy way of making a lot of noise and being very impressive. The really great players with two kicks use them infrequently, or they use them the same way you'd use a tom-tom to make a fill. I really lose interest with guys who use them in every song. It's like having a Ferrari and going everywhere at 180 mph. Eventually even that will become boring. But if you go back to 30 mph for a while, and then you go 180, then it's exciting. It's the same thing with two bass drums. When you use it when it's needed, it's devastating. When you don't need it, don't touch it. To me, because it's such a massive sound, it tends to obliterate everything else. So, if you're going to obliterate everything else, make sure there's a reason for obliterating it."

Curiously, when speaking with the author five years before the above conversation with Sam, Ian was more ambivalent about his role in "Fireball." "There are interesting moments," he told me. "The problem is, when you make the record, you listen to the damn thing so many times, and you routine the things many times, once you've got the takedown and you're happy with it, for a long time you don't want to hear it ever again. You've blown your cookies on it and that's it; it's done, I'm happy with it, now what's next? So, I don't really have the ability to go back and listen to those tracks in the same way somebody else does. I think you'll find most people are like that with songs they've recorded. It's only when you start to go back and play them live fifteen, twenty years later that you find interesting things in them. All right, that wasn't so bad. Now I know why I did what I did. It's like hindsight. But at that moment in time, you're just trying to get the damn thing right."

Once Paicey got the damn thing right, the rest of the band crashes in on cue, and it's a red-hot, white-knuckle ride to the finish. Weirdly, in place of an expected guitar solo is a bass solo from Roger. Lyrically, Ian calls this a tale of unrequited love, and it's merely another one in a long line of "magical, mystical woman" tunes by Purple and many other heavy bands deemed to be similar to them. "Fireball" would turn out to be a favorite of Blackmore's on the record, with the Man in Black also speaking fondly of "No No No" and "Fools" but little else on the record.

Music tablature book, 1972. *Pericle Formenti archive*

"Fireball" was issued as a single, in the UK backed by "Demon's Eye" and in the US backed by "Anyone's Daughter." It was the second of two singles from the album, first being the pre-LP "Strange Kind of Woman." "Fireball" wasn't an enthusiastic pick for single issue by any stretch, but given the weirdness of much else around it, it was tentatively floated, rising to #15 in the UK but not charting at all stateside.

"Demon's Eye" was a somewhat unwieldy and funky heavy metal riff rocker utilizing a 1950s boogie-rock chord structure but with ominous melodies. "Strange Kind of Woman" became a hit for the band, and interestingly, like "Demon's Eye," it's built from the ground up, using the blues rulebook, albeit with the band taking both tracks well beyond the predictable into this zone of making the blues interesting for people who don't have patience for the blues. The call and response between Ian singing and Ritchie guitarin' was inspired by Edgar Winter and Rick Derringer on the Edgar Winter's *White Trash* album, specifically "Tobacco Road." Of note, as alluded to earlier, Deep Purple didn't lean toward blues patter and patterning all that often. This idea of blues-based riff rock is more regularly attributable to the likes of Foghat, ZZ Top, and Status Quo, and of course most famously (and literally) by Led Zeppelin.

Curiously at this point—namely, pre-*Fireball* (but during the making of it)—Deep Purple were playing these ecstatic packed gigs of mayhem and destruction all up and down the UK and into Europe, and their two big songs—"Black Night" and "Strange Kind of Woman"—weren't on any of the band's full-length records. To clarify, "Strange Kind of Woman" would be included on the North American version of *Fireball*, while the European issue put "Demon's Eye" in its place—literally in its place, as the third track on the first side.

"Strange Kind of Woman" had as its B side a funky, jazzy, dated non-LP original called "I'm Alone." One might position this track fourth in line—stylistically and in terms of advancing quality—to "Hush," "Hallelujah," and "Black Night." The song was built quickly from the old "Grabsplatter" riff, with Ian adding a title he had kicking around from his Episode Six days.

And perhaps in testimony to the struggles the band endured with respect to gathering material, there were two other non-LP songs from the *Fireball* sessions that essentially fail by being stale. "Freedom" represents a sorry form of old-time rock 'n' roll, while "Slow Train," a marked improvement, is nonetheless flippant, punky, jammed out, and of ill construct. A positive reading might point out its energy and progressive shifts. All told, one could imagine "Slow Train" sprucing up the vibe of *Fireball*, but "I'm Alone" and "Freedom" are from another world that was long over with once "Speed King," "Bloodsucker," and "Flight of the Rat" were loosed upon the land.

Next up on both versions of *Fireball* was "No No No." "They were both antidrug songs," says Ian of this one and "Fools," also a *Fireball* track. "I didn't smoke my first joint until I was thirty-eight years old. We grew up in a drinking crowd, and it's rather like the mods and rockers, hippies or whatever. You would have one group doing marijuana, and the other group was doing beer and whiskey. And I was in the beer-and-whiskey crowd."

US white-label issue of "Strange Kind of Woman." *Pericle Formenti archive*

"No No No" points to a subtle increase in sophistication for Purple, who sort of bring back the texture and jazziness from their youths inside and outside Mk. I Deep Purple. Roger in particular leaves behind his "teenage eighth note" style for something much more artful and obtuse, even if he personally thought the song dragged on a bit long. There's blues, there's funk, and there's a defiance of the rock 'n' roll rules, with Purple proposing that there are no parameters. There's in fact the birth of Mk. II Deep Purple as a jam band. And fortunately, there was still riffing and exuberant loud playing by everybody. I'd have to disagree with Roger—this is a nice bit of stylistic diversion, widening the canon. If it's long, statistically, at 6:54, it's to make the statement that these are hot instrumentalists that need to be heard.

Additional to the "Strange Kind of Woman" story, that song was originally called "Prostitute," having been written during the Christmas period of 1970 at a rental the band inhabited just for that purpose on the Devon coast. Ian prefaces the tune on the *In Concert* live album with "It was about a friend of ours who got mixed up with a very evil woman, and it was a sad story. They got married in the end. And a few days after they got married, the lady died."

Years later, however, in conversation with me, Gillan put it this way: "'Strange Kind of Woman' was an amalgamation of various people. I got married to a . . . I probably can't say it—she was a lady of the night. And we were married for three months. Actually, we'd only known each other for about a few weeks. She was weird.

And it was a combination of her and a few other people in that." Which of course is closest to the truth, because Ian is on record elsewhere explaining that the lyric is the tale of his own odd relationship, in which he tried to take her away from her previous business into a more traditional one with himself, only for Ian to be, essentially, rebuffed in his intentions. He then quips that at least he'd managed to move up in the pecking order from Wednesday mornings to Saturday nights!

"Anyone's Daughter" is the one that really had the faithful up in arms. It's pretty much a novelty tune, a sort of old-timey bluegrass ballad, not heavy in any way, prefaced by a bunch of scattered chatter of studio detritus that the band found amusing enough to let stand. Like Uriah Heep's "Gypsy" of the previous year, it's a cautionary tale of a protective father tanning the hide of a horny, long-haired suitor. Muses Gillan, "'Anyone's Daughter' was a study in self-delusion, really. And hypocrisy. And the fact that you would use any position to get anything, including sexual favors, or a foot up in life. It was a tongue-in-cheek thing, really. But there's always a serious side to these things." Although Ian appreciated the bravery to do a song this radically different, he later considered it a mistake to stick it on the actual record.

Ian Gillan, Long Beach Arena, Long Beach, California, January 30, 1972. © *Marvin Rinnig*

"The Mule," when performed live, turned out to be a showcase during which Ian Paice could exercise his jam band rights to a drum solo, which generally took place in the early days during Purple's rendition of the Rolling Stones' "Paint It Black." But you wouldn't pick that up from the studio version here, because half of Paice's tracks for it were accidentally erased, and with his drums now in transit to Europe, a rental kit had to be assembled, and his performance was compromised. "The Mule is the devil," laughs Gillan, "and I think I probably had a few drinks when I wrote that." It's one of the stranger and proggier things on the record, and again, a track that demonstrates how willing to experiment Purple were after the blasting metal of the debut, along with the one-track-mind arrangements used to get to that place. The rhythm is a bit raga circa the Beatles, and Gillan in turn sounds sage-like while the band bashes about behind him.

Often considered a bit of a sister track to "The Mule" is "Fools," given that both seem to be off in a psychedelic haze. "Fools" oscillates between meditative stupor and big snarling power chords circa Black Sabbath, with Ian growling out thespian-like his wise words about a person who has died and simultaneously gained the realization that the world is run by fools. Ritchie performs a novel "cello effect" guitar solo, upon which his volume pedal plays a major role, recalling a trick he used in live renditions of Mk. I's "Mandrake Root."

And then it's off toward "No One Came," a groovy, blasting heavy metal rocker imbued with humor, but more so known for its insistent, pulsating heft. "I think what it is, is grabbing ahold of reality," explains Gillan, with respect to the lyric. "It's not about worrying that people aren't going to come to shows, but it's all these guys with cigars and contracts, flying around you, telling you how wonderful you are. And you know damn well that the minute things start slipping, they'll be on another bus. I think the idea with that was, we had all paid our dues and been in the business long enough to know that you had to work for what you get, and that there were going to be some rough times ahead. And in fact, there have been. And now we're through them. But the realization is, or I mean the punch line is, 'No one came for miles around and said, Wow' [laughs]."

Coming last on the album, "No One Came" raises the stakes and sets us up for the first track on *Machine Head*, which is "Highway Star." Both exude the confidence of a band firing on all sixes, improving on the heavy metal blueprints all over *In Rock*. It's also a song that helps build *Fireball* into an album that on paper may not be as impressive as *In Rock* but somehow comes off as more charming and personable, less cold. And then materially, the band is wildly more versatile on the current record; for example, far heavier with "Fireball" and far lighter with "Anyone's Daughter," with the light and shade of "Fools" serving as a microcosm of those two combined.

As it turns out, all that variety would polarize estimations of the album over the years, with a handful of hits becoming beloved chestnuts and a bunch more of it eliciting blank stares. Still, the sum of those disparate parts makes for a Queen-like or Zeppelinesque arch-1970s record where caution could be gleefully thrown to the winds, come what may, create, capture, and release.

Ian Gillan, for his part, quite liked the record, in large part because it was provocative, but also because he really got to stretch as a vocalist and lyricist. Glover, on the other hand, found the writing forced and contrived, with the pressure to follow up *In Rock* strongly and soon resulting in too much second-guessing in the writing department. Paice, conversely, figures the album wasn't heavy enough, whereas Lord was just pleased to put out something decent, given the internal and external stresses of Purple mania. Still, "It could have used another steamer," said big Jon.

And these opinions were verified by the fact that very little of the album was included in the band's live set, with the guys already starting to introduce *Machine Head*–bound songs such as "Highway Star" and "Lazy." Even the surefire winner of the *Fireball* bunch, the title track, was a bit tough to get around to due to Ian needing a second bass drum. Weirdly, it was "The Mule" and "Anyone's Daughter" that were mooted more enthusiastically over something like "No One Came."

Interestingly, Jon Lord figures that *Fireball* is the album he did the most writing for, but he cautioned that "it's difficult to write convincing hard rock material at home on a piano. I defy anyone to come up with the licks to 'Into the Fire' or 'Smoke on the Water' on a grand piano. In that respect, Ritchie Blackmore is invaluable, always has been and always will be. He is the spark that lights Deep Purple. I can't compete with him on that level. He sketches the bold strokes, and I do the coloring in. But that's my job as keyboardist. There's no other instrument that can add colors like the keyboard can."

As for Ritchie's reputation for being irascible? "Ritchie's like a terrier or pit bull. He gets hold of something and won't let go. He has a vision of what he wants, and he'll fight and fight until he gets what he wants. He's rarely wrong, and if he is wrong, he'll admit it with utmost graciousness. Until he's proven wrong, he won't

Long Beach Arena, Long Beach, California, January 30, 1972. © *Marvin Rinnig*

budge. I love him the way he is. Ritchie doesn't play the guitar the standard way; he has an odd way of looking at things. Different chord shapes than most guitarists would be able to come up with, or maybe wouldn't even want to come up with [laughs]. Because he's such an individual type of player, I have to be on my toes."

In the grand scheme of things, after so many decades *Fireball* essentially is framed as an oddball record, a representation of everything that was good about the composition of albums in the 1970s, and yes, the crazy uncle to another oddball record from the same band; namely, *Who Do We Think We Are!* By dint of that comparison, however, *Fireball* can count quite a few more converts, pretty much most fans and critics, and even the band now, agreeing that despite a shared weirdness, *Fireball* was resoundingly the most successful of the two.

And *Fireball* meant everything to the world's biggest Deep Purple fan among rock stars. "One thing I still think is really cool is that I still have my very, very first LP, and that's Deep Purple *Fireball*," says guitar legend Yngwie Malmsteen, pretty much considered "the next one" to Ritchie's "the great one." "I still have it. I got it on my eighth birthday. That's a long time ago.

"It fucked my life up," laughs Malmsteen, asked what it did for him. "No, seriously, that album . . . when my older sister gave me that record, my life changed. Forever. From that point on, there was no doubt in my mind what I was going to do. No fucking doubt in my mind. That was it. I was so determined from that point on. I was determined before, but especially that day. I got my first guitar when I was five, and I started playing when I was seven, really furiously. And maybe one year later, on my eighth birthday, well, not really a year later, but eight months later, my older sister . . . she buys records all the time; she always would bring records home, and I would listen to her albums. But she gave me Deep Purple *Fireball*, and it starts with those drums [sings it], you know, and I didn't know what the hell was going on. I was just freaking out! And the next week, I took my allowance, and I went out and bought *In Rock*. And I was . . . dude, that was it, man! Yeah, it was just . . . that was it! Yeah, yeah, I think it did a lot of damage, man.

"*In Rock* was the first metal album ever," continues Yngwie. "Listen to the beginning of 'Speed King.' It's like a fucking wrecking ball coming into your bedroom while you're sleeping, you know?! [yells]. It was. It's so good . . . 1969, man; it was recorded in 1969. And Sabbath, I mean, come on, I love them, don't get me wrong, and Led Zeppelin's great—how can you not like them? They

Left, an ad from the January 30, 1971, issue of the *New Musical Express*, and *right*, a gig ad from the September 11, 1971, issue of *Melody Maker*. *Martin Popoff archive*

were like the pioneers of everything. But Purple just had the one-over on all of them, because they had the greatest musicians, in my opinion, and the hardest sound. They were by far the heaviest band. I mean, listen to 'Into the Fire' [sings it], heavy, heavy, heavy, heavy. And 'Hard Lovin' Man,' oh God. 'Bloodsucker?' Serious stuff."

"I love, love, love Ian Paice," says another Swedish metal luminary, former Mercyful Fate and King Diamond drummer Snowy Shaw. "His drumming on *Made in Japan*, *In Rock*, and *Machine Head* was and still is absolutely fucking unbelievable. He was like Buddy Rich playing heavy rock—just phenomenal. At that time, he was the most technical drummer by any means, with tremendous groove and a wonderful laid-back jamming quality. I think Ian Paice has influenced more drummers than any other."

Final word goes to Yngwie, who reiterates the impact that Deep Purple had on him by adding a little bit of amusing environmental perspective. "Well, it's like this. When I was eight years old . . . see, I grew up in a country that was barren. I mean, there were a lot of trees, a lot of moose. There was hardly any TV, hardly any radio. I didn't wake up in a barrage of media like kids do today, in between the cable TV and the DVDs and video games and this online stuff. There was really nothing there. So, in other words, when I first heard Deep Purple *Fireball*, that was my first introduction to rock music. And what an introduction, eh? Those double drums. So, it had such an impact on me, and like I say, it completely decided my destiny. There was no single minute speck of doubt in my mind, in any fiber of my body, what I was going to do with my life. And actually, the year before, I saw Hendrix on TV, and that was huge, because that was when I first knew I wanted to play guitar. I saw him smash and burn the guitar in Monterey. But it was only that; it wasn't a musical impact, because it was on the TV news. 'Yesterday, Jimi Hendrix died,' and boom, there it is.

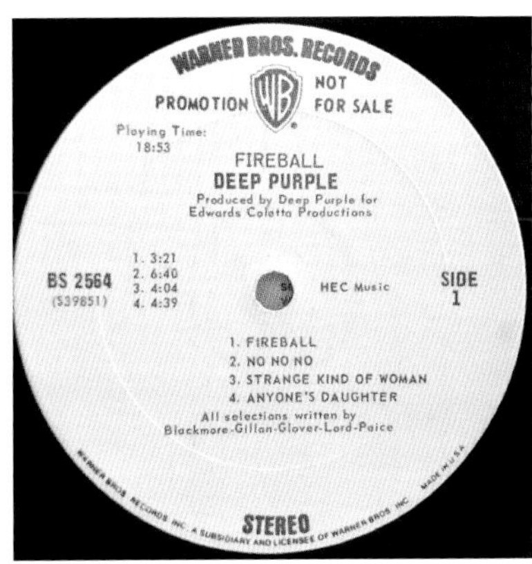

US white-label promo of the *Fireball* album

"So, I already had a guitar, and I started playing it that day. But when I heard songs like 'Demon's Eye' and 'Fools,' it was like a whole universe had just been opened to me. There was nothing comparable to that, around me. Nothing! I didn't see any other bands. I'd never heard Led Zeppelin or Black Sabbath; I'd never heard anything like that. And as I mentioned, a couple weeks later, I saved up enough money to go buy . . . which I didn't know at the time. I just wanted another Deep Purple album, and they gave me *In Rock*. That was the left hook, you know? [laughs]. And that floored me again! And I lived on those albums for many a good year. And as far as I'm concerned, looking back at it, I'm really happy that those were the albums I got. Because if I would've gotten maybe something else, my life would've turned out a little different."

Ian Gillan, Hamburg, 1971. © *Gladstone-dewiki, Wikimedia Commons*

Chapter 8

Machine Head

"How do you write a song?"

Record #3 for the Mk. II version of Deep Purple, *Machine Head,* would prove to be more of a fireball than *Fireball.* In 1972, the band's workload would get heavier and heavier, with bursts of creativity necessarily wedged in between live shows. Some of the bills made sense, but others looked kinda goofy. In the US, Purple found themselves sharing the stage with Faces—Rod Stewart had briefly been considered as a replacement for Rod Evans—as well as Matthews Southern Comfort. Life was becoming kaleidoscopic, with incendiary bouts of destruction taking place on the road, followed by the reality of having to pay up. As it turned out, the Deep Purple guys went through money like water, further causing rifts between members of the band as well as arguments with management.

But the mayhem turned out to be good for the art, with the guys carting around the likes of "Highway Star" and "Lazy" as evidence that friction and pressure among bandmates can often make for bouts of intense creativity. Offers Ian Gillan, with respect to the germination of what many consider to be Deep Purple's greatest song ever, "'Highway Star' . . . there were some journalists on the bus asking some very penetrating questions like 'How do you write a song?,' and Ritchie went duh, duh, duh, duh on an acoustic guitar and said, 'Like this.' And as we were driving down to Portsmouth, I started singing, 'Nobody's gonna take my car.' We did it in the show that night (September 13, 1971) at Portsmouth Guild Hall in England. So that evolved; songs just evolve. You don't sit down and write them as such."

And there it was, a thrilling new song in the set list, with Deep Purple deciding that futzing around and writing something in the studio and then placing it tentatively on your record was not the way to make rock 'n' roll. The new way would pay off famously, of course, with *Machine Head* becoming Deep Purple's unparalleled masterpiece, top to bottom, left and right.

The band had also decided that their most adjacent recording experience, that of *Fireball,* now, to their ears, sounded cold and clinical. Live shows were going down a storm the world over, from Europe to America and back again, from Australia

At the Palace Hotel, Copenhagen, Denmark, March 2, 1972. © *Jørgen Angel*

to . . . Iceland. Looking for a more organic sound for their next album, the band cooked up the idea of recording live onstage with no audience, choosing the casino in Montreux, Switzerland, for the task. Purple had played there before and liked the venue, but it was also picked for financial reasons, due to the Byzantine tax disadvantages of recording on home soil.

From this point the "Smoke on the Water" story, taking place "on the Lake Geneva shoreline," unfolds. The idea was for the band to record over the three weeks leading up to Christmas '71. But before getting down to it, "funky" Claude Nobs, organizer of the Montreux music festival, invited the boys to watch the last show before the winter shutdown. Purple had arrived just the night before. Frank Zappa & the Mothers began their set (a matinee performance), and Don Preston was into his Minimoog solo on a song called "King Kong," and "some stupid with a flare gun" shot a round into the wooden roof of the venue, which proceeded to burn "to the ground."

For his part, Don remembers it as a firecracker, which ignited decorative dried palm leaves on the ceiling. Other accounts have it as smoldering first in the space between the fake bamboo ceiling and the higher-up wooden roof. Fortunately, unlike the similar disastrous Station fire of 2003 during a Great White concert in which a hundred people lost their lives, there were no fatalities, since members of the crowd quickly grabbed Zappa's Orange amps and hurled them through the plate glass windows facing the lake, creating a large and easy exit route. Luckily, Deep Purple had been advised not to unload until Zappa's gear was taken out after the show, so they didn't lose their gear. Zappa's band recalls going back to their hotel across the lake and watching the venue burn, again, "to the ground," remembering it indeed as smoke on the water.

Ian Gillan remembers being in the crowd at that show, daydreaming away, admiring Zappa and, more specifically, the harmonies of Flo and Eddie, when over his shoulder he saw "two blobs of fire" tuck into the top corner of the venue. He also recalls that Frank took control of the situation by calming everybody down and talking them to safety, with Claude rescuing a handful of patrons who had run themselves into a dead end in the kitchen. Some concert watchers recall Frank's first words on the situation as "Arthur Brown in person!," whereas Roger remembers a deadpan announcement from Frank that ended in a loud "Fire!" and a quick exit from the stage. Glover tells the story of actually wandering back into the building to marvel at Zappa's two newfangled synthesizers. After he stepped back out, the massive complex, "eight to ten stories high," says Glover, erupted into "an inferno."

With this recording option extinguished, Nobs set the band up at a venerable concert hall called Le Pavilion, which allowed the band the construction of one track, "Smoke on the Water," before getting chucked out due to noise complaints. Then it was over to the Grand Hotel, where work continued in earnest. The band was able to rent the entire place cheaply, given that it had been closed up for the winter.

"The first thing that comes to mind," says Ritchie, "is that when we recorded 'Smoke on the Water,' we got kicked out of the studio that we were in—a makeshift ballroom—because we were making too much noise, and the police closed us down. So, we had to get this other place, and the only place around was an old broken-down hotel. So, the way we utilized the hotel is that we had the Rolling Stones truck, mobile, which was stuck outside, put into the courtyard of this hotel, and then the leads were run up the corridor. Well, they were through the reception, up the stairs, down the corridor, through a bedroom, then out onto a balcony, along the balcony, back through another bedroom, through a bathroom, through another bedroom, into a corridor, and that's where we were playing.

"So, every time we would listen to a playback . . . normally, when you're in the studio, it's like, 'Come and hear that one and see what you think, lads,' every five minutes. With that, it was such a trick. And we had to walk along a balcony, and it was snowing. There was like a foot of snow. So, you had to put your overcoat on to hear a playback, and walk . . . it was like fifteen minutes away. So, after a while, we used to say, 'It's okay, Martin,' who was the producer. 'We believe you.' Or we would hear it back through the cans because it was so far to walk. So that's how we recorded *Machine Head*; it was very strange. It was freezing. There was no heating in this hotel. We were kind of blowing on our hands to try to warm them up."

Indeed, the hotel's heat had been shut down for the season, so industrial heating had to be brought in. It was winter, the band was a few kilometers from Montreux itself, and they were ensconced in a drafty, deserted hotel. Lovely. To alleviate some of the running around—Roger's sequence of rooms that the cords ran through reads different from Ritchie's, but he punctuates his telling with a tally of twenty-nine doors!—Birch endeavored to set up closed-circuit TV so those operating the Stones mobile could see what was going on with the band. Of the £8,000 total recording cost, £5,000 was for the mobile, which was brought in from France. But the band worked quickly, finishing up on December 21 by working each day roughly from early afternoon, through the night, and into breakfast.

As Gillan explains, the band was getting along better than they had been previously, partly because of Ian's forced separation from Ritchie.

"I think because of the circumstances, it was quite an easy album to make. Because the circumstances were difficult. I mean, I'd been sick. I'd been off for, God knows, three, four months, with hepatitis, which everyone got. I just happened to get it particularly badly, in Chicago. And I'd been recuperating from that."

I asked Ian if that was legitimate hepatitis or "rock star not behaving" hepatitis. His answer puts it in a gray area. "Well, everyone got it. We all figured . . . in those days, everyone used to drink scotch and Coke. None of us were into drugs. We just didn't know anything about the drug scene at all. We all think we got it, believe it or not, from scotch and Coke bottles lying around, and everyone used to pick up each other's bottles with goodness knows what. So, we think it was contaminated from saliva or something like that."

Asked if the guys were eating properly, Ian says, "Oh yeah, but we were tired. But I mean, the fact that everyone got it at the same time . . . I mean, we didn't all misbehave at the same place at the same time. And nobody was into drugs at all—none of the crew, none of the band or management. But we used to drink pretty heavily. And so we were thinking that's how we got it. And I happened to go down with it particularly badly. So yeah, I hadn't been doing anything for a while, and we got there and the place that we were supposed to record in catches fire the first night, and we're playing catch-up from day one. So basically, our attentions were focused on other things, other than our internal squabbles. So, I would say, yeah, it was an easy album. It's always the case; you're talking about people's minds, and you just get on with it."

KB Hallen, Copenhagen, Denmark, March 1, 1972. © *Jørgen Angel*

Machine Head, issued March 30, 1972, on the band's new personal Purple Records imprint in the UK and Warner Bros. in the US, came wrapped in a gatefold sleeve, actually the band's fourth in a row. Adding gravitas to the album's bold, heavy metal title (which was Ritchie's idea), the wording was created by sinking actual physical type into the top portion of a sheet of soft metal. The lower portion, unbothered, was used as a mirror, in front of which the band was placed. It all looks like a bad acid trip, but nonetheless a distinct high school machine shop vibe is achieved. The back cover, showing an actual machine head from a guitar, is arguably more impressive, perhaps marginally more suited for use as a front cover.

Machine Head opens with the aforementioned "Highway Star," and yes, its lyrics—understandable given the way they were written—are the weak link in this robust track, one that is quite possibly the most beloved of the entire Deep Purple canon. Martin Birch's production on the song and on the wider album is the best Mk. II that would ever be experienced, easily surpassing anything from the archaic Mk. I lineup but also, arguably, eclipsing the tones and mix and sound picture afforded the Mk. III and Mk. IV albums. Instantly, with the song's anticipation-building intro, one notices thrumming, throbbing bass, drill-to-the-head organ sounds, and whacking snare cracks. Once Paice comes in for real, bass drum and ride cymbal join the impressive coterie of sounds.

Later on, as a sort of bonus on the rich sound picture we're getting and the muscular groove of what is clearly an anthem in the making, Jon and Ritchie dovetail together a solo section that widely considered the best thing either of them have ever done in this department. It's singable, melodic, memorable, and elegant and it's steeped in tradition, in classical music, and it's placed upon an insistent rhythm bed built craftsmanlike by Roger and Paicey operating effortlessly, of one grooving mind. Blackmore has said that this was one of the rare occasions where he worked out the solo in advance, utilizing an old Johnny Burnette run he hadn't visited in ten years, and adding some classical spice from Bach to create drama.

Bands all over the world were inspired by "Highway Star," and there were two pretty high-profile covers of it, done well before covers became commonplace. Southern rockers Point Blank had a minor hit with it as a live version added to their 1980 album, *The Hard Way*, and Metal Church stuck a frantic, thrashy studio version of it on their self-titled debut from 1984.

"Growing up it was like, 'Wow, how are they doing that?'" says Metal Church guitarist Kurdt Vanderhoof. "But they did. Basically, they are the forefathers of the heavy metal riff. Even though they had keyboards and everything, Ritchie Blackmore—plus Tony Iommi, obviously—was, for me and for most heavy metal guitar players, the one who invented the heavy metal riff. I think that is pretty much their legacy. And 'Highway Star,' oh boy, you're talking about driving a car down the highway, and they just nailed that whole vision musically, with that driving, really simple riff. It works perfectly with the subject matter."

On the technical end, to achieve the blessed sound of *Machine Head*, Martin Birch had set the band up in a T-shaped corridor with Paice's drums at the fulcrum, guitar and organ at two opposite ends, with the descending stick of the T populated by Roger and his bass cabinet facing a cupboard full of mattresses. The result was creamy, rich, organic sound light-years easier on the ears than the harsh and compressed midrange sound picture we got with *In Rock* and *Fireball*.

Second track on *Machine Head* is the angular and funky "Maybe I'm a Leo," the Leo being Gillan. It's a rhythmically tricky rocker that finds Ian Paice inverting the beat as the rest of the band stumbles through its amiable but thick chord changes. If you're a drummer, as I am, you'll be running the math on that one in your head for the rest of your life, while doing dishes, getting stuck in traffic, or typing and tapping out a Deep Purple book.

Front cover of the *Machine Head* album, US issue, along with the side 1 label for the original UK Purple Records issue

"'Maybe I'm a Leo' is one of those low-key songs," muses Gillan, "one of those understated songs. It's a groove. It's like 'When a Blind Man Cries' and it's like 'Move On' from the *Bananas* album. It's a similar, understated groove to those. It's one of those songs that if you put it next to the monster powerhouse numbers. . . . Deep Purple is not one of those bands that goes bang, bang, bang, bang. I mean, we do powerful rock songs, but we also work with musical texture, dynamics, and for us, rock 'n' roll means a whole bundle of emotions and a bundle of moods and a bundle of deliveries. And our idea of hard rock is to actually keep it under control. It seems so much more dangerous at that point. And I think 'Maybe I'm a Leo,' rather like 'Anyone's Daughter' and 'Blind Man,' like a lot of those slower, I don't know, thoughtful bits of material, it's never been a main stage song. We have done it quite a few times before, but it's always been one of those obscure tracks you put in between, just to sort of keep the dynamics of the show working. But it's a cool number."

Roger concurs, saying that he and Paice loved being the rhythm section on this one because it reminds them of the way some American musicians can play behind the beat or, in his actual words, "have a laid-back approach to playing without being lazy." The riff of the song indeed originated with Roger, who was inspired by John Lennon's "How Do You Sleep?"

"Pictures of Home" features a flurry of triplets from Paice to open the proceedings, with the band then collapsing into a gorgeous gothic rocker that is a favorite of many deep and discerning Purple fans. Lord's textured organ work percolates while

Paice swings. Ritchie's soloing is bluesy and Jimmy Page–like, to which Lord responds with dramatic runs, the two creating yet another battle royale as if their clash of swords on 'Highway Star' wasn't enough. Even Roger gets a solo, which . . . well, this seemed a bit wedged in to give the bass player a blow ("I can't remember very much about that song," said Glover years later. "The next three weeks passed very quickly once we started recording."). Amusingly, Ritchie recalls that when trying out the song live, folks in the audience were yawning, so it was summarily tossed in favor of more-fortified fare.

"Never Before" is famously framed as the album's weak link (and in this writer's opinion, you can toss on that pile "Lazy" and even "Smoke on the Water," at least the music at the verses). It's a chummy enough song, bouncing along to a mainstream hard rock riff and a chorus that approaches barroom party rock. But there's an element of the ordinary to it that most fans and critics notice, to the point where it gets singled out as the least inspired song on the album, the least necessary.

UK music paper ad for the "Never Before" single. *Martin Popoff archive*

"Management says, 'Well, you've got to write a single,'" laughs Gillan. "Now, all the previous radio play tracks that we had before were complete and utter accidents. I mean, if you just think about 'Never Before,' that was the only song on the album that was written to be a radio play track. And it was a total disaster. For some reason, we just never played it. And everybody got completely sick of it, because they considered it to be contrived. Actually, on reflection, it's a pretty good song. But our judgment about commercial material is so awful and so bad. For example, 'Smoke on the Water' was put on that album as a filler track. We needed one more track because we were short on time. And we thought, what's that other song? We had a backing track here that we called 'The Dan Dan Song' [sings it—dan dan dan]. So that was on a tape, and we didn't have lyrics or anything. So, we dug that out as just a filler track, and we thought that 'Never Before' would be the played track. So, it just goes to show, what do we know? Basically nothing."

Indeed, at the time, everybody loved "Never Before," Roger saying that it was swimming around in everyone's heads and that a lot of time and effort were put into it. Turned out to be a bit of a dud as a single, stalling at #35 in the UK, and yes, there's a timidity there that makes it fade away as pure filler on this flashy album. "Never Before" was issued on March 18 as a pre-LP single, in edited form, backed with "When a Blind Man Cries," a morose blues ballad that is a particular favorite of Gillan's. Ian explains that the lyric is about perspective, the idea of a blind person not complaining about his lot in life, but when he does indeed cry, then something really bad must be afoot.

Side 2 of the original vinyl album opens with the most famous heavy metal riff ever conceived—and one of the simplest, which is why it's so famous. Its stark obviousness, along with its evil twist, is why kids the world over discover the majesty and power of the electric guitar through its plunking. Once the band collapses into the song, though, the energy dissipates and it's all about texture. The verse is actually more strummy and jammed than riffy, with the band returning to their funky, jazzy, R&B roots for what becomes a respite, a placeholder, before we can all together enjoy that riff again, and now to the pulse of Roger's teenage eighth notes while Paicey goes sixteenth note on the high hat.

Asked about Roger Glover and what he brings to Deep Purple, Joe Bouchard, Blue Öyster Cult bassist and acquaintance of Roger's, says that he "just went to see Deep Purple a couple of years ago, and I was saying to myself that a lot of what I do is like what he does. I think [that] of all the bass players in sort of the hard rock era, Roger influenced me more than any of them. It's his melodic style but also his really steady hand, his keeping the bottom solid. And he plays with a pick too. Also, he doesn't overshadow the guitar. His job was like my job. I was there to support Buck Dharma, and I think he feels like he knew that was his job, that Ritchie Blackmore and later Steve Morse, that those are the guys. Those are the flashy guys, and you really want to make them sound great. And that's really a great tribute to creating a classic band. You've got to have the foundation.

"But 'Smoke on the Water'; it's funny, because later when we worked with Martin Birch, we all talked about the burning down of the gambling house in Montreux and all of that [laughs]. 'Did that really happen?' 'Oh yeah!' And he said that the hotel they recorded in, there was like no heat and it was dismal. I'm sure they had a sort of urgency there to get the music recorded so they could go home [laughs]."

"'Smoke on the Water' was basically an album track," explains Roger, who is credited with coming up with the title. According to Gillan, Glover wrote it on a napkin as he watched from the Europe Hotel, while Roger says that it was later on. "We didn't think of it as anything special other than a track on an album. But it was the first one we recorded after the fire. And it was the only one recorded in a different location to everything else on the album. The fire left us with nowhere to record, and we actually settled on a place two or three days later, actually another theater, in the town of Montreux. It's a beautiful theater as well, old, kind of art deco, gorgeous.

"So, we decided to do that, and the first day we got there, we had the truck parked outside and got in in the afternoon, set up all the gear. By late afternoon we were getting drum sounds and bass sounds and guitar sounds, took a meal break, and then by the evening we said, right, let's start recording.

"So, we started, and Ritchie said, 'I have this idea for a riff' and played that famous riff. And we knocked it into shape after a couple of hours. This will be a verse, this will be whatever, really knocked together. And by the time we actually started recording it, it was about one or two in the morning. And unbeknownst to us, the roadies were holding the doors shut against the police, who were trying to come in and stop us from recording because we were making a lot of noise. Actually, we weren't making a lot of noise; we were making our normal noise, but it was a lot of noise for Montreux, which is a sleepy little town. It's a quiet place where people go to retire, or at least it was then. It's getting more vibrant now.

"So eventually we stopped recording. We had finished the backing track, and the police came in and said, 'You have to stop this,' or words to that effect in Swiss. Is Swiss a language? No, I don't think it is. French it would have been. So that's when we said, we better find somewhere else. And that was actually a big problem because there was nowhere else. It's a small town, and in desperation we ended up at the Grand Hotel, which was closed up for the season, an empty space really. And there was nothing around it, so we could make some noise, and that's how we ended up there."

"It's the absolute, definitive biographical detail of the making of *Machine Head*," says Gillan, in summary. "It tells the story of the making of the album. Interesting concept. It just so happened that while we were in town, the whole casino burns down. We were watching Zappa do the last show ever in that wonderful building; yeah, it's a pretty amazing story. You say it's got a bad rap; I think people take it with a pinch of salt. There was a wonderful occasion in Australia where the whole of Australia played it. We had people in schools . . . they were mustered in, thousands, every network television station, radio station; they all joined in and had people in the studio with all kinds of banjos and ukuleles and whatever, and on the count of 1, 2, 3, 4, bam, the whole of Australia played this damn thing, while we were also joining in, playing it in the studio. It was amazing."

Adds Ritchie Blackmore on the song's germination, "I was jamming with Ian Paice at a soundcheck, because we often used to get to the shows early. I said to Ian, 'Give me a time or a measure that we haven't played lately,' and he put down that particular beat and I just went straight into that riff. It's related to a medieval way of playing, because in those days they played a lot in parallel fourths. That riff wouldn't sound the way it does if it wasn't played in parallel fourths. But Paicey and I just went through it, and it sounded like a backing track. I feel that we did things in Purple which were a lot better than that, that didn't go anywhere."

Assorted 1972 gig ads. *Martin Popoff archive*

Next up was "Lazy," a big, spirited blues jam with tons of soloing, interesting licks, and humorous Gillan yelps. But a blues all the same, to my mind, a coasting throwaway. But what do I know? Pretty much every Deep Purple fan buddy of mine loves it to death.

Notes Ian Gillan, "I think 'Lazy' . . . if you remember 'Wring That Neck,' from one of the albums prior to when Roger and I joined, it's just one of those. . . . Purple has always been a jamming band, and sometimes you never quite know where these things evolve from. You walk into the studio, and you hear Jon Lord playing the intro to 'Child in Time' one day, and the next day it's a song. And you hear 'Lazy,' and the next day it's a song. And you hear 'Smoke on the Water,' and two months later it's a song. So, these riffs and ideas, you never know quite how they germinate. But I think pretty much you can look in the Ian Paice / Roger Glover camp as far as the development of that swing rhythm goes. Paicey grew up with big band; his whole thing with Buddy Rich and all that—those were his influences when he started playing. So, if you listen to the swing stuff, you've got to put it right down to Paicey. When he started playing that shuffle, he's there, bang. Drummers never get the credit that they're due, really. But he's an important part of the band."

"Lazy," according to Roger, was inspired by Oscar Brown Jr.'s "Sleepy," or, according to Ritchie, "Steppin' Out" by Eric Clapton. Blackmore was none too pleased with his solo, having recorded it in pieces. But his fondness for the song remains intact, despite Ritchie not being much of a blues guy.

Machine Head ends with a reviving, resounding, and restoring symphony of flash metal called "Space Truckin'." Its riff was to become famous like that of "Smoke on the Water," and its character is similarly marauding and malevolent, titled somewhat toward that of Edgar Winter's instrumental masterpiece "Frankenstein." The song is also a classic drummer's workout, with Ian utilizing rapid-fire snare work to its fullest. For his part, Paice admits that he lifted a few bits from the Nice's "America."

"'Space Truckin" was like a road song around the universe," says Gillan. "Chuck Berry goes cosmic. At the time, it was amazing to think that there would be a time in the future when the space age would be a historical age rather than something very futuristic, and that's how quickly time has changed. But it was very exciting at the time. Sputnik was going around in the '60s, and people were shooting rockets out in a haphazard fashion, really." Ian's curious "Chuck Berry goes cosmic" comment is supported by Roger's assertion that there was a 1950s lyrical vibe to the song, and that he and Ian sat around firing back and forth silly little space puns.

At the song's incendiary close, Ian screams his nuts off. Asked if he can still sing *Machine Head* songs comfortably decades down the line, he figures, "They're all an absolute dawdle. Ten times easier than they were back in '71—much, much easier. I've found other parts of the range of my voice that were always elusive when I was a kid. I listen back to some of those albums, and I absolutely cringe at my vocal performance, not so much the performance, but the tone. And you know, working six cities a week, eventually you get the hang of it."

I asked Ian if there was a breakthrough point—or a breakthrough vocal coach perhaps—that taught him something along the way.

"No, I think it was basically the amount of work. I did all sorts of things, and I like to sing, so I tried all sorts of different styles. I used to find my top range . . . for example, 'Speed King,' oh boy, I love singing that song now. And I listen to it, and I go, my God, I'm reaching for those notes and it's all over the place. I mean, it's got an air of animal excitement about it, which I insist on keeping. But I'm just on top of it now, rather than underneath it, as I used to be, and I think it's just experience, to be honest."

As regards some of those high notes, sure, some of them are heroic reaching and some of them are screams. But some must surely be classed as "mere" falsetto.

"You know, I never quite know how to describe that," answers Gillan. "Some people call it falsetto; some people call it screaming. When I was in a band with Roger, before Deep Purple, called Episode Six, we had a girl singer, and every set she used to come out front and sing two or three songs, and I used to shift over to the keyboards and play keyboards. And then, of course, her harmony part was then missing because she was singing lead. So, I used to take her harmony part; it was a six-piece, six vocalists in the band, so there was a lot of harmony. So, I used to sing up there, and I hadn't sung up there since I was a boy soprano in the local choir.

"So, I found my range very easy to do that. And then, gradually, instead of calling it falsetto, I started singing up there, but full voice. So, it's basically like a controlled scream, in the screaming register, but it was actually singing. And it had to be clear, and it had a vibrato and it had a point of attack, and I was able to move the notes around quite comfortably. So, it was a style I developed just from necessity, really. But I never quite knew what to call it. But I still use it; we still do all kinds of stuff.

Promo poster issued by Warner Bros. in the US. *Pericle Formenti archive*

'Woman from Tokyo' has an awful lot of that in it. And in fact, there's some screaming on the new albums as well."

Celebrity rock critic Lester Bangs spoke quite sensibly of *Machine Head* (other than the gratuitous and erroneous MC5 reference) in his review of the album for *Rolling Stone*, writing that the band's "last three albums have finally found a comfortably furious groove for them to work in, making them prime contenders among the most searingly loud and heavy bands on both sides of the Atlantic. Deep Purple *In Rock* was a dynamic, frenzied piece of work sounding not a little like the MC5 (anybody who thinks that all heavy bands put out thudding slabs of 'downer' music just haven't gotten into Deep Purple).

"*Fireball* was more of the same," he continues, "if not quite as frantically effective. *Machine Head* bears strong similarities to both its immediate predecessors, lying qualitatively somewhere in between the two. And like both of them, though it delivers 'the Sound,' the rushing, grating crunch of a heart attack, it has its ups and downs compositionally. 'Highway Star' is a great opening track, quite similar both structurally and thematically to 'Speed King' and 'Fireball,' the openers of the two previous albums. The pace is blistering, almost too fast for comfort, with lyrics that take the primeval car-girl equation and turn it into something as breathtakingly homicidal as Alice Cooper's 'Under My Wheels.' 'Space Truckin'' is just as good, a sci-fi boogie that's the perfect answer to all the Kantnerian pomposities and turns out to be the missing link between them and things like Wild Man Fisher's 'Rocket Rock' (lyrically) and the Doors' 'Hello I Love You' (musically). Once again, the lyrics are ace, and never let it be said that Deep Purple don't have a sense of humor. In between those two Deep Purple classics lies nothing but good, hard, socking music, although some of the lyrics may leave a little bit to be desired."

Machine Head was an instant hit, reaching #1 on the UK charts and #7 on the Billboard 200. Additionally, it shot to #1 in Canada and all over mainland Europe. It received its RIAA US gold certification on November 6, 1972, and currently sits at double platinum. Black Sabbath and Uriah Heep now had themselves some serious competition, even if Led Zeppelin and the Rolling Stones were in another league.

"Musically, I don't think competition came into it," recalls Ian Paice, speaking with Sam Dunn. "I think the moment you start to feel you're cracking it is the moment you sold a few more tickets than the other guys. It becomes totally unimportant in the years, but at the time you think we did okay. Personally, I didn't take a lot of notice of Sabbath. It was something that I appreciated why it was successful and how well it was done, but it didn't appeal to me. Same with Queen. I know why it's successful, I know why a lot of people like it, I know why it's really well done, but it's not my music.

"Zeppelin was an obvious thing, why it was successful. It was brilliantly played, and they had chosen a style of music that was so blues based that it was immediately successful, and it opened up great vistas for them. They took blues and they made it hard. Cream had done a very similar thing before then. The Yardbirds, great British blues hard rock band. The precedents were there.

"But at that time, we were all working the same gigs, the same time, and you really didn't have a lot of time to actually listen to or wonder what the other bands were doing. One night, some time in about '69, Zeppelin and Purple were in the same town playing different halls, before it went mega. We were playing to like 2,000, and they were playing to 2,300 or something like that. Small theaters. So, you were doing it all the time. You were just having a ball and worrying about your own gig. You weren't worrying about other people."

Asked by Sam why this heavy-rock music was doing so well in the UK, Paice says, "Go back to where the music was invented, in North America. They forgot what they had. And we were enthralled by it. We changed it a little bit, and we sold it back to them. And they realized that—or maybe they didn't realize, but they thought it was something massively new—they had it ten, fifteen years ago, but they just forgot about it. We just took rock 'n' roll from the '50s into the '60s and translated it into something that made sense to us. And then North American audiences started hearing it from the radio stations, going, 'I really like that,' thinking it was something totally new, and it wasn't. It was just the way we'd seen their music of the decade before. It's an amazing thing when you think about it. We sold something back to North America that they invented.

"I think it spoke to young people because it had the aggression," continues Paice. "It had the emotion. It also had great musicality, and I don't mean musicality in the way you needed to be versed in the theory and notes of music. What you had to do was know how to convey what you were feeling to the person listening to it. And that's what that British revolution in the late '60s and early '70s did. I think we captured the emotions of another continent that nobody knew how to express, because it hadn't happened there the same way."

We can leave the word "competition" out of it, but it's interesting to note that all the "big four" UK hard rock acts of the day were peaking at this juncture, Black Sabbath with *Vol 4*, Uriah Heep with *Demons and Wizards* and *The Magician's Birthday*, Deep Purple with *Machine Head*, and finally Led Zeppelin with 1971's monstrous untitled fourth album. What's also interesting is that the entirety of the United States had absolutely nobody of note making this kind of music.

"He's a very close friend," intimates Gillan, when asked whatever happened to Funky Claude, immortalized by the "Smoke on the Water" line "Funky Claude was running in and out / Pulling kids out of ground."

"He does lots of things. He is on the building committee for the new Apollo Theater, the rebuilding of it. He still runs the Montreux Jazz Festival. He still lives in Switzerland. He has a house on top of a mountain overlooking the resort. We go there regularly. I speak to him on the phone a couple times a year. So Funky Claude is an old buddy. He is the guy who saved a few lives when the casino was set on fire. He has done all sorts of things. He has quite a few labels in Switzerland. It's a smallish country, and so you tend to get one company that has the franchise for Atlantic, Warner, and maybe Polydor as well, or something like that. He was a promoter and he was promoting our shows. As a friend, he arranged for us to have the use of the place. He was producing Frank Zappa at the time. He is quite a powerful man in Montreux. If he says something is happening, then the mayor says, 'Okay.' He has made so much money and raised the profile of the city of Montreux. Funky Claude is alive and well!"

Creem magazine ad for *Purple Passages* (December 1972), along with the album cover. *Pericle Formenti archive*

Six months after the release of *Machine Head*, North America was subjected to a double-album compilation of Mk. I material called *Purple Passages*. And so begins the endless stream of hits packages and live albums forever more. The album rose to #57 in the charts and, at the time, really caused a lot of confusion, given the contrast of the wobbly baroque music enclosed to the bluster and bravado of the band's current smash hit record.

The 1998 deluxe reissue of *Machine Head* on CD includes very little in the way of useful rarities, but there are bits and pieces of studio chatter, some amusing end-of-song flameouts, and a vibrant Roger Glover remix.

"Years ago, when CDs first came out, I was in my local record store," says Roger, with respect to the process he has been involved with sprucing up the Purple catalog. "I bought a CD player in Japan right when they first came out. I wanted to be first on the block. So, when *Machine Head* came out, I thought, 'Wow, this sounds like shit. No vibrancy, no dynamics.' So, I wrote the record company and said, 'I'm disgusted with this. If our legacy is going to be in this digital format, I want it to be good.'

"I had the grace of no reply and was very frustrated with the whole situation. Then EMI said, 'We're going to be doing some remasters; would you like to be involved?' 'Thank you very much; I would love to.' And they were very good; they let me listen to the tapes, and I had the freedom to do what I wanted. I think it's important to retain the mixes as they were, as I think the mixes are part of the character. You remaster it to bring out the best in it, but you don't really change the mix; you leave it all there as intact.

"But it's nice to take a fresh look and try new mixes, and of course you have to do new mixes for outtakes and songs that never made it, because they were never mixed properly in the first place. So, the whole idea of remixing something we did twenty-five years ago started with *In Rock*. Then we did *Fireball* and found a treasure trove of outtakes and bits and pieces, including a song that was never before released. Which is unusual because the old record company and management used to rifle through our past, and anything to do with Deep Purple, they used to throw out in one form or another. So, to find a song that was finished was great. That was a song called 'Slow Train.'

"Then *Machine Head* was next, and there were no outtakes, no alternative takes, no extra songs, except for 'When a Blind Man Cries,' which was a B side. So, I was doing them in order. For *Machine Head*, I decided to remix the entire album, so it consists of the old mixes on one CD, remastered, and the new mixes on the second CD. And I have to tell you, it's probably the most successful remix I've ever done. Wonderful sound. You've never heard 'Smoke on the Water,' 'Lazy,' or any of those until you hear the new mixes. *Machine Head* is the one I'm most proud of."

Chapter 9

Made in Japan

"Something that was priceless"

There's a lot of debate around these parts as to the merits of the *Made in Japan* album. History certainly records many smart people—fans, critics, rock stars—as calling it one of the greatest live albums of all time. Ask Yngwie Malmsteen about it and he'll set you up right (we'll hear more from him in a bit). I, on the other hand . . . just give me the songs in three- or four-minute bursts and I'm happy. But Deep Purple are a bit of a jam band, or at least they were then, back when it was in vogue. Zeppelin and indeed Rainbow created the same sort of "extended reinterpretations" of their hits and then slapped them on double vinyl. But nobody calls *The Song Remains the Same* or *On Stage* the greatest live album of all time.

Made in Japan is essentially the product of the *Machine Head* tour, representing the favored Mk. II Deep Purple at the heroic top arc of its game. The idea for the record was actually that of the band's Japanese label, Warner-Pioneer Corporation, which thought it would be a nice package to commemorate the first Japanese dates ever, each sold out long in advance, with Purple already being a huge entity there. The album was subsequently quickly slated for UK release and, reversing the trend, was issued at home first, on December 22, 1972, and not stateside until five months later. In the UK it was sold for the same price as a single album. The intention was not to issue it in the Americas at all, but once the label saw thousands of import copies selling at the then-high price of $10, they adjusted their strategy. Additionally, Roger Glover in particular decried the robust trade in Deep Purple bootleg recordings and hoped that the band issuing something official might "kill their market."

When you'd ask Jon Lord about his favorite Deep Purple album, he'd tell you, "*Made in Japan*. I remember that period well, and the band was at the height of its powers. That double album was the epitome of what we stood for in those days. It wasn't meant to be released outside Japan. The Japanese said, 'Will you please make a live album?' We said, 'We don't make live albums; we don't believe in them.' They said, 'Please, please make a live album.' We finally said okay, but we said we wanted the rights to the tapes because we didn't want the album to be released outside Japan.

The *Made in Japan* cover art. *Martin Popoff archive*

That album only cost about $3,000 to make. It sounded pretty good, so we said to Warner Bros., 'Do you want this?' They said, 'No, live albums don't happen.' They wound up putting it out anyway, and it went platinum in about two weeks."

Originally a double vinyl album, the set included but seven selections. "Smoke on the Water" was recorded at the Koseinenkin in Osaka on August 15, 1972. "Highway Star," "Child in Time," "Strange Kind of Woman," and "Space Truckin'" were recorded at the same venue the following night, while "The Mule" and "Lazy" were captured on August 17 at the Budokan in Tokyo. The remastered and expanded CD version of the album added "Black Night" (from Tokyo; an edit of this was used back during the album's original issue as a B side), "Speed King," also from Tokyo, and the band's rock 'n' roll revival "Lucille" encore from Osaka on the second night.

Roger Glover, in discussing his technical role with the reissue program, demonstrates the high regard for the album that is shared by many. "*Made in Japan*, I didn't have anything to do with, because to me there was no point in already remixing something that was priceless. The way it was is by far the best way it should stay. The three concerts from which *Made in Japan* was culled, they wanted me to remix those, and I didn't want to do that, because you already have the best album. All I wanted to hear was a remastered version of that, which has come out and it's great. That really is about the size of it."

Ian Paice tends to be in agreement. "From the old records, my favorite albums are *Made in Japan* and *In Rock*. *In Rock*, because it was a corner turned; there was a direction, and nobody really knew it was there until it smacked us in the face. And *Made in Japan* because it's still probably the ultimate live hard rock record—nothing really compares to that."

Adding a note about taking songs from studio to stage, Ian says that the tough nuts to crack "tend to be when you're bringing in new songs and when they're new songs that have fairly complex arrangements. The old ones sort of take care of

Japanese tour poster, 1972. *Pericle Formenti archive*

themselves. In the back of your mind, you know exactly what it is you've got to do, and you know what the changes are going to be. It's when you have a fairly complex new song . . . and that can be as simple as getting the tempo wrong. Because you haven't quite locked into it. And sometimes the recording tempo is nothing like the stage tempo. You can take the same tempo from the studio and put it onstage, and everybody thinks they're going to fall asleep. So, you have to change things. But that's the only time where you've really got to keep the brain cells happening."

Ex-Scorpions legend Uli Jon Roth can certainly appreciate what Deep Purple gets up to live, and in his description of Deep Purple's worth, you can see why musicians appreciate *Made in Japan* so much.

"I saw them live in '72 and thought they were great, particularly Ritchie and Ian Gillan. It was very unique, very musical—always. Ritchie was totally a trendsetter. His approach to playing the guitar was very, very unique, when he first came out, and it is still unique. There are very few people in the music business who were able to do like three totally different things and make them all work. You know, like

Purple, Rainbow, and then Blackmore's Night. It's a very unique gift that he has, a very musical gift, and a great popular gift also. Like, I couldn't write a riff like 'Smoke on the Water.' Some people maybe laugh about it because you used to hear it in every music store. But, you know, that's an achievement. And it's a gift.

"I always felt he was a guitar player who sounded exciting," continues Roth, who incidentally has a deeper Purple connection in that current Purple keyboardist Don Airey was with his solo band for five years. "Ritchie was never afraid to go close to the edge; there was always danger in his playing. And this is what I like. I like players who don't do the expected thing. They take chances and go for the dangerous moments and not just be self-complacent. I'm more fascinated by the aspect of creativity, in the making, and with Ritchie you always get that, this element of real excitement; it was always fresh. And even if they played the same songs for the umpteenth time, they weren't afraid to improvise onstage. Purple never played them the same.

"Another thing that I really liked about Ritchie is that he always has a great tone. He had very much his own tone, and I respond to that. I respect players that have a unique tone, a very good ear for sound. And he sacrificed the playability of the instrument for a great tone. Because it's not easy to do these sounds with an almost clean guitar, the way he used to play."

Gillan, who also plays a big role in *Made in Japan*'s explosiveness, also garners praise from Roth. "I mean, what can I say about Ian? Ian was fantastic from the beginning, when he did *Jesus Christ Superstar*—that was defining stuff. And I would say that if anybody in rock created the quote unquote rock sound that thousands of singers ended up copying, it was Ian. Before that, we maybe have Robert Plant in Led Zeppelin, but Robert was a bit more blues based, coming from that area. But Ian gave rock this kind of incredible bel canto edge, almost like an opera singer, in rock, without any of the opera kinds of sounds, but equally valid. And that is so hard to do for most people. I think he just single-handedly created that genre. That's my personal take on it. Or least he's the first one who really had it down to a fine point, with 'Child in Time' and all that."

In the weeks leading up to *Made in Japan*'s concert dates, Deep Purple was in a bit of a shambles. There were the ever-present squabbles in the band, but following up on tour cancellations due to Gillan's illness, now Ritchie had given out, due to a combination of hepatitis and what might be described as a mental breakdown. Ritchie would burst into tears at the thought of this life continuing, as he put it, being shuffled from hotel to hotel. Having just recorded their career-making album in the dead of winter, the band would spend January and February 1972 jetting back and forth between concentrated packs of tour dates between the US, Europe, and the UK.

It all came to a head during yet another US leg, in late March, with Ritchie summarily ordered to bed for some much-needed rest. After playing a March 31 date in Flint, Michigan, as a four-piece, a couple of replacement guitarists were considered, first being Al Kooper, more of a keyboardist and producer, known for his work with Bob Dylan. Kooper knew that he wasn't even close to right for the gig but rehearsed with the band anyway and actually had them convinced he was a worthy hire. Kooper thought more sensibly and declined the offer in the face of much begging and handwringing. He then suggested someone who would be better suited, Randy California, the flashy yet troubled guitarist for West Coast hippies

December 16, 1972 NEW MUSICAL EXPRESS Page 19

DEEP PURPLE

MADE IN JAPAN

後必用吏

Side One
1. Highway Star
Osaka – 16th August 1972
2. Child in Time
Osaka – 16th August 1972

Side Two
3. Smoke on the Water
Osaka – 15th August 1972
4. The Mule
Tokyo – 17th August 1972

Side Three
5. Strange Kind of Woman
Osaka – 16th August 1972
6. Lazy
Tokyo – 17th August 1972

Side Four
7. Space Truckin'
Osaka – 16th August 1972

TPSP 351

SPECIAL LIVE DOUBLE ALBUM FOR ONLY £3.25
This is the first ever "live" recording of Deep Purple's incredible stage performance. We think it is the best live recording ever made.

Available on Cassette and Cartridge.

EMI

EMI Records (The Gramophone Co. Ltd.) EMI House, 20 Manchester Square, London, W1A 1ES
A member of the EMI Group of Companies
International leaders in Electronics, Records and Entertainment.

New Musical Express ad for the band's first live album. *Martin Popoff archive*

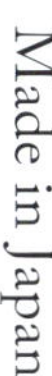

Spirit. Indeed, one show with Randy actually took place, in Quebec City, Canada, on April 6, 1972. Ian remembers it for the fact that California performed the "Child in Time" solo with slide guitar, and that the band did "When a Blind Man Cries," the only time Purple would perform it until the modern era.

Blackmore was back behind the Strat in late May, first for eight shows in twelve days in America, back to the UK, and then straight back to the States again for a fourth time that year, to play ten shows in twelve days. His strict diet of boiled fish and boiled chicken caused the crew to set him up with a portable cooker. Still, shopping for him turned out to be a hassle, especially because he was also on glucose, which couldn't be easily bought in American drugstores because it was used in the manufacture of illicit drugs.

Among all this, the band found time to retire to an Italian villa to try to work on the next studio album, again using the Rolling Stones mobile, which had to be parked outside the gates of the villa because it wouldn't fit under the arched gateway. Closed-circuit TV had to be instated once again to aid in communication. In the oppressive heat, the band managed to work up only two songs, "Woman from Tokyo" and "Painted Horse." The latter wouldn't make the album, but it was definitely worthy, being a slinky up-tempo popster with blues influence, harmonica, note-dense bass lines, and a novel falsetto vocal from Ian that the rest of the band didn't appreciate (it would be four years before the song surfaced in any form).

Ritchie and Ian were barely talking to each other at this point, with Ritchie hinting that he was about ready for a solo career, variously griping that the band had taken their sound as far as it could, or as far as their audience would let it, or that Ian's singing was holding them back. As well, Ritchie was the most prolific of all the guys with the groupies back in the US, and Ian broke the code of the road by bringing his girlfriend, Zoe, along. Zoe had the bad habit of calling home and reporting to the guys' various better halves. This Yoko situation, of sorts, got thrown onto the pile of tension-getters to the point where Gillan wound up traveling separately from the band, not to mention staying separately at hotels.

Having knocked the Italian session on its head, the band then worked to replace the canceled Japanese dates in May with mid-August dates, and these are the shows that would provide the source tapes for *Made in Japan*.

One recollection of those classic Mk. II days traipsing all over America comes from Wayne Bruce, guitarist for obscure southern rockers Hydra, of which the Purple guys were fans.

"Deep Purple were playing a show at the Omni in Atlanta, and they came to a club that we were playing called Finoccio's, also in Atlanta. It was the keyboard player, definitely Roger Glover, and Ian Paice, because they got up and played, and I remember that the song Ian wanted to do was 'Going Down,' because we were doing that well before the first album. And they had to switch the drums around because he's left-handed [laughs]. This would have been around '72. And I remember one time, I wasn't involved in this particular thing, but I certainly knew about it. They were going somewhere, and we had this equipment truck. They were going to a party, and they didn't have enough room in the front, so Orville Davis, our bass player, and, believe it or not, Roger Glover got in the back with the equipment. And this is a 12-foot truck, in the dark. I always thought that was funny. They were a big band at the time, but they didn't have any egos or whatever."

Interesting point Wayne brings up: that is, the fact that Paice plays a set that is essentially "backward" from normal. "I never even thought about it until I went to set up my first decent drum kit and saw that it was built for a right-handed player," notes Ian. "The tom mounting was in the wrong place. When you watch yourself in the mirror, you look right-handed, so you think you look just like everybody else. Had I gone for lessons, I dare say the teacher would have tried to get me to play right-handed. Had I done so, I think I would be a better player today, because I would have been training my weaker hand to play all the hard stuff from day one, and the independence my left hand would have would be amazing. Basically, I'm just a mirror image of every other drummer. The ambidextrous thing of changing over is the sort of thing that Simon Phillips and Billy Cobham have perfected. It must be very hard for them because they were set in their way of playing right-sided. Had I started being naturally left-sided and been trained from day one to play with the right, that would have all been there automatically. Any drummer who is naturally left-handed should try playing the other way around for a year, because the independence on the left side will be frightening.

"The only formal training was my father showing me what a daddy-mommy roll was," continues Paice. "He said, 'Practice that,' and I did, and that was it. Then I knew there was such a thing as a paradiddle. I didn't know what it was, but I found out from other drummers. Everything was just a variation of that. It's funny; when

Billboard ad used in the US to promote two Deep Purple albums at once

I do clinics, the first thing I say is 'Anybody with any technical question, just forget it. I'm not interested in it, and you can probably play more rudiments than I can. The thing is, I can probably play a bit faster and better than you can.'"

Made in Japan (the Japanese issue was called *Live in Japan*) was ably recorded by Martin Birch, who was by now considered an irreplaceable part of the Deep Purple organization. From the outset, Birch had declared the offered eight-track recording equipment unusable, due to lack of control over the balance, but you'd never tell by the rich sound he managed for the album. Both Ian and Ritchie showed their disdain for live albums by not even listening to the tapes (Gillan had an extra complaint: that his performances suffered due to having only recently recovered from bronchitis), leaving mainly Paice and Glover to champion the cause of the record, with both involved heavily in the mixing stages.

Made in Japan opens with a rendition of *Machine Head*'s flash first track "Highway Star," mercifully close to the original duration at just under seven minutes. But yes, just like a jam band, it positively creeps into view before exploding. This has become tradition over the decades. It feels like a live, real-time instrument check, sound check, and limber-up all at once, and fans love it. It's a spirited version, to be sure, but does it necessarily eclipse the steady class of the studio one? I think not, mainly because *Machine Head* is so gorgeously recorded.

"Child in Time" follows, with Paice getting quite busy for a ballad and Ian wailing his head off, something Jon Lord digs. "There are many," says Jon, of fine live memories. "The original *Concerto* night and California Jam, even though that wasn't with Gillan. Some of those shows in '71 and '72 with Gillan in his pomp and glory . . . sometimes when he sang 'Child in Time,' it would make your hair stand on end. I'd also say some of the improvisation battles I've had with Ritchie. I've had some glorious times."

There's an up-tempo and shuffling jam in the middle of "Child in Time," helping send the song to twelve minutes long.

"One of the earliest things we did together, Ritchie and I, was a track called 'Mandrake Root,' from the first album," begins Jon, speaking with Sam Dunn on the subject of improvisation. "We used it for donkey years as a vehicle for very long improvisation. There's another one called 'Wring That Neck,' where we would just go off, really, to see where it would take us. Luckily, particularly in the drummer we had, Ian Paice, Ian understood the shape of improvising. Because he was brought up listening to big-band music by his father playing that kind of stuff, as did mine, in fact. So Ian had already heard a setup, a tune that set up a chord sequence, and then various trombonists, saxophonists, trumpeters, etc. being let loose on the same chord sequence to see where they took it. And listening to great drummers sitting behind that, keeping the shape and the vision of where it's going to go live, is magic.

"Because it's quite a difficult thing to listen to a great improviser improvising alone. You've got to really like the instrument he's playing. Do you want to hear a solo trombonist all on his own for fifteen minutes? Well, good luck to you. So, I think what we had in the band was that Ritchie came out of an early rock 'n' roll improvising tradition. I had done more jazz and blues before Purple than actual rock. Like I say, Paice had this ability to listen and shape things for us. We had that wonderful freedom, which is both a gift and a responsibility, which is to go out onstage in front of paying customers and say, 'Hang on to your hats. You're going to like what we do here. We don't know what we're going to do, but we know you're going to like it.' So that, as I say, at the same time, is a gift and a responsibility. And we used that as much as we damn well could."

But there were naysayers.

"Yeah, there were nights when you'd get the occasional oik from the back, shouting out, 'Get on with it!' Which is fine. I think most musicians have been there. But that shouldn't stop you, and it didn't, because, like I say, we had the genuine belief that the improvisation was part of the music.

"And indeed, it was very often how we came up with the music. We would jam a lot. Paice would just start playing a rhythm, Roger would join in, and then Ritchie and I would go to see where it would take us. And Gillan would be sitting in the background doing the *Telegraph* crossword until something made him glance up. And he'd think, 'Oh, I like the sound of that,' and he'd start jotting something down.

"For example, that's how 'Child in Time' came around. As we've discussed, it was a vaguely borrowed riff from a band called It's a Beautiful Day, something they did called 'Bombay Calling.' But then we slowed it right down and started messing around with it. And I think within about half an hour we had a song. Likewise, with 'Highway Star;' that started with a jam. I think it might have even started in the back of a van with just acoustic guitars."

"So, you know, improvising was what we did. It's the way the band operated. I think when Purple started to try to become a more structured band, it started to be less Purple. That's my take on it. For example, once we get to albums like *Stormbringer*, Ritchie's last album in that era, and then on to *Come Taste the Band*. . . . I still don't think of that as a Purple album. I think of it as a Tommy Bolin and David Coverdale project, with me and Paice going, 'Isn't it time we stopped?' It's a very good album, but it's not Deep Purple. And again, later on when we re-formed the band, *Perfect Strangers* had a real improvisatory feel about it, like we were almost making it up as we were going along. But then the next one, *House of Blue Light*, was much more structured and therefore, although still good, I think less successful."

But you can go only so far with a studio album. Fact is that the huge reputation that *Made in Japan* enjoys is very much because it's the foremost document that represents Deep Purple as the greatest improvisational act in the hard rock space.

Jon draws further parallels between Purple with jazz.

"Yes, it's the spirit of adventure, the desire to push boundaries, the desire to see 'What if?' That's always a good phrase to put into a young musician's mind. What would happen if? Rather than, well, he did it, so we'll do it, but rather we'll do it this way. I think jazz is a more cerebral, more inward-searching medium, whereas rock is a more outward-searching medium. I'd say certainly the late '60s and early '70s, when there was no rule book in rock 'n' roll and when record companies were entrepreneurs; ah, those were the golden days.

"To go away from the written page and to just trust this sort of playful imagination, this other part of your brain that's able to make things up for you as you go along, that's a great moment in your life to discover that. It was discovering this idea in my teens, that I could sit at the piano and improvise. Although it was based in the way I was learning, which was a classical way.

"After college I ended up in my first blues band, but it was more jazzy blues, and I was being asked to improvise. 'Jon, you take these two choruses here.' Oh,

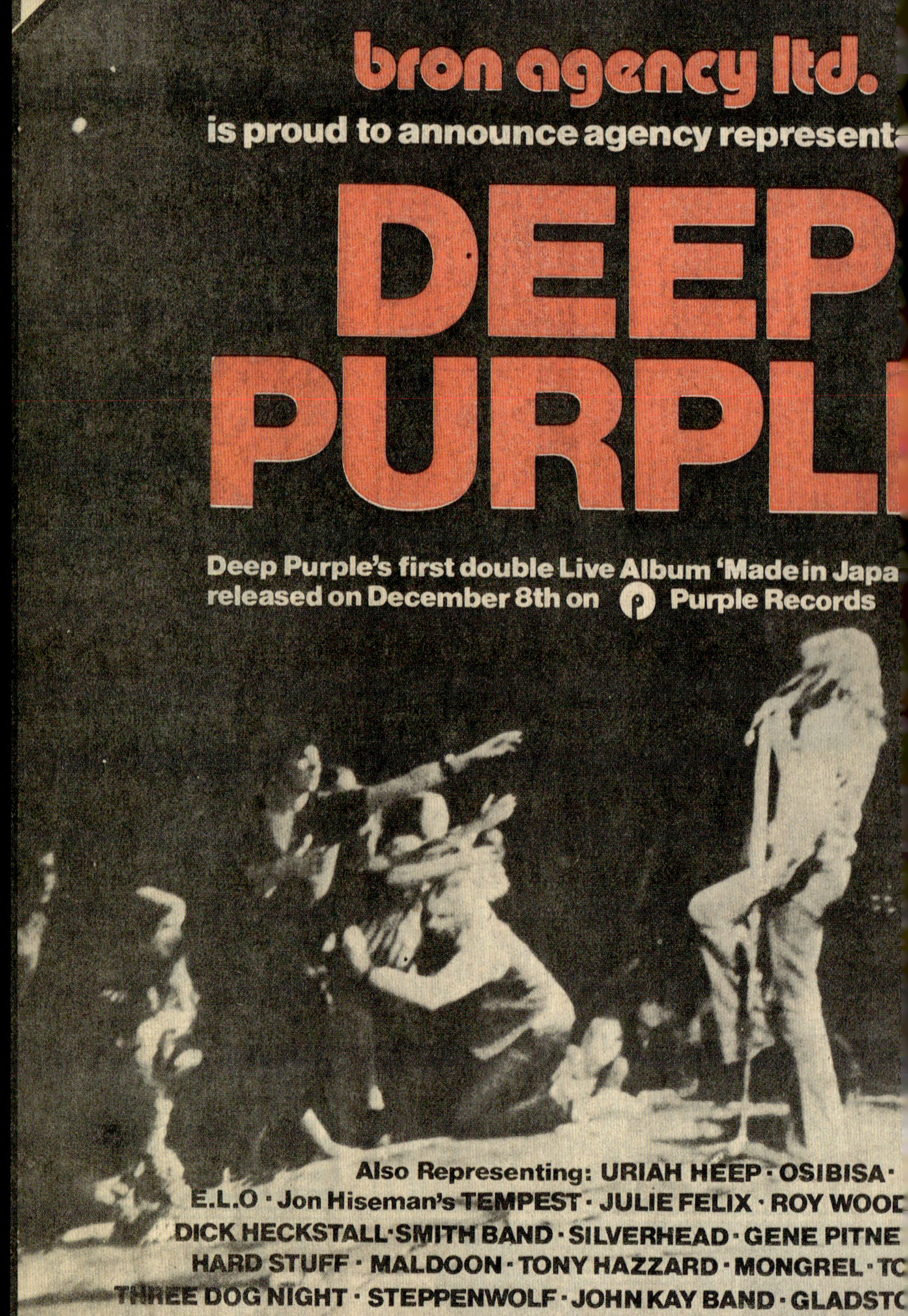

Gerry Bron's Bron Agency picks up Deep Purple, while taking the opportunity to promote *Made in Japan* as well. *Martin Popoff archive*

Page 60—MELODY MAKER, November 25, 1972

n of

ll be
P351)

IZZARD·
UNSHINE·
ASHTON·
MIKE MARAN

bang, you're off and running. So, then you start to listen to great improvisers. I had my heroes at the time. Dave Brubeck was a great hero. On the keyboards, Oscar Peterson. But then, players like Parker and Miles Davis and so on; I listened to the way they looked at improvisation in two massively different ways.

"And you start to see that if you keep your technique up, which is your servant, then you can ask your hands to go anywhere you feel they suddenly particularly ought to go. And one of the marvels of improvisation, I find, is that sometimes you actually look down at your hand and it's like another part of your brain goes, 'Why did it go there?,' and you realize you've just done something good. I don't think you can learn to improvise. You can help yourself be better at it by keeping your technique up. But if you're not a natural improviser—maybe people would disagree with me—but I don't see how you can learn to improvise. You have to feel it. You have to trust yourself. Some musicians—especially, of course, classically trained conservatory musicians—find it almost impossible to conceive going off the page."

"Some of Purple's predilection for improvisation came from Cream as well," adds Ian Paice. "Hendrix used to improvise, and Cream would improvise. Everything was extended. We've given you the song; now we're going to have fun in the middle of it. It wasn't just us; it was a whole movement of guys who can actually play that little bit better than guys who had been there before. Because they were two or three years older, and they just got better. And if you have that ability, if you didn't use it, you might get a bit bored. If you had this extra string to your bow, then you had to use it. Otherwise you're just playing the same thing every night.

A later-years ad promoting the *In Concert* album, culled from the same era as *Made in Japan*. *Martin Popoff archive*

"Again, I liken that to doing a Broadway show. If that's what you do, fine; I'm not putting it down. But that's not what we do. It gets harder the further on you are in your career, because you have so many more songs that people have an impression of in their mind from the CDs and the albums they have. And you can only change them so far before people start thinking you're doing it wrong. Before they knew the song really well, nothing was wrong. You could do whatever the hell you wanted. So, some of those things become more limiting the more accepted they become by the public.

"If you don't have that ability, it will never even cross your consciousness to do it. You will play the verse, the chorus, the middle eight, the verse, and the end, and that will be it. But if you have the ability to change something and keep the focus of the piece of music you're playing at the back of your mind, so you can come back to it, then why wouldn't you do that? And if you've got four or five like-minded people who have the same ability to just go on a complete tangent and then go, okay, back to where we were, that's a great art, and not everybody's blessed with it."

As for his view on the origins of improvisation, Paice says that "with blues, there's a lot of improvisation because it's such a simple format. If you're going to take a twelve-bar solo or you're going to take forty-eight bars, that in its own way is very basic improvisation. But jazz had a lot to do with that, because, again, you have a basic format of a tune, a template, and what you do inside it is up to the musician. As long as he has the quality and the inventiveness to make it work. I was in a band before Purple with a really good musician, but we were a cover band, and that's all we did. We wrote a couple of our own tunes, but you played the song. The thought of changing it was not there. When Purple started, I had that ability, and Ritchie and Jon certainly had that ability. So, between the three of us, if somebody looked across . . . Ritchie onstage would just look and go, 'Stop,' and he'd start doing something and we'd follow him. Now, you never know how you're going to get out of it, other than hopefully there's a lot of big eyes going, 'Now?' 'Yes!' But you have to have the ability to know we've got to go back to it. If you don't have that and you've gone off on this tangent and go, 'What were we doing in the first place?,' then you've had it."

Back to *Made in Japan* (and what they were doing in the first place), "Smoke on the Water" gets a little bit of an explanation at the beginning. And yes, this version sounds a mite heftier than the one on the hi-fidelity *Machine Head* record.

"The Mule" follows, sounding weak and out of place, no more than a vehicle for Paice's snare-dominated drum solo, which takes over soon and for most of the track.

"That's potluck," remarks Paice, asked about building the controversial beast known as the drum solo. "All drummers have their own tricks, and it just depends on whether or not they get the tricks in the right order."

As regards his own personal tricks, Ian figures, "The simplest one is just being able to perfect the daddy-mommy between the snare drum and the bass drum. If you get the placing of the notes right on two bass drums, it gives your hands time to do independent things, and the sound never stops. It's the sort of thing that people need two bass drums to do. You never develop that devastating power that two bass drums can have. You can fool so many people with what you're doing, because you have so much speed going. It's impossible for the audience to figure it out. If you've got two bass drums, the audience can see what you're doing. But when you've just got one foot, nobody can see how you can get two or three notes happening by sliding your foot forward on the bass drum pedal. People just don't know what's going on, and they think you're better than you are."

Defining the role of a good live rock drummer in general, Paice goes with "A lot of natural musical aggression initially and knowing when to control and when to let go. There are certain points in a song where you must hold back, and certain points where you must let go. You've got to know those instinctively. You have to have a lot of power, and you have to know how to conserve that strength because you're playing for an hour and a half or two hours. Very little of it has to do with actual drumming. It's a matter of how you look at the music you're playing. When

A gold-record award issued in the US by the RIAA. *Pericle Formenti archive*

you're playing rock 'n' roll, you're just driving along. You're not trying to be a virtuoso. You're just holding it together and hopefully making it swing. You've got your solo bit to be on your own and be clever. You've got to be sure that the band knows who is controlling it, and be sure they can hear you. It doesn't matter how many mics you've got on the kit. If you're playing quietly, all you're going to get is feedback. You must have that natural aggression."

And within the context of Purple? "To be exciting. Purple should never have worked. Basically, we had five egomaniacs. There was just a magical chemistry that allowed us to get some good stuff. I can't think of any other band that's been allowed that much freedom for all the members to do exactly what they wanted. We were just lucky that the chemistry was right, and people felt it. There was a real telepathy among the band members, and that meant I had a lot of freedom to play exactly what I wanted, where I wanted, and when I wanted. It wasn't even a matter of keeping time. It was a very exciting band."

Over to side 3 of *Made in Japan*, and half the side, nearly ten minutes, is taken up by "Strange Kind of Woman." Ritchie and Ian conduct their famed—and in this writer's opinion, notorious—guitar and vocal duel, in which Ritchie plays a lick and then Ian mimics it, which, again arguably, doesn't exactly result in what I'd call great music. The second half of side 3, nearly eleven minutes of "Lazy," features an imposing, distorted organ solo, inside of which Lord briefly riffs "Louie Louie." "Lazy" also includes a theme from Hugo Alfven's "Swedish Rhapsody #1," conjured during Ritchie's solo. Gillan plays harmonica, as he does on the studio version. There's more noodling, and the third quarter ends with a hot-dog break.

Side 4 is all "Space Truckin'," or rather five minutes of "Space Truckin'" and fifteen minutes of what amounts to sound check, including Ritchie performing his volume control / "cello" solo from "Fools." Paice is kept quite busy throughout. "That's just going for it, live onstage," says Ian. "With all the hiccups that may be there or the little blemishes. It's really strange. When you do something like that in a studio, the blemishes are so apparent because everything is so clean in front of you. But if you do those sorts of things onstage, with the wonderful wash that you get from a live stage sound, what are blemishes in the studio turn into bits of glorious humanity onstage. It's nothing like the machine; you're creating that music for that moment in time. The fact that it happens to have been captured on a recording device is neither here nor there; that's not what you did it for. You did it for that fraction of a split second, when it felt like the right thing to do."

"Audiences started to be standing at the time," notes Jon, speaking with Sam Dunn, on how the concert experience was changing. "I remember the first time I played in Amsterdam in a club called the Paradiso, not long after Ian Gillan and Roger Glover joined. They were all sitting cross-legged, smoking jazz cigarettes. So, we were getting a contact high at the same time, which was extremely enjoyable as I seem to remember. But you felt like saying, 'Please stand up!' It's awfully difficult to play 'Speed King' to a bunch of nodding heads going, 'Yeah, that's really cool.' It's not quite the reaction we wanted. So, there's a circular, somewhat symbiotic relationship beginning to take place between audiences starting to want more, and therefore musicians are trying to provide more, and the two are feeding off each other. I have no real knowledge of why it happened. I only know that it did, and I was there when it did."

And let's face it: Deep Purple were delivering heavy metal, especially as it was defined in 1972, no matter how much the guys pushed back on it.

"I first heard the term 'heavy metal' in '71, maybe '72," recalls Jon. "And I was quite annoyed by it because it seemed to me to have no emotion. It's heavy metal. Heavy rock, I'd heard, as opposed to hard rock, but then heavy metal . . . that seemed to be an emotionless, robotic kind of thing, which didn't fit the way I felt about Deep Purple. Until Ritchie left in '74, I always felt that Purple had, in spite of all the bombast and loudness and the dry ice and madness onstage, one foot just dragging back into the blues somehow. It was still that feeling that occasionally we were in touch with an emotion. A deeper, perhaps bluer emotion than just a heavy hard band."

Word salad, because there's no denying that until Judas Priest came along, or Ritchie bounced back with Rainbow, there was literally not a single band on the planet that was more heavy metal than Deep Purple.

Speaking more of the modern form, Jon says that "I think the first heavy metal I heard was concerned with power, speed, and volume. Certainly speed. Everything seemed to be wanted to be played quite fast. Some people say Purple had a hand in that, with songs like 'Speed King' and 'Highway Star' and so on. And I would accept that we could be one of the godfathers. But I defy the parenthood. That wasn't us. We weren't the parents."

Said Jon Tiven in *Rolling Stone*, reviewing the new live album, "*Made in Japan* is Purple's definitive metal monster, a spark-filled execution of the typical Purple style. Unlike *Five Live Yardbirds* or Humble Pie *Rockin' the Fillmore*, Deep Purple deems it unnecessary to play any new material on their live albums. The live versions of all the songs are played at a much-quicker pace than they were in the studio. As far as the artistic side of *Made in Japan*, Deep Purple have always been ace performers, rarely using any gimmicks other than their own volatile stage personalities. While Purple refuses to take themselves too seriously, all of the solos on *Made in Japan* are technically superior to most instrumental melodramatics one hears from supposedly more serious bands. Deep Purple is a tried-and-true '70s group that has proven itself time and time again, a favorite of many a serious musician. While we still have to wait for their next release to know if they are going to continue at even keel, the fact is *Made in Japan* is here, and it's everything it should be and more, and Deep Purple can still cut the mustard in concert—so be it."

And speaking of *Rolling Stone*, despite notoriously ignoring all things heavy metal (and progressive rock), in 2012 the magazine rated *Made in Japan* the sixth-greatest live album of all time.

Ian Paice attributes the magic vibe that Tiven picked up on to the band's spontaneity. "Like now, we didn't rehearse a lot then. I think a lot of the time we rehearsed onstage. We'd be looking at each other with great big eyes, going, 'What's happening next?' Basically, we'd just tune into each other and think, 'Okay, I don't know what it is, but it's going to happen now.' You'd lock onto that. And of course, if it happens once, it goes in the little gray cells and it can happen again. And it's just a slow amalgamation of all these little tricks that would happen by accident every night until they became almost an arrangement in themselves. Some of those things are so off the wall that to try to preconceive and concoct them in a rehearsal room or studio is . . . I don't know, for us, I don't think it was ever possible that way. It had to be of the moment.

"I think we were really lucky to capture those concerts," continues Paice. "I was in Spain about four months ago doing a radio promo for the remastered version of the album, and I hadn't realized that they had taken the encore tracks and tacked them onto the new version. I hadn't heard them since we put the masters up in Japan to see if the tapes were any good. When I heard the encore of 'Lucille' at the radio studio, I thought, that's very, very good. And you know why I thought that was really good? Because during the show, we were aware that the recording machine was going, and we sort of played somewhere between an absolute flat-out live show and with that sort of control that you would normally play with in the studio. But when the encores came, we forgot all about the machine, and we played exactly like we would just for the audience. You can actually feel the difference in the approach to the music. As soon as the encores come in, it's 'Okay boys, here we go!' It's just a totally different attitude."

And did we mention how much Yngwie Malmsteen deeply appreciates Deep Purple? "I'll tell you a funny story," begins the mad Swedish fret burner. "A couple of years ago I was playing in Stockholm, and my grade-school teacher came, and she brought some drawings because I was always drawing as a kid. And she shows me these drawings I was doing in the fifth grade, eleven years old, of my band playing—we would play in the school cafeteria, whatever. And it blew my mind, because that's how early on I started doing this. I had smoke machines when I was eleven years old! Let me tell you something: I was a freak! I was a freak!

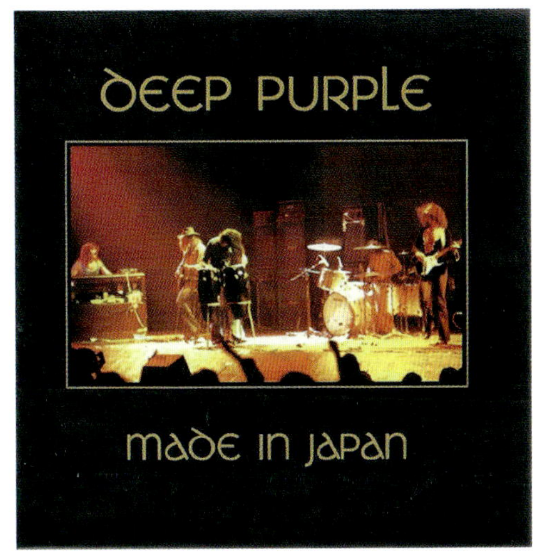

The *Made in Japan* reissue cover art

"But here's the perfect story about Deep Purple," continues Yngwie. "You're going to love this. Way back then, my uncle was in the R&D department at Philips. He was actually part of the team that developed CD technology, but also he was part of the team that developed cassettes as we know it. So, we had a lot of stuff in the house that maybe kids wouldn't have normally, and this was because of him. And one of things we had was a nice turntable, but also a cassette recorder, which was not very common in '72, '73; in Sweden anyway.

"And so, if you listen to *Made in Japan*, the mix is guitars hard left, and keyboards hard right. And I would put a little microphone in the left channel, on a cassette player, for my amplifier, and then I would put the LP on, and I would play it and record on cassette, but replacing the whole left side with my guitar. And I had studied *Made in Japan*—'Child in Time,' 'Highway Star'—down to perfection. When he switches the pickup selector, I would switch the pickup selector. I mean, it was exact! So exact it was stupid. And I was ten years old. And I would play this for my friends. I would say, 'Hey, check this out.' I would play them the cassette. 'Yeah, it's *Made in Japan*. So what?' I said, 'No, it's not.' And that's how fanatical I was. Just crazy.

Ritchie Blackmore in a calendar

"But a lot of people have the misconception that I got my classical influence from Deep Purple, which is as wrong as you can get. Because Deep Purple is blues. Don't fool yourself, people. Deep Purple is pentatonic blues—that's it. You can't get more bluesy than that. And God bless them for it; I love them—blues, you gotta have it. You've got to have blues. But my classical influence came in because I felt, when I was like eleven, twelve years old, I could play all this stuff as good as I thought I should be able to, and I felt like, well, I've really got to take this somewhere else. And that's how I got into more-baroque influences and stuff, eventually Paganini, as far as the solos go. But the impact they had, that band, and that those three records had on me, is undeniable. It is just fantastic, looking back at it."

Made in Japan proved to be a nice shot in the arm for Purple, having sold well and even spawning an improbable US hit in the live version of "Smoke on the Water," which zoomed up to #4 in the charts, aided by the fact that it was essentially a "double A-side" single coupled with "Woman from Tokyo." The ruse was such a success that the single was released in other countries, with worldwide sales eventually reaching twelve million copies.

Issued well before the golden age of live albums enjoyed by the likes of Blue Öyster Cult, Thin Lizzy, Ted Nugent, UFO, and Judas Priest, but especially Kiss and Peter Frampton, *Made in Japan* ultimately had more in common with the Fillmore sets of Humble Pie and the Allman Brothers, lending authority to the band as players, something the Purples always took pride in, as evidenced, obviously, by the eloquent words of Ian Paice and Jon Lord on the subject of improvisation. Still, any manifestation of onstage chemistry that might have been evident across four sides of *Made in Japan* did little to help staunch the flow of bile between what was beginning to look like two warring camps; namely, the new hires, Gillan and Glover, on one side, and then the old guard, Blackmore, Lord, and Paice, on the other.

Chapter 10

Who Do We Think We Are!

"Timing in music is potluck."

After a short tour of America with a version of Fleetwood Mac just as fractious as themselves, Deep Purple flew back to Europe to resume the recording of another studio album. These sessions would take place in October 1972 in Frankfurt, Germany, and the mood was ugly.

"That wasn't the happiest album for us to make," says Roger. "We were on the verge of breaking up at the time. It was a difficult album. You know, I think we've always had . . . there's this odd thing, several odd things. First of all, the odd thing about the first four studio albums, *In Rock*, *Fireball*, *Machine Head*, and *Who Do We Think We Are!*, is that all have seven songs on them. Now, how odd is that? Very, very strange. Obviously, time considerations; you could only get twenty minutes a side, and there was always one long song. And *In Rock* was fairly easy to make because we were fresh when doing it. *Fireball* was a bit of a struggle because we were following the success of *In Rock*, which was phenomenal. *Machine Head* was easy to make because now we had gotten used to the success, and we did it very quickly. And so therefore, *Who Do We Think We Are!* was difficult. And it seems to follow to this day. *Purpendicular* was easy, *Abandon* was difficult, *Bananas* was easy. And then in between, *Perfect Strangers* was easy, and *House of Blue Light* was difficult [laughs]."

"It was a period where the pressure of work was enormous," adds Paice. "There was tour after tour after tour, and during this time we were still expected to be coming up with new songs and have time to go in the studio and do it. And nobody really saw what was happening to us, least of all us, and definitely our management. And it's like, you can keep pulling water out of the well, but eventually you've got to let the well fill up again. And we were just emptying it. We were just taking all the reserves, and we were getting below the red line. And although *Who Do We Think We Are!* was not one of the bigger albums, there is some really great music on it. But emotionally the band was starting to go in separate directions; I mean, personally. And that was just because everybody was getting very, very tired."

In fact, right at the beginning of the sessions, Ian Gillan had tendered his resignation in a well-reasoned letter, also indicating that he would play out his obligations, which at that time included finishing the album and an almost comical number of tour legs. He picked a date of June 30, 1973, and said the decision was the product of six months' thought. His intention for the band to "quit while we're ahead" seemed to indicate his leaving would be the end of the band itself. Anyway, it goes without saying that an additional pall was cast over the *Who Do We Think We Are!* record cycle. This was not helped by the fact that Ritchie was isolating himself from everybody by keeping different hours, eating and sleeping out of sync with the boys. And when he was working, he'd reject ideas out of hand. Or if he was putting in his own ideas, he'd quickly change his mind and say that he was keeping that one for his solo project!

An interesting wrinkle to the tale of Gillan's resignation emerges from an interview that Roger gave at the time of the troubles, where he pulled Gillan aside and said that they should try to write a song together, top to bottom.

"So, the next night we went up to my hotel room with a guitar and worked out the tune and the words," explains Glover. "Later that night we went down to the studio and recorded what we'd written, while Ritchie, Jon, and Ian Paice were out playing pool." After the song was summarily shot down, Roger said calmly, "We discovered we couldn't write songs for Deep Purple." The inference there is that what was once a productive creative situation of give-and-take had gone sour, that his and Ian's services were no longer required.

Recalls Jon Lord with respect to the turmoil at the time, "We were getting ratty with each other, but that's the way you lash out when you're tired and emotional—you need to lash out. And Gillan must've felt we were lashing out at him just a bit too often, and off he went. Great shame, huge shame. We shouldn't have let him go. If we had had a creative and thoughtful management that would've said, 'Stop now. Ignore each other for six months and go away and lead your own lives. There's enough money,' then we might've stayed together."

The writing-credits issue was a sticking point as well. According to established Purple practice, the new record similarly had every song credited to the whole band. As Ian explained, it was Ritchie who was most bothered by this arrangement.

"Well, you know, if you spread the work . . . this came about in different times. It's rather like the Constitution in America. It's rather like the Bible. People take things word for word and never change. And of course, you have to change. The idea in the first place was that it was done that way because the music emerged very largely from jam sessions, and Ian Paice wasn't getting a credit because drummers never did, but he was a vital part of the process. We thought, well, why not just split it five ways? And that will work fine. So that's what we did, and it kind of stayed that way until Ritchie decided he didn't want to do it that way anymore. And that was it. So I think from then on, it was a bit of a question of 'Who does what?' And whoever is in the room. It's cost me a lot of money over the years; I can tell you that. You try to split a check five ways, instead of one way."

For the *Who Do We Think We Are!* album cover, the band went with an idea that was neither here nor there, although visually it possessed echoes of *Fireball*, with the band floating in the sky, this time appropriately in bubbles rather than as part of a comet. The inner gatefold played up the curious title, the idea being that the

The *Who Do We Think We Are!* cover art, US issue, signed by Roger. *Martin Popoff archive*

band was beloved by fans and bedraggled by the music press. As for the exclamation in the title, it's on the spine and the record label but not on the actual front cover. Two out of three is enough to make it official. I suppose without a question mark, it's sort of rhetorical. The guys in Deep Purple are not questioning themselves.

"Perhaps I can put this in a nutshell," says Ian, on whether he took the print barbs to heart. "We called one of our albums *Who Do We Think We Are!* because of the enormous amount of negative press we had when *Machine Head* was originally released. The reviews read absolutely awful. Of course, it turned out to be a very successful record. But the reviews and critique were unbelievable. So, we selected a few plums and put them inside the cover of the album, just to show that we did read our critics [laughs]. And we called the album *Who Do We Think We Are!* I think one of the reviews said something like 'Who do Deep Purple think they are? They did Deep Purple *In Rock* and then changed completely for *Fireball* and then changed completely and did *Machine Head*.' I forget what they described it as, but it was dismissed. So, we learned at a very early stage to be tolerant of it, but to realize basically that we don't give a monkey's toss. If we really worried about it, we wouldn't be here; we wouldn't be around. We are musicians. You know what musicians are like.

"I will say nothing about the press in the United States," continues Gillan, "but I will certainly say something about the press in the UK. It's completely different. We've had everything from unbelievably brilliant critical acclaim to those people that just hate the fact that we still exist. There is a guy called Ambrose Bierce, who wrote a thing called *The Devil's Dictionary*, back in the last century, and he was a bit miffed that he lost out to Samuel Johnson when the original dictionaries were getting written. And he wrote . . . let's see if I can get this right. As far as I remember, his definition of a critic was 'a position of some importance, reserved for those with the least ability in their chosen field.'

"And I think that's pretty much how we take it. You know, you either do it or criticize it. We have had criticism. And I think you grow up to respect it because you're in the business. You have to coexist with critique. It's not a bad thing; it's certainly not a bad thing. Bearing in mind, we don't do requests, and bearing in mind, we cannot bend or bow to current trends, never have done or will do. Most of it is fairly irrelevant. Our main critic is the audience. And believe me, we get some serious input. Certainly now, now that everything is available on the internet. We get some serious input from people who have loved Purple for many years and suddenly get angry because we've changed our style. Some of them get delighted because we have progressed.

"So, all of these things within the band are very important. But I do believe that most criticism, as we have come to know it, has nothing to do with objectiveness. It has to do with 'I'm writing about this subject, and so my words are important, much more important than the music you're making. So you better bend to my will and listen to what I'm saying.' I think we've gone through the days of being sort of dead

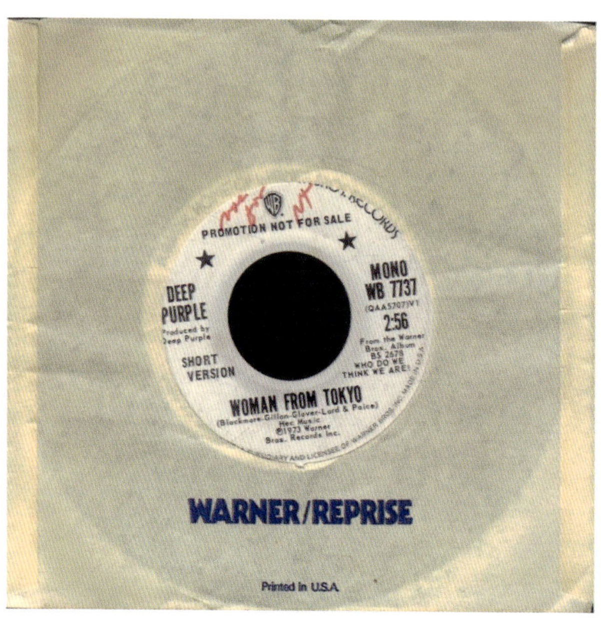

US white-label promo issue of "Woman from Tokyo," plus an ad promoting the single

angry about it. We basically don't take any notice of it anymore, because it's totally irrelevant."

Who Do We Think We Are! opens with "Woman from Tokyo," which, oddly, was written and tracked back in July 1972, before the band's trip of legend to Japan in August 1972. Ritchie is said to have nicked the riff from Eric Clapton's "Cat's Squirrel."

Says Gillan, "'Woman from Tokyo' is not about a woman; it's about the other way around. It's about our first trip to Japan, prior to that." So, it's a song that anticipates the event, with Ian blending the idea of a woman with the country itself, as the band got ready for an expected exotic wild ride, which they emphatically would get, from geishas to ecstatic adulation, to gifts of all sorts. As a parallel to "Smoke on the Water," it would be this album's hit single (of note, Tokyo is spelled Tokayo on the back cover, but not elsewhere), and it would be recorded separate to—and before—the rest of the album. The song is a beloved Purple track, but in this writer's opinion, a bit pedestrian, underwritten, intellectually light, essentially all those negatives one might apply to "Never Before." Still, it set the tone for an album that, like *Fireball* but unlike *Machine Head*, seemed relaxed and playful, which is in direct contrast to the circumstance in which it was constructed.

Next up was "Mary Long," an underrated rocker with a solid, insistent groove, one of those quiet tracks of quality that demonstrate the strength of this band and their ability not to slip too, too far, even on a record that band and critic and fan alike would decry as subpar. It would be the only track from the album to make the 1973 live set.

Stones in Australia
continues next week in NME
PLUS
Mary Whitehouse
on rock, sex and censorship

Published by IPC Magazines Limited, Fleetway House, Farringdon Street, London, E.C.4 at the Recommended maximum price sh (Westminster Press Ltd.), Uxbridge. (T.U.) Registered at the G.P.O. as a newspaper. Sole Agents. Australia and New Zealand., Go and Office Supplies Ltd., Subscription rate, including postage, for one year throughout the world £5.50. Dollar rate $15. Sen

Mary makes the news. *Martin Popoff archive*

"Mary Long is a composite name; it's a political song about the nascent stages of political correctness," says Ian. "Mary Whitehouse and Lord Longford were the two most prurient characters in the UK, and they would complain about anything that appeared on television. I mean, if you saw anything that was inappropriate or considered to be rude, or if anyone used a profanity, there would be major articles in the newspaper, and it was so boring, because they were writing about wonderful programs, cutting-edge stuff. So, I wrote this song called 'Mary Long,' and combined it with a lot of the hypocrisy I saw going on at the time. I always like to personalize things."

The Johnny in the lyric is Johnny Speight, writer of some of the good programming that Ian refers to above, and the reference to public money arises from the fact that much of the Whitehouse/Longford campaign was necessarily directed at the BBC, a public mother corporation of culture, much like the CBC in Canada or PBS in the US, only much more pervasive yet, at times, willing to push the limits of decorum as well.

"Super Trouper" maintained the sort of prosaic happy hippie vibe of the album's previous two tracks. Like, say, "The Mule" or "Living Wreck," it was a progressive-rock tumble of rhythms and texture and signals, ideas flowing out of the cornucopia that was always so easily filled by these players with so much to say. The swirling structure to the song, according to Roger, was inspired by previously mentioned southern rock classic "Going Down." The song's psychedelic vibe is underscored by experiments in tape flanging, along with the angelic backing vocals, rare for Purple. The title derives from a type of stage spotlight, and the lyric refers to a singer's self-reflection about what he has done with his life as he sings to that spotlight.

The last track on side 1 of the original vinyl, "Smooth Dancer," represents a shift in mood toward marauding, riff-mad heavy metal. Again, a quality level is maintained, even if there's a smidgen of feeling that the band had to force this one, that a box had to be checked off on the ledger waved about in front of those charged with writing a Deep Purple album.

Two ads for the new album. *Martin Popoff archive*

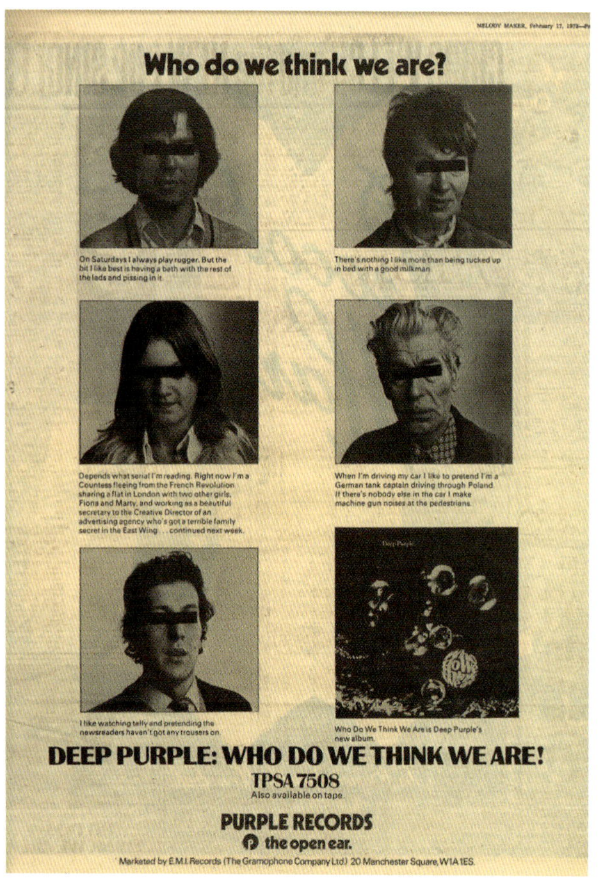

Great sounds, great performances, but the musical structure is something that a lesser band might have come up with on a good day, if tasked with writing an exciting modern heavy metal song strafed with power chords.

Explains Gillan, "'Smooth Dancer,' that's a love song to Ritchie, who was behaving like . . . well, I probably can't say it, but he was behaving badly [laughs]. I mean, we had all been sitting around for months waiting for him to turn up for those sessions. And he was . . . well, you know. So, it was a love song to him, saying, 'Would you please behave yourself?' But he didn't get it. Either literally or metaphorically. And I think it was about six years later when he actually found out . . . when somebody told him what the words were about [laughs]." The tip-off, if one was needed, is black suede, Ritchie's favorite at the time. "Smooth Dancer" was a brilliant choice of words because it applied to Ritchie in a half-dozen ways. Still, Ian's rant isn't entirely negative, since there's at least a half-hearted yearning there to work things out.

Side 2 is the great abyss of Deep Purple Mk. II sides. On an album that regularly gets overlooked, much of that overlooking is with respect to everything here. "Rat Bat Blue" valiantly tries to take one for the team, the team being the sense of unified but complicated purpose pursued by the first three tracks of side 1. The song dares to be progressive, rhythmic, and meaningful, with an abstract sense of idealism falling out of its musical proposals. I wonder if it's the title, or the fact that the bad blood within the band was about to be exposed, casting a pall upon the record, but "Rat Bat Blue" is forgotten, unjustly. There's complication and creativity here, but fans just didn't want to know.

"'Rat Bat Blue' actually came out of the sound that Paicey made when he did a drum turn," says Gillan. "He went 'rat tat tat tat,' and I thought, that sounds great [sings it again], so that's how it started, really. I can't remember what the verses are about, but it probably doesn't matter." In fact, according to Roger, it's about "picking up a loose chick for the night."

Turns out that it's one of Paicey's favorites on the album.

"'Rat Bat Blue' is a great track, and we're talking now, before the time of click tracks and metronomic timekeeping," explains Ian. "Don Airey was telling me the other day that if you put a beat counter at the beginning of 'Rat Bat Blue,' and although the song moves inside itself and it's human, by the end of the song it's exactly the same beat count. So that's something to be pretty proud of. If your internal clock is that good, that's okay. 'Woman from Tokyo' is a good drum track. So, there are good bits on it.

"But you can make the right album at the wrong time. And you can make the wrong album at the right time. You don't know. You're doing the best job you can at that moment in time. When you put this thing in the public domain, they actually decide if it's going to be a classic or not. They decide what's the one track that's going to hit them between the ears, and they're going to love it. But when you do a record, you can look back and say, yeah, we could've done it better. You couldn't. Because if you could've done it better, you would've done it better [laughs]. But timing in music is potluck. You can make a great record at the wrong time, and they'll ignore it. Had you made that record two years later, when maybe it would be more what's going on at that moment in time, who knows? But you can only do what you feel at the time."

"Place in Line," says Roger, was constructed like "Lazy" as an environment for soloing. As a matter of fact, one could view this album in total as one where Jon Lord gets to stretch out, including synthesizers here and there, although he realized they are best left to Keith Emerson and Rick Wakeman, preferring a Hammond or a piano to make his mark.

"'Place in Line' had to do with a book I'd read, and it was called *The Line*," says Roger. "And it's about this endless queue of people, in this line, and they had no idea why they were in this line. And it was just a new existence, because people being creatures of habit and wanting to find a comfort zone, they gather together. And it's endless. You spend your entire lifetime in the line, and I suppose it was sort of creating word pictures of going to heaven, I think, that sort of thing. And when you got there, of course, if you hadn't filled your papers out right, you were sent to the back of the line [laughs]. It was along those lines."

The song is a rote slow blues but then later a boogie blues. Gillan sings low and nasal like we've never heard, but up into the closing rave, he's back to normal. All told, this one's quite low on the creativity scale, save for Ritchie's modest and twangy solo and Jon Lord's profusion of note-taking.

Jon Lord, Selland Arena, Fresno, California, April 12, 1973. © *Jim LaMar, Wikimedia Commons*

Jon considered closing track "Our Lady" "quite surprising" in that it was devoid of solos and more concerned with lyric. The title came from Ritchie, who saw it on a church, and it is indeed kind of churchy (and even Beatlesque), thanks to Jon. It's a cozy fit to the hippie vibe of the record's opening tracks. Ritchie and Jon grind out a drone that pushes the song inexorably forward to conclusion, main conclusion being that this is one of the most obscure, least discussed, and least recognized Mk. II tracks ever recorded.

Ann Cheauvy's *Rolling Stone* missive on the album was none too kind. "Jeez, what an unsettling album! For the life of Reilley [*sic*], I can't understand how Deep Purple evidently lost the macho glory which made their *In Rock* LP such an Owsleyan mindfuck. Now that was an album—its kamikaze guitar and organ runs sped toward insanity with blazing intensity. It was rather melodic, too, for those who keep track of such things. The group's tried thrice to renew the assault on the senses, but each time they've come off like a fouled imitation of their earlier selves. Worse still, each outing displays less of the banzai spirit that once had critics crying asshole things like 'Power to the Purple.' *Who Do We Think We Are!* sounds so damn tired in spots that it's downright disconcerting. Now you might think it's impossible for a bunch of heavy metal mashers to sound like they've OD'ed on Sominex, but rest assured, this album will prove you wrong. Remember the two-stage construction of DP's earlier boogie beasts—songs like 'Speed King,' 'Flight of the Rat,' and 'Hard Lovin' Man'? And how the basic bitch of a riff served only as a launching pad for the Blackmore-Lord flights to musical nirvana? Don't waste any time looking for anything nearly as awe-inspiring here; the band seem to just barely summon up enough energy to lay down the rhythm track, much less improvise. Can metal men have iron-poor blood?"

I suppose so, but this band's problem, more so, was bad blood. As Jon explains, with respect to the imminent departure of Gillan, "I think Ian had that strength, and certainly a strength of purpose. I think in the end that's what drove him mistakenly out of the band in 1973. He has often said that he was an idiot to hand in his notice in '73. He just had this feeling that things weren't going as they should have been.

Gold-award promo shot, 1973

He now says, 'Why didn't I stay and try to change it from the inside rather than leaving and shouting at it from the outside?' He was as much an important part of the early story of hard rock as was Blackmore."

Chapter 11

Burn

"Obviously they thought I had something, God bless them."

What to do, what to do? Well, after losing their star vocalist and a man who was much more useful than just a bass player, Deep Purple do the unimaginable and hire a young hopeful who had sent in a demo tape to replace the former, and a proven soul singer from Trapeze to replace the latter. The result was a daring dark funk metal album that easily eclipsed its by-rote predecessor. *Burn*, issued on February 15, 1974, raised the ante, offering two new highly stylized vocalists instead of one not-so-stylish old one. Ritchie took a back seat to the grooves while Jon stepped forth, and yet, ultimately, it was the songs stealing the show.

But it almost didn't happen. With Gillan and Glover gone, it looked as if Ritchie would revive his idea of creating a three-piece with Paice, with Phil Lynott possibly as the third wheel, to bring the Babyface project back to life. Paul Rodgers, not yet in Bad Company, was also occasionally included in some of these musings. And then Jon Lord was pretty sure he was going to team up with Tony Ashton. Previous to that, at one point management and Jon Lord talked to Roger Glover about carrying on the name, which would require replacements for Gillan, Paice, and Blackmore! The tale of Roger's leaving, on the other hand, is just sad. Once Gillan had left, essentially Ritchie decided he wanted to fire Glover for no good reason other than the band's current state of "stagnation." Roger didn't wait to be fired, tendering his resignation as well.

"He saw which way the wind was blowing, so he gave notice that he was quitting," said Blackmore to *Circus* magazine, on the departure of Ian Gillan, but before the name of any replacements were made public. "If you're sharp enough and want to keep on as a successful band, you realize when you're stagnating. That is why there's going to be a change. There'll still be a Deep Purple, but it'll be three certain members staying together and two new members. We need more inspiration, more excitement, and a bit more imagination. There's a lot of managers who want us to go around touring for the next year, just taking in a lot of bread. But we're not going to take the public for a ride. We have to go to a higher level. We all hate each other. We always hated each other. We don't even get on when we played."

The new-look Deep Purple: *left to right*, Jon Lord, Glenn Hughes, Ian Paice, David Coverdale, and Ritchie Blackmore. © *Jørgen Angel*

Later in the same piece, Ritchie brings up the contentious subject of song credits, something that had rankled him from day one, but especially recently, given the five-way split of all these hit albums in a row. "I was writing about 80 percent of the stuff. But the credit was being split up five ways. I got tired of not getting the respect. Then I decided that we were stagnating. I told Ian, the drummer, that I wasn't happy with the way things were going for the last eighteen months. He didn't want any trouble within the group, so he calmed me down most of the time." Ritchie concludes the interview with the promise that "we'll still have the three members who have pushed Deep Purple the farthest and put the drive behind it. Hopefully the two people who will come in will push the band even higher."

Shortly thereafter, Glenn Hughes was hired, but still no front man. "Glenn is not just a bassist," said Ian Paice. "He's a very hard, harsh singer. Now what we're after in the way of a lead vocalist is something like a Jack Bruce or a Paul McCartney, a melodic singer who can add a mellow touch while Glenn belts them out. When we've found a singer, we're going to take a short holiday, find somewhere to rehearse, then drive across the continent with the Stones mobile studio to make the next album. Hopefully we'll whip out the LP by December and hit America again in January. And when we go back to the States, it'll be on a monster scale." It's amusing that most Purple watchers, contrary to Paice's assessment, would agree that in fact Coverdale would become the rough 'n' tumble voice of Purple, while Glenn provided the foil of sweetness.

"I was playing with Trapeze to four sold-out shows at the Whisky," says Glenn on the subject of his joining the band, referring to the Whisky A Go Go in Los Angeles. "Each night, a different member of Deep Purple was in the audience. I didn't know that Ian Gillan was leaving and that they were going to fire Roger Glover. About a week later, we played the Marquee in London. Ritchie Blackmore and Jon Lord showed up. They were snooping and asking questions. I was playing in Baltimore about three months later, and Deep Purple were playing in Madison Square Garden. They called me and flew me up there. I knew that something was going on.

"They asked me that night if I would join. I thought I was going to take Ian Gillan's place. They said, 'No, we want you to take Roger Glover's place.' They told me that Ritchie wanted to have two singers. I went, 'Fucking 'ell, who's going to sing?' They said, 'We've asked Paul Rodgers to sing.' I thought, 'Oh that's impressive!' Because he was the only other white, English guy who was in competition to me. They asked Paul Rodgers, and he said this: 'Why would you want me to sing when you have Glenn Hughes?' I thought that was a great compliment! Here is what they did. They went and got a Paul Rodgers soundalike in David Coverdale. He has the same blues qualities that Paul has. Basically, you had the making of a great vocal duo. That is how it happened."

As Glenn told me years later, "To be honest with you, Martin, that's probably one of the reasons I joined," meaning that he thought Rodgers would be his covocalist. "As we all now know, Paul, in the summer of '73, was putting Bad Company together, and he did a wonderful job doing that." Asked about rumors of threats from Peter Grant not to quash the Bad Company plans, Glenn confirms, "Yeah, there were, and I understand why. But that's a long time ago, and Paul is one of my favorite singers and a great friend of mine. But we talk about that scenario.

"But yeah, they were looking at me for about a year, checking me out, and came to see me a bunch of times. I was so naive; I was only very young; I was twenty years old; I had no idea. I didn't realize they were courting me. And when they asked me, I said no. I just did not want to be a bass player. I just wanted to be the singing bass player from Trapeze, where my heritage was started. And that's what I am today. I'm the singing bass player / lead singer. But I did think that the Coverdale/Hughes connection, with me being the secondary singer, if you will. . . . I've never had a problem in that role, because I always think I'm going to be a student of the voice until the day I die. I think that anybody who thinks that they are the finished article is bullshitting. So, I think what Coverdale and Hughes had to offer has never been reproduced by anybody."

I asked Glenn if it was Ritchie primarily making these personnel decisions.

"Yeah, first of all, he wanted Gillan out, and Gillan left. Definitely he wanted him out. Because Gillan was crazy back then; I think he just wanted to be away from the business. And Roger was let go in order for me to come in. Bruce Payne wasn't involved in that. Ritchie did everything. Ritchie ran that thing with a clad-iron fist."

On the subject of the politics of the band that Hughes was joining, Glenn explains that "they're all different characters in the band, with Ritchie being slightly darker. Ritchie—I can say this very respectfully—is an actor; you know, he gets in that Blackmore role. That's Ritchie to a tee, but off camera he's a very funny, kind, and considerate guy. But he's in that role of being Blackmore—bless him—and I respect that. Jon was a very kind, giving, generous human being and extremely funny. Ian was more guarded, if you will, more private. So yes, three different sets of characters. David and I became very, very close friends very early on. In fact, in the audition, we stayed behind while the band went to the pub, and came up with a few ideas. And when the band came back, they heard our vocals together. David and I have the same vibrato, so that really helped. So, David and I were really close, behind the mic and off camera too. We were always hanging out and always singing together. So, we created something special very early on. I came in in May, but they announced me in July. David joined fifty years ago this past August 14.

"We played for about an hour and a half," continues Glenn, offering more on the very genesis of the lineup. "And there was a lunch break. As I said, Dave and I stayed behind. There was a piano in the room, and Dave and I sat at the piano and we came up with an idea that would show the guys how our vocals sounded together. The guys came back, and we played them this little piece of music, which we came up with melodically, and they loved it. And then we continued on. That really eased David in. I think he'd had a couple of belts of Johnnie Walker. He was a tad nervous, as you would be, but he loosened up and the guys came back, and we played a couple more hours. But the thing is, Martin, we knew he was going to get the gig, but they didn't tell him for another week. But yes, what I did with David, I made him feel very welcomed. We're both northern guys from the north of England, and we have the same vocabulary, and we liked the same kind of music. David and I fell in love with each other from the moment he walked in the room.

"David selected the parts that he wanted to sing, and I always had second choice," continues Glenn. "Here is the trade-off to that: He knew that I had experience, and he knew that I had a gifted voice. The audience was always on him to be better than me. We didn't ever compete. It just so happened that he always took the first line,

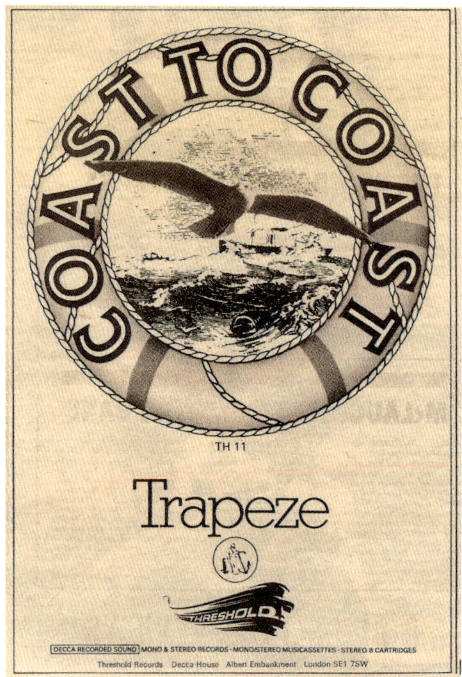

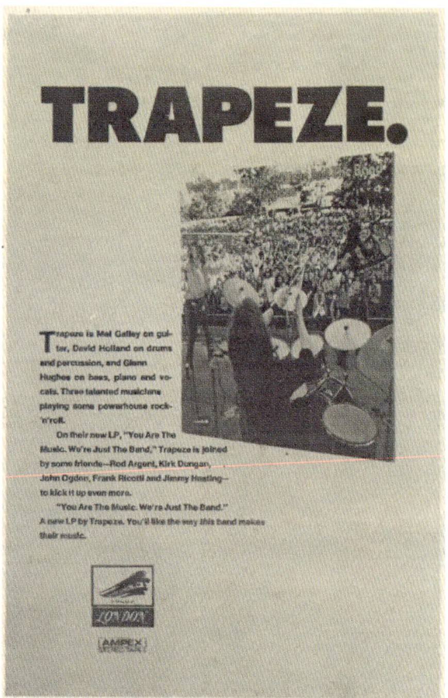

A trio of record ads for Glenn's old band, Trapeze. *Martin Popoff archive*

and I always had the second. I want you to relisten to 'Stormbringer' or 'Burn.' It was really an easy job for me. If I'm going to sing second, then I'm always going to do better! I've got this talent for doing that. I never, ever was in competition with David. I always thought that he made me sound good and that I made him sound good. I have no problems with David Coverdale. I used to know him, but I don't know him anymore. I taught him how to sing the vibrato thing. I brought him into my vibrato groove."

Asked if it was a tough gig overall, Glenn says, "I'm such a confident bass player and singer that it was really an easy job for me. I mean, I wasn't singing all the time. Ian Paice actually loved working with me as a bass player. Roger Glover is a very straight bass player, and I'm a very funky bass player. Paice really enjoyed that. I think it was very refreshing for them to take a different route. They were the number one rock band at the time. You couldn't have an Ian Gillan soundalike or a Roger Glover look-alike. That would be defeating the purpose of growth. I thought the albums that I made with David Coverdale, Tommy Bolin, and Ritchie Blackmore were brilliant."

"In '69, we were borderline hard rock," continues Glenn, offering a sense of his background with Trapeze. "In the Midlands of England, from the area in the north of England, there was still a heavy contingent of Americans like Beach Boys and the Beatles and the whole harmony thing. Between '67 and '69, there really wasn't much intense hard rock. And then Zeppelin and Cream in '68 started to raise their heads. When we started putting Trapeze together in early '69, we were also on the Moody Blues' personal label, Threshold, and the Moody Blues were extremely mellow. But we were sort of in the same genre as they were, with the big harmonies influence and Hammonds and the mellotrons. And then, of course, we switched. That black-and-white record and that first band was only around for nine months before we switched into the trio. We realized that America was going to be our calling ground, and we needed to go hard rock.

"I was from Cannock, which is near Stafford," adds Glenn, "70 miles north of Birmingham. Very, very good story. I'd sort of known Robert Plant from bands before Trapeze. I was in a band called Finders Keepers, which was the same sort of harmony thing. And John Bonham, I met. He came to one of my shows with Finders Keepers, and then with the trio as Trapeze, we would play at a place called Mother's in Birmingham, very influential place. Zeppelin played there, Black Sabbath . . . every major band played there. It was a huge club. Pretty much, I played there half a dozen times, and every time I played there, John Bonham would come, and he would sit in with Trapeze. And also, I'd see in the audience all of Black Sabbath, and there was Roy Wood and Jeff Lynne, all the local bands. Because Trapeze was a cult band that was about to make it very big, and then of course I left to join Deep Purple. But yes, Bonzo was a really good friend of mine. And Judas Priest were there. Actually, Glenn Tipton opened up for Purple, as the Flying Hat Band, I think they were called at that time, his band before Judas Priest. But yes, a lot of great bands came from Birmingham."

Speaking of Black Sabbath, Glenn would later work with the band for one album as well as Tony Iommi gone solo under the "Iommi" moniker. "Glenn comes with a lot of experience," says the Sabbath guitarist. "And Glenn is totally original in his soul; he's got great feel, and he can make things happen just purely by opening his mouth, and it comes out really soulful. With Tony Martin, on the other hand, I think it just takes . . . it's already been done by Glenn [laughs], if you know what I mean. Glenn was Tony's idol. Tony's a great singer; don't get me wrong. But I just found with Glenn, we bounce off a lot easier. He comes up with so many ideas."

Months on from the search for replacements, on the verge of *Burn*'s imminent arrival, Paice offered *Circus* an update to the earlier bit of press. "It's been a strange sort of seven months since the breakup. We already had Roger Glover's replacement in mind when he left. Originally, we wanted Paul Rodgers, but for personal and contractual reasons he couldn't do it. We spent three more months looking for a replacement for Ian. We just put the word around that anybody who would care to send a tape in, we'd give it a fair listen and judge it on its merits. We wanted an unknown. The best tape . . . that person would get the job."

Turns out that the best tape would be sent in by one David Coverdale, who had been working in a clothing boutique. On it, Coverdale did a swaggering reinterpretation of Harry Nilsson's "Everybody's Talkin'," and the band were taken by both his tone and his bravado. Jon Lord, after slogging through so many also-rans, remembers picking up the fateful tape, saying something to the effect of "If this isn't any good, forget it."

"He was shocked," said Ian Paice, regarding David and his hiring. "But he was also very happy. He had only played in a band in a semiprofessional way. You know, for beer money twice a week. This is the break of his life. He was one guy out of fourteen million, but he deserves it."

Before Coverdale got the gig, however, other semiknown names were bandied about. According to Lord, those included solo artist Jess Roden, Gary Pickford-Hopkins (from hard-hitting Purple Records act Wild Turkey), Graham Bell (Every Which Way), and Snips, from Sharks. But it was David, auditioning in mid-August at Scorpio Sound Studios, who nailed the gig, playing with the band for six hours and rattling through a number of Purple originals and every old rock cover the guys could conjure. Clearing up rumors of these other hopefuls, Glenn says, "No, and I love Jess. I don't think we actually auditioned those two. We may have spoken to them. Maybe you know more than I do. But we only auditioned—I hate that word, awful!—but we only played in the same room with David."

Coverdale recalls that the first song the band tried was "Strange Kind of Woman," his bluesier interpretation of the vocal finding favor with Blackmore, who barely had acknowledged Coverdale's presence in the studio, giving him a slight look and a nod after arriving with his wife, Babs, and two wolfhounds.

Recalls Coverdale, "Purple's office asked me to send a photograph of myself, which I thought was a bit daft. I wondered why they would judge a person's talent by his looks. The photo I sent down I had to borrow off my mother. It was one of me in my boy scouts uniform. They then asked for a tape of my voice, and the only tape I had was one of me singing at a party when I was drunk. I thought I'd had it, but I was invited down to London for an audition, and I got the gig. I guess what attracted them was the tone of my voice rather than what I was saying. I was just a local yokel, you know, local boy makes good and all that stuff. I'd never even been in a recording studio before we went in and cut *Burn*. Now I'm a local hero in Saltburn [population: 10,000]. They gave me the keys to the town; they also asked me for £25,000 to restore an old bridge, but I had to turn them down. Before Purple, the most I'd ever earned from a gig was a chicken sandwich and a bottle of Coke."

Coverdale was sent off into the night and didn't hear whether he had gotten the gig for nearly a week. Management was concerned about his funky style, not to mention his big glasses, his pimply face, and the extra few pounds he was carrying. Soon after, he'd be put on a diet (slimming pills, basically amphetamines!) and "get his eyes fixed" (contact lenses), and also sent off to the haberdasher for some flash threads. Frankly, we shouldn't dwell on looks, but it's hard to believe those original shots are of the same man who would become no less than a Robert Plant–rockin' Adonis within the course of a year or so.

A writing session at Blackmore's home impressed Coverdale when he found out that Ritchie had written much of the basics for the *Burn* album, ably double- and triple-tracking his guitars on a Revox reel-to-reel recorder. After looking for a place to record the band's important next album and ruling out setting up shop in Hamburg (seems this trip was more about a bonding bout of barhopping), Purple returned to the scene of their greatest triumph, Montreux, Switzerland. This is after concluding some writing sessions at Clearwell Castle, where Ritchie got to use his practical jokes on a shell-shocked Glenn Hughes.

Writing and rehearsing went well, despite Coverdale being deathly nervous at first. About half an hour's worth of new material had been cooked up, with the corollary being that most of it had to be playable in the live set, which Ritchie was intent on tarting up. "Smoke on the Water" was rehearsed as well, but with structural changes.

Also, at Clearwell on September 23, 1973, a press conference was called to announce the twenty-two-year-old Coverdale as the band's new singer. Into the fire indeed. At the event, Ritchie took a few minor digs at Gillan, mused whether there'd be more lineup changes again soon, and characterized the new lineup as "more into a blues-commercial pop thing. You could say a Beatles feel with a hard rock backing is the basic thing. We expect the vocalist to take on the part of a lead instrument, and that's why we're quite knocked out with matey there. Who knows? After the LP, I might be saying he's a shitty vocalist as well. I'm not going to say he's the best vocalist in the world, but when we heard him, we thought, 'Christ, he's good.' There are now two other guys involved, so it makes it more or less a new band to me. It's not Deep Purple anymore, although it's still the same name. Really, it's a completely different band."

"This time they had a big new convention center, which was ours for the month," said Paice, with respect to Montreux. The band arrived to begin work on November 3, 1973. "It was all soundproofed, so we had no problems. We were very cool about renting the center. We were on very good terms with the city fathers, and they gave it to us at a very low rate. And we didn't use all of it either. We recorded the whole album in the balcony. That's where the best sound was. The hall was used for regular functions in the evening because we were out eating dinner. When we came back to record, everyone had gone home."

"It was a convention center–type place," recalls Glenn. "And yeah, there was some spirited walking and running towards the mobile sometimes. And Martin Birch, what a great engineer and coproducer. What a wonderful kind, giving, and funny man. He was organically one of the greatest engineers I've ever worked with. And he was family; he'd been with the band for so long. Having Martin involved was so good for us, because he's a great human being and he was the glue that held it all together.

"But first we were at this centuries-old castle, Clearwell Castle, in the English countryside. The five of us, Martin, it felt like a brand-new band, when you have two new guys coming in. It was a great camaraderie in the summer of 1973. It was spectacular moment. We couldn't wait to start working on new songs. The atmosphere

David Coverdale, the man in the hot seat, KB Hallen, Copenhagen, Denmark, December 9, 1973. © *Jørgen Angel*

was electric, and the surroundings were amazing. I met Joe Cocker down there. He was looking at coming in after we left. Joe was an old friend of mine. I think Zeppelin were there at some point. It's a great place to either record or write music. All the songs were written in the crypt/dungeon, underneath the great hall. We worked on a new song every day, and we were in the flow. Musically we would play and work out ideas, and David and I would come up with vocal melodies that would later have lyrics. I remember it like it was yesterday. As you could imagine, Ritchie Blackmore was in full prankster mode—Jon had warned me, and he rigged my room one night with a speaker that was hidden, and had ghostly voices delivered to my bedside."

The sum total of *Burn*, save for "Burn" and maybe "Lay Down, Stay Down," is heavy rock, only in offhanded, oblique ways. It is a series of surprises, not the least of which is the astonishing vocal work track after track, with the crawling king snake of Coverdale dovetailing nicely with the springtime hummingbird verve of Glenn Hughes. It was a recipe for trouble, and trouble it eventually proved to be, with the band turning in one comfortable happenstance of an album and eventually two contentious follow-ups before they were to implode yet again.

Vocalist David Coverdale figures his favorite of the trinity of Mk. III / Mk. IV albums would be this first for the new configuration, pretty much matching the sentiment of almost every Purple fan.

"Yes, probably *Burn*, because it's the first record I ever made," explains David. "I remember being so keen. I knew Deep Purple was big in England, but I had no idea of the global aspect of it, so it was mind-blowing when I got that job. And the band was very supportive, and still, to this day, I applaud their courage in taking a risk. No question, I was completely unknown. Obviously, they thought I had something, God bless them. But the circumstance is, what a brave thing to do for a band of that size. But Ritchie and I did most of the writing on there. In those days they split everything five ways, which was their agreement, which Ritchie changed after the *Burn* record. There's a certain laziness. If you don't have to work, you don't contribute as much, and there was evidence of that. So, he changed that dynamic on *Stormbringer*, and Purple weren't very happy about that at all, the old guard. But anyway, what Ritchie said went. I wrote at least six versions of the song 'Burn,' I was so fucking keen."

Glenn couldn't help notice the risk as well. "When David and I came in, the band started to become more . . . I'm going to say soulful. Because we grew up in the north of England, we grew up listening to American R&B. Rather than try replacing Gillan and Glover with two look- and soundalikes, they replaced them with two totally different commodities.

"It was interesting. Obviously, I was in awe of Ritchie; my whole inspiration was Hendrix, that style of guitar playing," continues Coverdale on his impressions of the matchup. "And Blackmore was a phenomenal musician. I'd always worked with good players, but these guys were something else. And of course, they had the ego and the sound and equipment to put their money where their mouth was. So, working with Ritchie was a marriage made in heaven. And I was learning as I was going. I'm a good sponge, and I was soaking it all in.

"And the more comfortable I felt, the more comfortable I felt providing musical ideas, because I had been writing for a few years, just with local bands. And we

Press shot of Mk. III minus their honker on the Hammond

connected very well. Both of us were fans of medieval music, which was a modal concept, similar to Bach, and we both enjoyed similar acts or whatever. Then I would feel more comfortable putting in chord ideas and melodies. We did all the rehearsals at a place called Clearwell Castle in Gloucester, which was basically our second home. We rehearsed in a crypt, and I'd tape a cassette, because they had just been developed, and I would fashion lyrics out of those things. You know, the *Burn* album was really successful; it reestablished them in '74, '75. We were the most successful-selling act in the world, and then there was a collective sigh of relief that we maintained it by making the change from Mk. II to Mk. III, that they had maintained the success level, and so they could put their feet up. Which wasn't Blackmore's vibe, and it certainly wasn't mine. So, a bit of laziness crept in there in terms of the input into songs towards the end."

Burn was issued, like its three recent predecessors, in the home territory on the band's Purple Records imprint. "Yes, another scam," laughs Coverdale. "It's funny; when I joined Purple, I was going, my God, telling my friends they've got their own record company! But it was just a scam by the management. They would go get the advance, they would take their hefty percentage of the main advance, and they would take advantage of being the Purple record executives, and then they would give the band less percentages than they would have gotten from Warner Brothers or EMI, right? And the band would go, 'Look, we've got our own record company.' I'm sitting here in my office, which is loaded with platinum albums, and I'm looking at these records, Purple Records, purple with the big white P on it? So, we had our own record company, big deal [laughs]."

The album cover was a stunner, with famed photographer Fin Costello shooting specially commissioned candles in the guise of the guys, lit all occult-like. Apparently, the shot was rushed and meant only as a "demo" of sorts, and then through error, the demo slide was used for the actual cover. A second set of unused candles were later auctioned off. But the two sets were all that had been created for the very purple session.

Deep Purple's first Mk. III record positively exploded off the vinyl, kicked off with the legendary title track. "Burn" is a progressive-metal showcase, a power metal classic, a vocal tour de force, a percussive workshop, and from the get-go, blessed, ordained, baptized, and cursed with a corker of a riff.

"'Burn' was, for that lineup of Deep Purple, what 'Highway Star' was for the previous lineup," remembers Glenn fondly. "When we wrote the song, I realized that this song was going to become a trademark intro on tour and on the record. I knew it directly when we started to write the song. We just knew it was the one. There was no doubt that 'Burn' was going to be the opening track as well as the opening track on the live show, which it was. To me it was a major song to be involved with. I had parts to sing as well, and it was a really cool thing for me to get up there and sing to millions of people. So, it was the opening of a big door for me.

"We were down at the pub," adds Glenn, recalling the genesis of the flagship track. "We'd written all these other songs, and Blackmore suggested, 'Hey, we need to write a song about . . . about "burn."' And we all sat there going, 'Interesting.' So, we went back from the pub half inebriated and went down into the dungeon—we were set up in the dungeon there—and before one o'clock in the in the morning, we had written 'Burn.'"

Creative US ad promoting *Burn*, along with the back catalog. *Martin Popoff archive*

Deep Purple
BURN
#1
Deep Purple
Top Album Artists
of the year in the
U.S.A.
BILLBOARD
A new album on Purple Records
TPS 3505 Available on Cassette & Cartridge
Single from the album "Might Just Take Your Life."
PUR 117 – Released March 4th
Marketed by EMI Records
EMI Records Limited
20, Manchester Square, London W1A 1ES
EMI

Melody Maker ad plus the *Burn* album cover.
Martin Popoff archive

In fact, "Burn" came at the very end of the process, meaning that up to that point, the album as a whole would have been sort of half the piece of work it turned out to be. In other words, far and away the most-famed few minutes on the record didn't exist for the majority of the writing process.

"Yes, true. Again, we were having a drink and a conversation about, hey, you know, maybe we don't have an opening track. Because Purple were notorious for their great opening tracks. So, as I say, we went back from the pub and started playing, and immediately Ritchie came up with that riff and the song wrote itself. Jon came up with this

KB Hallen, Copenhagen, Denmark, December 9, 1973. © *Jørgen Angel*

KB Hallen, Copenhagen, Denmark, December 9, 1973. © Jørgen Angel

68

to know each other, the beautiful man that he is, was, and continues in my heart to be. He was telling me how challenging it was for him. Originally, in Mk. I, Jon was the primary writer. It was more pop with a little more classical stuff. When Ian and Roger joined, their first project was the *Concerto for Group and Orchestra*. As they were going around touring, the promoters would be going, 'Hey, where's the fucking orchestra?' It really pissed Ritchie off. He said, 'If we don't do a rock record, then I'm out of here.' That is when they did one of my favorite rock records ever, *Deep Purple in Rock*. I thought it was amazing. I don't think it resonated so much in the US, but in Europe it was huge.

"Jon said to me how difficult it was for him to play riffs on the organ and to sell a new song idea by playing a riff. He said Ritchie could just plug his Strat in and turn up the Marshall and play a really simple riff, and the way he plays, it must have made everyone go, 'Yeah!' I said, 'Don't compete. What about chords? Some of my favorite songs are like keyboard-oriented stuff.' 'Gimme Some Lovin" has no guitar riffs in it." Jon said, 'What about this?' He played me what became 'Might Just Take Your Life.' I said, 'I think that's fucking amazing.' The feeling I got from that was the Marvin Gaye song 'Heard It Through the Grapevine.' That was the blueprint for me to write that melody. That was a huge step for Jon. Whenever I had a dorky chord sequence, I'd give it to Jon, and whenever I had a guitar riff or something, I'd give it to Ritchie."

Adds Glenn, "'Might Just Take Your Life,' Lordy came up with that Hammond organ intro, and I just pretty much wanted to keep that chugging on the bass. It was really a very early '70s way of playing, and that pretty much dictated how the song went."

Commented Paice back in 1974, "It's about a cat who's sort of got everything together, and he's got a chick he's been hanging around with, and he's warning her he'll take everything. He's the kind of guy who takes everything he can, and he's just warning this chick that if she's not careful, he'll take her life as well. I don't know why David wrote it. Maybe there's something in David's character I don't know about yet."

Picture sleeve issues of the "Might Just Take Your Life" single

Conversely, Coverdale has said that the song was about Glenn and himself suddenly finding themselves in Deep Purple, with the lyric directed at those that had scoffed at the new guys being able to pull it off. Of note, even though "Might Just Take Your Life" was played only on the various *Burn* tours, David would revisit it during the early days with his next incarnation as Whitesnake.

"'Lay Down, Stay Down' was one of the first lyrics I wrote," explains Coverdale on another heavy track, one of the more joyous songs of Purple's back half before the first breakup, perhaps indicative of Whitesnake's future style, and once more a workout for Paicey. "Lay Down, Stay Down" (working title back at Clearwell: "That's Alright") is like the happy dumb cousin to "Burn," equally punchy but less ambitious, and definitely more gleeful, with tambourine and cowbell, plus amazing vocal trade-offs, which, again, serve as the true conceptual treasure of this album.

Mused Paice, again, back in 1974, "It's just a funky piece of rock 'n' roll, and you can't really say it means anything. We get an arrangement around this basic instrumental idea, and we put a track down. Then we give it to the guy who's going to sing, and see what he can write to the melody. You see, we do it backwards. Things will be the way they always were. Everybody has an equal say, even the new members. If one guy doesn't like a song, it just doesn't get played. If somebody feels strongly about something, they just put their point forward. If it's valid, we'll try to change things till everybody's happy. This group is three or four times as strong as when Ian and Roger were in the group. The whole thing got exciting again. Towards the end with Roger and Ian, it was getting like a job. There was no social life within the band. People would go onstage and they'd go back to the hotel and you wouldn't see anybody until the next day, when you got on a plane or something."

I asked Hughes whether Paice had a hard time nailing "Lay Down, Stay Down," given how busy and drum centric it is. "No, man. One of the greatest drummers in the world. His style in the early '70s was monumental. He was a very influential drummer, and he would just immediately kick in. He was very good. And 'Lay Down, Stay Down' was also written in that week, in Clearwell Castle. It's a Blackmore-style rock track, a very Deep Purple–sounding track and another great duet. That's the whole thing about that track; the beauty of the Deep Purple Mk. III / Mk. IV era, if I may say so, is the dual lead singers.

"That's a great live song. Again, it was a Glenn and David duet. A great tempo and riff. We needed a faster song, as you know, and it was great. Everybody played so well on that one. It showcases David's lower timbre and my higher register. It's setting the bar for what people should get to know as the new Deep Purple, what the new Deep Purple sounded like vocally."

I asked Glenn if it was a bit of an olive branch extended to Ian.

"Yes, but Ian was very, very forthcoming in what he wanted to play. Because we're brand new, fresh in that room, and it was like rehearsing and writing was all one. So, it was jamming and then writing, and then we found out how easy it was for the songs to come together. And the way Ian plays, he's a great jam drummer."

On the subject of working out his parts with David, Glenn indicates that "we had some moments together where, either in one of our bedrooms in the castle, we'd sort out who did what. Plus, Martin, it came together at the microphone. Because we have the same influences musically. David's bluesy and I've got the soulful blues stuff, as you know. We had no lyrics when we were singing—the lyrics would come

Japanese promotional poster from 1974

later. So, we were singing these melodies, making up strange titles, and we just went through it and the melodies, and the lyrics came together at the microphone."

Closing side 1 is "Sail Away," a true dark horse of a Purple track, with both Glenn and David trying to keep it low and sinister over a driving funky blues that sounds like Led Zeppelin's "Trampled Under Foot" slowed down, with perhaps a little "Boogie with Stu," "Four Sticks," and "Custard Pie" thrown in for good measure. Blackmore is wayward, while Lord is leaden and insistent.

"I think Blackmore and I sort of linked in that day in the rehearsal room and came up with that riff," recalls Hughes. "I think I might have come up with that riff, because it's a very Glenn Hughes riff. So, I was very excited with that. And of course, the Coverdale/Hughes connection on that is very strong, as a duet for singers. So that's a great blueprint for a sort of medium rock track with the dual lead singers. But yes, I think the riff is pretty much a Glenn Hughes riff. That vibe and that groove is something I would have played before I joined Deep Purple, in my band Trapeze. So, for me, that signaled that the band was grooving. It's an incredible song to play live. Everybody loves that song. But the thing is, we never played that one in Deep Purple. It's remarkable, isn't it?" Tambourine is again part of a Purple song, but the key feature is that not only does Jon use synthesizer, but Ritchie uses synthesizer guitar.

As for the curious Blackmore/Coverdale songwriting credit, Glenn says, "I don't know. I've had words with them about this. In my opinion, I did write that song with those guys. That's something I don't particularly care to talk about, because it's a sore thing for me. But that's definitely a song that I should have been credited for. And I wasn't okay with that. But that's water under the bridge."

Side 2 of *Burn* begins hyperactive and funky with "You Fool No One," a track that's closely related to the Yardbirds' "Still I'm Sad," given the strong yet slow 'n' uneasy vocal melodies.

"The whole influence on the vocals there were the early Cream songs, those wonderful Jack Bruce / Eric Clapton harmonies," explains David. "My favorite part on that is Blackmore's phenomenal guitar playing and, of course, Paicey's dominant drum pattern, which Tommy Lee stole for his drum solo. I remember we were recording in Montreux, in Switzerland, with the Rolling Stones truck in the basement, and we were like three or four floors up in this big convention center; I don't even know if it's still there. Anyway, Paicey is doing this phenomenal drum pattern, and we fell about laughing over something and he just got so fucking angry and stood up and stormed out and said, 'Look, mate—with sweat dripping off him—this ain't the easiest fucking drum pattern I've ever come up with! So, get it right!' And that was it; the next take, zap, done, five egomaniacs; it was great."

"That song was very influenced by the two lead-singer-harmony thing," adds Glenn. "David and I spent a couple of hours behind the scenes working on harmonies. I think that's one thing Blackmore really liked about me is that he would always thank me for bringing those harmonies into Deep Purple. Because those harmonies, it's still what I specialize in, bringing harmonies into rock music; it's what I've always done. So, I think he's grateful for that. But yes, Paicey came up with that drum groove, as you know, with the cowbell, and again that's pretty much it. Those vocal harmonies, I took one of the choruses and David took the other one, and those verses were very much, like I say, Cream influenced. That came from Jack and Eric, two friends of our band. I will definitely tip my hat to Cream on that one."

Side 2 begins to melt down a bit after this, rendering *Burn* slightly imperfect; mortal, if you will. "'What's Goin' on Here' came from a jam in the studio," says Glenn. Indeed, it's a casual honky-tonk boogie, unremarkable and casual, but saved by wondrous vocal acrobatics, soul for miles. Indeed, the band manages to come off as dashing, stylish.

"Oh yeah, that should have been either Glenn or me singing," notes Coverdale with regret, one eye on the train approaching full speed, so to speak. "One of the ridiculous things was that Glenn was such a talented singer, but Ritchie wasn't such a big fan of Glenn's voice. He liked my voice. He said, 'You have a great "man's" voice," which was a pretty nice compliment. And he didn't exactly get the same vibe from Glenn. There's no question that Glenn is extraordinary. Technically he can sing me into the ground. But I can connect deeper emotionally.

"But what happened is that prior to me getting the job, he really felt that he was going to be the lead singer and bass player, and that really is not what Ritchie was after. So, once they got the man's voice in—and Glenn and I have talked about this, I spoke to Glenn about it—it was ridiculous that I would sing a line, he would sing a line, I would sing a line, he would sing a line, I would sing a chorus, he would sing a chorus. It was just all over the place. One of the perfect examples was the song you mentioned, along with 'You Fool No One,' where we sing it together. But for anybody wanting to get their hooks into a song, to have this confusion of different voices coming in left, right, and center is more a distraction than a hook."

"That's a blues jam, a very simple twelve-bar blues," remarks Glenn, with respect to "What's Goin' on Here." "It's a Ritchie Blackmore guitar line, and everybody gets to take a solo. It's another Glenn and David, you know, romp-around, switch a verse, I'd sing a line, he'd sing a line. Again, we were establishing that there were two singers in the band. We wanted to take it away from Gillan and Glover and establish what the new Deep Purple should be. And I'm glad the band took that decision."

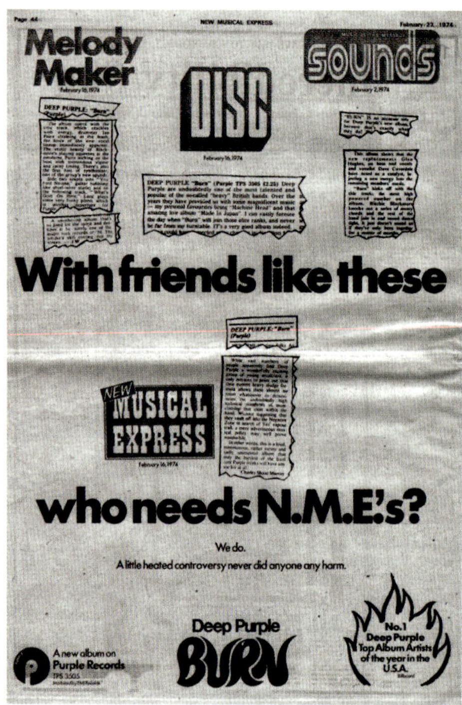

Another couple of ads, the first quoting reviews, the second promoting Deep Purple and Elf pretty much equally. *Martin Popoff archive*

Near to closing out, we get the innocently abbreviated nascent version of "Mistreated," a song that would spell hot-dog break at many a future Deep Purple, Rainbow, and Dio show as it got stretched to infinity. At seven minutes it's at least salvageable, with Ritchie doing some innovative things in terms of marrying classical music to the blues tradition. "Mistreated" was actually one of the handful of tracks held back from the *Who Do We Think We Are!* sessions, and it's the first song for which Coverdale completed his lyrics. Recording of the song was torture for David, however. An entire eight-hour shift through the middle of the night failed to yield a take that he was happy with. Picking it up again the next day, Coverdale nailed it on the second take.

"'Mistreated' was written before David joined the band," notes Hughes. "Blackmore played that to me at his home in Surrey when I first joined. In fact, first, the weekend I joined, I went with Ritchie to Germany. Ritchie and I went on a boy's trip in July of '73. The two of us went to Hamburg, one of Ritchie's favorite playgrounds, and Ritchie and I sat on a barstool for the weekend in some dark bar. We sat there back-slapping each other, and he was very, very kind and funny.

"And when we arrived back at Heathrow, we went to his house and we went into a room in his house, two guitars in that room, and Ritchie said, 'I have an idea for a song. Let me play it to you.' And we both sat there with guitars, and Ritchie played the introduction piece to what would become 'Mistreated.' And as he was playing it to me, a little voice in my head said, 'Everything is going to be okay.' It was just like that, because I knew when he was playing that great groove behind the verse of 'Mistreated' that Blackmore had come up with a beautiful new piece of music for the band. Ritchie wanted the new Deep Purple to be more blues oriented than the Mk. II. We didn't want to replicate or duplicate Mk. II. That was a big gamble and a big risk. It would have been easy for them to get a Gillan-sounding singer or bass player like Roger, but they wanted to go completely different. So it was a good idea to get more bluesy. And 'Mistreated' was a prime example of that. But yeah, I was just blown away by it, this half-time groove in F#. I played bass with him on that day, and I realized that, okay, if this is the kind of style *Burn* is going to be in, I'm really going to play bass, appropriately, on the album."

Underscoring this narrative and the style of a song such as "Mistreated" is the fact that on the road, the band played a rendition of Don Nix's "Goin' Down." "Oh yeah, and Don was a friend of mine," reflects Hughes. "That was a great, great song to play live, and another for our colead vocals. I believe we were down at Shepperton Studios rehearsing, and we just started playing it. It's a song everybody knew, and we thought maybe we needed another song to play, and we started kicking around that song. David and I started singing, and it was just magic."

Explaining to Sam Dunn the importance of the blues within the new Deep Purple, Glenn said that "if you look back and listen to early Purple, you'll notice Blackmore was playing in 3/5 back then, the 0-3-5 blues scale, and he was very much influenced by American blues players. You can hear that in the very early Deep Purple all the way through to my Mk. III era. You could hear Ritchie's influences, especially. He was the blues guy in the band, and you could feel that element. As you could with Tony Iommi, but he's more jazzy in Sabbath. But that element was definitely in Deep Purple, as it was in Zeppelin. And back in '71, '72, '73, that was an element in metal that came from the blues, really. Some people say it came from jazz or soul or whatever, but in Britain, it was definitely coming from American blues; hence Jimi and Tony and Ritchie Blackmore, and Jeff Beck, of course.

"The blues just seems to be a universal unspoken rule and language that people can understand regardless of understanding a lyric. With no disrespect to any blues players or artists out there, the blues, generally, musically, is an easier thing to play. There's normally three chords in blues, and it's a basic form of heavy metal, if you will. I think that's where we all started. My playing in a shed in my dad's garden, playing those blues riffs. But funny enough, I was at an age where my first blues education actually came from the Rolling Stones."

Once "Mistreated" was recorded, rank would be pulled over the fresh guys in Purple. David and Glenn, with Martin Birch's deft hand helping, had created this choir of voices in the outro that was to be their shining moment together. Once Ritchie heard it, all he could say was that the vocals drowned out his guitar solo. Birch meekly made the adjustment the boss wanted, and in the final, the vocals are buried. Truth be told, neither these backing vocals nor Ritchie's solo are all that impressive, although it is indeed easy to pick which one is louder.

Notes Ritchie, "That song was influenced by 'Heartbreaker' by Free. I get inspired by other people's songs and write something vaguely similar." Makes sense, since Paul Rodgers was floated as a replacement for Ian Gillan at one point. "Yeah, that's right, he was, for about a week. I think somebody was going to chop his legs off if he did leave, so he didn't. I think he was into a different type of singing, and he didn't want to follow Ian Gillan and all that screaming. Rodgers wasn't into that; he was more into blues. With *Burn*, we had about a year off, and I had the excitement to start again. Just before that, I was ready to kind of leave myself. We were just working and flogging ourselves to death. I was sick all the time. Luckily, we changed two members, and there was new blood. Then again, *Burn* was great, and *Stormbringer* became a bit funky, souly, smooth."

Continues Ritchie, "I was listening to some of our old stuff recently, and I thought I was better than that. It's very sketchy and it's very clinical. At the time, it was the best I could do, because we had three weeks to get an LP together, and there were so many egos involved. But I go through the same sort of things as Jeff Beck; I'm never happy with what I'm doing. And I can't get really excited talking about myself. And that's why I can't talk about somebody else even to slag them. That's why I don't do interviews—what can you say about yourself? 'I do this, and I do that. Yes, our new LP is great and we're touring.' Everybody comes up with the usual crap: 'With this new LP of ours, we're going in a new direction.' We're not going in any direction; we're just going along. If people don't like it, it's too bad. I certainly wouldn't change to suit the radio play that's gone down in the last three years, all the Fleetwood Macs and Eagles and all that business."

Finally, *Burn* ends with a mess of an instrumental called "'A' 200" (working title: "Touching Cloth") which is a dated, almost Mk. I–sounding synthesizer showcase set to a rudimentary "Bolero" rhythm, which would be nicked for Iron Maiden's "The Ides of March" intro seven years hence (which in reality came from Samson—long story). This one was written during the recording sessions at Montreux, if it can be said to be written at all.

"Ritchie wanted to give Jon a song where he could stretch his muscles," notes Hughes, adding that "Jon Lord is the diplomat, the analyzer. He was probably the backbone of the group, actually. At the end, when a lot of decisions were made, they were by him, because he was the more stable person, I thought, at the time. Ian Paice was definitely the engine in the group. A young Ian Paice, there was no finer drummer. He and John Bonham were the two best drummers around. And he was my roommate in Purple for about a year. I love Ian Paice." Of note, A 200 was an ointment, its ad proclaiming "Crabs on crotch, lice on head, one thing's sure to knock 'em dead. A 200."

So, we had an olive branch to Ian, and now we have an olive branch to Jon.

"Yeah, it absolutely was," says Glenn. "Looking back, we may have had a moment where we were going [that] we need to feature Jon more on this record, and very quickly came up with that 'Bolero' on the drums. In fact, that song may have come together in the Rolling Stones mobile. We may have not even rehearsed that song at Clearwell. I think it came up when we were in Switzerland, if memory serves me correct."

I asked Glenn if the band had some cool, new synthesizer gear no one else had.

"Yeah, the ARP Odyssey—he had two of them. Jon was really not a synthesizer guy in the mid-'70s. He later became one. Also, I think the ARP Odyssey was the first synthesizer. He didn't have one in Mk. II. So, he was brand new on "'A" 200,' and of course we used it more on *Stormbringer*. But yeah, the ARP Odyssey was Jon's new weapon."

Ritchie shows up sparingly although quite effectively in this one, turning in a dirty and aggressive solo that grinds away at the otherwise slight construct of the thing. No surprise that the composition was never formally included in Purple's live set, although Jon was wont to throw a sample of it into live renditions of "Space Truckin'."

Burn did well out in the marketplace, hitting #3 in the UK and #9 in America, going gold instantly, although it's never been certified any further. It generated no charting singles, although "Burn" has become one of the band's five or so most celebrated songs, not that you'll be hearing it performed live by the Ian Gillan–fronted version of the band.

Rolling Stone's Ken Barnes called Deep Purple's eighth album "a passable but disappointing effort. David Coverdale sounds suitably histrionic, like Free's brilliant Paul Rodgers. But the new material is largely drab and ordinary without the runaway locomotive power of the group's best work. The title track is a notable exception, attractively energetic, with appropriately speedy instrumental breaks. And 'Sail Away' is a Free-like mesmerizer. 'Mistreated' again sounds like that lamentably extinct group but is flaccidly lengthy. Much of the LP is skillfully wrought and likable, and the new lineup has potential. But the Gillan/Glover spark that created 'Highway Star' and other memorable Purple smokers is regrettably absent."

Back inside the workings of the band, the happy circumstance of having such an embarrassing wealth of vocal riches was sure to cause disaster eventually, and that is exactly what happened, although as David explains, it was more the strong blues and soul musical tastes both of Glenn and him that would eventually drive Ritchie over the rainbow. Then there were hard drugs.

Reveals Coverdale, "Initially, Glenn and I got on very well, and then it tended to go south somewhat, given the more peripheral indulgence that went on. It was actually a very, very tough time. I left Deep Purple, which was pretty much a well-kept secret out of respect for Jon Lord and Ian Paice, but it was really degenerating very badly in terms of the shows and attitude. A lot of drugs and alcohol were rearing their ugly heads. There was a great deal of disrespect for the legacy of Deep Purple, which I still maintain.

"Ritchie and I always got on well, and I think what alienated Ritchie from me is that I didn't do Rainbow. He came up with all his songs, which at that time, the whole climate was that you had to progress, and I just thought his songs were *Machine Head* songs. And one of the things that I wanted to bring to Purple was blues. And Glenn of course was a huge soul fan, and I loved soul music as well.

"The year that I joined Deep Purple, my most-played records were Sly and the Family Stone *There's a Riot Goin' On*, Stevie Wonder *Music of My Mind*, and Donny Hathaway *Live*. I mean, nothing to do with rock, but I loved rock, in the sense of the early Allman Brothers, original Fleetwood Mac, Jeff Beck Group. So, I thought it would be entirely appropriate, without compromising the identity of Purple, to inject more of a blues element, more of an emotional element instead of motorbikes and whatever and planets and 'We had a lot of fun on Venus.' I can only write about what I know. But of course, the great soul element started to creep in. And that was not really where Ritchie was at, at all. The essence is always songs, with me utilizing the three elements that I feel are very appropriate to my expression, which is rock, soul, and blues."

After the frothy chemistry of *Burn*, things did indeed deteriorate until the end was well on nigh. "Well, you know, Glenn and I would stand together; that's when I first came up with the expression the Unrighteous Brothers," says Coverdale. "When I actually left the band, Glenn wasn't told. I'd flown over to England for Ian Paice's wedding, and he was going, 'Oh, Dave, I've got all these great ideas; we've got to use our voices more' and all of this. And I go, 'Glenn, hasn't anybody told you? I'm out.' And he was utterly shocked. And I was like, we blew it. It could have been incredible, but we blew it. Which is one of the reasons now, if I feel that kind of negative energy creeping into any scenario, even private ones, let alone professionally, I change it. If I can't see the light, I change it because there's too much compromise. It really is a difficult pill to swallow."

And even though we're getting ahead of ourselves, given that true dissolution happened well past the *Burn* period, Ritchie's oppressive control over the band was already causing at least rounds of raised eyebrows. Onstage, the guys were informed that no one comes over to his side any further than the bass drum—stage right (their left) was Ritchie's terrain. Once offstage, Ritchie would travel in a separate limo and sometimes even have a second room in a separate hotel to get away. He didn't talk much to the guys and preferred to be either alone or with the roadies. His relationship with Babs was deteriorating, and she was no longer on the road with him as much as she used to be, allowing Ritchie, one of the most dedicated swordsmen in the band, to let loose much like doppelganger Jimmy Page.

"I think the first gig we did with David was maybe in Denmark, 10,000 people," recalls Glenn, with respect to kicking off the Mk. III touring duties. "He jumped in with both feet. David Coverdale was a charismatic guy, even before he was famous. He was perfect for the role. There was no problem with his voice, but he was very green in the fact that he had never done any arena shows. He had never been on a stage bigger than a club stage."

Indeed, as with Mk. I a lifetime earlier, Denmark got the first look at the new Deep Purple, as part of a six-show run the band conducted as warm-up, even before the album was issued. Openers were a poor man's Deep Purple Tucky Buzzard, on Purple Records. The first gig was in Copenhagen, after the band and its gear didn't arrive in time for an earlier scheduled show at Aarhus, where four thousand had congregated for the event, only to get the word at 6:00 that the gig was scrubbed. Coverdale recalls himself as incredibly nervous, even after getting a bunch of booze down, with the rest of the band equally on edge, given that they hadn't played for fully six months prior.

Partying at the Revolution until 4:00 a.m., the band members were not in good shape for the next day, which had them booked into a local studio to try to knock off a B side. With Coverdale AWOL and in no shape to sing anyway, the band worked on what would become "Coronarias Redig." The working title for the song had been the more functional "Drunk at the Revolution." Once Coverdale showed up, he and Glenn provided some backing vocals, but the song didn't get past the status of fairly structured instrumental, funky, hardish, with Glenn's bass runs and Ritchie's slide being the highlights. Ritchie's guitars were eventually laid down at around 4:00 in the afternoon, with Blackmore sitting in the control room to do his deed. In the end, the song was pretty much a long guitar solo on top of a decent Lord-counterpointing funk rhythm. The band was kicked out by 6:30, given that the studio had been booked by another act for that time.

"That's a Danish word that really does mean anything at all," says Glenn of the odd title. "I think it might be a street name. We had a one-day session in the studio, in Denmark, and we didn't have time to do the lyrics, and we just came up with that title. We didn't finish the track, so it basically was an instrumental."

"Coronarias Redig" was dutifully issued in the US as the B side to "Might Just Take Your Life," which stalled at #91 on the charts (the band had pushed for "Sail Away" to be the first single). In the UK it was used for the backside of "Burn," which summarily failed to crack the Top 100, even though it was Deep Purple's first UK offering in two years. Echoes of this impromptu instrumental track can be heard within epic Rainbow ballad "Catch the Rainbow."

Crazy with the travel plans, the band flew off to Sweden the following day to play their second gig plus receive five gold records, and then it was back to the Revolution in Copenhagen to see another Purple Records signing called Silverhead, a bruising blues / glam rock outfit fronted by future famous actor Michael Des Barres. A few shows and press conferences later, the band was in Germany, where EMI Germany gave the band engraved watches for sales of *Made in Japan*. Glenn Hughes found this particularly embarrassing, having, of course, nothing to do with the album. The label also took the opportunity to announce a compilation album titled *Mark I & II*. Next up was a full European tour, but this was scuttled after Jon was laid up with appendicitis, which, after infection extended his hospital stay to three weeks, also wound up causing a delay to the start of the US tour.

Like Led Zeppelin, Purple was sufficiently flush enough to hire a private jet, a Boeing 720B passenger liner deemed Starship I, to take them around the stadiums they were filling stateside. Tour guide John Coletta rationalized the $4,000 a day habit as necessary, due to the heavy schedule and also to the fact that flight itineraries at the airlines had been chopped by 15 percent, making all the band's city hopping that much more challenging.

"I just loved it," muses Glenn. "You know, back in that time, you didn't have a luxurious jet. There was nobody that had ever been on a luxurious jet with its own library and, you know, shower, bar, keyboard. No one had had that, so nobody really knew about it. So, when we had that plane for those two tours, it was awesome, because it was the true rock 'n' roll lifestyle. I mean, you can't imagine it getting better than that. I don't remember ever having to wear a seat belt, because, you know, different flight regulations. You could pretty much do whatever you wanted on that plane. We were all together on the plane, and it was a great feeling to have that power and that luxury behind you."

Deep Purple had been christened America's top-selling artist by this point, and US adulation for the band didn't miss a beat with *Burn*, despite the new sound and the new guys contouring it. Lester Bangs was impressed as well, having caught the band at their inaugural two-night stand at Cobo Hall in Detroit, and then jumping on the plane with them for a trip to their next stop.

The live show got a favorable notice from *Rolling Stone* as well. Gordon Fletcher, addressing the March 8, 1974, gig at the Capital Centre in Largo, Maryland, wrote that Hughes and Coverdale "are no caretakers. Their arrival has added a new dimension to the group's sound, supplying a depth and emotional range heretofore missing from the band's material. To emphasize the fact that this is a 'new' band, Deep Purple began their show with 40 minutes of selections from their just-released *Burn* LP.

Though initially perplexed by the lack of familiar standards, the capacity crowd was soon responding to the new material with rocking enthusiasm.

"'Burn' and 'Might Just Take Your Life' displayed the band's new vocal capabilities, with Coverdale and Hughes using their voices to counter, complement, and prod each other into stunningly effective harmonic patterns. Though it was dedicated to Linda Lovelace, the real star of 'Lay Down, Stay Down' was guitarist Ritchie Blackmore, whose extended solo was filled with jazz-tinged subtleties not usually heard in a 117 dB onslaught. 'Mistreated' spotlighted Purple's new 'free' sound, with Coverdale rendering an impressive vocal interpretation as Blackmore spat out tortured blues licks. Though they encored with Don Nix's 'Goin' Down,' on this night Deep Purple proved that they are a band still on the rise. The addition of Coverdale and Hughes has made a good group a great one."

Purple was now commanding $20,000 to $40,000 a night in the States, with the high point of the '74 campaign being California Jam on April 6, where Ritchie jabbed his guitar into an expensive camera and had his amps blown up. It's a maximalist Purple moment captured on film, but one can't help but view it as juvenile and petulant as well. The foul mood was exacerbated by disorganization at the event. Dealing with 400,000 people frying in the heat instead of the expected 60,000 had everyone on edge, and there were headliner politics going on between the event organizers and Emerson, Lake & Palmer (also on the bill were Rare Earth; Black Oak Arkansas; Earth, Wind & Fire; the Eagles; Seals and Crofts, and Black Sabbath).

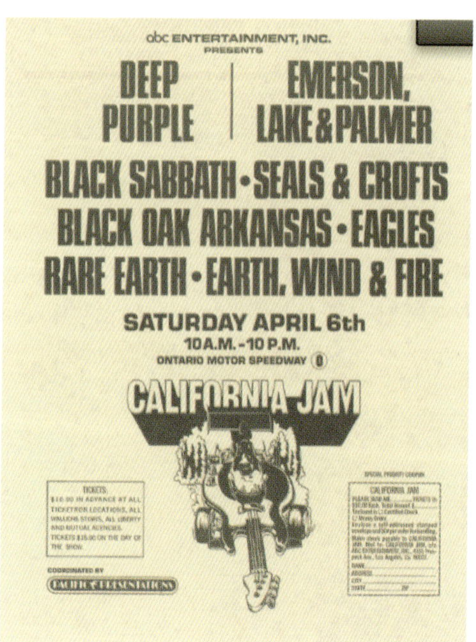

Two notices promoting California Jam. *Martin Popoff archive*

ELP was a late add as a second headliner and were supposed to close the show. Purple had been booked for six months, with ELP added just two months before kickoff. Then again, ELP were pulling their own petulant fit that if they were forced to go on too late, they'd live by the letter of the contract that said they could leave without playing at all—and keep their fee.

But pressing the schedule to tightness, Ritchie refused to go on before sunset, locking himself in his trailer. Purple had the big lit-up rainbow by this point, and it wouldn't have been that impressive in broad daylight. Plus the band had just arrived. The event was actually running ahead of schedule by twenty minutes, and so it was put to the band whether they could please get up there and start while it was still light out. Ritchie fumed all night and eventually gave in (sort of) but then had it out for anyone who rubbed him the wrong way for the rest of the night. The ABC cameraman was just an unfortunate victim in his way. Ritchie really wanted a go at the guy who pressed them to get onstage, now, and tried to do so by using a threatening count of thirty, after which Purple could consider themselves wiped off the show's schedule.

UK dates were to follow, with additional seeds of Purple's demise planted when backup band for the jaunt turned out to be Elf, fronted by future Rainbow vocalist Ronnie James Dio. At any opportunity proffered, Ritchie expressed his disdain for the conditions in which he was forced to carry on his career as the Man in Black. Circumstances would worsen as writing sessions for the band's controversial next album would find Ritchie missing from some of the song credits for the first time in Purple's long, tumultuous reign.

But we end this chapter on an amusing note, with a view from the crowd. "As luck would have it, a friend of mine sold me a ticket for the *Burn* tour concert at the Kursalle Theatre, situated along the seafront in Southend on Sea, Essex," recalls fan Martin Newall. "I made my way there only to find out that it had been canceled, and a band called Greenslade were filling in for them.

"Fortunately, we were informed that the Purple concert was only postponed, and our tickets were still good. So, a few weeks later I made my way back to Southend. When I arrived, it was obvious it was on, as there was a mass of people everywhere and a buzz in the air. Entering the large lobby, the walls were totally covered with what seemed like thousands of *Burn* album covers and posters—a nice touch which added to the overall excitement.

"I walked into the theater to see massive black-and-white 'Marshall Amplification—Loud and Proud' posters all around the hall. It looked awesome along with the towers upon towers of Marshall PA equipment that seemed to touch the roof. After the opening act had finished—I think it was Thin Lizzy with Eric Bell on guitar—Purple hit the stage to the sound of Blackmore playing the 'Burn' riff, and the place went wild.

"There are three things I remember clearly: (1) The volume was earthmoving, (2) Glenn Hughes seemed to be carrying most of the vocals, and (3) the way Blackmore dealt with the naked woman who ran onto the stage! This happened during the encore. We all kind of looked up in amazement as this naked blonde young woman ran onto the stage, only to see Blackmore place the neck of his guitar between her legs, wrap his arm around her back and carry her off the stage to his left! That's my big Blackmore story. I know it sounds a bit much, but it is true."

Chapter 12

Stormbringer

"We changed the spin on things dramatically."

Come record number two for the surprise Deep Purple Mk. III incarnation, despondency was starting to set in, most notably on the part of Ritchie Blackmore, who would be casting his eye about for a solo situation in which to sink his teeth. But *Stormbringer* got made, and much to the chagrin of Purple purists, it got made kind of funky. What distinguishes the album, however, is its almost invisible status, or its underrating, if you will, as a fierce vocal showcase, more so than *Burn* or the subsequent *Come Taste the Band.*

"I can definitely remember that Linda Gray from *Dallas*, her husband did the artwork for *Stormbringer*," recalls Glenn, with respect to the album's gorgeous illustration and typography, most notably as applied to the band name, resulting in a new logo that would be used regularly throughout the ensuing decades. "There was no other alternative art. You may know different, but looking back, to 1974, I can't remember if there was. And I don't think anybody had any say in the art. I believe it was left to the Warner Bros. art department. If someone came up with something now, I have total control over it, but then someone just came up with an idea and we liked it—very simple, I thought."

Issued on November 8, 1974, *Stormbringer* would arise from a return trip to Munich, Germany. Purple was in that class of British rock star that had become tax exiles (i.e., having to work for a period outside the country due to tax rules back home). Meanwhile, Jon Lord had just spent some additional time on classical work in that city with the Munich Chamber Opera Orchestra. An album called *Windows* was recorded, issued, and ignored, much like *Gemini Suite* was back in 1971. Previous to this session, in October 1973, he had been to town for a repeat performance of "Gemini Suite," quietly building a classical career that would regularly be attended to until his death in 2012. Both Coverdale and Hughes tagged along for the *Windows* session. Actually, there would be a third album for Jon Lord in 1974; namely, *First of the Big Bands*, as a duo with Tony Ashton (of Ashton, Gardner & Dyke as well as Family and Chris Farlowe fame). Ashton had also helped out on *Windows*, along with guitarist Ray Fenwick of the Spencer Davis Group. All the above would conveniently find a home (of last resort?) on Purple Records, with *Gemini Suite* actually preceding the first Deep Purple album proper, *Machine Head*, on the band's vanity imprint.

Print ad from *Disc* promoting *Stormbringer*, plus the album cover itself. *Martin Popoff archive*

Purple Records, as mentioned, also included Silverhead and Tucky Buzzard on its roster, but most significant would be Elf, who issued *Carolina Country Ball* on Purple in 1974. Hughes totally dug Elf live. "Oh, God, yes. They were fantastic, absolutely fantastic. Ronnie Dio has had a well-deserved career. Ronnie Dio is a tremendously gifted metal performer, entertainer, whatever you want to call him. He's got a great voice and he's a super guy, really good, good person, and I've got the greatest admiration for Ronnie; I love him to pieces. Oh yeah, but Ronnie is part of the family. Elf was opening up for us all the time."

Elf would soon form the nucleus of Ritchie Blackmore's Rainbow, with Ian Paice and Roger Glover having produced Elf's self-titled debut album, on Epic, in 1972. "Roger was more the producer," clarifies Ronnie. "That's what he wanted to do. He was very involved in the studio and learned a lot from Martin Birch, just like I did. And he started to do a little bit of production on his own. I think Ian was more there because either Ritchie or Ian Gillan had come down with hepatitis, and the tour had stopped that they were just about to start, and they had nothing else to do. Roger, musically, really wanted to do it, and Ian didn't have anything else to do. So, he came along with Roger. He has good ears, and he helped with the drum sounds, which were good. But I think it was more Roger than anything else, proven by the fact that Roger produced all the albums after that, by himself, without Ian. So, I think it was a product of the times. And Roger is brilliant, absolutely brilliant."

And speaking of Roger, here he was up into the tail end of 1974 with a big, weird concept album called *The Butterfly Ball*, the fanciful project including Glover's replacement, Glenn Hughes, singing "Get Ready," and David Coverdale on "Behind the Smile" and, more pertinently, "Love Is All," which was sung by Dio and became a minor hit. The following year, the laborious and layered musical potpourri was brought to the stage, interestingly, with Ian Gillan replacing Ronnie's bit. Relates Roger, "The fact that when I first did *The Butterfly Ball* at the Albert Hall in 1975, Ronnie didn't come . . . that posed quite a problem for me at the time. And the reason he didn't come the first time is because of the various politics that were going on. He had just joined Rainbow. In fact, there was kind of a division between him and I at the time."

"I didn't do the live show," affirms Ronnie. "At that time, we'd just put Rainbow together, Ritchie and I, and he felt it was not something that I should do, that we should be concentrating on the Rainbow thing and not be sidetracked by that. It was his band, and he was another one of my heroes, so I figured he knew what he was doing. In retrospect I'm quite glad I didn't do the show."

But we are getting ahead of ourselves. First there is *Stormbringer*, and you'd never know that Deep Purple were becoming a funky blues band, given the panoramic heavy metal majesty of the opening title track, a song that grooves large, riffs malevolently, and gets downright artful come chorus time.

"Oh my God!" recalls David Coverdale. "I wrote two songs which could be termed heavy metal or whatever. I've never embraced the expression heavy metal, because all my themes are emotional. But I wrote two songs to keep Ritchie Blackmore happy, which were 'Burn,' which is, I still think, a classic, and 'Stormbringer,' which basically, if you look at the lyrics, they are more or less sci-fi poems. But it never felt comfortable for me to have those. In fact, I think that's where Ritchie got the name Rainbow from, the hook in 'Stormbringer.' 'Burn' I can enjoy any time of the day, but I don't really go for 'Stormbringer.'"

"That was the second album with a song as the title cut," notes Hughes. "I thought it was another great classic, but I wouldn't call it a heavy metal song. I would call it more of a classic rock song. Call it what you will. Back then I guess you'd call it heavy metal."

After that bombastic calling card, however, things get slinky and R&B-ish for "Love Don't Mean a Thing," where Coverdale delivers a lascivious, proto-Whitesnake vocal. Ritchie, however, is barely himself.

Turns out he's even less himself than we suspected. "I love that track," notes Glenn Hughes. "I'm going to tell you. I'm going to give you a real exclusive here. We were on the road with Ritchie, the last American tour with him, the *Burn* tour. We were in Chicago and Ritchie had met this Black guy, and he was playing in either a bar or a subway, and he was singing this song. And basically, Ritchie took for the vibe of 'Love Don't Mean a Thing' from that song. Maybe he borrowed it, if you will, just a piece of it. And funny enough, if you listen to the vibe of it, it's funky. It's very funny when Ritchie says he hates funky music. Because when you listen to that track, the groove that is laid down is funky, but even his vibe on it is funky! And 'You Can't Do It Right (with the One You Love)' is also funky! So 'Love Don't Mean a Thing' is funny, because Blackmore fans, when he talks about how he doesn't want to play this music, he's doing it on that track."

It's way out of character for Deep Purple though. "Sure. The *Stormbringer* album is when I was well and truly involved in the band," agrees Glenn, indicating that a power struggle was on. "I mean, I was with *Burn*, but with *Stormbringer*, we toured about a year, and we were really at our height. Blackmore at the time was thinking of leaving, and I think the genre of the songs that David and I were writing, like 'Hold On' and 'You Can't Do It Right' and 'Holy Man,' it was becoming a little more apparent that it was becoming a crossover group.

"Because Ritchie always built his songs around the Bach guitar playing, and I really respected Ritchie for that because he was an originator, the first true innovator of that kind of music. But I've got to tell you, man: on *Stormbringer*, I was firing on all cylinders as a writer and a singer and a player. It's a great record! Listen back to it. I had a lot of fun recording it, at Musicland in Munich, and we finished it up at the Record Plant in L.A., where we did 'Gypsy' and 'High Ball Shooter.' Funny enough, I rerecorded 'High Ball Shooter' for one of my solo albums. So I have good memories of recording *Stormbringer*, in both Germany and L.A. It was a great time for the band, and it was a great time for me, and I thought I sung really well on the record."

"I would say halfway through the record, or even before we started, he was looking to leave anyway," continues Hughes. "I think he had gone as far as he wanted to go in Deep Purple. You know, I think the format of Gillan and Glover and all that stuff was a great metal band, whatever you want to call it. But we showed very strongly on *Stormbringer* what it was all about. And I like change in music. I don't want to make *Burn* II. Led Zeppelin did a really good job in their careers of making different records every time out. So that's how I feel about *Stormbringer*—it's a different record."

"Holy Man" is an underrated track on the album, one that, like "Soldier of Fortune," struck a convincing blues rock chord, along the lines of an exciting new band called Bad Company. As well, it's the lone track on the album that is sung solo by Glenn Hughes.

"I distinctly remember Ritchie doing the guitar solo," recounts Glenn. "You didn't really suggest too much to him. But I did ask him, as I had written the track, if he wouldn't mind playing a bottleneck. He looked at me, and rather than take a bottleneck up, he picked a screwdriver up and played it, almost in defiance. And the funny thing is, he played it wonderfully. I mean, he didn't react mean to me. He looked at me like, 'Hmm, okay.'

"But as I've said in the years since, Blackmore didn't like the way the band was going and the way the interaction was. The thing is, when you get two guys in a band like Coverdale and Hughes, we changed the spin on things dramatically. And the thing is, with Ritchie Blackmore, bless him, I have nothing but good things to say about him, but Ritchie had a problem with singers: Ian Gillan, Ronnie Dio, Joe . . . he just has a problem with the color they bring to a band or whatever, the ego, whatever you want to call it. But 'Holy Man' is a song I'm really proud of because it's the first song I got to sing solo on with Deep Purple. It's a great song. I think the tone I used to my voice is very innocently sang. It's a tone I hadn't used before, so I was very excited by that."

"Ritchie was—and is—an immensely versatile musician," adds David, and we connected immediately. My muse is Jimi Hendrix. Jimi Hendrix harnessed all of the elements I still utilize today with hard rock; namely, rhythm and blues, soul, melody, and great riffs. And Ritchie was that style of guitarist, this Hendrix-style

The disgruntled banjo player, Brøndby Hallen, Copenhagen, Denmark, March 20, 1975. © *Jørgen Angel*

guitarist, even playing a Strat, or whatever. So, I was in awe and sat at his feet. We actually wrote a great deal of music of the *Burn* album at his house outside of London. Ritchie and I initially got on amazingly well.

"But he became more disenchanted the more that the funk aspect came in, through the *Stormbringer* record. There was a huge collective sigh of relief when the *Burn* album was #1 on both sides of the Atlantic. Because Mk. II had been an incredibly successful band. But as I know now, from my own experience, success doesn't necessarily breed content. So, there was a great deal of discontent and dislike for musicians and that kind of stuff. You have a choice. You stay together like a lot of artists do, like in any personal relationship. You stay together for the kids, or you choose personal happiness. And that's what their choice was."

"Fascinatingly enough, I had most of the music before I actually joined Purple," begins David Coverdale, when asked about "Holy Man" by Jeb Wright. "I was too nervous to present it to the band. When Ritchie and I first sat down for him to play me demos, slowly but surely, me presenting him with some ideas of mine, as you could imagine, it was extremely intimidating. He is totally open to my ideas and, of course, took them to amazing fucking heights, being the breathtaking musician that he is.

"Both of us were big fans of Traffic. You know when you have talks about what bands you like? Another one, Ritchie was always like, 'Do you like Jethro Tull?' He has always loved harnessing folk music. But 'Holy Man' was like my 'No Face, No Name, No Number.' I don't know if you know that one. It's a beautiful Stevie Winwood song from the Traffic days. It was very, very funny. I played the idea to Jon, and he added that beautiful synthesizer passage that's on the original. I didn't use that on this version. That was Jon's contribution to the song. Glenn wrote the lyrics for the chorus. I wrote all the rest of the stuff.

"It was very funny because Jon Lord and Ian Paice said, 'Oh, David, there is no way Ritchie is going to play that guitar riff on the chorus." I went, 'Oh. Why? I think it's cool.' They just laughed. Ritchie played it without hesitation. I sat with him while he did the beautiful slide playing, using an Eveready battery or something. He would just use anything at hand. He is an extraordinary gifted melodic musician. To finish up on 'Holy Man,' I wrote the verses about Glenn. I am not sure he was even aware of it, but he surely is now."

Remarks Ritchie, comparing blues with classical, and more specifically whether blues has helped him with renaissance music, "Blues doesn't really help. Because obviously with blues, you're bending notes. And in those days, you never bent the notes. It was always trills. And I learned, when I was learning to play guitar, to play trills, because I had classical training. So, I kind of went back to that. In fact, the only thing that blues has to do with it is the relative minor keys, of which the lutes often play. But again, you cannot bend the notes or play a blue note, or seventh . . . especially major sevenths, which are kind of frowned upon. There are a lot of limitations to renaissance playing, as there is in blues playing. In blues playing, you very seldom play the majors. You always keep it in the relative minor keys. So, I'm attracted to the fact that it's limiting. It's unlike jazz, where there are no wrong notes, and musical possibilities are endless. But with blues and renaissance, you can have a few notes that just don't fit."

From that quote, and from his spare, clean playing on "Holy Man," you get the impression that Ritchie isn't really committed to the concept of the blues. He seems somewhat outside himself, airy and ethereal. It's like it's not really his domain, and he's standing outside himself watching this other guitar player approximating the blues.

Closing out side 1 is another track indicative of the album's funky vibe. "Hold On" is a bubbly, galloping cross between pop and R&B. Ritchie's guitar solo is considered by Purple watchers as the most absurd of his career, with the Man in Black turning in a flippant bit of country picking that left them all baffled. The solo would be cut in the control room in one take, and it's fully amusing to one and all who grasps what it means about what was going on within this band of battling brothers.

These two tracks—in a row, no less—would mark the first time since the Mk. I era that Ritchie would not be included in a song's writing credit. Further diminishment came with the fact that Ritchie's guitars had been laid low in the mix throughout the album. Blackmore hadn't bothered to show up for much of the mixing, so the other guys took advantage of the situation. And for once, it didn't seem to bother Blackmore. His mind was elsewhere—in stereo: his six-year marriage was on the rocks, and he knew his tenure in Deep Purple was on the rocks as well.

"David Bowie was actually with me when I recorded the vocals for that song," recalls Glenn, musing about the fateful "Hold On." "Stevie Wonder came in and heard me sing 'Love Don't Mean a Thing.' He was in the next room recording and I had met him, and he came in. He was my hero, as you know. Iggy Pop was in there, Bowie . . . I had a lot of friends in the studio; I had a lot of friends in L.A. at the time. The Record Plant was filled with spectators and well-wishers. For me, it was recorded at the height of my love, flower power, peaceful state." Additionally, Jon Lord used to tell the story of Stevie Wonder coming in while Coverdale was singing "Soldier of Fortune." Stevie was part of an entourage of about six people, and David, not being able to see who was out there and rattled by the commotion, had said, "Whoever it is in there, fuck off!"

But again, this was a song that was at odds with what Blackmore wanted to do. "Ritchie didn't like the super-groove thing that David and myself, and actually Ian Paice, were doing," reiterated Glenn, speaking with Sam Dunn. "And Jon Lord is now playing a Fender Rhodes keyboard. So, some of this stuff, 'Love Don't Mean a Thing' and 'Hold On,' they were very melodic classic rock songs. It wasn't *In Rock* kind of music. Look, every band evolves. I mean *Technical Ecstasy* from Sabbath is a completely different album. You look at albums from Yes or Rush. They have a moment where they just go completely off to another place. *Stormbringer* was an album of great songs, but it wasn't *Machine Head*."

Just like side 1, side 2 opens loud and proud with a fast-paced rocker. "Lady Double Dealer" presages the metallic side of Whitesnake, along with the clutch of happy and hard rocking party songs that Deep Purple would come up with through the 1980s and 1990s.

Asked about "Lady Double Dealer," Hughes begins with another look at his roots, in effect, pointing out that a song like that is an aberration for him.

"You know, when I joined Deep Purple, I had to put my head in. If you listen to the last thing I did before in Trapeze, it was *You Are the Music . . . We're Just the Band*, and that smacks of Glenn Hughes now really finding his Americanisms, his

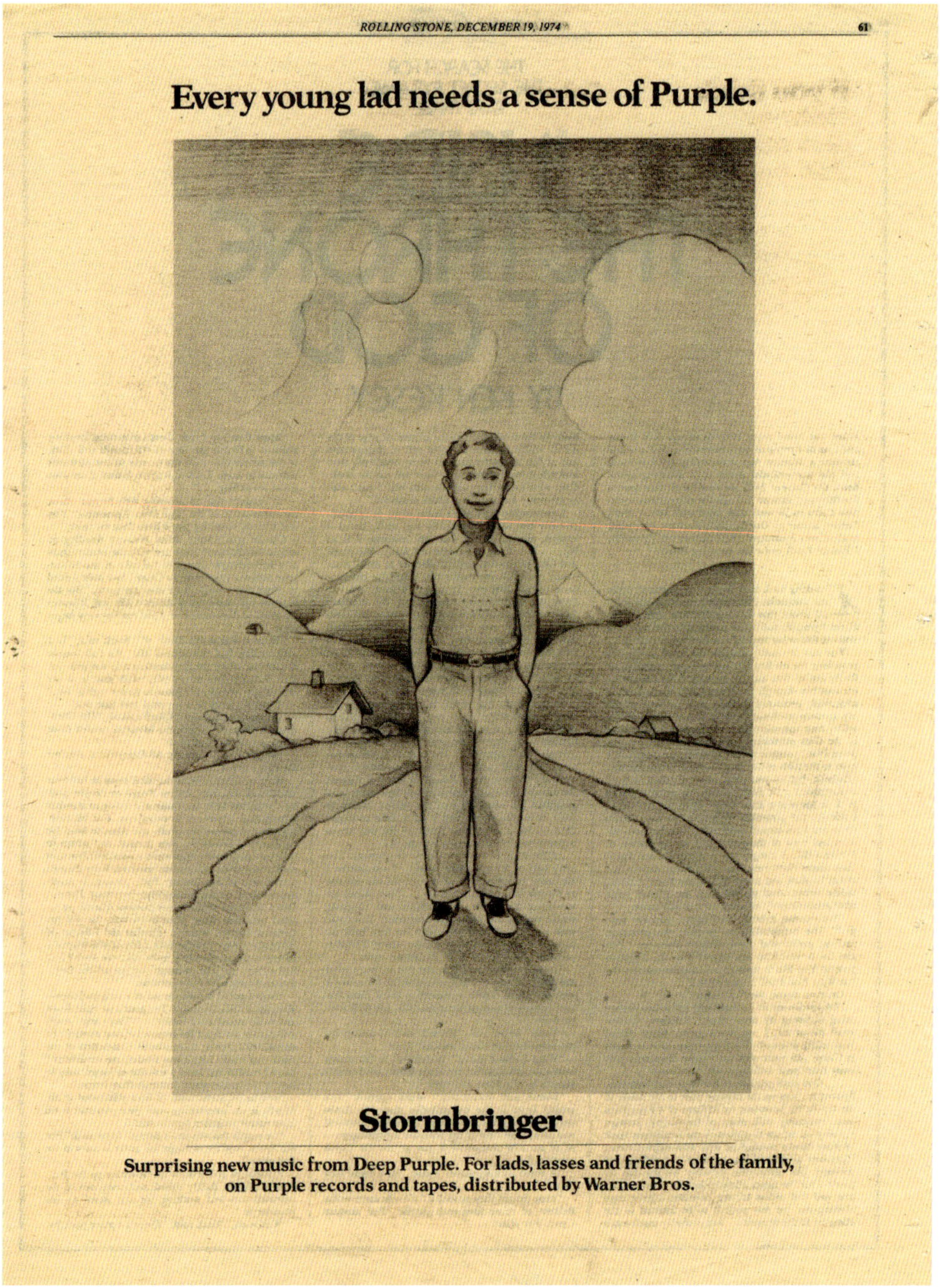
ROLLING STONE, DECEMBER 19, 1974
61
Every young lad needs a sense of Purple.
Stormbringer
Surprising new music from Deep Purple. For lads, lasses and friends of the family, on Purple records and tapes, distributed by Warner Bros.

Advertisement
WARNING
STORMBRINGER
IS COMING

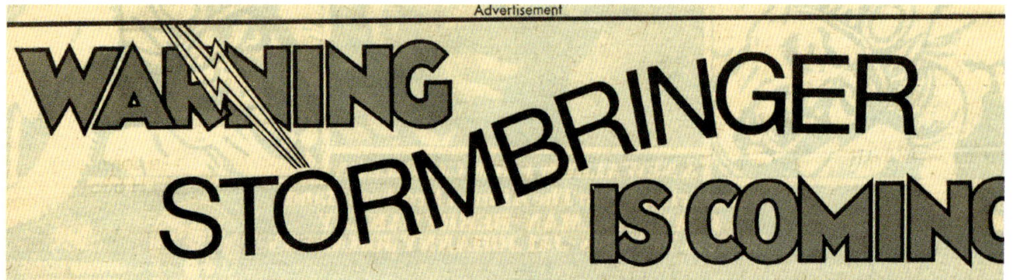

Arguably the best Deep Purple ad ever, plus a teaser ad. *Martin Popoff archive*

R&B roots. If you listen to my work with Trapeze, I was really going away from rock into R&B, a really different approach. When I joined Deep Purple, I realized I was taking a step backward musically to play more-traditional rock. Which I was over with by the time I joined Deep Purple. So, I had to go backwards a little bit, for things like 'Lady Double Dealer.' I don't know, it's really just another album cut. I thought it was a good song. But if you listen to the way the songs are formatted on the album, you'll hear my influence. And then you'll see in the reissue of *Burn* that I was really credited on all those songs as a writer. You'll see that there's a lot of influence from me, as far as the groove and the way that Ian Paice and I . . . a lot of things I wrote, they could not have been done with Roger, because it was a different kind of feeling. And the answer to your question is, you know, 'Stormbringer' and 'Lady Double Dealer' aren't heavy metal songs to me; they're more hard rock, you know?

I asked Glenn if they were bones thrown to Blackmore to keep him happy.

"No, not really. I think the album needed those songs, because if you take away those two tracks, the album would be even more of a David and Glenn record. You know, by *Stormbringer*, we were flexing our muscles. You've got to remember; I was the leader of my own band for years before I got to Deep Purple. And when you're a leader of the band, writing and producing and doing what I was doing at an early age, I was still in that headset. And I must say, as a five-man group, Deep Purple, we were all our own leaders. We were all very, very much strong individuals. But at the end of the day, it was Ritchie's last call on a lot of the stuff we did.

"But he was obviously losing his power. And I'm not taking anything away from Ritchie Blackmore, because he was Deep Purple. Without Ritchie Blackmore, there would not be a Deep Purple. He's sadly missed. Steve Morse is an amazing guitar player, but Ritchie . . . you see, the Deep Purple that is playing right now shouldn't be playing. It's ridiculous. You know, when I go see my old group . . . it was just abysmal. It was just abysmal. It was just . . . the band were playing intensely, and then Ian just isn't singing anywhere near like he used to do. And that's all to do with his smoking and his drinking. It's just . . . the band is playing to the best of their ability, and the band is not like they used to be in the '70s. It's just a very polite band now. It's not dangerous; it's just limp. Ian was just egotistical. He thought he was great, and he's not. He's got a lot of balls to be out there fronting that group."

Next up for *Stormbringer* is "You Can't Do It Right (with the One You Love)," which bridged the harder sounds from *Burn* with the funk stylings of *Stormbringer*. It's a medium rocking track which, like "Lady Double Dealer," would have fit well on an early Whitesnake record. Reiterates Glenn, "'You Can't Do It Right,' my God! I'll tell you what—Blackmore? He plays funky on that track! I'll tell you what; check it out, play it again. That little son of a bitch, he plays funky on it! And that guy, he hates Black R&B! And he plays it really well. So, I love that track."

"High Ball Shooter" follows, and to most fans it's the third-best song on the record, in terms of straight solid rock value, especially when it gets to the triumphant climax of a chorus. "The Gypsy" is another underrated track, scintillating in its sonic brightness but morose of disposition, weary through Coverdale's worn and bluesy vocal, with beautiful harmonies from Hughes singing high.

"Those two were written at the Record Plant in L.A.," explains Glenn, "because we recorded in Musicland and we came to L.A., and those songs were recorded there and written in the studio. And I've got to say, I loved that three- or four-day session we had in L.A.; those two songs turned out really good. 'High Ball Shooter' was another Purple-sounding song which featured the two of us going at it. And 'The Gypsy' has a very midpaced, Blackmoresque vibe on the lead guitar, and I think the vocal sounds really good on that one."

No surprise that "Stormbringer" and "Lady Double Dealer" made the new set list, but "The Gypsy" did as well (and only those three), with the tune gaining new life as a driving, co-lead-vocal showcase, heavier, faster, more histrionic.

Closing out the album on a dour note is "Soldier of Fortune," a dark ballad with tasty guitar work and a mournful solo vocal from Coverdale. "It's a very simple, straightforward melody," notes Ritchie. "Sometimes you just kind of follow on these melodies. David Coverdale wrote the first part, and I think I wrote the middle part. It was a very natural process. I like writing naturally as opposed to getting to rehearsals with a riff, and everybody throws in a chord because they want to be involved in the writing credits. I've been through all that, and it's ridiculous. But 'Soldier of Fortune,' I came up with the title, because I saw it written in a magazine and I didn't really quite know what it meant. But it was a very simple, straightforward melody, just one of those that fits."

"'Soldier of Fortune,' I love it," adds Hughes. "David loves that song, and I think he still sings it a cappella in concert."

As Coverdale told me, "Ritchie and I wrote that at Clearwell Castle in Gloucester in the Forest of Dean. And I think, initially, I was disappointed when it got the lyric, which was very mature lyric for a twenty-one-year-old, twenty-two-year-old; Ritchie was hoping I would write something like thirteenth-century warriors or mercenaries coming back covered in mud and shit from the Crusades or something. I'm going, fuck, you know, I haven't had any experience like that—not in this lifetime anyway, darling. Hah! But 'Soldier of Fortune,' I usually sing a little bit of that in my Whitesnake shows around the world. Looking for a pin drop in the big arenas and stuff. It's a very special song."

As David told Jeb Wright, "The rest of the band didn't buy off on 'Soldier of Fortune' at all. It was the only time I saw Ritchie really angry—well, no, I saw him angry actually a couple of times. We actually cut a demo after they passed on doing 'Soldier of Fortune,' to show them the vision of what we had. To this day it's one of the biggest classics of that time period, of Glenn's and my Mk. III association. But Ritchie walked out of the studio with me and said, 'That's the last time I ever fucking do that. If they don't trust that I don't know what I'm doing, then fuck them.' I think that was one of the seeds that led to him saying, 'Fuck it; I'm moving on.' Trust is an immense issue when you're working with a band, certainly when it comes to a vision."

Ritchie himself covered "Soldier of Fortune" with Blackmore's Night—but so did progressive-metal legends Opeth. As it turns out, this idea of younger bands appreciating Coverdale/Hughes-era Deep Purple is a bit of a trend.

Says Michael Amott, guitarist for Arch Enemy and Carcass, "Ritchie Blackmore can be one of the world's best guitar players ever, when he wants to be, when he's in the mood. He's kind of uneven, isn't he?"

Adds Carcass bandmate and coguitarist Bill Steer, "Yeah, but he's an interesting guy because he really polarizes people, with his antics onstage and stuff. Sometimes it's a bit strange seeing a guy trying to play his guitar with his foot. But on his records, he's very tasteful, honestly. I mean some of those solos, they are just ironclad, just really great moments in the music, such a massive part of the song. And obviously, without Ritchie Blackmore, you wouldn't have somebody like Yngwie Malmsteen. Me and Michael, around the time we were doing *Heartwork*, we were massively into Purple, but the things we got into were the albums with Coverdale and Hughes, the funky albums."

"I didn't go grow up with those," explains Michael. "I was a massive Purple fan, but I grew up with the Gillan stuff, *In Rock*, *Made in Japan*, and then you played me *Burn*, and I went, 'Holy shit! Glenn Hughes was in Deep Purple?!' I had no idea, because I grew up basically listening to different stuff. I didn't grow up on Deep Purple. I'm too young for that. Coverdale . . . I knew him from Whitesnake. I didn't know he was in Deep Purple. I freaked out. And then I got totally into that as well."

"It's just an interesting thing," adds Bill, "because as a kid, I worshiped Gillan in Purple, and then I got burned out on it, I suppose, as many people do. You don't want to listen to 'Highway Star' every day. And then I got fixated on the *Burn* album. Especially the fact that everyone was saying it was shit. Everyone was saying, 'I love Purple, but Hughes and Coverdale fucked up that band.' And I was just mystified. It was like, how can they make music this good, and the lineup gets slagged to shit? Then when we exhausted those albums—*Burn* and *Stormbringer*—then we had a big thing on the Tommy Bolin record, and that was a different thing, because obviously Tommy Bolin is a fantastic guitarist, but much looser than Blackmore. Blackmore has a very artistic approach. Everything is crafted, and there's a very even vibrato and all that stuff. But Bolin is just a different approach, quite druggy, but there are some jazz influences creeping in. But supercool, nonetheless."

Alan Niester from *Rolling Stone* was lukewarm on the band's shocking change of direction, writing in his review that "Deep Purple has attempted to prove, firstly, that replacing the departed Ian Gillan and Roger Glover with David Coverdale and Glenn Hughes has in no way weakened the highly successful and profitable Deep Purple sound, and, secondly, that to continue to sell albums, the band need no longer rely on the unique but overdone speedo-riff rock that made the five albums from *In Rock* to *Made in Japan* quadrillion sellers. While the two newcomers are just as competent as their predecessors (as witnessed on the title cut, one of the few real throwbacks to *Machine Head* days), the attempts that the band has made at diversifying its sound have been only partly successful. While the group-penned 'Hold On' should rightly be considered one of the neatest, most accessible, and rockiest songs they've ever done, slower-paced stuff like 'Holy Man' or the Uriah Heep–like 'Gypsy' hardly rate above the commonplace."

Stormbringer's stylistic left turn would cause the destruction of Mk. III Deep Purple. Ritchie would leave to form Rainbow, with the remaining now-somewhat-rudderless foursome hiring fairly unknown quantity Tommy Bolin—an American!—to fill Blackmore's black boots.

"Ritchie just became . . . he wasn't mean, he wasn't angry, as he can be," recalls Hughes on the beginning of the end. "He just sort of disappeared into the woodwork a little bit. It all happened in a matter of . . . it was on the last American tour, which I believe was with ELO backing up, while I think it was Elf in Europe or another one of the Purple family bands. Anyway, he told us, even before we did the European tour, that he was leaving. It was all in a matter of three months that he was gone."

"It started when I wanted to do a song called 'Black Sheep of the Family,' by a group called Quatermass, that a friend of mine was in," explains Ritchie, on his shocking split from the band. "And I took it to the band, Purple, and I said, 'What about playing this song? It would really fit into our repertoire; it's a great song.' And that was met with a lot of reluctance along the lines of 'Well, if we don't write something, we're not going to play it,' which I thought was incredibly narrow-minded. 'But yeah, it's such a great song!' 'Well, yeah, it is. But it's not one of ours.' And I kept thinking, that's not right. So, we were on tour with Elf, and I went to the studio, and Ronnie said that he would sing it. He heard the tune, and he said, 'Yeah, I'd sing that, sure, okay.' So, I did it with him. And that's the first song I did away from Purple.

Elf ad from November 21, 1974. Ronnie James Dio is second from right.

"And we got along so well; we did it very quickly, and we had the guy from ELO playing with us, actually, as well, the cellist Hugh McDowell, and it went so quickly. It was so refreshing working with Ronnie; he was so up and excited and positive. So, after that, I suddenly realized that this might be the way to go. Because we were getting very stale as Purple in about '75. Things were getting . . . everything was a business meeting. A lot of briefcases and men in suits walking about with lots of money. It didn't have much to do with music anymore, and everybody was becoming very isolated in Purple. Even Jon, for instance, who was kind of very independent. I would only ever see him onstage.

"Drugs started coming into the band," continues Blackmore, "not from my angle, but from a couple of the others. And then they wanted to become more of a soul band, getting into this pseudo-soul stuff, which . . . I've never been into soul music. You know, the Motown stuff? It's never done anything for me. I can respect that it's good music, and in those days, nearly everybody loved it. I was the only one where it didn't do anything for me at all. And they were going that way. And I thought, this is no longer rock 'n' roll. This was after *Burn*. It was *Stormbringer* where it came to a head, where I realized that I was in kind of a pseudo-soul band. And that's when I thought, I want to be with a group of musicians playing rock 'n' roll, you know, symphonic rock. And that's why I got Elf involved. And obviously, I kept

Ronnie, and we realized that when we started to go on the road and were rehearsing, that the rest of the band didn't measure up, his band. So gradually, one by one, we had to fire them and get other people who were better. Not that they were better; they were just different musicians for the style that we wanted."

Contribution was key with Ritchie, and even though the songwriting-credit problem was largely cleared up in and around *Stormbringer*, it was still an issue that rankled.

"Yes, everybody has to contribute. I've been in bands when someone has just sat there and said nothing. And all of a sudden, they're going, 'I want writing credits.' And you go, 'Well, what did you write?' 'Well, I changed the C to a D.' 'That's it?!' And they want equal writing credits. That's a whole other problem. When Deep Purple was going, for instance, three of us were writing; two were not writing. And never five of us. But we credited it to five, just to keep everybody happy. But that began to wear thin after about the fourth record. I kind of put my foot down and said, 'He who writes, gets.' Enough of this charity stuff, you know?

"It was funny; I noticed [that] Eddie Van Halen, who I respect as a person and as a guitar player, said the same thing. In one of his interviews, he said, 'Oh, we all write.' And I felt like saying, you know, I don't think so. That's Eddie probably writing with the singer. But I didn't know. I just felt it was. And then later on, when they broke up, Eddie was complaining that 'well, nobody else wrote; it was all my ideas anyway.' And I could relate to that. So, it's amazing what you have to do. You have to be very democratic if you're in a band. Otherwise, heaven forbid, if somebody doesn't get some writing credit that's in the band, all sorts of eruptions go down. That's one of the most difficult things to control in a band, because everybody thinks they're a writer. And some of them don't write a note. They're just there to have a coffee, you know?"

"Blackmore never really mingled with anybody in Purple," says Hughes, who speaks of the end. "He never really . . . that family of Purples, on tour, Ritchie was totally separated from all of us. He never really spoke to us at all. He continues to be the same way, he does, Ritchie. But he did mention a couple of times in passing that he thought Ronnie was a great, great singer, blah blah blah. So, when he formed Rainbow, it wasn't really a surprise.

"Look, you know, people have always said when Glenn Hughes and David Coverdale came into Deep Purple, we changed the sound of the band from being a straight hard rock metal group to making bluesier, more soulful, intelligent-sounding music, I thought. When you replace guys like Gillan and Glover, you've got to come up . . . you don't go with two soundalikes. I don't sound like Roger Glover, and of course Roger doesn't sing. And I certainly don't sound like Ian Gillan, and neither does David. I think it was a really bold move to replace those two and have us have a top five record all around the world with *Burn*. The *Burn* record stands up for itself; it's brilliant. But Ritchie, midway through the *Stormbringer* tour, realized that the end was nigh for him, because the power was being taken from him, in the music. Because it had all been written by all of us guys. And he just didn't understand and like what he called shoeshine music. And as I said, if you listen to *Stormbringer*, to tracks like 'You Can't Do It Right' and 'Hold On,' actually, Blackmore plays very funky. He didn't like it, but he played great."

I wondered if Glenn was privy to any of Ritchie's dalliances with the dark arts.

"Yes, I did a couple of things with Ritchie. We had a couple of séances, where he freaked on one of them. He was really freaked out. Some shit started happening. Oh, he was really awful. If you're in the dungeon of a fifteenth-century castle and shit starts flying around the room . . . you know, he was freaked. I think I was high, but I was freaked too."

And did he believe what he saw? "Oh yeah! Absolutely! I've seen and heard things in my lifetime. Whilst I've been clean and sober, I've seen things that . . . there's no doubt about it, there's another dimension out there."

But then, of course, Ritchie always kept everybody guessing by mixing the earnest spiritual quests with practical joking. "Yes, numerous times. Horrible things I can't really talk about. But some stuff; the first day at Clearwell Castle, he rigged my room up with a microphone, and he stayed up overnight making evil noises, clanking stuff, tapes going on. Yeah, he did that quite a few times with people."

"One can never be convinced of anything," said Ritchie, asked about life after death. "It's really a case of the blind leading the blind when it comes to other realms, and anyone who tells you they 'know' or that they are an 'expert' has no idea. One thing I can tell you that I don't believe in is giving money to organized religions. Everyone has his or her own path to follow. Too much blood has been shed in the name of religion, so obviously that is not the right way to go. I do believe in life after death. Only weak and feeble minds that are afraid of confronting possibilities are scared off by these thoughts and ideas."

I asked Coverdale to confirm rumors that Ritchie might have wanted him to run away with him to Rainbow. "Initially he presented me with these songs," says David. "And I said, 'These seem like *Machine Head* songs.' You know, if you listen to Rainbow, other than Ronnie's vocals, they are very *Machine Head*–like, songs that could have easily been Gillan era, Mk. II as it's called. And I felt it was going back. Like I said, the climate at the time was about moving forward. And of course, I was getting me licks in doing the blues and soul elements.

"It wouldn't have worked. Ritchie took a band called Elf, who were on Purple Records, and they basically did what Purple would not have done. They did everything Ritchie wanted. 'This is what I want; this is the kind of lyric I want; this is the theme I want,' and that was it. They didn't argue with Ritchie. It was basically a band of puppets, of course, until Rainbow *Rising*. Once you get Cozy Powell and Jimmy Bain in, Rainbow *Rising* was a fucking corker of a record—you know, really good.

"Years later, I of course had the pleasure of working with Cozy, God rest his soul, and I would see Jimmy Bain around all over, and Jimmy was a very talented writer. But Ritchie wasn't opening the shop to having other people put their stuff in there. I think it could have been significantly more successful had he been more open-minded about other people contributing in the songwriting department other than trying to keep complete control."

"I never spoke to Ritchie after I started playing live with him," continues Hughes, who underscores David's description of Ritchie with respect to control issues. "He made an imaginary chalk line down the front of the bass drum and said, 'If you ever cross this side of the stage, I will hit you with my guitar.' I did cross it one night, and he reached over and played my bass with his left hand. He told David Coverdale and me not to come near him onstage. Basically, it was like five guys onstage that did not communicate with the guitar player. There are a lot of guitar guys like that.

A trio of satin backstage passes from 1974

Yngwie Malmsteen, George Lynch, and other metal guys are that way inclined. They are like, 'Don't talk to me.' Michael Schenker is another one. You just can't communicate with them. I don't work with people like that anymore. I won't work with people who won't communicate with me on a real level. I don't have time for people who are not loving and nurturing. Looking back on my life, it was all crazy. We were all young, and we were into all kinds of shit. I look back and I thank God that I am over that period. Blackmore isolates, as we all do. But Blackmore isolated and didn't communicate with anyone. Ever. Never. That's Ritchie Blackmore."

"It was fine, absolutely fine," reflects David on the *Stormbringer* experience. "The disenchantment was predominantly Ritchie's. It was interesting. Purple was five egomaniacs fighting for the spotlight. Everybody had an opinion. We didn't do certain cities in America, because one member of the band refused to play there if there wasn't a Benihana restaurant. Everybody, really, their opinion counted, no matter how superficial or whatever. But if someone said, 'We don't want to do this,' we wouldn't have done it. *Stormbringer*, to me, is a great album. A colleague of mine many years later, Steve Vai, said that was a pivotal album for him in terms of inspiration and influence."

Speaking with Sam Dunn, Glenn continues itemizing why Ritchie took off. "By the time we were making *Stormbringer*, Ritchie had already got it in his head that he was going to start making the Bach-influenced medieval music. It wasn't meant to be. So, he took his foot off the gas, completely, and I think halfway through *Stormbringer* is when he started thinking about, well, there's a guy called Ronnie Dio and there's a band called Elf. I'm thinking maybe the drummer's good, and the keyboard player is good too. And he did a great thing by getting Ronnie to sing with him.

"But that medieval, I call it, or whatever, seventeenth-century music, Bach-influenced music, classical-influenced music . . . let's be clear: he is the go-to guy in guitar for the end of the last century that did it wonderfully. Blackmore circa '70 to '77; we should remember the greatness of that."

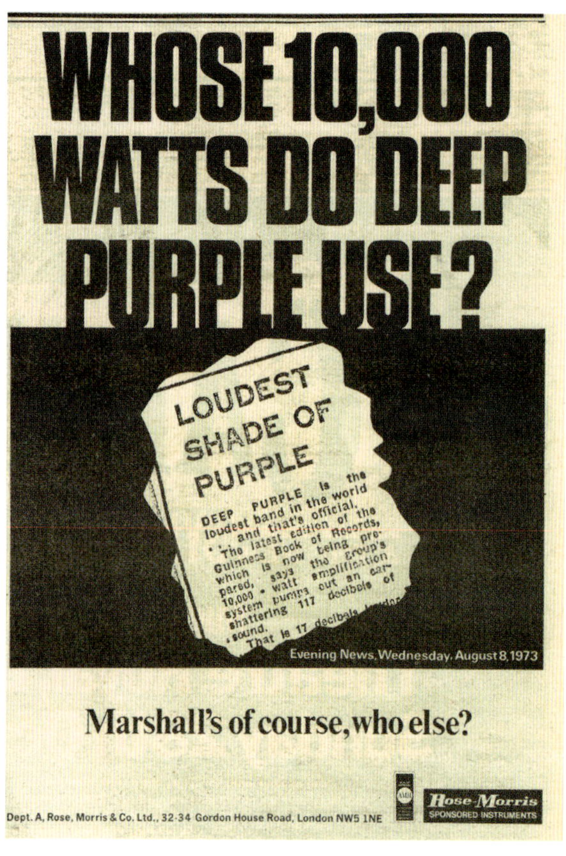

Deep Purple makes the *Guinness Book of Records. Martin Popoff archive*

In parallel, it just seemed to be part of Ritchie's history that band configurations were constantly in flux. Glenn: "Yes, since that period, up until he stopped playing electric guitar in the early '90s, whatever band Ritchie led, he would change personnel every two or three albums. Ritchie likes to have new blood. I think it's a good thing for certain people to do that. He likes to keep people on their toes and keep people guessing. He's one of the last great rock 'n' roll characters from England that we have."

"It was such an extraordinary and extreme circumstance for this Cinderella aspect of coming out of nowhere," muses Coverdale, speaking with Jeb Wright. "I got this opportunity and was literally, no pun intended, being thrown in the deep end. Thank God I swam, but it was with the help of those guys. The five egomaniacs fighting for a spotlight came later. Jon taught me grace, charm, and to look further than just a C chord. He taught me to look for a C minor, or a C minor seventh, that kind of thing. Ritchie taught me to watch what tempos get people out of their seats and start dancing on the dance floor. Not that Deep Purple was particularly a dance group, but rather what tempos, what kind of drum patterns, for instance, resonated with people. That was a very simple thing, but it was advice that was worth millions. I meet twenty-one-year-olds now and go, 'How in the fuck are you going to do this?' These guys nurtured me. They took good care of me, and that's why my gratitude is eternal to them. That is the primary reason that I wanted to tell Ritchie Blackmore this to his face.

Chapter 13

Come Taste the Band

"We were the toxic twins of the band."

It's a wonder that an album got made at all, given the judgments clouded by drugs, the power struggles within the band's intergenerational ranks, and the expectations of the Deep Purple public beating down upon them like the hot sun. *Come Taste the Band* is a qualified success in spite of itself, because, quite surprisingly, what stumbled out the other end of its factional, fractioned process is a record growing in stature among Deep Purple fans as the perfect stranger of the catalog.

Despite an unexpected toughness, the soulful sounds of *Stormbringer* would remain, sensibly, given that Ritchie Blackmore was gone, replaced by a new junior member in Tommy Bolin.

"Well, here's the thing," says Glenn Hughes, reiterating his love for incongruous influences. "Most guys my age, when they were turning twelve, thirteen, fourteen, in England, they were listening to the Beatles and the Stones. I was listening to Otis Redding, Wilson Pickett, little Stevie Wonder, Al Green, Martin Gaye—those were my heroes. So, when I first started, you've got this guy from England who was in a rock group called Trapeze but had this unusual American-sounding voice. It's like blue-eyed soul with a rock influence."

As discussed, it would be a mutual respect and interplay and heritage between Hughes and David Coverdale that would overpower the disappointing *Stormbringer* album. It was the last straw for Blackmore, who proved his traditional Deep Purple values and left to create the early Deep Purple–loving sounds of *Ritchie Blackmore's Rainbow*, *Rising*, and *Long Live Rock 'n' Roll*.

This left Deep Purple to either pack it in or persevere. Persevere they did, hiring the twenty-four-year-old Tommy Bolin from Sioux City, Iowa. Bolin was best associated with his work for James Gang, having made two records with the band as the second replacement for Joe Walsh. He'd also played with fusion drum wizard Billy Cobham as well as appeared on records with his own soft-rock band, Zephyr. There was also an even earlier band called Energy, plus a plethora of diverse collaborations in the jazz world.

The entry into the ranks of Purple was promulgated by Coverdale, who had heard Bolin from one of those Billy Cobham records. David was suitably impressed, and relations intensified when it was discovered that Bolin was currently unencumbered with any one band.

"There were three names on my list of proposed musicians," David told Jeb Wright. "The first one was Jeff Beck. I am the biggest Jeff Beck fan in the world to this day. I didn't know him as well as Jon and Ian, and they both said, 'Oh my God, after the challenges of Ritchie.' Jeff was horrid about showing up in the early days with the Yardbirds if there was something fun on TV. They felt that would be like jumping out of the frying pan into the fire. The second name I had was Rory Gallagher, who I love. Certainly, he could have done proud, but he had a beautiful career, as we all know, God rest his soul. They couldn't see that.

"Then I said Tommy Bolin. They said, 'Who?' I said, 'I don't know what kind of image this guy has. I've only heard him on Alphonse Mouzon's *Mind Transplant* album and on Billy Cobham's *Spectrum* album. Paicey was, of course, a big Billy Cobham fan, and he says, 'Do you have anything of his?' I went back to my hotel room and came down with a compilation cassette that I'd made and presented this stuff, and they said, 'Fuck, he's great.'

"The word went out, but we couldn't find him for, I don't know, over a month or six weeks. We found him living about 2 or 3 miles from me in Malibu. His image, as we know, was breathtaking. I must own up that once I was at a party with Bonzo and Tommy, and *Spectrum* was on the fucking record player. I went, 'Oh, I love this lick of yours,' and Tommy goes, 'Oh, that's Jan Hammer.' I went, 'Oh, sorry.' Then I was going, 'Oh, but listen to this one, Tommy. I really love this one.' Tommy goes, 'That's also Jan, David.' I was like, 'Oh, for fucks sake.'

"By that time, he was in the band, and I loved him dearly of course. I was very challenged by how he treated himself, sadly. He was a beautiful and fragile soul. I never considered him a replacement, like I don't consider Joel Hoekstra as a replacement for Doug Aldrich in Whitesnake. I don't look for replacements. Ritchie was so iconic that it was, I think, very challenging for Tommy to hear in concert 'Where's Ritchie?' That is completely understandable."

As for losing their guitarist, David told Sam Dunn that part of the reason Blackmore left "was also to have musicians who basically did as he told them. He couldn't do that with Purple, regardless of the power that Ritchie held sway within the band. And it was significant; he was a huge creative source for what Deep Purple was. But you can't turn around and say to Ian Paice, 'I want you to play like Bonzo.' You can't turn around to Jon Lord and say, 'I want you to play like Keith Emerson,' or whatever that he was hearing in a particular composition. These guys would turn around and say, 'Are you baked?'

"Basically, he took a great band that we had on Purple Records and a wonderful singer, my dear friend, and he's sadly missed, Ronnie Dio, and did great—fantastic. Ritchie actually spoke to me about leaving. That's how close we were. And he played me a lot of the songs that we'd actually passed on for the *Stormbringer* record that ultimately became part of *Ritchie Blackmore's Rainbow*, and he did great. He got what he wanted, so that was fine. And then when I did my thing with Whitesnake, we had a very healthy competition going on.

David Coverdale, Long Beach Arena, Long Beach, California, February 27, 1976. © *Marvin Rinnig*

"I listened to some of it," continues Coverdale, asked by Sam what he thought of Rainbow's music. "Of course, I was good friends with Roger and Cozy Powell, God rest his soul. So difficult with so much loss now. I thought they were great songs, the way they worked on the first Rainbow album, and the second one. With respect, I lost touch after that. Ronnie was a lovely man, an astonishing singer with a beautiful voice. I'm honored to have known him, and I knew him from the days of Elf on Purple Records. We had a couple of bands we would take out with us, and I always sat chatting with Ronnie. Always admired his voice, very much so. He was very approachable, and people loved him dearly, I think. But to be honest, I'm the last person to ask about legacy. It's the last thing I think about, what people brought here. I know that I miss Ronnie as a friend and as an artist."

"Look, here's the deal," begins Hughes on the chemistry within the band at this strange time. "Tommy Bolin joined Deep Purple in, I think, June of 1975. In June and July, we basically rehearsed in Los Angeles, writing the songs, pretty much three-quarters of them. We wrote a couple in the studio. Then we went to Munich, to Musicland Studios. Tommy Bolin had moved into my home in Beverly Hills. There were definitely two camps being set up, maybe three camps being set up. There was me and Tommy to one side, David alone, and then Jon and Ian.

"And it was very obvious when we went to Germany that it was me and Tommy hanging out. It was basically . . . if you listen to the album, there is definitely a Tommy and Glenn influence on the one side, and Coverdale is doing the big voice in the middle. I wouldn't say it was tense. Tommy and I were younger, and we were more free-spirited. We were the toxic twins of the band. We were young, and we didn't know what the hell we were doing as far as that's concerned. But that's what we did. But I thought the music was great.

"Tommy, bless him, was the opposite of Ritchie," adds Glenn. "He lived at my house. We were 'mates' in many ways. You can imagine what it was like. We were rocking and rolling and totally out of our minds. He was totally creative. The deal is that Tommy was sick. I didn't know he had a problem with the heavier narcotics that he was taking. On a personal level, he was wonderful to live with and very childlike in his quality. He was a brilliant, innovative guitar player."

Asked if David was wild as well, Glenn says, "I wouldn't like to comment on that. All I can tell you is that David was a weekend warrior."

The early rehearsal sessions of which Glenn speaks were at a place called Pirate Sound, commandeered by an erstwhile Purple engineer named Robert Simon. Before they found Tommy, with Paice and Lord down in the dumps, Coverdale and Hughes drew up a wish list for the band's all-important guitar slot, which included Rory Gallagher, Jeff Beck, Clem Clempson, Harvey Mandel, Wayne Perkins, Mick Ronson, and Bolin. Much of the list matches that pondered by none other than the Rolling Stones, who had seen Mick Taylor quit on the band less than a year earlier, and much of the list never got beyond someone throwing the name out there for consideration of an eventual call. Humble Pie's Clempson was in fact brought in to try out while the band worked on new material, but as discussed, it was Coverdale's admiration for Tommy Bolin through Billy Cobham's *Spectrum* album that got the ball rolling.

"Clem Clempson was the only other guy, from Humble Pie," recalls Hughes. "He also came and stayed with me, while we auditioned him. The only thing wrong

Tommy Bolin, Long Beach Arena, Long Beach, California, February 27, 1976. © *Marvin Rinnig*

with Clem . . . Clem was a great guitar player, but he didn't have the charisma to replace a Ritchie Blackmore. We needed strong charisma. And when Tommy Bolin walked in with his multicolored hair and his strange clothes and the way he spoke . . . just the way he held his guitar, just the way he looked was enough, and the way he played. Not taking anything away from Clem; he just didn't have the charisma to be the lead guitar player in one of the biggest groups in the world at that time."

Given that Bolin was based in Malibu, "3 miles down the road," made it easy to give the young gun a whirl. Roadie Nick Bell was dispatched to track him down, beginning with a phone number proffered at the infamous Rainbow club.

"When Ritchie left, I wanted to discontinue the band," recalls Jon Lord. "But one day, David Coverdale showed up at my house in Malibu with two bottles of wine and, with great eloquence, persuaded me to carry on. I felt that Ritchie was the heart and soul of the band, and I wasn't ready to back down from my decision. But then David said, 'I want you to hear something,' and he played the *Spectrum* album. I was blown away and utterly entranced by this guitar player."

And then, explains Lord, came the meeting. "This glorious young man walked in with red and green hair and this beautiful, wide, friendly grin. On his arm he had this stunning woman who was wearing one of those crocheted dresses and absolutely nothing underneath. Tommy plugged in, we jammed, and boy was it good! This guy could really play. But it was a totally different style of playing from Ritchie. It was untutored. His technical ability came from within. But he was like the little girl with the curls: when he was good, he was very, very good, but when he was bad, he was horrid."

"I wanted out as well," says Glenn, even though history has it that Ian and Jon were most despondent. "But David Bowie convinced me to stay in. He was staying at my house at the time. He was making a movie called *The Man Who Fell to Earth*. And when Tommy was auditioning, he came down with me and thought it would be a good idea to get a guitar player, like a Tommy Bolin, somebody completely different to Ritchie Blackmore. And no, you know, I must say, I wasn't really intrigued about carrying on either. I mean, I could've definitely just gone back to Trapeze or gone on and played some different kind of music. But David convinced me to stay in the band."

Bowie hadn't suggested any guitarists. "Well, no. I mean, we only auditioned two, which was Clem Clempson and Tommy Bolin, and no, David Bowie didn't suggest anybody."

As Jon Lord alludes to, Tommy and the band hit it off right away, and, curiously, it was Ian Paice who felt a quick musical kinship first. Bolin, for his part, says he was hesitant about joining an English group, finding most of them "sterile" and their jokes repetitive. Still, Bolin quickly found that the guys had assimilated much of the same funk and blues roots that he himself had grown up with; namely, the likes of Sam and Dave, Motown, and R&B. Bolin also recalls that he was forced to perform for the first time for the Purples after "a couple days" of no sleep, apparently having lost track of time due to "songwriting." After searching for an excuse to delay the audition for a day, he decided to buck up and just get the job done.

Scott Cohen from *Circus* talked to Tommy in 1976 about the years leading up to his adjoining with the Purples. "When I got to L.A. and was with the James Gang, I got the opportunity to write a lot, to play in front of large audiences, make some money, but it got to a point where I had to leave. The lead singer wanted to do something else; the drummer wanted to be an accountant; the bass player was sick of touring. Then I joined another band, then I took a year off to look for a lead singer; I spent money and threw it away. Then I ran out of money. I said, 'Fuck it; I'm going to do it myself,' and so I did. I got a contract and then I got an offer to play with Deep Purple. I had heard two songs by Purple, 'Smoke on the Water' and some other song. I don't like English bands. They're too structured. But when I'm with Purple, I'm totally with Purple; when I'm doing my thing, I'm totally doing my own thing."

Bolin also explained how music was part of his life from an early age, relaying, as well, a sense of how his guitar vocabulary would become so diverse. "When you come from the Midwest, you have a more open mind than if you come from the West Coast or the East Coast. At that time, you had vagrants, rich kids, and everything. My family were all musicians. When I was five years old, my father took us all to see Elvis. I had a leather jacket and combed my hair back. As I said, I've always been surrounded by music. That's all I wanted to do. I really wasn't interested in school or anything.

"I started off on Hawaiian steel," continues Bolin. "I didn't want to, but for some reason the guy said to start on Hawaiian steel. Mr. Flood was his name. He tuned the guitar to the E ninth, which is the real Hawaiian, but I would never play it—I'd always stand in front of the mirror at home and put on the records and pretend I was playing rock. Mr. Flood didn't know Elvis. He liked Hawaiian music. So, I left that and started taking lessons from this lady, Mrs. Sullivan, who had an unbelievable collection of guitars. She had tons of them. And she was very country and western. I started off reading, and the first song I learned how to read was 'On Top of Ol' Smokey,' but I thought, this isn't it either. So, then I went to another place, the music store where all the bands hung out, all my local heroes, but what they taught me wasn't it either. Finally, what happened was I started playing along on Rolling Stones records."

During June and July 1975, Deep Purple spent jamming, with the guys suitably impressed with the scope of Bolin's talents, not the least of which was a strong predilection toward songwriting, proven by his concurrent crafting of his first solo album while now ensconced with Purple. Bolin had wanted his new mates to play on what would become *Teaser*, with Glenn asked to sing the whole record. But contractual limitations quashed that idea, although Hughes wound up sneaking a small bit of himself onto a track called "Dreamer."

Paice tells an amusing tale of the band's relocation to Musicland, whereby arriving jet-lagged, an assistant had managed to pick up some sleeping pills so that the guys could slumber well and start fresh the next day. Bolin, as it turned out, eyed the bag, gulped them all down, and proceeded to hit the sack for a full forty-eight hours.

"I got along really well with Martin Birch," recalls Glenn, asked about both Martin and the Munich experience. "He was a one-on-one guy. Doing vocals or whatever, Martin was very, very proactive in my career. He really was a friend and a fan of mine. And I was of his, because he really was one of the greatest engineer/coproducers at that time. Wonderful, wonderful man, and never a bad word to say about anybody. He was a really good human being, great fun, and great to work with. And Munich, oh God, I mean, we went there twice, once with Ritchie and once with Tommy. And we created some great music in that studio. We wrote a lot of

Glenn and Tommy, Fairgrounds Arena, Oklahoma City, Oklahoma, February 17, 1976. © *Rich Galbraith*

The Toxic Twins, Fairgrounds Arena, Oklahoma City, Oklahoma, February 17, 1976. Supporting on the night (and much of the tour) was Nazareth. © *Rich Galbraith*

the songs on *Stormbringer* and *Come Taste the Band* in that studio. I really did love those sessions, where you could actually be in your hotel room upstairs and come down to the studio. Wonderful place, and one of the greatest cities in the world. We adopted that place. I mean, Germany was very popular for Deep Purple."

The record that resulted, despite heroic drug taking on the session, was essentially a battle royale between the three youngsters in the band against Paice and Lord, who were aboard as bemused onlookers. The band's Mk. II creative engines, Gillan, Glover, and Blackmore, all A-type personalities, were now gone, leaving the two nonwriters from the early days watching their band spin away from them.

Come Taste the Band would be recorded once again by Martin Birch, from August 3 through September 1, 1975, subsequently appearing in the shops on November 7, 1975. The engineering credit would also go to Martin, and the "final mix" to Birch and Ian Paice. Whoever was responsible, it's a solid production palette that was achieved.

Also, serendipitously, the rock was back, pleasing a large portion of the fans who were turned off by the timid arrangements across much of *Stormbringer*. But the funk also pulsed freely, given that Tommy was significantly aligned in his tastes with Coverdale and Hughes. *Come Taste the Band* sounds pretty much like a late 1970s or early 1980s Whitesnake record, touching down on, say, *Trouble*, *Lovehunter*, and *Ready an' Willing*. Logically, it's a bit more raw, but it's consistently rocking and full throated, although conspicuously leaving out the classical influence Ritchie took away with him to Rainbow. There's nothing grand or epic here. *Come Taste the Band* sits somewhere between stadium rock and high-volume funk. It's an urban rock version of Deep Purple.

The action develops with "Comin' Home," which is both energetic and anthemic, rousing us in preparation for the album experience, sort of like Aerosmith's "Sick as a Dog" or "Draw the Line," but, most adjacently, that band's "No Surprize," given the shared boogie rocking vibe.

"'Comin' Home' was a last-minute addition to the album," says Glenn. "It was thrown together at the last minute, not

An ad from the *New Musical Express* promoting the new album and tour, along with the *Come Taste the Band* album cover. *Martin Popoff archive*

one of my favorite songs." Indeed, Hughes had not even played on the track, replaced on bass by Bolin while Glenn was "busy," sent off for treatment after having "freaked out in Munich." In fact, Glenn claims to have not even been aware of the song having been recorded until he got a finished copy of the record. Bolin had also initially recorded the bass parts for "Gettin' Tighter" for the same reason, but for that one, Hughes was able to come in at a later date and perform his duties.

"I was asked to go home," reveals Glenn. "It was suggested that I go home, because the tail end of *Come Taste the Band*, I started to dabble in coke, and I started to miss a few things and I started to become, well, quite a lot unfocused. I was having trouble with my girlfriend at the time. It was my fault, not hers, really, but basically the cocaine devil started to hit me in '75, and that's when it sort of backfired on me. So, towards the tail end of *Come Taste the Band*, I went back to the UK, and I went into some sort of rehabilitation. It wasn't a rehabilitation place, but I went to do . . . let's just say I was detoxing at that time. I was sent home for my own health. At the time, in the press, we said that I had hepatitis, but it was all just a cover-over of the fact that I was sent to clean up."

While drinking was prevalent in the band, Tommy was on the heroin, and although Glenn was accused of being on it as well, he at least lays claim to his longer-range problems (this is more so in the 1980s) being "coke and booze. But really, seriously, seriously, for the longest time, I was asking God to remove these problems from my life. And in time, God removed them. But I didn't particularly want to work with my friends like Tony Iommi and Keith Emerson and all the people I know, Dave Navarro and John Frusciante, all the people I work with now, and Brian May and Roger Taylor. I didn't particularly want to be around my heroes and friends because I was really losing the battle with drugs. And when I got clean and sober, I was granted all these great wishes again to work with my friends who I love dearly. And today, years after Purple, I have a great bond with all these people I just mentioned."

Although Glenn never did wind up with a heart attack from all the coke he had been hoovering up into the 1980s, he indicates, "I did have a slight problem on the last day of my using, when I thought I was having some serious problems with my insides. And I just checked in before it was too late."

"Lady Luck"—written by Bolin and Jeff Cook, a bandmate from Tommy's Zephyr days, and in Bolin's live set for a number of years—and "Gettin' Tighter" showcased the band's new funk style, comparatively more combative and aggressive than the staid presentations we got on *Stormbringer*. "Gettin' Tighter" would be the album's first single in America and one of the band's least successful singles commercially, although the song is creatively quite inspired and has fared well in the estimation of the fan base over the decades. The UK got "You Keep On Moving," and both singles were backed with album track "Love Child." Both were issued six months after the album's release date, and neither single charted, although the album itself would rise to a #19 placement in the UK, and #43 in America. And although *Come Taste the Band* became a bit of an oddball in the Purple catalog, it still sold quite well. There's an award presented to Tommy Bolin by Purple management that is displayed in his hometown of Sioux City, Iowa, that cites two million in sales for the record worldwide.

Which, if accurate in the tallying, underscores the fact that Deep Purple was a global band, picking up sales all over the world, and proportionally more in some

Tommy and Strat, Long Beach Arena, Long Beach, California, February 27, 1976. © *Marvin Rinnig*

of these secondary markets such as mainland Europe and the Far East. Case in point, if one examines the official Recording Industry Association of America documentation (sticking to Mk. III and Mk. IV), one notices that *Come Taste the Band* didn't even break gold in the US, with *Burn* and *Stormbringer* duly reaching gold but not platinum. Two million copies of *Come Taste the Band* sold worldwide sounds like an exaggeration, but it's entirely possible given the band's uncommon reach.

Again, that's because Deep Purple were a European thing, says ardent fan and Metallica drummer Lars Ulrich, who also adds a respectful treatise on Ian Paice's place in the world.

"Man, anybody who knows me, I can talk about Deep Purple for longer than you can [laughs]. Purple was the first gig I ever went to, and probably, if you're going to break it down to one band, Deep Purple is the band for me. Where I grew up, Deep Purple were the true kings, the true heroes, as opposed to Led Zeppelin, who were more in America. And Ian Paice is obviously . . . when I was ten, twelve, thirteen, fourteen, the first drum kit I got was basically set up exactly like Ian Paice's configuration. Ian Paice has been one of my all-time heroes and inspirations in what I do.

"But I would say that what he did in Deep Purple and what I do in Metallica are two different things. There was a looseness in Deep Purple, almost a progressive, jazzy kind of feel. A lot of the drum fills come from more of a syncopated school, where I go a bit more for power and try to do stuff that works a bit more with the rhythm guitars. But with Deep Purple, there is so much space to do a lot of super, psycho jazz stuff or whatever.

"But as for somebody to watch, somebody to listen to, somebody who I could just be completely awestruck by, I think Ian Paice is probably the best hard rock drummer of the last thirty years. And also, I would say probably one of the most underappreciated hard rock drummers, maybe because the personality was not as big as Blackmore or Gillan or Jon Lord, but also compared to some of the other drummers that were the drummers in some of the peer groups at the time. I don't want to mention names because I don't want to be disrespectful, but Paice . . . I don't know, he just feels underappreciated. I mean, I've been flying the flag for them for the better part of thirty years now. But obviously, I don't think in America they quite left their mark. Talk to Europeans, and you can talk Deep Purple all day. Talk to a lot of Americans, and it's mostly about the two other bands."

Indeed. And as reinforcement that America didn't care, the album's #43 chart position in the States would be the lowest the band would notch since way back in 1970, with the advent of *In Rock*. One wonders if we had seen one too many lineup changes. Was the loss of Ritchie, the fiery heart of the band, insurmountable? And why replace him with an American? Deep Purple was supposedly an English band through and through. Head chasing tail, vicious circle, train out of control . . . all the clichés apply.

Back to the album at hand, Glenn recalls that "'Lady Luck' was a song that Tommy had brought in. I think he wrote that when he was in James Gang and then he brought it in, and Coverdale obviously took a shine to it and wrote some lyrics to the music. David brought a definite Coverdale approach to it, but it was an unlikely Deep Purple track.

Ian Paice, Fairgrounds Arena, Oklahoma City, Oklahoma, February 17, 1976. © *Rich Galbraith*

"'Gettin' Tighter' was a song that Tommy and I wrote in my home in L.A., and that added a little bit more funk to the album. And you know, look, that's what I added to Deep Purple. It's a heavy-rock band, and my influence is a bit more on the funk side, so I was excited to bring that element into that song. And I think the song, funny enough, when I go to play, people still ask to hear it, and I still play it to this day. It's a Glenn Hughes song."

Glenn addresses the album's highlights and lowlifes. "I'll tell you what, I think the opening track is boring. I like the instrumental 'Owed to 'G',' I like the ballad, I like 'You Keep On Moving.' 'Love Child' was cool, and of course I love 'Gettin' Tighter.' I just think the overall sound on that record is way, way different from anything Purple had done before, and I prefer *Stormbringer* as an album—love it, love it, love it. But I love the album *Come Taste the Band*; there are a couple of great moments on it." Of note, the "G" in "Owed to 'G'" is George Gershwin, inspiration for the track, or more so, the totality of the fused "This Time Around" / "Owed to 'G'" situation, and, in fact, maybe even more so, the sweeping drama of "This Time Around."

Elsewhere, "I Need Love" is a funky track—or perhaps a clunky track, with Paice slamming a tom-tom instead of snare for a swampy, gutbucket vibe, and with Tommy contributing slide (Hughes: "That's one of Tommy's—great riff, great song"). Side 2 opener "Drifter" predicts a Ted Nugent vibe circa 1976 and 1977, and also the swagger of future Coverdale vehicle Whitesnake, rent soulful with a bit of Bad Company.

"This Time Around" finds Jon Lord playing all the instruments while Hughes sings. There are organ washes, electric piano, and synthesizer bass parts, making for an impressive full band texture on this spooky track of sophisticated, melancholy melodies. Says Glenn, "We sat alone in the studio one night, in Munich, and we just came up with that song. I was really intrigued by the minor nine chords, and I asked him to write a song around minor nines and major sevens, which are my two favorite chords. And it worked great."

"You Keep On Moving" is a strong closer, proposing a funk, blues and heavy-rock synthesis that works well and serves as a metaphor for the album as a whole. Ian provides some busy drumming, and Tommy creates choppy dialogue with himself. "'You Keep On Moving' was a song I wrote with David for the *Burn* record," notes Hughes. "We never ended up using it. So that was a song written in '73 that finally got used in '75. It just wasn't right for the *Burn* record. David and I wrote that up in his flat in Redcar in Yorkshire."

And "Dealer"? "Good song," says Glenn. "It's a song I initially sang on, and then my vocals were taken off about a week later; I don't know why. But I sang on it, on an original version with different lyrics, different melody. But I went back to the UK for a week, and when I came back, David had sang over it [laughs]. I was kind of disappointed by it, because my version was definitely more soulful.

"That wasn't about dealers at all," continues Glenn, "but yes, when you're famous, a lot of people want to get to you, especially drug dealers. It happens with every major band. People just try to give you things, and that song is written about that story. And years and years later, obviously when I got clean and sober, I look back at that, and I thank David for writing that. Regardless of what people think, David

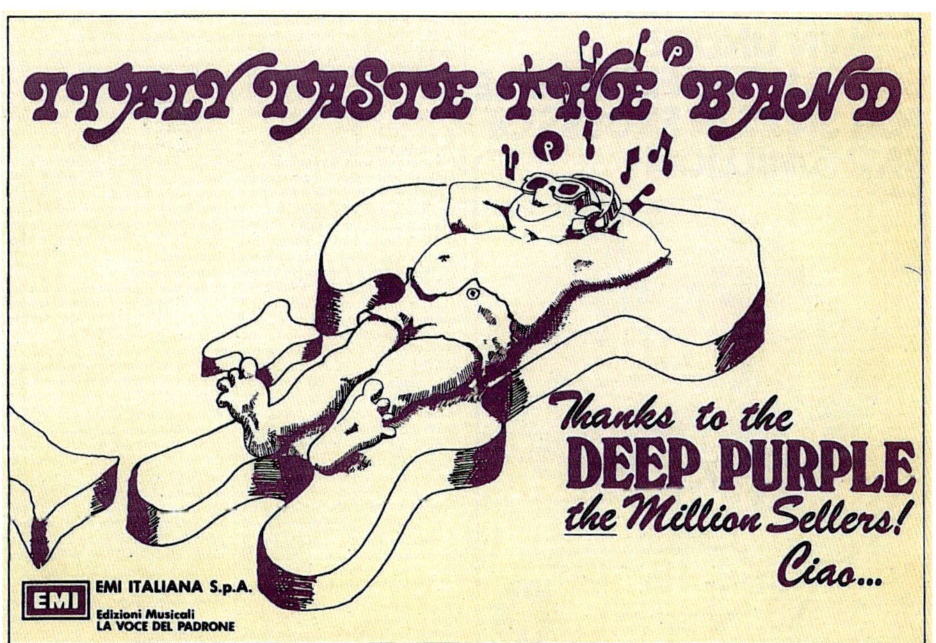

Italian ad for the album. *Pericle Formenti archive*

and I have a long, long friendship, and we only want the best for each other. Early in the game, in '75, he was only thinking of the best for me."

"And a year later, we lost Tommy because of drugs. Tommy Bolin . . . he lived with me for three months, before he joined the band. Tommy Bolin was a very sweet, kind, philosophical, hippieish, generous, loving person. There wasn't a bad bone in his body. The only thing was, Tommy was riddled with drug addiction. I had no idea he was into the morphines and the other stuff at all. We talked about it, and he joked about it, but I hadn't realized my friend was actually getting to be hooked on the stuff. But Tommy and I also have stuff we wrote together. He was a great guy. If he would have been alive today, we probably still would be working together in some aspect. I mean, we definitely would've done something after Deep Purple. But, I mean, I was sort of into my disease as well. The cocaine was definitely drug of choice in the '70s, for people who could afford it. So, I was in my own head at that time."

Ian Paice, when asked about fond memories of drum performances over the course of the whole catalog, surprisingly mentions this song, "Dealer," as a peerless piece of personal achievement.

"Sometimes they're not the most obvious tracks," begins Paice, the beating heart of the band and, pertinent to this record, a crucial tie-in to Purple perpetuity. "Sometimes they're not the tracks that people think you go for. I've always said, if I do a track with a lot of fast drumming on it, it may be very impressive, but the great thing about fast playing is that if I make a mistake, you'll probably never hear it. It's gone past your ears so fast, I'm the only one who will actually know what happened there. But if I make a mistake playing something fairly slow, everybody knows it's happened.

"So, for me, sometimes the really great tracks are where I've actually had time to let the fills breathe, the notes come through, with each note being clear and exactly

Rich's most iconic shot of Tommy, Fairgrounds Arena, Oklahoma City, Oklahoma, February 17, 1976. © *Rich Galbraith*

where it needs to be rhythmically, in the formation of the piece of music it's in. And sometimes it's not the whole track; sometimes it's just a couple of drum fills. For example, on one of the albums we did after Ritchie had left, and Ian and Roger had left, we did with Tommy Bolin and Glenn Hughes and David Coverdale, was a track called 'Dealer.' And the drumming on that, you know, I will play that to anybody and say, 'That's pretty good.' And again, the very, very fast track 'Burn,' you know, that's a pretty good drum track, but then I can take a really slow thing like 'Living Wreck,' off *In Rock*, and it's not that the drumming is difficult; I just love the feel, and I love the sound of it. It's just something that is different and special to me.

"So, I can go on taking bits and pieces all the way through, and that's lucky. You know, 'Fireball,' for the uninitiated, it's very impressive, but it's not a difficult piece to play. What was great about it was that it set the song up so perfectly, and that's more important than being a clever drum part. It was exactly the right piece of music for what was going to follow it; so that's nice, you know?

"Because just being a drummer isn't enough," continues Paice. "You've got to be a musician. You've got to understand what it is you're trying to help. You're trying to help this piece of music be something else, take it somewhere special. And sometimes just playing along to it doesn't do it. You've got to find that little thing that changes it. And you don't do it every time. It doesn't have to be for every track, but every now and again you find this little rhythmic hook inside yourself, and that's what makes it a different drum track and one of those tracks you look back on and go, 'Yeah, that one was okay.'"

I asked Ian if "Might Just Take Your Life" fits his parameters of a slow track with a clever thing going on.

"Yeah, that's the idea. It's just got a nice feel. And when you're playing medium or medium-slow things, it comes down to the feel. It's not like playing something slow, medium slow in a jazz situation. Rock 'n' roll is a little more basic than that, when you're playing slow. It's got to just feel right. But it's got to feel right in a way that has power, and it has to have a swing inside it. And you're having to create this without using too many notes. So it's a different discipline, to try to find it.

"It wasn't so much David, but the influence of Glenn," muses Paicey, looking back on the band that created *Come Taste the Band* and, in part, the two before it. "David was the new kid on the block, and he was very malleable. He was just enjoying the vibe of being in a big rock 'n' roll band. Glenn's influences were so different, although on the first album, *Burn*, they were kept under control. When it came down to the second one, *Stormbringer*, I mean, Glenn can't help it. He likes the music that he likes, and that was starting to change it. So, it was starting to change from being a hard rock 'n' roll band to something a little more funky, which Ritchie hated. And Ritchie, being true to himself, just went, 'That's it; I'm off; I don't like what's happening; I don't think I can get it back to what I want it to be.' And I think he saw the way that, if I had my own band, I can control the way I want it to be. And I think that's why Rainbow was formed.

"Look, I know the impression people get if you say you're a metal band," continues Paice, "and that's fine if you are a metal band. But if you're not, it's something you really don't want to be tagged with. It's like if someone said, 'Yeah, Purple, they're a really good jazz combo.' You've got to be just as annoyed at that. Labeling things. . . . I know everybody has to have a label so they can rationalize it, but we always

The Lovehunter, Fairgrounds Arena, Oklahoma City, Oklahoma, February 17, 1976. © *Rich Galbraith*

said it was just a hard rock 'n' roll band, and sometimes it didn't even need to be so hard. But that was the idea behind it."

Back to the record: for its day, *Come Taste the Band* was indeed a fairly heavy album. And given the lack of competition at the time, you may as well call it a heavy metal album, again, by the standards of 1975. But despite a return to the temperature of *Burn*, Deep Purple's fortunes were nonetheless on the wane. Indeed, Tommy Bolin's solo album, *Teaser*, received as much attention, if not more, as did Blackmore's new band with a demon named Dio. But there was some pounding rock on the album that deserved to be heard, particularly "Love Child," featuring one of the band's biggest dinosaur stomp monster riffs of all time. All told, taken as a whole, the album was communicative, connective, and celebratory, unlike its two arty but melancholic predecessors.

Circus magazine's Jim Brodey considered the merits of *Come Taste the Band* in a paired record review with *Teaser*, saying, "*Come Taste the Band*, the first Deep Purple disc featuring the complete, whirling, furious, hurricane-pitch tempos of Tommy Bolin's plunging guitars, is a fine record, easily worthy of the band's past recordings—and a pretty solid reply to anyone who still thinks that Purple without Blackmore ain't Deep. Not only is it Deep, it's also dense. There are so many guitar tracks that it sounds as if Bolin is doing everything. The guitarist makes mincemeat out of his solos, continually bombing in from behind Coverdale (who reacts to the new push by really getting it not only on, but under, and pretty high indeed).

"The group backs Bolin very well," continues Brodey. "His favorite guitar effect is a low, growling whine that sails on top of the backup vocals. He then opens this up into a frightening rage that encompasses everything in its majestic stride. But while Bolin's force breaks down the walls of your mind, there's a mellowness here, too—something for which Ritchie Blackmore had no use. The album's major surprise is the lone instrumental, Bolin's own 'Owed to "G,"' a jazz rock cut complete with some contemplative John McLaughlin–esque riffs that must have sounded very far out while being recorded, booming out of a West German Studio.

"If the Blackmore daze are gone, it's just something we're going to have to forget—or at least remember only when listening to the old LPs. Bolin is clearly in control now, having written or collaborated on all nine tracks of *Come Taste the Band*, thereby taking over another position Blackmore held so dear, that of chief composer. Even though the whole band makes the music, the spotlight will be on the guitar player. And most of the pressure. But if this album is any indication, we're going to be getting a lot tougher records from the new Deep Purple."

With respect to *Teaser*, Brodey remarked that "it is the debut of a new crown prince of flaming, space-age, blues guitar, orbiting somewhere in the common universe of such well-established heavies as Rick Derringer, Joe Walsh, and Peter Frampton on the rock side, and such giants of the guitar as John McLaughlin and Jimi Hendrix, with whom he shares several tendencies. If *Come Taste the Band* follows the usual super-tight pop format of Deep Purple's previous English (loud) blooze material, *Teaser* aims for far-wider realms, demonstrating that Tommy B. can not only rock hard and heavy, he can also fly. Released from the constraints of Purple's formula, Bolin literally lifts off from Mother Earth with an excellently recorded item sure to plug up any remaining holes you might have about him deserving Ritchie Blackmore's position in that band. On the strength of his own LP, we'd have to say he probably won't be with any group that does not bear his name for very long.

"If Bolin picks at already well-established riffs and pieces of other people's music," contends Brodey, "he uses them in ways which are new. Clearly, his utilization of harmonics puts him high above the Joe Walsh, static-as-melody school of playing, but as yet he hasn't developed a strong, personal style. The crowning glory of the Cobham set, the thing we remember most—his incredible speed—is underplayed here. When Tommy Bolin begins to come out of his shell, growing as his progress thus far indicates he surely can, we'll really have something to scream about. You can bet on it."

With Tommy touting *Teaser*, Jon Lord had also whipped up a new solo spread, having missed nary a beat, traveling north from Munich, with Martin Birch in tow, to Oererckenschwick to record *Sarabande*, his best-received (least daunting?) solo work. The album was recorded with the Philharmonica Hungarica Orchestra, but also with future Ian Gillan Band drummer Mark Nauseef and Andy Summers, soon to simplify with the Police.

Turmoil in the Purple ranks had begun to fester, particularly between Coverdale and Hughes, first centering on writing credits and, later, the lead vocal slot within the band. "I got along with David fine. I don't know if he got along with me very well," offers Glenn innocently. "As far as the friendship was concerned, it was deep. As far as the musicianship was concerned, I think it might have been fragile, to say the least. Because when I joined Deep Purple, I did tell them that I would not be joining as just a bass player who sings the oohs and the aahs. So, they knew that going in. And like I said, 'Dealer,' I actually sang. And I went to bed one night and the next morning I came back, and David sang it. And I went, 'What the fuck?!' I guess I was voted off the track, and I sang it like a motherfucker! It was brilliant. On *Come Taste the Band*, I sung two songs, 'Gettin' Tighter' and 'This Time Around,' I think, and the rest was like double vocals. If you know anything about Purple toward the end, I think we did an hour-and-forty-five-minute show, and David was offstage for about forty-five minutes because the band was jamming, and I was doing a lot of singing. And I think he was a bit pissed off about that."

So, there was an overt power struggle for lead vocal slot. "Well, you know, really, I wasn't pushing that!" says Glenn. "I'm just a progressive person onstage, and I liked to jam. Tommy and I were doing that, and also Jon Lord, and Ian Paice is a ferocious drummer. And I just think the David Coverdale thing, although he was the singer, he could have stayed onstage and banged a tambourine or something. But he was offstage."

Politics was also getting out of control. "You have to understand that Tommy was living at my house, so a lot of those songs were written at my house. And that's why I was getting pissed off. And I'm not pissed off at Tommy. I'm not going to mention the guys' names in Deep Purple. There was some very, very heavy jostling for 'I wrote that word! I wrote that syllable!' It was very, very cutthroat. And maybe I should have been more that way. I was very uncutthroat.

"I mean, I was going to leave the band when Ritchie left, and it was a very bizarre situation. Ritchie and I got along reasonably well, but he didn't like my Black R&B influences, although we spent a lot of time together. But credits-wise, I'm going to tell you the truth. I was fucking ripped off on that record. [Note: even worse, according to Glenn, was the *Burn* situation, which he couldn't go into for legal reasons.] Because when the credits were going down, I was actually on vacation for three weeks in Bermuda. When I got back and saw the credits, I was going, 'Wait a minute, I wrote

Tommy Bolin, Long Beach Arena, Long Beach, California, February 27, 1976. © *Marvin Rinnig*

. . . wait a minute?!' But I have no sour grapes. Those sour grapes will kill me. I don't have any resentments in my life. I just probably wasn't inclined to fight back then. Deep Purple is a big part of my roots and always will be."

Come Taste the Band would be the last studio effort from Deep Purple for another eight years. Despite its status as the album with the most compromised lineup, or certainly one of the top three, it's viewed as a noble and, on balance, successful effort. Fans appreciated that the band valiantly tried to strap all manner of power chord and guitar lick onto songs that, structurally, strongly reflected the funk, jazz, and blues preferences of the youth contingent in the band. And this was all achieved while the experiment in having two strong lead vocalists in the band was going pear shaped, predictably.

Oh yeah, and the name of the album? Do tell, Glenn. "You know what it was? Tommy was drunk one night, and there's a song that goes 'Come hear the band, come taste the wine.' It's an old '40s song, and he said it backwards and then went, 'Oh, wait! That's a great title.' I don't know who recorded it, but go check it out."

The song was in fact from the musical *Cabaret*, and then it was tasked to the Castle, Chappell & Partners company, who had previously done *Fireball*, to portray the idea photographically.

Those who would find it necessary to check out Deep Purple in a concert situation were offered various degrees of quality on any given night. A fan revolt quickly grew as word spread about Tommy Bolin's chemicals and chemistry within the band. Embraced he was not, and that only exacerbated the problem.

Even Coverdale was prone to expressing concern, telling *Melody Maker* midtour, between gigs in London and Leicester, "I still think we're asking too much of our audience. We start giving no-nonsense rock with no subtleties. Then we go on to the solo spots, where everybody does their own things. It's really unnecessary to overindulge to the point we do. I think we should just go on and play to the people. I'd rather be regarded as an entertainer than a prima donna. The messing about can be done in the studio.

"I don't see Purple as a group, you see," continues Coverdale. "It's a concept. The musical interests in the band are so diverse and so stretched out that the idea of rock can sometimes get lost. Sometimes people put in their alternative interest, and that can take away the essence. It's frustrating as fuck, to be honest. Being a part of a concept can be very limiting. If you're not an instrumentalist. I'd rather run around the stage than be sitting in the dressing room having a smoke when somebody's doing the solo bit. You've also got to remember that Purple is five instrumentalists, five egomaniacs fighting for the limelight.

"If Tommy wants to blow it, he can blow it," remarks Coverdale, ominously, on the subject of fan heckling. "He got a bit uptight at Leicester. He was doing a solo piece, and it could only take one guy or chick to shout 'Blackmore' to throw it. For two years I was answering questions about Ian Gillan. It's something you have to live with and get over. The thing about Tommy is that he's been replacing people all the time. He replaced Joe Walsh in the James Gang and then Ritchie in Purple. I suppose he's got a bit of a chip on his shoulder. It's all a matter, really, of maturity and believing in yourself. Tommy is a gypsy nomad in guitar land. He can either show breathtaking genius or be very boring and mundane. Usually, he's breathtaking."

Jon Lord, Fairgrounds Arena, Oklahoma City, Oklahoma, February 17, 1976. © *Rich Galbraith*

"We did this disastrous Far Eastern tour," recalled Jon Lord in 1999. "I discovered that Tommy had a rather serious drug problem, and, probably as a result of that, something had happened to him. I'll never know what it was, but it caused him great difficulty in playing. Then one of our trusted helpers, Patsy, was murdered in Jakarta, Indonesia. It appeared that he had fallen down an elevator shaft, but we knew that he was murdered. We did two nights in Jakarta, where, so we were informed, we would be playing to about 20,000 to 25,000 people a night. But the first night we played to about 90,000 people; the next night we played to over 100,000. It was after that first night that Patsy was murdered. The promoter never paid us. He took all the money and had us deported. He had our tour manager, one of the roadies, and our bassist, Glenn Hughes, locked up on suspicion of murder.

"Tommy seemed to be able to cope with all the problems he had when he was on home ground," continued Lord. "On occasions, he played absolutely sublimely. But then we went to Europe, and he didn't do so well. By the time we reached the UK, he completely lost it. It was not entirely his fault. There was some opposition from the British fans to seeing their favorite British group with an American guitarist. He won them over on a couple of nights, but usually he ended up shouting at the fans. On the last concert of that particular run, in Liverpool, Ian Paice and I met backstage and decided to quit the band. About ten minutes later, David Coverdale came into my dressing room and told me that he was leaving. I informed him that there was no band to leave. It was a rather ignominious end to what had been a wonderful few years."

Gig notice for an important New York City show

Backing up a bit, Bolin's action-packed but brief time playing live for Purple had begun in, of all places, Honolulu, Hawaii, back on November 2, 1975, after which Tommy rested off the effects of a smallpox shot at the hotel pool for a week, "watching everybody swim." From there it was off to New Zealand for two gigs on November 13 and November 17 and then to Australia—Bolin and Lord were seen out jamming at the local clubs nearly every night—and on to the fateful stop in Jakarta of which Jon speaks, and then more traumatic times in Japan.

The Australian leg found the band doing what rock 'n' rollers do best. Tommy regaled *Circus* magazine with a tale of fun times at a club called the Stormy Summer. "This chick comes over and starts wiggling in front of me, and everybody's yelling, 'Tear 'em off with your teeth!' But she was so high up I couldn't reach her. She didn't bend down, so finally I took my hands and ripped 'em off." Back to the hotel, and

. . . "there were like 25 people at the party. Between the 25 of us, we got together only $16 for this chick to do a show. She was thrilled. Sixteen bucks for her was like a zillion dollars. She did her strip show, and then Glenn did one. We didn't have to pay him."

Having woken up with two strippers the next morning, Tommy says, "I had to do an interview, and we're all in bed naked, and this guy calls and says, 'You've got an interview in two minutes.' There was really nothing I could do, so I said, 'Okay, send him up.' He came up and he was wearing these annoying Bermuda shorts and high socks and half-beaten Beatle boots and a madras shirt that wasn't quite bleeding. So, he comes in, and I said, 'Sit down,' and he sat down but he would not look at me. He just kept glancing over, like every ten seconds."

In Jakarta, the story at the time, as told to *Circus*, seemed to be that Patsy Collins, a "hired bodyguard" (actually appointed by management to be Tommy's personal bodyguard), had been drinking and had gotten himself locked in the hotel stairwell after arguing with a couple of roadies. Yanking on doors, he had somehow opened one to a dark and empty elevator shaft and plunged to his death six floors through a maze of scalding hot-water piping.

In a further nuanced difference to Jon's story above, the two roadies, as well as erstwhile manager Rob Cooksey (but not Glenn Hughes), were arrested and thrown in jail on suspicion of murder. A $500 "fee for photocopying of their passports" got them out the next day, after which Jon began speculating over Collins's murder at the hands of locals.

For his part, Glenn said that after the first show, a few prostitutes had been sent up to his room, and the roadies were fighting over these girls, One of the road crew, known as "Paddy the Plank," had hit Collins, who had stormed out of the room and was later found dead, in Glenn's estimation, having fallen down the shaft.

Pan forward to 2008, and Glenn plainly supports Lord's assertion of murder.

"I was the only guy in the band who was thrown in jail," explains Hughes. "The other two guys were Neil Slaven, my assistant, and Paddy Callahan—he was one of the bodyguards. We were thrown in jail because Patsy Collins, our lead security guy, was found dead. You know the story, right? So, I was the first person to get thrown in the jail; it was me, and then the other two guys followed. It was a horrific, a threatening scene. And I'll tell you, because, when you're in a Third World country . . . we were the first band ever to play down there. You know, needless to say, you've got to ask questions why we even went there. Some shenanigans happened where we were thrown in jail, and the key was basically thrown away. And then we were let out. Eventually we were let out because either the promoters or the government had gotten the money back from us. It was really a tale of evil, and we were the ones who had to suffer, and of course Patsy Collins, who was really a great security man, a professional, hired security guy, was murdered."

And Glenn's theory as to what happened to him? "Well, I was the last one to see him. There were some chicks, ladies of the evening, in my room. The promoters had sent some girls up, and there was a party going on, you know, some boys having a good time. There was a little . . . it wasn't really a skirmish; it was just some kind of backtalk or something, but nothing outrageous. So, I mean, he was in my room, and he left to go to his room. He was on his way to his room, and then four or five hours later, you know, the police break down my door. What I believe happened is

Up close and personal with Tommy, Long Beach Arena, Long Beach, California, February 27, 1976. © *Marvin Rinnig*

that he was captured, leaving my room. And that could have been me or anyone else in my party. We were surrounded by really great security, but down there, it was dark, and it was strange. And you know, you don't . . . Patsy was a big guy, and he was a real professional. It must've taken four or five people to take him down. You don't just fall down an elevator shaft, when you are a professional bodyguard—you just don't do that."

With the band's manager in jail, back at the venue a full-scale riot had broken out when police had to battle 20,000 fans who were attempting to storm the Soviet-built 100,000-seat venue. Rubber bullets, rifle butts, and Dobermans were used in the brutal crackdown.

What happened in Japan, according to Glenn, is that Tommy, after being relatively clean for the trip so far, had a reaction to heroin and lost the feeling in his left hand, which is why on the later-issued *This Time Around* live recordings, Jon Lord does much of the soloing. This was Tommy's first trip to the all-important Purple stronghold of Japan, and at one point the shows were almost called off. The ensuing ragged sets would add fuel to the argument that the band was spent. The theory about a bad heroin reaction also goes back to Jakarta, with some theorizing that with management or Collins not around to protect him, it was there that Tommy got some bad dope. Tommy, for his part, said that he had pinched a nerve making a fast exit after the chaotic first night in Jakarta. He had grabbed a huge armful of guitars, and he and the rest of the band had been crammed into a security van, which then beat it out of there. It is conceivable that an injury could happen under those circumstances.

Up into 2008, Glenn sticks to his story. "What I think happened was . . . Tommy was very close to me, as you know. Tommy had gotten into Jakarta, and he might have spoken to the promoter about getting some kind of opiate drugs. Tommy was more into the opiate drug thing. And what he'd done, he'd gotten some morphine or heroin derivative or something like that, and what it had done, Tommy had fallen asleep, and he had fallen asleep on his arm. And you can imagine, when you fall asleep on your arm, it becomes really numb. Well, imagine doing that for about eight hours. And that's why he couldn't move his arm. That's what he told me, and I've got to believe that's what happened."

Bolin figured an acupuncturist might help the situation in time for the shows. "The dude had like this cardboard piece of electronic stuff that went 'bzzzzz' all over my arm." As he went for a spot to stick his first pin, Tommy says, "I think he missed. In fact, I know he missed. It was stuck in the old main vein. I said, 'Forget it; I can do it myself.' Then he stuck me with a piece of electricity with clamps on it and said, 'Okay, I'll be back in five minutes.' The needle was just spinning around and spinning around. It looked really strange with just a needle sticking outta your arm, and nobody else around. It was really stupid looking at it."

Things went okay for the start of the first night's set, but then his arm gave up the ghost in "Owed to 'G'." To prepare for Osaka, he kept his arm wrapped in an electric blanket. Another doctor was then tried, who massaged Tommy's hand into the best shape it had been in since the accident. This was fortunate, because Tokyo was to be filmed and recorded for European TV as well as a possible live album, with Martin Birch in attendance to twiddle the knobs.

The final Tokyo date was issued in abbreviated, badly edited form as *Last Concert in Japan* in March 1977, with an eventual CD issue including the entire show, with the eccentric bits flowing better in context with the more complete showing. Highlights of the CD issue, titled *This Time Around: Live in Tokyo*, include "Wild Dogs," a solo track from Tommy's *Teaser* album, as well as all manner of *Come Taste the Band* tracks we rarely get to hear, including "Drifter," "Love Child," "Gettin' Tighter," "Owed to 'G'," "I Need Love," "You Keep On Moving," and "Lady Luck"—fully seven of the record's ten tracks. There's also a fool-around instrumental jam version of "Woman from Tokyo," a profusion of Jon Lord soloing, and a weird "Georgia on My Mind." "Smoke on the Water" finds David fooling with the vocal melodies to the point of distraction.

With respect to covering the Ray Charles classic, Glenn explains that "Purple were renowned for jamming, and sometimes we would play this and that, and one night Jon Lord just started to play the chorus to 'Georgia on My Mind' when I was doing my bass solo. So, you know, there I am, David wasn't onstage, and I just started to sing it. Funny enough, it was in Georgia itself, Atlanta, Georgia, where Trapeze were very, very popular. So, he started to play, then I started to sing it, and man, people still to this day want to hear me sing that. It was a pretty groovy version.

The Japanese-issue *Last Concert in Japan*

There were some interesting things going on, and yeah, we wanted to do 'Wild Dogs' of course. But I think even prior to Tommy coming in, I think I sang 'Georgia.'"

The album originally was scuttled with respect to European and North American release due to sentiments that it was hacked together illogically and jarringly, that the mix was bad, and that the creatively best bits from the show were not included. Mexico picked up the album for release, however, and an early Japanese CD issue kept the original bad premise intact. The ultimate CD issue is remastered from the original tapes, although the "Lazy" recordings could not be found, resulting in that song being inserted in sequence from the original finished recording. The film footage of the event has never been found.

"All I know is that the CD is the long version of the vinyl that came out years ago," remarks a dismissive Hughes. "I think it's called *This Time Around.* I just want to say to anyone who is out there that I don't know anything about this. It was not a great concert for Deep Purple. I remember Tommy's hand was severely damaged. We were all impaired alcohol-wise. We are drunk, and we were all throwing up. You want an honest interview, I'll tell you—we were all drunk, and I don't pride myself on that. But I can't stop these things from coming out."

Remarked Lord just after the chaotic tour, "I think we can afford to relax a little bit. We know that it works. We should be able to get into some really nice things and experiment a bit with what we are. With Tommy, people didn't know what to expect, so we were able to be free again. What's come out of it, to me, is a good extension of what we were. It proves that the band will always be this kind of band, but we're trying to extend the variety of the things the band is capable of doing. And with Tommy, the contribution is also a personal thing as well. He's a much more happy, outgoing person than Ritchie was. It's made the band a different place to be."

The enthusiasm would be short lived, with the US tour going fine. But the bad reception afforded Bolin in England, and the confrontations that resulted, impeded any further momentum. The drugs were still there, and now Tommy had a mildly successful solo album to think about supporting. It was management who declared the band dead, in July 1976. It was all too much: Bolin had blown Wembley, Hughes and Coverdale were bad on other nights, and the European Blackmore cult was relentless.

"The audience hated Tommy!" sighs guitarist Pat Travers, who was part of the London scene in those days. "They wanted Ritchie. There was only one guitar player in Deep Purple, and that's Ritchie Blackmore. Nobody could take Ritchie's place in Deep Purple, and here comes Tommy, this funky American guy, and it was tough for Tommy. And I think he had injured his hand as well at the time, so his ability to play was impaired. Later that year he died, and Glenn . . . I was in the studio recording the *Makin' Magic* album, and I was doing the song 'Stevie,' and I asked Glenn if he would come in and sing backing vocals on it. Then Tommy died, and the night before they flew out of London to go to Tommy's funeral, that's when he did the backing vocals for 'Stevie,' so it's very emotional. Yeah, I didn't include all of the wailing and moaning, but he was definitely doing some strange vocal expressions. There was a lot of anguish in it."

"Only in the UK; nowhere else in the world," says Glenn, palpably bitter about his home country's reaction toward Bolin. "When you are replacing someone like Ritchie Blackmore, and you're actually firing on all cylinders as a band and you've got to replace him, and you get a guy who is not really from the rock world but is from a different kind of energy . . . you know, Blackmore and Page and Beck and Clapton were the gods of that period, and if you replace one of those guys, you're going to get some disparity, so it was slightly difficult for Tommy. He handled it pretty well, except in England, which was really tough. Wembley was bad. It wasn't great. I mean, at that point, the band were . . . it was going down pretty quick."

Asked what he figured the state of Deep Purple was at the time he first started hanging around with Glenn in London, Travers agrees with Glenn that "it was the twilight of that band. I think the show I saw was the second-to-last one, and the next night, I forget where they played, but that was it. They were done. Tommy Bolin and Glenn had alienated themselves pretty much from the band at that point. And nobody was really happy. Like I say, I was in the UK at the time, and they did not like Tommy Bolin. You know—at all [laughs]. So, it was really tough for Tommy."

"But David never really suffered from that," adds Glenn, with respect to confidence issues or negative reaction such as heckling. "David, when he first came into the band, was a little green, but he developed, as we saw, right in front of us, developing his own style. Which took him to Whitesnake. He became pretty strong at the end of the *Burn* tour and into *Stormbringer*. We weren't the new boys anymore. He's a strong character."

Cleaning up helped Coverdale get over. The new clothes, the contact lenses, getting fit.

"Well, I think he wanted to do that for himself," says Glenn. "I mean, David, from the get-go, was very professional. Obviously, he hadn't worked in this genre before, ever. So, you just need the blueprint of how to do it. I'd been on the road for three or four years with Trapeze, and in Purple, David and I had been—and were—the very best of friends. You know, people ask me, were there problems and this and that? I think if you interviewed David, he would say there's never really been any problems with him and I. My singing, to him, didn't deter him from his goal, and his singing didn't deter me from mine. We were a great team. We were the greatest vocal duo in rock. And I think we still are—when you look back—the only two singers that were sort of really dominant in that role."

Coverdale has great respect for Deep Purple's legacy, but he says, "Sadly the management doesn't. They're just scraping the barrel, putting anything and everything out. I have no dealings with them at all. For such a powerful musical band, I have absolutely no say in what is done with the material, none. Even though I see money, I consider it an insult. And usually when I go out and promote a new record, usually they will turn around and tie in something from the past, which is confusing to people, thinking there is a new record or whatever. They'll take advantage of the fact that I am out there promoting stuff.

"I kept getting asked about a record called *Days May Come*, which is basically the audition and rehearsals tapes when Tommy Bolin joined the band. Yeah, go figure. Literally, I'm in a room now with drawers full of past materials and ideas for songs, and I thought I was the only one because I was the principal writer. We would cassette everything in rehearsal, and I'd take it home and try to make songs out of them. So, I thought I was the only one who had these tapes, cassette tapes, to the point where . . . I don't know if you remember, Geffen Records, about ten years ago did a box set of Tommy Bolin, and they heard I had this stuff and they were offering significant money, and I said, 'No, these are fucking cassettes!' It doesn't make any sense. So, to this day I haven't heard this record, but people are buying, like, 'The Orange Juice Song.' If I'm just jamming on stuff, I'm making up the words as we go along. Go figure."

The album David is referring to is *Days May Come and Days May Go: The California Rehearsals, June 1975*, first issued in 2000 as a single CD and then expanded to a double in 2008. It's pretty much as David describes it, fairly casual but surprisingly well produced. And there's lots of superlative playing on it too, with the album becoming a significant part of Tommy Bolin's limited canon. It's understandable that David is dismissive of it—it's a little hard to jam as a vocalist, especially if you haven't written the lyrics yet.

As discussed, Tommy was getting significant push as a solo artist, to the point of distraction. "I just wanted to blow my cookies all over the record," said Tommy of *Teaser*, making the press rounds. "I'll go as far as to kill myself to have this album go gold. Some of the tunes are four and five years old; I knew they were good then, and now they're getting airplay. I'm not saying they were ahead of their time, but I am saying they must really be good tunes. They wouldn't play them five years ago, though—let's put it that way. I put every amount of effort that I could into it. Maybe more."

Official news of Deep Purple's split filtered over to America three months after that July 1976 date that is cited. It became common knowledge in mid-October, when *Circus* published these whitewashed words from manager Rob Cooksey on the matter. "Having had so many personnel changes over the past eight years, we felt rather than rearrange yet again, it would be better to stop while the going was good. It would be a lie to say there were not some personality differences. Everyone wanted to pursue his own career, and David and Glenn Hughes have been driving me mad wanting to make their own albums. Jon Lord and Tommy Bolin had already done so, and there was a feeling that their best stuff was being siphoned off for their projects at the expense of Deep Purple. The reason for the split is simple. Their talents have outgrown Purple. Their music has matured from the heavy rock that has made them famous."

And Tommy's take on the subject? "It was mainly a management thing, where a couple of people in the group were saying it was the fault of a couple of other people in the group. It's a lot of bullshit. I guess what happened is that now Jon Lord and Ian Paice just did an album, and David Coverdale is doing an album. It's weird. Now, I'm not too close to any of them, except for Glenn Hughes. The only hassle I'm having right now is trying to find a fuckin' house. I'm staying with Linda Blair. She's doing *Exorcist II* in Connecticut, and she's letting me use her house. Everyone from New York's moving out here, which is probably why it's so hard to find a place. People from New York used to go to Miami—the older ones—and now the younger ones are coming here. I guess that's the difference between the generations."

"The first gigs were the best," noted Tommy to Jim Green of *Rock*, in what would be one of Bolin's last interviews ever. "They got progressively worse. It was not much fun anymore, and when you're not having fun, it's not worth doing. They didn't need to do it; they didn't need the money, and talentwise they could do anything. A lot of things just got distorted, like stories about each other. After the tour, they never called and we never talked. I don't know, but I believe a band should be a band. I think Purple became frustrated and wanted to do more 'Smoke on the Water'–type, straight-ahead, kill-their-ears, beat-'em-to-death music."

With respect to his then-promising solo career, Tommy explained that "*Teaser* also got much more airplay than *Come Taste the Band*, and I had to do interviews both for that and for Deep Purple too, because the others were kind of anti-interview-ish. I gotta spring my cookies somewhere. I replaced Walsh, I replaced Blackmore, [and] now I just gotta be me. How do you stop someone from growing?"

"The band broke up through sex, drugs, and rock 'n' roll," adds Hughes. "It just spontaneously combusts when you start believing that you are God and everything else. Coverdale really couldn't take it. Towards the end, I was onstage more than he was. He was offstage because I was doing my funky R&B stuff. There was a lot of jamming. Coverdale really wasn't happy. I think that Tommy and I were running amok. It was becoming more of a jam band than a heavy-rock band. The players were growing apart. Tommy and I were rapidly turning into something that was not Deep Purple. It was Ian Paice and Jon Lord in the end. Coverdale was doing his thing, and Tommy and I were doing our thing.

"There were a lot of things going on in the band that are very personal to me. Not just to my health but to my principles. There was some shit going on with women that was really inappropriate. Let's just say there was some swapping going around. I have never really talked about this. It was just really inappropriate, and I was the one who got hurt. It was disgusting. It was really a blow to my ego. Let's just say that I could never rejoin a band where my ex-girlfriend was married to the keyboard player! It was brutal and very inappropriate. I do forgive them. A lot of people were hurt. I've gone on with my life since then. I've seen the guys, and we've made amends. It was a long, long time ago. I'm very happy with the music that I brought to the group. I thought my performances were great. Cal Jam is there for everyone to see! It was a good moment in my history.

"Here's the deal: there are two sides to the coin," opines Hughes, asked if his reputation with Purple can be a bit of an albatross. "Deep Purple, over twenty-seven years, has monetarily paid for my life. The machine is still going on. I have wanted to break away and do pop and R&B for years, and it has been difficult to do because I have the moniker of ex–Deep Purple bass player / singer. Sting broke away from the Police and had a successful solo career because he took some of that with him. I can't take part of Deep Purple into that area, because it won't work. I have to make jazz and R&B records on the side. I have a very good rock career."

Asked whether he was ready and willing to let Deep Purple go at that time, Ian Paice explained that "what should have happened was, when Ritchie said he wanted to quit, we should have said, 'Let's just stop and look at this.' He, Jon, and I should have sat down and said, 'Look, if it's because of Glenn Hughes and David Coverdale and what they're doing, then let's change the band again or let's just take two years off. We'll all do what we want, come back in two years' time, and look at it again.' That's what we should have done, because if we had, it would have continued through to now, and we'd have had a lot of fun all along. We would have done a tour every two years, made a record, and still had a nice social circle. But when Ritchie left, we were a bit silly. We were determined to carry on, and we brought Tommy Bolin in. As good a player as he was in the studio, he was hopeless onstage. When he got on a big stage, he just seemed to freeze up. Instead of playing a solo, he'd end up shouting at the audience and arguing with them. Plus, there was his personal problems, which didn't help at all. That's when it became too much."

And the subtle change within Deep Purple from a guitar-centric band to a vocal-centric band didn't help Ian's mood either. "I find it a lot easier to play with a lead instrumentalist rather than a lead vocalist. There's a lot more freedom. With a vocalist like David, what he's doing is so all-encompassing that there is very little space left for anybody else to do much. When you're doing a solo, then you can let go, but when what you're selling is basically an instrumental thing with lyrics, there's the freedom to do certain things. In guitar-oriented bands, just by virtue of the fact that they're thinking along the same lines as you are, they give you a lot more freedom and leave a lot more gaps. With singers, it's their thing and they're out in front doing the whole thing. Really, you just fade into the background. There's nothing you can do about it, and there's nothing the singer can do about it.

"The last year was not fun at all. It was pure fun until Gillan left, because he was very funny on the road in those times. You never knew what he was going to do next. You never knew if Ritchie was going to turn up. It was just very exciting. On the night something went wrong, it was terrible, but when you look back on it months later, it's hilarious. That was good. From the time David and Glenn joined, it wasn't the same. The fun had left."

As we move toward the end, Tommy Bolin, on tour supporting his second solo album *Private Eyes*, would be found dead in bed in Miami on December 4, 1976, after a multiple drug overdose at the age of twenty-five. He had just played a solo gig with his band supporting Jeff Beck. Bolin was to be buried in his hometown of Sioux City, Iowa.

Willie Basse, guitarist for 1980s metal act Black Sheep, worked at the Record Plant in San Francisco, meeting many of the stars of the day. "Tommy was great, man, and I was with him the day before he died," begins Basse. "He was on his way to superstardom. It's just unfortunate that we lost him. Remember, he was sort of like the fill-in guy. He played with Joe Walsh and the James Gang, and then he replaced Ritchie Blackmore in Deep Purple, and he also did that album with Billy Cobham, *Spectrum*. And that was groundbreaking, but it was still instrumental. And then he got to doing his solo stuff. He did a couple of solo albums, and it was just like . . . if he had done that tour that he was getting ready to do, it would have been superstardom as a solo artist."

As for Bolin's state of mind at the end, "Everything was great, you know?" laughs Basse. "There was like some drugs on the scene that were, you know . . . I actually thought it was coke, but it was China White heroin. I know that's what he died from. But he was a great man, just a nice guy, and just loved to play, and not a lot of stuff got under his skin. He was just there to play. God bless him, and I love him. I miss him dearly. Because he was like unegotistical, just one of those special people. The beauty of his soul comes out, I believe, in his playing and his music.

"I think a lot of it was in his hands," reflects Willie, asked to articulate Bolin's sound. "And I think he was deeply connected to his soul. He was able to express that, like Jimi Hendrix. I was just looking at some of the original Woodstock footage, and it was like, how does a guy in his midtwenties gather that kind of information and those skills? It's got to be some kind of anointing or special connection to other forces that be. And the same with Tommy. Just talking about the substance of the material, it's like, how can he get all that information in his twenty odd years? It amazes me. There are certain ones, certain special ones."

"I was 3,000 miles away, sitting in a restaurant, when the news came on the radio that Tommy had died," recalled Jon Lord. "I was devastated, although I must admit that I was not surprised. That was the path he had chosen. I had never seen anybody do to themselves what Tommy did to himself. I just wish he had someone around him who would have held his hand. Sometimes I feel guilty that we didn't do more. But I'm not sure what we could have done."

Adds his predecessor, Ritchie Blackmore, "I don't envy Tommy Bolin for trying to take my place in Purple. He was a uniquely talented player, and it's unfortunate that he never had the chance to develop with the band the way that I did. His death was an incredible loss, not only for Deep Purple but for guitar fans as well."

"I think there's always a structure of media who will take an antiposition," muses Ian Paice, asked by Sam Dunn on whether the media eventually turned on Purple. "If something becomes super-successful and they've had nothing to do with it, they'll take a position of 'Well, it's crap.' They'll take every opportunity to decry it. Hey, you can't please all the people all the time. Yes, it was a change when it was happening, but it wasn't dangerous. It was fun. It may have had a few kids thinking about things they didn't think about before, it may have burst a few eardrums, but at the end of the day it was never destructive."

On the topic of whether Deep Purple, now calling it quits, were misunderstood, Paice figures, "I think we misunderstood what we were doing half the time. Ask any guy that came out of a band at that period, 'What were you doing?' 'We don't know. It just felt right at the time.' Maybe a few songs said a few things you felt needed to be said. But it was never destructive. It was pure, unbridled emotion. The ability to get in deep, whether that's excitement, beauty, aggression, pathos, humor—it can do all those things. It takes good players to do it, but it can do all those things."

Final word on the *Come Taste the Band* chapter in Deep Purple's long history goes to David Coverdale, who told Dmitry Epstein, "Regardless, it was a very successful album. I never involve myself in who liked what or didn't. I'm always busy with the next thing in my life. I haven't heard *Come Taste the Band* for many years, to be honest, but I have good, positive memories of writing the songs with Tommy Bolin. It was a challenge, coming up with stuff after Blackmore left, but I feel we pulled it off. I embrace challenge—it's more interesting. A musician must make the

Tommy Bolin: death by misadventure, Fairgrounds Arena, Oklahoma City, Oklahoma, February 17, 1976. © *Rich Galbraith*

music he or she wants to make. It's up to others if they want to join in the journey or not. If I spent my time trying to please everyone else and not me, what would be the point of that?"

The 1976 tour book. *Pericle Formenti archive*

Chapter 14

Made in Europe

"This album could well represent an epitaph."

Deep Purple's last official album of the 1970s draws us back to the Mk. III era of the band, despite arriving in the shops after the demise of Mk. IV. As well, *Made in Europe*, issued in November 1976, arguably marks the first of many archival live albums and compilations to come, flooding the market from all manner of licensed situation, left, right, and center. And why would we call it the first? Well, that's because it's the first posthumous release, framed doubly so by virtue of the record featuring Ritchie Blackmore and not Tommy Bolin.

But let's face it: for many, Deep Purple had died with Ritchie's leaving. Bringing Tommy in was one lineup change too many. The jarring arrival of Hughes and Coverdale was enough, but at least they were English. Plus, there was the anchor of Ritchie, one of the band's chief songwriters, gone, and with him, a comfortable centering. Sure, during Mk. III, Ritchie managed to hold it together for two albums, but the stylistic swing of the second one was like an extra lineup change in and of itself.

In any event, here we had *Made in Europe*, blessed with a crazy heavy metal album cover, along with the band's best logo, that of the *Stormbringer* album brought forward, and still in use today. The back cover liner essay by Geoff Barton and Pete Makowski underscores the disappointment many felt with the Bolin run, indicating that Ritchie's "departure broke up the all-powerful guitar-keyboards-drums triumvirate, and, to many fans, things were never the same again." Geoff and Pete drive the stake in by adding that "this album could well represent an epitaph, a final testimony to the greatness that the Deep Purple name implied."

The final dates for the Mk. III lineup came at the tail end of a twelve-date European tour. In the end, Ritchie recorded his final notes to self at the Palais des Sports, Porte de Versailles, Paris, on Monday, April 7, 1975, having informed the band he was definitely leaving, just before hitting the stage. That show is represented here. The other two shows on offer were Graz and Saarbrucken, and the reason they were captured was precisely the thought that the band could implode at any moment, allowing for one more live album out of the mess.

New Musical Express ad for *Made in Europe*. *Martin Popoff archive*

Of note, as the tour had kicked off, Ritchie was in Munich working on what was to be *Ritchie Blackmore's Rainbow*. The guys, as a result, made their way to Belgrade, Yugoslavia, separately and had to hold a press conference without Ritchie. Two shows were played, March 16 and 17, at Belgrade and Zagreb, respectively, both in sold-out venues that held a mere six thousand punters (Ritchie later dismissed them as warm-up gigs). For this last jaunt, "Might Just Take Your Life" and "Lay Down, Stay Down" were dropped from the set to make way for obvious rocking

Ad for the first Rainbow album, plus tour dates. *Martin Popoff archive*

Stormbringer material, but also for "The Gypsy," as well as the "Going Down" cover and the perfunctory "Smoke on the Water" and "Highway Star."

Copenhagen was next on the list, March 20, with Gothenburg, Sweden, up the following night, and then into Germany for a series of dates to close out the month. It was at this point that management (already privy to Blackmore's plans, although the band didn't quite know for sure) was able to book the Rolling Stones mobile in order to record the back end of the tour. The band had used the aforementioned gear on all their studio albums since and including *Machine Head*, as well as *Made in Japan*, the album that would always eclipse the one at hand in fan estimation for all of time. Four shows would be recorded, two in Graz, Austria (April 3 and 4), and then Saarbrucken the following day and finally Paris on April 7.

Dive into the grooves of *Made in Europe*, and the evidence therein was of a Deep Purple that was still great, a band, dare I say, more fiery and sophisticated than the one that cut *Made in Japan*. In some manner, this is Ritchie's and Ian's album. Blackmore is captured clear and carnal, with Paice just killing it on "Burn" and even finding a way to make "Mistreated" interesting (things you never heard at a Deep Purple concert: "Play 'Mistreated'!" and "More, Ritchie, more!"). "Mistreated" includes a half nod to old chestnut "Rock Me Baby" but is over with at just over eleven minutes. Side 1 closes with "Lady Double Dealer," again, with Paice both fully groovy and busy within the framework of staying very musical.

Over to side 2 of this single vinyl album, and we're confronted with a nearly seventeen-minute-long and very funky "You Fool No One," turned into a jam, with Jon constantly percolating and Ian furiously busy, and even more so when it comes to his drum solo. Ritchie is on fire, slipping in bits of the Yardbirds' "Still I'm Sad," which would surface on his first Rainbow album. There was also a curious spot of a half-formed song as well as a soft blues, and after the drum solo, a big, loud blues windup. The album closed with a slightly bluesier, greasier version of "Stormbringer," which meant that, neatly, all five selections on offer were from the Mk. III era of the band. The bulk of *Made in Europe* is considered to hail from Saarbrucken, but there is splicing, editing, and apparently some overdubbing going on, not to mention crowd noise massaged in as a tape loop.

"I never listen to them," dismisses Ritchie, referring to both *Made in Japan* and *Made in Europe*. "They're old, dead, and buried. I think both of them as live LPs are rubbish. But compared to all the live albums that are put out by other bands, I think they were brilliant."

Wrote Alan Niester of *Rolling Stone* in his review of the album, "For the most part, the material here lacks the drive and cohesion of *Made in Japan*, the group's earlier live set. Blackmore's aimless diddling about on 'Mistreated' may have been passably interesting live, but it is wasted space here. Jon Lord's fooling around on 'You Fool No One,' Ian Paice's drum solo, and the extended audience reaction which closes the album add to the padded effect. The only interesting moments occur on 'Burn,' the seven-minute opening cut. It's a well done, solid rocker, but its fascination stems largely from how hard vocalist David Coverdale tries to mimic his popular predecessor, Ian Gillan."

As David told Dmitry Epstein, there was a wee chance that he might have ended up in Uriah Heep. "Actually, it was not really an audition. I never had any intention of going there. I just jammed with Heep for fun. Nice guys, but it was never a career consideration. I knew what I wanted to do, and I did it. Still doing it, as a matter of fact. Heep was too similar musically to what Purple were doing, and I definitely preferred Purple! I really did know what I wanted to do."

It was a good time for Purple to exit stage left, because right around the corner was punk rock.

"The punk thing was huge," remarked David, speaking with Sam Dunn. "When punk started, I was twenty-six years old and called a dinosaur in the music press, which was fascinating to me. But thank God, I ignored it and soldiered on. I had remarkable support from an audience. I was led to believe there was no audience for my music until I put together . . . to save face, I called it a Back to the Roots tour, after playing in stadiums throughout the world. I'm playing to 300, 400, 500, and I find out there was like ten times as many people outside saying, 'Why the hell are you playing in a small venue?' So, it was a huge learning lesson to me that the music press doesn't exactly represent what is happening on the street, you know? So, with Whitesnake, even at the height of punk, we flourished and always have.

"When everybody says, 'What's your advice? to anybody, it's do what you want to do. And if you don't have the support for it from the corporate music business or whatever, you really do have to do what you want to do. That's the only way an audience is going to buy what you're doing. And after being the principal writer for Purple, I found that my writing for personal expression was getting in an ever-decreasing spiral. I tried as much as I could to be loyal to the Deep Purple identity, writing 100-mile-an-hour songs like 'Coming Home,' 'Stormbringer,' and 'Burn,' stuff like this, but really, I wanted to do different things.

"So, the way Purple degenerated in the last two years or so, and on a social level, not only musical level, it was very easy for me to leave. I did the UK tour in '76 as a favor to the acting manager at the time. It was an immense lesson that you don't do favors of that magnitude. We should never have taken that band to the UK the way it was. It was in gross disrepair. It needed redecorating immensely. But I had plenty of time and no support whatsoever from the Purple management. They still considered me a new boy, so I was living in a beautiful big cuckoo clock of a house in Bavaria, writing songs that I still draw from now, and boy were they wrong. But the circumstance was I wanted to harness those elements—hard rock, rhythm and blues, soul, all the stuff that I loved—without being too diverse to be difficult to

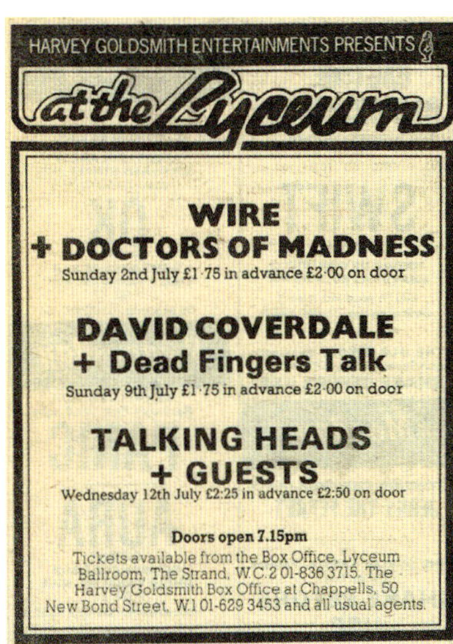

Where David Coverdale would go next. *Martin Popoff archive*

lock into. I wanted the creative umbrella of Whitesnake to be able to sing my Wilson Pickett–style songs, but just louder. And most of the time I've achieved that.

"Still, punk was not only necessary, it absolutely had to arrive because rock had started to take itself awfully seriously and had forgotten, perhaps, some of its roots. Punk arrived with this huge breath of mad, fresh air and swept that away. And I think what it brought back to the mix was 'Yes you can.' 'I only know three chords!' 'Well, it doesn't matter—you can do it!' And for a while, it was almost like you were wearing a badge saying I can't really play. But of course, you can only do that for so long. There's nothing wrong with virtuosity, and I've gone full circle here. There's nothing wrong with it if it's at the service of music and at the service of emotion. But rock'n'roll is still open to people who are learning to swim while they're drowning. It's still there for them."

We'll close this chapter and move on with a quick recap of the chronology. *Come Taste the Band* was issued in October 1975, and *Made in Europe*, November 1976. Deep Purple threw in the towel three months early, in July 1976, and come December 4 of that year, Tommy Bolin would be dead, having gotten to see the release of *Made in Europe*. It would have been a wistful experience, reflecting on how he's not on the record. Indeed, a live album with Tommy on it, called *Last Concert in Japan*, would soon see release—granted, in Japan only, but nonetheless officially. But Tommy wouldn't be around to enjoy it, having left us four months before the album's March 1977 release date. *Last Concert in Japan* would be dedicated to Bolin, and perhaps most graciously, it would contain a Deep Purple performance of "Wild Dogs" from *Teaser*, Tommy's final album.

Chapter 15

Perfect Strangers

"Would anybody be interested?"

Dip the Man in Black into the paint tin—to mix or, nay, invent metaphors—and there's bound to be a myriad of gray areas. Nothing comes easy with Deep Purple—until Ritchie Blackmore is gone, anyway. Well, that was the conundrum that various broken pieces of Deep Purple were considering back in 1983. That band had been long gone fer dead, having bowed out back in 1976 with a lineup that wrinkled noses, hooverings of blow notwithstanding.

And for the band to rise again, there was going to have to be a wholesale decimation of the midtier hard rock aristocracy of Great Britain. First the band Gillan, and then Black Sabbath, would have to crack, but also Rainbow and Whitesnake. That's a lot of daggers brought to the matter, and a lot of still-hopeful bands saying never mind to potential fame and fortune

On a case-by-case basis, we can start with Ian Gillan. Essentially, Ian had to break with two bands amid two attempts at making a Deep Purple reunion happen. The first trouble happened after his Gillan band's *Magic* album and tour dates, and the second after the incendiary stint he drank (and stripped) his way through fronting Black Sabbath, resulting in a little demon of a record they like to call *Born Again*.

"I was very satisfied by the way my band Gillan was doing," begins Ian back in the day, doing press for *Born Again*. "But then things started to happen. I developed nodes on my throat, and my doctor said that it would take at least three months' rest to get my health back. The other members of my band didn't want to wait three months before beginning work on another album, so they branched out on their own. That's when I decided to call it a day with that band. I thought the chances were excellent for Purple to get back together for a few gigs. I even went to America and stayed with Ritchie and Roger for a while to work out some details. But then problems started to arise. Ritchie began to see that it would be impossible to have a simple reunion. He was asking for a flat rate of $1 million for every gig we were going to do, and that price had been met by a number of promoters in South America. But then Ian Paice had the opportunity to join Gary Moore's band, and Ritchie was advised to prepare material for the next Rainbow album instead of taking the time off to rehearse and tour with Purple."

Prophetically, he added, "The idea is still viable for some time in the future, but not now—I have other things to keep me busy at the moment. I must admit that I was disappointed by the failure to get a Purple reunion together, but in retrospect, it probably was the best thing for me."

Ian tells the amusing tale of the first attempt to put the band back together. "It came about first of all in 1983, when we had a meeting in New York to discuss the possibilities of re-forming. This is when drinking doesn't actually pay off, because within ten minutes, Ritchie Blackmore and I told each other to fuck off, and I ended up joining Black Sabbath for good money! But the seed was sown then. Ian Paice was involved with Gary Moore, Jon Lord was with Whitesnake, and Ritchie had another tour lined up with Rainbow.

"Previously, Jon and I met in a Spanish restaurant in Reading, and that was the first Deep Purple reunion meeting. There had been press speculation about us re-forming, but until 1983, we had never spoken about it at all. That was the year we started speaking to each other again. We all live within 30 miles of each other; yet, we never saw each other. We never socialized at all. We lead different lives, and we're a diverse bunch of characters. If you decided to put five guys in a band, you wouldn't pick us! But there is a strange chemistry that has always worked when we are on the road and in the studio. So, in 1983, we started to think about Purple in a different light and realized this was the best band any of us had ever been in. For the first time in all those years, we were free to say, 'Let's sit down and talk about it.'"

But as Ian says, the demon alcohol was also involved. "Yeah, but as I told you, it also caused some trouble. I think drinking is essential. And it certainly is creative. It's a natural English trait. When I was in Paris, I was drunk all the time and able to speak French fluently [laughs]. When you have a drink, the barriers come down, and you tell people what you think. The truth comes out, and you get to know other people's personalities. Professionally it is no good. You lose your sharpness. Consequently, we all go onstage sober, and the drinking starts from the moment I go onstage. My first beer is always as I walk onstage. I tell you one thing; Ritchie has a strange way of checking whether he's sober or not. His theory is that if you eat bread, then it soaks up the booze. You watch Ritchie onstage, going behind his amps with a whiskey bottle in one hand and eating dry bread with the other—it's just an incredible scene!"

So yes, much was going on with the implosion of Gillan, and to recap, the Purple thing didn't work the first time. But then after the Sabbath situation, it was pretty clear-cut why Ian was on his way out of the Sabbath camp—namely, that a deal got put together to finally make Purple work. Granted, Ian wasn't at his best on the Sabbath tour, nor was his personality that well suited to be part of Sabbath in the first place. Finally, there had been some bad vibes over various decisions taken with the *Born Again* album; namely, its album cover, its muddy mix, and then its subsequent lukewarm sales and mauling by the critics. Amusingly, these days there are throngs of Sabbath fans that adore *Born Again*, even though it remains divisive and grist for animated debate.

"That was the craziest year I ever had in my life," figures Ian. "It was just unbelievable. I went out for a drink with Tony and Geezer in a place called the Bear Hotel in Woodstock, which is in Oxfordshire in England. It's halfway between Birmingham and where I used to live. And I had a car wreck on the way there. Someone drove into my car. So, I parked what was left of my car outside the hotel, went in, and had a stiff whiskey. Tony turned up a few minutes later, and we went

Ian Gillan as part of Black Sabbath, Circus Krone, Munich, Germany, September 22, 1983. © *Wolfgang Gürster*

into the restaurant, and we started drinking. I can't remember much, but apparently, they poured us . . . they dragged us out from under the table at about 7:00 so they could open the restaurant for the evening. So, they got us home, and the next day I got a call from my manager, who was pretty pissed off and said, 'You know, Ian, if you're going to start making serious career moves, I think we should talk about it first.' I said, 'I don't know what you're talking about.' He said, 'Apparently yesterday afternoon you agreed to join Black Sabbath and record an album and do a tour.' So, I said, no I didn't. And he said, 'Well, you signed papers.'

"So anyway, whatever. I never regretted it. It was a fantastic, great experience. We spent God knows how long at the Manor Studios, Richard Branson's studio in Oxfordshire, near Oxford. I lived in a tent for the duration. I mean, it was just wild, fantastic. And then we did a tour, which lasted a year. This was '83 or so, and then I went straight into *Perfect Strangers* after that, the reunion of Purple. And Tony and I are still good buddies. In fact, it was only last Monday or Tuesday I was at his house. He's doing some work right now on a studio album, and he phoned my manager in Barcelona airport on his mobile and said, 'Help, I need some lyrics; can you get hold of Ian?'

"Geezer Butler was totally responsible for destroying the production on that thing," figures Ian, on the notorious *Born Again* sledge of wanton destruction. "I've got the rough mixes. It sounds sensational. Geezer took it away to London to another studio. Next thing I hear was on plastic, on vinyl. I couldn't believe it. He just obviously cranked the bass up, not only the bass guitar, but I can't even listen to it. It's just a disgusting production. We were told it was unplayable on the radio."

Over in Rainbow land, management and the Purple alumni in the band were working their own career machinations.

"We toured the album all over Europe, Japan, and South America," says vocalist Joe Lynn Turner, referring to *Bent Out of Shape*. Joe would soon figure more directly in the Purple story as the band's front man for one record. "And then we came to the States. It was a limited tour on that particular record, and I'm not entirely sure why. We headlined. And then what really happened was that the manager, Bruce Payne, got an opportunity to put Purple together. Only a couple years ago did I really find out the truth about this, and so did Ritchie, which is really surprising to both of us, that we were really played and duped. The manager told Ritchie, 'Well, Joe wants to do his solo album for Elektra Records, and he doesn't want to do Rainbow anymore, so we have this opportunity to do Purple.' Then he came to me and said, 'Ritchie wants to do Purple, and he doesn't want to do Rainbow. He'll come back to it at some point in time, and you've got your solo career, so shuffle off and have a good time.'

"And the band was never really communicative, so Ritchie and I never went up to each other and said, 'Hey, what's your fucking problem? How come you don't want to do another record with Rainbow?' Because I found out later that he was disappointed that I didn't want to continue with Rainbow. And I did! I would have easily put off the solo record for one more Rainbow album. We were duped, because there was a lot of money involved in the reunion of Deep Purple.

First photo, Joe looks to Ritchie for answers; *second photo*, Joe gets his answer as Ritchie raises the axe and . . .
© *Martin Popoff*

"And then they put out an absolutely fabulous album, *Perfect Strangers*, and I always felt like a part of that. It's like, 'Well, I helped, because I didn't get in the way.' I took a sidestep, and I helped to put this band back together. I always felt a little part of the reunion, and I think rightfully so. But at the same time, I really felt we were going to get back together at some point in time and continue this. But as we all know . . .

"I think Bruce was pretty amenable to us," continues Joe, softening. "I thought he was a great manager, and he did what was best for the band at any given time. I look back and, of course, you're always clashing at some point. There is just one thing that I still have a bit stuck in my throat, and that was the end of Rainbow and the beginning of Purple, what happened there. It's a story that basically he got what he wanted, and I suppose that's the way you do it politically. He wanted Deep Purple to re-form.

"Like I say, I was doing a solo album for Elektra, so I was on top of the world. You know, he told Ritchie that I was just more interested in solo recordings, and Ritchie got a bit upset, and Ritchie went and proceeded to do the Deep Purple thing. So, the truth really is that he kind of played as both against each other, in a way. Because the real truth is Ritchie thought that we would do at least another album; that's what I figured. Bruce had promised me that Rainbow would get together and that we would do another album. It never really happened. So, I guess he was just being a manager, and getting what he felt was best for himself and the band and everything else."

And Ritchie's take? Legendary UK journo Dave Ling was brave enough to coax an answer out of the Man in Black.

"When I had been onstage with Rainbow for quite some time, I came to realize that many people only came to watch because I had played in Deep Purple. Rainbow was my responsibility, and at one time I grew tired of that because I had to do everything myself. The rest of the musicians were only making money. That's what made them extremely lazy, and quite a few changes took place. When I was fed up with this, I visited Gillan during Christmas and asked him to come and sing with Rainbow. He immediately said no, and then we got drunk.

"Then it remained quiet for a while. Some years later he organized it himself. My own singer was getting on my nerves, and I knew it would be hard to find a new one. This boy was . . . I don't like picking on other musicians, but sometimes I do . . . he was an enormous obstacle. He was a nice guy, but then he started taking drugs and he thought he was the best. I observed this for a year and then told him to quit. I was walking around with this Purple thing all the time and then decided to let Rainbow die. I thought it was time to return. When Ian had left the band, we did have more respect for what happened in 1972–74. We were a lot younger and rebelled against everything and everybody, whatever we did. It took us ten years to look back and to be able to say, 'Yes, it was really good.' That's how we got together again."

And with Ritchie came Rainbow bassist and producer Roger Glover. That left Ian Paice and Jon Lord as the crucial bits of the Mk. II puzzle. Ian Paice was out of Whitesnake and now touring as part of Gary Moore's band. Jon arrived directly from Whitesnake, with Coverdale then capitalizing on huge changes to his lineup that would take the band high up the American charts for the rest of the 1980s.

"To me, it's basically a different suit," mused Coverdale, on the proposition that Whitesnake breaks into two eras, demarcated by the bluesy UK unit versus the Americanized hard rock of the hit-bound band. "When I was with Purple, I learned to tailor the style of music I was writing for the identity. But within three years that became an ever-decreasing circle. So, when I formed Whitesnake, I wanted Whitesnake to be able to embrace a plethora of styles under a particular creative umbrella called Whitesnake. I wanted to do hard rock, R&B, blues, and, if necessary, with good commercial hooks. And I've done very well harnessing that. I got to a period in the early '80s where I knew it was time to take Whitesnake to the next level, which was going to be more the style that Hendrix created for the blues. He made the blues more electrifying. My colleagues at that time weren't of the same vision, which is why I moved on to players like John Sykes, who could assist me in going to that next level."

"Whitesnake was the funniest band I've ever been in," recalls Ian Paice, happy with those times on a personal level but not creatively, given the limitations of the band's traditional song structures. "I never laughed so much in my life; it was great. The band was totally irreverent toward David, but not in a nasty way. Just seeing the funny side of everything.

"I mean, I'll give you an instance. I think we were playing Hammersmith Odeon, or one of the big London theaters, anyway. I looked across, and Micky Moody and Bernie Marsden were basically holding each other up back to back, laughing so hard. If they hadn't been there, they would have fallen over. And I couldn't work it out until Bernie looked at me, and he sort of motions to me to look at David. And David's at the front of the stage there, throwing all these wonderful shapes and thrusting the pelvis and extending the mic stand as part of his personage and doing this whole repertoire. And I looked at the audience, and the first fifteen rows, it's just pubescent young men. There's not a chick there to be seen [laughs]. And Bernie and Mick each had hooked onto this, and it just made them laugh. And within two minutes, I'd gone, Neil had gone. And David never knew. I mean, throwing all these sexual suggestions to a bunch of fifteen-year-old boys, which was . . . well, it was funny."

Even funnier was the idea that at one point in the early 1980s, there was a proposal for Purple to re-form, but with Coverdale fronting the band. Then, also in the early 1980s, there was a meeting between the Gillan-era version of the band, sans Blackmore. And the stall at the point before the Sabbath album? Ostensibly, the idea was to give the very promising Joe Lynn Turner version of Rainbow one more shot at breaking America proper, with an additional tour of that territory. There was also talk of a spirited disagreement between Ritchie and Ian over publishing monies that culminated in Ian pouring a beer over Ritchie's head—it seems that Ritchie wanted 50 percent and the other 50 percent?—sort it out among yourselves. In any event, into 1984, a reported $2 million to each party involved got the ball rolling, and the band soon found themselves ensconced in idyllic Stowe, Vermont, to figure out how to get along again.

Jon Lord emphasizes that it was more for the music than the money. "I was working in Whitesnake at the time. But when I heard that Gillan and Ritchie had actually sat down and agreed to do the project, I couldn't resist. Deep Purple is in my blood. We each made significant contributions to the music world and to that band, and naturally we want to recapture that feeling again. There's unquestionably an energy we all have when we get together. When I start trading runs with Ritchie, we push each other to excel. Each of us needs that, and in Purple we're surrounded by musicians who will nurture our individual needs.

"We've matured, that's for certain," continues Jon. "In the past, we were always filled with petty disputes and jealousies. So far, at least, those haven't been apparent. Naturally we're all very excited about this project, and we want it to be enjoyable as well as profitable. The money really isn't an overriding factor for us. We know the demand for Purple to tour is incredible, but we're doing this strictly because we found that we enjoyed working with each other more than anybody else. It's fun to see how we've each grown over the years.

"There were the biggest grins I've ever seen on five faces the day we got together. It was a super day. Funnily enough, for the first week we didn't play any of the old stuff at rehearsals. It was almost like we were afraid to, you know? We didn't want to spoil what was happening by just being nostalgic. The amazing thing was nobody could remember what key any of the old stuff was in anyway. Lots of arguments about that. But when we did find the right key from our records, we discovered to our great joy that Mr. Gillan could still sing them in the same key. I don't know how he does it. I think it's tight jeans!"

In Stowe, a pastoral playground for the privileged that is based on a ski hill and arts and crafts, the band had found a neutral location that calmed their nerves. Rolling hills, hot-air ballooning, authentic restaurants and pubs (tip of the hat to Richard and Dawn Hughes), lush greenery, fancy cars, and places to play soccer . . . it felt a bit like aristocratic England, except for that ski hill. Sure, the band could still get a bit squirrelly on the drink, but if this had been something attempted in central London, you figure the whole thing could have gone off the rails. Of note, the resulting record, *Perfect Strangers*, would be the band's first album ever made in the US of A.

"We also found an English pub run by a mad Englishman," recalls Glover, with respect to the aforementioned Richard Hughes, proprietor of the Pub at Stowe. "We used to hang out there most nights. We spent many an evening in there, sipping English beer and reminiscing about old times. It was a very enjoyable album to make. If there was any pressure, it was well concealed. We tried to make it as natural and nonpressured as possible. Several people brought families and children over,

The Cow Palace, San Francisco, California, January 31, 1985.

and we basically spread ourselves around the town and rented condos and houses or whatever. But most of the time we spent together. In Stowe, people accepted us as just a bunch of long-haired idiots that rented the house up the road. Stowe is a small town, and most people didn't give a damn who we were."

Stuart Smith, Englishman, consummate guitarist, and recording artist in his own right, was a good buddy of Ritchie's starting (gradually) in the 1970s. After moving to Long Island and staying with Ritchie until he found his own place, Stuart was asked to come along to Stowe, eventually joining the payroll as Ritchie's PA, or "personal assistant." Soccer was of course part of the job description.

"When we got up, we would go play soccer," remembers Stuart. "It was always the band against the crew. I was always on the band side, and the crew always used to win, probably because they were in better shape than the rest of us [laughs]. But I remember, every time we would go down to the pub after soccer and have a drink, there was a blackboard when you went into the pub, and every day the crew would write, you know, Crew 5, Band 3. And the day we actually won, the crew was really pissed. So, I went to the pub first, and I'm in the process of writing, you know, Band 5, Crew 3, and Colin Hart, from the road crew, came up behind me and pushed me. And he didn't see Ritchie there, and Ritchie just slammed him into the wall and said, 'Don't you ever push my friend!' Yeah, Ritchie . . . for everything negative that is written about Ritchie, Ritchie is one of the greatest people I've known in my life, very intelligent, incredibly funny. Always playing practical jokes. We used to play them on each other until it got to the point where we called truce on each other and concentrated on other people."

Besides soccer, Stuart also had to necessarily wear the hat of Ritchie's driver. "Yes, I was driving Ritchie, because he hadn't passed his driving test at that point. But yeah, everyone had their own cars. It was great; it's a very nice place. Beautiful neck of the woods, and it was the summertime of course. I understand it's more of a ski town, but it's very beautiful, as was the house, the Horizons house, where they were recording. And then everyone would have condos within a few miles' area.

"But yes, I taught Ritchie to drive. He never even learned to drive until I came out to Long Island. I would take him out to shopping malls; he had bought a new red Mercedes, and after him and his wife, Amy, broke up, I mean, he was trapped at his house. He'd be calling me to say, 'Stuart, can you do me a favor? Can you take me to the supermarket?' And I'd say, 'Ritchie, this is ridiculous. You've got to learn to drive.' And I would take him to parking lots late at night and teach him.

"One of the funny things was, we were going to go off to . . . I believe it was Rhode Island, to see this old girlfriend of his who was singing in a band, Shoshana, and who sang backups on the first Rainbow album; we're going to see her at this place she's playing. And I remember turning up, and he was in his driveway, in the Mercedes, with the door open, and his foot . . . he's driving the Mercedes up and down on the gravel, with his foot on the gravel of the driveway. And I walk up and turn off the car and go, 'What are you doing?' And he says, 'Well, I'm practicing driving.' And I say, 'What's with the leg?' 'Well, if it gets away from me, I can stop it.' 'Ritchie, this is like a 400 hp car. Your foot . . . that's what the brake pedal is for.' It was so funny. It was hilarious."

"You know that pub was like an episode of *Fawlty Towers*," laughs engineer Nick Blagona, a Canadian back on the case after working with the guys in Rainbow. "We

The Man in Black, Maple Leaf Gardens, Toronto, Ontario, April 1, 1985. © *Martin Popoff*

literally took over the pub, and Ritchie and I used to have a good old time playing practical jokes on the patrons of the pub. The reason was . . . I think it was the World Cup of soccer that was on, and the pub, because the owners were English, British, it was built like a British pub. But the thing is, we had a satellite dish, and they had cable. And so, we knew the scores before they got the scores, so Ritchie would bet with people, and everybody couldn't believe how accurate Ritchie was. Ritchie played this whole thing that he could see the future, and all this mystical bullshit that he was into [laughs]. I mean, he didn't bet a lot of money. It was five bucks here, ten bucks there. But people just couldn't believe that he could actually get the scores like that, because they didn't realize that we had this special satellite on the truck that picked up directly from Europe. So that was pretty funny.

"They had already had meetings without me," explains Nick, asked about first hooking up with the band. "I wasn't there, obviously, because there was no need for me to be there. How it worked was, they flew me in, and then I met Roger in Greenwich, and we both drove up to Stowe, Vermont. And I walked in, and everybody was joking at the pub; that's how it all started."

"We wanted somewhere off the beaten track," adds Gillan. "This was, don't forget, the reunion of Deep Purple. It was a very sensitive time, and we wanted to be deep in the countryside away from the journalists and the media people who might just want to get involved before we were ready. We just wanted privacy and a quiet atmosphere where everyone could relax and spend as much time as we wanted making a record. And a couple of the guys were up skiing there, at Killington or whatever. Somebody went through there and said, 'Hey, this would be nice.'

"And anyways, we found this guy called Richard Hughes, who used to own the Pub at Stowe. He's now a good friend of mine. He lives in Portugal. I think he's about to buy a castle in Scotland, but he's just one of those wacky guys. And he fixed us up with everything, accommodation and renting the hall, wherever it was that we had the Playhouse [Note: this is now referring to the return visit for *The House of Blue Light*]. And we had this house that had a great basement, so we got the mobile truck up there and set the gear up in the basement and wrote and recorded the album. We have many happy memories there. We had some crazy times there. I know that Stowe doesn't seem like the environment for crazy times, but we really did [laughs]."

Ian Gillan, Maple Leaf Gardens, Toronto, Ontario, April 1, 1985. © *Martin Popoff*

"Yeah, we did the hot-air ballooning and all that kind of stuff," confirms Nick. "We had a film crew follow us for *Perfect Strangers*. I have no idea where that stuff is. I've never seen any of the documentary or me being interviewed, or the band being interviewed. But for a good two or three weeks of the process of making the record, we had a full film crew. Never knew what happened to it."

Some of this obviously got used for the "Knocking at Your Back Door" video. Nick knows this but adds, "There was a whole documentary made. And I have no idea where it is. Neither does Roger. Because I talked to Roger a few weeks ago. Because Roger is in a very peculiar situation right now, in this particular month [I interviewed Nick in June 2009]—not only is he becoming a father, but also a grandfather [laughs]."

"Yeah, they were there all the time!" confirms Stuart. "We occasionally would watch this stuff. Some of it was used on the video, where they are playing soccer there or were in the pub, and I remember somebody at the pub had owned a balloon, and they were taking members of the band and crew up. Ritchie and I were saying, 'We're not going in that. Something horrible is going to happen.' And when it landed—it might've even been Ian Gillan in there—it came down in these trees. And they filmed it, this big crash into the trees in the middle of the woods. They couldn't control where they were landing. So yes, there was a film crew around, but I don't know what happened to the footage."

Other than the hot-air ballooning, Nick says recreation basically consisted of "soccer and drinking. I played goalie. We were all good or bad, you know. Ritchie was a great soccer player. But we would play . . . like at Stowe, Vermont, we used to play against CHOM FM in Montreal, or in Germany against the Scorpions. It was great exercise, but Ritchie's rule was, every second day we would play soccer. You know, being at Stowe in the summertime, and having every second day off to play, it made the album longer to work on, but it was a lot of fun."

"It's a super part of the world," adds Jon. "Far enough away from the city to avoid temptations, but close to a town with a couple of bars and nice restaurants, so you can get out and relax for a while. It's a fabulous place for us to go. In the past, a great deal of the problems were attributable to management. I'm not passing the buck, but we were very much treated as a property, the sort of thing that you wound up and made money. We were sent out on the road with no real thought about longevity or what the pressure might do to the band.

"So, to get back together in 1984 was terrific but nerve-wracking. It was an idea we had all resisted in various ways. There'd been a long gap from 1976 to 1983, and during those seven years there have been various blandishments. We were offered a million and a half bucks to do one album and a concert—I mean each! This was in 1981. So, you can see the prime mover behind re-forming was not financial. If that had been the reason, we would've done it before. We got back together for a far less starry figure. The thing was that it worked, it was great, and we had a wonderful time."

Spring rehearsals (ah yes, the optimism of spring) and writing at Bass Lodge led to recording at a different outpost of rural resplendence called Horizons, beginning July 10 (rehearsals had ended on July 3). Expectations for the results were high, now that the cat had been let out of the bag back on April 27, when UK radio legend Tommy Vance had announced the reunion to the world. Bass Lodge was owned by the Von Trapp family, subjects of the classic 1965 movie *The Sound of Music*. The July 6 move to Horizons was necessitated due to the Vermont State Authority deciding that there'd be too much noise ringing throughout the valley from the elevated location that was Bass Lodge. A mobile studio (or rather Le Mobile Studio, a mobile from the famous Le Studio, north of Montreal) was set up outside the new manse, commandeered by Nick. The record was pretty much laid down in a quick month.

"Yes, we used a mobile truck and had a tremendous amount of fun," recalls Nick. "We did the recording in the basement, of all places, in a large estate in Stowe where they were rehearsing the album. I walked in and listened to it and said, 'We should just stay here and do it, because it sounds good.' Luckily enough, the basement, although it had wood and a fireplace and a relatively high ceiling, the drums sounded awesome, in this little room. And everybody was quite happy with doing it there, and that's how we did the record. We basically took almost every second day off to play soccer. And then we moved the whole entourage to Germany. Ritchie wanted to be in Hamburg, and so I found a nice studio in Hamburg, and we finished the record there. We mixed there, and we did some overdubs with Jon and Ritchie, but it was basically done.

"The songs were all done live off the floor, and then Ritchie would do the overdubs that particular evening. He would sit in the truck, and we would set up the amps, either in a garage or in the building, and how it would be, it would be like a night in the pub. We would talk about everything, politics and so forth, drink scotch and coke, or beer or whatever was going, and then he would do a solo, and then we would chat a little more, and so he would end up with four or five solos, and then Roger and I would sift through them the next day and make a composite of the best of each solo. Then Ritchie would come in and listen to it and either say yes or no, or he liked a little part of this and so forth, and that's how we'd construct the solos. But it was a really easy record to do. We laughed a lot, and you can tell by the album that it was fun to do."

"I saw a lot of the whole process," adds Stuart. "Generally, it was Ritchie. Ritchie would come up with the riffs. He was always the one who would come up with a killer riff that would start it off. He would just start playing and the band would join in, and someone, usually Roger or Jon, would go, 'How about go into here?,' and the song would come together like that. And generally, Ian would be hanging around. He really wouldn't do much singing; he would just be hanging around and listening and making notes. Then he would sort of disappear for a time, and he would come back and try something with the song and then go away again and work on it some more.

"I remember that 'Wasted Sunsets' had started off much faster [sings it as almost a gallop]. That's how it started off, and someone at some point said, 'Let's just slow this down.' And when Ritchie did his solos, he liked to be outside and see the stars. So, they had a door on the side of the mobile, but with the lights, there were so many insects and mosquitoes and everything, so they built like a mosquito tent around the door, and Ritchie would sit outside and play, looking up at the moon and the stars while doing his solos. With his compulsory Johnny Walker Black and Coke. They actually built a structure of wood, built like an extension to a house, really, and he would sit out there with his guitar and his scotch and Coke."

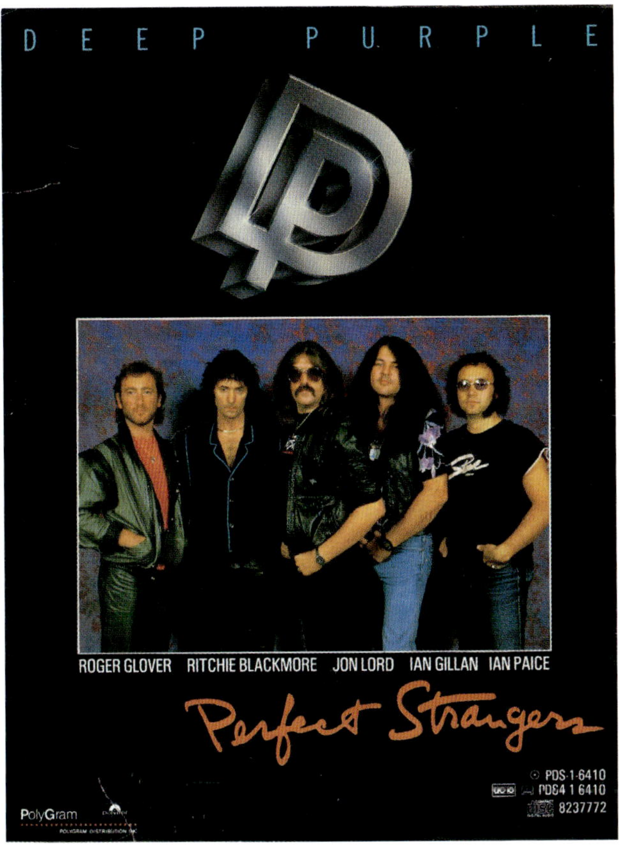

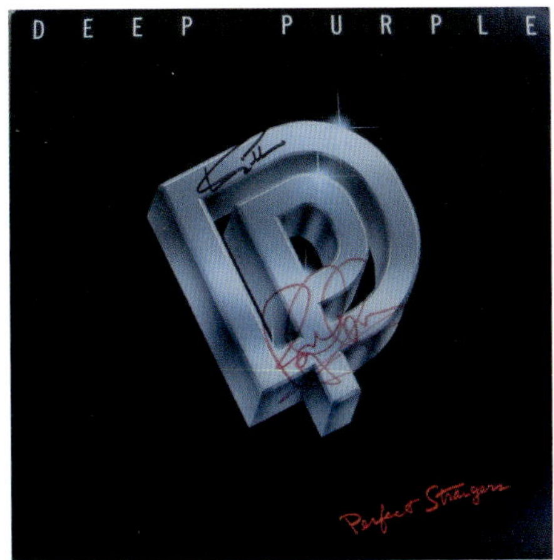

The *Perfect Strangers* album cover, signed by Roger and Ian, plus a color ad for the album

As indicated, mixing took place in Germany, in September, at Tennessee Ton Studio, built by the legendary Michael Wagener, who began his prestigious run there with Dokken back in 1979. Following its completion, the band got busy at the Antico Room in Bedford, England, preparing to tour their forthcoming opus, due to drop in November 1984. Gillan is quick to dispel rumors of a $2 million advance for the making of the album, claiming it was closer to half that, with the money being burned up pretty efficiently in the making of the album and preparations for the highly anticipated tour. Still, the band's new contract was rich, with winning label Polydor said to have prevailed with a four-record deal worth $10 million, although what that means in the rough 'n' ready rock 'n' roll business makes for a complicated computation.

"I think we had a kind of phenomenon," explained Roger back in 1988, articulating the business climate for the reunion. "A band that didn't exist anymore, but whose albums still sold consistently and were still played on the radio, and whose members were still very active in the music business, playing in various different bands. So, it's not really a quantum leap in anyone's mind to think that if you can just get those five people back on the same stage, you can make a lot of money. This reunion came about, basically, because of Ian Gillan, and it's the first time it came from someone in the band. As a matter of fact, his first overture was turned down. He came out to see Ritchie and me in 1983, just before he joined Black Sabbath. He didn't really want to join Sabbath; he wanted to re-form Deep Purple. But at that time, Ritchie and I were just about to make a new Rainbow album."

The ex-Rainbow guys, Roger and Ritchie, Maple Leaf Gardens, Toronto, Ontario, April 1, 1985. © *Martin Popoff*

"It's difficult to throw away a career you've spent many years building for something that may or may not happen. No one realized how we'd get along together as people, let alone as musicians, because we did break up in a fairly bitter way. There was a question mark about the reunion. To throw away a career like Rainbow for a question mark, at that time, seemed wrong. So, we said no. Ian went ahead and joined Black Sabbath and didn't like it a bit. He called up again in early '84 and said, 'Do you want to reconsider?' Finally, we said, 'All right! Let's finally have a meeting about it—all five of us.'

"After the initial 'Hello, how are you?,' we settled down to the business of the day, in terms of figuring out whether we did or did not have a reunion here. And the first thing we decided was that we were going to make music together to see if it still worked, because if that didn't work, there's no point in continuing. We went up to Vermont and we started jamming. Five minutes into the first jam, there were smiles on everyone's faces. It was fantastic! As a matter of fact, there was so much magic in that first jam that it would be impossible for me to describe it to you without sounding really stupid. It was wonderful.

"Anyone who can say that Deep Purple just got back together because they ran out of money . . . I mean, there's nothing I can do to stop someone from thinking that. But that was the basis of most of the reunion rumors that came our way. We got offered enormous amounts of money to re-form at various points in the last six or seven years. And to be quite honest, I was totally against it. They were all the wrong reasons for doing it. There had to be a good reason, and money wasn't it. Sure, it's nice to make money. It's hard to turn down $2 million or $3 million a show, you know. I'm not trying to say that I'm such an idealistic person and that I'm not above being swayed by money. But it's true. Every single one of us turned down offers."

And in the famous-last-words department . . . "At this moment, I think a Deep Purple without any one of the five of us would be unthinkable," pronounced Glover. "I think the whole reason why this reunion is working is because it's those five people. If there was any one substitution, I don't think it would have the same credibility. Now ask me this question a couple of years down the line, and you might get a different answer; because then I think we will have reestablished ourselves and the name of the band, and it might not matter so much. But certainly, the magic would go out of it for me. There's something about us five people that you cannot define. I feel that if you change the chemistry, you change the band, you change the sound."

Directly post–*Perfect Strangers* production, Gillan had said much the same thing. "The chemistry between us is back. Each one of us is playing better than ever before, and the enthusiasm is incredible. It's probably more apparent than when we first got together way back in 1969. *Perfect Strangers* is the best album we've ever done. If I played it once, I've played it forty times. I'm that proud of it. We used to say we'd re-form every Christmas and then we'd be broken up by Easter. This time the timing was right. None of us were feeling the magic with our individual bands that we felt with Deep Purple, so we decided to try again."

Ian also tells the story of being the first to show up for work in Stowe, wondering if the whole thing had been a joke and he was going to be left holding the bag. But then Ritchie shows up with Paicey, then Roger, cigarette in hand. Jon Lord was last

Jon Lord, Maple Leaf Gardens, Toronto, Ontario, April 1, 1985. © *Martin Popoff*

to arrive, since he had lost track of time reading a book. Ian Gillan relates that a piecemeal jam ensued, and not some old Purple number, while he sat watching and listening from the corner, feeling damned privileged to be playing with these guys.

"It's luck," added Paice. "Luck and chemistry. As soon as we got back together again, things happened very simply and very easily, no problem. It was a revelation to capture the Mk. II Purple once again. It's very refreshing, the ideas we came up with, the songs we wrote, and now the tour. There really isn't a minus to it. It works. We're having a wonderful time, and we believe people want to see and hear what we're doing."

"It was brilliant," agrees Jon. "It was one of the best years of my life; it was such fun. If you see the video for the song 'Perfect Strangers,' which was filmed when we met up in the studio, the smiles were real and even Ritchie smiled! That was a wonderful year. We had enormous fun writing and making the *Perfect Strangers* album, and the first tour was great. We started at the end of '84 in Australia and appeared at Knebworth in 1985."

Perfect Strangers, issued on October 29, 1984, turned out to be the perfect record for the times, deeply evocative of the band's legacy but also tight, modern, and efficient. Apparently, Blackmore had insisted the band listen to Yes's bright and hard-charging comeback record *90125*, as if to say that this is the standard to which we have to rise. But Purple didn't want to come off as clean as all that. In terms of milieu, the record arrives at the tangle of three nexus points in heavy rock: (1) the New Wave of British Heavy Metal (NWOBHM) was ending, (2) hair metal was starting, and (3) most of the heavy 1970s bands were enjoying pretty decent success because of these two youth movements.

The idea of hiring a big-shot outside producer was raised, but in the end the job fell to the dependable Roger Glover, with vague ideas that the band wanted a *Machine Head* for 1984, rather than something too starkly modern.

"I actually said at the re-formation of the band that I didn't want to be the producer, even though I had the experience," explains Roger. "And I said that we should get someone else in. But Ritchie, who's very astute at times, said, 'It's going

A couple of *Perfect Strangers* promotional items

to be difficult for you not to produce this band, isn't it?' And in effect that was quite right, because I can't just sit back, do my bass part, and go home. So, it started like that, but then the niggles started: this wasn't right or that wasn't right, and I was trying to listen to everybody's point of view. But in the end, I had to say, 'Okay! Either I get to do it my way, or we get somebody else in to do it.' And of course, typically Deep Purple, a decision was never made—we were still having fights about it. But in the end, I did it the way I wanted. You have to be strong as a producer; otherwise it'll go nowhere. As a result, I now feel stronger and better as a writer and a producer than I ever did. It's just unfortunate that I don't feel the same way about my bass playing."

"It is the same rawness that was in the early stuff," said Ian Paice to *Modern Drummer*, back before anyone had heard the album, "but with a passage of ten years, so it's 1980s music instead of 1960s and 1970s music. It's a genuine extension of what we'd done before, just played a little less frantically. We still seem to be getting the rawness and aggression coming through, which is the trademark. I don't know; when I hear the old records, they're still nice, but that was then. I hear what we're doing now, and it's definitely today. It's not a trying-to-live-in-the-past sort of thing. That would be a huge mistake."

Ian also gives his take concerning putting the reunion together. "Basically, what happened was that Jon and I thought there was still a possibility of getting the

Ian Paice, Maple Leaf Gardens, Toronto, Ontario, April 1, 1985. © *Martin Popoff*

Purple thing back together, so we started making quiet inquiries about the interest on the business side amongst record companies, promoters, and such. What we didn't know was that at the same time, Ian, Ritchie, and Roger were doing exactly the same thing in America. Of course, business people do talk to each other, and the next thing I knew, I got a call from the manager of Rainbow saying we were both going at this from different angles on different sides of the Atlantic.

"When we realized that all five of us, in fact, were interested in doing it, we were not going to do it as a nostalgia thing or a hit-and-run job of going out on the road for a year, making a lot of money, and then forgetting about it again. The consensus of opinion was that if we were going to do it, we were going to do it properly—a straight continuation of what we were doing ten years ago. We were going to do it very seriously and look at it as a two-and-a-half-to-three-year project, and that's where we are now. It was most important that we didn't do it just for the money. We had to find out that we still liked each other, and it would work again when we started playing together."

The next stage after the meeting was to set up a rehearsal area for about a month," continues Paice. "We went up to Vermont, where it was quiet, and it worked incredibly well. At that point, we knew there was nothing really to stop us. We got on very well, and the music came very easily again. Before we rehearsed, I was a little apprehensive, wondering if it—meaning us—had changed too much. After a couple of days playing together, it was the same kick. That's the magic that happens, with the possible 'hiccups.' If Ritchie, God bless him, gets a huge buzz on his amp, he'll turn around, take the guitar off, and go home. He says that if he can't play properly, he won't play at all. I'm prepared for that happening this time around, and I should just sit back and let the world go by instead of worrying about it. I'm hoping it won't happen at all, but I have to keep my mind open to the possibilities of things going wrong. The general mood is that optimism is too small of a word. It's very exciting."

Ritchie defended his reputation for practical jokes once the band got over to Hamburg, Germany, for the mix of the album. Partner in hijinks Stuart Smith lives to tell the tale.

"When we arrived at the airport, we rented these four-seater Mercedes; they're like Volkswagens over there—there are tons of them. Roger Glover and Colin Hart, I think, were out with us that night, and they parked in front of us, and it was by this park. And so, Ritchie and I are at the bar, and we decide to go on to another one, but we wanted to do this prank on Roger and Colin. So, we were about to leave, and I got these two girls to go over and talk to Roger and Colin. Just as we were about to leave, they come over and start talking to Roger. So, Roger wanted to stay, because these two good-looking girls were talking to them. We said, 'We're playing a trick; can you keep this up for ten or fifteen minutes, and just talk to them?'

"So, Ritchie and I go out, we get the jack out of our car, and we jacked up Roger and Colin's Mercedes—because it's the same car—and we take the wheels off, and we take them and lay them flat, and then lower the wheel onto the tire, which is lying flat, the hub that holds the wheel, onto the actual wheel itself lying on its side. So, they come out, and the car is totally on sort of the four lying-flat wheels, sideways.

"And some old lady walking a dog saw us doing this and thought that Ritchie and I were stealing the thing, so she called the police. And the police came after we had gone, and they left a message on the windshield saying, 'Someone is trying to steal your car; we've taken the lug nuts; come to the police station.' So, they had to head over to the police station to get the lug nuts, and then they had to go back. And he got to the last wheel they are putting on . . . they got to the last one, and Colin is probably doing all the work. Roger's probably just standing there, the car being jacked up, and he's exhausted, leans against the Mercedes, and crash!—off the jack, onto the wheel, the hub. And they couldn't get the jack out, so they had to get a tow truck out to get the car up to put the wheel on. So, they were up half the night with this practical joke that we pulled."

And while we're on the subject, back in the USA: "I think the last one we did on each other, before we turned our attention to everyone else, was Ritchie thought it would be a great idea to put my apartment up for rent in the *Penny Saver*. He put 'Six room apartment available, overlooking the ocean, call Mr. Smith until 9:00 a.m.,' knowing that I was probably up with him till like four in the morning. So of course I get all these calls, and he thought this was a really fun idea.

"And then when he went on tour with Rainbow, I was looking after his house, feeding the cats and that, and I got to know the local cop. And for my birthday, Ritchie gave me the guitar he used on the solo of 'Stone Cold.' He only used it on the videos for 'Stone Cold' and 'Death Alley Driver,' and so he gave me a guitar. So, I got to know the local cop who patrolled the area, and we became friends. And when Ritchie came back from tour, I said, 'I'll come around for dinner.' And so, I called this cop, and I met him up the road, and we got the guitar, and we put it in the trunk. I got into the back of the cop car, and we drove into Ritchie's driveway. Ritchie saw a cop car with flashing lights, and he went and hid. And his girlfriend, who was in on this thing, said, 'Ritchie, there's someone at the door for you. Ritchie!' And the cop goes to the door, and he says, 'Mr. Blackmore, we pulled over Mr. Smith on Bay Avenue here, and it turns out that in his car he had this guitar, and he says you gave it to him. Is that right?' And he says, 'Yeah, I gave it to him for a birthday present.' 'So, you gave it to him, then?' 'Yeah definitely.'

"And then he says, 'Well, I'm afraid I'm going to have to arrest you then, because it's on the hot sheet as a stolen guitar.' And Ritchie, who hates authority, just . . . and you see him onstage, he never even sweats. Never breaks a sweat. He was dripping! It was so funny, and this cop kept it up for five minutes. Because I told him he was going to try to worm his way out of it and get the management to confirm that it's his guitar.

"So, he brings him over to the police car, and I'm like, 'Great, Ritchie, thanks.' And he says to me, 'Look, you go down to the police station, and we'll sort all this out.' And the cop goes, 'No, no, you don't understand. Mr. Smith is free to go. You're the one who's under arrest.' And he literally kept this up for five minutes, in Ritchie's driveway. And Ritchie is just absolutely sweating at the prospect of having to go to jail. And he's thinking he's going to be there for the weekend, because this is a Friday or something. And so anyway, the cop gets his clipboard out, and he's reading, right? 'You've got the right to remain silent. You've got the right to an attorney.' He's reading something I've written. 'Anything you say will be taken down in writing . . . and advertised against you in the *Penny Saver*.' Ritchie's going, 'Yeah, yeah . . . and then it's like, 'You bastard!' [laughs]."

Stolen guitars notwithstanding, *Perfect Strangers* would go platinum for sales of over a million copies in America four months after its release. The tour—unsurprisingly for these blokes, a world tour—would also be an immense success. More importantly,

Two-page ad for *Perfect Strangers*. *Martin Popoff archive*

despite good-natured tongue-in-cheek wordplay such as "Perfect Wheelchairs," the album was a critical success. The band could hold their head high while performing these anthems on the stages of the world to crowds who, unsurprisingly, were salivating, at least through the early dates, for nothing but the old hits.

But back to the record: the front cover art was a dud. But that enigmatic title . . . it said so much.

"We thought about so many titles," recalls Glover. "We had this one called *Cods Wallop*, but we had passed on the *Perfect Strangers* title until Bruce Payne, our manager, phoned me up in the middle of my sleep one morning. The title came from Ian Gillan, but it's not about the reunion. It's about something different. But when Bruce called me at three o'clock in the morning, saying that he was thinking about it and he couldn't sleep, that *Perfect Strangers* would be a good title for the album, I told him that we had already rejected it. Now, getting a decision out of this band is not the easiest process in the world. There's five people with totally different views of what it should be. It's not the easiest to get together and make sure of some unanimous decision. I told him I'd think about it more, and we called around and we weren't really for it that much, but no one was really against it, so it became a unanimous decision. But in retrospect, the thing is it was a good title for an album. It alluded to the fact that we had been strangers for eleven years. I think it worked out well enough."

Opening track on the record is the lyrically sly and slight but musically much-grander "Knocking at Your Back Door." And with an opening musical sequence themed like a shark attack from *Jaws*, an entering redolent bass line from our resident "teenaged eighth note" bassist, plus a smash of drums from Ian Paice playing as straight as he ever had, Purple for the 1980s was off to the trot. All that was left was for Ritchie to saw his way into the fray with a sublime melody and for Ian to regale us with a bawdy tale of not much consequence, life as an absurd carousel ride, save for the pretty obvious deep and direct meaning of pleasuring oneself when and where one can.

"Well, it's whimsical, it's humorous," points out Ian. "There's this guy named Red Beard, from a radio station down in Texas; he phoned me up after it had been played on every radio station in America and said, 'Is this what I think it's about?' And I said yeah. And he said it's amazing; every radio station in America is playing a song written about anal sex, and they don't even realize what's going on. And I was like, 'Well it's not in-your-face anal sex; it's just a joke.' It just came about with the lyrics. It's no big deal. But it's a humorous thing and not meant to be offensive. And I think it was just an afterthought. It certainly wasn't what inspired the song."

"Great riff! Ritchie really is the riff king!" adds Roger. "We'd had that one for a couple of years; I've got tapes of us jamming over that riff in Rainbow, but we couldn't write anything over it that was satisfactory at that time. Best to save them for another day."

"Knocking at Your Back Door" was issued as the first single from the album, achieving a #61 placement on the Billboard chart and an equally paltry #68 in the UK. Nonetheless, it became a Deep Purple classic, living on in the set for decades and becoming a classic rock-radio staple. Helping its reputation was its placement as the first track on the album, as well as the fact that it was accessible, sensibly structured, and yet lengthy, at over seven minutes, allowing for its conservative hooks to sink in. It was personable enough to serve as a calling card for the album, which got to #17 stateside and a whopping #5 in the UK. Ritchie's solo on this one is one of the most diverse and hook laden of his career; it is also both sweetly musical and brilliantly noise tainted. What's on offer is everything he learned as a guitarist on the three Joe Lynn Turner–era Rainbow albums.

"Under the Gun" reemphasizes many of the signals and characteristics established on the album's sprawling opener. It's set to a similar and similarly simple midpaced bash. Just the right dose of Blackmore's Egypto melodies pulsate in mirrored tandem with Jon Lord's signature Hammond grind. And there's a second tough, wrangled guitar solo in a row from our man Ritchie, who is fortunately hard at work establishing *Perfect Strangers* as the receptacle of some of his most visceral and aggressive soloing ever. And if the first six-string salvo within "Under the Gun" isn't enough, the man's outro jam puts salve to the salivating. It's no surprise that Blackmore often cites "Under the Gun" as his favorite solo guitar performance on the album.

Next up is "Nobody's Home," which deftly marries cowbell party rock with one of Ritchie's twisty, note-dense riffs. Jon Lord follows the scale play while Ian Paice rocks 'n' rolls. Jon takes a nice, traditional Lordy solo before the band collapses back into the song's barroom verse music. "Nobody's Home" is credited to the entire band. It's the only track designated as such, with the balance of the album's tracks credited to Blackmore/Glover/Gillan after a round of hard-won diplomacy approximating the true chain of events. Anyway, we're hard 'n' heavy so far, and with a sameyness that is more comfortable and solid than concerning.

Side 1 of the original vinyl ends with a perfect four for four with respect to wall-of-sound *Machine Head* rock. "Mean Streak" is framed upon a subtle heavy metal shuffle, set to a bobbing bass line from Roger and yet another track of Paicey doing little more than keeping a beat. Like the last song, Ian's on about a woman doing him wrong, while Ritchie expresses himself through fluid runs.

Over to side 2, and the album's title track takes over the record with authority. Jon Lord's organ intro is legion, arguably the most celebrated of his entire canon. It sets the stage for a propulsive rhythm and a rare and interesting situation in which Ian Gillan and his vocal melody is more Egypto or Moroccan (roll) than what Ritchie is doing on the guitar. The usual order of things is restored later, however, when Ritchie turns in a brilliant "Led Zeppelin on steroids" riff bounced over an odd time signature. And if that wasn't a bulging enough bag of goodies, the song's chorus is a seductive inviter, its lush melody and Ian's lyric conveying a certain sense of age-old wisdom, in this case, earned by Deep Purple like that of Fleetwood Mac and that band's interpersonal turmoil.

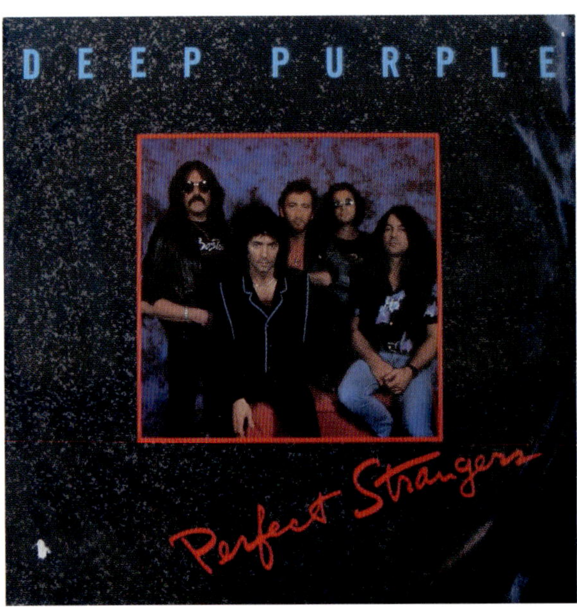

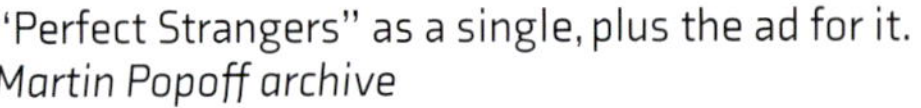
"Perfect Strangers" as a single, plus the ad for it.
Martin Popoff archive

Figures Ritchie, who brought this riff forward from as far back as Rainbow's *Difficult to Cure* sessions, "'Perfect Strangers,' there was a heavy riff that had that kind of chromatic tone that was almost like a kind of heavy Turkish riff, again. In Rainbow, there was 'Gates of Babylon' that I was pleased with. And there's more of a Turkish solo. I've always been interested in Turkish and Egyptian scales, Moroccan scales. I'm trying to remember. But yes, I was always more into the arpeggio classical Vivaldi stuff. So, when it came to a solo, I wasn't so preoccupied with blues. You know, I liked the blues playing of certain people, but I also liked classical music. So, I wasn't 100 percent into blues."

Mused Gillan twenty years on, "'Perfect Strangers' is one of those songs. . . . I was going through all the lyrics that ever meant anything in my life, and I think the idea is that there's a certain amount of self-analysis in 'Perfect Strangers.' It was difficult, the reunion at that time in '83. We had all carried on with our careers, our own music. And in families, you always have rows and disagreements, but there's some kind of spiritual bond or tie to hold you together or at least make you want to give it another shot.

"We were all doing okay individually, but having got together, there were two questions. Individually we were confident with our own abilities and contributions, but there was that nagging doubt: Would it work a second time? And the answer to that was yes and no. And the other thing was, would anybody be interested? And the answer to that also was yes and no. And had we been able to rekindle the flame, with that thing you call, whatever you like, a love affair in torment? I think it might have been great. But there again, if you look at quantum theory, would we be where we are now had we been successful at that time, or would it just have prolonged the agony? I don't know. It's just a different way of looking at it. So, I think what happened with 'Perfect Strangers' and the lyrics, it pretty much told the story of the album and the making of it and the reunion."

When I clarified with Ian whether he thought it was a successful era for the band, he says, "No, I don't think it was successful, really. I think it was pretty commercially successful, but it depends what you value, really. I suppose it was perceived as being successful. I thought it was a period that sowed the seeds of our destruction. And the whole thing exploded, just blew apart, and it was just a miracle that it ever happened again."

But there was indeed a time there when Ian and Ritchie were getting along again.

"Oh yes, with *Perfect Strangers*, that was no problem at all. He had his occasional bark, but I'd bark right back at him in his face. But the relationship was okay. I just wouldn't sing what he wanted me to sing. He wanted me to sing like Joe Lynn Turner [laughs], which, I just used to burst out laughing at him. He didn't like that. He wants his courts to be full of respectful servants. I respect him if he respects me.

"'Perfect Strangers,' I think, is one of the most interesting songs on that record because it was truly about the reunion. And we had changed, our lives had changed, and we were meeting again as if we were perfect strangers. But there's a twist in the tale there, of course, because the perfection actually lay in the fact that the music still existed. The deal we made when we got together for that record was that if the magic wasn't there, we would quietly go back to where we'd come from and carry on with our lives. And that's why we did it in secret, up in Stowe, Vermont. But within five minutes of everyone cranking up in a jam session, I was looking around the room and there were smiles on everyone's faces. I knew then it would be all right."

Stuart Smith says that in the dining room, the band had put up a big sheet of paper on which everyone was invited to add proposed titles for the record. He doesn't recall if *Perfect Strangers* ever made the sheet, but he does recall that "when we were in Germany during the mixing, in Tennessee Ton Studios, Ritchie showed me the lyrics, and he said, 'These are interesting; this is Ian's take on reincarnation.' And I believe that's how all that came about."

Even if the heart says that "Perfect Strangers" is the album's best track (it is pretty much a catalog favorite of Roger Glover's as well), the head might pick "A Gypsy's Kiss." This one picks up the pace, with Ritchie turning in an action-packed, note-dense riff somewhat akin to "Burn" and other "circular" riffs of his canon, such as "Lady Double Dealer," "Sensitive to Light," or "Danger Zone." But then he steps back for the verse, at which time Ian spits his venom over angled textures from Jon Lord. Come solo time, Blackmore impossibly turns up the stuttering aggression and then gangs up with Jon Lord in classical mode. Then he gives way to Jon, with the immortal "Highway Star" solo construct coming inspiringly to mind.

Finally, nearing the end of the damn record, it's ballad time, with "Wasted Sunsets" somewhat dropping the ball on the quality end of things. It's as if the band is exhausted by the bluster of the previous six tracks or, conversely, has collapsed into benches at the airport. In fact, Deep Purple never excelled at the standard ballad thing, although that's not to say they haven't written some pretty songs of a softer nature, with the best results achieved once Steve Morse joins. This one, however, sounds a little too safe toward what might have been expected of a power ballad in the high-pressure mid-1980s. In congruence with the rest of the album, it's conservative.

Ian, however, has always been quite fond of "Wasted Sunsets," even if most of the lyrics were actually Roger's. "Well, it's a fantastic ballad," begins Gillan. "We always, Roger and I, wanted to do it with Deep Purple, but Ritchie wouldn't do it. I'd say that's a drinking song. 'One too many wasted sunsets.' And I think probably the analogy there is to do with previous band breakups."

The album proper winds up with "Hungry Daze," a tight, coy, halting rocker that wouldn't be out of place on the odd-man-out Rainbow redux album, *Stranger in Us All*. Surely, it's back to the rockers, but this one's more like Egypto pop, given its pert rhythmic advancement. The lyric is an autobiographical reminiscence of sorts, with a classy, complicated instrumental passage reinventing psychedelic rock for an age supportive of synthesizers and other glossed-up studio tricks.

The headbanging minions, fully bulging at the time and feasting on the waning years of the NWOBHM, were ready for this new Purple proposal. And so was the press. Wrote John Swenson from *Circus*, "If Purple had faltered on *Perfect Strangers*, the buzzards would have picked their bones clean before you could say 'boring old fart.' Obviously, the group was mindful of the challenge, because *Perfect Strangers* is the most calculated album Deep Purple has ever made. While the record is not exactly nostalgic, there is no risk-taking; the band plays carefully to its strengths. *Perfect Strangers* works. Blackmore proves once again that he sounded better with the Deep Purple rhythm section hurtling along with him than he ever did on his own. Jon Lord's organ work rivals the finest moments of his past. Bassist Roger Glover and drummer Ian Paice actually sound better than ever together, in part due to Glover's increasingly formidable production skills. Ian Gillan's voice has become richer over the years, so those high-pitched shrieks now have less edge but more feeling. The Deep Purple of *Machine Head* was fueled in part by bitter fighting among group members over musical direction. On this record, those same musicians actually sound as if they're enjoying each other's company."

And despite its aversion to hard rock, the venerable *Rolling Stone* couldn't ignore such a milestone event, even if Deb Frost's review was less than effusive.

"Excepting the title cut and the rambunctious but less effective 'Knocking at Your Back Door,' the material consists of hastily knocked-off jams that allow guitar demigod Ritchie Blackmore to whip out his finger exercises in public. The band spent about six to eight weeks recording this comeback. It doesn't sound as if they spent much more time thinking about it either. Blackmore's Strat has such a great roar that you're willing to just let it reverberate in your eardrums for a bit. And it's nice to hear Jon Lord's unsynthesized organ squalls, Ian Paice's meaty pounding, Gillan's howls and whispers, and Roger Glover's solid bass lines once again. Even though, it's 'enough of the soundcheck already—where are the songs?' Instead of Glover, an outside producer might have forced the band to tighten up its licks and arrangements. Then again, did Deep Purple ever have more than one or two really good, concise numbers on an album? Maybe they're just making the kind of record they always did, the only kind they know how to make."

Two additional tracks revolved around the album proper. "Not Responsible," used as a remastered CD bonus track, is a hefty metal rocker with a couple of speeds and a grinding presence bolstered by a growly Gillan vocal. Again, Ritchie is impressive come solo time, putting a stamp on 1984 as arguably his best year at this component of his game.

"Son of Alerik," on the other hand, is a lengthy instrumental, disciplined enough but essentially a jam. Roger says that it was cooked up on the spot as the band was waiting to get on with the business of making a video. Mischievously, the band was making the video crew wait and wait while this song, it was hoped, was about to come to an end. The song was issued as a B side to the "Perfect Strangers" 12-inch, only in the UK and Canada, and exists also as a 7-inch single version.

As alluded to, the tour for *Perfect Strangers* has to be viewed as a success. There was indeed a great deal of appetite for the reunion. First off, reunions weren't as legion as they are today; second, metal was big; and third, this was a rock-solid classic lineup reunion with nary a substitute. "Destiny brought them together again" was the hyperbole used on a sticker affixed to the cellophane on the front of the record, as well as on the face of the tour program. And even though David Coverdale had joked that "overdrafts brought them together again," the boys did indeed pull together a ripper of an album, followed by an energy-filled, sold-out tour of everywhere.

Purple started their traipsing in Australia and New Zealand, where, even before the rest of the band arrived, Ritchie got in trouble by starting a noise war with a hotel—along with the bodyguard of one of its guests, Eric Clapton.

"Yeah, that was my idea," recalls Stuart Smith. "I believe that was at the Hyatt in Perth. Ritchie and I checked in, and we said, 'Look, we want a floor that is reasonably quiet. We sleep in late, and we don't want to be kept up by the disco until four in the morning, and we don't want to be woken up by the cleaning crew at seven in the morning.' So, they put us on the top floor, all very well, until the morning comes, and they neglect to tell us they're doing construction on the hotel, and they start these jackhammers at seven o'clock in the morning. And we were, I mean, just pissed! We asked for other rooms, and on that day, they were full up or something, and I mean, the next day we were woken up again. And this is like a nightmare. Especially if you've done that flight from New York all the way to Australia. Exhausted.

"So, we complained about this and said, 'Look, can they start later?' 'Oh no, sir.' And they've got the signs all over the hotel saying, 'For your convenience.' They'd

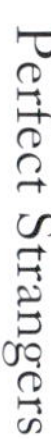

The "Deep Purple Open Air '85" show at Maimarktgelände, Mannheim, Germany, June 29, 1985. Also playing were Rodgau Monotones, Roger Chapman, Mountain, and Meat Loaf. © *Wolfgang Gürster*

done it like, 'Renovations Starring the Construction Crew' and all this sort of thing. They had these notices all over the hotel. And we're just pissed off about this. So, we actually did find one room in the middle of the hotel, and we rented it in the name of Mr. J. Sessions. Jam Sessions. And we got to know a load of the locals. Because every time we fly into a place, we'd meet them after the show and say, 'Hey, do you want to play soccer the next day?' It would be the band against a load of fans. And so, we talked these fans that we met at this music store into bringing in all this equipment, drum kits and Marshall stacks, into this hotel room in the middle of the hotel. So, they set it up, and Ritchie and I are out drinking and having a good time. We come back to the hotel at about three o'clock in the morning, and we bring these local musicians in and have one of the roadies hold the doors: 'Don't let anyone in!' Charlie, I think it was.

"And so, we just started playing. And this is three o'clock in the morning. For some reason, we thought we would just let the hotel know what it's like to be woken up like us, in our twisted drunk way of thinking. So anyway, after about five minutes of this, the door is suddenly almost coming off the hinges. Charlie opens it, and there's the biggest guy you've seen in your life comes in, in his jeans, and he looks at us and goes, 'One more note and there's going to be trouble.' And we're like, holy shit! What we didn't realize was that the room we booked . . . in the room next door was Eric Clapton, who was playing the next night. And that was his bodyguard, Alfie, who thought that we were doing this to wake up Eric.

"So anyway, in the morning . . . and what we'd done as well, is that Ritchie—it's very funny—he'd written out this thing, copying the hotel's sort of notice that they put up, 'For your convenience.' He wrote, 'For your general annoyance, and for our profit, we are reconstructing the hotel, starring the.' It was very funny the way he worded it. And we had the girls at the desk . . . they photocopied about fifty of these and stuck them all over the elevators. And in the morning, the next day, we're coming down to leave, and there's Alfie, Eric Clapton's bodyguard, sitting there. We went over and said, 'Look, we're sorry about that. It wasn't meant for you.' And we explained about the construction crew, and he said, 'Oh, I know; they woke me up as well.' So, he was cool about it."

Stuart says that in Australia, well-regarded hard-boiled boogie band Rose Tattoo was the opening act, not that Angry Anderson and the boys got to rub shoulders with Purple very much.

"Not really. I mean, Ritchie didn't hang out. And he would stay sort of separate from the band, from anyone connected with us, really. Ritchie and I would go off on our own. And occasionally we would go out with Roger Glover, Ian Paice, and Colin Hart. And we did a few séances. Jon Lord was with us for a séance once. But we didn't really hang out with too many of the bands. I remember Ritchie would always like to go out and see the opening acts, sit and watch them for a while before he went onstage, to get himself in the mood. And I remember once he was out without his pass. I was with him, and I'd said I was going to go back and have a drink or something. I walked back, and it's getting like ten minutes before they're due to go on [laughs], and Ritchie walked back, and the guy wouldn't let him in. It was one of those old guys who would've been in the theater for years and years. He's got his uniform and his cap and he's saying, 'Well, I'm sorry; no pass, you can't get in here' [laughs]. There was this whole hullabaloo, and I came out and said, 'No, no, no—he's the guitarist of the band.' [laughs]."

There were "a lot of women," says Stuart, and pretty much by design. "That's right. One of the ideas that I had was that when we first arrived in Perth, I had met this model on the plane, and she gave me her card, and it had her modeling agency on there. So, when we arrived—I'm trying to think if it was the next day or the day after—I called the modeling agency and I said, 'Yes, I ran into one of these girls on the plane, and she said they would like to come to the show. So, we'd like to invite any of your models as our guests, for the show.' And so, the backstage was just besieged with beautiful girls [laughs]. I tell you what: this became a thing I would do every time we flew into a different place. I would open a Yellow Pages and find a local model agency in town and invite the girls. So, the backstage was like a Victoria Secret show."

Another Aussie story revolves around having George Harrison (a close chum of Jon Lord) join the band onstage for a solid but long rendition of 'Lucille,' with the quiet Beatle in pink jacket punching out a nicely phrased solo and the whole band bopping and bobbing along. Recalls Stuart, "Yes, that was in Sydney. I remember, the band was playing, and I ran backstage for something. I don't remember what it was, but I ran into the bathroom and knocked George flying. He was coming out of the bathroom. He was very cool: 'Hi, I'm George.' 'Hi, I'm Stuart.'"

After eleven dates in Australia and one in New Zealand (two of three New Zealand dates were canceled), it was America for forty-two dates, plus six in Canada, commencing January 18, 1985, in Odessa, Texas, with Giuffria as support. Next, in May 1985, the band racked up seven shows in Japan, followed by June and July spent in Europe, where the highlight was a very wet Knebworth festival headlining gig on June 22 in front of 70,000. Mountain, Meat Loaf, Scorpions, UFO, Mama's Boys, Blackfoot, and Alaska were also part of that party. Finally, after a month off in the summer, straddling July and August, the *Perfect Strangers* tour came to an end back in the USA, final gig being the Texxas Jam in Dallas on August 24, where the Purps were joined by Scorpions, Ted Nugent, Night Ranger, Bon Jovi, Victory, and Grim Reaper. At one point, Ian received the news that the American portion of the tour alone had grossed $7 million.

With respect to the set list, Purple was as playfully ragged as they had been in the 1970s, with most songs including jokey little tossed-off bits of popular and classical music, resulting in endless light relief (and come solo time, hot-dog breaks).

"There's always something different going on," figured Roger circa 1985, nonplussed at infiltrating the classics with comedic asides. "I can't stand to see bands that have rehearsed to such perfection that they're like machines. You know, at a certain point in a song—maybe halfway through the chorus—they'll walk to a certain spot on the stage and then they'll be picked up by one of the lights. And they'll always acknowledge the crowd at certain points, or the lights will be put on the crowd at certain points. It's too worked out. I've seen too many bands like that, and that's really only cabaret. That's not live music. I think rock 'n' roll is live music. It's living and breathing as you play it and is subject to change."

On the material and quantifiable side, most of the expected classics were there, while from the new album, one could variously hear "Under the Gun," "A Gypsy's Kiss," "Nobody's Home," "Knocking at Your Back Door," and the title track. All told, it was a triumph. although with slivers of doubt around whether the guys could keep it together, and even doubts expressed in the previously cited record reviews, this idea that as efficient as *Perfect Strangers* was, it was still a little bit safe, something this band emphatically in the past was never about. These very same doubts were cast upon Black Sabbath with respect to *Heaven and Hell.* As great as that record was, it was at least lightly denigrated as a bit commercial and even "dumbed down" compared to the creative explosion that pockmarked the Ozzy-era albums. Judas Priest stepped into this as well with *British Steel.* Still, the circumstances surrounding Purple obviously differed. A decade of the music business had whizzed by since Mk. II had last worked together, and that's an eternity of hard rock. These were five old rockers significantly changed over the years, with each having made a boatload of music in the interim.

Speaking with the eminent Geoff Barton from *Kerrang!* back in 1984, Ritchie expressed a level of satisfaction with safeness, or at least consistency.

"You see, I've always admired AC/DC," begins Blackmore. "I don't like them particularly as a band, but they've stuck steadfast to their own brand of straightforward music through thick and thin. To my mind, when they first started out, AC/DC sounded incredibly dated, but then suddenly the rock 'n' roll world turned full circle, and the band took off. And that was just great. They kept hanging on to their principles until the right time came along. In a way, you can draw a parallel between Purple and AC/DC. We're just going to go out and do what we're best known for, which is playing sophisticated rock, not heavy metal. And hopefully there will be a few people out there who will like it. Maybe it's got to the point where the public is just so sick of disco music; I don't know. Perhaps the time is right for Deep Purple once again. It's almost as if no one will dare play our kind of music anymore. It would be nice to think that we can convert a few people back into liking hard rock instead of feeling that they have to dance to everything."

Japanese tour poster

Asked by Geoff whether virtuosity was lacking among Purple's competitors, Ritchie says, "Uh huh. Without wishing to revel in my own artistic values, there is an art to playing heavy rock 'n' roll. It's no use just cranking up the volume and being loud; there is a trick to it. There are dynamics and certain progressions that you can play, but you don't hear much of that today. I think Van Halen are interesting. I don't particularly like them as a band, but there is a lot of movement, a lot of color to the material they produce. Led Zeppelin too; now they probably defined the term 'sophisticated rock' with things like 'Kashmir' and certain scales they would hit—that was incredible."

Barton noted that Ritchie once hoped that *Perfect Strangers* would be as good a comeback project as *90125* by Yes.

"Well, who wouldn't want to return with as strong as album as *90125*? It's a great record, it's got a superb sound, and I like Trevor Rabin. One of the best guitar solos I've heard in a long time is 'Owner of a Lonely Heart.' That actually moved me. It made a real change to hear someone actually doing something adventurous with a guitar, instead of just running frantically up and down the fingerboard and saying, 'Wow, impressive, huh?' The sound of that guitar synthesizer is very exciting, also. So much so that I actually went out and bought one."

Would he have liked Trevor Rabin to have handled the production of *Perfect Strangers*? "I'm not so sure," says Ritchie. "We did think about various producers, but in the end, we said no, let's get Roger to do it. We don't want a glossy sound. We want the album to be an '80s version of *Machine Head*. And I'm quite pleased with the end result. I think we've struck the right chord."

"I really don't know exactly what I think of the album at this moment in time," counters Roger, in the same piece. "Normally, I can't listen to any LP I've made until it's been on release for about six or seven years. Only then can I start to give it any kind of serious, honest appraisal. Having said that, I thought, I must admit, I never liked much of what Deep Purple did in the old days, anyway! I never thought it was that special. I had a great time with the band and all that, but I could never understand why people bought the records. But that's just me being supercritical, I guess.

"I was sure that the first album and tour would generate an enormous amount of interest based solely on curiosity. And to me, for a band to simply capitalize on this curiosity value is not a good enough reason to re-form. What we needed was sufficient strength and motivation to go beyond that, to make people buy the second album and see the second tour. It sounds absurd, I know, but we're in the strange position of knowing we're going to be successful. It's whether we can carry it through the next time around. That's the real crux of the matter.

"For six years or so, I'd been fighting vehemently against it. I went into the initial meeting we held in, at most, a kind of 50/50 frame of mind. But when we finally sat around the table, all five of us—this sounds stupid—but almost immediately I could detect a certain magic feeling, a definite spark of excitement in the air. And so, I quickly went from 50/50 to about 70/30. And then after we'd spent some time playing together, I became 100 percent in favor, really; it felt that good.

"The parting of the Mk. II lineup was not pleasant," continues Glover. "It was fraught with all kinds of tensions. But I guess it always felt . . . put it this way, it's kind of like when you're eating a meal halfway through, someone takes your plate away, and you're still hungry. I suppose I felt with Purple that deep in my heart, I wanted to finish that meal, but in the back of my mind, I thought it might be a mistake, because the meal might have turned cold. Ha! This analogy is getting beyond me. The real reason I'm here now is because I enjoyed myself when we first met and jammed together, and I felt that, yeah, we had something good to say.

"Purple is like an old love affair, and love can be very close to hate. We've had our good and bad times, and yes, I'm sure that this will be the case once again this time around. But there's got to be friction. There's nothing worse than being surrounded by a bunch of yes men, yessing themselves to death. Friction was the thing that caused this band to split in 1973, but friction was also the thing that gave us the success we enjoyed in 1973. Like I say, it's love and hate. When it's love, it'll be good. When it's hate, it'll probably be disastrous."

In the end, there was magic and excitement around the guys very much making a success of the reunion. Whether they could pull it off a second time remained to

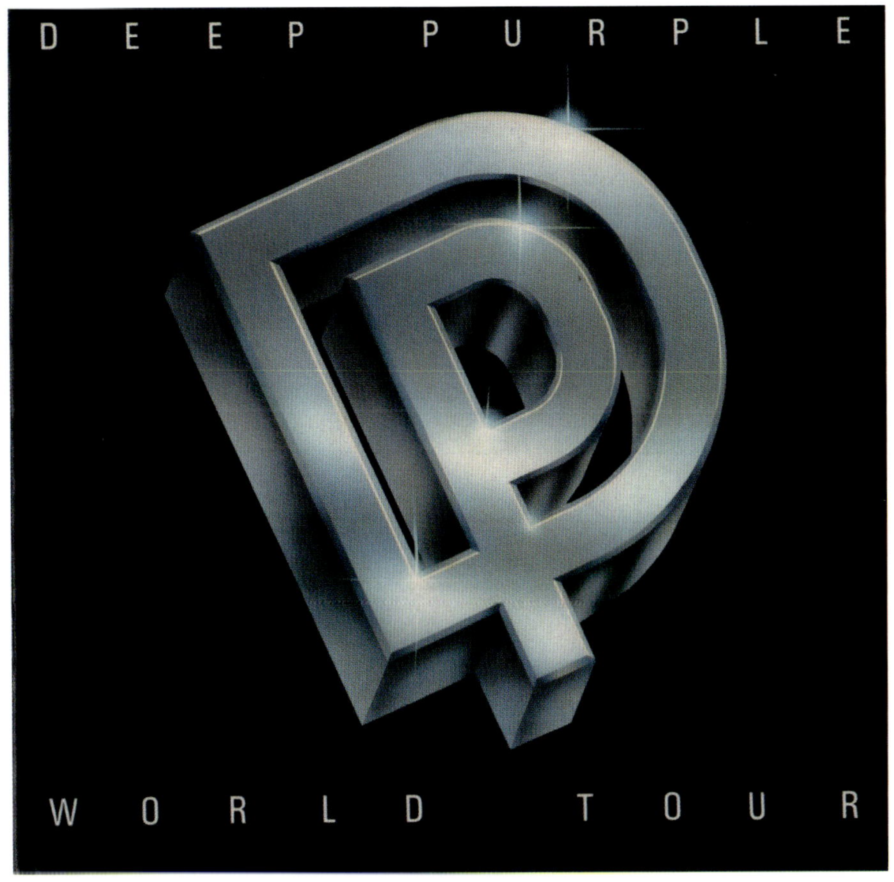

Tour book plus a trio of backstage passes

be seen. The solid footing supplied by *Perfect Strangers* and the subsequent ambitious tour would be tested, not only by the pressure to produce an even better follow-up album, but by the reality of so many brasher, younger bands doing huge numbers in the suddenly exploding heavy metal realm. To be sure, Purple never wanted to compete with anything as base as heavy metal, but the choice wasn't exactly theirs—fans decide who fits in what camp. And with storming records such as *Perfect Strangers*—one ballad among the lot—it wasn't exactly as if Purple were disowning heavy metal, even if both Ian Gillan and Roger Glover continued to disparage it.

Chapter 16

The House of Blue Light

"We were going into a nosedive with Ritchie in the band."

With *The House of Blue Light*, we're right back into that somewhat maddening compartmentalization that goes on with both Ian Gillan and Roger, but more so with Roger, of Purple albums falling into pairs of an easy album to make turning out good, followed by a difficult album to make turning out bad. And so it goes that with the follow-up to *Perfect Strangers*, the band was once again bickering. Roger and Ian accused Ritchie of being dismissive of their work, while Ritchie accused Ian of too much carousing and not keeping his eye on the ball.

"*Perfect Strangers* is a good record; *House of Blue Light*, I can live without," says Paicey. "Again, with *Perfect Strangers*, there was harmony in the band, everybody was really excited about getting together, and the ideas flowed. Ritchie was . . . he was workable. He wasn't easy all the time, but he was workable. And the thing between Ian and Ritchie had totally subsided; everything was sweetness and light. *House of Blue Light* was very difficult. The old animosities were starting to rear their ugly heads. Some of the music that Ritchie was insisting we play was not probably as good as we would have liked it, and it was starting to get to the point where if somebody else did have an idea, Ritchie wasn't very interested in listening to it. So, I don't look at that record with any great fondness at all—*Perfect Strangers*, I do."

Asked what the paramount problem was between Blackmore and Gillan, Ian figures, "They see life two different ways. Ritchie's picture of the world is totally different to Ian's. The difference between the two people is Ian doesn't mind that Ritchie sees the world differently from him. Ritchie does mind that Ian does see the world differently to him.

"*House of Blue Light* was a horrible album to make," recalls Gillan, with a palpable shudder. "It was horrible. I mean, professionally we can all do our craft. We can craft songs, we can write, we can perform, we can get through it. That doesn't mean to say the spirit's in it. There are a couple of albums like that, which I think have good material. *House of Blue Light* and the *Who Do We Think We Are!* period . . . they're quite similar. To me, they're cold. I never play them. I just don't get a good feeling

Ian versus Ritchie, Monsters of Rock,
Pforzheim, Germany, August 30, 1987.
© *Wolfgang Gürster*

from them. I hear the songs every now and again, and I know they're okay. I like the songs, but I don't pick the albums up and fondle them with affection, like I do some of the other stuff. I occasionally take these records out and say, 'That feels good.' I can feel the spirit on them, but those ones, I wouldn't call success. That period, I would call it a qualified success, really. It's like looking at an album of holiday photographs when you just had one miserable time and everyone's arguing, and it's been raining from the beginning to the end. But of course, there were magic times there.

"So, *House of Blue Light* was a hard record to make. I look back at the Purple career, and you know, the band are good musicians, they're professional writers and performers and whatever, and you never go into the studio thinking you are going to do anything other than your best. You give 100 percent. But this was a horrible situation; it was not pleasant, like I say, just like *Who Do We Think We Are!* or *Battle Rages On* for that matter. I'll tell you; it was recorded in Stowe, and it was damn difficult. *Perfect Strangers*, we were all on our best behavior, and it was quite nice to be back together again.

"But I've got to tell you: Ritchie . . . talk about the fly in the ointment; he was troublesome during the recording of *The House of Blue Light*. We came up with songs like 'Mitzi Dupree,' which Ritchie hated, but Roger and I thought it was so refreshing. We captured something that was just a jam one day. 'It was in the wrong key' and blah blah blah [laughs]. And I thought, well, Roger and I were writing the lyrics, getting so involved in the whole thing, and Ritchie said, 'Oh, it's crap!' and it shouldn't be on the record. I mean, I used to room with Ritchie in the '60s and '70s. I have a great deal of affection for him as a guy, but we've had some difficult times. I don't want to go into all of that. I wish him well, really. But we were going into a nosedive with Ritchie in the band. We were approaching terminal velocity. Absolutely. We were aiming for the ground."

Ian has also acknowledged that he was being difficult as well, and Ritchie heartily seconds that, saying that it was the other way around—if he had an idea, then Ian would quash it. In any event, between the two, Ian said he could see a "nervousness" creeping into the situation, with Jon Lord noting that the writing was beginning to be brought in separately. "It started again during the recording of the next album," recalls Jon, of the rift. "Things began to crack again."

Still, not to be contrarian, but this writer finds that *The House of Blue Light* sounds more worked upon, and that doesn't necessarily make for a bad record. *Perfect Strangers* sounds like the demos of *The House of Blue Light*, rawer and thus less readied, although in total it's a better, more deliberate batch of songs. But there's more detail here, more to munch on to lasting effect, even if studio craft doesn't exactly compensate for the diminished songcraft.

"I mean, I'd love to remix it, actually," says Roger, somewhat refuting this premise proposed. "Actually, there are a lot more good ideas on *House of Blue Light* than there is on *Perfect Strangers*. *Perfect Strangers* has held up as a great album, but I don't think it is. I think it's just got a couple of killer tracks on it, and it was of the moment. There's a lot of throwaway stuff that we could've done better."

Hitting Ian Gillan up with the idea that *The House of Blue Light* sounds more polished than its predecessor, he responds that "the '80s seemed to be the time of big productions. It really was a time where people were concerned with sound. I'd have to say, to a certain extent, that this was the state of uncertainty. I look back on those times and I think what happened. What I thought happened in the '80s is that people lost musical identity, and production took over, radio took over. Music became diminutive; production became larger. 'This is a Bob Rock production' or whatever. Everybody was concerned with how they could get access to a certain sound."

But yes, the band was back at Stowe, after looking into other locales—perhaps this was akin to going back with the high school sweetheart. The Mobile was used once again, this time at the town's Playhouse, with mixing to take place at Union Studios at the hands of Roger and Harry Schnitzler. Once again, the production credit went to Roger Glover and Deep Purple.

"We basically ran out of time in Stowe, Vermont, because we were using the Playhouse," recalls Blagona, who was engineering. "The Playhouse is traditionally empty in Stowe, Vermont, until the latter part of the summer, when they start rehearsing for their theater groups. Roger had a studio down in the basement, but we just decided to . . . because of the complexity of it, we continued doing voice-

DEEP PURPLE

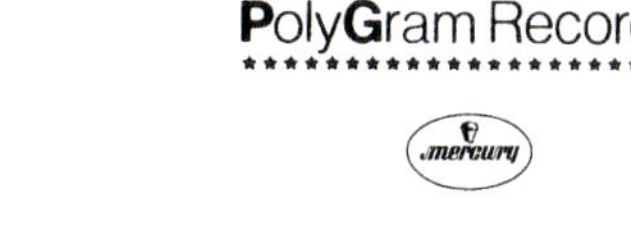

A couple of label promo pictures from this period

overs at Roger's house. So, Ian and I drove through the New Hampshire / New England area down to Greenwich, and Guy Charbonneau, who owned the truck, still owns the truck, drove it down, and we all met down there, and we hooked it up, continued working through that particular summer.

"I've never been witness to the conflicts that Ian and Ritchie had," says Nick, staying out of that particular rat's nest. "I didn't ask any questions, so I don't know what went on. I just enjoyed Ian's company a lot, and Ritchie's company to a degree. I usually stayed away from him, because he was very much a manipulator, you know. I mean, the joke about Ritchie is that the reason that Ritchie was such an asshole is because he was in his preminstrel period [laughs].

"Everybody had their foibles, and Ritchie definitely had some very strange foibles, but Ian was down to earth, and I've never seen anybody have major arguments. It was all done very subtly. It was none of my business, and I never got into why. I never asked questions, because as an engineer, I usually don't get involved in this. Even if they asked me to get involved, I never did. It was just personality conflicts. Ian is my dear friend, and I don't understand what the problem was, because I got along with Ritchie too. Roger and I were already close friends from our time with Rainbow, and Roger and I sort of hung out together, and I stayed with him in Greenwich, Connecticut. So, we had a very close relationship. And then as soon as I met Ian, it was of course love at first sight—we got along like ghost busters. So, it's a very long time that we've known each other."

As the guys have said, making the record, in the fall of 1986, two years and a bit after a more pleasant Stowe stay, was a chore. Roger and Ian set up their own windowless playhouse within the Playhouse. A minor war had erupted over 'Mitzi Dupree,' and the final version of it had to be the original demo, due to Ritchie's lack of cooperation on rerecording it. Ian says that everyone had thrown in the towel well before the record was done, and that Roger and himself tucked tail and took what they had to Roger's home in Greenwich, Connecticut. With the recording mobile parked out back, Nick presiding, he and Rog finished "Mad Dog," "The Spanish Archer," "The Unwritten Law," and "Bad Attitude." It was then up to Roger to mix the thing, which he did under extreme stress at Union Studios in Germany. All told, the album took triple the time it took to crank out its predecessor, roughly April until August, with the mix happening in late September.

"We started recording in Massachusetts," explained Paice, on the press trail. "But the place we were working in was a little too rural for us. There were no bars open past ten in the evening, and the place we were staying had four beautiful rooms, but only one bathroom. So, we decided to go back to Stowe, Vermont. Originally, we hadn't wanted to do that because we didn't want to have the ghosts of the last album hanging over our heads. But we managed to get going, even if it did take us a great deal of time. The results are some of the best we've ever gotten."

"The last album was quite easy for us to do," added Lord, also back in 1987. "We got a couple of tracks like 'Knocking at Your Back Door' done right away, and from there it was easy. This time we had a lot more difficulty getting the material together. We spent three and a half months in the studio, which is much longer than we normally do. We go by the law of diminishing returns; the more time we spend on a particular track getting it right, the less energy there is. We'd gotten a lot of material together almost a year ago, but when we got back together and listened to it again, we realized it wasn't that good. So, we had to start from scratch.

"Our basic sound is very simple," continued Jon. "It's all based on guitar and Hammond organ. Of course, we do things with those sounds that are interesting, and we utilize them in good songs, but the sound itself is simple. I think we're the best at that particular style, and we feel very comfortable with it. On the new album, we brought in a few new elements, such as having Ritchie play guitar synth. But the bottom line is that musically we'll never stray too far from home."

"Why should we?" agreed Paice. "We've been very successful with that sound, and we're quite happy with it. The idea of changing just for the sake of experimentation seems a bit silly to us. Nobody else sounds like Deep Purple, though many have tried. We have something unique and special, so why shouldn't we keep it?"

"They're great. I mean, they played well, and my job was just to capture the right feel soundwise," says Nick, intimating that the actual recording of *The House of Blue Light* wasn't as onerous as the guys remember it. "You know, it was all very simple. There was never anything very complicated—at all. *House of Blue Light* was easy to record; it was just a very long process of choosing songs, getting rid of songs, redoing songs. It was pretty screwed up."

I asked Nick if songs were completely jettisoned and replaced.

"No, they were the same songs. They just couldn't get the feel right. And Ritchie was very obstinate about not liking this, not liking that, whereas the rest of the band liked it and so forth. So, they basically acquiesced to Ritchie. I guess that's where the conflict happened. So, we just spent long hours redoing songs. I never asked questions. As long as they paid me—which they paid handsomely—I didn't complain. My job was to record. And sure, I was very creative as an engineer. I'm coming up constantly, even today, with new sounds. Even today I tend to push the envelope in an engineering sense."

And, says Nick, there was no talk of direction or mission with Purple. "No, never. They knew what the direction was—it was a guitar/Hammond sound. They had a sound, and every member of the band contributed to the sound because of who they were. There were never any discussions at all when anybody sat around for dinner or went to the pub. They knew pretty well; it was all set in stone."

Wrapped in another cheap record cover, *The House of Blue Light* was labeled with a title recycled from the lyrics to "Speed King." That in itself is no disaster, but Roger did regret that it was a lukewarm choice after the fact, given that he always liked to be inspired by a predisposed—and, he hoped, conceptually unifying—title all through the record-making process.

In any event, *The House of Blue Light* starts on a dramatic note. "Bad Attitude" opens with Jon Lord pastiching the emotional palette of his "Knocking at Your Back Door" and "Perfect Strangers" intros. The song proper is menacing, much like "Perfect Strangers," even providing a similar Middle Eastern–toned break structure, although this time buttressed by more-modern synthesizer sounds all around (not unlike Robert Plant on *The Principle of Moments*). Indeed, these were positives and not negatives, with the band exploring '80s production values and coming off class instead of crass.

"'Bad Attitude,' sure, I remember the video," laughs Gillan. "It was the best video we ever made. That was after recording it, of course. But it started out at a football match. Ritchie was playing up front, and I was in goal, and I let in a couple of goals, and he hadn't scored any, and we were down 2–0. I missed a goal, let in a goal, and

Sweet color ad for *The House of Blue Light*, along with a Japanese issue of the album

The US 12-inch promo version of "Bad Attitude"

he shouted something about my goalkeeping abilities, and I screamed at him up pitch, and he turned around and said to me, 'You've got a bad attitude!' And I was like, well, when you score a couple of goals, you can make some constructive criticism about my goalkeeping ability, but as of yet, you haven't scored a damn goal. Actually, it was a little more ferocious than that [laughs]."

"The Unwritten Law" ranks even further up the production scale, with Purple going for additional very modern synth patterns, a rare tribal beat, and even a moderate drum solo to close the track. Still, its highlight is the manic syncopated jazz scat of the intro. Roger recognized this composition as the most progressive thing the band had written to date, with Gillan explaining to *Kerrang!*'s Mark Putterford that it's "about the clap. I mean, there is a code, know what I mean? If you've got a dose, you don't go spreading it around. It's a general comment on how people should have a little more responsibility. We tried to think of other unwritten codes to include in the song, but I can't think of any at the moment! I nearly killed Ritchie when I heard that riff—it's the most difficult riff I've ever had to write for. I was going 'round for ages going 'diddle-id, diddle-id' behind his back. Still, it's a different vehicle, and that's one of the great things with this album—without doubt it's my favorite album since *Fireball*."

"Call of the Wild" finds the band in barroom rock mode, rollicking along, using that guitar/keyboard chemistry, Ian rattling on about fast women, and the whole band colluding on a shameless pop chorus. "Yeah, that's a telephone call about this bird," says Gillan. "Oh, it's a cheap pun, really, but it's an interesting lyric and it has an interesting chorus. We thought it was too soft and sloppy at first—it nearly got rejected, strangely enough—but when it was finished, it seemed to have a nice edge to it. It sounds like some of the more accessible songs Purple have done in the past."

Pedestrian to be sure, but a valid direction, or pit stop, along the versatile trajectory of songs that Purple offer up on any given day. The label viewed the song as a single, with Roger calling it a tribute to 1950s rock 'n' roll, although the resemblance is many times removed (thank God). Quips Ian, "Unfortunately the worst with 'Call of the Wild' was the ridiculous million-dollar video we made in New York. It was a simple song, really. Man, I wish I had the lyrics in front of me, but now you're talking about good music, nice song!

"That's got to be about the management," laughs Ian, asked about "Mad Dog," a classy rocker with new guitar tones and indeed novel phrasing from Ritchie. This one's a quick rocker, but once again in the band's strangely relaxed style, as witnessed across both of the first two reunion records, especially rhythmically. Look for the

Assorted "Call of the Wild" configurations

starkly futuristic synth solo from Jon on this one, but also a slippery bit of work from Ritchie late in the sequence.

"Black & White" kicks off with Ian on harmonica (no guest stars needed—Nick says that the only "ringers" Purple ever used were professional German footballers!), with the song percolating along like a cross between "Hush" and "Hungry Daze." "One of my favorites on *House of Blue Light*," says Glover. "Strange how you go against the fans. It gets panned a lot by the hard-core fans. I absolutely love it; I think it's a great song. I don't understand what they don't like about it—killer groove, great lyric; it's a really unusual tune. It's got a lot going for it, and no one likes it. I guess I must be wrong."

Lyrically, the track is a smart, enigmatic analysis of the press and how the truth isn't automatically what falls out of their scribbles. Or as Ian puts it, "That's about newspapers, you know, the newspapers that I love so dearly, the filthy press, as I call them." Indeed, Purple always got their fair share of barbs from the press, but in getting to know the guys, you get a sense that their concerns are more elevated than those revolving around their petty rock career. Readers, they are, and there are bigger fish to fry than the errant ramblings of pronouncers on Deep Purple records. Incidentally, "Black & White" was one of the record's proposed or working titles (or both), with more-casual ones being *The Acid Test* and *It's Not That Bad!*

After the "Speed King" reference in the album title, "Hard Lovin' Woman" constitutes a second tribute to the band's seminal *In Rock* album, with that record containing a blitzing, ground-zero metal rocker called "Hard Lovin' Man." This isn't quite that classic, but the song's somewhat pedestrian, circular arch-Blackmore riff gives way to what is a pretty cool verse arrangement. Plus, it's fast, if not entirely convincing, given the naff lyric. Actually, the lyrics emerged from the song's title, "Hard Lovin' Woman" being one of many titles Roger and Ian had written up on the wall inside their makeshift workspace / war room / skunk works.

"That means El Bow, as in if you give somebody the El Bow," laughs Ian, succinctly summing up a lyric that is one of the record's best, especially with respect to the phrasing and musicality of the words. "If you give someone the 'Spanish Archer,'" elaborates Ian, "you give them the elbow, and so that song is about giving some lump the heave-ho. I don't actually think this song should've been included. I mean, it isn't properly arranged. It's just a series of verses with jamming in between, and it wears on me. But everyone else disagrees with me—which is par for the course anyway, ha!—so it's been included."

But it helps that the man's regaling is set to a languid power metal spread, replete with Middle Eastern melodic bits out of both Ritchie and Ian.

Next up, "Strangeways" is somewhat the follow-up to "Hungry Daze," if a bit more heavy metal. Major Turkish or Moroccan tones pad like a black cat through this one. It's a solid, classy rocker on an album that, by this point, one pretty much has to call underrated.

"Mitzi Dupree" we've heard a bit about, and essentially it's the album's big departure, a full-band slow blues, over which Ian tells the tale of a stripper known for shooting ping-pong balls from her muscular loins. There's adequate riffing to the song to make it interesting, and the honky-tonk piano from Lord helps the cause as well. It's a left-field fit to the record, but if anyone can dress up the predictability of blues to the point where it works, it's Purple, and yes, even here in the aforementioned quasi-demo form.

"Actually, it's a true story," explains Ian. "I was on a plane going to Salt Lake City when I was in Black Sabbath, and I saw this most amazing boiler—oh, a sensational lump!—so I went over to talk to her and she said, 'Hi, I'm Mitzi, Mitzi Dupree.' And I thought, 'Wow, what a great name!' I was in love. Anyway, it turned out she was going up north to a mining town in Canada to do a show. So, I asked her what she did, and she told me that she did a show with ping-pong balls. Now, I've actually seen women do this before, in a small room behind a kitchen in Bangkok, and it's absolutely amazing. There was this Siamese girl onstage, and there were five Italians in the front row, all with a glass of wine each. She bent over backwards and—pop-pop-pop-pop-pop—these five ping-pong balls were fired out of you-know-where, and each one landed in a glass—I swear to you! This bird also pulled out fifty double-edged razor blades from the same place, all attached to a bit of cotton. She signed autographs, she did paintings . . . it was unbelievable! And this was what Mitzi did.

"But 'Mitzi Dupree' is a dead live song. It came out of a jam, and we just recorded it for reference. I played it afterwards and thought it was great. I couldn't stop singing it. So, I said to Roger, 'We've got to do something with it.' And he said, 'Well, we can write on it, but we don't have to play it again because everyone else hates it.' So, we wrote the lyric and I sang it to the jam tape, and Roger and I decided to leave it like that, because it sounded so natural and spontaneous. It's a great track."

Closing the record is a fast rocker called "Dead or Alive," and perhaps as metaphor for the vague dissatisfaction many felt with the album, this one's a bit underwritten, badly arranged, and badly mixed. In fact, maybe it's also badly produced, with speed having a tendency to amplify shortcomings. In this case, braying synths and a turgid drum sound conspire to suggest the term "dated." Still, it's testimony to Purple that they never fell headlong into the commercial pitfalls of record making in the 1980s. They didn't glam out, they didn't set up with a raft of outside songwriters or coke spoon producers, and they didn't start using electronic drums and every new 1980s production gizmo that came along.

"'Dead or Alive' is a pile of shit," Gillan told *Kerrang!*, winding down toward the end of his track-by-track analysis with Putterford back at the launch of the record. "It's just not any good. Don't ask me. No, it's going to be good onstage. Maybe that's why it's on there. I did write it, but under protest, I might add. I think everyone else likes it, but I don't. So that's it; ten tracks on the album, and that's more than

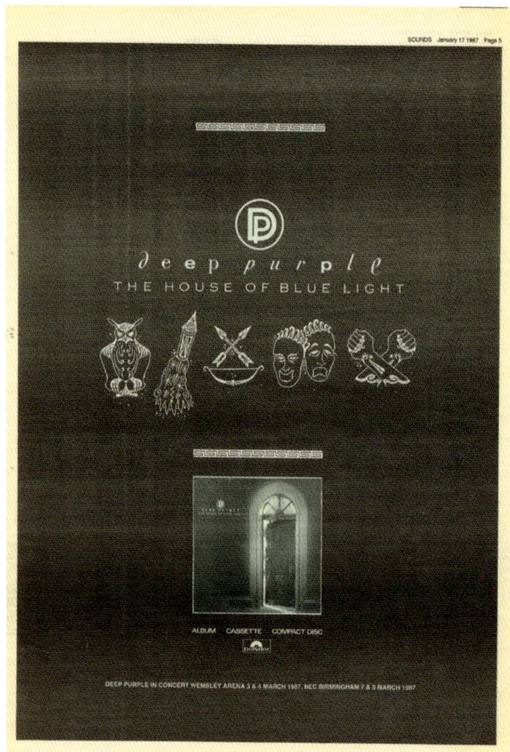

A couple of large-format black-and-white ads, one for the album and one specifically promoting "Call of the Wild." *Martin Popoff archive*

you usually get on a Purple album, so . . . I'm pretty pleased with it. I would say 'delighted' but I won't, because I feel there should only be eight tracks on it. Still, it is a good album overall."

Reacting to the supposition that *Perfect Strangers* might have been a bit safe, Ian figures, "That's a fair comment. I don't think *Perfect Strangers* was intended to be safe, but when we got back together after so many years, we just played what came naturally to us, and were so knocked out by what was coming out of our jams that we just decided to put that on the album. Y'see, an album is a collection of songs which record how you are at that particular time, and to do anything else other than lay down how and what you feel at that time is to go into contrivances; it becomes artificial, it becomes difficult to live with, and it doesn't wear well."

Asked whether *The House of Blue Light* was different, then, Gillan says, "Not much, because the chemistry of the band only allows us to go into certain areas. For example, if Roger and I are doing a project, we can go off in any direction we want to, and if Jon is doing something solo, he'll have no boundaries to restrict him either. But within the parameters of the band, you can only stretch so far. I think people confuse progression with change, and half the time they want you to change in order to progress. But I think you progress within yourself more than anything else, by pushing yourself a little more each time. I don't mean singing higher or louder or faster—I'm sick of all that. Heavy metal drives me bonkers—it makes me vomit—but we're just trying to improve on your previous efforts."

Which is a roundabout way of saying that *The House of Blue Light* was pretty safe too, although with respect to both records, let's not get too fixated with that. There are fine Purple compositions all over both records, and if anything, I'd like to steer history away from the ossifying happenstance that the first is looked upon as good and the second one as bad. I'd say *Perfect Strangers* is a tiny bit less exaltable than its very high-horse reputation, and that *The House of Blue Light* is much, much better than its lukewarm reputation.

Curiously, *Rolling Stone* "officially" (meaning that this is the composite view of two different reviewers, one per comeback album) gave the thumbs down to *Perfect Strangers* and the thumbs up to *The House of Blue Light*. After David Fricke qualifies that "except for a couple of outright duds on side two," the record is "as good as this band has ever been since its 'Smoke on the Water' salad days," he goes on to say, "The band has spiked its old hammer-and-anvil sound with a little future tech here and there: 'The Unwritten Law' features subtly deployed electro-handclaps and percolating sequencer amid its clenched-fist chorus and Blackmore's loco fretwork. But it's only when Purple turns on the retro-charm full blast that *The House of Blue Light* really goes up in flames. 'Hard Lovin' Woman' and 'Dead or Alive' are both body-slam rockers in the old Blitzkrieg spirit of 'Speed King' and 'Fireball,' while Paice's sledgehammer-of-the-gods drumming and Blackmore's punch-your-lights-out chords keep 'Call of the Wild,' with its atypically poppy hook, from turning into neo-Boston fluff."

Adds Fricke in conclusion, "Fortunately all that crash 'n' burn also obscures most of the album's lyric embarrassments. Although Gillan is hardly the Alan Alda of heavy metal, 'Mitzi Dupree,' a heavy-plodding blues, may be a new low in rock-star sexism. But aside from the rather purple poetry, the ho-hum Armageddon stomp 'Strangeways,' and a notable lack throughout the album of classic Blackmore psycho-chicken-scratch soloing, *The House of Blue Light* is a surprisingly strong return from the tar pits."

"*The House of Blue Light* was a weird album and hard to put together," reflected Jon, three years after the fact, sticking to the band plot of putting down this more-than-creditable follow-up. "*Perfect Strangers* pretty much wrote itself. It was so glorious because it was great to be back together after being apart for so many years. We had grins from ear to ear. Then we did the *Perfect Strangers* tour, and we were second in ticket sales to Bruce Springsteen. Then the management and record company said, 'It's time to do the next album, guys.' We made the massive mistake of trying to make our music current. We discovered that people didn't want us to do that. They wanted us to do what we do best. We're Deep Purple—loud, proud, pure, and simple.

"Forgive the immodesty, but I thought *Perfect Strangers* was a perfect album," continued Jon. "It said everything about the band that needed to be said. We weren't trying to be a super-new '80s band, and at the same time we weren't just a nostalgia act. On the second album we made a few concessions by using sequencers, but looking back, we liked the album a lot. At the time, we weren't too sure what we were doing; we were a bit confused. We always do one good LP, a confused one, and then another good one! So, *House of Blue Light* was like the '70s LP *Fireball*, which set us up to do *Machine Head*, which was our biggest ever. The next new LP will be the biggest too!"

And Ritchie's assessment, at the time, of the second record? "George Bodnar of *Kerrang!* recently asked me the same question, and what I answered was that I like the new album. He said that in that case, it had to be a very good album. I wouldn't go as far as saying I'm excited about it, but I do play it quite often. And that's very unusual for me. Especially Ian's singing surprises me. He had an operation on his vocal cords and his voice sounds very full now, and I'm very pleased with it. We did spend quite a long time recording it; some tapes had almost worn out because we used them so much. After we had recorded the [first] album, many people asked us what we would do next. Everybody thought it was just a one-off thing. It was interesting to watch the reactions. Everybody automatically assumed I was going to re-form Rainbow."

Reacting to Roger Glover's comments in the press that *Perfect Strangers* was an album recorded for the fans, and then, dispensed with that, the band was going to spread their wings, Ritchie says, "Roger Glover talks from his ass. Roger is a nice guy, but he makes many comments he later regrets. We didn't make our latest album for the fans, but for ourselves. Our fans are our fans because they are okay with this, and not because we write what anybody would want to hear. Our fans want what we want; otherwise, we wouldn't have any fans."

Final word goes to Ian Paice, who looks back on the *House of Blue Light* era for us from a vantage point of thirty-three years later.

"Tough record," sighs Ian. "We were in a place where we thought we were recording, that the room sound would be good to record, and when we got into it, it really wasn't. It was hard. There was no thrill about going into what was this makeshift studio every day to try to get something that we would be happy with. Everything was sort of a compromise, and every track took a little longer than it should've done. And generally, when that happens, you're driving uphill all the time. It's not easy. Because the best records happen when you get it in the first two or three takes. It might not be perfect, but they're perfect because they have the fire, they had the freshness of the imagination. When you've done something fifteen or twenty times, you may get it exactly right, but you listen back to the first two or three takes and it loses something. And that's what *Blue Light* was to me—it was a tough record."

As for relations with Ritchie, "Not bad, but it had been better. There were obviously cracks in the wall. That's just the way that is, man. Sometimes, it doesn't mean either one is wrong or either one is right. Sometimes, people just don't get along."

Chapter 17

Nobody's Perfect

"I thought we were better than that."

The tour for *The House of Blue Light* saw the rot of old seep into relations between the Purples, not to mention between the Purples and the outer world. At the band's second Wembley show, Ritchie refused to come out for the band's "Smoke on the Water" encore, leaving Jon Lord to carry the load of that monumental riff on organ. On another occasion, in Paris, the band decided they weren't going to do an encore, in part to tick off *The Old Grey Whistle Test* people who were filming. It seems that two years earlier, an interview with the organization had their side chiding Ian and Jon that Purple were re-forming only for the money. Well, having their filming restricted was one thing, and then when the band didn't come out for the encore, Ritchie surprisingly did, launching into "Smoke on the Water" with a roadie at the drums, before knocking the night on its head. *The Old Grey Whistle Test* folks managed to cobble together a show, using footage of "The Unwritten Law" from Cologne, during which Ian seemed to be having one of his rough nights.

So, having squeezed in about half the work on a fine duo album called *Accidentally on Purpose*, to be issued on February 15, 1988, Ian Gillan and Roger Glover quickly found themselves dragged back into Purple work, touring with the band in America and then Europe in August and September. It was a stark return to heavy realities after putting together a good chunk of the sunny, tropical side project at Air Studio in Montserrat, now an obliterated fond memory of many an upper-crust rocker, due to a volcano that wiped out the island.

So yes, fans weren't digging the new material, and the new record hadn't charted as high as *Perfect Strangers*. Nor was it selling well in North America, which depressed ticket sales. And then to make matters worse, Ritchie managed to break a finger, when, on May 30, 1987, in Phoenix, he blew a shift trying to catch his guitar. Over in the other warring camp, Ian and Roger had been traveling by bus, separate from the other guys, continuing writing sessions on their record. Now they took the opportunity to go into New York's Minot Studios and the Power Station to finish *Accidentally on Purpose* with some of America's most esteemed studio hotshots.

Monsters of Rock, Pforzheim, Germany, August 30, 1987. © *Wolfgang Gürster*

Pearl

Back in Purple world, fans had been noticing that many of the tour dates, both in the US and in Europe, were being recorded, and indeed a double live album called *Nobody's Perfect* was to be the average, not very exciting or excitable result of this bickering hodgepodge of a tour. Even the assembly of the album was cause for argument, with nobody being able to agree about which versions of songs to use. Roger was naturally enlisted as the producer (again, credit would go to "Roger Glover and Deep Purple"), seeing the project through. And no Nick Blagona this time: "I was busy in Australia doing an album, and I couldn't do it. It was an impromptu thing."

One bright spot was the amusing cover art by Aubrey Powell of Hipgnosis fame (the company was now defunct), which subtly brought to view items that weren't perfect. An added layer of irony might be represented by the fact that when it came to album covers, Deep Purple was much more distant from perfect than anybody out there, save for AC/DC, Def Leppard, and Foreigner.

Comparisons with *Made in Japan* were inevitable, given the inclusion of many of the tired old anchors and albatrosses of the Mk. II catalog. Ian warily took notice that things hadn't changed much at all, save for the band getting slicker. "Highway Star" sounds rushed and smeary, "Lazy," deconstructed and then similarly harried by the stopwatch and impatient coach. "Smoke on the Water" bobs refreshingly, but something about the way Lord's keys are mixed in—here and elsewhere—sounds more thin and clattery than grinding and rich.

Representing the modern era are a couple of tracks from each 1980s album. "Hard Lovin' Woman" fits and rocks (spot the "Under the Gun" riff), with Ian turning in one of the album's better vocals. "Bad Attitude" makes the double vinyl but not the CD. "Knocking at Your Back Door" gets an electric piano solo at the front, played for cheap laughs and played for four minutes. Once into the song proper, all the grandness, the aristocratic tilt and languish of the song as it exists in studio form, is lost. And finally, "Perfect Strangers" (introduced as "Perfect Stranglers") brings back into focus the fact that Purple in the 1980s carried with it some considerable level of substance.

So yes, if one hadn't noticed that *Nobody's Perfect* wobbled badly, there are constant reminders from Gillan that this whole rock 'n' roll circus is a bit of a charade. His "parody of a front man" routine is indeed refreshing, and he is laughing with us, not at us. Still, one can envision why Ritchie gets upset at the guy. Then again, Ritchie has the same sort of disdain for the clichés of the mad, mad business of rock. And I guess the problem is that each of them presses the serious work ethic button at different times and places. As Purple hit the road and then hit it again, one town to the next, it is not hard to smell the smoke as it swirls up from the friction as Ritchie and Ian make each other's own entirely private decisions of when they will play the clown or not. Sometimes it's onstage, sometimes off, sometimes in dealing with each other, the press, their audience, their crew. Anything could happen.

"There's always a reason why I do it," explains Ritchie, asked about his moods by Geoff Barton back in 1984. "I don't just do it because I enjoy upsetting people. To start with, most lead guitar players are sensitive individuals, unlike, say, singers or bass players or drummers, who tend to be more brash and extrovert. And this sensitivity can turn into destruction. Sometimes, I often say to myself, I wish I wasn't so sensitive, so tuned into the way people feel. You see, I pick up on the way people conduct themselves, and if I get a negative feeling from someone, then I'll respond in kind. It's very difficult to relax. And I think that uptight feeling, that feeling of

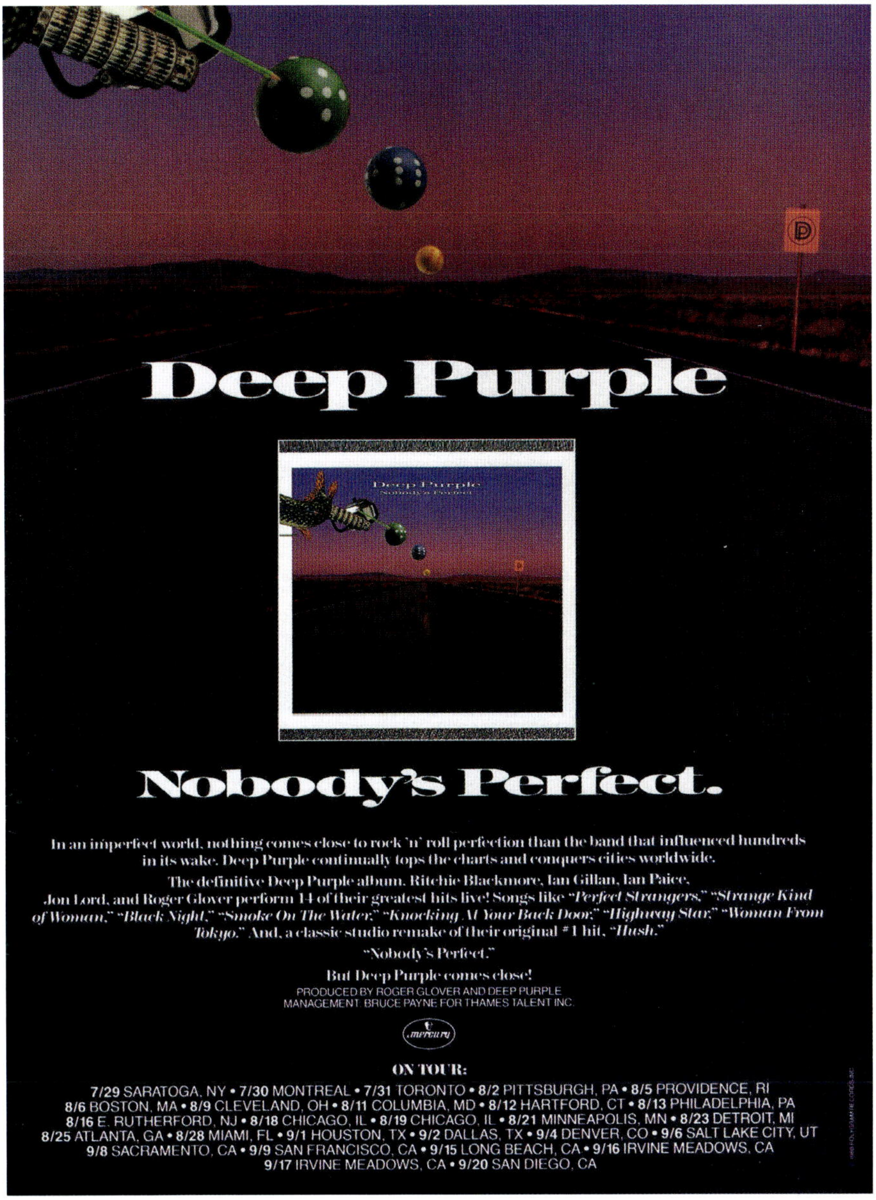

Deep Purple

Nobody's Perfect.

In an imperfect world, nothing comes close to rock 'n' roll perfection than the band that influenced hundreds in its wake. Deep Purple continually tops the charts and conquers cities worldwide.

The definitive Deep Purple album. Ritchie Blackmore, Ian Gillan, Ian Paice, Jon Lord, and Roger Glover perform 14 of their greatest hits live! Songs like *"Perfect Strangers," "Strange Kind of Woman," "Black Night," "Smoke On The Water," "Knocking At Your Back Door," "Highway Star," "Woman From Tokyo."* And, a classic studio remake of their original #1 hit, *"Hush."*

"Nobody's Perfect."

But Deep Purple comes close!

PRODUCED BY ROGER GLOVER AND DEEP PURPLE
MANAGEMENT: BRUCE PAYNE FOR THAMES TALENT INC.

Mercury

ON TOUR:

7/29 SARATOGA, NY • **7/30** MONTREAL • **7/31** TORONTO • **8/2** PITTSBURGH, PA • **8/5** PROVIDENCE, RI
8/6 BOSTON, MA • **8/9** CLEVELAND, OH • **8/11** COLUMBIA, MD • **8/12** HARTFORD, CT • **8/13** PHILADELPHIA, PA
8/16 E. RUTHERFORD, NJ • **8/18** CHICAGO, IL • **8/19** CHICAGO, IL • **8/21** MINNEAPOLIS, MN • **8/23** DETROIT, MI
8/25 ATLANTA, GA • **8/28** MIAMI, FL • **9/1** HOUSTON, TX • **9/2** DALLAS, TX • **9/4** DENVER, CO • **9/6** SALT LAKE CITY, UT
9/8 SACRAMENTO, CA • **9/9** SAN FRANCISCO, CA • **9/15** LONG BEACH, CA • **9/16** IRVINE MEADOWS, CA
9/17 IRVINE MEADOWS, CA • **9/20** SAN DIEGO, CA

A couple of artsy ads for the aggressively nonartsy *Nobody's Perfect* album.
Martin Popoff archive

being on the edge, can be very frustrating, especially when you're on the road. I just need the slightest provocation, and I'll be off.

"When the pressure's on and I'm touring, I get incredibly moody because I feel there's so many people who aren't doing their jobs, people like the guys who do the lighting, the spotlight operators, and so forth. They just don't give a shit. I go to do a solo and I'm in the dark or whatever. Everybody's after a quick buck. They're so lackadaisical. There just isn't any discipline."

Geoff then reminds Ritchie that it's hard to achieve perfection.

"I know, I know, but that doesn't stop me trying to get as near to it as possible. I mean, I take the instance I mentioned to you about not being spotlit when I take a guitar solo. When that happens, it throws me for about a minute. I think, that's incompetence. And then all sorts of thoughts start running through my head. Why did he do that? Was it incompetence? Did he do it on purpose? Why didn't he do his job? What's going on? All those kinds of weird thoughts."

Ads for Deep Purple at Wembley. *Martin Popoff archive*

"You know, it's a case of value for money. The kids pay their money, and they don't want to see a shabby, semiprofessional show. Monitor mixes too. They're another one of my great bug bears onstage. Picture the scene. You're out front; you're all fired up; the audience is with you; they're jumping around. You start playing, and suddenly all you hear is 'Errrrrrr!' That messes me up, and I get very strange when I get pissed off, very weird. I kind of retreat into myself and become extremely self-destructive. I say, all right, if the soundman's going to behave like an amateur, then I'm going to play the next song behind an amplifier and show him what amateurism is really all about. It's very much a case of cut off your nose to spite your face. I'm a firm believer in that, and it gets me a terrible name. If we're doing a bad show and I'm playing badly myself, then sometimes I'll deliberately play even worse, because I'm so disgusted with what's going on. It's weird, isn't it??"

And it feels like all this second-guessing and all the mind games are rifling through the grooves of *Nobody's Perfect*. Ian wisecracks his way through song introductions, and then once he's singing, sometimes he offers an eyewinked parody of Ian Gillan. Ritchie can joke around too, through his six strings, or simply sound off. And as mentioned, Jon isn't above taking the legs out from under the grand reputation of Purple's catalog either. The rhythm section can only hold on and hope they don't blow a shift during whatever games are being played up top.

"The band doesn't necessarily have one leader," notes Roger. "As it happens, Ritchie is responsible for directing many of the jams we perform onstage, so we look to him to signal when he's finished playing a solo. We try to change our jams every night. Sometimes they can go for five minutes; the next night we can play for fifteen. That's why he looks like he's in charge onstage. There's no denying that he's the main catalyst behind the band, but we all have our roles to play."

Stuart Smith takes a stab at the cause of all the dissension within Purple's ranks over the years. "It's hard to know, because it started long before I was ever involved in the whole thing. But Purple, for me, was a band that carried the seeds of its own destruction, as it were. They were all brilliant at what they did; they far outshone, musically speaking, the other musicians of the time who were getting a lot more credit. I mean I heard them do things on nights that were just astounding. And you know, it's sort of like jet fighter pilots. When you are that good, part of what comes with being that good is having the confidence, bordering on arrogance, to be able to do what you do. And Ian, somewhere along the line, I don't know what it was . . . they used to be good friends. They actually used to room together, in the early days. But somewhere along the way, it became sort of like a competition. They were trying to outdo each other. The song 'Smooth Dancer' was Ian's take on Ritchie at the time. Ritchie is a very hard taskmaster, and when they got back together for *Perfect Strangers*, everyone thought all the old things had been forgotten. We'd actually went around for dinner at Ian's house one night!

"But Ritchie's sort of main complaint, I guess, was that Ian would sometimes forget the lyrics. This is from what Ritchie has said, and this is common knowledge. Ian would say, 'Oh, I'm not feeling too good, Ritchie; let's not do "Child in Time" tonight.' You know, it's a taxing song. Ritchie would go, okay. And then the next morning, Ritchie would be heading to the plane, and you would see Ian in the bar drinking, or on the plane having a brandy, and then the next night, 'Oh, not feeling too good.' So, Ritchie would actually want them to do it. As I said, who knows? Even between Jon Lord and Ritchie, there was that musical competitiveness, but it never got to the stage that it did with Ian. And between two people, there are three stories—there's one side, the other, and basically the truth in the middle. And who knows what that will ever be?"

Jon tends to acknowledge that there was indeed a subplot in the band, with respect to Ritchie and himself as musical competitors. "When we started, we were both very young; both of us wanted to have the upper hand, and the music was our battlefield. Sometimes I really felt that we were at war, especially onstage. Sometimes, when I came out after a 'fight,' my pulse was beating so fast that I thought, 'No more Purple!' Which is probably the reason I still listen to classical music only, in my cloakroom after every gig. In case you're interested, come backstage this evening, and I'll show you the tapes I have in my suitcase—pieces of Beethoven, Schubert, Tchaikovsky, Mozart. Without Mozart I'd probably be dead and buried for ages! But I have other things as well—Miles Davis, Led Zeppelin, the Eagles; I'm a big Eagles fan. Ritchie is at least a very big friend of classical music. But onstage, he knows how to hide this side of his personality [laughs]. Onstage the slogan is always 'Whose fire is burning better this evening, his or mine?'

"That's the territory on which we've fought for a long time," continues Jon, referring to hard rock up against classical. "But what came out of it was sometimes very exciting, wasn't it? I mean, if you know that deep inside your heart you have to tolerate a person, that he is your fate, then it can be heaven or hell for you, but you have to cooperate also. It was never that hard on me. For Gillan, I believe, it was a

Pearl

A montage of shots from Monsters of Rock, F.C.P. Stadion, Pforzheim, Germany, August 30, 1987. Also on the bill were Dio, Metallica, Ratt, Cinderella, and local heroes Helloween.
© *Wolfgang Gürster*

lot harder; he has suffered a lot more. But I don't want to pretend to be a white mountaintop who looks out over things. The only thing I know is that the nice phrasing 'They have parted company because of musical differences' is a lie. Things like that look good in the press, but with Deep Purple it was always personal differences. We can't help having five genuinely different egos—we are egoists! [laughs]. I mean, when we met for the first time, we didn't get along very well. But we concluded that we were equal, considering our skills, and that we could make something special together. But this was only possible on the basis of compromises, and sometimes these compromises are more to the satisfaction of the one than to the other. Sometimes Ritchie got a larger part, sometimes I, sometimes Gillan."

And where do Roger and Ian Paice fit in? "Ian stayed out of it most of the time—a very wise decision, I must say! [laughs]. And Roger always tried to negotiate. In the end, Ritchie got most of his way most of the time. When I look at it nowadays, this was probably for the best, because Ritchie is without a doubt the cornerstone of the band—he defines Deep Purple. He is always 100 percent convinced that what he wants is the only right thing to do. You have to learn to handle that, especially when you think that he's wrong. But we did all right by it."

"Ian was Ian," adds Stuart, who, like Nick Blagona, doesn't really think that Gillan's "benders" at the pub had a whole lot to do with the problems between Ritchie and him. "I thought he was a very funny guy. When he'd get very drunk, he would occasionally do up his hair like a samurai and take all his clothes off and sit at the bar. And as I said, I never had any problem with Ian. And again, I think a lot of the whole thing between Ritchie and Ian . . . I think a lot of the drinking thing was the fact that Ritchie can be very intimidating. And I think a lot of it was him sort of needling Ian, so he would drink more.

"Because I remember going to the House of Blues and seeing Deep Purple play, when Steve Morse first joined, and Ian was just singing brilliantly and looked like he was having a lot of fun up there. There wasn't that air of tension. But there again, that's what made Deep Purple so exciting, that air, that tension, where you never quite knew what was going to happen, on the night. You can sense it. And I don't think the fans all knew that there was anything so much between Ritchie and Ian. They thought of it as Ritchie being his moody self, which he built a persona and an image on. To be sure, it's a part of him as well, but it's also because Ritchie is just a very shy person. He's very shy, very intelligent, very funny, and he doesn't let a lot of people in easily.

"Ian, I've known actually for years," continues Smith, asked for a profile of Paicey and Roger Glover. "When Deep Purple first broke up after *Come Taste the Band*, I called Ian, introduced myself, and said, 'Hey, would you want to get a band together, if you're not doing anything?' And so I went to his house, played him the stuff, and we thought we'd give it a try. So, I got a studio together in London, and we all drove . . . I actually drove out the night before to his area, Henley-on-Thames, [and] stayed in a hotel that night, and we drove down together. It was myself, Paul Martinez on bass, and Elmer Gantry, I think, singing. And it was really good, good-sounding stuff. But then Ian got the offer from Whitesnake, so that sort of killed any chance of that happening. But he was a great guy; I've always liked Ian. And Roger, I consider him a friend as well. He was very much a mentor in ways; I'd ask him certain things about recording, and he taught me a lot; very philosophical. The band called him the Stinking Hippie. I mean, he was very much like a hippie, very poetic, very creative, and you know, I think he had a lot to do with the writing process, from what I would see. Ritchie was the one who would generally come up with the riffs, and Roger would be the one to take it to other places. And a great producer—I mean, phenomenal producer."

Elsewhere on *Nobody's Perfect*, "Woman from Tokyo" and "Strange Kind of Woman" (in this writer's opinion, two of the band's most pedestrian, underwritten, and overrated songs) are similarly thin and casual compared to the rest of the album, although "Strange Kind of Woman" does achieve the level of lively, jazzy, five-way conversation the Purple guys so often pride themselves on as a differentiating factor between themselves and base heavy metal plodders. Look for the nod to Ian's bizarre *Jesus Christ Superstar* past inserted within the song's inevitable diversionary jam.

Speaking of plodders, the album closes with a February 1988 live-in-studio remake of "Hush," one of those impossible oldies the guys seem to perennially think is more magical than it is, if only they can get it cooked and seasoned properly. The track was issued as a single and rose to a paltry #62 on the UK charts.

Nobody's Perfect CD cover signed by Ian Gillan, Ian Paice, and Roger Glover. *Martin Popoff archive*

After a launch party for *Nobody's Perfect* at Fort Frankenstein in Frankfurt, Germany, at which the guests were dressed in Renaissance garb (ideas for Blackmore's Night no doubt taking seed), Purple found themselves canceling a planned US tour after just one warm-up gig and one date proper, a massive tilt with Aerosmith and Guns N' Roses at Giants Stadium in New Jersey. The demand just wasn't there. "I wouldn't dress up in medieval gear," says Lord, of the launch. "That's more Blackmore's territory. It was our last record company's idea, which might have something to do with why they are our last record company!"

In Europe the band fared marginally better, playing dates in Germany and Italy, where *Metal Hammer* caught up with Ian Gillan putting on a brave face: "Whatever we do is done as honestly as possible. I don't care how dangerous it is, but it has to be honest. When you are in a group, you have to do things a little bit different to the way you do them on your own. And with Purple, the chemistry of the personalities is such that . . . well, we have always been regarded as a dangerous band, and that is because we don't ever agree on anything! But there is a basic honesty in this band. The majority decision rules: that has always been a code within Purple, even if it means I don't always get my way!

"If the spark ever dies, that will be time for the band to split or for me to quit," continues Gillan. "I gotta tell you that the last world tour was the best we ever did. The atmosphere was electric; everyone was doing his best, even though Ritchie broke his finger. We were like Liverpool FC playing at their best. We are all in a band because we enjoy playing music. Deep Purple has always been a live band more than anything. We tend to work in two-year cycles: one you're writing and recording, and the next touring. We did our tour last year and unfortunately missed a lot of America because of a broken finger. So, 1988 was supposed to be a recording year, and we were going to do only a mini tour of the States. Europe was excluded. But there were all kinds of politics going on. Basically, we were better off in Italy and Germany doing a few shows before going back into the studio and writing again. I think we have to get back onstage and do some work and get things into our minds about how we are going to do the next album. You can't do that just coming from holidays. You gotta work hard.

"I hope the album will have a strong live feel. The music itself just takes its own course. We have already got three of our good ideas that came out over the last six months. Before we go into the studio, we will be going into rehearsal to spend two or three weeks jamming and writing. Then we'll go into the studio. The last album took a lot longer to make than we wanted, mainly because we didn't start it the right way. It went on for months! The best albums we ever made were done quickly. This time we're gonna do a much-quicker and fresher LP."

And Ian's assessment of *Nobody's Perfect*? "Our idea was to have a tape recorder on throughout the tour and put out a live album. It filled the gap, because we weren't ready to do another studio album. Our show, apart from current material like 'Perfect Strangers' and 'Knocking at Your Back Door,' has been based around our old stuff, and pretty soon we're gonna start changing it. But how are we going to drop 'Smoke on the Water,' 'Child in Time,' and 'Strange Kind of Woman'? It's very difficult. We just have to make the show longer and bring in new stuff. I'd like to think [that] some of the older songs we're gonna play are gonna sound different, but it's hard, and the only way to revitalize them is by mixing in new stuff. Personally, I love the older material, and I'm sure the kids want to hear them too.

"But I was very pleased with *Nobody's Perfect* because it was honest," answers Ian. "No studio overdubs. Tracks like 'Child in Time' had a new lease on life. When we reunited, we couldn't deny that a lot of people would come to see us because they wanted to hear 'Smoke on the Water.' So, *Nobody's Perfect* is a 1987 version of songs that were written in 1969. For instance, if you listen to the *Made in Japan* version of 'Smoke on the Water' and compare it with the one on *Nobody's Perfect*, they are two totally different songs, with a different spirit."

All told, the *House of Blue Light* tour was quite exhaustive, with January and February 1987 spent in mainland Europe, closing off in March with six dates in the UK, with Bad Company as support for most of it. April and May were filled rock solid in the US, with Bad Company again as main support, up until Ritchie's accident caused the cancellation of the last five dates of this leg. August and September 1987 found the band playing scattered dates throughout Europe, with an actual *Nobody's Perfect* campaign taking place in late summer / early fall of 1988, with the likes of Zed Yago and Guns N' Roses backing up, but Aerosmith topping the bill in the US.

Ritchie found himself with a new PA (personal assistant) in Europe, a New Englander by the name of Frank Morgan, who, all told, took the rift between Ian Gillan and his boss in stride, just as the band seemed to.

"You know, those things had been going on," begins Morgan. "As you probably know this, one time Ritchie and Ian Gillan shared the same room when they were on tour [laughs], so that always shocks a lot of people. But you know, the big thing is, the fallout with those guys, again, they all have tremendous egos and everything,

An assortment of satin backstage passes from the tour in support of *The House of Blue Light*

especially when a band is placed onstage. I'm a musician, by the way, a bass player. But Deep Purple was pretty much set up . . . it's Ian Paice, Jon Lord, and it's Ritchie. And they put a singer and a bass player there—that is the defining sound of Deep Purple. Ian Paice's way and style of playing the drums, a left-hander drummer, his high-hat sound. Of course, Ritchie's sound, and Jon Lord's—that's what makes up the Purple sound.

"But Ritchie . . . okay, I'm the guy who doesn't drink or do drugs. I'm in the restaurant business and have been a restaurant owner, so I do know people well. And despite everything I've ever heard about Ritchie Blackmore, it couldn't be . . . you know, you always get a raw deal from the press. The guy's very down to earth. I'm a big boxing fan, and he was into boxing. Ritchie is like a semipro soccer player [laughs]. And he likes to talk about world politics, the relationships between the Brits and the Americans. He's a very good guy. But if you don't do what he wants, then you got a problem [laughs]."

In an amusing tieback to the "Knocking at Your Back Door" video, the band convened for the beginning of European tour duties the same way they began *Perfect Strangers*—at the bar.

"Ritchie and Ian Gillan were always separated, but when the *House of Blue Light* tour first started, we all went to Frankfurt, Germany, to the Grevenbroek Kempinski Hotel, and each member of the group would show up, and you know, each day somebody would come into town. Ritchie and I, I think we were the first ones in the town, and then you'd all get out to the pub at the end of the day, and as each group member would show up, they would all meet in the bar. One night it would be Ritchie and I, then Jon Lord, then Ian Gillan came into town, Ian Paice, and Roger. Everyone got along, chatting very nicely, in the bar. The shenanigans started mostly onstage."

And then came rehearsals, which, again, mirrored the way the band made records. "You see, there was a gap. They recorded that album, *House of Blue Light* . . . it was pretty much done in '86, early part of '86, and we didn't get into Germany until the early part of '87. That's when the rehearsals started for the tour. I think it was at a little place called the MTV Studios in Germany, but it had nothing to do with the TV show. It was where the band and all the equipment was set up, and that's where they would rehearse and figure out what material to play and not to play. They have so many songs; there's always an argument, on every tour, which songs are in and which songs are out. But they got on very good. The band would start rehearsing, and Ian Gillan would show up once the band got warmed up. But Ritchie, when they were rehearsing, he doesn't play a lot of guitar solos, because he wants the arrangement of the music to sink into his head, you know what I mean? Because he hasn't played the songs in a while. And that's what keeps them fresh. Also, they forget parts and they have to relearn them. But that's what keeps the songs interesting, because you find a new way every night to play the same old song, as I guess most musicians do.

"I never saw any drugs," continues Morgan. "The English are drinkers. Johnny Walker Black and Coca-Cola—that's the signature cocktail. And the guys were very fun. Whether I was hanging out with Roger . . . because I was from Richfield, and he lives in Greenwich, Connecticut. They're all really nice, down-to-earth guys. Once they accept you and they know you're not a moron, then they open up and talk to you. I would put Ritchie to bed at night, and Tammy, and then go to the bar and hang out with Ian Gillan and Roger Glover. They were just really nice guys. They knew I was the biggest Beatle fan in the world, so we were able to talk about the Beatles, Paul McCartney, bass playing with these guys [laughs], because they were fans of those guys too. There's no doubt that Ian Gillan was a wild man. But I thought he was always on the money. There's no doubt about it. They would all go out and have their drinks, but I never saw him be sloppy drunk or anything. These guys are very classy guys."

There were other Beatles connections as well. "Yeah, first off, Ritchie always has an English Tudor of some sort. You know, the House in Redding, Connecticut, he wanted to build a nightclub in the basement, because he liked to entertain. So, I got all my carpenter guys in Richfield—Bob Schneider, John Simone—and we built what we called Blackmore's Night Club in his house in Redding. After we did all that, he had a beautiful bar down there, pool tables, and dance floor with the crystal, you know, the big chrome ball there. Joe Lynn Turner came over a couple times when they were patching things up. That was before he was in Deep Purple. He did come by once with his wife. Roger would come over all the time, because we would organize soccer parties, soccer games. Roger lived in Greenwich, so it wasn't that much of a ride over to Redding. So, Roger and Ritchie, yeah, they got along really well.

"Ritchie's a very cool guy. Christmas parties, Ritchie liked everybody to get involved with music, and at the Christmas party, he would play the acoustic and he would have a keyboard player and a singer. He always loved people singing around the bar. Ritchie would play Beatles songs and other little ditties that you would never hear him do, only to friends and stuff. Ritchie loved the Beatles too. He and Tammy did go, supposedly, to visit George Harrison one day, at Henley-on-Thames, the big house he had where he had got stabbed. And Ian Paice and Jon Lord are brothers-in-law. They are both married to a set of twins, and those two were very, very friendly with George Harrison. And George Harrison, I think, came to Roger's wedding too. I was out of the picture by then, but they were very friendly with George Harrison. And George, as you know, guested once on the *Perfect Strangers* tour. George was the only guy that Ritchie ever let onstage.

"But these guys are really classy guys with integrity," underscores Frank. "They're really cool guys, and I sat down with Ian Gillan, and he would tell me he went and saw Paul McCartney a few times, when they were with Wings, and he was disappointed when they didn't play enough Beatles songs. But they all complimented Paul. A little off topic, but I also remember Ian Gillan would say things like, 'In the early days, you know, we listened to every little word that Ritchie Blackmore ever said. But when we got back together, it was more like, let's have our own thoughts on things.' But he did at one time have them under his spell. I wouldn't call it a spell, but he was the guitar player, he was the man—no doubt about it."

As for pastimes on the road, Frank says, "Ritchie always told me Jon would stay in his room during the day and read his books; he loved to read. He would come out occasionally to play soccer, but not all the time. And on the soccer field, the daytime, I mean, Ian Gillan, Ritchie Blackmore, Roger Glover, and Ian Paice, they all got along very well playing soccer together. No deliberate hits or knocking each other out or anything [laughs]. I was quite impressed with these guys. Because I can't stand the drug use, and they just liked to go out and have a few drinks and have a good time. You've got to remember, back for *House of Blue Light*, they were all about forty-two years old, all about the same age, except Jon Lord; he's the oldest. So, they are all within a few months of each other.

"One thing I remember . . . we were on the tour, and I would have to go through these books and look at these people's names, but there was one promoter, I think his name was Thompson. He just did certain gigs over in the Denmark area or the Scandinavian countries. And I think they were at a Chinese restaurant one night, and they had like the little ponds with the water and the lights and all that, and Ian threw him in there [laughs]. Ian Gillan . . . I'm 6'2", and he's about 6'2", you know, and he was tall, lanky, and the guy was in good shape [laughs]."

I asked Frank if Ritchie ever tested his patience in terms of his PA job; you know, "Go get this" or "Go get that"?

"No, but he played a few shenanigans. I think he did more shenanigans in the past, because he knew I was so impressed with him, because I was a tremendous Rainbow fan and a Dio fan. The way we met, you see, he came into a restaurant I was working in, in Richfield, Connecticut, and I was a bartender. I've been a bartender for a million years, besides being an owner, and I had eyes for rock stars because I had another good buddy of mine . . . you see, same story; I was best friends with Ace Frehley from Kiss, who is my neighbor [laughs], and Ritchie Blackmore is my other buddy. So, you know, they both would come visit me at the restaurant at separate times. I wasn't caught up in the drinking and drugging, and they knew they were going to be driven around safely, and I introduced them to good people, and they were in safe hands with me. And they knew if other people got too close to them, I was like a built-in bodyguard. Very nice guy, 'Back off; you're getting a little too close here' [laughs]. And they are complete polar opposites, of course.

"I don't talk to these guys much anymore," muses Frank, "but we never had a fallout, and I really don't chase them either. We had our time together. They recycle their entourage all the time, most of these rock stars. Because if you're hanging around someone all the time, you hear the same old stories, the same little skits and the same little tricks. So they recycle the entourage so the new people are constantly impressed with the little tricks [laughs]."

And speaking of tricks, "He would send me on a wild-goose chase sometimes," laughs Frank. "We would be in Germany. When we were off the road from Deep

Purple, we would stay in these wonderful castles, all over Germany. And some of them are closed in the wintertime, but they would open them up for Ritchie Blackmore. Very interesting [laughs]. So, we'd take our little excursions, when the band had a day or two off. They would pretty much play four nights in a row, sometimes five, and they would have to have two days off for everybody to rest. So, we would go to these wonderful, wonderful castles, and Ritchie would tell me, 'Meet me in the courtyard.' I'd go out there; there's nobody around. Also, he would get food delivered to his room, and then I would open up my door, and he would take the tray and everything, and the little car, put it outside my door, so when I opened my door, dishes and everything went everywhere.

"Another one . . . Ritchie knew I wasn't crazy about flying, so sometimes he or even Colin Hart, the tour manager, who is a wonderful guy [laughs]—he was with them from Rainbow, Deep Purple, and everywhere; he's no longer with them, unfortunately—but sometimes it would be 'Okay, Frank, meet you in the lobby.' We had to leave at a certain hour. And I get down there; they would already be gone. Or, if you miss them, 'Where the hell were you? You were supposed to be here half an hour earlier!' And they would put me on a little puddle jumper, and I would have to fly to the destination by myself, because they knew that would wig me out [laughs]. So, little games like that. And yeah, 'Meet us down the courtyard; we're gonna have a snowball fight.' You walk down, walk around; there's nobody there."

A nonexclusive shop, to be sure, Frank was also brought into Ritchie's spiritual experiments. "Oh yeah, I did all that stuff with him. We had our séances. And I think they worked. Especially the one at the Dalhousie Castle in Scotland, where he had the big rock photographer, Ross Halfin, and this other journalist came along, and they were doing photo sessions with Ritchie in the Dalhousie Castle. Ritchie was like Tony Iommi, very steeped in séances and stuff like that. So, there was one room in the Dalhousie Castle that they didn't rent out anymore because too many weird things would happen. So, we tried the séance one day, and nothing was happening, so Ritchie gave us all books to read up on the history of the Dalhousie Castle and stuff.

"So, the next day we tried another séance, and we rented that room, which Ritchie told me nobody ever rents. I'm only going on what he said. So, we did a séance up there, and I remember I had a red jacket, and to dim the room, Ritchie threw my red jacket over the light, and then we got a small little coffee table, and we didn't have a Ouija board. We had kind of a notepad, and he cut out all the numbers and the alphabet on pieces of paper, and I went down to the bar and got a little port glass and we put it in the center of the table. So, it was Ritchie and me, and I think one rock photographer and this girl from France that was there, and maybe one or two other people.

"But anyway, Ritchie would have the notepad, and he would talk: 'Is there anybody there who would like to talk to us?' And then suddenly the little glass starts moving. Everybody put their fingertip on it in the center of the table, and me, I'm stone sober and all this, but I have an open eye for these things, because my restaurants were haunted. Suddenly the little glass starts moving around. I would try to stop it, but it kept moving around [laughs]. Ritchie would ask it questions, and you would stop and look at the letters and rearrange the letters to be yes or no or some answer of some sort.

"But long story short, it's always about an earthly spirit, somebody who has died that doesn't know they've died, and they remain earthly. That's what I was always told by Ritchie. It was forbidden in those days for the royal family of the castle to date somebody who was a servant in the castle, and so it ended up being Catherine and James, 1678. That's what we got out of it. And I think Catherine was still looking for where James was [laughs]. That's what I remember. And also, I would have to open up my tour book, because I keep everything . . . there was one other hotel in Germany, possibly Hamburg, but Ritchie's girlfriend at the time used to feel the walls, with the tremors and stuff. Some people have that gift, you know, when they grab your hand, and they can tell you stories and stuff. She was into that. So, I can't count it in or count it out. It was an experience."

And there are the same sorts of stories that Stuart told us, says Frank, regarding Ritchie and his lack of driving.

"He never had a license. So, when you are Ritchie Blackmore's personal assistant, you see, you always have a hotel room that is adjacent to his so you can communicate and give him a little privacy and alone time, so you don't have crazy people and they're having a party next door when he's trying to sleep. As I say, he never drove, so Ritchie travels independently from the rest of the band. So, when we would be on tour, it would be Ritchie and me and his girlfriend, which at the time was Tammy. It would be the three of us every day, and then the other four band members would travel with their assistants. They would take the tour bus and this and that. But we always had a private car."

Frank also found himself with a ringside seat to the band's onstage warring. "One time playing at the Playhouse in Scotland, a little theater that all the rock groups hit, I guess Ian Gillan wanted to do an encore. Ritchie was already leaving, and they got very mad at each other. But we took off, and Ian Gillan was so upset, because I think Ritchie didn't want to do the encore. That was a big one. So yeah, sometimes he would walk off. He's been doing that for years, and then the band would play 'Smoke on the Water,' without Blackmore on guitar. I guess he'd been doing that for years. He was just ready to go. He just didn't think they were coming back on. The car was already waiting, and as his assistant, I had to have the car all ready to go, in case this guy wants to do an encore or wanted to take off."

Asked about the band's considerable popularity during that time, Morgan is pretty emphatic. "Oh yeah, worldwide popularity. You've got to remember; they played the entire world. They tour from Istanbul to South Korea to places that Led Zeppelin or the Rolling Stones wouldn't go. That's why they have a diehard following, very much worldwide, even to this day, for touring. They tour the entire world, and very few bands do that. All the places were packed. But the venues over there aren't the size of here. So a 12,000-seater over there is a pretty good size, and when you get into London, the great indoor/outdoor place, Wembley, we played the Wembley Arena inside, and they played that two or three nights in a row. That was all sold out. Yeah, that tour, I mean every seat, everywhere we went . . . and then they would play the 3,000-to-4,000-seaters, some places in Germany, but they would also play 12,000- and 16,000-seaters too. There are beautiful venues out there, especially when you got up to Denmark and Sweden, where a lot of those places are all hockey arenas."

After grinding it out to the end of the *House of Blue Light* tour, Jon Lord, doing press around this time, suddenly found himself fighting rumors that the band was about to split.

"We are still five extremely strong characters. It's not an easy ride. There is still some occasional whitewater. Just before a gig is the most critical time. If you are recording and things go wrong, you can go off for an hour, or even a week if necessary. But at a concert, things sometimes get said. We're not so sophisticated that we can't go onstage in front of that number of people without feeling extremely nervous. I still get dreadful butterflies—oh yes. In the old days one used to solve it by pouring booze down one's throat. I don't drink before I play anymore, and we have never been a chemical-abuse band. Well, the only chemicals we've abused have been hops, barley, and malt. We are a perfectly straight lot now. We only celebrate after a gig. The fruit of the vine is more our mark. But before going onstage, it is a touch critical."

We'll close with an interesting food-for-thought kind of comment from Roger, who is speaking of events between the two studio albums: "It was interesting when we first went back to the old albums to learn the material for the tour. We had actually forgotten most of the songs [laughs]. When he started listening, Ritchie turned to me with a pained look on his face and said, 'I thought we were better than that.'"

Chapter 18

Slaves and Masters

"Jesus, there's going to be a lot of flak because I was in Rainbow."

Roger is wont to muse, and wholly without humor, that Ritchie's broken finger seemed to set off a chain of events not unlike the butterfly effect, where the smallest ripples can amplify into cataclysmic changes. Roughly concurrent, Gillan and Glover were somewhat preoccupied with the sometimes world music, sometimes flippant, sometimes old rock 'n' roll oddity of their duo album *Accidentally on Purpose*, which prompted a few TV appearances, the highlight being an arch-1980s full-band rave-up for the song "Dislocated," which can be classified as jazzy postpunk. "Clouds and Rain" was also represented with a lip-synced performance. The album opener was indeed an elegant choice for a single, a late arrival and one of four. It's an epic, intelligent sort of ballad, soul-replenishing, really, like the title track from Roger's solo album *Mask* from four years previous.

"How that worked was that everybody was so tired, and probably pissed off with *House of Blue Light*," relates Nick with respect to the diversionary record from the two Musketeers. "Roger and Ian weren't happy about that record. At the same time, Ian had to fulfill a contract with his record company to do a solo album. And we were sitting around, and he said, 'Well, Roger, how about if we do it together?' And I said, 'Well, how about the Caribbean? That would be a good place to go, to relax, to write the songs there.' George Martin had a recording studio in Montserrat, so in July we went down there, and they started writing, and I just played golf and swam until they came up with a song, and we started recording it.

"We moved to New York to do the rest of the overdubs, and we decided to go down in November again to finish the album. So, we went twice to Montserrat. I really like the record, and strangely enough, we finished the record, and the record is out, and the unfortunate thing is that when the record came out, the record company Ian was signed to went bust. But people really loved the album. And you know, I'm sitting in a movie theater watching *Rain Man*, and there was their recording of 'Lonely Avenue' in the movie. And nobody knew about it. Roger didn't know about it; Ian didn't know about it. So, I called them up and said, 'It's in the movie.'

So that was fun. They drive down in the Buick, and out of the radio is a song called 'Lonely Avenue'—it's an old Doc Pomus tune."

But "Clouds and Rain" is the record's true jewel . . . "Yeah, the reason 'Clouds and Rain' was there, when we arrived . . . I mean, most of the songs were autobiographical. 'Clouds and Rain' was because when we arrived in Montserrat in July, it was one tropical storm after another. So, it was pretty tough to even get there, because we had to stay overnight in Antigua and wait and so forth. Same thing with 'Via Miami,' because Ian lost his luggage in Miami, so there was a song called 'Via Miami.' That album was basically to get the frustrations out from being on *House of Blue Light*. And we just wanted to have fun. We didn't even think about the direction. They left the sound up to me and they loved it, so there wasn't any problem there. We just had an outrageously good time. It was like a holiday, and getting musicians who you like to work with, you know, like Dr. John, Joe Mennonna, and on it goes. We had a constant smile on our face."

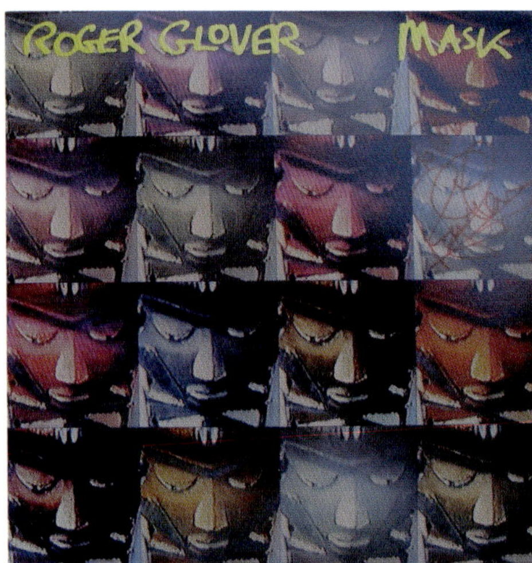

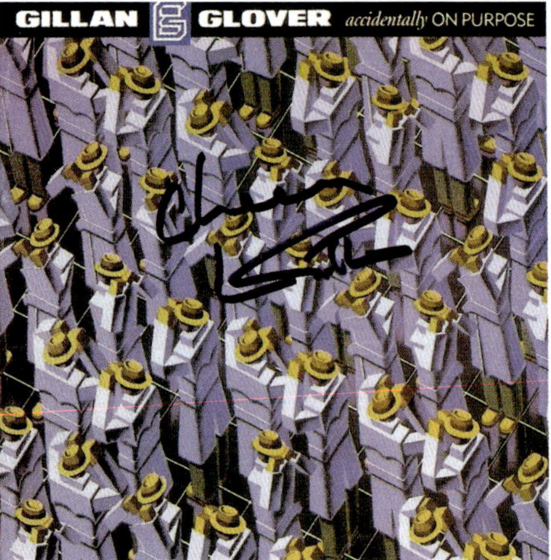

Roger Glover's *Mask* album from 1984 (signed by Roger) and Roger and Ian Gillan's *Accidentally on Purpose* album from 1988 (signed by Ian). *Martin Popoff archive*

Incidentally, Nick was also on board for the aforementioned *Mask*, issued by Roger in 1984. "Yes, well, how *Mask* worked out was I was living with Roger, and I kept noticing his poems. And I thought, my God, these poems are great! So, I kept hounding him and said, 'You should do an album; you should put these poems to song.' 'Well, I don't have a voice; no, no.' And I said, 'Oh well; think about it.' And then Rainbow was playing in Montreal, and I went to see them, and Roger and I went out to dinner. We went to Moishe's Steakhouse or someplace like that at eleven o'clock and I let him have it again. 'Jeez, Rog, let's do it.' And he says, 'Okay, let's do it.' So, I came back down to Greenwich, and we started doing pre-pro, and that's how the album happened. All of that happened at Bear Tracks studio in Suffern, New York. It was probably a forty-five-minute drive from Greenwich to Suffern. It was a recording studio owned by Spyro Gyra, the jazz group."

A punctuation mark of sorts was put to the business end of things, with Purple's Polydor deal laid to rest and BMG picking up the pieces. Both labels were based in Germany, perennial anchor nation to the band's prospects.

"We have changed to BMG, or Mercury in America," said Jon in a contemporaneous interview. "It seemed like a good idea for a change, because I don't think our band and PolyGram saw eye to eye anymore. They didn't give us the feeling they still thought Deep Purple was a current band. We still believe it is, and when we got back together, we didn't intend just to do one album and split. In fact, if ever we do disappear, we are going to do it loudly! Our management came to us one day and said they thought it would be better and they had a fabulous offer from BMG, so we took it. Quite a few of the people who were at Polydor when we re-formed are now at BMG, so in a way, we've moved with them. BMG are another of those huge German conglomerates. But as you know, Germany has always been good for us, careerwise and recording company–wise. Germany seems to be the center of the rock universe. It was an amicable split, and there is no point in a group and record company staying together if there is no feeling intellectually and emotionally between them. It doesn't seem to make an enormous amount of sense. It only means the company would be forcing an artist to make something, and the artist wouldn't be trying their best.

"Our records have always sold well in Germany," continues Jon, "and they were among our first supporters. Ritchie always had a big following there. He had created a mystique with a band called the Three Musketeers, believe it or not! This was in Hamburg just before Purple. Gillan and Glover were vaguely known for Episode Six. Purple started out playing clubs in Germany, and from there our fame spread by word of mouth. Ritchie destroyed an amplifier, and Gillan did his high-octane scream; suddenly people realized our band was different, and it was Germany that first picked up on that, followed by the UK."

Jon Lord and collaborator Tony Ashton at the Hotel Post, March 1990. © *Menerbes, Wikimedia Commons*

Meanwhile, despite Lord's optimism, Ritchie did nothing to sugar-coat the possibility that Purple was on the rocks. Rumors swirled around putting Rainbow back together, or of Blackmore working with powerful shrieker Lenny Wolf from Kingdom Come or perhaps Brian Howe from the compromised modern-era Bad Company lineup.

But of course, they soldiered on, although broken, mind you. After not being able to agree on recording the next album in New York, with Blackmore and Glover now living within proximity of the city, or in L.A., the band had decided that relations were irreparable between Ritchie and Ian, and that Gillan would have to fall on his sword. Ian remembers that moment somewhat ruefully as having taken place while the band fulminated at Stowe about what to do next. Having put the guys down one time too many, everybody stormed out of the room, leaving himself and Roger, who took the opportunity not to support his longtime mate and working partner in and out of Deep Purple. Ian also recalls, during those drink-fueled few days, arriving back from the pub wearing nothing but a couple of plastic bags on his feet hitched up to the knees, crashing through the door, and shattering himself into a glass case full of more glass and falling asleep right then and there, smack in the company of an arguing Blackmore and his then girlfriend, Tammy.

Among many differences between Ian and Ritchie, one was purely musical. Ian wanted to take the band in more of a spontaneous, artistic, progressive direction (he would later get his wish), while Ritchie was still glowing with a fondness for the commercial hooks of his 1980s Rainbow records—his particular wish would be granted right now, through the crafting of the very next Deep Purple record.

In any event, there was a bit of a moving-along, with tracks that compromised the commercial for a pronounced Purpleness, presented in demo form to Ian for consideration. These rough tracks would become "Wicked Ways," a brisk arch-Purple romp; "King of Dreams," the record's Zeppelin-like centerpiece; and "Slow Down Sister," a rockin' extra that didn't make the album proper. Nonplussed, Ian chose instead to hit the road as Garth Rockett and the Moonshiners, playing an eclectic mix of solo stuff past and present, and covers that comforted Gillan and reminded him of his extensive early rock roots. As Ian recalls it, the millions of reasons above came down the phone line from manager Phil Banfield as Ian sat at his desk in his tranquil England home studio, after which he hung up and muttered, "The bastards have fired me."

"Deep Purple was a highly tuned moneymaking machine," mused Ian, speaking with Garry Sharpe from *Metal Forces* back in 1990. "The guys didn't want to tour in Britain at all. I think they were shit-scared to coming to Britain, to be honest, like a lot of bands, because they couldn't make much money here. Knebworth on the first tour, Wembley, NEC, and Edinburgh on the second tour. That was no good. It made me feel disgusted. The thing with playing major venues is that it's all over too quickly. I like to be on the road.

"They've been very evasive on statements as to exactly what happened," continues Gillan, on his firing, although given the history, the give and take, that seems too strong a word. "Basically, Bruce Payne, the manager, phoned my manager and told him the band wanted another singer and that was it. I got no phone calls from any of the guys in the band. To this day, I've only spoken to Roger. They put out a statement saying we've parted due to musical reasons. But that's a load of bullshit. I don't know what the reasons are. If I was singing crap, then someone could have come up to me and said, 'Ian, you're singing crap.' I mean, we all went up to Ian Paice and said, 'Ian, you're playing crap. Pull yourself together.' If I'd been writing shit songs, I would have thought they'd come to me and said, 'Ian, don't like your writing these days. Ian, you're drinking too much.' You know, okay, I'll bear that in mind. I'll stop drinking.

"Strangely enough, when I spoke to Roger a couple of months after this happened, he was very uneasy on the phone. He said, 'Look, man, I don't know what to say. Honestly, it was beyond my control.' I knew that. I knew Roger didn't want me out of the band. He was so upset. Roger is my best friend. I've worked with him for twenty-four years. So, we made a pact that day. I said, if it means that we can at least talk on the phone, we won't discuss Deep Purple at all. So, I've spoken to Roger probably a hundred times on the phone, and neither of us has mentioned Purple."

Adding meat on the bones, Ian says, "The facts are that Purple's manager was Ritchie Blackmore's manager, and there was a great deal of unpleasantness when the band was re-formed in terms of my manager, who was to look after the European side of things. Much as Bruce Payne has vowed that he's been acting in the interests of the whole band, I'm utterly convinced that he had Ritchie's interests first and foremost. I don't want to start a slanging match. I've got a great deal of affection for Jon Lord and Ian Paice. I'm just trying to rationalize it as I see it. I think it was my turn to be out of favor. Everyone else has been out of favor. It's a volatile situation. There are difficulties with Ritchie, his playing and his drinking and whatever. Lately, we had tours canceled because he'd throw the guitar up in the air and forget where he'd put it, and it would land on his finger and the tour would be canceled. Then you would catch him eating a loaf of bread backstage, because somebody had told him that bread sobers you up, which made it easier for him to drink more whiskey.

"There was a lot of rumors flying around about me and my supposed drinking habit. I never touched the drink before I went onstage. Going onstage was like going into the pub for me, and yet, I think those rumors were to divert attention from, well, Ritchie's got problems. So, I don't know what happened, but I have to assume the seeds were sown by Ritchie and that Jon and Ian had no alternative but to go along with it."

Losing Gillan, the rest of Purple went through a prolonged period where a whole bunch of nothing happened. But eventually a bunch of discussion was generated about looking for a replacement. Paul Rodgers, Ronnie James Dio, and Doug Pinnick from King's X were discussed, while Jimmy Barnes, Kal Swann, Brian Howe, John Farnham, Terry Brock, and Jimi Jamison were said to have actually auditioned.

In fact, Jamison, of Survivor fame, had done more than auditioned. He had recorded with the band in September 1989, and as far as Purple was concerned, he had the job. But Jamison had just recorded his first solo album, and, as Jon Lord tells the story, Jimi's record label had Italo-American connections of a certain sort and had strongly advised Jamison not to join Deep Purple.

"We auditioned Jimi, who had been the lead singer in Survivor, and he wanted the gig so much," adds Lord, leaving out the Mafia reference. "He sounded fantastic, and we had some wonderful rehearsals, but then his management told him that he couldn't, as he was going to be big on his own. He really would've been great in the band, I can tell you. You want to hear him sing 'Highway Star'—it was absolutely marvelous. We did things like 'Sail Away' with him and a couple of others like 'Maybe I'm a Leo' that he did brilliantly. I think he would've been just brilliant for us. I didn't want Joe in the band. I thought he was totally wrong, and that's not with hindsight. I fought against it."

But the job did eventually fall to a familiar name and voice, Joe Lynn Turner, the longest reigning and most recent of Rainbow crooners.

"Rainbow was defunct, I was doing solo stuff, and, to make a long story short, I got a call," begins another Italo-American (and also of that ilk is Ronnie James Dio, who had been discussed as an option). "They wanted me to come up to Vermont. It was the eleventh hour, the last minute. I had already heard that they already had a singer, a friend of mine, Terry Brock [Note: from Scottish AOR band Strangeways]. To make a long story short, they said, 'Look, we're not really sure.' I think he's from Atlanta. He really sings great. He's a great guy and we're still friends today. But I

Rainbow at the Baltimore Civic Center, November 8, 1983. All three of these guys—Roger, Joe, and Ritchie—would be in Deep Purple for the *Slaves and Masters* project, prompting the nickname "Deep Rainbow." © *Rudy Childs*

think they had him in line after months of auditions. But they call me up at the last minute and say come up there. And I'm like, Jesus, there's going to be a lot of flak because I was in Rainbow. And Ritchie says, 'I don't give a fuck.' So, I went up there and I went in, and what it was was a country club that was closed up for the winter. They had rented out the area of the bar and just set up right on this red carpet, moved all the tables, had a mobile unit to do the demos.

"And as I came walking in after a four-and-a-half-hour drive from New York, he started the riff to 'Hey Joe.' And I just went straight up to the mic, picked it up, and started singing 'Hey Joe.' After that there were a few casual amenities, because I didn't really know Jon and Ian that well and just said hello, hello, hello, and then they went into what became later 'The Cut Runs Deep.' And I just started singing some lyrics I had, which was 'The Cut Runs Deep,' and they were all just eyebrows raised going, 'This fucking guy is the guy.' Because nobody had gone in before and just adapted right to it. But I was made for it because I had grown up with them and had been in Rainbow, so I was ready for this. It was a natural thing for me. So that was it; they said, 'You're in the band.' Jon and Ian opened their arms to me, and it was really great."

Frank Morgan, by this time having moved on, nonetheless puts a bit of a different twist on the tale of Joe's joining. "I wasn't actually working for Ritchie by that time, but I was a close friend of his. But the deal with Joe Lynn Turner coming back . . . the Deep Purple reunion was not supposed to last that long, see? Then they decided to stay together, and then Ritchie had an allegiance to Joe Lynn Turner, and that's why, for some unknown reason, whatever started between Ritchie and Ian Gillan, he was able to convince the others, because he still had status in the group, to get rid of Gillan and bring in Joe Lynn Turner, to kind of help his buddy. Because he left him in the wind there. So, I think that was part of the reason for getting Joe Lynn Turner in. He had to convince the others. He didn't really fit in, in my books, anyway.

"Joe was in a band called Fandango," continues Frank, filling in the backstory, "and Ritchie . . . they were out on a record, and he was playing a club in Norwalk, Connecticut [laughs]. And you know Joe—doesn't have a hair on his head. He had rheumatic fever as a child, so he's got a great wig of hair. Really nice guy. If you go back to *Kerrang!* magazine and things like that, there have been little shots of him as a Mr. Clean, and then suddenly with a hairpiece on. So that's nothing new. Over the years, whenever I run into people, they ask me about Deep Purple: 'Do they have a hair on their heads?' It's like Gene and Paul Stanley of Kiss. Not completely bald, but they want the youthful look, so they wear some extra hair. Ritchie—same thing. He's been wearing it for years. He's got the absolute best-looking hair in the world. He's paid enough money for it. I never actually saw him with it off. But he told me about it, because I was dating an older European woman that was Ritchie's age, and he was dating young Tammy, who is closer to my age. So, he liked my girlfriend from Belgium, and I got on very well with Tammy. So, he invited my girlfriend and me back to the house, and we were just sitting there having drinks, and I go, 'God, I hope that when I'm forty-two, I hope I have a head of hair like you.' And I grabbed a curl on the top of his hair, and I didn't know at that time [laughs]. And he never said a word to me until we were on tour six months later, and then I was finding out, because his hairdresser, Cindy Drucker, would show up and do his hair, and that's when he told me. And I was 'Okay, well, it looks beautiful; don't worry about it.'"

When I asked Frank if he seemed touchy about it, he said, "No, just touchy on breaking the ice to me, because he knew I was so impressed with him, and he had beautiful hair. This guy out of California does hair units for him."

What Purple had now gained with Joe in commerciality, they lost in sound projection, figures Frank. "You know, when you're in rehearsal and some guys need a PA, and other guys have such a loud voice that when a band is playing you can still hear them singing? That's what Ritchie said about Ian Gillan. He said that his voice in his prime was so powerful.

"Did you know Paul Rodgers was supposed to audition for Deep Purple?" asks Frank. "And did you know they tried to get Ronnie Wood in the band as a bass player one time? Because Ronnie played the bass on the *Beck-Ola* and *Truth* albums with Jeff Beck and Rod Stewart, and he got on with those guys really well. And Ritchie was also friends with the bass player in the Average White Band, who was also in Paul McCartney's band, the blond-haired guy, Hamish Stuart. This was back when Ian Gillan and Roger Glover were going, and they were trying to find replacements. And Ritchie loved Ronnie James Dio. Ronnie James Dio, to me, and Ritchie, he's an opera singer that does rock 'n' roll. He's got probably one of the finest voices in all of music, and Ritchie, if you think about it, Ritchie has selected some of the finest vocalists in rock 'n' roll. He is a spotter of talent. Anybody who has ever played in Rainbow, or those Deep Purple lineups, you know, they have a career."

The exiled Ian Gillan, touring with his solo act, Longhorn Club, Stuttgart-Wangen, Germany, December 2, 1991. © *Wolfgang Gürster*

On the promotional trail once the record was done, Joe was filled with a bit more bravado about why Purple made the decision they did.

"Ian would give them a hard time, and they got sick of it," explains Joe. "He's got his own solo album out now. The guys in Purple told me, 'We've never really had a singer.' I go, 'Well, you had Ian Gillan.' They go, 'He's not a singer's singer. He's a stylist.' I go, 'Aah, I see what you mean, a stylist as opposed to a singer—it's two different things.' They wanted somebody who can really sing and write songs, like what we did on this record, as opposed to the *House of Blue Light* record, which was no songs and really yielded nothing they could bring to the stage. I grew up listening to Deep Purple. I grew up in a cover band that played Deep Purple and also did originals like Deep Purple. I've been singing 'Highway Star' and 'Woman from Tokyo' and 'Child in Time' since I was seventeen years old. I have an affinity for this band. I know where they're coming from. Now, I do not sound like Ian Gillan—I never tried to, I never wanted to. I can't say I never liked his voice, because I really do like Ian's voice. He's incredibly gifted and he has a wonderful style, but I'm not that style. I'm much more of a hard rockin' blues singer than a high-pitched operatic screamer.

"I was honored, and I was flattered, but I said, 'Do not take this as an insult, guys. Give me ten days to clear up my legal hassles with my band and labels. If you've waited two years to find a singer, you can wait ten days and let me get my heart together and see what I want to do.' I didn't want to burn my bridges. After about a week, I knew. I just thought, 'What, am I stupid not to just jump at the chance?!' But I had to sit down with the boys in Purple and say, 'Are we going to be true to Purple? Are we going to have the hard rockin' blues image come out? I really don't want to scream.' I had my own rules. In other words, the possibilities had to be weighed out and the other opportunities cleared. And when I realized that they were ready for anything, that they were going to be real collaborative of what I was going to bring to the band, I said, 'Yup, I'll do it!'"

Once they got down to doing it—mostly at Greg Rike Productions in Orlando, Florida—*Slaves and Masters* took from the end of 1989 until about June 1990 to finish, eventually seeing issue on October 22 of that year.

"That was a terrible record to do," recalls Nick Blagona, once again on the docket as engineer. "In my opinion, that wasn't Deep Purple at all; that was like Deep Rainbow. That whole album had a strange feeling about it. I mean, I'd worked with Joe. I'd done a few Rainbow records and knew Joe very well, and both of us lived together in a condo in Orlando. But it's not the same without Ian. Ritchie always liked Joe. And so, you know, Deep Purple became an American pop band. They sounded a bit like Foreigner, with the catchy hooks and so forth. I mean, a lot of people like the record, and I like the record, but to me it wasn't a Purple record. I never understood how Joe could fit into Deep Purple. Joe is the perfect American singer and was perfect for Rainbow. In fact, Rainbow had their biggest hits with Joe, with 'Stone Cold' and 'Street of Dreams,' but particularly 'Stone Cold,' again, sort of a Foreigner thing.

"In fact, 'Stone Cold' was such a big hit that I was quite surprised. Going back to that time, I was in New York making another record when I called up Roger, and Roger said, 'I've got to meet with you. I've been trying to find you.' 'Okay, well, do you want to come down? I have a couple of days off.' So, we went down to New York to have dinner; he came down from Greenwich. And he says, 'Deep Purple is going to re-form, and we would like you to engineer.' And I said, 'Well, I'm honored.' But I said, 'You know, Rainbow's just had a hit record here. Why blow that off?' And he says, 'Well, we're really Deep Purple. Rainbow is just, you know, to kill time, basically, until Deep Purple re-formed.' So that's how *Perfect Strangers* came to be."

Blagona is emphatic that no one should consider him as coproducer on any of the Purple projects. "No, definitely not—I was the engineer. Although I was free to help produce the record, and I was like the extra member of Deep Purple. But yeah,

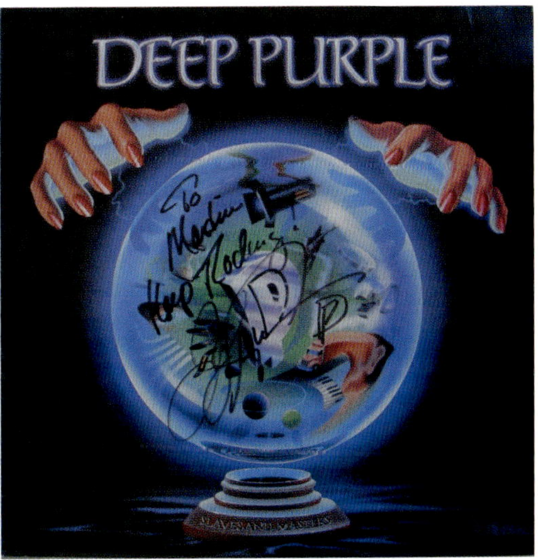

Nice ad for *Slaves and Masters*, along with the album cover, signed to the author by Joe. *Martin Popoff archive*

that record was grueling, because we spent a lot of time doing that record, and then they didn't give us much time to mix the album."

Otherwise, the album was made much the same way as the previous couple. "Yes, same thing. You just record them as best you can. Ritchie always liked my guitar sounds; I get sounds very fast. So, there wasn't any talk about where we were going to go songwise and so forth. I just gave them a great sound. I don't think it was any more live off the floor than the others. I think we always did live off the floor. We never did drums by themselves. Except *House of Blue Light*, which was a difficult album to do. Because Ritchie was being very difficult. We ended up redoing a lot of drums, and people weren't sure about the songs, and we were redoing it. That was one long album, and very expensive because it took almost ten months to do. *Perfect Strangers*, on the other hand, was a joy to do. Everyone loved each other, and we had a great time. It only took about three months."

As for Nick's assessment of Roger as a producer, "He was great. Always got the best out of everybody. And we really enjoyed working with each other. We were friends too, so it helped a lot. And you know, with Roger and I, he didn't have to say anything to me in terms of drum sounds, guitar sounds, bass sound. He was always happy with what I was doing. So, there was never any 'Can you do this; can we try this?' I was the one who would say, 'Can we just try a little of this, a little more compression and so forth?' And he'd go, 'Cool, whatever.' Because I'm always very fast; there isn't any wait time. So, it worked out very well—no disagreements. And actually, in all my career, I've never had any disagreements with anything. I don't know what it is to have that. Because I'm always trying to keep my head."

Although the *Slaves and Masters* album cover was another amateurish nonstarter, the title has an interesting background story.

"Roger was drawing a few things, because Roger is quite an artist," begins Joe. "The reason it became *Slaves and Masters* is because we had this huge board in the back of the studio that we would write titles on. There was everything from *Fuck Your Mother* . . . everybody was starting to take the piss out of everything. But that was one of the things somebody wrote down, because of the constant repetition of the slave tape and a master tape. That's actually where it came from.

"Because it had a life on different levels. When somebody says slaves and masters, you can think of world domination or sexual things; it had a lot of levels. So, when we saw *Slaves and Masters*, we said, 'Well, this is just really apropos because we had an overabundance of slave and master tapes.' And they work like this: For example, you'll record the drums on a master reel. And then what you'll do, in order to keep the sonics on this particular 2-inch tape . . . you don't have to do it anymore with digital, because of ProTools, which is another way of recording. Digitally, you don't lose any generations playing the tape back and forth. Every time you spin that tape, rewind that tape, play that tape, run that magnetic tape across the heads, you'll lose tone, quality, etc., top, bottom—you'll lose it. So, the more times you run that master tape through those heads, in order to do overdubs, vocals, guitars, whatever, you're really diminishing the quality of whatever was on that tape. So, in order to keep perfect quality, you'll take a master tape of the drums, for example, which are very important, and then you'll take another twenty-four-track machine and make a copy, which is the slave, and then we'll work all our overdubs, running them back and forth over the slave. This way, when we transfer the vocals and/or guitar, bass, back over to the master, the drums are fresh. So, you get all the sonics and the sound—hence slaves and masters.

"So, Roger was doing all kinds of artwork, and we all had our opinions of what it should look like. But we threw it over to this guy. Roger had seen an artist in some magazine that we obviously got in touch with, and this guy came up with this thing which I thought was a very clever concept, with the world and all kinds of things going on in the world, with the hourglass and time running out and things like that. Which took on another level of meaning to slaves and masters, which is really what we were going for, to have many different levels. In fact, we had soccer teams, with shirts made up with slaves and shirts made up with masters. So, you had the slaves against the masters.

"We had an album title suggestion board on the wall in the studio, that we treated as a joke box, really," says Roger with respect to the titling, speaking with Dave Shack from *Metal Forces*. "Some of the titles were like *Same Difference*, *Deep Shit*, *Does It Make Any Difference?* In the studio, we used two digital machines, which are linked, and these are always referred to as the slave and the master. And so, one day I wrote *Masters and Slaves* on the board, and after a discussion, we agreed that we liked it, but we turned it around so as to be humble! It's interesting to see people's reactions to it, because it says a lot about them as to how they perceive that relationship.

I mean, we're all slaves and masters to something. Are you a slave or a master, for example?"

Asked by Dave about the hiring on of Joe, Roger says, "Well, Ritchie had always kept in touch with him. They'd always been at Christmas parties together and things like that; not close contact, but in touch. And in truth, his name did not come up for a long, long time. We'd almost settled on someone before he came into it. But in the end, it just felt that everyone just sounded like they want to be Robert Plant at the end of the day, and I didn't want that. The thing about Joe, though, and I have thought about this in relationship to Rainbow, is that he didn't possess his own voice back then. He had an amalgam, a hybrid of voices back then. But after his audition for Purple, what impressed me most was just how his voice has grown since then. I don't think he tries to emulate other people anymore. He's a lot more like himself now, and that's why he got the gig."

As for being able to detach himself from the band in order to produce the record, Roger opines that "it wasn't easy, but after working on *House of Blue Light*, I knew what I wanted to do this time around. It wasn't for a while that I actually asserted myself on this album. In the end, I slammed the gauntlet down and said, 'Do you want me to produce this album or not?' And everyone did. In fact, it was Joe that helped me make that decision. At the record company conference in Monte Carlo, me and Joe got totally trashed and ended up having this stand-up, knockdown fight that finally showed me that I had to assert myself."

Joe picks up the tale, explaining that "the thing was that we had so many hang-ups about one another, and they all just came out. The conversation was slurred and disjointed, but I was saying, 'Don't bring your fucking pomposity down on me, Glover. Don't you dare turn your nose up at me.' And Roger was saying, 'You're a fuckin' maniac and you're a wimp, and you're not doing this and you're not doing that.' But in the end, we just ended up hugging and crying a little bit. For the first time ever, I think we both understood one another. That was the turning point, and from then on, I said to Roger, 'I'll back you on anything.' So, he went back to the band with an ultimatum and from then on he produced the album, and he produced it damn well."

When Dave Shack frames Roger as the spokesman of the band, Roger says, "I don't mind at all. What interests me is that Ritchie never says anything. He never does any interviews, apart from a couple of guitar magazines. Yet, most of the questions I get center on 'What's he like?' I told him that the other day, and he just laughed. To be honest with you, I think it's better for the interviewers that they don't talk to him, because he doesn't particularly care to explain himself—he doesn't feel any need to. People's perceptions of him are then built upon their interpretations of him, often wrongly, but he doesn't mind that. He's dead easy to work with on a musical level, because he knows exactly what he wants, and he goes about it, and he achieves it. But having said that, everyone still gives him the respect he deserves. So, with him, you always know where you are. If he doesn't like something, he'll say so, and he doesn't pussyfoot around."

The Roger Glover–produced *Slaves and Masters* turned out to be a fine Deep Purple album. It's underrated in the extreme, and upon repeated plays, sophistications are unearthed, rock-solid songwriting is on display, and the evidence of both is in how many times it can be spun over the years without fatigue or loss of relevance.

Ritchie did indeed prove that a warm, personable, commercially tilted Deep Purple album could be a good thing.

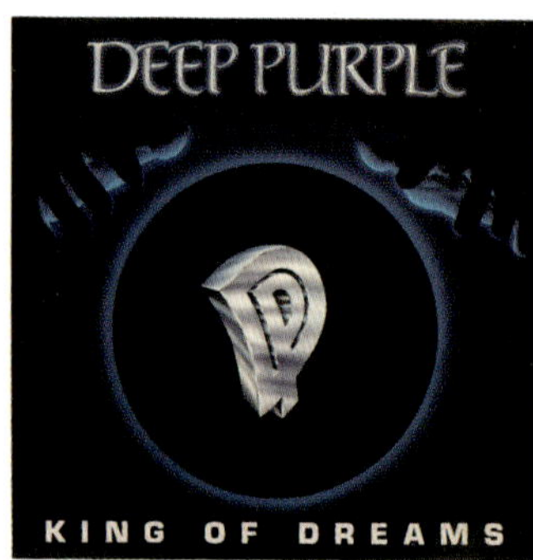

The "King of Dreams" picture sleeve single, along with an ad promoting the song

Opening the album, however, Blackmore gives nod to legacy, not in the way "Stormbringer" played odd man out for the metal fans all those years ago, but in the way "Perfect Strangers" gave link to "Gates of Babylon."

Explains Turner, "'King of Dreams,' well, let's put it this way: half of it's about me and half of it's about Ritchie. And that's the absolute truth. The chorus is all Ritchie. Look, 'I'm a real smooth dancer?' Hello? Black suede? You know, go back to the old Purple song 'Smooth Dancer.' That was about Ritchie too. And I believe the verses were pretty much about me at the time. I was into my complete magical mysticism shit, and I was doing all kinds of weird stuff with that. And I really felt that way. I didn't care if anybody thought it was right or wrong or indifferent. I really felt I had certain powers that I could at least place upon myself and project to the world, and that's called the power of intent. And intention goes a long way, so the verses were me, the choruses were Rich."

The video for the track had a rough time of it, however. "That was banned!" recalls Joe. "The 'Street of Dreams' thing was the psychiatrist and hypnosis, which I'll never understand what they were talking about, why they banned that one. And then in the 'King of Dreams' video, it was the fact that we were promoting suicide, that this guy jumps out of a Ferris wheel car at the top of the wheel, him and the girl, and he jumps, and he disappears, actually, because he becomes a puppet again. I can't understand any of this. It's the same thing as the situation with Sponge Bob, that he's kind of advocating gay activism. Give me a fucking break! Are you kidding?! The kids love Sponge Bob! And he's gay now?! These right-wing conservatives, I gotta tell ya, man, I'm done! So done with this shit."

"I wanted that solo to evoke a certain mood," says Ritchie, with respect to his sophisticated, dream-evocative slice of heaven conjured on guitar for this one. "It isn't meant to be a pointless exercise in speed; that's why it's very sparse. I was trying to make it an extension of the vocal melody and have it express something that was connected to the bloody song. I didn't want to just show off some trick I'd learned at the music store on Saturday morning."

"It was just a floor, four walls, and a tin roof," adds Joe, setting the scene for the album's construction. "We put up some dividers, set up, and started to play. 'King of Dreams' was a jam. We never played it twice, never played it three times. We were trying to get 'The Cut Runs Deep.' We were going after it all afternoon. Ritchie was getting tired because Ian kept fucking up, so he said, 'I'm going outside to play soccer.' So I said, 'Hang on!' And he started playing this riff, and everybody kicked in on it."

Legend has it that Roger found the tape a couple of weeks later, liked it, and implored Joe to add a title and some lyrics to finish it off.

"I usually go in trying to sing all powerful," adds Joe. "But Roger says, 'Lay back. No high notes.' The kids want that nowadays, but he says, 'Fuck what the kids want. Give them artistic value.' He made me grow up. He gave me my soul back."

"The Cut Runs Deep" is another deep, dark, and delicious rumbler down toward a Rainbow's pot of gold. And like its predecessor, there's a hint of blues, mostly brought by Joe and his Paul Rodgers jones and tones, but also Jon Lord, who can't entirely shake the blues from his blood for the blue blood of classical. Chorus, verse, guitar tone . . . this one achieves a claustrophobic heaviness without pulling out cheap heavy metal ploys.

"Roger had the title for 'Cut Runs Deep,'" explains Turner, who also includes the audition story, again, with new nuances for your entertainment. "He just had a title, and it was very cool—where he placed it, and everything was very cool. And I just turned around and sort of wrote the lyrics and the melodies to the verses. It was one of the songs that when I first walked into the so-called audition for Purple . . . they already had a singer. They were looking for months and months and months, and they finally picked a singer, who I'm just going to leave out of this because he's a friend of mine.

"They were going to go with him, and at the last minute Ritchie goes, 'You know, we should give Joe a try.' And they raised their eyebrows about associations with Rainbow and all that, and Ritchie was like, 'Screw that; it doesn't matter. I mean, the guy's just a good singer, good writer,' and whatnot. So, they called me up at the last minute. I drove up to Vermont and walked into this, I guess it was a country club bar, that was not in season at the time. Because it was a summer-type-season thing, golf, I suppose. It was the ski season. So, they rented it out quite cheaply. This is the kind of thing Purple does. They always find weird places. So, I just walked in, and Ritchie started playing 'Hey Joe.' I just grabbed the mic, didn't even say hello to anybody. Just started singing, and the second thing, after a few handshakes, Jon started playing the signature piano riff to 'Cut Runs Deep.' And I came up with the chorus, immediately. Just started singing. And I think Jon liked the way that was going, and of course they had the riff. So, we just put all this together, and it's just one of the first songs we'd ever written. So, I think that was a convincing factor, that things came across that easy."

True to the tale and tradition, this track finds all five band members in on the credit, with Paicey, one imagines, added to make it a tidy five. And to uphold the second half of the recent tradition, the rest (save for the Turner/Held/Greenwood of "Too Much Is Not Enough") get the traditional three-way citation: Blackmore/Glover/Turner, with Turner in place of Gillan, of course.

"You do see Ian and Jon showing up in the credits here and there," explains Joe. "Were they truly part of any of the songs? Yeah, you know, I would have to say sure. 'Cut Runs Deep' and everything, Jon had the whole signature piano riff. It's not to say they didn't contribute. It's just to say that when you are really songwriting, it's a concentrated effort. And when you sit in a room and you go into songwriter mode, that's an exercise in itself. One of Ritchie's main problems with the guys was that he felt all these years that he pretty much carried the band with his riffs and his signature guitar sound and so on. And that they just accepted part of the publishing

DEEP PURPLE

MISTERS PAICE, BLACKMORE, TURNER, LORD AND GLOVER
INVITE YOU TO HEAR "SLAVES AND MASTERS."

The classic guitar of Ritchie Blackmore. The driving vocals of Joe Lynn Turner. "Slaves And Masters," the first album from Deep Purple in four years, featuring "King Of Dreams." A masterful display of hard rock, from the band that started it all.

On RCA Records cassettes, compact discs and albums.

A couple of more ads promoting *Slaves and Masters*. *Martin Popoff archive*

as much as he did, so he gave them equal share. I guess we could say that familiarity breeds contempt, in this situation. And he was totally pissed off about anybody who didn't contribute, really contribute and write. Because if you don't, you don't get any money. He was fed up at this point in his life. And I can't blame him, because he made everyone quite rich. Very wealthy. And he looked at that and said, 'After all I've given and done, to get shit from these guys just doesn't seem fair.' So that really kind of piled on his resentment. And I can't blame him. You know how it goes with friends and lovers. It gets pretty inside it all."

Part of the allure of "The Cut Runs Deep" comes out of abstracts deep within the production—this time credited to Roger Glover alone—and the performances he gets out of the guys. It's a cogent argument, says Ian Paice: "What we realized was that we sort of got lost in the technology of the '90s, trying to do things we weren't good at, and other people were: making super-high-quality technical records at the expense of the performance. On *Slaves and Masters*, we made a conscious effort to start making records again like we did twenty years ago. We'd all be in a room, play it together, and try to get it right! I think we got about 50 percent of that back. The next one will be even more live, and hopefully the sound will reflect that more. The magic is getting five people to perform at the same time. The prime example is *Made in Japan*. By today's standards, it's not brilliant quality, but that's not important. The atmosphere and emotion of the night is still obvious to people who listen to it."

As for the band's new singer? "The thing that's different is that Joe has the ability to sing anything well," remarks Paice, "and because of that, it opens up more possibilities than there were before. I mean, Ian was a great rock 'n' roll singer, David was a great blues singer, but Joe has the ability to do any and everything. So, where there were certain limitations on what we could do before, at the moment anything we can think of he can do, which gives us a lot more. The excitement that can happen onstage becomes more varied because we can do something totally off the wall. Sometimes Ritchie will start something, a piece of music that has never existed before, and Joe will sing something; he has the ability to ad lib and be totally spontaneous about it and create a song from nothing. We couldn't do that before, so it just gives us more things to do."

Asked in the same 1991 interview to describe the guys and their personalities, Ian offers that "Ritchie is the simplest—a black-and-white character. It's good or it's bad; I will or I won't. He's there or he's not. There's no middle ground. He's still a terrible practical joker and at times he can drive you crazy; at other times you love him. Jon is a lot more introvert than people think. They see a very polite gentleman, but he tends to keep a lot of his emotions inside. He lets it out through his music. He's a very restrained man. And Roger is just a hippie, a leftover hippie. He lives his life for artistic things. Joe, I don't really know that well. He seems to be a party animal, enjoys his life to the full. When it comes to music, he's a total professional. Me, you'll have to ask somebody else!"

"Musically, I would say the singer doesn't drink as much," laughs Ritchie, also on the subject of Joe Lynn Turner. "But seriously, the older I get, the more I want to hear melodies. We really worked hard on constructing good, memorable songs and interesting chord progressions. That's what excites me at the moment. It also helped that our new singer writes and sings great melodies. With Joe, we didn't have to rely as much on heavy riffs. When I was twenty, I didn't give a damn about song construction. I just wanted to make as much noise and play as fast and as loud as possible.

"There is a big showbiz side to Joe," adds Ritchie, "and sometimes I think it might be a bit hard for him to turn that off. I think he was serious about it as much as he can be serious about that stuff."

A Purple singer from the past, in later years, became an on-and-off collaborator of Joe's. That would be one Glenn Hughes, who has made records and performed live shows with Turner on many occasions. Says Glenn, "Well, you know, funny enough, probably on solo work or anything outside of the Hughes Turner Project, we're very sort of different. When we work together in the studio, we are very, very generous, if you will, to the point of . . . we're both listeners and we're both giving and we both sort of support each other. When you've got two lead singers in a band, on paper it looks like it could be a nightmare. It probably would be, if it wasn't two lead singers that weren't generous in their support for one another. He is a really passionate guy—obviously: he's Italian. He's emotional, but I think I am as well. But we come together as a strong duo."

Back to the record at hand, dial up the third track and you get an entertaining, event-filled blues like "Lazy" for the 1990s. The song slinks into view, but come chorus time, it's cooking along pretty good, with a late modulation knocking it out of the ballpark.

Joe Lynn Turner performing with Over the Rainbow at Rockweekend, Mohed, Sweden, July 9, 2010. © *Micke Mejdén, Wikimedia Commons*

"Yes, 'Fire in the Basement' was the modern 'Lazy,' so to speak," says Joe in agreement. "It has the blues riff and it's a shuffle. And when Roger said, 'Fire in the basement,' I said, 'You know what we're talking about here? Why don't we just write metaphorically about a house, sort of a person is like a house, the bottom floor, the basement, what have you.' And it was all about this guy visiting this girl's house, and it's all totally sexual innuendo."

Side 1 of the original vinyl ends with "Fortuneteller," although at this point, the track sequence of the CD version of the album diverges. This one is firmly in the "Deep Rainbow" zone, being a moody, mystical but still weirdly commercial semiballad, more or less "quiet" save for a slightly more intense arrangement come chorus time that recalls "Hungry Daze." Ritchie's solo is of his new wayward bent, but a little dirtier than usual.

"'Fortuneteller' was something I had from the Fandango days," says Joe, referencing the four-record RCA act he headed up pre-Rainbow, essentially from 1977 to 1980. "And what we did was, we really kind of rewrote it. Because it was such a good idea. Ritchie just put some very mystical chords behind it and what have you, and Roger came up with some great melodies and lyrics. That was a real collaborative effort. Still love that song to this day."

With respect to the band's working methodology in general, Joe explained that "there were no songs written. Ritchie had some riffs written and some ideas of how things should go. We didn't have any titles or lyrics, any melodies or song structures. So, we took the riffs and made them songs. Roger and I had notebooks filled with titles and lyrics. We found it strange that we could come together with our notebooks and come up pretty much with the same stuff. Sometimes we'd write from scratch with a couple of beers, and boom!—a song. Most of the time, the whole band wrote together, but sometimes it was just the three of us. It came down to what was best for the band. Most of the lyrics were all true, I might add. It was all very personal. When people ask me what most of the songs are about, I say, 'My girlfriend.' But that means it could be anyone's girlfriend, wife, lover, mother. It just means you have an emotional situation. You're getting together or breaking up, and you write about it. I have to believe in what I'm saying to do a good job. I like the message to really be out there."

Over to side 2, and "Truth Hurts" emerges as a dark semiballad featuring some trenchant Blackmore work, while Joe digs deep into his bluesyness. I guess it's a fairly logical outcome that Free was the one band that Joe collected in his youth with some degree of seriousness. "Yes, for sure, and Paul Rodgers and I've become pretty good friends and all. He's my mentor. He's my favorite singer, or at least one of my top favorite singers. And I've got demos, outtakes from the Law and the Firm, just songs. He demo'ed up two of my songs, got him singing that, so I'm like really proud of that. But 'Truth Hurts' . . . ooh, ow, yes, that was again personal experience about my breakup at the time with my ex-wife. I was going through an amazingly emotional time, as all people do with divorce. It was very difficult. And the phrase 'Truth hurts' was always running around in my head, and I kind of said, 'There's a song here somewhere.' And it pretty much explains anyone's betrayal and breakup."

Different versions of the "Love Conquers All" single

"Love Conquers All" is pretty much a true-to-form power ballad like "Wasted Sunsets" from two records earlier, and "Truth Hurts" from only a few minutes earlier. Still, it's appropriately dour, like Renaissance music meets Foreigner's "I Want to Know What Love Is."

"That song was kicking around in my head for a long time," recalls Turner, "and Ritchie wrote this really moody piece. It was this whole 'love and leave on the road' thing, and all these magical lyrics. I remember Jon not wanting to do this song. He was in the studio, and he said, 'This is a load . . .' or 'Oh, this song sucks large' or something like that. And I pushed the talk-back button and went, 'Why don't you just shut the fuck up and play the song.' You know, it was one of those things. I told Jon Lord to go fuck himself in the studio. I said, 'Really, Jon? Just play the right fuckin' parts and I'll sing it so fuckin' emotional that you won't be able to keep your eyes dry.' Ritchie turned around on his stool, and he was laughing. I'll never forget that moment. Jon was so flustered. They started to lose control, and their egos were so massive at that point.

"I'm not demeaning Lordy in any way, but what I'm saying is that there was some tension about the direction we were going in and what was happening. Meanwhile, that song happens to be a lot of people's favorite song. I mean, it just came out great. But there was that tension going on back then. And it finally erupted when we tried to do the second Purple record. But I think it came out to be a brilliant song, and it's still one of our finest moments."

"Roger did some real Herculean work at the time to keep everything together," counters Lord. "Sometimes he went to Joe, sometimes to us, always to try to bring us together musically. But it just didn't fit. There was this beautiful piece which

Ritchie and I had written, 'Love Conquers All.' We once played it late at night; that is, Ritchie and I played it together. It was very sad, very melancholy, it was introspective, but it was absolutely a Purple song, a bit like 'When a Blind Man Cries' or the quiet parts in 'Child in Time' or 'Wasted Sunsets'—a ballad of the kind we sometimes play, a blues ballad.

"But then Joe appeared and turned it into some sort of cabaret song. I mean, Joe's vision on this band was not our vision. He wanted to make something out of the band which it couldn't be, and we wanted to change him into something which he couldn't be. It was a marriage made in hell, not in heaven, and this hell became extremely hot very quickly. I continuously said, 'No, no, no—what are you doing to the song? What is this gonna be?' The feeling wasn't right from the beginning on. I had really tried to steer the piece into a different direction; I had, for example, put in a string quartet. I wanted it to sound a little more sour and not so sweet. The term 'sweet' could only have been used in a blues context for this piece. It was a sweet little blues, if you know what I mean. But it was not sweet as in sugary, and Joe sang it like it was a real kitsch ballad! [laughs]."

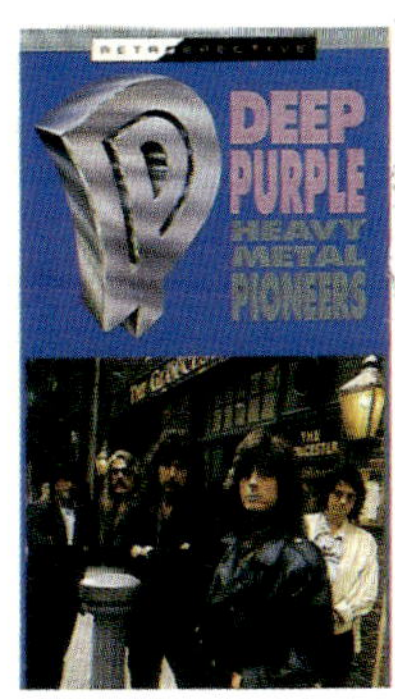

The *Heavy Metal Pioneers* VHS video from 1991, along with a Japanese CD issue of *Slaves and Masters*

Adds Roger, on his approach to bass on the track, "When I was driving around London last week, I had some Motown on the tape machine—Diana Ross. Listening to the bass playing, it encompassed the entire feel of the song; the bass line provided the counterpoint to the melody more than anything else. Relating that to my own experience, it's very difficult to play in a band, produce it, and mix it, because I always tend to play myself down and play everyone else up! But with those thoughts earlier, regarding the position of the bass line in a song, on this mix I sat down and tried to work out what the key elements of the songs were, what makes them work. And on 'Love Conquers All,' it's the bass part, because it outlines where the chords are, and the guitar is just keeping basic time. So, I could definitely put that down to a Motown influence."

"Purple has to work hard to come up with something every time," continues Lord. "To come back to *Slaves and Masters*, the album seemed quite okay to us at the time, and some tracks—'Truth Hurts' or 'Breakfast in Bed'—I thought were interesting. I said, yes, okay, I can live with that. But in the back of my head, I kept hearing Gillan sing, and I can't imagine any other singer for this band. This is enough of a formula to me: Gillan's voice and Ritchie's guitar! If there is something like a formula, then it's Gillan's voice and Ritchie's guitar. The rest is of minor importance. The song structure does not play any part. Ritchie comes up with the matching riff, and Gillan will do justice to every song. I mean, *Burn* was really a good album, but I don't know what Gillan would have made of it."

Backstage pass, autographed door sign, and gig notices for both Purple and Ian Gillan as a solo act

There's more concerning Joe's allusion to the "second" Purple record in a moment, but first, let's look at "Breakfast in Bed," which represents the album's brightest, most AORish collection of chords. Blackmore picks delicately, sometimes playing arpeggios and sometimes just dovetailing in licks, like he does on *Bent Out of Shape* and *Stranger in Us All*, combined with warm transitions between sections that bespeak of Bad Company.

"'Breakfast in Bed' is one of my favorite songs ever," says Joe. "And why? Because it really was raining out, at the time [laughs], when I said, 'The rain's coming down.' It really was about 'Won't you take this pain from my head?' It was about my wife, now, who is now my wife, and we fell in love, and she just gave me so much comfort, so much forgiveness in her hands, and so much mercy, and I just felt so comfortable with this particular soulmate. And it really just came off spontaneously. Actually, Roger had the title, but he didn't want it to be about a relationship. And I said, 'Well, what the hell can it be about? Eggs and toast and tea?! You know, what are you talking about?!' So, I went off and I just wrote it. I said fuck this, and I brought my rendition to him, and he just had to . . . he couldn't deny the fact then that it was a great song at that point. So, it's still one of my favorite grooves, favorite recordings, the way it opens up, the way it just moves along, the sentiment, the way it's sung, everything, the way it's played. Love the song."

Penultimate track "Too Much Is Not Enough" is one of the songs that Paul Rodgers had borrowed from Joe for a run-through. "He was going to do it on a record, and I just got sent his version," enthuses Turner. "And it's quite startling when you hear your favorite singer singing one of your songs, you know? It's kind of like, whoa. But Ritchie had heard it, and he saw the magic in it. However, I don't believe, in my opinion, that Purple did it justice. I really think they should have swung it more and whatever. I think the demo is better than what we did. It's still a reputable recording, but that's how that came about. Ritchie really loved the song, and he said, 'Look, it's a great song,' but I don't think we did it justice."

The song is credited to Turner/Held/Greenwood. Explains Joe, "Oh, Bob Held, if you look on my solo albums, he's still my writer and coproducer. Bob Held and I have been friends for thirty years. He's a very strong utility guy. Bobby can play bass, which he did on my recent solo album, *Second Hand Life*. He wrote some songs. He sat at the board, did a little engineering. He beats me up when I need it, because I get out of my mind. He's just an all-around great friend who is extremely talented and necessary as part of the project."

And Greenwood is Al Greenwood, ex-Foreigner. Of note, this track was intended for the next solo album from Joe, with Turner indeed getting around to tackling it on 1998's *Hurry Up and Wait*. Aesthetically, the keyboards in "Too Much Is Not Enough" are a bit braying, but all told it's quite a triumphant-sounding track. A bit of cowbell from Paice doesn't hurt either, nor does Glover with his slinky bass lines.

Last track is the album's heaviest, with "Wicked Ways" being a grooving fast rocker that, again, demonstrates the hot playing and production all over this underappreciated record.

Slaves and Masters tour book

Lyrically, "'Truth Hurts' and 'Wicked Ways' . . . both of those are very personal to me," says Joe. "I met my girlfriend, wife now, Theresa, down in Orlando when we were doing this. She was out for a Mötley Crüe / Warrant show. She was friends with the guys. And I didn't want to go to the show. I just tried to stay away from the rock scene a little bit and just do what I had to do with Purple. But I ended up going to the show, and I was backstage with Jani Laine, and I fell in love. So, the 'Wicked Ways' song, Ritchie had this huge epic, and I just said, 'I've got a good title: "Wicked Ways," and he loved it. And it was really about Theresa. I mean, it can be about any girl, or guy for that matter. You can turn it around. You know, when you write songs, you try to write them for every man; they're not just personal songs. But they have to come out of some sort of experience, an a priori experience, and that was mine. I just said, 'I love your wicked ways,' because she was very hot and very cold and nobody's fool. That's the first line; that's how that happened."

Unfortunately for Deep Purple, in the harsh light of the rock 'n' roll marketplace at the time, fans were beyond caring about the band. It was Tommy Bolin all over again; in other words, one lineup change too many. Which is a pity, because *Slaves and Masters* is a creditable album, charming even, hair let down, played by a band that seemed relaxed, even though we now know otherwise. Perhaps they knew that there were fewer eyes on them this time, and performed without restraints or baggage.

"I really liked *Slaves and Masters*," reflects Blackmore. "A lot of Purple purists put it down, but I think they put anything down that didn't have the exact lineup they liked. But to me, that was very good. It was very melodically sound, to me. And of course I like melodies. Whereas I'll put on things like *Fireball* . . . I don't even own *Fireball*. I didn't like that at all. It was done under duress, with lots of traveling, and we were in the studio for five minutes at a time. I didn't like that."

"I think with my involvement, we opened it up a lot more, and there was so much more that we could do," says Joe, with regret. "I did my versions of all the Gillan shit. *Slaves and Masters* is still one of Ritchie's favorite albums to this day, and it's one of mine as well. I think it's a very underrated album. As you know or may have read, jealousy crept in by the other guys, and it was just getting too much for me to handle. I went through a rough period where I went out and did a lot more drugs and drink. I started to drown myself in that shit. They say they fired me, and I say I quit. Of course, Ritchie was in the middle of it, and he just said you guys are fucked for doing this. We were writing the next album, and if I was to tell you what that album was going to be like, it was going to be superb."

At the time, unsurprisingly, Joe was more optimistic and argumentative about his chances. "I don't replace anyone. I start something new. I've got this 'I don't give a fuck' attitude. I come in and I write, and I make my presence known, and usually the bands are more successful than they've ever been. The only pressure is the fact that critics and the fans give you a lot of shit. Like, I met this guy the other night who said, 'I love you and everything else. But I'm a fan of Ian Gillan with Purple.' So, I said, 'Well, good. Go buy those records. Have you heard the new record?' And he said no. And I go, 'That's real intelligent. Why don't you at least give it a shot, borrow it or something? You might like it, and if you change your mind, you might grow a little bit.' I was not insulted at all, because it doesn't matter to me. If I'm good enough to be with Ritchie and the boys, then I'm good enough. It's not like I have to worry about every Tom, Dick, and Harry's opinion. I think this is the reincarnation of a really great band."

"I will never say a bad word about Joe's time with the band," reflects Ian, decades down the line. "Joe gave us something invaluable. He gave us an eighteen-month period where we stayed together as a band, and they got Gillan back in the band. Had Joe not been there, I think it would've all fallen to pieces then, because, quite honestly, there was nobody out there we could get who could sing. And one thing you can say about Joe is that he can sing. It may not have been, from a purist's point of view, the right thing to do, but for the life of the band, we needed to have a way of existing, to keep going. And Joe, God bless him, he gave us these very precious months to actually be able to get Mr. Blackmore and Mr. Gillan back together again.

"I think it's one of our better-sounding records from that period," continues Ian, asked to sum up the production values of *Slaves and Masters*. "But we were still dealing with the dilemma of really try[ing] to keep everything in-house, doing it all ourselves. And with Roger taking over the mantle of producer, it's almost an impossible situation when you're in the band, to do it. Because you try to keep everybody happy. Generally, that ends up with nobody being happy. You need an external point of view on something as complex as a record. You need somebody who has no vested interest other than making it sound as good as it can, to make the music as complete as you can."

The guys must have liked the record at the time, because a number of songs from it were performed live, including no less than "Truth Hurts," "The Cut Runs Deep," "Fire in the Basement," "Love Conquers All," "King of Dreams," and "Wicked Ways." Other wrinkles included Rainbow tunes "Long Live Rock 'n' Roll" and "Difficult to Cure," plus "Burn," now that someone more inclusive of the catalog was handling vocal duties.

Touring for the record was minimal, recalls Joe, despite the vote of confidence reflected in that set list. "We did tour it, but when we came to the States, we ran into roadblocks, because of the Gulf War that was going on. I mean, we did Europe twice, we did Japan twice. But when we came to the States, instead of playing the Gardens, we wanted to play in better-acoustic places, so we had three nights at Radio City, and then we went down to Philly and did the Spectrum, which, again, is like a boom-boom room. And then, for whatever reason, Bruce Payne just pulled the plug on it and said we're going back to Japan, and we played Japan again twice. And it was just like wheelbarrows of money. I guess he felt that the sales were not as strong in America at the time because of the climate, and that our best bet was to go down to South America and Japan and Europe. Like I said, we played each place twice. It was incredible. They couldn't get enough of us down there. So, we only did a short tour, I think a couple dates here in the East and a couple on the West Coast, and that was it. We never got to the Midwest or anything."

"God, we did all the dates through the Gulf War, for sure," explained Joe, on a different occasion, filling in some detail. "I mean, they were all over Europe, and then we went into the States. The States, really, because of the war, was in kind of a quandary, so we did like the East Coast, but we never really got out much past that. And then we went back over to Europe again, and we played there for like the second time. Because we were the only game in town. All the bands were canceling, all the bands were running scared, and I remember standing in Scud missile holes in Tel Aviv with a gas mask on and laughing my ass off. Because there was really no threat. Oh no, it was amazing. We went around twice, because everybody was canceling. There were no bands coming around. So, we just raked it in; it was unbelievable, what happened."

Asked if the band was as big as ever or now relegated to smaller venues, Joe says, "No, the only reason we ever played a smaller venue is for acoustic reasons. We didn't want to play a boom-boom room and would play two or three nights in a smaller venue, rather than one night in a larger venue. No, I don't think the band was losing any of its popularity, at that point anyway. I think fans were interested to see what the hell I had to offer as well, so it was novel for them, and I think that increased curiosity, to a degree. We just had no problem selling tickets."

Indeed, the *Slaves and Masters* tour found the band hitting Europe hard in February and March 1991, with all-girl hair band Vixen as main support. They closed off that leg with three up-country UK dates and then a five-night stand at the Hammersmith Odeon in London. The US leg, as Joe states, consisted of eleven northeastern dates, plus a one-off in San Diego with Vixen and Winger backing up. Next it was six dates in Japan, Singapore, and Thailand (contrary to Joe's take on it, Japan was visited only once), followed by a month and a half break before seven Brazilian dates in late August 1991. Four scattered eastern European dates led into the final two stops, both, as Joe alludes to, in Tel Aviv, Israel, where Turner was touched by the hand of God.

"I remember, it was on the Lake of Galilee, big festival, and something very interesting had happened. I had walked into a porta-shed. We were talking about Jesus walking on the water and everything else. Ritchie and I, of course, we're into the supernatural stuff, and we were like saying, 'Well, look at the sandbars. Anybody could have seen that—if he actually did do this—basically, that he could have been walking on sandbars.'

"I remember my girlfriend at the time telling me, 'You better not talk like that; you're on holy ground' and everything. And I went into the porta-shed to take a piss, and the next thing you know, I heard a huge crash right on the porta-shed, which made me go, 'Whoa!' Then I heard some kind of yelling from outside, and when I finally zipped up and came out, the strings of lights—they were big party lights in the backstage area—one of them just came down and smashed right into the porta-shed I was in. So, Ritchie looked at me like, 'Oh! What the fuck was that?' I looked at him and I'm just going, 'God; maybe that was a sign.' You know, we were laughing. We didn't know what to make of that. But my girlfriend, immediately, who grew up in a Christian family, she said, 'This is a direct . . . he's telling you to knock it off.' And Ritchie and I, we just looked at each other, raised our eyebrows, and went, 'Whatever!' Funny stuff. To this day we'll never know."

Chapter 19

The Battle Rages On . . .

"It was an artisan's record."

There would be no second Deep Purple album for Joe.

"As we progressed, obviously what happened was that the egos and the seniority kicked in, and there's now this new kid," explains Turner. "People are starting to call it Deep Rainbow, it's the Ritchie and Joe show, all this kind of crap. Animosities really built up. And there were wars over the publishing. Ritchie was really tired of giving away all the songs. He had told me some really inside stories, about the old Purple, *Machine Head*, etc. I mean, he would write all this stuff, and these guys would just take credit for it, and he was fed up with that. And he just said, 'Look, if you work, you get it. If you don't work, you don't get it.' And we tried bringing these guys in to write certain musical passages or whatever. This is pretty much Jon and Ian, because Roger was quite involved with lyrics and producing, so there was dissension. But we ended up turning around and giving them 15 percent for no reason at all. So, we wanted to share the wealth, but at the same time it was just throwing them a bone and saying okay. And I guess they wanted more, and they felt put out.

"In the meantime, they felt threatened by me and Ritchie because we were palling up again," continues Joe. "Now there were three guys from Rainbow and four guys from Purple, so what the hell do you expect? It was crazy. Now I'll shoot right to the end, when we were already doing a second album. Some of the tracks are coming out amazing. We really wanted this thing to be strong, so we called in great writers like Jim Peterik from Survivor, who wrote all these hits. And Jimmy was really, really great. He understood where we were going and the heaviness of it all, and we were really writing some great songs. And again, the other guys got very, very jealous. So, you could cut the tension with a knife. It was this thick. So, it finally got to a point where it just snapped and there was a whole big fight and an ostracization of each other and all this other crap. Apparently, somebody had to go down—the sacrificial lamb, as Ritchie put it—and that was me.

"So, what happened was they said, 'Look, we want Gillan back,' and Ritchie said no way! And they said, 'Well, we don't want Joe,' and he said, 'Look, what do you want me to do?' And he came to me and said, 'They're putting you on the block; they're hanging you.' I said, 'You know what? It's just as well because I just can't deal with all the fucking backstabbing anymore.' These guys were really starting to . . . one minute it was 'Hiya, mate, nice to see you,' and the next minute they're just tearing you up. So, I couldn't deal with that emotionally, and I started to get more into drinking and drugs just to cover it, mask it up in my life. You know, I was on top of the world, and then I was in the shitter! It was like, I couldn't deal with this.

Joe's first album after his time with Deep Purple, 1995's *Nothing's Changed*, along with a signed copy of 2003's *JLT*

"So, the best thing to do for me was to back off and leave. And we had all these great tracks, vocals to them and everything else, and it was really a crying shame. I was so disappointed, I actually quit the business for about four years and just watched my daughter grow up. I was just fed up with people and the whole business and everything. It really, really disappointed me. So, I was the sacrificial lamb, and they asked Ritchie to get Gillan back, and he hates Gillan. To make a long story short, six months later they were still looking for a singer.

"And BMG finally went up to Ritchie and said, 'Look, if you let fucking Gillan back in, we'll give you like $1 million for a solo deal.' So that's a lot of money. So Ritchie went, okay, fine. So, Gillan came back in, [and] Ritchie signed his contract for a million dollars, all by himself, which is a nice chunk of change. And they got Gillan in, and they made that album, which I think only has one or two good songs on it, *The Battle Rages On . . .*, which is a fucking awful album I think—sorry. We call it *The Cattle Grazes On . . .* So, then the tensions obviously got so thick with that. You know the story; they were sending notes, they weren't talking on these live dates, and Ritchie quit. And that's when they got Satriani and finally Steve Morse."

Asked whether Ritchie was supposed to deliver a solo album to BMG then, Joe says, "Well, he did, in a way. He made that other Rainbow album, *Strangers in Us All*. He used that money with Doogie White and those guys and made that album. And let me tell you, those guys, Greg Smith from Alice Cooper's band, John O'Reilly . . . those guys were all in my band. I mean, the only other guy was Doogie. Paul Morris, everybody else, they were in my band. They were like the Joe Lynn Turner All-Stars, and we were playing gigs in the Midwest, whatever. And they all came up to me and went, 'Um, is it okay if we join Rainbow?' And I said, 'You know what?

Far be it for me to hold back anyone's career. But be warned—be fucking warned—because this guy, he's a master of deception, and you're going to have to watch your ass.' And two years later they were like, 'You weren't kidding!' Everything from merchandise to per diems to their actual salaries, everything, they had to go to court and sue each other. Oh yeah, they said, 'Boy, were you right!' And I said, 'No, I just have experience. I don't have the magic ball or crystal ball; I just have experience' [laughs]. Crazy stuff. They were suing him for the shirts.

"So, I guess Ian and Jon felt threatened," recaps Joe, "because it was the Ritchie and Joe show; it was Deep Rainbow; it was this, that, and the other thing; and they felt that they were being overshadowed by the two of us. Which is strange. It was, as you can tell, jealousy and ego—they prevail no matter how long or how great your career is. And if you don't evolve past that, then you're just going to carry that forward. And that's what happened with these other guys. And Purple is still going; I don't know if you can still call it Purple. I think that maybe they just put out one of their better albums in years, *Bananas*, but at the same time, I don't know where they got the title [laughs]. You can do a critique on it. But Ritchie, again, yeah, he can be strange, and he can be moody. Oh, I'm sorry; moody if you're poor, eccentric if you're rich. So, he's eccentric. But not in a terrible way. There's a lot of misconceptions about Blackmore. And I really don't want to pull the veil back and expose those things, simply because I think he wants to keep it that way."

Ritchie and his then life mate, Candice Night (they are now married), had both said that Joe had written some really good songs for what was slated as the follow-up to *Slaves and Masters*.

"Yeah, well, you should have seen it . . . that album was really coming along," says Joe, in elliptical agreement. "We were really onto something there. We had Jim Peterik as well coming in and doing writing. So, Jimmy and I and Ritchie and Roger, we were all putting our heads together, and we were coming up with some phenomenal material. And yes, there were a few tracks that apparently were left over. But no, they changed the arrangements and changed all the melodies, and that's when that *Battle Rages On* . . . album came about. Or, like I say, as we affectionately call it, *The Cattle Grazes On* . . . [laughs], which I didn't think was a good album at all. It really turned out wrong. That was the point where they were throwing me out, and Ritchie wanted me to stay, and they were like, no, and Ritchie was like, yes. And then he wanted to keep these songs, and they said no because Gillan wouldn't sing anything I did. All this kind of crap went down. It was a mess.

"The song itself is a real kicker," says Joe with respect to "Second Hand Life," the title track of his 2007 solo album, but one that, says Joe, "Jim Peterik and I wrote back in the days, when we were writing for Purple, for the second album. 'Stroke of Midnight' [also on *Second Hand Life*] came out of that, and Ritchie had emailed me, and that's why that song is on there. But that's another story for later. So, we were writing, and Jim was there writing for us, with Roger, myself, and Ritchie. We tried to get Jon and Ian to write, but they were totally disinterested. But to make a long story short, we were out for dinner one night, and I was telling Jim that Desmond Child had handed me this book for this community he was living in in West Virginia, a handbook, and this particular song, 'Second Hand Life,' the meaning of it is we don't want a handed-down life. We should learn our own lives and live our own dreams and follow our own heart. It's a very thought-provoking song. So, Jim and

I said, 'Let's write it,' and it came out in about twenty minutes, we demo'ed it up, and I've had it in the vault for about fifteen years now.

"And 'Stroke of Midnight' was a track, again with Jim Peterik, Roger, and Ritchie, which we wrote for the second Purple album that never came out. A lot of songs were written. The reason Jim Peterik was called in is that he's a song doctor. Aerosmith had Desmond Child. So, as we were writing 'Stroke of Midnight,' that became one of the signature guitar riffs that Ritchie wrote. It's a blues song, but at the same time it's got a very commercial edge.

"When I say commercial, that was our intention," continues Joe. "What Aerosmith had done with Desmond was really sort of commercialized their sound a bit more, made them more radio-friendly and accessible, and they had huge hits with 'Dude (Looks Like a Lady)' and 'Rag Doll' and such. And we thought that Purple was in a similar position, that they were an underground band, but not necessarily inaccessible. So, with the history and the fan base worldwide that Purple had, we could bring them into a higher echelon, more visibility, obviously more radio play . . . hello? And that was the intention with Jim Peterik. Jim is a fantastic writer, for anybody who doesn't know—Survivor, Pride of Lions, and whatnot. He's written for everyone in the world, all these huge stars, all kinds of music, so he is a real consummate professional. So, Jim was our Desmond Child.

"So yeah, to recap, we went in to make the second album, and that's when the shit hit the fan. We were already back down in Orlando. The philosophy, to give you a quick overview, was [to] become even a bit more commercial, à la Aerosmith. And our way to do it, or at lease Bruce Payne, the management, and Ritchie, our thinking was, get another great writer in like Jim Peterik. And Jim came down and started writing songs with me and Ritchie and Roger. And what happened at that point was that Ian and Jon just started to freak out. They just started to lose control, like the band was slipping away from them, and they weren't necessarily in agreement with the commercial attitude.

"However, I don't know if they had their heads screwed on properly, because this could've worked. And it could work like it worked for Aerosmith and a few of the other bands, Def Leppard and everyone else. So, what happened was, because of the—let's just say—egos, jealousies, and fears, the band just kind of went to pot. We were recording and we had a bunch of stuff done, and the next thing you know, I'm being the scapegoat. And Ritchie has always called it a scapegoat. He always says, 'Someone hadda go down, and Joe went down for it.'

"The history of the band after that is that for seven months, they looked for a singer. Ritchie did not want Gillan, and BMG gave him $1 million on his own, henceforth to do the Rainbow album after that, and he took it, and they got Gillan back in the band, made a terrible album, and that was it, man. Ritchie quit, as you know, but he really left before that. He was just sending notes back and forth to everybody. He wasn't talking to anybody. After I'd gone, it went right downhill because Ritchie was totally not into what they were doing, and really said, 'That's it. If Joe is gone, I'm out of here. We had a great team here, and now it's not going to work, so fuck it.' And as I said, for seven months they looked for a singer, until finally he gave in when BMG offered him a nice deal. And that's how the other Rainbow came out, and of course we know what happened with that—it didn't make much noise.

"So yes, as we went along, the other guys got upset about all this: (a) they didn't want to be involved in the writing, but (b) they didn't want anybody else to write! They thought the band was getting away from them and that they were changing into something different. Which we really weren't. We were just trying to sort of bring them up into the '90s. Because you can only go so far with the '70s sound. And to make a long story short, it erupted, and it was a lot of backstabbing and jealousy and hate, and as you have it, I quit, and they said I was fired. But Ritchie was completely on my side.

"Now, one of the tracks on *The Battle Rages On* . . . is called 'One Man's Meat,' and that song, 'One Man's Meat,' is the track 'Stroke of Midnight.' You see, a song . . . many people get confused. A music track is not a song, and until there's music and lyrics on it, it's not a song. Other than that, it's just a musical arrangement, not a song. There's no title, there's no nothing. There's nothing you can sing to or whatever. So 'Stroke of Midnight' was the actual song that he recorded, and to my knowledge, I was told by Blackmore's personals that he would play that before the Purple gigs toward the end, which really pissed off Ian Gillan. You know how Ritchie is. So, this is kind of a funny story. So, when I started into the *Second Hand Life* album, I was originally looking for Candice, to sort of return the favor for them doing 'Street of Dreams,' and I said, 'Look, why don't you sing on this hauntingly beautiful ballad I have called "In Your Eyes"?' And I wanted her to be the kind of ghostlike female voice behind there, singing the refrain and whatnot. And they were in Florida at some Renaissance fair or something and they couldn't make it, so the emails came back fast and furious.

"So, I mean, there are no problems with us," says Joe, meaning himself and Ritchie. "I always get asked that question, but I didn't look for a future. I was just looking for a present. And just getting along. I mean, he did invite me to his Christmas party. I was in the studio, but I couldn't go. That was a big first step. And we promised to get together sometime when we both had some time. There have been a couple of emails, 'How are you doing?' and whatnot. Other than that, no, I'm not looking for a future with Ritchie."

In the vaults from those years, "Of course, there are other songs," says Turner. "In fact, Ritchie wanted me to do another track which we called 'Lonely for You,' a really up-tempo-type commercial track, but very strong. And Ritchie was really going in that direction. He really wanted that direction, and he got nothing but flak from the other guys. And again, he didn't feel that they deserved to give him any flak, because they weren't contributors or songwriters to begin with! So, things got a little out of hand, as they can."

Other titles and working titles thrown around at various stages included "Lost in the Machine," "Little Miss Promiscuous," "Just Don't Call It Love," "Put Your Money Where Your Mouth Is," and "Vicious Circle of Friends." In any event, with Joe pushed out of the picture in August 1992, Purple weren't necessarily quick to call Ian back. Mike DiMeo of Riot and the Lizards fame briefly entered the picture.

"In '93, Blackmore had asked me to join Deep Purple," explains the consummate New Yorker and even more consummate hard rock crooner. "I mean, we started recording the record. This was before it was called *The Battle Rages On* . . . , but it was some of the same songs that are on that record. Roger Glover and myself started working on some stuff. But at the time, BMG wanted Ian Gillan back because it was the twenty-fifth anniversary, and all this political crap started happening, so I got the boot."

Mike's ally in the tangled web seems to have been Ritchie. "Yeah, he's the one who originally called me. I still have the demos. The same songs that are on that record with Ian singing, I have with me singing with different words and different melodies.

"When you've been doing that for so many years, with these guys, it was like clockwork to them," continues DiMeo, on the personalities in the band. "Very talented. I think Jon Lord didn't like me from the get-go. I was twenty-three years old at the time, and these guys would be like forty-eight, forty-nine years old. From the get-go, he didn't like that idea. But Roger Glover was really cool; Ritchie was pretty cool too. But it has a lot to do with political stuff, and at that time in my life, I was happy to be there, but I was definitely unsure whether it was going to happen. And Ritchie kind of changes his mind pretty fast. Before he had told me, 'Oh, you're going to be the singer in Rainbow; you're going to be the singer in Rainbow,' and when I got back from touring, he had left Deep Purple, and he had gotten another guy for the new Rainbow [laughs]. I didn't even question it at that point."

And as for the *Battle Rages On . . .* sessions, "The music was already recorded when I got there," explains Mike. "All the tracks were done. The only thing . . . they went to Red Rooster in Germany to finish the lead guitars and stuff. But when I met Roger in Connecticut, we went to a studio and started doing vocals; you know, the tracks were there. And they were talking to Joe Lynn Turner at the time to do the record, and they said a lot of different things, but for some reason he wasn't going to do it. And then I started doing it. But the tracks were pretty much there. I think what they did is that they just sent the tracks over to Ian and let him do what he wanted to do."

"The basic bottom line was they wanted to have Ian Gillan back in Deep Purple," explains Ritchie, "and I didn't want to have Ian back because he wasn't singing very well. I wanted a new singer. The rest of the band . . . it kind of went to the committee meeting as usual, and they all decided that it would be better to have Ian back. And I'm saying, 'Yes, but he can't sing.' And they're going, 'Ah, but it doesn't matter. The fact is we'll be all the originals.' And I said, 'Well, I can't work with those conditions.' And this went on for a couple of months. And I remember the manager saying, 'Is there any way you would work with Ian Gillan?' And I said [laughs], 'Only if they would pay me a lot of money.' And the management immediately said, 'How much?' And I told him what I think I should have got, which was like ridiculous. Just doing it. I made up a figure, and I think that within the hour, they came back saying that the record company would pay it. So, I was like, 'Okay, I'll make a record with him, and I'll do some touring.' For that money. So, I was becoming a mercenary. Working for money. And wait, and then they said, 'And also we'll throw in a solo deal, and you can record any music with whomever you like as well, afterwards.' That was part of the deal. So, I went okay."

"And they also offered for him to play with the German national team too," adds Candice Night, during our shared interview. "That was a nice little perk. Because Ritchie's such a fan of theirs."

"Yes, I wanted to play soccer with the German national team. I wanted to go to their warm-up. So that's . . . I was doing the whole thing for money. But of course,

The legendary lineup:

Ritchie Blackmore, Ian Gillan, Roger Glover, Jon Lord, Ian Paice.

Promo poster for *The Battle Rages On . . .*, along with the author's CD booklet to the album. *Martin Popoff archive*

when you're doing something for money, it doesn't usually last. And I think we were on the road for about a week before Ian and I fell out with each other. And it was more from the point of view of . . . I just . . . his singing was not right, you know? He was croaking away there. And I thought, music is too valuable for me. The singer is so important. If I'm backing a singer, the singer's got to be able to sing. I can't just close my ears and eyes and take money for playing. So that's when I fell out and said, 'That's it; I'm leaving."

"There was a lot of money floating around, and I thought, well, it won't be for very long," was how Ritchie put it in a separate chat. "But being the lazy person that I am, I stayed with them much longer. I enjoyed some of it, you know, but after thirty years of playing hard rock, I was getting stale. I found myself not playing anything that I was impressed with. I was coming up with riffs, and that was it. Some of Rainbow was better, because that was more my kind of band; I was kind of leading that band. But with Purple, you don't lead it, because there are five guys. There was a lot of music that I didn't like which we were playing. It's like anything else—after a few years of something, you get tired of the same thing. Sometimes it's not them as much me. I get bored with the same setup."

But at least a record got made, and then issued, on July 19, 1993. After all the years and all the bitterness, what does Blackmore think of *The Battle Rages On . . .* ? "It was strange, because all the backing tracks, to be quite honest, I thought were very good. We finished the whole record. . . . Can you imagine? We had like nine or ten backing tracks, and I was listening to it on the ferry, coming across from Long Island, thinking that's really good. But when I heard the finished product with the singing, I just went, ugh, that's terrible. And I just really went off the whole issue. So, hearing the backing tracks, I felt it was very good and interesting, and when I heard the finished product, I just was very embarrassed by the whole thing. You remember that, Candy?"

"Yes," responds Candice, "and you know, the interesting thing is, actually, before they got Ian back in the band, you probably know, Joe Lynn Turner was in the band. And Joe had actually sang on two of the songs. They had two completed songs that were great, great songs, very bluesy, kind of commercial melodies. And one of them was called 'Lonely for You,' and the other one was 'Stroke of Midnight.' And they were in the can, totally done and complete, and they sounded amazing.

"And that's when the management started saying, 'Maybe you should get Gillan back,' and that's really when they started that whole rift, and everybody started going their own separate ways. And one of the stipulations to get Ritchie back together with Purple in its entirety, you know, with Gillan in it, was that they keep the lyrics and the melody line of those two completed songs, because they were such brilliant songs. The ideas that Joe had come up with and contributed were so great. It turned out that when Purple wound up recording vocals, with Gillan, they weren't anything . . . I think it turned into 'Anya' [Note: actually, 'Time to Kill'] and 'One Man's Meat' or something. And Ritchie just went and said, 'What's going on? What happened to the original lyrics?' That was one of the stipulations. And apparently management had never even mentioned it to Gillan, to keep it the original way. So, there was a lot of miscommunications that were kept from each other. It was a bad situation."

Adds Ritchie, "It was amazing because I said to management, 'Have you told Ian about singing that song?' He said, 'Yes, I've spoken to him and he's in agreement with it. He's going to do that song, you know, the way that you've done it; it's great.'

Cassette copies of the album. The Music Giants issue is unofficial, with the other two shots being the Canadian release, inside and out.

But of course, it came down to the crunch, and Ian had not even been spoken to. Ian didn't know anything about it. So I was very angry at the management. And that's when the rot really started setting in—it was down to management, really."

Remarks Candice, "They were manipulating band members against each other. They don't really converse a lot."

But of course, the Purple guys are first and foremost working men, and second, professionals—it's an amusing dynamic one sees within progressive-rock titans Yes as well. At first, Ian likened Purple to an ex-wife he couldn't very well remarry. Still, with talk of this being the twenty-fifth anniversary of the band, and the commercial failure of another couple of solo albums in *Naked Thunder* and *Toolbox*, sanity, reality, and logic (and logical place in the world?) prevailed. Ian Gillan was back in the band, and a record got made. And to be sure, *The Battle Rages On . . .* has more than its fair share of disparagers, just like the two records before it. But given the band's prodigious talents, even a Deep Purple album framed as subpar is going be built on a sturdy foundation. In other words, very much like Aerosmith, despite what one thinks of the songs or the direction on any given project, there's a confidence-establishing level of effort and craft put into the final product.

As has become tradition, Deep Purple open their new record with a dramatic instrumental flourish, with the album's title track—an evolution from a working version called "Lost in the Machine"—serving as one of the most dramatic of the band's career. It's but a brief mystical, moody, and muscular stop-start volley, which leads into a signature Middle Eastern–tinged riff from Ritchie and a ton of swaggering Led Zeppelin–proud moves from the band. A dramatic conclusion to the track finds Ian Paice and Jon Lord shining in an instrumental culmination of swirling Purple tectonics. Unfortunately, necessarily, it can only be downhill from here.

"That's a great drumming track," muses Ian Paice. "I mean, we did that five or six times, and that's the only time the drum tracks came out like that. And I don't know where it came from, because when we tried to do a take after that, it had gone again. Everybody was so happy with that track. But I said, 'Well, let's just see if I can try to get a better one.' And we just went back to whatever the hell we were doing before it, and it had no relation to the way that drum track came out. I don't know where it came from; I don't know what I was thinking when I got it, but that's one of the ones I really like. It's hard to put into words. When you do a track and it's easy to play, generally, it's because you've got exactly the right part and you're happy with it.

"I think the title track is a class above everything else on the record," continues Paice. "But yeah, I remember, from my point of view, we were going over and over the track, and it really wasn't working. I was playing it one way, and I couldn't think of anything else to do. That little light went on and we did another take, and the drum part totally changed. And that's the track you hear on the record. I thought I could do better, and I went back in the studio and that switch turned off again. Like I say, the only time I could play like that was that one time, for five minutes—that's when I had the revelation of how to get that part right and correct, and then it went away again. I just say thank you for those five minutes."

Ian Gillan is quite fond of "The Battle Rages On" as well (note the lack of the annoying ellipses), acknowledging Jon's stamp on the writing and also admiring that the parts worked well together. He remarked in early 2009 that "strangely enough, 'The Battle Rages On' has been proven to be one of the absolute highlights of the show recently, because we brought it back into the show about six months ago, on a rotation thing where we're always trying out these new songs, and songs we never played before. So, there it was, and we looked around at each other and went, 'Wow, that's great.' And it's been in the show ever since."

It's interesting to note that Jon tended to say that Roger wrote the lyrics for the album, with a more accurate picture being that the "work" was a collaboration between Roger and Ian, over a period of seven to eight weeks. Nonetheless, Ian acknowledges that this one was Roger's idea, the concept being that the fall of the Berlin Wall resulted not in an end to wars, but instead, business as usual.

Track 2, "Lick It Up," sounds like a Kiss song, but not like the one with the exact same title. It's more like one of their stripper rock deep tracks written by Gene, made a bit funky by a busy bass riff that locks in with what the rhythm guitar is doing. The chorus is hideous, but the verse is sophisticated of melody and therefore a bad match to the hair metal chorus, but welcome just the same. Ian has called this his favorite track on the record, quipping that "it just felt dirty to me!"

"Anya" is the album's second and last "gypsy-hearted" arch-Purple rocker on the album, and it's one of three tracks on which Jon Lord garners a cowriting credit, with the very classical intro piece accompanying Ritchie on acoustic being his biggest contribution. Lyrically, it's a bit of a soul sister to the title track, examining the hopes of eastern Europe after the fall of the Iron Curtain. To the author's surprise, "Anya" was played live at the band's show in Toronto on August 25, 2024.

The "Anya" CD single

"I had only written the intro after the song had basically been finished," points out Lord. "When we were recording the backing tracks, we noticed that something was missing, and Ritchie and I conferred what it could be. Then we discovered that the beginning wasn't right and that the ending wasn't perfect either. And we often work this way. In this case, I recorded my test version and Ritchie recorded his. Then we tried to combine the both of them, and as you can see, it worked. It would be best to create a synthesis, right? But Deep Purple has always worked like this, from end to beginning. This means, as soon as we've finished a song, we determine whether the beginning and ending are right. Often, we conclude that the song as such is okay, but that the beginning is not quite right and the ending could also use some revision.

"Personally, I don't like fade-outs," continues Lord, who adds a harpsichordy bit to the end of "Anya." "They are replacements for a real ending, the confession that we couldn't come up with one. At least at concerts, one has to come up with one, especially when one plays as loud as we do from beginning till end. You just don't have a fade-out. That's why we design a song most of the time like this: an intro, which grabs you, verses and choruses, which are not disappointing, and finally a chord, which guarantees that the song will actually be remembered!"

Asked about his lack of songwriting credits through and through, Lord draws a long pause.

"I'm sorry for not answering your question right away, but I don't want to say anything wrong, since this is very important to me. Let's put it this way: my contribution to this album was principally playing the organ, not writing. This is because Ritchie had very clear ideas from the beginning on what the riffs and chords would look like, and his ideas were so convincing, I didn't want to ruin them. But I have helped out on a couple of arrangements and got credit as a cowriter for those, and that's okay.

"We in Purple have always had very precise and fair rules," continues Lord. "It's not like in other bands, where everybody's fighting on who gets the biggest share. We really try to treat each other fairly. I have always considered it to be harder to write for Deep Purple than for myself. It doesn't matter how important the organ has been for Deep Purple from the first day on—the guitar is the center of Deep

Purple! I mean, I know how a guitar works, I can also play a few chords, but of course it is easier for me to write on a keyboard. Two or three pieces on *In Rock* and *Machine Head* were created on the Hammond, but the biggest part arises from ideas Ritchie developed on his guitar, and from then on, we discussed how to fit in the Hammond. Because, of course, the Hammond has always been an essential part of the Deep Purple sound from the beginning on. I believe we are really the only big rock band that has always worked with a Hammond. There were always these three elements: Gillan's voice, Ritchie's guitar, and the organ."

Unlike the title track, "Anya" is not a favorite of Paicey's. "When tracks are difficult, it's probably because you haven't got the right part. And sometimes, by the time you've actually made the record, you never really found the right part; you've just found the part that would do it. And some of those later records, they've got tracks I really like on them, and some I really don't like at all. But there's nothing else I can do about it, other than what you hear now. One of those is 'Anya,' which I hate. Because I didn't really like the track, and everybody else did, I couldn't find that spark that was inventive. So, I just played it. And so, if I never hear that again, that's great."

Roger's explanation of how the "Anya" intro got put together differs from Jon's, mostly with respect to issues of timing. In a nutshell, Roger says that Jon cooked up an intro, Ritchie didn't care for it, and Roger recorded forty minutes of Ritchie noodling away on acoustic. The next day, after Jon asked Roger what Ritchie thought of his intro, Roger delicately proposed piecing together a cogent sampling of Ritchie's acoustic work for Lord to accompany. All told, Glover figures the process cost him an entire day's work.

Final (succinct) word on the track goes to Ian, who still maintains that "'Anya' was great. Ritchie said he wanted a Hungarian influence, so I wrote about a Hungarian girl called Anya."

Producing the record was one Thomas Panunzio, with many engineering credits to his name, but as a producer, known more for postpunk, hair metal, and, well, all manner of eclectic nonstarters on the edges of both. Iggy Pop, Gene Loves Jezebel, Joan Jett, Jeff Healey, Link Wray, Lions & Ghosts, Hericane Alice, Beat Farmers, Nuclear Valdez . . . it was a strange mix, but certainly intriguing and demonstrative of range.

"How did I get involved with this?" laughs Panunzio, clearly bemused himself at his memories of this job. "From what I was told, from the management, Ritchie Blackmore was in a club one night, and a Joan Jett record came on. They played a Deep Purple record, and then a Joan Jett record came on after that, and he thought the guitar sound was great, and maybe the record was louder or something. And he said, 'Who did that record? Get that guy.' So they called me, because Ritchie wanted me, without even meeting me, to do the record.

"I had actually worked with him years before as an assistant engineer," continues Thom, "when it was Rainbow. Cozy Powell was the drummer, with Martin Birch, the famous producer, and Jimmy Iovine was the assistant. I was just starting to work at the Record Plant, and Jimmy had asked me to come in to help him. It was a Saturday. And he left. He left me there, and it was probably the worst session I was ever involved in, because I knew nothing. And I was left there with an outside engineer who didn't work for the Record Plant; he was an English guy, and he never

Roger Glover, Ritchie Blackmore, and Ian Paice, live at the Zenith, Nancy, France, October 18, 1993. © *Fredamas, Wikimedia Commons*

worked in the studio before, so the assistant was supposed to know everything, where to plug things in and stuff. And Ritchie was awful to me, because I was so green, and I couldn't do anything he asked me to do. And then he came back a year later and trusted me as an engineer, and I worked with them just for a couple of days. But he didn't even know that I was the same guy. And so . . . we met [laughs]."

"So, they asked me to do the Deep Purple record," continues Panunzio, "and I said, 'OK, what's the situation?' 'Well, Ritchie doesn't want to go far from his house; he lives in Connecticut, and we've got the studio picked, and the guy's got the board from the Record Plant in Studio A,' which was the room I worked in for many, many years and actually booked out solidly, because it was my room solely. So, I went up to where they wanted to do the record, and the way they wanted to do the record is they wanted to cut everything live. And this was one big, like, barn. And I said, 'You're not going to be able to make the record you want here. There's no isolation; you can't all play live in one big room and have isolation and have it sound right.' This is not Bearsville yet; this is some unknown studio in Connecticut.

"But what attracted me was, of course, Deep Purple, so I would've flown anywhere to see where they wanted me to work. But also, they were telling me they had the board from the Record Plant, where I spent half my career working on up until that point. So, I basically said no, and I went home. And I don't know, maybe it was six months later, they called me back again and said, 'Would you consider doing the record at Bearsville?' And I said, 'Most definitely. That's a great studio. We can do what we want. I can make the record you want there.' So, I flew out to Bearsville and brought my engineer, Bill Kennedy, who I don't think lasted through the whole time—they scared him away, literally.

"But what happened, the reason Ritchie chose Bearsville was because there were six soccer fields there. So, I immediately had to learn how to play soccer with Deep Purple, which was a little bit different than what I remembered in high school [laughs]. He was very serious about soccer, and he's a great, great soccer player. Great soccer player. And every day at five o'clock, no matter what was going on, he would put down his guitar and start stretching, and we would all go and practice soccer. And if we didn't go and practice soccer, he didn't come back after dinner, to make the record. So, it was basically, you know, if you don't play soccer, we don't make a record. So, I got to be real good at soccer. I'm pretty fit and always have been, so it was easy for me. It was a lot of running, but I was a jogger and whatever, bicyclist, surfer, so I could hold my own. So, Ritchie and I . . . that's how I became friends with him, by really making an effort, and he appreciated it. I still have a pair of cleats he gave me, to play, and we played a lot of soccer. But that was really the reason we went to Bearsville [laughs]. I thought it was because it was a great studio; it was because it had so many soccer fields. There was a lot of soccer going on."

Serious soccer. In fact, laughs Thom, "There was Colin, the road manager, and then there was another guy who was a roadie, and he was in charge of the guitars. And I remember, I told Ritchie he needed to change his strings, because the string sounded dull. He called Colin to change the strings, but Colin was out getting us food or something, or taking care of business, and he said, 'We've got to wait till Colin comes back.' But meanwhile, his roadie was still there. And I said, 'Why don't you have so-and-so do it?' And he said, 'No, I'll wait for Colin.' And when Colin came back, I said to him, 'What's up? You know, the guitar roadie can't change the strings?! We've got to wait for the road manager to come in?!' 'Oh no, don't let him touch the guitar.' Whatever this guy's name, I don't remember [laughs], but he doesn't know anything about the guitar! And I said, 'Well, what's he doing here?' 'Oh, he's a Swedish hockey player.' And that was like, you know, very close to soccer. And I can see his face, but I don't remember his name. But he was a great soccer player, and that's why he was there.

"And then we would play . . . what was the town? We would play Woodstock; they had a team in soccer, and we would always beat them. So they were getting frustrated. They brought a ringer in from, I think, Kingston, which was the big town nearby. And we continued to beat them, but it was more like five to three rather than fourteen to one [laughs]. And one day I asked where Colin was, because I needed him, and he said, 'Oh, he went to pick up so-and-so at the airport.' And I said, 'Who's so-and-so?' He says, 'It's Ritchie's friend, who's coming over to visit.' So, we went outside to just hang out and get out of the studio for a minute, and a car pulls up with Colin, and this guy gets out of the car, and he's in full soccer gear. He's got a soccer ball, and he's whirling it on his finger and bouncing it off his head and doing the whole thing. It turned out, he imported a guy from England. He brought in one of the Olympic soccer players from the English team. So, like I say, I mean, that record was more about soccer than anything else [laughs]."

"I myself at first also thought that Thom was a very strange choice," muses Lord, on the new New Yorker in charge. "But it later turned out that it had been exactly the right choice for us. Thom is very reserved, very quiet, but he loves rock 'n' roll, and he brought along his own engineer, Bill Kennedy, a guy in his thirties, who clearly wishes he was still in his twenties, with a punk hairdo and a fifty-cigarettes-a-day voice. He insists on raising the recording volume, until right below the point on which everything distorts! [laughs]. Ritchie warmed up to him very quickly, not just because he recorded very loudly, but also because he's a very good engineer—he hasn't screwed up one single track. It was also a very classic studio. I don't mean a studio for classical music, but a studio that was built especially for the kind of classic rock 'n' roll Deep Purple plays—the Bearsville studios in New York."

"Bill Kennedy was an assistant at A&M Records at the time," adds Thom. "For many years, I did all my own engineering. Basically, I started as an engineer and became a producer, and that was kind of the step up back then. If you were an engineer, the next step up was to become a producer. Nowadays it doesn't happen as easy. Producers are more guys that make beats or write songs or whatever. Back then if you were a good engineer, you could become a producer. And I became a producer, but I was still known for my engineering. People wanted me to engineer their records, but they hired me to produce them. Bill was my assistant at A&M. And I knew, because I already had a meeting with them, that I was going to need . . . I was going to an outside studio; I didn't know who the assistant was going to be. So, I wanted to go with an army; I wanted to be prepared.

"So, I brought Bill with me. Bill lived across the street from A&M Records, in the strip joint Crazy Girls. And that's what we called his office. I mean, he literally lived there, and he eventually married one of the girls, but he was a real rocker. He always wore tight pants, Beatle boots, long red hair, a leather jacket, and a black T-shirt. Didn't matter if it was 110 degrees in the summer, he had his leather jacket. He liked things very loud, and he smoked cigarettes and drank, which went well with Deep Purple. It was great to have him out there, so I didn't have to go out sometimes, with some of them, and I could go to bed and not stay up all night drinking and be okay the next day. 'Oh, I'm not going; Bill's going to take you' [laughs]. He was a real, real rocker and still is. He was a great engineer, and he did some Alice in Chains stuff with me. He was Canadian; he came from Randy Staub and Bob Rock, that whole school. And Ritchie really like him."

Continues Lord, "This studio has this enormous recording room, built almost entirely out of wood, about 15 meters high, a bit like Abbey Road #1—you can put a whole orchestra in it. Ideal to get a fat drum sound. All backing tracks were recorded there, and most overdubs. It was the best possible situation for us, since we could really work as a band. Thom has really made it work. His musical contribution had its limits, but he hadn't been hired for that anyway. I mean, nobody tells this band what the songs should look like; when we're good, we're good, and when we're bad, we're bad—I mean really bad!—but we're good or bad in the Deep Purple way. What Thom did for us was produce the backing tracks in such a way that the band sounded like a band. That was his job; the rest, the second session, was Roger's work."

Referring to the second session, at Red Rooster in Germany (Thom is gone by this point), Lord points out that "that was for the vocals. And that's a story that tells you a lot about how Deep Purple functions—if it functions! After these first three weeks, Ritchie and I were sitting together in a room, and he looked at me for some time and said absolutely nothing. Then I couldn't take it any longer, and I asked him, 'What's the matter; do you have a problem?' And he said, 'I think we all have a problem. Be honest; you're not satisfied!' 'No,' I said. 'I am satisfied with the backing tracks, but still, something is wrong.' Then he said, 'And what's the problem called?' What should I say? I said, 'The problem is Joe, right?' I just knew that was it."

Which of course means that the band had sailed through most of the heavy lifting on *The Battle Rages On* . . . with Turner still very much within the ranks of Purple.

"Yes, and it was really a problem," continues Jon. "None of us wanted to be the one to show Joe the door, but at the same time, everybody knew that it wouldn't work with him. So, Ritchie said, 'Okay, we have a singer whom nobody wants, right? Help me out here!' I knew exactly what he was thinking at the moment. He didn't want to be the doorman again, the bad guy. My heart was pounding in my throat, for I thought the next thing he would say was 'Let's get Gillan back!' But then he just said, 'We'll have to start looking for a new singer; don't you think so?' I thought, oh man, not again! So, I talked about it to Roger and Ian Paice and said, 'Joe is really not the right singer for us; what do you think?' And both of them said, 'Yes, we should see if we can get Gillan back!' But this shouldn't become an anti–Joe Lynn Turner interview, for Joe really has a super voice; he is a great singer. But he just isn't a Deep Purple singer—he is a pop rock singer; he wants to be a pop star, who has girls at his feet as soon as he comes onstage [laughs], and I wish him all the luck."

Ian Gillan, Jon Lord, and Roger Glover, live at the Zenith, Nancy, France, October 18, 1993. © *Fredamas, Wikimedia Commons*

On why *The Battle Rages On . . .* ultimately ended up featuring the Mk. II lineup, Lord says, "It's really easy: we have made our best records in this lineup. All the records we have made without Gillan, for example, were not the records we could have made with him. The amazing thing about it is that in the beginning, Ian seemed like a stranger in the band. He didn't know what to do with his wonderful voice. Roger is somewhat like Ian's interpreter. I mean, Ian comes up with really weird ideas in his singing, just to see if they can fly. But then they crash and burn, and Roger's task is to extinguish the fires and to pick up the pieces. What I want to say is that nobody in the band knows in which direction Ian wants to go with a song—except for Roger! Ian needs Roger to explain it to the rest of the band. They are really the perfect team.

"I had the feeling that we had to prove something with the new album," continues Jon. "We had said to ourselves that when we were to record an album for our twenty-fifth anniversary, it had to be a real Deep Purple album, not some surrogate Deep Purple album like *Slaves and Masters*. We did one three-week session, we then took two weeks off, and then we did another two-week session, and with this, all the backing tracks and principal overdubs were ready. But to come back to your question, the first reason that Deep Purple always made new starts is that we always said to ourselves, 'Let's prove ourselves to the people once again and make another really good album!' With *The Battle Rages On . . .*, we wanted to show that we can deliver better things than *Slaves and Masters*, which was really not a Deep Purple album at all. It carried the name, but the sleeve was deceiving.

"We can never be sure that there'll be another Deep Purple album," cautions Jon, in closing. "I mean, we ourselves know best, that the band has been working in situations in which we'd ask who'd leave this time, for the umpteenth time [laughs]. That's the reason why we have made every album, aware of the fact that it could be our last. We'd never want people to say, 'What a lousy album. They should have thrown in the towel ten years ago.' We've reached this point a few times, but that's the way it is—sometimes the fire is there; sometimes it is not. You can't just go into a store and buy something to light it, like, 'Oh, sorry; do you happen to have a Deep Purple lighter on offer?' [laughs]."

Back to the lead singer intrigue, producer Thom Panunzio, in fact, thought all along that the singer on *The Battle Rages On . . .* was going to be Ian Gillan, which of course turned out to be the case, just not when Thom was brought on board!

Japanese CD issue of the album

"That's right. The other reason I wanted to do Deep Purple was because they told me it would be the original band, right? I said I'm not interested in doing the record unless it's all the original members, because that's the only thing that's really going to matter at this point. You want to make a comeback. You want to make a great record? People want the original Deep Purple. That's going to make more of an impact than anything. Later I did the Black Sabbath *Reunion* record, and we put the original band back together. They knew how important it was to have all the key members. The lead singer is most key, except for Ritchie, in that band. But you've got to have Ian.

"Anyway, they said it would be the original band. So, I got up to Woodstock, and I think the only person that was there the first two days was Roger. Roger was there first, because he was really the most involved, because he was the producer before me. He came and he was tremendous, he was just great, and then Ian Paice came, and then Jon came, and then Roger left, and then Ritchie came, and then the whole band wasn't there, so he left, and so it took five days to get them all in the room. Once I got them all in the room, we had to build some walls, because Ritchie played so loud, and he didn't want it to go into the drums or whatever. So, it was a big to-do to get this thing going. Took about a week before we actually hit the record button. We were up there about a week.

"But I was assuming Ian was going to come," continues Thom, "and we were going to start getting some sounds, maybe even start getting down some tracks, a couple tracks, before he got there. One day Joe Lynn Turner shows up, who I know

The two Ian Gillan solo albums from just before he rejoined Deep Purple, 1990's *Naked Thunder* and 1991's *Toolbox*. *Martin Popoff archive*

really well, because he grew up in my neighborhood. I knew Joe from the old Jersey days. And he comes in and I go, 'Hey, Joe, how you doin', man? Great to see you; what are you doing up here?' 'Well, I thought I'd get up here, get in a couple extra days, and start, you know, warming up my voice, get going, learn the songs.'

"And all of a sudden, I realized, he's going to be the singer. Well, Joe Lynn is a great singer, and he's a good friend of mine, so I would never do anything to sabotage him, throw a wrench into him. But I went to Ritchie and said, 'What the hell, man?! I thought this was going to be the original band!' And he says, 'I'll never work with Ian again,' or something to that effect. And you know, I thought, oh shit. I'd already gotten into it, I couldn't back out now, I couldn't fuck Joe Lynn Turner, and so we made the record with Joe Lynn, and he did a fantastic job, and he really broke his balls to keep it together and put up with all the craziness and stay healthy, and, you know, sang great! And come up with lyrics and everything else. We made the record, and when the record was over, or right there before the record was over [laughs], they said, 'This isn't working; we're going to bring Ian in.'

"And I'm like, oh my God, that's really hard to do after the fact. Do we have the right keys for him? You make a record with the lead singer in mind, you know what I mean? You don't just cut tracks and say, 'Okay, who's going to sing on that?' It's like I was saying, how are you properly going to do that? And so, we all went home, because he wasn't there anyway, and then I got a call from Ritchie saying that he wanted me to go to Germany for Christmas, for the Christmas holidays, and record Ian. And at that point, I had to decline [laughs]."

"Well, that's always been a sore point with Purple," notes Ian Gillan, asked about the keys on this record. "I mean, the thing is, part of the glorious process is that you tend . . . you can go anywhere you want. If it's too high, you can start lower. You can write in a relative key. The only thing is, if it's too high, and you want to start on a tonic note and follow what might be a natural melody, there comes a time when you have to go down because you can't go anywhere. And that means you end up with a 'Hey hey . . . ,' a kind of tail-away blues, shouting style. But it may not be what you wanted to fit in with it. But that gives it rough edges as well. That's another difference when I'm writing my own stuff—it's always in the right key.

"But yes, *Battle Rages On* . . . was the most excruciatingly difficult record to make. You know the story on that one—the songs were all written, and I had to rewrite songs over backing tracks that had been used with other songs. To this day, I've never heard the other songs. But needless to say, they had to be different. So, it was an absolute . . . that was pure craftwork; that wasn't art at all [laughs]. I did my best. I had no idea what Joe Lynn Turner had sung; I hadn't heard anything. They took his voice off and everything else off and just played me the backing tracks and said, 'There you go; there's the album; write it. Write it and sing it.' So, imagine, taking an album by any artist and removing the songs and just leaving the instrumentation, and saying to somebody, 'Write. Write an album over that. But it's got to be different to what it was before.'"

"I don't really know who pulled the plug on Joe," reflects Thom. "I'm just assuming that Ritchie had to be . . . you know, Ritchie is the boss. Maybe those guys complained so much that Ritchie said okay. And it very well might have been, because in the beginning, Ritchie said to me that Ian was not . . . that he wasn't going to work with Ian. Or he wasn't going to be the singer. That was the line: 'Ian wasn't going to be the singer.' And so, when he said, you've got to come to Germany in the middle of Christmas, the middle of winter . . . and I spend Christmas with my family, every year, to this day. I go back to New Jersey from California for Christmas, and it's unacceptable if I'm not there. That's pretty much when I walked away from the record."

Thom reflects further on the firing of Joe. "I couldn't really say, but Ritchie really ran the band. And Ritchie is a great, great talent, and once you get to be friends with him, he's one of the best friends you can ever have, and one of the most fun guys. I love the man. I've so much respect for him, and I hope you put that in the book. He's a genius guitar player. He and Jeff Beck are two of the only guitar players that came out of that whole thing, who were that innovative, you know what I mean? You never know what they're going to play next. And he would always talk about Jeff that way, and that's the way I felt too. He was just wonderful, but he could change his mind and get sour on things easily, you know? He just didn't feel it was right, or decided he didn't like Joe anymore, or it might've been a mutual thing. Actually, Roger was very involved with the decision-making as well."

Concerning the pretty persuasive analysis from Joe, that Ritchie was in fact his ally in the situation, Thom is easily swayed.

"Nobody ever told me that they didn't like Joe, but it was like a message from management that . . . and that very well might be; I don't really know. It seems to me that from what I saw, not too many things happened that Ritchie didn't want to happen. And if Ritchie wanted it to happen, it usually happens; you know what I mean? Nobody went out and played soccer in fucking hailstorms because they wanted to. Except Ritchie. A quick funny story on the whole soccer thing, not to dwell on that, but one day we're out playing soccer, and it started to hail the size of golf balls on the soccer field. And I'm thinking, 'Thank God—we can go back in and get some work done.' But Ritchie insisted we continue to play soccer in this hailstorm.

"And Roger Glover, who was the goalie, slipped because it was so icy, and there were hail balls all around. He slipped and fell on his wrist and really hurt himself. We stopped playing soccer, we went back to the studio, and we decided to take a dinner break then. And because Roger's wrist was hurting so bad, Colin took Roger to the hospital. So, Ritchie actually went back to Connecticut, not just home. We decided not to work that night because we decided Roger wasn't going to be able to work. And what happened is they come back from the hospital, and Colin comes back to the house and tells me that Roger's wrist is broken. I'm like, 'Oh fuck.' His right wrist.

"So the next morning, I wake up and I see Ritchie's car out in the driveway the next morning, and I walk over to the little cabin that he's in, in Turtle Bay or Creek, whatever, and I knocked on the door, and I said, 'Ritchie, you know when Roger fell yesterday and hurt his wrist, it was a lot worse than we thought it was.' And he says, 'Really?' And I said, 'Yes, his wrist is broken.' And he goes, 'Oh my God,' and he puts his hands over his face. And I go, 'Yeah, I know. Isn't it awful?' And he goes, 'Who's going to be the goalie?' [laughs]. And he was not being funny. I mean, that kind of sums up his humor."

Further pressed on whether he saw any spats between Joe and either Jon Lord or Ian Paice (the most likely adversaries for Turner), Thom says, "I don't remember seeing any spats. Jon Lord isn't someone you spat with. Jon Lord is a real gentleman, and he's the kind of guy who, if he has something to say, he'll say it, but he's not somebody who will . . . you know, he's very proper. He's a real English gentleman. And he is like history, you know what I mean? In some ways, I enjoyed his company the most. At night I would sit around with him, and we would drink some wine or something, and he would tell me how Jimmy Page brought him in to play on 'You Really Got Me,' and the producer didn't want him to play, and that's why you hear that piano come in only on the second verse, which is really where that comes in.

"I could sit and listen to him talk all night. I enjoyed him. I enjoyed them all! They were all great guys. Roger was incredibly helpful because he had such great production skills. Ian was one of the sweetest, greatest drummers you ever want to meet, and play on your record. Ritchie was . . . Ritchie is a real rock star. I mean, he is a unique individual; there is no one I've ever met like him, and I would consider him a good friend, no matter what went down on that record. He's the kind of guy who I would always be friends with. Even though I haven't talked to him for a while, we stayed in touch for many, many years. Him and his girlfriend Candy. But Jon Lord was like . . . well, he was the oldest; he had been around. He's history. He was just a pleasure, a real English gentleman.

"I would have probably stuck it out, if it wasn't, I have to go there for Christmas, to Germany, to record Ian. If they would've said, 'Look, this isn't working for us; we want to put Ian on the record,' I would've gone along with it if we could've done it here in America or Bearsville or whatever. If they could have at least waited. I would've gone to Europe if they could've at least waited until Christmas was over. But they were not happy that I didn't go, and there was some bitterness, and they didn't want to pay me all the money, and meanwhile I used what they gave me. That's all I could do, was to use Joe. And we did a great job with Joe, and whether they were happy or not, everybody worked hard, and nobody seemed to have any regrets until the end. Maybe somebody should've said something before the record was completely done. And what they did, I do remember them saying, 'We can get this guy; we can get that guy,' and I remember them saying now, 'It's got to be Ian.' And then they went back to Ian."

The "Time to Kill" CD single

Back to the record at hand, the fourth track is called "Talk About Love," and fair enough—it's a heavy, blues-tinged rocker with a hooky chorus, a perfect example of a dud for Purple but a solid album track for anybody else.

Same thing with "Time to Kill," which pits a party rock chorus against a regal and aggressive riff sequence at the verse. Ritchie colors the space behind Ian's vocal like Billy Gibbons might do with himself. This one is a pure Gillan lyric, revolving around the idea of using downtime to work on solving one's problems. It was yet another track that Ritchie didn't like, with Blackmore pushing Gillan to use Joe's old idea for the track. Ian, to get through the making of the record, says he completely ignored anything Ritchie had to say.

"I know they were going for something that they could get on the radio," says Thom, with respect to the commerciality of "Time to Kill" and other bright spots on the record. "They wanted success, they wanted to make a great record, and I don't remember . . . it seemed to me like the songwriting was done in the studio. Now, they might've had some ideas or songs when they walked in, but pretty much everything was worked up in the studio. I don't remember anything about any songwriters or anybody telling me this is a song they did with somebody else, or something we worked up with somebody else."

But the funny thing is, despite all this talk of trying to be accessible, it's hard to see *The Battle Rages On . . .* as an AOR record, even to the extent that *Slaves and Masters* was. Deep Purple were supposedly reaching even further than last time for that brass ring, but the results are fairly claustrophobic, oppressive, heavy, and English.

"Yeah, I agree. Joe would've been a good choice for making a more commercial record than Ian, but I wanted a heavy, real Deep Purple record, but one that could get on the radio and have hits. I mean, 'Smoke on the Water' was played once a day every day, since it was a hit on the radio. Somewhere in the world, every day, 'Smoke on the Water' is played—that's a fact. I remember Ian was telling me, showed me pictures of his mansion, and I said, 'How do you even keep up the upkeep?' 'Just from my royalties on "Smoke on the Water."' That's a heavy, heavy song. Sorry, this is Ian Paice. I never met Ian Gillan. I never met the gentleman. I never had the pleasure. I would love to. I wish he was there the first day. Not to say anything against Joe, but that would've made the whole thing right. Joe did a great job. Joe worked his ass off and he did a great job, but maybe it wasn't the record, I guess, that they wanted."

Arcing back to the record they got, "Ramshackle Man" is a heavy blues of the sort the band finds itself trapped into doing from time to time, out of habit perhaps, usually with middling results.

"'Ramshackle Man' was about how I felt at the time, trying to let loose," notes Gillan. "That album was done at a difficult time because the band was fractured. I was being forced back into it against my will at the time, but I'm glad I did, in hindsight. Ritchie hated the very idea that I existed, let alone coming back into the band. And it was very fractured. That album was probably the most heavily crafted record we'd ever done. There wasn't a lot of inspiration, except for the occasional bit like 'Ramshackle Man,' which Ritchie refused to play onstage, because it was only a jam in the studio. He refused to play a decent guitar track on it or change the key to something that might be singable, in the human world. Very difficult album: it was an artisan's record, I would say."

And of course, quite oddly, Ian's gotten himself a disconnect when it comes to recognizing the producer of *The Battle Rages On . . .* "Who's that? Oh, no, he was the guy who was there before I came back into the band. They did about four or five songs with Joe Lynn Turner, which I've never heard to this day. But they gave me the backing tracks. They took the vocals off and gave me the backing tracks, and I wrote new songs out of them."

I asked Ian what he makes of this gripe of Ritchie's that Bruce was supposed to instruct Ian that he was to sing Joe's lyrics, but that in the end, Bruce didn't relay the message.

"Yes, I remember something like that. I don't know what he said or what went on. All I know is that it was a very painful process and not particularly pleasant. But I know that my manager in London, Bruce, plus Roger, Jon Lord, and Ian Paice, all wanted me back in the band. It was the first time they were going to stand up to Ritchie, who was being a dick."

And Ian's thoughts on the deal sweetener for the Man in Black; namely, the offer of a solo deal? "I don't know, mate. I don't know what his business is. It's never interested me, to be honest."

The Battle Rages On . . . continues its perfunctory march to close with the obligatory fast rom. "A Twist in the Tale" offers up yet another "Burn"-derived riff from Ritchie, this one also comparable to Rainbow's "Spotlight Kid."

On recording Blackmore, Thom says that "what we did with Ritchie; he would be down on the floor, but his equipment would be up in the loft, all walled off. But he was playing live. I mean, we tracked everything live. We brought in carpenters to actually wall off the room, and a lot of the stuff he played was live. Ritchie didn't just lay down a rhythm track to go back and play the lead over. A lot of it was very spontaneous, and it was always original. He very rarely played the same thing twice. Again, he's very much like Jeff Beck. That's the way Beck is, who I never had the pleasure to work with, but I've been a big fan.

"And actually, Ritchie gave me more history about Beck than I had ever known myself. But he's real. That's the best adjective I can use for Ritchie—he's real [laughs]. And sure, we went back and fixed things, and there are solos I know we overdubbed, but what I thought was the real magic was when those guys were all in a room together and they played. There aren't too many bands like that, with that real original sound, and Jon Lord with a B3 going through the Marshalls. That sound; nobody does that. People try to copy it and stick an organ through Marshalls now to copy him, but nobody gets the sound he gets. They're all amazing, amazing musicians.

"But it was very well worked out," recalls Thom, "and everybody really worked hard and was part of it, including myself, to make sure that we had a real interesting record. And you know, it was definitely a different record, with Joe Lynn. So, the record that is out now, I mean, you can't change the lead singer and have it be the same record. I don't know if they—I'm sure I knew back then, but I don't know now—if they did any other overdubs musically, other than just to add Ian's vocal. But I'm sure they had to do some backgrounds, and I guess the keys all worked for him, which is really, really lucky. Because in those days, they didn't have ProTools, where you can change the key without completely screwing up the sound of everything, and the speed. But those are the tracks that we tracked.

"We didn't really invent anything, as far as the technical part of it goes," says Thom, asked if there were any innovations from his own hand. "It was basically get it on tape and get the sounds, the real sounds of the band. Later on, I had planned—because I was going to mix it—I had plans to do this or do that, but as it turns out, I didn't mix it. But we tried a lot of different things, things with the keyboards, and spent a lot of time with Ian's drums, moving them around, mic'ing them differently, putting the mics far away and close, and making tunnels for the bass drum, and double-mic'ing things. We spent a lot of time on that, because Bearsville is a great studio, and one of the reasons it's great for a band like Deep Purple is that it's a big room, so you get that big live rock sound. And that's really for the drums. Everything else is baffled off; you could be in a closet. But the room is about the drums, because you want that big, ambient drum sound."

The tour book

Further on the significant heft of the record, Thom says, "Deep Purple to me is a heavy band. They had big hits, but they are a heavy band, and that's the way I heard them, that's the kind of music I made, and that's the way I recorded drums and guitar. That's why they hired me! As I say, they really hired me because Ritchie heard a Joan Jett record, from what I understand, played in the club next to a Deep Purple record, and liked the way it sounded.

"I think that Deep Purple has a sound, and they've established that sound from the beginning of their career, with 'Hush,'" figures Thom. "And I think *Battle Rages On* . . . is very much a real Deep Purple record, and that was really my goal. Because originally it was supposed to be the original band, I wanted a real Deep Purple record. I felt that they'd wandered off the path at times and done things that didn't remind me of what Deep Purple really was. So, my goal was to capture what the band really sounded like, not to change their sound or influence their sound too much, but just record it as best we could get it.

"The arrangements were more what we worked on. And we all worked on most of it together. I spent a lot of time in the studio with them just working through the arrangements, and they all had great ideas what to do, so it wasn't like pulling teeth. Usually, I do preproduction with a band before I go in, and we work out the parts, work out the songs, but that's not the way they work. I had to work the way they wanted to work. You don't change a band like that. A new baby band, you go through preproduction, you come down, you get the songs, but Deep Purple or the Rolling Stones or Bruce Springsteen or any great band that's been established for years, you don't tell them how to record, you don't tell them how to write, [and] you don't tell them how to arrange. You just try to help them reach their vision. Which, at times, we did, but at times, I think we were looking for it, you know? But I thought by the end of the record, we all had something everybody was happy with. Apparently not, because they erased all of Joe Lynn Turner, so . . ."

Next up, "Nasty Piece of Work" is a doomier, more successful bastardization of the blues premise, akin to what folks thought Sabbath did (but did so rarely). The lyric for this one is courtesy of Roger, and Jon Lord gets his third music cowriter credit on the album.

"Solitaire" finds Ritchie synthesizing his classical melodies with his pop rock predilection. This one sounds like a *Stranger in Us All* song. Ian's singing of the song is an octave lower than planned, something that had been put down to a fortunate accident.

"One Man's Meat" is some sort of stumbled reprise to Rainbow's "L.A. Connection"—namely, a slow and funk hard rock stomper—and really a fourth track that cozies up to hard blues, a style that turned out to be a philosophical fit to the future singer of the record, Ian Gillan, more so than it was a fit to what Joe does. Frankly, Joe and the other Purple guys don't give Ian enough credit for what he can do with bluesy rock. Roger had said that this is one of the tracks he had Mike DiMeo sing on, back when its working title was "24 Hours." On the lyric, Ian at least prides himself on not completing the cliché of the title with the inevitable reference to poison.

But back to "Solitaire" for a moment: this one has an extensive keyboard solo from Lord, something of a return, says Jon, after the more modernized sounds used on *Slaves and Masters*, which he now regrets. "Yes, and I have only noticed afterwards that this was a mistake, since it was exactly that—besides Joe Lynn Turner's voice—that made one question the identity of the band. But at the time it seemed inevitable to me, since the songs we had were not right for organ. It had to be synths."

Further on *Slaves and Masters*, Jon explains that "it was simply the case that I looked at the songs and searched for places to fit in the organ, but there were no such places. There were only places in which sometimes a fill was lacking, for which synths are much better. But there was no room for organ solos. On *The Battle Rages On . . .*, this was no problem, thank God. There was enough room for the Hammond. I was very happy about this."

"I dug the grind he got out of things," recalls Santana and Journey keyboardist Gregg Rolie, adding to the accolades for Mr. Lord that crop up often. "I liked the rhythm playing. The soloing that Jon Lord did was, I don't know . . . what do I want to say? It wasn't as blues based as I would do, I guess. But I loved it. I loved the grind he got out of the stuff, I love the music, and a lot of what he played. I thought they did a really good job."

I asked Gregg about the Hammond and its legendary unwieldiness.

"Well, let me put it this way," laughs Rolie. "I had to sell my hot rod, a '55 Chevy, to get a stupid Econoline van. I had the first van for Santana, but I had to have it because it was the only way I was able to get the instrument around, to gigs. I kind of stepped down a notch, the way I looked at it. But that's what it was. I mean, we had to have it. The other thing that was pretty funny is that because that van was what we hauled all our stuff in, when it came time to load and unload that Hammond B3, the funny thing, the rest of the guys in that band disappeared. You know, I even loaded it myself.

"I've talked to other keyboard players that had the same problem. Nobody wanted to pick it up. It weighs 250 to 300 pounds, some ridiculous thing. It was heavy, and to move it . . . for instance, the Fillmore had no elevator, and you had to carry it up the stairs. Thank God by that time we were big enough where somebody actually did that for me [laughs]. But there were times I had to move that thing by myself, and it is big and cumbersome. One of the first synthesizers, really. And it had a sound all its own. I've had young people ask me now, 'What is that?' [laughs]. Which I find hilarious. But they've never seen or heard it. Or they've heard it, but they just didn't know what it was.

"It required a certain amount of electricity," continues Rolie, "or it wouldn't go up to speed, and it wouldn't hit A440. So, you had to make sure that happened. I had that problem before. If it sits in the heat too long, things like that, it's kind of temperamental that way. But as far as once it's in and on, no, I had very little problems with it."

"Jon Lord was a Hammond and Clavinet player," remarks Van der Graaf Generator's Peter Hammill, who adds an amusing Purple anecdote from way, way back. "He's much less of an organist. I think his function . . . he obviously wants to be the Hammond guy, which is kind of the top keyboards bursting through. I don't think he was a structural player the same way that Hugh Banton is in our band at all.

"If you are talking about organ players of that era, I think you'd be looking at Emerson, Brian Auger, and Zoot Money," continues Hammill. "But I would say Emerson and Auger were the guys, and Georgie Fame, from an entirely different area. And actually, Graham Bond was the man, plus Vincent Crane—okay, there are quite a few. But those are the guys who were organists, while Jon Lord was a bit more of a keyboard player at that time, I guess.

"We did play with Deep Purple, in the Ice Stadium in Munich, in '69. We all flew over there on a chartered plane. It was one of these big German festivals, and we all flew there, and there waiting for us on the tarmac was a German oompah band. And Senta Burger, who was a hot movie star at the time, was obviously there on behalf of the festival, undoubtedly to welcome Deep Purple—it wasn't us! [laughs]. But we happened to be the ones at the front of the plane. So, we came down the steps first, and we were greeted. But we were very impressed with Purple, I'd have to say. Not very loud, but nobody was very loud. But they did make an impression."

Ritchie's impatience with Purple, once the record was done, was palpable whenever he talked to the press. Speaking with *Kerrang!*'s Anders Tenger, he was quick to begin taking jabs at the band's inadequate singer.

"I think the main thing was money. Ian needed some cash, so he called us up. Okay, let's do it. No, after twenty-five years, we get back together every five years or so and do our thing. The rest of the band wanted Ian in. I said I'd go along with that. I didn't know how Ian was singing or behaving. I heard his solo albums later, and I wasn't very impressed. But he has identity. Ian's like glue. He puts things together. I wanted to bring somebody else in, but I was voted down by the other three.

"Ian and I haven't always had this love/hate relationship," continues Blackmore. "He always refers to me as his hero, and I blame myself for Ian being the way he is today. We were in a club back in 1971, and just by accident I knocked him off his chair, and he fell backwards and hit his head. He really did. He changed from then onwards. He became very aggressive, solemn, and intense, and it wasn't Ian. But nobody sings like he does."

Ritchie's nemesis in action. © *Tom Wallace*

Asked by Anders if they've buried the hatchet, Ritchie says, "No, we still have a hatchet. One of these days on the road, I'm going to attack Ian Gillan in a back alley. He's bigger than me and probably a better fighter, so I'm going to do it with a few friends of mine, and we'll beat him up, but he won't know it's me.

"Yes, it's possible. Friction causes something," reflects Ritchie, on the idea that good art can come out of its makers butting heads. "You can almost make an analogy to marriage. Friction causes passion. It makes a good marriage. That's how we are. We're not the best of friends, but I think we make some good music. Any band that's been together for twenty-five years is going to get a little tired of each other. It's strange that the band has been together for so long. Maybe in ten years, we'll be coming back in our wheelchairs. Here we are again after Mk. 14. I don't care. I just want to play. I don't care who is in the band, as long as they like to play too. I suppose this particular lineup is my favorite. The '74 period was a strange lineup with David Coverdale and Glenn Hughes, still a good lineup, but not one of my favorites. Ian Gillan, although not one of my favorite friends, is a great singer."

On conjuring songs, Ritchie relates that "studios are like being in the dentist chair. I love to play music, but not in a studio. It becomes too formal. I like to take control in the studio, but it would be nice to hear some good ideas from the others. It doesn't usually happen. I tend to write on the spur of the moment, because an idea, to me, is enthusiasm; that's all. In the beginning I used to think that an idea had to consist of this and that, but it doesn't. It just has a groove. It's just a groove, something you feel good about. There were days fifteen, twenty years ago when I felt it had to be a perfect riff and perfect middle eight and perfect hook. But songwriting isn't about that.

"It's amazing that we've conned the public for so long," continues Blackmore, mischievously. "I'm still very unfulfilled. I feel that I haven't really said anything yet, but I will someday. The twenty-five years have gone by very quickly. I don't think we made history in music or anything earth shattering. We were a band thrown together, and we produced music, nothing more than that. Originally, we were copying Vanilla Fudge. We loved them and Hendrix and a bit of Cream. We were just blending their elements."

Asked to defend the mystique concerning his public persona, Ritchie says, "It's something that's always there, because I don't quite understand who I am or what I'm doing. I'm involved in the mystical things. For twenty years, I've been studying the paranormal. Not black magic; I'm talking about séances and communications with spiritual realms. I wear a lot of black clothing, and I'm a very quiet person. I believe in thinking rather than speaking. I don't know if I have anything to say and, if I do, if I should be saying it; I don't quite know where I'm going. So why should I be shouting my opinion at people? My life at home is very simple. I love to exercise. I love to kick a ball around and play soccer. I wake up with my cats. I love animals. Then I tune into my satellite system and try to pick up some soccer games. My ultimate goal would be to live on a cobbled street near a German castle, listening to medieval music."

Finally, Mr. Glover offers a few words on the whole *Battle Rages On . . .* debacle, his first thought being that "I wanted to get a producer since 1984 [laughs]. We've never managed to settle on one. Well, once we did. *The Battle Rages On . . .* was started with another producer, but it ended up somewhat disastrously, as far as he was concerned. And Ian Gillan was coming back into the band as well, so we didn't need yet another voice on the same ship. Again, I took over and finished that album."

And what was Roger's impressions of the final result?

"Actually, not bad. For me, I have to temper it with my memories of the time. And my memories of the time are really totally colored by the fact that somehow, we managed to get Ian Gillan back into the band, which was an unbelievably major coup. I didn't ever think that would happen. Ritchie was pretty entrenched in his views. And Ian did it under protest, but there were various political goings-on that enabled him to come to that decision. However it was done, he did come to that decision, and we had Ian Gillan back in the band, and it was wonderful for Ian and I to be able to write again. The only problem was that most of the backing tracks were already done. So, things like putting them in the right key for the singer was a luxury that we didn't have. So, we basically had to write songs to whatever was there. And some of it was fun, and some of it was difficult. We came out with some great songs. I liked 'Anya'—that was a great song. Actually, there are quite a few songs on there that I think stand up."

"Ritchie is the biggest prankster there is," laughs Thom Panunzio, who closes this chapter on a light note with more stories of guitarists gone wild. "It's funny, but the English guitar players . . . Tony Iommi, also. They are jokesters. They love to play jokes on you; they have a great sense of humor; they are so much fun. They would have a séance. First of all, I'm not one to believe in crazy shit, but I remember for years, I heard that this Turtle Creek place is haunted. Before I went up there, I was hanging out with Living Colour; they'd made a record there, and they said, 'Man, don't go there, don't go out there; that place is spooky; there's fucking ghosts there, no question about it; you don't wanna be there.' I heard this for years, from lots of people. I'd been up there before but never stayed there for a length of time."

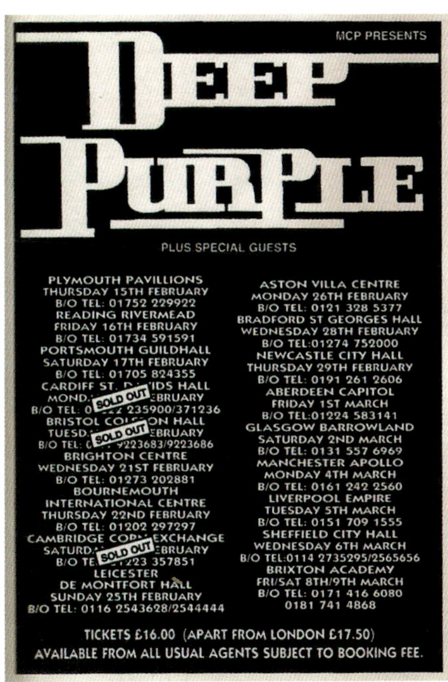

Tour dates advertisement.
Martin Popoff archive

And to clarify, this is the living quarters at Bearsville Studios. "Yeah, Turtle Creek. There was a barn, which is the only thing that's left of Bearsville right now. Eddy Offord used to record in the barn, used to put the speakers right in front to him, and the band right in front of him, or all in the same room. It's almost like recording a band playing in a club, live. He's an old English producer who used to work up there; he used the barn for recording, and he would actually do his tracks in there. That's all that's left of Bearsville now.

"But Turtle Creek was haunted," continues Panunzio, "and there were things that happened there that were unexplainable, that Ritchie couldn't have done. My engineer, Bill Kennedy, got so spooked. There were houses—maybe there were three;

I don't remember—and they were actually divided, so there would be like one family in one side of the house and one family quarters on the other side. And my engineer and I shared one house, and he was so spooked that after about a week, he slept every night on my couch, on my side of the house, with his clothes on so he could run out, and to the point where he did leave. Because, you know, Ritchie is into all that stuff, and because he's a prankster, he made it even more crazy [laughs].

"Every Thursday night they used to bring in an English cook and have a proper English dinner, in my house. I had the biggest quarters, and it had the big dining-room table and kitchens and everything, and everybody would be there for dinner that was up at Bearsville with us. There was nobody—whether it was the assistant engineer who worked for the studio, to the roadies—everybody would be in my dining room, every Thursday night, having dinner. You were crazy to miss it, because it was great food, but you were also kind of like expected to be there. Things were discussed and whatever.

"Well, what I found Ritchie had done . . . after a couple of practical jokes, I got on to him, but he took a ghetto blaster and turned it on ten, and he took a ninety-minute cassette and recorded horrifying screams on it, on the reverse side only. It was an auto-reverse cassette, if you know what that is—plays one side, then flips the cassette and plays the other side. So, it would literally play almost ninety minutes of silence before it got to these horrifying screams."

"And he would hide the ghetto blaster up in the rafters in the attic, which was very inaccessible. You had to pull down the stairs, and it was all dirty and there were no lights. Nobody would ever go up there. And he put this ghetto blaster up there, and we would be sitting at dinner, and everybody was there, so it couldn't be somebody who did it; everybody was there for a while. So, it would play ninety minutes before it got to this, and then all of a sudden you would hear the screams coming from this fucking attic. But you didn't know where it was coming from; you just knew it was upstairs somewhere, because there are bedrooms and stuff. So, you would go up there, and you would see nothing. And also, Colin Hart was definitely afraid of spiders. One night he hired one of the guys, one of the helpers, a gardener or something, swept all of these spiders out of the barn, and they put them in Colin's bed. And Colin got into the bed one night, and there were all these big spiders there. But that was Ritchie. You'd never know what to expect."

As for the story of Bill Kennedy's sad departure, "There was an apartment that was attached to the studio," explains Thom. "It was part of the same building the studio was in. And Bill moved into that apartment. One night they got Bill really drunk, and he went to bed, and what Ritchie had done was he planted a remote-control car. He had two of them. He had one in this dresser, this wooden dresser that there was nothing in, and then he had another one that he took the body off and put this skull on it. And when Bill got into his bed, Ritchie was on the other side of the wall. Ritchie had an apartment up there also, so his apartment was right, you know, on the other side of the wall, and the remote worked through the wall. Bill was in bed, and all of a sudden clunking in the drawer, boom, boom, boom, and he jumps to run out, and all of a sudden the skull goes shooting across the floor. Bill didn't take the practical jokes or the supernatural well. He's a scaredy-cat and he disappeared [laughs]. That's the last we saw of him."

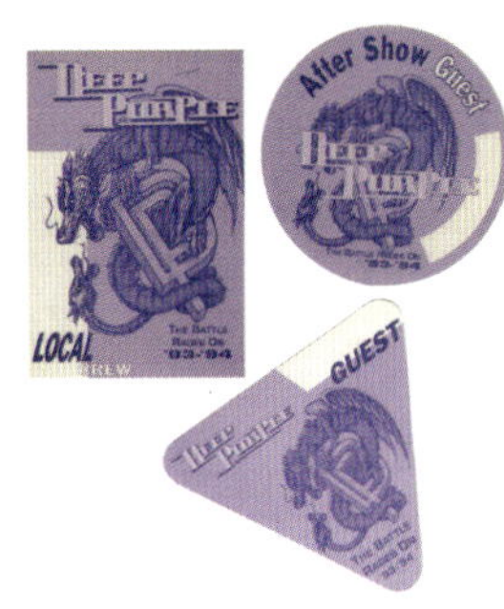

An assortment of backstage passes

The end result of all this was another conservative Deep Purple album, like *Perfect Strangers* and *The House of Blue Light* but dimmer of purpose. And then once you know about its fractured construction, you begin to perceive that there's less joy in its making.

Some of this emanates from Paul Elliott's three-out-five-K review of the album for *Kerrang!*, most pertinently for the fact that it's more about the business of Purple than any reason we would want this record.

"Ian Gillan is now enjoying his third stint as singer for legendary heavy-rock group Deep Purple," begins Elliott. "In between times, Ian has indulged in an erratic solo career and has also fronted Black Sabbath during Sabbath's darkest days. Deep Purple are something of a soap opera—Gillan's new autobiography trades heavily on the rivalry and power struggles within the band—and *The Battle Rages On . . .*, Purple's twenty-fifth-anniversary album, is similarly melodramatic. Gillan has quit the band twice due to personality clashes with guitarist Ritchie Blackmore. But much as Blackmore and Gillan needle each other, they also need each other together.

Deep Purple sell out major concert arenas throughout the world and shift a few albums into the bargain, but individually, they struggle. Gillan toured clubs with his last solo flop, the bizarrely titled *Toolbox* album. Presumably, the sting of failure was enough to drive him back to Purple and Blackmore.

"Under the circumstances, *The Battle Rages On* . . . (an ironic title, perhaps?) is a good record. After a quarter of a century, Deep Purple sound amazingly strong. The rumbling title track and the old-fashioned rock 'n' roller 'Ramshackle Man' are especially vibrant. At their best, these cunning old foxes can still craft fine, classically styled heavy rock, as on the epic and insidious 'Anya,' which borrows a little from 'Stranded' by Blackmore's Rainbow. Blackmore riffs and solos with typical good taste and economy, while Jon Lord puts in a sterling performance on the Hammond organ. An old tart he may be, but Gillan doesn't sound like he's marking time here. Deep Purple's last album, *Slaves and Masters*, featured journeyman Joe Lynn Turner on vocals. It seemed like a bitter end for the band, but Gillan is back yet again, and Purple live on! The band's fans and accountants weep with joy."

Thinking back on those times in 2020, Ian Paice admits that "all of us knew that we were on borrowed time."

Chapter 20

Come Hell or High Water

"A perverse delight in being destructive"

With *The Battle Rages On* . . . rising to a hopeful #21 on the UK charts but petering out at #192 in America, the guys tried to put on their best game faces and promote the damn thing. In fact, a world tour was put in motion, to include Europe, America, and Japan. Not only were Ritchie and Ian traveling separately and not talking to each other, but they would try to trip each other up onstage. Ritchie was occasionally inclined to massage a lick from *Jesus Christ Superstar* into "Black Night," reminding Ian that he sang for the Savior back in 1970. As for Jesus, Ian would tacitly withdraw support from Ritchie by walking off during his guitar solos. Not that Ritchie took his own presence seriously either. He oscillated between wrecking guitars, disappearing from the scene himself, or, on his fateful last night, shaking hands with fans from the lip of the stage.

Ian, likening Deep Purple to a wonderful meal—with himself and Ritchie playing the fork and the knife on the side—mused about the situation.

"I don't know; I've often thought about this. I see and I've always seen Purple as being five members with no leader, and everyone puts in, and what's best comes out—there's the songs, and we just enjoy ourselves. I think Ritchie saw his role as being more dominant than that. I think he saw his role as being more clearly defining within the direction of Purple. And he did probably, I think knowingly or unknowingly, kind of subjugate the rest of the band into a sort of support role, really.

"And I think if you analyze the music over the years, I think you'll see the obvious contributions of Jon Lord and the rhythm section, Roger and Ian, and the others in the band. Even though you could hear everything on the records, the writing root became narrower and narrower. There was always this focus on this riffy stuff. I found that became very limiting in late '72, when we were doing *Who Do We Think We Are!* I think the songs were fine, but the spirit of the band was gone. All of a sudden there's four guys living in a house together and Ritchie's down the road, and he wants to be separate from the band. I mean we were all assholes when we were kids, but you try to grow out of it a bit and get more productive in your life.

"Ritchie's behavior's been pretty well documented," continues Ian. "He despised the audiences; he would walk off in the middle of a show; he would refuse to do encores and seemed to have a perverse delight in being destructive. Now it's hard to weigh up, really, because we need characters. You know, heaven forbid we should be living in a boring world where everyone does the right thing. I'm talking about rock 'n' roll here, not politics or society in general [laughs]. So, there's plenty of room for eccentrics, but when it becomes self-destructive, it's very difficult. You know, I'm a much-weaker character than Jon or Ian and Rog. They stayed and supported and fought to keep the band alive. What can I think of? It's like an unhappy marriage, and you're staying together for the sake of the kids. Well, the kids have grown up and left home now, so we're enjoying ourselves."

So, the band did manage to get a bunch of Europe under their belts, although twenty-four North American dates in July and August 1993 were summarily canceled. And then it came to pass: Ritchie announced, on the eve of the first UK show, that he wouldn't be Deep Purple's guitarist when the band were supposed to visit Japan. To put a lock on it, he ripped up his visa. It must have been a hard grind—late September through mid-November, the band chalk up fully thirty-seven shows. In any event, a disastrous show of tantrumness would mar the band's Birmingham date as the bedraggled collective limped through a clutch of Scandinavian stops, with no apparent change of plans in the wings as regarded the Japanese leg. Ritchie's last show would be Helsinki, Finland, prompting the next night in Moscow, November 18, to be canceled. Stepping back a bit, the June 11 stop in Gothenburg, Sweden, found the band headlining something called the Göteborg All Star Festival, on a bill that included ELO, Kinks, Uriah Heep, Electric Boys, Georgie Fame, and a half dozen more you ain't never heard of, most of them likely locals.

Anyway, before Ritchie fell out of the band, a live album, recorded in Munich, Stuttgart, and, surprisingly, Birmingham, was patched and dispatched to capitalize on the fact that yes, Mk. II had risen, at least temporarily.

Come Hell or High Water would turn out to be anticlimactic not so much because of the bust-up having already passed—and, as such, documented in the liner notes—but for its dull track list. Nine generally too-long tracks are on the docket, too long to be sure, because what kind of band jams if they aren't communicating on an artistic level? In any event, the old-timey hits—"Highway Star," "Smoke on the Water," "Child in Time," "Speed King," "Black Night"—dominate, with "Child in Time" surprisingly winning the day with heretofore unforeseen power, much of it welling up from Paicey.

Come Hell or High Water CD booklet.
Martin Popoff archive

Peel the onion back, and it's nice to try to get along and sing along with "Anyone's Daughter," while the 1980s get the nod with that era's best track, "Perfect Strangers." Acknowledging that there's a new album, Purple cough up a good choice in "Anya," but a less convincing one in "A Twist in the Tail." Early on the tour, the band also floated "Talk About Love" and the tempestuous title track. In the covers department, the boys brought back the Stones' "Paint It Black," to be used in medley form.

Ian found himself on the phone with Israeli press in December 1994, having to talk up yet another live record of ill circumstance . . . "I must be completely honest with you. The only reason that I'm ready to promote this album is that I'm the only Deep Purple member that could be reached by telephone right now! I'll try to do my job the best way I can and express my opinion about this album. The truth is that I'm not an adherent of live albums, and not very keen on this one. Mostly, I hate live albums that include old stuff that was recorded in the past and released on previous live albums. The audience has an inclination to conservatism. If you release one good live album, it is considered that all your live albums are good, and this is silly."

Gillan goes on to say that after *Made in Japan*, "A few more live albums were released, and they are not worth the raw material that they are printed on. I think *Nobody's Perfect* is the most shameful album that we ever released. I can't justify its existence. Over the years we made some wonderful albums, but we also made some to be ashamed of. When I came back to the band in 1993, after *The Battle Rages On* . . . , we decided to spend a year together and write new stuff and to try to rebuild the band. Of course, we didn't know that Ritchie was going to leave us at that time. I honestly didn't like the fact that Ritchie was leaving the band, but I'm only one of five, so I didn't want to rock the boat and make waves. We started to work to schedule and decided not to break up. I think that this album is important for all Deep Purple fans, just because it's the last album with Ritchie Blackmore. That's the only reason that I keep this album. I didn't listen to it yet, but yesterday I visited a club, and the DJ played a bit of it for me; I think the producer did an excellent job."

On Ritchie's predictably dramatic departure, Gillan explains that "he started to disgust us all, so one day I decided to ignore him. I did things and said things that I thought were good for Deep Purple, without referring to him at all. He almost had a heart attack. He started to understand that we were all enjoying life. He didn't like it. Then one day during a successful tour, he announced, 'That's it; the tour is finished.' He ordered the crew to pack. Fortunately, we weren't scared, and I told the staff not to follow up Ritchie's order. I thought if the banjo player is going home, it's no reason to end the party. We all decided to search for a new banjo player. The truth is that we had to do this a long time ago. We realized that all these years, we were just the megalomaniac's accompaniment."

"Not my favorite gig," says Roger, about another incident toward the end. "He didn't want cameras onstage; he was throwing water all over the cameras. It was his way of . . . I don't know what he was doing it for. I think he was just protesting various things, one of which was the presence of cameras. And what happened was, he actually drenched my wife and Ian Gillan's wife, who happened to be standing right next to the camera. I looked around and saw my wife with a towel and a look on her face that just wasn't too happy. And they were just drenched. I was very angry. The whole band was very angry. Really, it was very difficult to focus on the music. I wasn't sure whether I was going to put my guitar down, hit Ritchie, and just leave for good and let that be the end of it, or whether to just try to get through to the end of the gig and somehow sort it out, which is what we did. Professionalism prevails, I suppose.

Ad for the album and the video. *Martin Popoff archive*

"The management, he was unhappy with," continues Glover. "All sorts of things. Who knew what he was unhappy with? If you don't talk, it's very difficult to know what makes one unhappy. There was not a lot of communication with Ritchie. He sort of kept his own counsel, and the four of us, you know, well, what do you do? The guy's uncommunicative. So not a lot was said. And we'd been so busy traveling and doing gigs that, in fact, we found it difficult to confront the issue ourselves for about a week. But then we started talking about it. 'What are we gonna do? What are we gonna do? Maybe we can get him to stay.' And I think at that point, that's when Ritchie tore up his Japanese visa. He did it to underline the fact that he'd made his mind up. It came out of the blue that Ritchie decided to leave. And then he told the crew that they were fired. It was right in the middle of the tour. We had about two or three weeks left of the tour before Japan, when he announced he was going to quit."

"During the long years that the band has existed, for a long time we did everything to destroy the band," continues Ian—as clarification, this is long after excising Blackmore from his life. "We devoted a lot of time to family feuds, the dirty laundry always washed outside, and we created an image problem and negative public opinion. I still think that we can bring the band to the big days like we used to twenty years ago. We must cherish the good times we have; in a few years we will be very old, and there are a lot of good and positive things that can be done. I would rather live in Deep Purple's light than in Deep Purple's shadow. I've never seen Roger Glover and the other members so happy. Last week he hugged me with much affection on the hotel staircase, the place that we were in. He said that he can't wait for Christmas to finish, in order to start recording our new album."

"I think we've had two very tumultuous people in the band, sometimes together, sometimes separate," muses Lord. "Ritchie and Ian Gillan are both spiky people. They mix like . . . I was going to say milk and Jack Daniels, but that might even mix! But oil and water is too common a cliché to describe how they don't mix. I think that's been the root of it all. Initially, it wasn't, of course—'69, '70, '71, going through '72 was pretty reasonable. I think everyone was still young enough to be able to very quickly put differences behind. That became more difficult as years went by, I guess. In '73, Ian Gillan actually left because I think of an artistic dispute with Ritchie. Artistic dispute . . . you don't get artistic disputes in rock 'n' roll [laughs]. I mean, they just fell out. They are oil and water; they just really do not mix. You know, Ritchie is a very strong-willed, strong-minded, difficult, spiky man. It's made life difficult sometimes. But we've made some great music along the way. So now that we don't have that apparent conflict, I hope that we can continue to be just as exciting without the personal conflict, for as long as we're sure we can do it."

Adds Roger, "It all ended in Helsinki with a handshake and a smile and a drink. I think Ritchie was happy to be going. In retrospect, he did us a huge favor by just leaving. He could've hung on and made life really difficult. It could have ended in far-worse circumstances than in fact it did. The fact that he left, and left us to carry on, was in fact a huge favor. Unfortunately, bad behavior has a way of exacerbating things, and Ian Gillan wasn't doing himself any favors then. You know, it's not just an Ian Gillan / Ritchie axis this whole thing revolves around. There are various other axes within the band that tend to grind against each other from time to time. There are friction points between various members of the band, but they're nothing great. They're things that, at the end of the day, we still throw our arms around each other and say, 'Hey, I love ya, man.' And that is everything. But there's got to be some friction. If you've got creative people together in a band, you're going to have disagreements."

Ritchie's longtime bud Stuart Smith reenters the picture, with a glimpse into Ritchie's state of mind at this juncture. "I know he used to call it, on the tour, *The Cattle Grazes On*. I wasn't around too much during that time. I would spend Christmases with Ritchie, but we would try to sort of not talk about the business end so much. I was living in L.A., and he was living in New York, and I would go there. I remember once, around the time when he left Purple, I think I was out there for probably about ten days, and I generally go a couple a days before Christmas Eve, because he had a big Christmas Eve party, and then I would leave a couple days after New Years Eve.

"And then about two days later, he said, 'You know I left Deep Purple.' 'Yeah.' 'So, what do I do? Because I've got a record deal.' And I said, 'What do you mean what do you do?!' See, Ritchie led a life that was totally insulated from the business end. He rarely ever met the people at the record label at all, he doesn't know anything about the business as far as that went, and so he said, 'You know, Bruce is no longer managing me.' And I said, well, I know a guy named Joe Boyland [died March 7, 2009, at the age of sixty-one], who manages Lynyrd Skynyrd and Bad Company at the time, in New York, so I called Joe, and he came out to Long Island and met Ritchie, and it was sort of taken from there."

Ritchie, of course, would resurface with a new Rainbow lineup and, in the fall of 1995, issue the slightly watery *Stranger in Us All*, touring it into 1996 and then knocking "Ritchie Blackmore's Rainbow" on its head once and for all. He'd then begin a strange yet prolific and ongoing chapter in his life as half of Blackmore's Night, alongside his then girlfriend and now wife, Candice Night.

"Tammy was in the picture before I met Ritchie," explains Frank Morgan, getting the girlfriends straight for us. "So, they must've been together right after the *Perfect Strangers* tour. He met her down south. Ritchie lived on Long Island. He's always floated between Long Island and Connecticut. So, he had a lot of friends in Long Island, and they used to come up and play soccer. And he had this one fellow Mike, who used to drive a van; I think he worked in a nightclub down there.

"Candice was part of that group," continues Frank. "He was breaking up with Tammy, and he was getting on very well with Candice, and that's how it started. As you know, Ritchie has a great ear for talent, and once again, he heard her singing skills and turned her into a star [laughs]. Just like he did with David Coverdale, Joe Lynn Turner, you know, all these guys. Ronnie James Dio was a sensation in upstate New York, and actually an opening act for Deep Purple, as Elf. But Ritchie, what he's doing right now, he's always wanted to do. He's always wanted to make music with a loved one, you know what I mean? Just to share not only his wife or girlfriend, but to make music together. And he dreamed of playing medieval music. The first Blackmore's Rainbow album with Dio, they were doing medieval-type rock 'n' roll, 'Sixteenth Century Greensleeves,' all that great stuff. He was heading in that direction."

I asked Frank to what extent Ritchie was in love with guitar in particular, or whether it was in fact this renaissance kind of music that was most important to him.

"Oh no, no, he loved guitar. There was a time when he dropped the guitar for a few years and just played the cello; I think it was the cello. I'm not sure when that was; he lived in Germany for years too. That's why he loved Germany so much. So, it was kind of like George Harrison—he didn't totally give up the guitar, but he was so into the sitar for a little bit there. And Ritchie was definitely into the cello there for a little bit. Plus, he always loved the turn-of-the-century instruments, the little guitars, mandolins. But as we all know, he's one of the best rock guitarists in the world."

Backtracking a bit, at the end of the European tour there was the matter of whether Deep Purple would live on, and whether they could snap back to some semblance of life fast enough to honor the band's Japanese dates.

"Those Japanese shows were a contractual obligation," notes Jon. "Had we not gone to Japan, we would've been sued. Not only us, but Ritchie would've been sued. Joe Satriani was marvelous, and we asked him to join and he said, 'Yes, as soon as I've made these two solo albums that I've been paid for and haven't done yet!' We asked him how long would it take, and he said about eighteen months, and we thought that was the end."

A couple of Joe Satriani ads, one promoting guitar strings and one promoting his *Time Machine* album from 1993

Ah yes, Joe Satriani, at the time thirty-six years of age and pretty much the most successful instrumental ax shredder in history. Commercially speaking, Steve Vai might have something to say about that, and maybe even Jeff Beck, but yeah, Joe had a nice little cottage industry going there. Later, he'd be part of a pretty buzzing hard rock quintet by the name of Chickenfoot, no longer balding, as he was during his Deep Purple jaunt, but for years, head fully shorn. These days he's in a closely adjacent situation, playing Van Halen hits, also with Sammy Hagar and Michael Anthony.

Purple also considered hiring Michael Schenker, who demurred nonetheless because he couldn't see himself playing someone else's solos. Satriani turned out to be a perfect choice, though, given his acceptability to Japanese audiences and promoters (the legendary Mr. Udo insisted on a marquee name), plus the fact that he learned the set list rapidly and accurately. Still, fully 2,500 Japanese ticket purchasers exercised their option to receive a refund, unsurprising given Ritchie Blackmore's nearly mythical status among guitarists and hard rockers in Japan.

"Yeah, it was very unexpected," begins Satch, reminiscing about those days. "It was one of those afternoons where I got a phone call, and my manager said, 'Hey, how would you feel about replacing Ritchie Blackmore in Deep Purple?' And I remember saying, 'Don't ever call me with one of those again,' and I hung up. And then about a half hour later, I called back, and I said, 'What did you say now?' [laughs]. And he said, 'Oh, this is the deal. Ritchie Blackmore has walked out, and they are desperate, and they called to see if you'd like to do it.'

"So, I thought, well, I'm going to get crucified by the fans. Because you can't replace somebody like Ritchie Blackmore. But I thought this is a chance of a lifetime to play with one of my favorite bands of all time. So, I said okay, I'll do it, I'll try it. And Roger sent me cassettes, I think, of their last show in Stuttgart, so I could learn the live show. A week later I was in Tokyo, and we started the tour; we did a short tour of Japan, and a few months later we did a two-month tour of Europe. I had the time of my life. Those guys are just an amazing, rocking band, a great bunch of guys. But it was mentally very difficult to replace somebody that is one of my idols, Ritchie Blackmore, a guitar player that I've grown up with. In my mind's ear, he has a sound and a style and is an institution all to himself, so it was just very hard to get around that. When you are onstage and you are playing 'Highway Star,' your brain wants to hear Ritchie, but instead it's hearing you [laughs]. Very hard."

I asked Joe how he navigated the decision to stick close to Ritchie's solos versus striking out on his own.

"You know, it was actually pretty easy to make that decision. Because it seemed to me, like when you do 'Highway Star,' it's so important to do exactly what he did. Because that song has got an ensemble feel to it. A lot of the solos are harmonized and play with vocal lines, so you can't really stray, you know? And the one thing I got from the tapes that I got from their last show was that Ritchie was doing the same thing, where if they were doing 'Woman from Tokyo,' he would pretty much stick to the script, from what he did on record. And then there were other songs where he would really take artistic license and play something entirely different. So, I took that as my cue, that I should react the same way. Being a guitar player, I can understand his reasons for doing that. So, if I was doing a long improvisation on like 'Hush,' you can do whatever you want. If you are doing 'Child in Time,' you can do kind of whatever you want. But when you are doing 'Smoke on the Water,' why not celebrate with the audience and play exactly what Ritchie played?"

The band's set list in Japan was quite yummy, scooping up another couple of *Battle Rages On . . .* selections in the blustery title track plus "Ramshackle Man." For obscurities, bluesy ballad "When a Blind Man Cries" was also featured, as were "Maybe I'm a Leo" and "Pictures from Home." There was even a nod to Joe's presence through a run-through of his semihit "Satch Boogie" from 1987's *Surfing with the Alien*. Over to Europe, and the band pulled out of their magic bag "Fireball." All told, the Satch version of the band played the six Japanese dates, plus twenty-six more in Europe, shutting 'er down on July 6, 1994, in Bayreuth, Germany, that country once again getting blanket coverage given its support of the Purples over the years.

And the story of Joe's leaving? "Well, you know, I always felt that I was helping them out. That was the first tour. And the second tour that came up, I was really psyched about doing it, and I really did think that I could get over my philosophical problem of replacing somebody like Ritchie. But as the tour went on, I realized that I just couldn't. And so, I remember, I think we were in Barcelona, and Roger had asked me, officially, you know, that if you want, the door's open. We would love to have you be our guitarist. It was a very difficult offer to turn down, because I was so close to them at that point. And you know, you always feel like you've got to be crazy to turn down something like being in a great band like that.

Industry-related ad for *Come Hell or High Water*. Martin Popoff archive

"But I was pretty straight up with him. I said, I've just got this ghost of Ritchie hanging over my head [laughs], and I just can't shake it. And having a solo career is like having . . . it makes you feel like the luckiest guitarist in the world. I just couldn't see having to turn my back on it, to be in a band where I was truly, in the mind's eye of everybody on the planet, replacing Ritchie Blackmore. I remember my friend Steve Vai, he came up to me and said, 'Boy, if you can ever avoid replacing a famous guy, do it.' Because he had that for most of his career. He was replacing people who were huge, and he had to struggle to keep his identity in these other bands. It can be draining."

There was a bit more to it than this. Yes, Joe had an eye on his solo career, but so did his record label, firmly, with Satriani's *Time Machine* compilation, issued in November 1993, doing well on the charts. All manner of contractual restriction was causing problems, and a time commitment conflict with Purple's New Zealand dates sort of put the nail in the coffin.

Purple wouldn't miss a beat, however. The band quickly found a new guitarist in forty-one-year-old Steve Morse, former member of Dixie Dregs, Kansas, and his own Steve Morse Band. Additionally, Steve was a pilot and, on a personal level, a slight and soft-spoken master of the ax in more departments than we'll ever know.

"You know, it's funny; Roger and I were talking about guitar players who we think would be great, and Steve's name came up," says Joe in closing. "And we were both thinking it would be great, because he's so different. I've known Steve for quite a while, and he is a monster musician, a great guitarist, and he just comes with such an original sound. But I could understand why they would really gravitate to somebody like that.

"And so, I sort of said, 'Hey, if I were you, that's where I would go.' I wouldn't go towards somebody who was trying to be like Ritchie Blackmore. That would be a big mistake. Every guitar player who was a Ritchie clone was knocking on their door. And that's not really what they're about. They've always been about moving forward and writing interesting songs and making records that have a life of their own. And so I think they needed someone who was as unique as Ritchie, in their own right, and also someone who was a—what would you call it?—someone who had volumes and volumes of stuff that was original, someone who was good at writing on their own, and also as an ensemble. They needed a prolific original guitar player."

Chapter 21

Purpendicular

"I've never been fifty before in my life."

From the morass of the mind games, after Ritchie Blackmore and Joe Satriani, it's really quite inspiring how quickly and confidently Deep Purple reemerged. Folks sort of downplay or forget the fact that really, the band deftly and efficiently made a single personnel change, not disbanding temporarily, not missing a beat. Instead, *The Battle Rages On* . . . came out in 1993, they toured with Ritchie and then Joe in 1994, squeezed in a live album for 1994 as well, and here they were with a sparkling, spanking new record just into the opening months of 1996.

The band's first post-Blackmore record would be a game changer, a strident demonstration that Purple wasn't painting by numbers but could grow and mature and provoke and write renewed, despite being elder statesmen. They were now unencumbered by including the appropriate number of circular, widdly-diddly "Lady Double Dealer" riffs or ticking off the boxes for a blues number, a track with high BPMs, a commercial track for radio, and perhaps a shared Lord and Blackmore solo. The formula, quite evident across the three Mk. II reunion albums, was over with. Although, let's give props to the "Deep Rainbow" album, *Slave and Masters*. Among the 1984 to 1993 canon, that one takes the most chances, embodying the highest level of fearlessness—that is, until the wonderful Steve Morse era of the band begins, represented by a first bold salvo called *Purpendicular*.

But wisely, before any attempt at writing a new record was to be ventured, the band's new guitar picker, Steve Morse, was to be tested with some live dates away from the glare, in exotic climes such as South Korea, South Africa, and India, a campaign that took Deep Purple Mk. VIII through the spring of 1995, winding up more than enthusiastic enough to create some new music together.

"The only common factor about all banjo players is that they are all fuckin' mad," joked Gillan, speaking with the author right at the beginning of this journey. "But some are madder than others! But I've heard Steve is a very nice guy, and I know he's a great player."

Asked about the fact that hiring an American might compromise the chemistry within the band, Ian adds, "Not in the slightest! I don't think there's any parochial value in it at all. For God's sake, there was hardly any English music we listened to when we were kids! I deal with the so-called heritage that we have very respectfully. I think it's something to be proud of, but I don't think it's something to gloat over to rest on your laurels. If you are an individual artist, people can accept you adjusting and changing throughout your whole career. But there's something about groups—you're expected to die young or give up gracefully and quit! For most of the people who enjoy doing their stuff vocationally, like painters and writers, it's a life's work. Wonderful things have happened in the past, but we're looking for good things ahead.

"We did the last European tour on a tour bus," continued Gillan. "I spent many a happy year on tour buses with various reprobates from all over the world, and I love it, but I've never done a tour with Deep Purple on a bus before. Many a morning I'd sit sharing a bottle [of] wine with Jon and watching the sun come up over the Spanish countryside or looking at the lupins in Sweden. Because you're on a bus, you're seeing the countryside, you're stopping at the pit stops and eating sausages and crap, you're not getting enough sleep and you're probably drinking too much, and what the hell? We'd play cards and do nothing in particular, just enjoy each other's company, and it was great. It was a band again. Suddenly, you don't feel like, 'Oh God, we're the grandfathers of rock 'n' roll.' You think, 'Hang on, we're a fucking good band!' And we're proud of it again.

Steve Morse in Dixie Dregs, June 16, 1992. © *Bill O'Leary*

"I think the title is quite pertinent," concludes Ian, circling back to the coda of a live album discussed last chapter. "Come hell or high water, the band will always go on—this time, I think, very much for the better. It's sad it had to happen this way, but I see the light of life in everyone's eyes again, and it's been a long time since anyone walked this way!"

With Steve Morse now duly road-tested, it seemed as if enthusiasm and hope for the band rolled right into the writing sessions, with Ian and Rog responding immediately with a raft of lyrics that belied a new maturity, even a degree of seriousness, of reflection.

"Interesting, really, that you mention that," Ian told me, shortly after *Purpendicular*'s issuance on February 5, 1996. "Because a couple of years ago, Roger and I were, I think, in Portugal. We were walking on the beach, talking about things as we do; philosophizing about this, that, and the other; and putting to rights the problems of the world, like we'd been doing since 1965. The topic of the day was naivety, basically what makes young kids' music so powerful? Because we were looking at the lyrics, for example, of 'Black Night' and the stuff we wrote in '69 and '70. And we were saying, we can't even figure out what it means, but it sounds great.

"So, we thought, you know, when you're at that age, you're immortal. You don't think twice before you say anything; you just do it because it's cool. And as you get a little older, you start thinking about everything before you say it, so everything becomes a little more considered, not just in songs but in life itself. You get a little cautious, or not exactly cautious, but experience in life tells you to weigh things up a bit before you speak. And the consequence is that in a very slow process, you end up, your songcraft improves enormously, you think you're writing better songs, and in fact you probably are. But what you're writing is probably becoming a little more boring as you become more and more remote from activity, if you're trying to write about fast cars and loose women and all that.

"But of course that's not the reality in your real life anymore. You're doing things on a far more philosophical level. But naivety is lost, and we figured that—and said to ourselves—we'd happily replace it with all these conclusions: 'If you're going to write something about love, just make sure it's not oversentimental' blah blah blah. And then we'd go into this process of analyzing everything.

"I remember sitting bolt upright in bed a few days later and saying, this is ridiculous, just nonsense—of course I'm naive. I'm just a naive fifty-year-old. I'm not a naive twenty-year-old. But I've never been fifty before in my life, so what are the things we should be writing about? Let's not try to play this sort of 'from memory' stuff anymore. Let's write about the things that really make us angry, just like we used to, but it's different things these days. Let's go for that. So, the stories can of course be more anecdotal because we've experienced a lot more and are a lot more spiritual. Your spirit develops; you're a lot more philosophical. Also hopefully, there'll be humor in it. But having said all that, the point is really not to care about it and really concentrate on making the words sound good, or to put the sound of the words before the meaning of the words. So anyway, after a long process, we finally figured out [laughs] where we'd been going up the wrong path."

Makes sense, because sure, the lyrics to *The Battle Rages On . . .* do have that "play-acting the rock star" feel to them—and maybe from memory, like Ian says. It's sort of "What would Deep Purple do?" The same can and can't be said about *Perfect*

Strangers and *The House of Blue Light*, given the guys' relative youth and the rock star excitement of the time. In other words, the Purples were closer to their debauched rock star years than they were far from it, and the business was different in the 1980s, especially with the arriving hedonism of hair metal.

Additionally, says Ian, "I think we're in a different situation now, of course, now that we have Steve. It's a whole different approach anyways. Everybody's standing about 2 inches taller, and there's a very positive air of expression. What we are hearing is people's individual voices coming through, much like it was in '69, '70, '71. And it has been remarked to me that some of these lyrics could have come from some of my solo stuff. It's probably just because we're all expressing ourselves a little more naturally these days, so you would spot the difference. Instead of being this sort of worked-out program, being limited, doing the best we can under the circumstances, it's almost anything goes now. The more I talk about this, the sort of easier it gets to understand, because obviously over the last six months or so, we've had to think this through quite carefully."

Asked about making the connection with Steve Morse, Ian explains that "Joe Satriani sort of did his stint with us, and we had the best we could from Joe over six months. But he was committed for another world tour and an album. There was never any really serious conversation about him staying on permanently. So, we had to start writing the lists out, you know, 'Who are we going to look at on a permanent basis?' I think the manager said, 'Well, send me a list of who you think you would like to be in the band.' And there was only one name that was on every single list, and that was Steve Morse.

"I think as an individual, I certainly got Dixie Dregs stuff and some of Steve's solo stuff in recent years," continues Gillan, on what first impressed him about Morse. "I think we just all respected him as a guitar player. And when we met him, it became very evident that what became most important really was the personality. You know, he's got a great sense of humor. He's sharp and intelligent. He's very focused. He's adaptable. He's enthusiastic about the history of Purple; you know, he grew up with it. He's been in a band since he was thirteen years old. And so, he's completely familiar with the old stuff. And in fact, he's held us very much on track as far as keeping the vitality in the music. And at the same time, he's got an awful lot to offer. He's very, very versatile and he plays as he speaks. He said at a press conference once, I believe [laughs], 'It's no crime to be good at more than one thing.'"

"It was Roger who said he'd seen this brilliant guitarist called Steve Morse," adds Jon Lord, "and we all immediately said yes, as he was on all of our lists. So, we called him up and the rest is history. We jammed . . . actually we did a concert in Mexico back in early '94 to see if we liked each other, and it was brilliant. It's a joy playing with Steve Morse."

"I've been a big fan of Steve's for a long time," said Roger. "I went to see him play six or seven years ago down in Florida, when we were doing the *Slaves and Masters* debacle . . . um, album. Sorry. But Steve blew me away with his live abilities. And Dixie Dregs before that; I remember listening to Dixie Dregs' *Unsung Heroes* sometime in the early '80s. It just stunned me, the amount of musicianship involved. So, when we were looking for a guitarist, his name came to my mind. I said, 'Well, why don't we try him?' So, we made an inquiry or two, and they came back very positive. So basically, we went in at the deep end with him. We did a gig, or a couple of gigs, in Mexico, which is somewhere we'd never been before. It was fairly large

Steve Morse, Universal Amphitheater, Los Angeles, California, August 30, 1998. Supporting on the night were Dream Theater and Emerson, Lake & Palmer. © *Tom Wallace*

It was Roger that got the ball rolling with Steve. Los Angeles, August 1998. © *Tom Wallace*

scale, a big arena-type place. And we did a press conference. So, we actually saw Steve under a certain amount of pressure. You really don't know someone until you've seen them under pressure. He handled himself very well at the press conference. He could talk; he's very eloquent. And he handled himself great onstage. So, we thought, 'Well, this guy is great.'"

"Two things," begins Morse's more succinct answer on how all this happened. "One, a Dregs tune called 'Take It Off the Top' was used in a BBC intro for a radio series for fifteen years, and so they felt like they knew me from that [laughs]. And then Roger saw my trio play in Orlando, and he's the one who suggested that the band try me."

"We went into a sort of writing session in January of '95," adds Jon. "We just sat in the studio and jammed, basically, for a couple of weeks, and ended up with a whole bunch of material. Of course, some of these were Steve's ideas, this, that, and the other. Then we went away, each with a copy of that. Came back a couple of weeks later and started to weed it out, as it were. It was so easy working with him. He really is an incredible, easygoing, genuine, good guy. Which, as you may recall from our past, we're not used to having good-guy guitarists [laughs]."

Roger, ever the artist and abstractionist of the band, could immediately see the potential. "Right from the first day, it became obvious that this was going to be a whole new ballgame than what we'd known for years and years and years. There was no fear in the studio. Everyone could speak their mind, and everyone came up with ideas. Music just erupted out of us. We could not stop writing music—I've got tapes and tapes and tapes. It was actually kind of hard to stop writing. Steve's input was infectious. When you write a song that you don't have to think about it, when it just appears, that's usually the best type of song. If you have to work at a song and you're struggling with it, no matter what the end result, it's not going to sound organic, for want of a better word. I have this theory, which says that the atmosphere in a studio somehow gets into the very grooves of the record. It's got nothing to do with the precision of the music or the playing or the quality of the songs or whatever. The atmosphere that's just in the studio somehow conveys itself. I believe this to be true. It was a happy record to make, so therefore, I think there's a good feeling about the record. There's a wholeness to it, an organic quality, if you like. It sounds like it was meant to be.

"But we decided to actually do some more gigs before we made the record," continues Glover. "Just to sort of cement Steve's relationship in the band. To that end, we called our manager and said, 'Look, we just want to work somewhere in the world. Just book some tours.' So we went to South Korea, South Africa, and India, on a sort of little 'round-the-world leg. It was great; we matured very quickly as a whole new unit."

Steve Morse figures he first picked up the guitar seriously back in 1966. The family had moved from Ohio to Tennessee and then to Michigan and finally Georgia. Early bands included the Plague, Three, and Dixie Grit, all with his older brother Dave. "It was just the opportunity of having a guitar. My brother brought one home that he had borrowed or rented, and I just thought that it was so cool. I played other musical instruments a little bit, but when I saw the guitar I said, 'That's the thing!' The Beatles were probably part of it, the Chuck Berry sound; it's just that rhythm that everybody loves, ya know?!"

And the sound that he's developed over the decades? "I think you put together your own sound based on how free you feel to be yourself. I remember some kids were more concerned with learning a solo note for note when they were learning to play, and I was more concerned with learning the atmosphere of the solo and kinda doing my own little adaptation. Just having that kind of attitude started me on my way of being less of a session player and more of an individualist. I like to be good at both, but I remember some of my friends were better at that."

"He's just an insanely good guitar player," says Vinnie Moore, top shredder in his own right and longtime UFO guitarist until Phil Mogg retired the band. "His technique is just amazing. And I think his composition is really good. I mean, he's written some amazing stuff over the years. I was influenced by a record called *Unsung Heroes*. 'Cruise Control' was on that record, and I listened to some of the other tunes on there also and thought, 'Wow, that's a pretty serious composer.' I don't know the Purple albums, though, I'm sorry to say. But I know the old stuff, and they are one of my favorite bands. And Ritchie was actually one of my big influences. I remember when I was a kid and I found out that Ritchie Blackmore had the same birthday as me; wow, I freaked out."

Ad promoting a Steve Morse solo show at the legendary Rock 'n' Roll Heaven in the author's hometown, Toronto. *Martin Popoff archive*

With respect to his early impressions of the Purple sound, Steve says that "the first thing I noticed was the combination of organ and guitar, weaving those lines together. There are some interesting lines in like 'Wring That Neck,' where it's like a fast shuffle. And then in 'Highway Star,' when that came on, Jon had a classical approach to doing the solo, but it was so heavy and in such a straightforward rock setting. Jon really knows how to voice things on the keyboard to where it fits with the guitar, and I enjoyed that very much, and I noticed it way back then. And Ritchie, he used a combination of vibrato and a really strong left-hand technique to get a very aggressive sound, and that was kind of new for then. And the way Ian would scream, really high. And then after I heard 'Highway Star' and then some of the early Van Halen with David Lee Roth, I could see a lot of influence there."

"That's quite a tricky question!" thunders Jon, asked to explain what Mr. Morse brought to the process that was missing with Ritchie. "It's difficult to answer without sounding like I'm criticizing Ritchie. Ritchie's onstage commitment could be sometimes movable, shall we say, whereas Steve's is 100 percent total. What Steve doesn't have is the astonishing freedom that Ritchie was very often capable of displaying, that astounding trip outside of what you expect into what you don't expect. Steve doesn't quite have that, not in Deep Purple anyway. But what he does have is utter commitment to the band and to its legacy and to what it stands for."

"He was absolutely a driving force," says Gillan, with respect to Steve's role on what would become *Purpendicular*. "He was an equal member with everyone else.

Ian Paice would get in . . . it was just brilliant watching this, because I keep making comparisons with the old days. But we hadn't done this for a long time. Paicey would come in about noon, just play for half an hour, and Steve would be there. They'd be jamming for a while, and by the time everybody ambled into the studio about 1:00—this was five days a week for about three or four months—it was like going to the office. Six or seven hours a day, total focus on the music.

"Then Roger would come in and say, 'Well, I've got these tapes,' and he'd be recording everything. We wouldn't just be jamming endlessly. There'd be a lot of thought going into this idea, that idea. Steve would come in with an awful lot of ideas. So, Roger would capture them on ADAT, and Roger had a quarter-inch analog running nonstop. So, every now and then we'd focus on an arrangement that would be coming together, and I'd start singing a bit of gibberish over something that felt good, and we'd come back to it three days later and everything would gradually come into shape. Eventually we ended up with over twenty songs, I believe. It's the first time we've ever had to cut down."

The author's *Purpendicular* CD booklet along with an odd travel-related ad. *Martin Popoff archive*

As alluded to, *Purpendicular* was issued in February 1996, having been recorded over a two-month period the previous summer at Greg Rike Productions in Orlando, Florida, also home for much of the work on the preceding two studio albums from the band. The mix was also conducted in Orlando, at Parc Studios, by the album's engineering team of Darren Schneider and Keith Andrews.

"It's completely coincidental," says Ian, on recording in Florida and having the band's new guitarist based there. "Totally bizarre. We'd used that studio in Orlando quite a bit in the past. Basically, it's great fun, because you can go canoeing, swimming, play tennis, whatever you want to do in the mornings, because that's what Orlando's like. In the afternoon, we'd work, and then in the evening you can go out to the strip clubs or the bars or whatever you want to do. And it so happens that Steve lives in Ocala. So, he used to commute to the office every day."

Given the state of classic heavy music at the time, Purple found themselves without a major label deal stateside, instead signing with busy and aggressive upstart CMC, sporadically derided as the Cheese Metal Cemetery, given its patronage of Slaughter, Dokken, and Warrant, with each turning in somewhat alternative-influenced records for the label, who then wrapped them in shoddy graphics. *Purpendicular*'s album cover would be a dud as well, but thankfully the band, on the music side, was full-blooded independent in their record making, eschewing any thought of trying to please the grunge- and hard-alternative-crazy music industry of the mid-1990s.

Asked about label dealings, the notoriously business-blind Gillan draws a blank. "Well, now you've got me struggling here, because I live in England, and I don't really know what's going on. I'm not really involved with any of the label setups. I decided years and years ago that one thing I really couldn't understand is the mechanics of this business. So, I leave that to management. All I do know is that we changed labels over here, and anything I can say is that from our offices, they seem very excited about the approach that the US record label's taking. They seem to be keen on the effectiveness of their campaign etc."

Purpendicular, Deep Purple's fifteenth studio album, opens with a lighthearted hard rocker of funk propulsion called "Vavoom: Ted the Mechanic." At the lyric end, Ian goes to the bar and drinks with a guy named Ted, who tells him about his

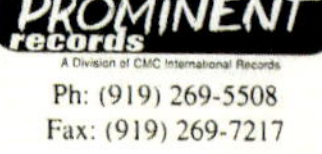

Promotional 8" × 10" presenting the new lineup. *Martin Popoff archive*

simple life, ending with "The banjo player took a hike / What's that song I used to like?" The main narrative is of this guy blowing off steam.

Ian knows of which he speaks. "I spend all my life on the road with musicians, and when I get home, I like to spend time with my wife, my family, and my friends, who are a combination of fishermen, social workers, farmers, etc. I've even got a hippie policeman in our town. We have friends who all appreciate the same things in life. There are lots of musicians living around, but we don't get together much for that reason. Because, you know, when you're together on a bus, on the road, you develop an incredibly cruel and vulgar sense of humor. You develop a strong, passionate bond with each other, and you become very defensive, like brothers in the face of a pretty hard existence.

"And you just can't take that kind of attitude back into your house. You know, you can't be cussing and swearing all the time, not in front of my twelve-year-old daughter. And I appreciate the other side of life. That's great. It balances—a bit of this and a bit of that—and it works very well. Everyone's a family man. Steve's got a little boy. Roger's got a family. Yeah, we've all got families. I'm just checking [laughs]. Yep, everyone's got families. Ritchie doesn't have a family, not any kids, not current ones anyway [laughs]. But yeah, Jon Lord and Ian Paice and myself live in England.

CD single artwork for the single pairing "Vavoom: Ted the Mechanic" with "Sometimes I Feel Like Screaming." *Martin Popoff archive*

Roger's lived in Connecticut for about seventeen years, and Steve Morse, of course, lives in Florida."

The "Ted the Mechanic" lyric (the "Vavoom" bit seems to have been cast aside over time) does perpetuate and demonstrate Ian's power of observation, distilled down into a combination of the humorous and cryptic.

"I don't write lyrics in advance, but I do make notes on things," explains Ian. "So, if I've been to the Soviet Union or I've been to Bolivia or to Calico, a ghost town in California where I've had these experiences, or get drunk in Nashville with an old songwriter . . . these things happen and they're very romantic, or I always view them as being very romantic, as potential inspiration for songs. So, they get written down, pretty much in journal form, together with any observations that might add some color to it. And when you get to a certain song that gives you a certain feeling, and you get more involved, I go, I know, let's get out this book here and flip through the pages, and I go, 'Oh, right, yeah.' Normally there's enough to get you started. It may not necessarily be the literal transfer from book to lyric, but it just might act as a catalyst that sends you off in another direction whatsoever. Very difficult, really. Pretty much nothing's prewritten in lyric form, but there's an awful lot of preparation done."

True to form, Ian tells the tale of hitting the pub to try to get some writing done back for the *House of Blue Light* album, whereby, instead, he falls into a few drinks and conversation with this Ted the Mechanic character (although his name wasn't Ted, nor was he a mechanic), who proceeds to tell Ian his life story, with Gillan then dutifully writing it down on napkin after napkin.

The second track, "Loosen My Strings," is a haunting semiballad, inscrutable, expertly obscured, and musically sophisticated, an effect that is hard to achieve in ballad form. Although maybe it's more of a laid-back and melodic full-band rock song, with a heavy beat, if that's possible, the full band punching on through this tale of . . . unease in the dead of night, regret in the morning, sanctuary yearned for at any hour. Roger tells the tale of tuning up for the day, when Steve came along and provided accompaniment to his pitched positioning of the notes. It was this spontaneous and fecund creativity out of Steve that the band found most refreshing about their new strange situation.

"Soon Forgotten" is a heavy, surging progressive-rock monster of a song pumped full of regal authority by Jon and his Hammond. Ties to Purple's legacy can be pondered through the song's weave of classical and Middle Eastern melodies, and Lord claims further ownership of the song through a memorable, hummable organ solo. Fully creative in this new "mature" conceptual space, it's an example of a Purple track that is textured so elusively that it's hard to put a label to it as to how point-blank heavy it is or isn't. Lyrically, well, Ian's in a similar purgatory that he was experiencing on "Loosen My Strings," but it's progressed to more of a fugue state. It's heated up and there's more of a sense of panic.

It's all quite literary, which comes as no surprise. "We're all avid readers," says Ian. "There's funny things as well, though, that aren't by a direct route. I mean, Steve Morse is sitting upstairs in the bus, playing his guitar twenty-four hours a day, or okay, sixteen hours a day. And when you're talking to him, he's practicing. So, Roger and I will be doing crossword puzzles all day long, and Steve, after a while he realized, 'Hey, you're practicing too!' 'Yeah, that's right.' So, anything interesting that happens,

The wordsmithing team. Los Angeles, August 1998. © *Tom Wallace*

Classy UK ad promoting the album and tour dates

whether it's in a book, which may subliminally or subconsciously trigger something, an interesting thought, or a fresh approach to things, or whether it's a conversation or experience . . . I mean, I've had the wildest things happen to me in parts of the world where musicians or Western entertainers have never been. And you see things and go, 'Wow!' And that's where, from their point of view, you think, we are so bigoted in our approach to life. We all think we're right. We all think our way of doing things is right. Yet, the other guys think we're crazy. It's very interesting. You also have to be careful that you don't get into lecturing mode. You just soak it up and see how it goes."

Strength to strength, "Sometimes I Feel Like Screaming" is another passion-filled semiballad, and it's "semi" given its rumbling, purifying, but quite heavy chorus, strapped to a melancholic verse structure, over which Ian tells a tale of loneliness on the road, or again, more like ennui, a feeling that the road, kaleidoscopic as it is, can't replace human connection and the familiar.

"It's fairly effortless, yes," says Ian, asked after the state of his "screaming." "I've always thought about singing in the most natural style possible. If you force yourself into a range or into a style that's uncomfortable, it's going to be a struggle, without any doubt. But I was lucky. I had about eight or nine years of, being in my formative years, singing every possible style, so, by the time I found my voice and joined Purple, I was fairly comfortable with what I was doing.

"We're still playing that," continues Gillan, on that song (albeit a long time ago now). "That's become very much part of the show. People adore it, and I do too. It's a real rock 'n' roll song. It's a road song. It's about, you know, the frustration of getting back in your hotel, and there's a message from your wife in a language you can't understand. It's just a 'while you were out' type of message. It's about the dirty clubs and the night streets and the back alleys and all of those sorts of things. It takes me back to . . . it may sound bad, but to be honest, when I was sitting in the beer cellars of Munich, Frankfurt, Cologne, back in '65 and '66, and when the whole world had gone to bed apart from the night people, we would sit up playing blues and drinking beer and listening, swapping stories with waiters and dancers and prostitutes and musicians.

"And they were the best and most honest bunch of people I've ever met in my life," continues Gillan, "because we had a mutual trust, and an understanding of why we were there that late at night. Because nobody comes home from school or business and goes to bed at six o'clock. We had to wind down a little bit. And I think some memories of that are probably included in 'Sometimes I Feel Like Screaming.' But a lot of it, if I had to describe the way I write in artistic terms, it would be impressionism. You get a little glimpse without it being brutally honest."

"Cascades: I'm Not Your Lover" provides a welcome typical Purple romp, with Morse and Lord locked in signature ax-to-organ battle across what is an up-tempo sort of blue-collar rocker. In fact, Steve was instrumental in getting Jon's sound nice and dirty, having put the keys through one of his guitar effects. A highly structured "Highway Star"–like solo completes the circuit.

"'Cascades' is obviously taken from the guitar," notes Ian. "Steve, when he walked in the studio, it sounded like Niagara Falls or a trickling brook, depending on how intense he was playing at the time. Lyrically, I think there was something quite biographical about that [laughs], about my ex. But we'll leave it at that."

Next up is "The Aviator," a real step off the norm for the band, into a Celtic ballad feel. Remarks Steve, "What surprised me with *Purpendicular* is the way the band responded to weird stuff. I was just playing the little guitar themes from 'The Aviator' while we were sitting around. We do a lot of sitting around in the process of recording. It's like touring—you spend all your time waiting. Very few seconds are done with the red light on, with the actual recording happening. So anyway, they heard me playing that idea and said, 'Hey, we can actually use that.' Because I really wanted Deep Purple to do more of a Led Zeppelin branching-out thing. Jimmy Page would always reach for weird folk roots and acoustic things, playing steel guitar and everything. So, I thought Purple could really use some of that, expand it. And they totally went for it."

Lyrically, Ian and Roger present a subtle and deft homage to Steve's aviation skills, couching their presentation in imagery surrounding freedom, dreaming, innocence, and even the mystical.

"Rosa's Cantina" percolates upon a "Hush"-like groove welling up from Paicey, while Gillan turns in one of his celebrated "Where in the world am I?" tales that would be far less credulous coming from anyone but Ian. Again, strength to strength, the guys just attempt new things and succeed at them, with crackling, vital, gorgeous production and hopeful, joyous performances supporting the rock-solid songwriting.

"A Castle Full of Rascals" finds Ian poetically venting his spleen over politics, one of his preoccupying thorns, be it of the strictly British variety or concerning Brussels and the EU. Brexit was far in the future at this point, and unsurprisingly he has keen opinions about that too, having taken this issue on as a bit of a hobby.

In fact, he'd been writing, on and off, a book on the subject of the European Union, fictionalized, mind you. "I did most of the second half," explained Ian, now twenty-odd years back. "The first half was mostly my buddy. It came out of a . . . you know, it's the usual story. It was just a mistake. I was trying to write a novel, and I was also working on a screenplay at the same time. And it was crap. You know, I'd never written anything in long form before. Anything I'd ever written had been essays or lyrics or poems or short stories or letters. And so, writing something long, I was just finding it quite a challenge. So, somebody said, 'Why don't you, uh, just start with your own thing, the usual life story?' So that's what I did."

Musically, with "A Castle Full of Rascals," Purple draw up another rocker, with Ian and Roger perhaps unwittingly perpetuating the band's status as some manner of "heavy metal" band through all these loud, bold songs up into what are supposed to be their twilight years.

"Hey Cisco" and "Somebody Stole My Guitar" go there as well, giving cause to scratch one's head at those who feel egregiously disoriented by Steve Morse guitaring for the Purps. I mean, not only is *Purpendicular* sufficiently electrically charged, but riffs and rhythms and melodies . . . many of these are not unlike what one could expect out of a Deep Purple record with Ritchie Blackmore, albeit a Blackmore in more of a universal and rock 'n' rollsy mood and not fully moat rocking to the minstrel gallery. Additional to "Hey Cisco," Paice turns in a rare double bass drum performance. Picking their way through the barrage, the band members hit chords and then leave spaces, turning the song into an American-feel party rocker not unlike "Get Up" or "Hot for Teacher" from Van Halen or similar "OTT" (over-the-top) songs from Diamond Dave's *Eat 'Em and Smile* album.

"We decided that we wanted to do a fast shuffle," says Jon. "I just worked on that little collection of riffs that make up 'Hey Cisco' until we felt comfortable, and we felt comfortable real quick. That's been a trademark in Deep Purple, and Steve was very, very happy to fall into that. He's really a most amenable chap, because he does understand that there are big shoes he has to fill.

"But in filling someone's shoes, you don't actually have to slavishly imitate what they do by any means. We wouldn't have wanted that. We could have put a thousand guitarists in who would have been only too happy to get paid for imitating Ritchie Blackmore. That's not what Steve's about. He's about bringing a lot of his own vibe to the gig. It worked for me very, very well. He's a joy to play with. What Steve has taken on board—which is a compliment to him—is he's realized that Deep Purple carries a certain baggage with it, you know? A certain amount of history that leads an audience to expect certain things. As a result, while he's trying to remain his own man as a lead guitarist—which he has succeeded at, I believe—he's also tried to weave in some phrases and some ideas and some boogies and feels that will make you feel like you are listening to Deep Purple."

On the lyrical front, "Hey Cisco" concerns the story of Clayton Moore, the actor who played the Lone Ranger, being denied his rights to inaugurate the opening of grocery stores because the studio had the intellectual rights to the Lone Ranger character. In the end, it's somewhat of a truncated and abstract vignette because it's a hard concept to get across with so few words. Nonetheless, art and poetry fall out of it, a good set of lyrics, so the story becomes secondary.

Also for "Somebody Stole My Guitar," which may as well be the dusty, alcohol-soaked tale of a different long dong of a night at Rosa's Cantina. More pointedly, Ian talks of being inspired by a visit to a ghost town saloon in Calico, California, while traveling with his tour manager Al Dutton, imagining getting locked up in the place with the ghosts of gunslingers.

Elsewhere on the back half, "A Touch Away," however, is another strident, rich, realized ballad. Sure, it may be sacrilege to laud ballads within the Purple canon, but one would have to concede that in this department particularly, Purple had grown by leaps and bounds. Both "A Touch Away" or "The Aviator" could sensibly be argued as several levels more advanced than either "Child in Time," "When a Blind Man Cries" or "Wasted Sunsets," either creatively at the music end or intellectually with the words.

Purpendicular closes with "The Purpendicular Waltz," and thankfully, despite that very unpromising title, it's a proper song and not some tossed-off closing instrumental. On the contrary, "The Purpendicular Waltz" turns out to be the album's most progressive and arguably heaviest-metal track, with Lord and Morse locked in doomy unison for the odd-time verse, and then a chorus that splashes into a place of comparatively sunny melody. There's a sense of musical adventure all over this song, navigated confidently by the band's collective but quiet firepower.

"It doesn't pay to do that," says Steve, asked if any of this vibrant new material gets brought in fully formed by himself or anybody else in the band. "Because you've got to be able to write on the fly, to have the band do the stuff. Things change quickly. Ian would say, 'Well, I like that feel,' after one or two bars, and you go from there. Which, if you bring in the whole thing, which they've done—Roger and Ian have done a bunch of that, where they've written some ideas and brought it in—but I can tell you, if it ends up being someone bringing in a song and that's it, then it's not going to sound as much like Deep Purple. But 'Purpendicular Waltz' was close. Well, actually it wasn't, because Ian had this demo [sings it], which we changed, changed the feel of that, and then added a bunch of different parts. So I don't know if there are really any. 'The Aviator' was pretty much that track, except there was no singing. It was just a little tune I used to play for my boy, and he would dance around to it."

Not that any of this fecund creativity mattered in a world that had forgotten the dinosaur bands. To be sure, guitars were very much alive out there in the music industry, but postgrunge and alternative and hard alternative were more about churning punk rock loudness than delicate interplay between keyboards, six-strings, or, God forbid, harmonica. In other words, rock bands were still popular—there are shockingly almost none in the charts today—but in 1996 it was much more of a youth movement. It's a bit of an abstraction, but certain music theorist buddies of mine, such as Rich Davenport, make a pretty good case for the concept of classic rock not arising until the early years of the 2000s, in part symbolized by the return of Bruce Dickinson to Iron Maiden, followed by Rob Halford coming back to Judas Priest.

Purpendicular got to #58 on the UK charts and missed the Top 200 in the US entirely. Its lack of impact was no doubt due to the dog's breakfast of the band's

Roger, minding his "teenage eighth notes." © *Tom Wallace*

label deals in each market shackling the record promotionwise, as well as a bad album cover, the muddiness of import sales, and a confusing bonus track situation—it was America that actually got one, the pedestrian but still serviceable "Don't Hold Your Breath."

"Well, to me it's got great spirit," remarks Ian, asked to look back at *Purpendicular* from a vantage point a dozen years on. "It's a fantastic tour into another universe, really. And I think it's as significant a record as *Fireball* was, insofar as it really opened up the writing room to allow in the new ingredients. And one of the most important ingredients wasn't actually the musical skills; it was the relaxed nature and the embracing of new ideas. The beginning of a kind of maturity for Purple. I thought that was very important.

"And we didn't get it all straightaway, because having somebody new in the family, it takes a little while. But the initial impact was superb, absolutely superb. I'm not sure we actually handled ourselves well in the studio. I'm not sure we ever have done. It's the only thing I've had disagreements with the guys about. I always think we're a bit too haphazard when we make our records. You never quite know what's going to happen. And this idea of not making any plans before we go in is okay—to a point [laughs]. It does put a lot of pressure on. But that was a significant album, not only in the musical history of Deep Purple, but as a social document too."

Meanwhile, "Pretty much finished it, just before this one," said Ian, referring to his considerably less newsworthy solo album *Dreamcatcher*, another in a long line of frustratingly playful and nonrocking efforts from a man who likes to provoke.

"I'm keeping it in the bag until there's a convenient gap, because I don't want to necessarily tour it or anything like that. I'm just going to do a couple of audiovisuals, and I shall just probably do a quick around-the-world three-week promo tour and then back into the Purple business. It's all acoustic. It's a very spiritual thing. I was walking on the beach, and I always sing, and I always have sung since I was in school all day and all night when I'm walking down the street, or when I'm in the bath or whatever. I enjoy singing.

"So anyways, I had never written a song or never had sung any of my own songs, because all the songs I had ever written had been written with electric guitar, keyboards, drums, and bass in mind. And those kinds of songs aren't the kinds of songs you sing when walking down the street. Not these rock songs, anyways; well, not for me. So, I went home and wrote a whole bunch of stuff, and they've got pan pipes and flutes and hand drums and acoustic guitars and things like that. And obviously they lead in a different direction lyrically as well, so it's quite a spiritual thing."

On another occasion, with regard to the *Dreamcatcher* concept, Gillan explained to me that when he walks around singing songs, "I realized I wasn't singing any Deep Purple songs, or any rock songs, and I thought, well, maybe I should write something that is melodically led, or lyrically led. The process when writing with Purple . . . the whole key is the groove. The band is cooking in the studio; it's all improvisation and it's groove-led or whatever. Vocals are really the last thing on the agenda. So, I just got together with my buddy Steve Morris and started writing this stuff. But it was what you would call a hobby or a spare-time activity. It's nothing that is in conflict with the Purple job or anything; it's just one of those things that you love to do. It's an expression of joy which comes out. I had this thing with my dad, which turned into a song called 'Gunga Din.' And then I had a song called

'Sleepy Warm,' which is about waking up in the morning, and my wife was so, you know, sleepy warm. It was just like, 'Hello!,' you know [laughs], just that lovely thing in the morning, when you just wake up in the morning and say hello. Just that beautiful moment of waking.

"So, I saw all this beauty in the things I wanted to write about, and you couldn't write these songs with a five-piece rock band. They were something that could be accomplished with something gentler, without constraint. It's hard to explain. It's just a natural thing, really. I did an album with Roger Glover in the '80s called *Accidentally on Purpose*, and it was the most enjoyable thing I've ever done in terms of musical expression because it was done without the constraints of a rock band. It's pretty exciting when you get that freedom to write songs.

"I'm in New York at the moment," continued Ian, at the time running down the balance of *Purpendicular* plans, offered here to show a sense of the bouncing around that these guys do when longtime manager Bruce Payne is left to his devices, filling up the band's dance card, much to the quiet desperation of . . . well, mostly Steve Morse.

"What we're planning at the moment is, we're in the middle of a tour right now. We're going back to Denmark at the end of this month to commence the sort of open air, the summer dates, early dates for Europe. We're finishing at the Montreux Jazz Festival on July 9. Deep Purple and ZZ Top, which is the twenty-fifth kind of anniversary of doing 'Smoke on the Water' in Montreux, so it's going to be a night to remember. They're having a big fireworks display to re-create the burning down of the place—it's going to be a great night. And then we're going to do a few free shows. Because we switched labels in America, things have been delayed. I think they're planning to do some free concerts, four or five in the summer. And then we're going to take the summer off with our families. Just going to have a nice vacation. And then start touring again. I should imagine North American business will recommence in the fall."

True to the above snapshot, Ian had indeed been on a bit of a press duties break when he spoke to me about *Purpendicular*, with the band being away from their highly intensive live campaign, taking off April 5 through to May 29. However, prior to that gap, the band had blanketed the UK in mid-February into March and then covered various western European countries up until April 4 with a date in Hungary. Back at the end of May, the guys hit the road pretty much rock solid up until the aforementioned Montreux date. After seven weeks off, it was back to exploring every nook and cranny of Europe, followed by Japan in late October and then Canada and the US to finish out 1996.

"It's been great," mused Steve Morse, a couple of years into it, looking at where the band had gone in such a short time, specifically the new territories back when he had just been shot out of the cannon.

"When I joined the band, they decided they were going to play all the places they'd never played before, these places that Ritchie didn't want to go to. It was like this whole new beginning because, first, these people had never seen the band with me, and we still had four of five of the original guys from the 'Smoke on the Water' days. It's worked out incredibly well. We have been expanding huge markets everywhere, with North America being one of the more forgotten ones. So that actually improved; we worked on it for two tours here, and it got better."

Time for a tour tale from behind the Iron Curtain. Steve says this happened in Kiev, which . . . well, a few of the details don't sync up with the official tour record. Anyway, there's definite comedic value to it.

"We were playing outdoors in a stadium there," laughs Steve, "and we were flying from somewhere in Russia, or the crew and equipment was flying on an airliner. We had leased the whole thing, but the problem is, when they got there, due to a language barrier, they'd been misinformed about the size of the cargo door, and we had all these cases that couldn't fit in the plane. So, they ended up leaving the cases in Moscow and just putting equipment and bare wires, amps heads, and stuff all inside the plane, on seats and stuff and in overhead compartments inside the plane.

"And when the roadies got there and got ready to get on the plane, they were looking at the plane and they noticed that some of the tires were bald [laughs]. So, they started this whole panic thing, and just about the whole road crew refused to get on the plane, and the gig was that day. And so, the plane takes off, and it's an old Aeroflot plane, and it makes it there.

"So here I am in Ukraine, and I get the call—my roadie isn't there, and two other roadies for setup weren't there, and stuff has just been thrown onto the stage with no cases. It's like, there's nothing organized. And this was supposed to be a summer tour, like a late spring tour. I've got a little blue jean jacket and T-shirt, and it's getting really cold, and I go up to the stage, just trying to organize my wires for everything. No one can help me, no one can understand me, and there are no roadies. Just this barren wasteland of wires, tripping over millions of wires and pieces of equipment upon equipment. And the crew that did make it, the crew that did get on the plane, they were there, but they are hooking up their own stuff. And I'm going around picking up wires all across the stage, just seeing if I can recognize this. And well, I haven't been doing this even with my own rig, so I don't know what color goes with what, and I'm having to figure out ways to wire it up.

"Meanwhile, I still don't have 110 volts, because they use 220 there, and it starts snowing. So, I'm shivering, just really cold. The audience is coming in, and I hear some guys, 'Hey, Steve, why you setting up equipment?' And I'm still scrambling trying to get it to work. I mean, it was so bad, at one point I had to move six cabinets, amps, 2 feet over, just so I could reach the chord. It was one of those days. There are all kinds of things like that that happen, but this was one thing after another. So finally, I got everything to work, everybody else is long gone off the stage, and people are taunting me from the audience: 'What you doing? Why you set up equipment? Say something.' And my hands are frozen, meanwhile."

So, they're thinking that the new guy has to set up all his own equipment.

"I don't know what they're thinking. It must've been funny. And then the band pulls up in a limo, behind the stage, and they come up onstage like it's time to play. Well, I can't move my fingers—it's too cold. So, this one roadie who did come, on the plane, gets me some steaming-hot water. And I put my hands around it as usual, and I end up scalding my hands [laughs]. And then trying a little bit more carefully, I'm trying to warm up my hands a little bit so I can start playing in the snow."

Fortunately, things usually ran more smoothly, and given the band's advanced years and eons logged together, well, it often could look like the proverbial picture of domestic bliss.

"Oh, the guys have a routine, for sure," chuckles Steve. "They carry lots of luggage and have CD players, lots of books; like, they carry their own libraries on tour. And when we're on a bus tour, the whole band would be downstairs. We have double-deckers, and they would be downstairs just drinking tea and doing these cryptic crossword puzzles, from the *Sunday Times*. And they would have the old *Oxford English Dictionary* there, and some of the stuff is incredibly difficult to do. Ian has really got a talent for that; he loves to do that. They all sit around, and they will help each other, and they will occasionally watch a video. I generally stay upstairs and look out the front window, generally try to see things, practice my guitar. But on the road, I know Roger and I always go walking if we have time, in any city, exploring around, to get the flavor of the area."

And back to the music, answering the age-old question surrounding a new guitarist's approach to some of the most sanctified solos of all time, Morse figures, "I just try to listen to what Ritchie did, and to realize that they wanted somebody totally different in the band, not to copy him exactly. So, I just do my own take on it, what I think would sound good. And if it's a well-known solo or something, I'll try to capture that, the essence of it anyway. And working with Jon . . . Jon Lord really is an amazing musician, and mostly because he can hear and improvise anything on the spot. In every set we have a spot where just he and I will play, but I don't know what chord he's going to play next, and I don't know what melody I'm going to play next, and we just kind of work together and close our eyes and just listen and try to read each other's mind—it's so cool to improvise like that."

A couple of backstage passes

Or as Steve explained in a press release at the time, "This band is a unique animal. Roger and Ian can put down a track like they were born in Nashville, while Jon Lord is like, 'Just play whatever you want and I'll be there,' and that's exactly what happens. There's a lead singer who entertains the band as much as the audience and includes us in the front sale thing. That is what I love about the stage show—there's no competition. We're a band."

"I think the rest of us, over the years, sort of accepted our fate, as it were," adds Roger. "But all of a sudden, we found that we've got a whole newborn enthusiasm.

We all suddenly started playing much better than we played in years. The feeling in the room and those first few weeks were so similar to what I remembered the band being when I first joined it in 1969, which is an eruption of music. A very vibrant, happy atmosphere. Just very relaxed, very happy, and very productive. And the Deep Purple that you see today is nothing like the Deep Purple that was in existence three years ago or four years ago or five years ago. When people say it's the best record we've done since *Perfect Strangers*, that's how I feel about it. Somehow, we got lost for ten years, and we suddenly found ourselves again."

In terms of the *Purpendicular* set list when the band packed their lunches and went to work, according to Steve, the guys were keeping it interesting.

"Yeah, that's something that they are constantly fond of doing. It's really whatever Ian Gillan wants to do that night, what we play, because he's got to sing it, and he's gotta have the stamina for it."

And the response to yet another guitarist in the fold? "It's been great from the beginning," says Roger. "Because there had already been a year since Ritchie quit, and a lot of people knew that Joe Satriani had done part of the tour to finish, and they were ready for the fact that Ritchie was not there anymore. And Ritchie's been very good about it too, as far as I know. He's had every opportunity to slag me or the band, and he's just pretty much turned into his own new project and kept his energy there, which is great."

"I think there's been a rebirth in the band," reflects Ian, guardedly. "We certainly don't want to decry anything we've done in the past. But what we're saying now is, hey, we're fifty years old. We've had our fun in that direction. This is something we've never had the chance to do before. And it's music, it's our music, we're speaking with a very clear voice, and we'll see what happens. We never look at it in terms of how or where it's going to sell. And to a certain extent, it becomes very cyclical. Who knows? You coincide with public tastes, or you don't. As long as you don't bow to convention, you won't get lost in the morass of what goes on. Just stick to your guns, stick to what you believe in. Carefully progress, and make sure your music's vibrant."

From a vantage point of twenty years later, Roger still looks back with fondness upon what would be the first of many records with Steve Morse.

"A couple of months ago I played *Abandon*; I hadn't listened to it for a long, long time, and it kind of surprised me—I liked it. But *Purpendicular* is definitely my favorite of the era. There's such a glorious memory of being in a band again, after all the shenanigans of Purple over ten years that brought us down. You always do the best you can, but there was a feeling that we'd just gone on a long slide down for ten years. Gillan out, Joe Lynn Turner in, and suddenly Ritchie left and what are we gonna do? Joe Satriani helped us put it off for a year, but then when we finally got Steve in the band, we couldn't stop writing. It was an absolutely magical experience."

Chapter 22

Abandon

"Is there a dress code?"

As if to prove the band's new vibrancy, Purple toured the living daylights out of *Purpendicular*, hitting all points on the compass through 1996 and 1997. The campaign represented a subtle shift in the band's identity, into that of a "working band." The records won't be selling in large quantities ever again, and ticket sales would be down accordingly. For the next little while anyway, it was going to be a harder sell. And yet, the band had so much renewed vigor, despite the grind, that there was a spring in the collective step. But yes, this was the start of a sense that Purple worked for a living, took it to the people, filled that lunchbox and emptied it at lunchtime. At the end of the day, they got on a bus and did it all over again the next day.

And they didn't let up on the swell record making either. Tired as they must have been, the creative taps were flowing hard, to the point where it became sensible to say that this is the best the band ever were, or the most mature and substantive, whatever specific and compartmentalized positive a fan might want to apply, if he or she thought a blanket "best" went too far. *Abandon* supported and strengthened that idea, equal to or arguably over and above *Purpendicular*, even if the guys in the band have framed it as one of their apocryphal hard-to-birth records, a struggle, the inevitable chore of a project after an easy one.

One is first introduced to the album through its cover art, not of crucial importance to the tale, granted, although it's a good opportunity to hear from album cover designer Ioannis, who provides some insight into what it's like to deal with the Purple camp.

"At the time I was working with Yngwie Malmsteen's manager, Jim Lewis, and I had just finished doing *Alchemy* for Yngwie. And next door to Jim, literally, was Deep Purple's manager. There were a couple times we said about going over there saying hello and getting together, and it was like being in the right place at the right moment. 'Let's get together,' and then he's off to India or something [laughs], and then you don't see him for another year.

"And then I get a call from Yngwie's manager: 'Hey, listen, the other day, Bruce walked in here and he just got the record cover back from the record label, and he's horrified. It looks terrible. And he asked me if I had any ideas of who to use. Can you come down here for meeting?' I was like, yeah, fuck yeah. The first album I ever bought was *Machine Head* when I was a kid, so I was just in awe of these guys. So, I run down there and there's Bruce, their manager, and there's Roger Glover. So, we sit down and we started discussing it, and Bruce says, 'Look, we're really in big shit here,' verbatim, you know [laughs]. And 'This thing looks like crap,' and he shows me the cover. I wasn't going to respond to somebody else's artwork. I was like, okay, if he doesn't like it, he doesn't like it. At least I know what not to do."

Asked to describe what had been supplied, Ioannis says, "I guess what the guy had done, or the agency, is that they simply had taken the words Deep Purple, and the title *Abandon*, and they basically just did a whole lot of Photoshop filters and effects, to make it 3-D. And to Bruce, it just looked like one of those cutout albums. They're Deep Purple. And a lot of the greatest albums of all time are not the greatest covers. But to them, they always really wanted to have something different or original, at least in their minds. So, I asked them, what was their idea? And they had an idea about throwing yourself with abandon. And Roger was saying, 'If you really break down the title, it sounds like "a band on."' So that was a cool approach, that way: a band turned on. Especially because of their music and everything.

The *Abandon* cover art, along with the CD art for the US advance. *Martin Popoff archive*

"So, we talked about what would it be like, and Bruce said, 'What about the idea of somebody just diving into a pool of sharks, you know, not caring?' And I started thinking . . . I know every fricking album cover by heart, that's ever come out; I'm a fanatic. I go to record stores, and I just collect. I started thinking about Gamma and then Def Leppard *High 'n' Dry*. And I'm going, 'Yeah, I'm pretty sure it's been done somewhere.' But they were really keen on the idea of somebody diving, and I said, 'Well, how about somebody just diving into nothingness?' Like somebody just diving off . . . well, back then, they hadn't fallen down, but somebody diving off the World Trade Center? Somebody taking a dive into New York City, like the person just doesn't care. So, the idea of a diver, diving from the top of this building in New York, into New York, as though he's going to hit water. It seemed kind of cool. And we had to be really careful, so it wasn't like somebody was committing suicide. It had to be a very surrealistic picture.

"So, it was a series of black-and-white photographs that were shot and pieced together and tinted with a heavy blue, to tie in with the name Deep Purple, and the story very loosely continues within the packaging. There's a point where the guy is touching the area, and there are like ripples of water created. So now you're really not sure if he's diving into New York, or he's diving into a reflection of New York City in the water. I always liked that idea of it being just enough doubt, something for the mind. And Roger loved it. I had given him like four or five ideas, but that was one of the main ones. They went with that, they pieced it together, and I lived out one of my greatest dreams.

"Roger wanted to do the tour books and everything else," continues Ioannis. "He wanted to take over the art. So, he came down to the office. I'm sitting there, sitting next to the guy who helped cowrite 'Smoke on the Water' [laughs]. And he's like, 'Hey, can we get something to eat?' or whatever. And I'm like, 'Yeah, there's a Greek diner right down the street.' Okay, great. So, we're in his BMW and we're driving down. And we're sitting there, and at one point me and my brother look up at each other like we're in surreal land. We're sitting here with Roger Glover in a Greek diner having Greek salad [laughs]. At one in the morning."

And both Ioannis and Roger are in Connecticut. "Yes, and then suddenly he's inviting me over to his house for tea. You know, house in the loosest sense of the word. Palace is a better description of it. It's one of these places in Greenwich that costs about $9 million, and he's got a bigger recording facility downstairs in his basement than most recording studios are. But it was weird, because I had forgotten all the bands Roger had done—*Butterfly Ball*, Nazareth, Judas Priest—so I kind of lived out my dream there. But the amount of work we did a few years later that occurred out of this thing was just unbelievable. So, I was pretty psyched.

"He's done well," continues Ioannis, who also cracks up over another culinary story of Roger making a McDonald's run for the guys during another late-night work session. "It's great, because Greenwich and Westport, Connecticut, are like the Beverly Hills of Connecticut. It's a very high-end area; a lot of superwealthy people live in the area. It's one of the top areas. It's so cool, because on the one hand, he's Roger Glover, the bass player for Deep Purple, but here he is on the cover of *Greenwich Time*, one of the most upright citizens. You know, the board of directors; one of our famous citizens, Roger Glover, this kind of stuff. He's just a terrific human being. He hasn't changed; he's still an old hippie. He wears his bandanna, and he has his worry beads with him and wears hemp and stuff. Him and his wife love the Indian food.

"All his kids listen to Radiohead," chuckles Ioannis. "His kids never go to the gigs. His son is a huge Radiohead fan. And I look at him and I'm like, 'Do you realize who your father is?! Do you have any idea how huge of an impact this man has made on the music you listen to?' It's just unbelievable. One of my treasured moments out of that was, we went out, we were sitting one night with the manager, me and my brother George. And I don't how the conversation went, but we told him that when we were kids, we got rock 'n' roll wherever we could get it, and one of these magic moments was the California Jam concerts that aired on ABC. And it was the first time we got to see Black Sabbath and Deep Purple, because back then, they came to play in your town, and we were too young. Our mother refused to take us to see Black Sabbath, because we were too little. Or you read in *Creem* magazine and saw what they looked like. So, we were so psyched.

"So, we were recalling our fond memories of how we got up in the middle of the night and made sure our parents didn't wake up at midnight. We turned our TV on, and we put headphones on. And Bruce says, 'Oh, I'm quite glad you guys have fond memories of California Jam. Let me tell you my fond memories of California Jam.' And he goes into a story, dude, about Ritchie Blackmore and about what happened that night. Oh my God, it was fucking unbelievable. It was just 'Holy shit; these guys have lived some really heavy times.' Again, it brings into perspective who you're dealing with and how big and what a legend these people are. It's a cool thing, just to sit there and have a coffee with them."

"There's two meanings to the word 'abandon,' as far as I know," reflects Ian Gillan, critiquing the cover art. "And one of them is to be left behind on a desert island or something like that. But the really original meaning of the word 'abandon,' there's an expression, an old English expression that says, 'to do something with gay abandon.' And of course, a whole section of the community has hijacked the adjective. And of course we have to say, well, that's not fair. To do something with abandon means to do something without any care. It's not looking before you leap. It's flying like a bird. To be abandoned means to be freed without fear of consequence. And I think that's really the mood of the music."

Writing team Roger, Ian, and Steve. © *Tom Wallace*

Past the steely-blue wrap and into the new canon of songs, *Abandon* opens with a vigorous drum groove, accompanied by a bulbous swell of electrics. "Any Fule Kno That" (the spelling is a nod to Geoffrey Williams's *Molesworth* books from the 1950s) finds Gillan essentially rapping over a note-dense swirl of a Ritchie-like riff out of Steve. Ian chides the industry (welcome back "Moronica, Queen of the Biz") for its focus on celebrity and paparazzi press, and not the quality of the music itself. Come break time and the song becomes panoramic. It's a convincing and rocking way to open the album, but given the intensity of many of the songs that follow, it's not outsized and obvious as a Deep Purple album opener. In other words, in the spirit of the band's productivity at this point, it's not as patently the best song on the album, compared to how quite a few other Deep Purple albums play out.

Ask Ian about how the music business is treating him, and this song comes firmly to mind. "On *Abandon*, listen to the first song, called 'Any Fule Kno That.' I don't know if you've ever studied the English language, but there's a phrase; twenty-five years ago, we were playing with this little toy, this grammatical game called an oxymoron. Now, for example, it might be jumbo shrimp, you know? Or in Ian Gillan's humble opinion [laughs]. Or military intelligence. You take this train of thought a little further, and you come to the music business. Doesn't really go together. It's kind of an uneasy relationship. And this song is all about the music business. So, the idea of the oxymoron led me and Roger to think about things like 'Woman from Tokyo' and 'Strange Kind of Woman.' Let's turn it into a euphemism, and all of sudden we've got Moronica, Queen of the Biz, and Flash Harry and 'Tin Pan Alley Fat Head Larry don't know shit / Just trying to keep her happy.' So, we get into all of this stuff, and yeah, basically, the relationship with the business has never been all that good. We despise it and they despise us.

Two single versions of "Any Fule Know That"

"If I could just give you one little story. My wife tells me, 'Ian, don't do yourself down. Be a proud man; you've done some nice things.' And I go, 'But Bumble, you've got to listen to me. We're treated like dogs.' She says, 'No you're not—be proud.' And I say look, I was in Monterey, in Mexico, and I closed my hotel room door, and there on the back of the hotel door there's the rules. And I look at clause 3, subsection 2, and it says, 'It is strictly forbidden to bring into the hotel, number one, guns, number two, animals, number three, musicians' [laughs]. So, you have to take things tongue in cheek, have a little fun, and accept what you are, where you are, and you look at the whole situation. So, everything I write is from that perspective, which I hope is far enough up the hill to be able to look at things from a reasonable point of view."

Remarks Steve, comparing his two records with the band so far, "With *Purpendicular*, there was a range that was kind of undefined, of what was going to be Deep Purple. I guess I was bringing in more outside ideas, and the more weird ideas, to start working on. Like 'The Aviator' was one, and 'Sometimes I Feel Like Screaming,' things that I wouldn't have thought they would have liked. And the second album with them, it was more like guitar, bass, and drums that the songs were worked up on, because Jon was doing his solo recording at that time. So, he didn't join us until late. Jon eventually caught up with us, but the songs were pretty much sketched out by then, so they are more-heavy, riff-oriented things. And possibly some of that was me just saying, 'Here's what I think might work with the band.' But the best stuff comes from not thinking. So, I'm not sure what was the best thing to do, or to have done. I think we had more time on *Purpendicular*, so that was crucial as well."

Roger had expressed something similar, in that there was an unspoken agreement that the album was going to be heavier than *Purpendicular*, more in keeping with the hard-charging attitude of the road and the road set list.

"It's a very exciting time for me, being back with Purple," Ian had told me, when *Abandon* had just launched. "Everything is great, you know; we have the family back together again, and everybody feels strong and therefore confident, and therefore expressive. I think to be expressive is the first requirement of any artist. I don't mean to make this thing sound so grand. All I can say is that it's a lot of fun."

As he continues, Ian revisits the concept first covered in the previous chapter about writing as a middle-ager. But in the current telling, he offers some new perspectives. There's some repetition here, but it's a crucial element of understanding post-'95 raison d'être of Deep Purple.

"Well, you know, I think as you get a little older; sorry, I hate to be . . . have you got a moment or two? [laughs]. I remember talking about this very subject with Roger when we were down in Portugal a few years ago. And we started talking about songs such as 'Black Night,' stuff that we wrote when we were kids in our twenties. We were thinking about lyrics, when we started Purple. I've known Roger since '65, like five years before Purple, and we started thinking about what is it about these lyrics that had such power when we were kids?

"Of course, when you're a kid, you feel immortal; you just blurt them out; you don't think twice; you just say what you think. So, there's a kind of naiveté about what you write. Then all of a sudden you're fifty years old, and you think, my God, how can we recapture that naiveté? And then all of a sudden you think, to hell with it, we've never been fifty years old before—I'm now a naive fifty-year-old. So now you do think twice, and you have to embrace that experience of life, enjoy it as a songwriter and as a performer.

"So, you sit down, and you think, 'Well, hang on a second—where do I stand in my life?' I feel tender, gentle, and strong and all those things, and I can look back over the days of my mother and my father and my grandfather, and now I have a daughter and everything, and my life is pretty rich, and I've traveled around the

Steve Morse on the West Coast, August 30, 1998. © *Tom Wallace*

world a thousand times. So, these are the inspirations that lead you into the music that is your next record, really. It's very exciting.

"And I remember as a kid not any of the words that were told to me by my father and my mother and my grandfather. But I remember the smells, you know, the shaving soap they used to use when I was a kid. My father used to shave with this Palmolive and put this shaving cream on his chin. And then he used to take this brush and put it on my chin when I was a little boy and shave me with a bladeless razor. And it was just a wonderful feeling, you know, looking up to my heroes, to adults, just looking up at these people and saying, 'You know, these are my heroes.'

"And if I could aspire to the nice thoughts that they had, I'd be doing well. You know, I was a lucky person. I had a wonderful family and a wonderful environment to grow up in, and it just inspired me for future life. And when you get to a certain age and look back on those things, you treasure those moments. I think everyone does. It's not a thing you have to deny; it's a thing you have to treasure."

Ian goes on to compare the new album with its predecessor. "Okay, first of all I would say *Purpendicular* is an absolute first. It's Steve Morse's first album with the band, and it's a statement. But I have to tell you, I look back to when we were on the road, and I think back to when we made Deep Purple *In Rock* back in 1969, then *Fireball*, and then *Machine Head*, then *Who Do We Think We Are!*, and then the records we made in the '80s. And I was talking to the audience the other night, and I said, 'Thank you so very much for listening to our new songs. These new songs one day will be old songs.' Like the songs from *Perfect Strangers* and *House of Blue Light*, those were once new songs; now they are old songs. 'Highway Star' was once a new song; now it's an old song.

Ian Paice promo shot

"The thing about this new album, I have to tell you, I really think it's fantastic. The only reason we make records—and this may sound strange because of the way the industry works—the only reason we make records is because we write new songs. It's kind of a demo of what the audience can expect on the next tour. And you know, we're doing seven songs off this new album in our current show. But this *Abandon* album, in my opinion—and it may not be everybody's opinion, and it does have to stand the test of time; we may find out in ten years that we were wrong—but in my mind, *Abandon* is the best record we've made since Deep Purple *In Rock*. Absolutely. I mean the songs, they're unbelievable. 'Almost Human,' 'Evil Louie,' 'Fingers to the

Bone' . . . this stuff just fits in so well with all the classic songs. I mean, we have twenty-year-old kids out there, and they know every single word to the new album. It just fits in so perfectly with the old show. I mean we have 10,000, 20,000 people showing up every night over here in Europe, and it's unbelievable."

Validating that glowing review, *Abandon*'s second track, "Almost Human," brims with youthful vigor. Ian Paice provided a roiling shuffle beat, over which Ian sings an abstract paean to whiskey. And, of course, whiskey makes you do crazy things, such as roll up a newspaper, stick one end up your butt, light the other end on fire, and do as many laps around the parking lot you can before being singed by the flames (yes, Ian's actually done this). Toward the end of the track, there's a reference to being in a bar, getting up to leave, and finding yourself stuck to the floor by old beer. Which means you have to stick around for another round.

"My absolute favorite song on the new record is that one," says Ian (while Steve plumps for "Any Fule Kno That"), "and it's about a man singing into his glass of whiskey. If I can explain it to you, which I can't, because we don't have enough time, the absolute essence of that song is so vivid in my imagination about what happened in my local pub one night. Every song on this album is a true story. Every single damn song.

"These lyrics are not veiled at all," adds Ian. "First of all, from a mechanical point of view, there are two aspects to lyrics. First of all, it's my language [laughs]. The first responsibility, and I'm going back to 1965 now, back to when I first met Roger, back to the craft, the first responsibility of lyrics is to have them sound good. We talk about the melodic value of words. You can sing absolute gibberish, but it's got to sound good. After that, you can have fun as a lyricist. You can work on one or two or three levels; you can bring people in to enjoy the story, so they can see where it's going. But all of these songs are actually very heartfelt."

"Don't Make Me Happy" is a shaggy, late-night blues like "When a Blind Man Cries" and "Love Conquers All." Ian demonstrates his little-discussed prowess with respect to the art of vocal phrasing, especially as it applies to the blues genre. Yet, even this one has its muscular moments, with the chorus getting angry while Jon Lord punishes the Hammond. Interestingly, the track is in mono, given that a technical problem occurred with the stereo version, and fixing it might have delayed the album by two months.

"Seventh Heaven" is *Abandon*'s anchor track, its tour de force, a crushingly heavy song and arguably the apex of the Morse-era catalog thus far. Roger admires the song's "raging spirit," which is a great way to describe it. It's a roaring lion of a song.

"You know what that's about?" says Ian. "Well, that's about Steve Morse. It's being in seventh heaven. The last verse goes something like, 'I get down on my knees and kiss the ground,' and it's like, my God, when this guy came into the band, I mean he was the only guy we wanted, and you know what his condition was? We said, 'Well, Steve, we'd like you to join the band; let's check it out, let's have a rehearsal, let's see if we get along well.' He said, 'I have one question: Is there a dress code?'"

Without Ian telling us that, you'd never know what the lyric is about. Instead, we'd just revel in the poetry of it, especially the elliptical first verse, not that there's much more to it. This is a case where the wordsmith essentially steps way and witnesses the embarrassment of riches that is this band. Although one more point:

armed with that brief explanation, now the first verse looks like a description of what a nightmare it was dealing with Ritchie.

Assembling the record, says Ian, "We'd never discussed anything. Day one, we turn up, Ian Paice, Steve Morse, they turn up at midday, they start arriving, [and] they start jamming, jamming for an hour or so. Jon Lord turns up, pours a cup of coffee or makes a cup of tea; I show up; we're watching the football or reading the paper, blah blah blah; we work from twelve to six o'clock every day, five days a week. Roger Glover and I sat up all night working on lyrics, and we just carry on until it gets done. If only we could record the album six months after we've written it, it would be unbelievable (i.e., if we could have recorded the album now). It's really dangerous what's going on onstage."

"Not workwise but in terms of schedules," answers Steve, qualifying the sense of "laxness" he experiences recording with Purple. "The schedule was lax. In fact, there was an emphasis on not worrying about expenses, time, stuff like that, and we definitely, definitely let some time go by [laughs]. I mean, we would be doing things like . . . Roger would do a perfect take on one bass, and I would say, 'That sounds great, Roger!,' and he'd say, 'Yeah, I don't know—let me try the blue one' [laughs]. We'd go, 'Got it, yeah!' 'Yeah, but I don't know if I like the tone on this one.' And Ian would basically come in every day and try a different cymbal and redo his entire drum part, stuff that was not so much them not being able to get it, but it was more so they could experiment with tonal details. And Jon would come in and get a really good take down, and you know, he won't do too many takes. When he's in there to record, you gotta press the button [laughs]. Jon doesn't waste any time in the studio. He also wasn't there for part of it.

"Things are actually really good for the band right now," continues Morse. "We've been steadily doing better. And financially, I'm as pleased as I can be. And you know, if things had gone the other way, it would've been really easy to point the finger at me. But things are going good for whatever reason. We feel great playing together; that's the main thing. And you know, I think it's the most perfect job in the world for me, and the only thing I would change, ever, is just to make the tour legs shorter, just because I have a little boy now, and I don't want to be gone that long. But I would never say stop touring."

Of note, *Abandon* was recorded, as was its predecessor, at Greg Rike in Florida. The recording happened in two main chunks, in the fall of 1997 and the spring of 1998, a typical interruption for this band perennially surrounded by live dates. Inherent in Ian's comment about how he wished the album could have been recorded six months later, generally speaking, the band's songs at this point had no chance to be routined live, having been, for the most part, invented in the studio.

Next up is "Watching the Sky," an angular progressive-rock opus with circular logic and a dropout to a quiet psychedelic verse before more ensemble explosions. Lyrically, there's a man experiencing a full disconnect, perhaps from society, perhaps from a relationship. In any event, he's stunned. Saxon has a "Watching the Sky" too, and it's very much as good as this one.

"Fingers to the Bone" proposes a novel pastiche of soft Celtic rock sentiments from Steve against an oppressive straight-eight rhythm strafed by monotone power chords. The result is a dark semirocker, with Jon Lord turning in a rare piano solo (accompanied by wistful and distant harmonica), and Steve playing both acoustic and electric of many shades. It's definitely one of these modern-day Deep Purple songs that wonderfully confound genre classification, given how it's literally in the middle of two different genres at the verse alone, and maybe a third for the chorus.

"Jack Ruby" is a jumped-up funky blues, a light moment on the album. It's the closest thing to filler on a record full of astonishing triumphs. The song has roots back to the *Perfect Strangers* reunion sessions, with Roger and Ian Paice cooking up a 6/4 rhythm and jamming it out into temporary oblivion, only to be revived fifteen-odd years hence.

A couple of gig ads

"She Was" is another ominous and very heavy rocker, its pregnant pauses allowing for organ and guitar counterpoint, its lyrics fairly inconsequential . . . female temptress and all that. Late in the sequence of events, Steve and Jon get to duel cleanly and real laid-back over a roiling slow burn of a rhythm from Paice and Glover.

There's similarity between "She Was" and the album's next track, "Whatsername," with both being thick and almost forced from a riff standpoint, a bit of 'What would Ritchie do?' Lyrically, again, we get a temptress tale, and as Ian suggests, not all that veiled. Further, "Whatsername" has a bit of a driving "Mary Long" vibe. Both do a bunch of heavy lifting toward this idea that the guys wanted a heavier album this time, likely helped along by Jon Lord not being present the whole time.

Toward the tail end we get "'69," which finds Ian feverishly name-checking various fond memories from the early days (note the reference to "Hallelujah," Ian's wobbly first song with Purple from way back). Additionally, there's a very condensed version of a story in which Ian passes out in his plate of spaghetti in a pub, wakes up, tries to make it to the men's room, but throws it all up on top of two bar patrons rolling around on the floor and beating the daylights out of each other. Ian's contributing to the fight has the effect of putting an end to the tussle.

"The interesting thing about Purple is that we didn't all start because we liked the same kind of music," reflects Ian, offering another view of the year 1969, through the subject of influence. "We didn't all start to be this kind of a band. Purple started,

JON LORD

Jon Lord 8" × 10" promo glossy

or ended up as it was, in '69, when Roger and I joined, because it was the kind of people we wanted in the band. It was the kind of attitude that we wanted in the band. It just so happens that it is very diverse. Jon Lord's background is classical. He studied musical composition at the London College of Music. He grew up with Jimmy Smith, the Hammond organist, and he had a great jazz influence. Ian Paice grew up in the Buddy Rich school of music, so he brings a big-band, swing feel from his heritage into the band. Roger Glover is all things folk.

"I grew up with the young Elvis Presley and then graduated into all the rockers like Fats Domino and Ella Fitzgerald. I got into jazz stuff, plus I had a weird background with the church choir, and my grandfather was an opera singer. Ritchie bore his English rock 'n' roll, which was very prevalent with the English guitarists. Steve brings in his southern root and his southern rock plus his jazz and classical training. He also has many years' experience playing with different people. When you get all of that together with a band that has been around for a while and put the freshness into it, it becomes a special thing."

To expand upon what Ian said about Steve, his main gig had been instrumental (and improbable) southern fusion act Dixie Dregs, with whom he'd recorded eight albums back to 1976. There'd also been five Steve Morse Band albums, one Steve Morse album, and two records with Kansas, 1986's *Power* and 1988's *In the Spirit of Things*, on both of which he was a major contributor to the writing.

"Steve brings a whole lot to the band," continues Gillan. "He has revitalized everyone else as well. When the ingredients are right, then it all works. You can go around and say, 'You and you and you and you' and pick the best in the field, whether it's music or sports, to make a team. In a football team you can pick the greatest goalkeeper in the world, the greatest striker in the world, and the greatest defensive men, and you will have a crap team because they will all just be playing for themselves. If you get a balanced team with the right amount of experience, intelligence, [and] youth and the right coaching, then it works beautifully. A team which normally wouldn't stand a chance can do very well because of team spirit. I think in a band, it is very important that the family feeling is there. That is what we thrive on. Deep Purple is a family again, and Steve has made that possible by playing his part. Not only musically but in a human sense.

"We have done two albums with Steve, *Purpendicular* and *Abandon*," continues Ian. "We have a clear idea of where we are going next. We are going to take some big strides technically and productionwise. We are going to work with an outside producer, which will give us some outside objectivity that we have not had for a long time. I think we have learned a lot about how to approach the next album, and we are very excited about it. I can't talk too much about it, because everything sounds like a self-serving comment. We have got a title for it, which of course I can't tell you [laughs]. We should be recording in the autumn.

Ian at the congas. Roxy Open Air, Ulm, Germany, June 20, 1999. © *Wolfgang Gürster*

"There are a million things to come out of this band musically. After we did Deep Purple *In Rock*, we did an album called *Fireball* that freaked out the record labels. They said, 'What is this?' We said, 'It's our new album.' They said, 'But it's nothing like the first album!' We replied, 'Correct!' They went on and said that we had to do something like it, or people wouldn't buy it. It was a transition. It was a springboard to *Machine Head.* That's exactly what it was. Record companies have no conception of the creative processes. They want everything to be the same, so they can sell albums. When the record sales drop off, then they just get rid of you. That's the way it was, the way it is now, and the way it will always be. We decided a long time ago that we were going to be expressive. Like everyone else, our mood changes from day to day.

"One of the major things that I can say is that we have matured in a pretty exciting way, dignified if you like," continues Ian. "None of it has taken away the dynamics of the band. It is quite the reverse; it has improved the dynamics because there is that thing called confidence. We went through something in the '80s that was very difficult. Our fans have always been totally supportive and very, very loyal, but you had the whole industry and media thing that started in England. They called us dinosaurs. No matter how well you are doing, it does make you think a little bit about the aging process.

"Like I say, I had quite a long conversation with Roger, who is my writing partner. We talked a lot about this, and it was very important that we made that step from writing about fast cars and loose women in every song. Well, not every song, but we were thinking about it all the time! My wife said to me that the average man thinks about sex forty times a day, and I said, 'I can't understand how they keep losing concentration!' [laughs]. It was true and it is still true now, but somehow there is something undignified about a mature guy ranting on about his dick! It's teenage and youthful behavior.

"I think people expect a little more from us at our stage. You do it with a twinkle in your eye. You hopefully have learned to express yourself in a way that is just as interesting. Don't try to do what the kids do. Try to act your age. I think that is exciting. I got my hair tied back every day because it was getting in my beer. The only time I would let loose is when I was onstage, so I cut it off! It was one of those things. Suddenly, I started thinking that we had always had thoughts about this, and that our lyrics have always been expressive, concerning things that affect you emotionally, intellectually, and spiritually. We decided to work on that. We decided to use this medium that we have to be expressive.

"Being expressive is a phrase that I keep coming back to," reflects Ian, digging into the topic. "As I said, if you feel confident within your surroundings, within your group, then people respond to you and things escalate. This applies to anyone; if you feel confident, then you behave well, you drive well, and you act 'confidante.' You have a good circle of friends, and you trust each other. All of those wonderful human things kind of develop in a way that you don't have to make a big deal about it. It's just there, and it enables everything that you do to be done to your satisfaction. You get messages."

Back to the record, the second-to-last track on *Abandon* is "Evil Louie," with Ian offering a kaleidoscope of inscrutable words, seemingly disconnected lines, but all of them action packed. Again, it's a slow, heavy rocker with big drum windups. There's a middle eight that Ian Paice found the hardest thing to do on the entire record.

Closing out the fifty-five-minute album, we get a remake of "Bloodsucker" from 1970, now called "Bludsucker"—the tale has it that the band was jamming it in the

Ian's literary partner. © *Tom Wallace*

studio, and manager Bruce Payne heard it and thought it good enough to poke onto the album.

"Well, that's a weird thing," chuckles Ian. "That was on Deep Purple *In Rock*, written in '69. We escaped and did a few dates while we were in the studio. We did some shows at the House of Blues in Chicago and Atlanta and Los Angeles, wherever. People would come up to us and say, 'Oh, I love those new songs you've written, "Seventh Heaven" and "Bloodsucker."' And it was kind of interesting because we had the feeling that Deep Purple has been rediscovered. I don't know if it's our innocence or natural being or whatever it might be, but there was a kind of connection.

"I'll tell you a story. When we finished recording *Abandon* and the tape arrived at my house, my buddy came over and we were playing pool in my house. I played the album and said, 'What do you think?' And he said, 'Wow, it sounds like your first record,' which was really interesting because we recorded this song 'Bloodsucker' as well, which was on our first record. So I was like wondering, well now it sounds like '69. Or does '69 sound like now? Or has Deep Purple finally found its voice again? Anyway, doing that song just seemed like a really nice thing to do. And you can also just put aside the analysis and say, 'Well, it's a fun track' [laughs], or it's merely a connection to '69."

Touring for *Abandon* featured bills with both a reformed Emerson, Lake & Palmer and, conversely, Dream Theater. Neither pairing resulted in good enough ticket sales. Again, being on CMC/BMG in the US for a second record had the band in that mid-indie zone, and the climate for this kind of music—classic rock, as Gillan disdainfully calls it—wasn't as hospitable as it would be later with the rise of *Rock Band* and *Guitar Hero* (and, as we discussed, major old bands re-forming).

"Have you seen what's going on on the net?! Have you read any reviews?!" said Ian, down the line to me midtour, painting a prettier picture. "Take a look at some of them. The whole tour is sold out; we're doing 10,000, 15,000 a night. People are going crazy. They're loving it. And all I see is twenty-year-old kids, and they know the words to the new songs and to the old songs. Dream Theater played with us in Italy; they're great guys. But we won't see them again until we get to the States. The opening band for us right now in Germany is Rage. They're huge in Germany, right? Fantastic, great band. The first US leg is August, all of August. And then I guess we'll be back, because this tour is going to be . . . I've got on my day sheet here that it runs up till the end of October, which is the second European leg. So, we finish here in Spain, and then I go home and get ten days off, and then we go to the States. I'm taking my wife, my daughter, and her school friend on the whole of the American tour, which means Canada too. We're going to see the sights, have a great time."

South America, North America, everywhere in Europe, Russia . . . Purple, unsurprisingly, toured these "second wind" years with abandon, reaffirming themselves as one of the premier bands of the world, an inspiration for what Iron Maiden would become in the first decade of the 2000s.

"We just came off the road in Russia," begins Roger, asked if he had any examples of snafus that occurred, perhaps due to a language barrier in exotic locales.

"It was a whirlwind tour, and normally your equipment is sent by truck overnight. Well, this was from Japan to Korea to Finland to Russia to Greece. It was ridiculous, and it cost so much to ship stuff that we only ship certain amp heads and guitars, and particular personal equipment. And the bulk of the equipment the promoter

Assorted backstage passes, for the immediate tour and a few after

would get there. Now, Ian Paice uses Pearl drums, so it's really easy and simple to say, 'Get the local Pearl guy to supply a kit.' We turned up in St. Petersburg, Russia, minus our luggage. We get to the hall only to find that the equipment we've got is unbelievably no good. I mean, Paicey's drum kit was all different colors. They had cobbled it together from all the different club bands; it was somewhat less than professional. And Jon's organ, the same way, the speakers, the same thing. There was only one speaker in one of them, out of the four. That kind of thing goes on. And when we said, 'Look, this is ridiculous; this is not what we asked for,' I don't remember the exact wording, but they turned around and blamed us. I don't know if that's a translation problem or maybe that's just Russia, I don't know."

Asked if anyone in the band was known for lavish spending on the road, Roger chuckles that "someone was very extravagant, but it wasn't one of us. In Moscow, there was a guy who was wooing us. He wanted us to consider him as a promoter. And to that end, apparently it costs about $15,000 to get your company name printed on the ticket. Because sponsorship is very big in Russia. And that's your name on the ticket and probably up on the wall somewhere. You know, insurance companies, tobacco companies, banks—they're all kind of joined in, and that's the way it works in Russia; it's a big sponsorship country.

Abandon tour book

"This guy figured that instead of spending the money getting his name all over the place, he would take us out for a meal. And he must have spent fifteen grand on the meal. I mean caviar, buckets of it, the best vodka, vintage brandies afterward. It was amazing, and the spread was unbelievable. A pig with an apple in its mouth, all glazed over and sitting on a plate waiting to be carved. Which, you know, didn't particularly go down well with me—I'm a vegetarian. I didn't even want the apple after that. But it was just overboard. I don't think I've ever had such an expensive meal. God knows what it cost."

I asked Glover whether he ever got the vibe that the money being thrown around in Russia came from the criminal element.

"Not so much the money, but you definitely get the feeling that things are being run behind the facade that you see. It's most noticeable in security. There's usually a lot of security, and they are very heavy-handed, I mean, to the point of really annoying us. We would come out of the hotel to get into the van, and there would be maybe half a dozen fans there. They want autographs, and you see them being pushed aside really too violently for our taste.

"And everywhere you go, there are big burly guys. We went to a club in St. Petersburg after the gig for a meal with the promoter, and it's almost embarrassing to walk into a place like that. I mean, we're huge stars there, and I'm not used to acting like that. But to walk in and have these big bouncers just rough people up just for looking at you, it's all a bit over the top. And you realize that's what they do all the time. In Kiev, when we played there a couple of years ago, there were a lot of news reporters and fans at the airport. They got us out a side door and whisked us off. We're driving into Kiev, and a Mercedes pulls up alongside us and the window comes down and a big TV camera comes out, trying to see into our limo. Whereupon the enormous 14-foot security guard in the front seat—I kid you not—whips out this equally enormous gun, this handgun, and lowers his window and just points it calmly at the driver. But you say, 'Where are we?' I can't say I've seen it in action, but you do get the sense that there is a lot of Mafia hoodlumery around."

The threat of being kidnapped must be an issue as well. "Not that I know of. I remember going to India, and I remember going up to my room after going down to the coffee shop, and there were two guys standing outside of my room. I didn't know who they were, whether they worked for the hotel or what. And they started walking toward the elevator, and they fell into step behind me. And I said, 'Excuse me,' and they said, 'We're your security.' And I said, 'Well, I'm just going down to the coffee shop,' and they said, 'Well, we'll stay with you,' and I didn't check them off. And they slept on the floor or sitting on their chairs outside of the room all night. And apparently—I was talking to the promoter later—they had about fifty security guys for us. And every single one of us in the band had two guys all the time."

Steve offers another tale from far-flung nether regions of the world. "There's always something crazy going on. We finished our last tour in Korea, there was a typhoon coming in, and Dream Theater was playing before us there. They pretty much got to do their set, and when we began playing, it was starting to rain. The

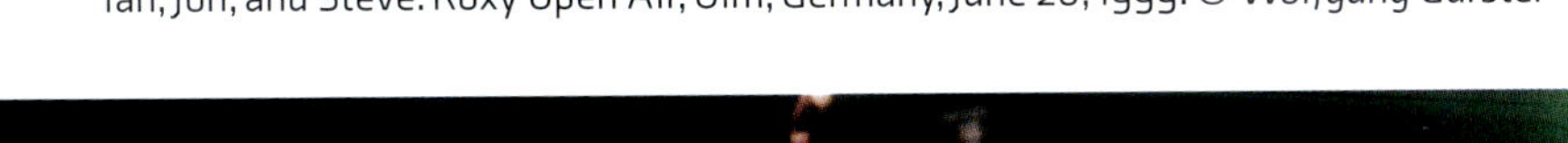

Ian, Jon, and Steve. Roxy Open Air, Ulm, Germany, June 20, 1999. © *Wolfgang Gürster*

rain was coming in sideways, so we were in the rain, playing. We kept playing, and the drums, every time he hit, we'd see just sheets of water come off the heads of the drums. And Jon would slide his hand up and down the keys when he was playing his solos, and you could see a rooster tail of water.

"My guitar stopped working; I had to switch to another guitar, because it'd just literally like totally shorted out. And the same thing happened with Roger's. We had my pedalboard covered in plastic, as if that was going to do any good. But it was real slippery, and I was slipping trying to move the pedals and everything. Ian was just out there singing and getting soaked, and he was happy, because he loves stuff like that. We kept playing until our equipment wouldn't work anymore. We used up all the guitars; they all got shorted out. The only drag was because it was the last day of the tour, everything immediately got thrown into boxes, shipping cartons, as it's raining down with this typhoon, and it got shipped on a boat for like a month, totally wet, so everything got ruined."

Dream Theater's Mike Portnoy wrote about the situation on the band's website, saying that the hurricane was going full bore before they went on and after they left the stage, but it remained pretty much clear for Dream Theater's performance. Many bands' sets got canceled, quite the unfortunate situation for the country's first big rock festival, with 30,000 fans in attendance.

"And then shifting channels to a gig recently," continues Steve, "we're playing somewhere in Switzerland, we get there and ride up this incline, a railroad, for like a mile and a half, and it's snowing! And the only problem is it's an outdoor gig! So, we're playing in the snow [laughs]. It was just so bizarre. And the dressing room, which was the little station where the trains come, and they work on them and put grease on the wheels and stuff—that was the dressing room. The snow was too deep to walk to the stage, and we just had like regular clothes on; we weren't dressed for the outdoors. They had one of those big snow cats that they use in ski resorts bring us from the 'dressing room' to the 'stage,' and the stage was just a wooden platform with plastic around it [laughs]. And the snow's blowing in our faces, and you can't feel your fingers. It was just so bizarre! So yes, we do some weird gigs."

And some weird songs, such as Thin Lizzy's "The Boys Are Back in Town!" "Well, we did for a while," notes Roger. "It was just a bit of fun, really. You know, it's great to be in a band with Steve, because he's always thinking along different lines than the rest of us. We've known each other so long, and Steve comes in with a whole different outlook. And he suggested we use 'The Boys Are Back in Town!' as an opener, and we were all like, 'Yeah, sure!' And then we were 'Wait a minute; that's not such a bad idea.' Off-the-wall ideas are great like that. So, we just did it for a laugh. We didn't intend it to stay. It's only a verse and a chorus anyway, not the whole song. It's just a way of opening the set with a little groove, you know?"

Backstage at the band's June 19, 2001, stop at the Molson Amphitheatre in Toronto (with Ted Nugent and Lynyrd Skynyrd), Ian and I chatted, with Gillan expressing relief that this "band he loved in torment" was no longer in torment.

"Yes, it's gone. Because history changes every day, doesn't it? I mean, circumstances change every day. That's why it's futile to be dogmatic in life and stick to an opinion. No matter how the world is changing around you, you've got to adjust to it. So, we've had our divorce, and that was a long time ago. It was a love/hate relationship, and it was a difficult family to be in, but now it's not. All of us except Ritchie are still in the band. Steve has been great; he's a very vibrant contributor to everything that we do, and he's also got his own definitive personality, which gives that edge. He's vital. But we had some good times, and we look back on that with great affection. Just to think that a lot of people thought that it was the aggression that created the spice that made it work . . . in fact that's totally wrong. It was the difficulty and the aggression and the disappointment in the personal relationships that destroyed the band, not only internally but also publicly. And I think we all feel a lot easier with life now, and we can get on with our music. It was torment, but it's not anymore."

On Morse, Ian points out that "he's internationally known. I don't know why it takes longer in America to become accepted—it's his own country. But you know, Steve was voted number one guitar player around the world by guitarists five years running. And on the sixth year they made him ineligible for the poll, and Joe Satriani won it the year he actually played for us, the year before Steve joined us. Steve is generally accepted as being the maestro. He's part of the family, and yeah, seven years and it's run by in no time at all. It's wonderful."

On the side, Mr. Morse had put out an interesting record in 2000 called *Major Impacts*, where he wrote songs in the style of his influences (*Major Impacts 2* would be issued in 2004).

"It's stuff that was part of my really early life of playing. Interestingly enough, it was the record company that came up with that, Magna Carta. They're quite a good label to work with, and they came up with the whole idea themselves, and it seemed like a good idea for me. I sort of made a list mentally and then just thought of which of them gave me an idea of where to start. A good starting point for me was to think of one tune that I really loved. Like the Keith Richards one; I was thinking of his rhythm guitar in 'Start Me Up' or even 'Street Fighting Man' or 'Brown Sugar' and then 'Honky Tonk Women.' There was a really neat, kinda funky country thing that he did that I really loved. That was kind of like the verses of the tune, and then it rides out with a different feel, kinda like 'Gimme Shelter.'

"The Led Zeppelin thing. When I saw Zeppelin live in '69, I was struck with the song 'Black Mountain Side,' which Jimmy Page played live. I thought it was so cool that this really heavy-type band had taken the time to do this acoustic-type piece, along with the open tuning. And then I kind of incorporate some of the Indian-influenced melodies that he does. Then I wanted to have a heavy section and then combine all those things together at the end. And I like Rush a lot. We got to open for them in the '80s, the *Power Windows* tour. They were a pleasure to listen to every night. Alex, one of the things he did that I thought was so cool was to come up with these nice big voicings and then come up with a melody out of a chord voicing and incorporate that into a part. I've listened to a lot of guitar players that play with just a trio, and it's a tough gig to do for any guitar player. Eric Johnson, Jeff Beck, and Alex Lifeson all played in trios at some time."

And back in Purple land? "You're right—we don't have a new album out anywhere," laughs Ian, asked about "touring" a record, *Abandon*, that by this point was now well on nigh three years old.

"But we started this tour in February [actually March] in Australia, and we finish in the UK in November [actually, the last date turned out to be September 8 in Turkey; then the World Trade Centers fell, and the band didn't play again until February 2002]. It's a fun year; we had a lot of interesting projects, and we just took what came along. It's not promoting an album or anything like that. We just like to work. We just like to play. We've done a lot of things. We did a benefit in India for the earthquake fund. A couple weeks ago I was singing with Pavarotti in a benefit for the Afghani kids in Pakistan. I can't remember what else we've done this year. There were a couple of concerto tours early, where we played with orchestras and

Ian Paice, California. © *Tom Wallace*

other bits and pieces. Then we were going to do some US dates, and they suggested we put this tour together, to put these two tours together to do one tour. It's been fabulous; I've enjoyed every minute of it."

And the Purple guys were playing for seventy-five minutes. "It's better than the first package tour I played on, where we got four minutes to open the first half and seven minutes to open the second half," laughs Ian. "It's pretty good, impact stuff. You think of festival bills, summer bills, and all that stuff; you don't want people to be playing two and a half hours—it's a pain in the neck. Obviously, everything brings a problem. If you haven't got any money, that's a problem. As soon as you start earning money, you've got to pay tax—that's a problem. And when you headline the show, you get to do two and a half hours, and that's a problem. And when you have to cut it down to seventy-five minutes, that's a problem.

"Altogether, they're good problems to have, not difficult. Even cutting the show down to two and a half hours is very difficult with the kind of catalog we have, and the kind of new stuff we like to bring in. But because of the nature of the band in terms of improvisation, it's not. It's not too easy to work the discipline in terms of exact timing. That's the most difficult thing, to cut down some of the improvisation. So, what we've got is a little expanse and contraction point, so we can feel free to break loose in the middle of the show. And then we can shorten it in the end if it's gone on too long in the middle. It's a terrific thing.

"I think there's an awful lot spoken about 'Oh, we got our money's worth because they did two and a half hours.' Two and a half hours of what? If the conditions are right, that's great. If the band is really kicking, that's great too. But I've heard two and a half hours of rubbish that I only wish was half an hour. Long time ago, on average, we worked out that the best set for the audience, their attention span, on a good night, was just leaving that little buzz of excitement at the end instead of draining people to the ground so they just want to get out of there and go back home, was an hour and a half, ninety minutes. So that's only fifteen minutes more than what we're doing now."

Reflecting on the big classic rock billing on the eve at hand that day, Ian chuckled that "Lynyrd Skynyrd told us they don't do well in Europe because the beer isn't cold enough. But I've nothing but good things to say about them in terms of their professionalism and demeanor backstage. I have a lot of time for them. The thing is, both acts mean it. They mean what they do."

On the subject of these "compromised" band lineups, worst offenders being Thin Lizzy and Foreigner, but yes, somewhat Skynyrd, Ian is energetically dismissive of criticism sent their way.

"No. I'll tell you what. We never think that. All those kind of comments were going around about Lynyrd Skynyrd. You know what? They're fantastic and the whole audience loves them. And we had all these comments about, well, you know, half of them aren't there, and it's all-new people and goodness knows what. You know, they're brilliant. And I think, I hope, that Thin Lizzy will be brilliant [laughs]. We have a lot of bands that we've worked with over the years. And it's very rare these days to have the entire unit still together from how it was originally conceived. I'm looking around at the Stones; I'm looking around at Floyd; I'm looking at Jethro Tull; I'm looking at Status Quo; I'm looking at every band there is, including Deep Purple. I mean, the interesting thing is, a lot of people say Deep Purple isn't the same as it was, because it's not the original band. Well, in actual fact, when Roger and I joined in 1969, already the band had changed; it had lost two original members. So, let's keep it in perspective. In actual fact, what we have got is . . . we lost a few fans, and we've gained a few—things have changed.

"I look back on all the bills we've been on in the past," continues Ian, back on track about the range found within these packaged shows. "The first one I mentioned to you was with Dusty Springfield. We were doing four minutes to open the first half and seven minutes to open the second. And I think if we were ten seconds over or under, we were fined our fee for the night. After two nights running, we were off the tour. It teaches you a lot about the professional side of things. Outside of the genre of rock music, I've worked with Dusty Springfield, Sammy Davis Jr., Tom Jones, Pavarotti as recently as that, George Benson, Taj Mahal, you name it. We've headlined the Montreux Jazz Festival a couple times, and we've done things with the London Symphony Orchestra.

"To me it's all music, and it just doesn't necessarily embrace the whole sphere of rock music but to touch on it every now and again. You touch on a little of this and a little of that. But it's great, because I love Fats Domino, Brooke Benson when I was a kid, as well as Ella Fitzgerald and Ray Charles, as well as Little Richard and Chuck Berry, Cliff Bennett, Art Tatum, all of these influences that came in. It's great to work with all these people. And that's why I detach myself, not aggressively, but I detach myself as much as I can from that term, heavy metal. None of us from that generation, us or Led Zeppelin, ever thought of us as heavy metal. It was an invention like a lot of things from the media. I'm not knocking it. We just don't actively jump in there to participate in the genre. I just don't like the phrase. It's a phrase I particularly detest because it's the least musical form I've ever heard in my life."

Chapter 23

In Concert with the London Symphony Orchestra

"Right, you stand here; wait your turn."

On September 25 and September 26, 1999, Deep Purple played with a symphony orchestra. Sure, many bands have done that, but as we all know, (a) Purple did it first, and (b) they actually cooked up a whole album of material for the occasion. History records it as a bit of a pompous debacle, so here they were trying to make things right, plus adding a bunch of pizzazz.

Ergo, what we got was the full "Concerto" from thirty years back—the anchor of the new set—plus some of Roger's *Butterfly Ball* material, as well as a weirdly positioned "Wring That Neck," picked as an Ian Paice showcase and played very jazzy. Later on, commendably, there are three Steve Morse–era songs and then the closing "Pictures of Home" and "Smoke on the Water" tribute to the single Deep Purple album that has become part of the wider pop culture fabric.

But that's the DVD. The CD version of the album includes "That's Why God Is Singing the Blues" from Ian Gillan's *Dreamcatcher* album, "Take It Off the Top" from the Dixie Dregs album *What If*, and the somewhat silly "Via Miami" from the Gillan Glover album *Accidentally on Purpose*.

"The whole album—or should I say the event—was conceived on the bus, whilst touring," explains Roger. "It was a lot of fun; we knew we wanted to do something different. The whole idea of doing the 'Concerto' came lateish. We were actually looking for something to do extracurricular, as it were. The 'Concerto' appeared because the manuscript turned up, so we were trying to figure what else to do. So, the idea came up to sample from our solo careers. We mooted and bandied that about the bus, and of course we all have varying careers. Ian Paice of course is the one who has the least in terms of albums to pick from.

"But the rest of us certainly have been very active over the years. I didn't know whether to do something current or something old. And then somebody said, well, *Butterfly Ball*—and get Ronnie [James Dio] in. Ian Gillan said that. Now I hadn't seen Ronnie for quite some time. And it just so happens that on that tour, we were doing a couple of gigs with him. He was really up for the idea, so it wasn't much of a decision after that. The fact that when I first did the *Butterfly Ball* at the Albert Hall in 1975, Ronnie didn't come, and that posed quite a problem for me at the time. I was a little concerned that he wouldn't come this time either, but he was actually really up for it.

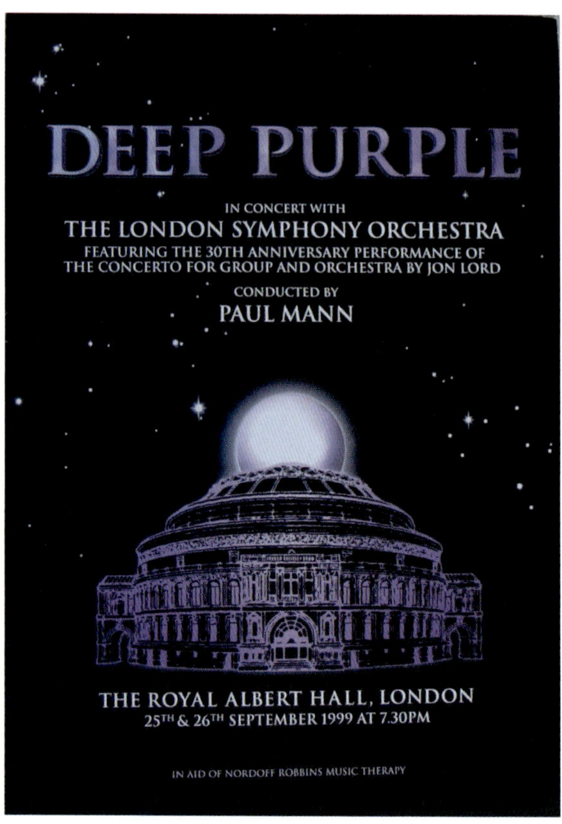

A couple of posters promoting the show

"The reason he didn't come first time is because of the various politics that were going on," continues Roger. "He had just joined Rainbow. In fact, there was kind of a division between him and I at the time. But for him to turn up this time was absolutely fabulous. There was really no question about what songs to do. 'Love Is All' had to be one of them. We did consider 'Homeward,' only because Ronnie said he loved that song, which is a revelation to me after all these years, to have the singer turn around and say he loved the song. But we just thought 'Sitting in a Dream' was probably better."

Each party in Purple was given a ration. "Yes, we only had two songs each maximum. So, for Ronnie to come over and just do one song didn't seem right. But yes, I wouldn't have minded doing something from *Mask*, probably 'The Mask.' But with Ronnie coming over, I just wanted to utilize him the best we could."

And frankly, seeing Ronnie sing so effortlessly and powerfully and precisely, that's the highlight of the disc right there. It gets your mind racing around the idea of Ronnie singing classical more often, and it also raises that age-old question: Why was Ronnie never part of Deep Purple? Elsewhere, Ian shows up in his famous all-white sorta East Indian dress to do a raw, quick, tight "Ted the Mechanic." Jon Lord is clearly loving the opportunity, conductor Paul Mann is omnipresent (Mann had a huge part in bringing the rebuilt score to life), and there are always myriad performers to watch, from horns and strings to backup singers.

"'Via Miami' was a fun thing to do," continues Roger, asked to pick favorites. "It was great to hear that. I also have to say 'Ted the Mechanic' has really become one of those new Purple classics, if you like. I heard it the other day for the first time whilst watching the video. The video is actually on this record. If you put it in the computer, it's like a DVD, a video clip of 'Ted the Mechanic.' That's even on the American Spitfire copy, although it doesn't say that on there. It's a well-kept secret. It's on the first disc. Stick it in your computer and it will pop up. I played it for the first time, and I looked at it and said, 'Wow, this is great stuff.' I was blown away with the sound and the visuals going with it. And I played it for various members of my family, and they were just knocked out. I just think this is one of the nicest all-around albums we've ever done. It's got a real warmth to it, and it sounds great—it sounds like the occasion it was."

Asked if there were any moments of chaos during the shows, Roger laughs and says, "Were there any moments when there wasn't any chaos? No, pretty much it went according to plan, although we didn't have a plan, so it's fairly hard to tell. It's unusual for us to go onstage and do that much new material in one fell swoop. So yes, it was a bit fraught with tension, and memories were stretched. The real chaos was not so much in the music, but the staging. We spent four or five days rehearsing beforehand, and then we moved to the Albert Hall and then we immediately had problems. Because the stage is obviously big enough for an orchestra, but it's a little small for us. So just arranging us on the stage crammed in front of the orchestra was a bit of a problem.

"But by the time we had sorted that out and had our first rehearsal with the orchestra, all was well. By the way, they were just superb, never put a foot wrong, a collective foot wrong, that is. The first rehearsal was great, but there were lots of stops and starts between songs, this, that, and the other. And the second rehearsal was just the afternoon of the first day, and again with stops and starts. So, the whole idea of it being continuous was just something that was the chaotic part—there, I thought, we would fall down. Because no one knew when to go onstage, how to get onstage, when to leave, and so on. And I was somewhat nervous about that. But I have to say that Charlie, our stage manager, was absolutely brilliant. He became the military man and barked his orders out off of his list and said, 'Right, you stand here; wait your turn,' and it was great. You need to be told what to do."

Asked about tracks that had been picked but discarded along the way, Roger recalls that "I think Ian Gillan went through a couple of changes before he settled on 'That's Why God Is Singing the Blues.' I think he wanted to do 'Gunga Din' from the last solo album. But at the end, I think he thought it was too ambitious. The only real regret on the album is that Steve's 'Night Meets Light,' which I thoroughly enjoyed, I enjoyed mixing it, it came as a bit of a blow to me when it got left off, and I'm sure it's a blow to Steve. But unfortunately, these things happen. It was kind of a corporate decision. Those higher up deemed it the one that was the best to go, probably because it was an instrumental, and the only other instrumental was Ian Paice's. You couldn't take Ian off."

Speaking of Steve Morse, here's his impression on how the album got constructed. "Well, Jon and the guy who reconstructed the score—I can't remember his name

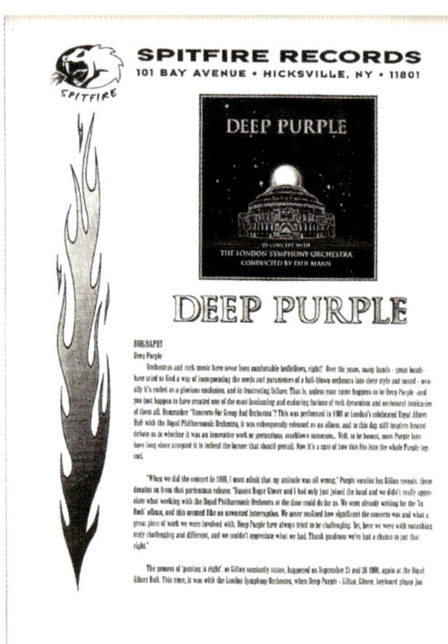

SPITFIRE RECORDS
101 BAY AVENUE • HICKSVILLE, NY • 11801

DEEP PURPLE

IN CONCERT WITH
THE LONDON SYMPHONY ORCHESTRA
CONDUCTED BY PAUL MANN

DEEP PURPLE

BIOGRAPHY
Deep Purple

Orchestras and rock music have never been comfortable bedfellows, right? Over the years, many bands - great bands - have tried to find a way of incorporating the needs and parameters of a full-blown orchestra into their style and sound - usually it's ended as a glorious confusion, and in frustrating failure. That is, unless your name happens to be Deep Purple -and you just happen to have created one of the most fascinating and enduring fusions of rock dynamism and orchestral intricacies of them all. Remember "Concerto For Group And Orchestra"? This was performed in 1969 at London's celebrated Royal Albert Hall with the Royal Philharmonic Orchestra, it was subsequently released as an album, and to this day still inspires heated debate as to whether it was an innovative work or pretentious, overblown nonsense... Well, to be honest, most Purple fans have long since accepted it is indeed the former that should prevail. Now it's a case of how this fits into the whole Purple legend.

"When we did the concert in 1969, I must admit that my attitude was all wrong," Purple vocalist Ian Gillan reveals, three decades on from that portentous release. "Bassist Roger Glover and I had only just joined the band and we didn't really appreciate what working with the Royal Philharmonic Orchestra at the time could do for us. We were already writing for the 'In Rock' album, and this seemed like an unwanted interruption. We never realised how significant the concerto was and what a great piece of work we were involved with. Deep Purple have always tried to be challenging. Yet, here we were with something truly challenging and different, and we couldn't appreciate what we had. Thank goodness we've had a chance to put that right."

The process of 'putting it right', as Gillan succinctly states, happened on September 25 and 26 1999, again at the Royal Albert Hall. This time, it was with the London Symphony Orchestra, when Deep Purple - Gillan, Glover, keyboard player Jon

US press release for the symphony project. *Martin Popoff archive*

[Dutch composer Marco de Goeij; a herculean task for which Jon is eternally grateful]—listened to the old recording. He and Jon Lord corresponded about that and got together. Then Jon Lord and the conductor got together off and on for over a period of months, just part time, working on it, and the conductor gave him some advice about arrangement, assigning the strings and changing a few octaves here and there to make it easier to play.

"When we got involved, it was maybe three or four times before the performance," continues Morse. "So, he went into London into this tiny practice room where . . . well, actually it was a studio, and the conductor, Paul Mann, he's there playing the score, sight-reading the score with one hand while he flipped the pages with the other. He would play the sections where we were going to come in and just . . . we didn't have any music; we had to write our own. Basically, the hardest part for me was trying to figure out when you're supposed to come in, because you had to read the music before you came in. Because the only thing is, I found out, what you play on the piano doesn't necessarily . . . you've got to look at all the possibilities that can happen with the orchestra. Because you can only play one or two voices at a time with one hand. But he did a good job of giving us an opportunity to get ready for this."

In terms of rehearsal time, "The background singers came to one or two rehearsals, and the horns to one rehearsal, just the five horns, and I worked with an arranger. In fact, the guy who is playing violin, they cut it off the album; it wasn't Deep Purple,

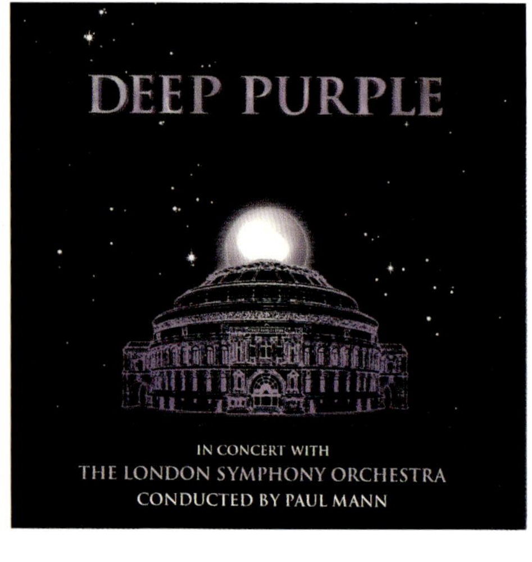

CD and DVD issues of the concert

but he did a nice orchestral arrangement. That was done via files and email, where I said, 'Here's what I think would work good,' and he took it and worked with it. Anyway, the final rehearsal was the time when we got to hear all the guests and singers and everything. That was at the actual Albert Hall itself, because that's when I know Ronnie Dio came. We just had stand-ins before this. The songs were not difficult, but the orchestration was a real challenge. And Ronnie, the only thing was, I'd suggest maybe a key change, to make it easier to sing. But I think more spur of the moment, he decided on singing on part of 'Smoke on the Water' and stuff like that. It all felt quite [an] informal thing. We were like bumping into each other.

"Oh, lots," says Steve, asked about highlights. "First of all, I got to sit right next to the conductor and hear the most perfect stereo image of an orchestra [laughs]. That was great. And then just seeing Jon get his piece done properly, which he's very proud of—that was a highlight for me. He's not a keyboard player that toots his own horn very much, or at all, really. He's just phenomenally talented, but he's always preferred to stay in the background."

Shortly thereafter, the original and much-derided *Concerto for Group and Orchestra* album from 1970 was attentively remixed and reissued.

"I don't think it was a calculated move by the record company, but I can't know what they were thinking," mused Lord, just after he would leave Purple, to be replaced by Don Airey. "But, as you quite rightly identified it, the rerelease has nothing to do with me or Deep Purple. It was an issue settled by the record company themselves, because when we recorded the thirtieth anniversary of the 'Concerto' in 1999, for a different company, it did incredibly well. I think they genuinely believed that what they had in that original album could be made into something excellent. And indeed, I have to say that the remix is astonishingly good. I'm actually thrilled with it. The differences between the original recording and the new mix are enormous, particularly in orchestral detail. Hidden inside that original rather bad mix is a glistening performance by the Royal Philharmonic, who actually suffered some criticism from their fans, who accused them of playing like children. Now, through the benefit of the new mix, you realize the orchestra played like heroes. The whole performance—the band, the orchestra, the conducting—was of a very high standard. It's great to see it vindicated."

In closing, Lord reflects about the trend for heavy metal or classic-rock bands to perform select shows with orchestral backing.

"Well, I've never been a great fan of using the orchestra as a giant backing group for a rock band," cautions Lord. "I'm generally not into doing that. When I wrote the 'Concerto' in 1969, it was a genuine attempt to write something for two opposing forces,

Backstage pass

to try to see if there was any way they had some kind of common ground. It was a terrifying experience, because it was something that had never been done before. Looking back on it now, we must have been out of our minds to think that it would happen [laughs]. But because the band and most of the orchestra played it for what it was—an honest and emotional piece—we got away with it. If the 'Concerto' proved anything, it proved that it's a difficult area that isn't one you should treat lightly."

Chapter 24

Bananas

"We can definitely do different."

Would it be considered a slip in momentum that Purple would take fully five years to craft a follow-up to *Abandon*? Were they surrendering themselves to the nine-to-five grind, the concept of being a working band that goes out and plays the hits? Were they losing their creative fire? It seemed that way, with so many live shows in the years following the release of *Abandon*. But the sense of drift was to heighten further, when in mid-2002, ever-present mainstay and elder statesman of the band Jon Lord announced his exit.

"Yes, I have officially left Deep Purple," said Jon, after a brief spell of being replaced by Don Airey for a string of dates but then actually returning for a leg. "If they ask me to come onstage with them in a couple of years as a guest to do a few numbers, I'd be thrilled to do it, because we're all great mates. There's no acrimony, angst, or anger. These guys are my best friends. As for the confusion, that was my fault for not going on the record; I actually didn't step out and come back. I was going to do my farewell tour in February around the UK, but Ian Gillan caught the flu, so of course he couldn't soldier on without a voice [laughs]. That tour had to be postponed, but Purple went off to the Far East and America, two tours that I had never wanted to do, so I stepped out for that. When they put the UK gigs back in for September, it was only fair that I at least make an appearance, since many of the fans had kept their tickets. So, we came up with a plan that I would do the UK leg, and that would be it for me [laughs].

"I have to say that Don Airey is a trooper," continued Lord. "He's a marvelous man for dealing with the situation the way he did. It is now his job playing keys for Deep Purple, so for him to step offstage and let me take the glory was one of the most selfless, unegotistical things I've ever witnessed in a musician. I'd like to thank him publicly for that.

"I wasn't about to sit around and wait for it to finish," said Lord, venturing into his reasons for bowing out. "I have to believe that I've made the right decision. I don't have sleepless nights anymore, but I did at first, asking myself if I knew what the hell I was doing [laughs]. I know now that I've done the right thing."

Looking back from a 2009 vantage point, the band's new tinkerer of the ivories, Don Airey, says he and Jon kept in touch in the ensuing years.

"You know, I've kind of been friendly with Jon for a long time, and at one stage, I actually would call him up every year, just reporting for duty, and he wanted to know how I was doing, how it was going. Now, not so much. But yes, there was a bit where his final tour got canceled, because Ian Gillan was ill, so he came back in, by the time I joined the band. He had a contractual obligation to do the tour, so we did it with two keyboards. I did the first half of the show, and at the end of the keyboard solo, I kind of disappeared and Jon popped up, playing 'Perfect Strangers.' And then he kept playing, and I joined him for 'Smoke,' and then we both shared the keys on the encore. It was a wonderful thing to stand behind him and watch him play Hammond. He's a magical player. And we did it recently. Ian Paice does a charity gig every year called the Sunflower Jam, and Purple played, and he said, 'Would you mind if Jon . . .?' I said, 'Of course not.' So, we did the same thing again—Jon sat in for a couple numbers. Quite an education."

Articulating the difference in Jon's style versus his own, Don figures, "He's just got such a touch with the instrument. He gets a sound, and I don't know how he gets it. He just seems to stroke the keyboards. He uses drawbars a lot more than I do. I'm much more of a Keith Emerson school of 'Less is more.' But Jon, he's always coming up with sounds and always pulling the drawbars and adjusting them, and I don't do that so much. First time I saw them, I was a classical-piano student at Manchester College, and I went along, and it changed me. I went, 'Well, I want to do that' [laughs]. That was Mk. II, and they were marvelous. Jon Lord was just so great that I couldn't believe what I was hearing."

The motivation for the maestro to be leaving Deep Purple was an admirable one indeed. Basically, facing down his own mortality, he's got one last dream to fulfill. "I've got another way of looking at things now. Deep Purple has been an enormous part of my life, but I reached a time in my life where I decided that I had to get on with this other stuff; otherwise I'll never do it. If I don't, I'll lie on my deathbed in my nineties, staring heaven in the face and saying, 'Why didn't I do it?' As for my new focus, rather than calling it classical music, let's call it a less rock-oriented way of writing, a more gentle way. It will be less electric in the physical sense of the word, but I hope it'll still be exciting. There are elements of both rock and classical music in the material I'm writing now, because those elements exist in me."

"I'm getting used to not being in Purple now," said Jon to *Record Collector*'s Joel McIver. "It was a wrench, but it's been nearly three years, so I'm starting to get really used to the idea of not being in the band. I still see Ritchie Blackmore every now and then. In fact, it's my turn to buy dinner—although it's his turn to buy the wine, which means he loses out with the way he and I got through it when we get together. We're quite old-fashioned; we write letters to each other, although my handwriting has deteriorated after years of signing autographs. I've never understood why people want thirty or forty albums signed all at once. But it's one's duty to stick around and do it as much as you can."

Further on his justifications for leaving the band, Lord cited, "The incessant touring, plus—if I'm honest, which is the only way to be—a slight feeling of getting tired with playing the same-old same-old, were the reasons behind my leaving. I honestly felt that I wasn't fulfilling my role in Purple as well as I should have been,

Don Airey, Deep Purple's new tinkler of the ivories, at the Molson Amphitheatre, Toronto, Ontario, Canada, June 18, 2005. © *Nick Soveiko, Wikimedia Commons*

Roger and Steve, Molson Amphitheatre, Toronto, Ontario, Canada, June 18, 2005. Also on the bill, April Wine, Mountain, and Tricky Woo. © *Nick Soveiko, Wikimedia Commons*

although of course I'm a professional and there is a level beyond which I will not go. I also felt that if I didn't get on and do my own music at some point, then I'd never do it—I felt that time was rapidly running out for me. I didn't feel it was fair to split my intent between Deep Purple and my own material, and I reached the point where something was going to have to give. Some things just have to be written—you have to get them off your chest. The band were extremely understanding. They knew what was going on better than I did, I think. Ian said that it was the most friendly leave-taking in the history of the band. They're my best friends, to such an extent that they will be friends for life.

"I wrote them a letter," continues Jon, asked about his method of announcement, "and faxed it to them and my management, saying that I felt that we were touring too much and that the emphasis of the band had changed. Touring everywhere that God made possible—or promoters anyway, who are sometimes synonymous—and that there was no time for anything else. So, in my letter I asked them if there was any way we could take a year off, because I really had to get on with my own music. And I got a lovely letter back saying that's not how we see it. It really was a charming letter; there was never any animosity about it.

"That was what I wanted to do, but they didn't feel that was fair to them or to the fans," continues Lord. "Don had already done three tours with us when we all had flu anyway, so it wouldn't have been fair to him to say, 'Hi, Don, I'm back now.' It was very scary at first, being out of the band. I had done solo work before, but always with the band as a support system. It was so difficult because Purple was my band—me and Ritchie started it. But back in '74, when Ritchie formed Rainbow, I actually left and was persuaded to come back by David Coverdale. There have been two things that David has persuaded me to do in my life that I felt were innately the wrong thing to do, and that was the first thing. The second thing was joining Whitesnake, and while I'm not ashamed of anything I did in that band, it felt a bit like running on the spot. David had pestered me for about three months, saying, 'Come on, lad!' and all that—although of course he doesn't speak like that anymore; he's the Roger Moore of rock 'n' roll. But I wasn't doing much in 1978—although Paice, Ashton, Lord had exploded, I must say—and so I thought I'd do it."

"I don't know; we just believe in it," shrugs Roger, asked how the band can keep up such a touring schedule. "The band seems to have an energy of its own, and we're just hanging on. Purple has been lucky enough to have a great deal of fans around the world who have stayed with us. I don't think we're popular in the conventional sense, but we remain a live draw because we're a live band. The records are a necessary evil! Recording isn't the same as going onstage because you're not in the moment, with that magic and the adrenaline rush of where you put your fingers during a solo. You do things you never thought you were capable of."

Back in the world of such "necessary evils," the guys would be asked at various junctures (certainly by me, repeatedly) about the mounting possibility of new music one day. But given their way of working—intense collaboration and spontaneity—there was usually not much concrete that could be promised.

"The new stuff is interesting and is really good because we have all worked on it together in the same room, and we hadn't done that since some of the early songs of *Purpendicular*," said Steve in 2000. "We got Ian jamming with us on the microphone in the same room when we're coming up with ideas, so instead of him feeling like, here's another song idea that just got thrown down in your lap, he's there to help you push it in the direction that is comfortable for him. So, it's a really good thing. It's hard for me to judge; I don't notice much difference from album to album. I couldn't give you an objective opinion because I get so far into the music. I could sit there and play all the songs on the album, but I don't hear much stylistic difference between them; it's just all music, all tonal music, no big deal. I'm not good at categorizing."

"It takes about two years of talking about it before we can arrange to start doing it," Steve told me, also in 2000, but on a different occasion, in May. "It's like, 'Oh, we've got this coming up; oh, I've got this coming up; oh, I've got this coming up. As soon as we get done with this, well, no, after Russia . . . well how about after that?' [laughs]. I guess the whole idea is to not . . . well, the manager has got one idea, which he's vocalized very clearly, which is if you just make another rock 'n' roll album, then they'll just treat it like a rock 'n' roll album gets treated these days [laughs], which is kind of like a coaster for drinks and things.

"The idea is that he would like to see us do something that is different, and we can definitely do different [laughs]. We've got quite an eclectic range of musical tastes in the band. I guess the question is, how different do you want to go? You can't really put words to describe what's going to happen, other than to say that it's not going to be as much as a 'This is who we are' attitude, but more a 'Gee, I wonder if this is too weird?' kind of attitude. We're starting our creative session in a few weeks, down in Florida. So, we'll definitely come up with a few ideas, some new ideas, because that's definitely what we do. I spew ideas quickly when we work together, and they're usually good and they're well organized, because Roger takes care of that. He's like the natural record keeper."

But as alluded to, Roger had pretty much decided he wasn't going to produce the thing. "I think Roger could, of course, but he's sick of it," notes Morse. "He's been working that way for so long on each album that I think he'd like to just see what would happen with a record producer. Everybody has put in their name, for their favorite producer. But this is one of those cases where I'm not really up on all the discussions that are happening. One thing I do know is that they are set on getting a producer. They basically said, you know, we've got a really good producer in-house, but if it takes an outside producer to get everybody to show up at the same time on the same day, then let's do it [laughs]."

Cut to a year later . . . "We started working on some stuff and then got together again and worked on some additional stuff," says Steve, with the update. "The thing is, Purple just tours on a continual basis. Everybody lives in different countries, thousands of miles apart, and we just haven't yet got back together to work on the album. As I said before, they decided to have an outside producer for the first time in a long time. And that takes a lot of planning and getting the right person. So, it's even more of a scheduling difficulty.

"Roger is a natural organizer of the musical ideas that get thrown out. I'm one of those people that spews ideas in all directions. Roger captures some of them and remembers or takes them and categorizes them, and he's a large, very important piece of the puzzle. He's a very musical guy too; he helps with all kinds of stuff in the songwriting process. But he's sick of being the producer without any authority. But yeah, I'm really one of the worst people to interview about albums. Because even though I work intensely on everything I do, I have a real matter-of-fact approach to a project like that. I feel, sure, it's going to be good, but I also know the guys change their minds a lot. There's no way of telling. Anybody who does tell you what an album is going to be like is full of . . . energy [laughs], but not so much full of realism."

"All I can tell you," offered Roger, during that same visit with the band, "is that there's a great enthusiasm in the band for making a really, really great album, a spectacularly different album that will be bold. It will be strange, it will be different, but there's nothing much written. We've had a couple of writing sessions, but I can't really tell you much about it. I would definitely rather not produce. I didn't want to produce any of them, starting with *Perfect Strangers*, as a matter of fact. The very first meeting for the reunion, I said, 'Excuse me, I don't want to produce,' and look what happened [laughs]."

At the time, Roger was finishing up a new solo album that would emerge in 2002 as *Snapshot*.

Asked for a bit of info on it, Roger tells me, "It's impossible to tell you a little bit. I have to start and tell you a lot. I'm just about to mix. We've got fourteen songs. The two main people throughout the album are a drummer called Joe Bonadio and a singer, organ player, sax player, all-around good guy called Randall Bramblett. He's actually just got a new record coming out on New West Records, sometime in the next few months. I don't have any deal yet. I decided to make the record and have finished product to do a deal with, rather than a couple of demos. Because I'm not a big-name act. I'd rather go with a company who really believes in what I'm doing. And I'm willing to promote it as much as possible, probably do a club tour or at least a couple of dates, something along those lines, film it. But I really need to find a record company who is going to support it with me."

As for Purple and record labels, "You know, we don't actually make the business decisions in the band. Bruce Payne does that. But right now, there's no decision being made. CMC are a good label—don't get me wrong. If for some reason we're not with them, it's not because of their performance."

Snapshot would be a comfortable roots rock record reflective of Glover's love of folk, rhythms, singer/songwriters, and that whole Bramblett / Little Feat vibe—southern pop meets avocado mafia. Interesting names associated with the record would include Warren Haynes and way-back original Rainbow keyboardist Mickey Lee Soule, who of course hails from Elf, the band befriended and then produced by Roger. Soule also guested on Roger's *Butterfly Ball* and *Elements* projects (and projects they were).

As for Ian, prodded with details on a new Purple record, he was saying, "There've been a lot of quotations. And actually, I'm keeping totally quiet about it now. I don't have to be reminded—I know what I said. And in actual fact, the less said, the better now. I just want to make the music and get the album done. We're very excited about it. And I'm not trying to be . . . there's just no point talking about it yet. You can say whatever you like about a record, and if everybody talked about it, you would have a #1 record. It's easy to talk about music. But to write it and play it is another story. So, we're very excited about what's going on. There will be some technical changes. I'm not trying to be mysterious, but we don't actually know what the answers are yet. We've focused on a few areas we need to improve on in terms of getting more objectivity to the writing and the performance in the studio, and also to the technical

Ian playing a mean air guitar, at the same Toronto show as the previous two shots. © *Nick Soveiko, Wikimedia Commons*

side as well. There's quite a lot of fresh ideas that will be coming in. And that's all I can say, because nothing has been nailed; there's no producer been named; no studio has been booked; no songs have been written. There are bits and pieces flying around in the air that will no doubt become songs one day, but nothing has been sewn up."

"But at the same time, there's a general feeling in the band that we really want to stretch out on this album," counters Roger. "*Purpendicular* was really a wonderful period of rediscovery and the breaking of a lot of the old barriers. We just wrote where our instincts told us to, and came up with some great songs. I think it was a real breath of fresh air, and the fans certainly seemed to like that one. *Abandon* was more of a retrenchment, strangely enough. But it's hard to tell before an album comes out what it's going to be, before you started it. With *Abandon*, we just had a really long tour, and we were road-worked in. And there was a feeling that we really wanted to get back to basics and do a rock album. So that's what *Abandon* was—it was pretty much a rock album, and I missed the eclecticism we found on *Purpendicular*. Especially now, since the 'Concerto,' with all these different kinds of music opening up. It was always there, but it has opened up in fans' eyes, as well as ours, that we can actually do anything we like. There's a great sense of excitement and anticipation of what the next record is going to be. Ian and I have done a little bit of writing so far, just about a week's worth, just to get some vague ideas. And we're not limiting ourselves in any way, shape, or form. There's no reason why Purple this time around just can't go nuts."

Asked what the function of an outside producer would be, Roger laughs and says, "To take the burden off me. I think we've always been a sort of self-contained band, and for better or worse we've always given ourselves ridiculous handicaps under which to work, location being the main one. You know, setting ourselves up in the cellar of a ski house or a castle in France or a hotel corridor in Switzerland or a villa in Italy. For God's sake, why don't we just go into a proper studio with a proper producer and do a proper album? I've gotten to the point where I just want to get a great-sounding album without all the headaches that go along with trying to make . . . how do they say that? A silk purse out of a pig's ear. Although I enjoy that, it's an unnecessary added stress. Just for once I would love us to do an album like the old-fashioned albums in a proper studio with a proper producer. And I have no idea where. It depends on the producer, really.

"We'll certainly be writing in Florida. I think it's also important to get some objectivity I cannot give to the band. I can give them the benefit of my hindsight and my experiences. After all, I'm only a member of the band. Not only that, I'm just the bass player as well, the bottom of the heap [laughs]. So, getting people to listen to what I have to say without necessarily arguing with me would be also a luxury."

Thorny point there, and perhaps there's a bit more to it than the guys let on. Same day, same backstage area, Steve made a bit of a side remark to me that it seemed as though when he came up with an idea—sort of on anything, not strictly musically speaking—it got shot down. And one gets a sense that Roger was feeling exactly the same sort of persecution complex about himself.

In any event, somehow, an album called *Bananas* would finally emerge on August 25, 2003, with fans immediately wrinkling their noses at that title, along with the odd—or oddly random—cover art. One-name graphics guru Ioannis was brought

Bananas CD booklet and the printed CD itself

back to assemble the artwork, although he had less input this time versus his work on *Abandon*.

"Yes, in this situation, *Bananas*, Bruce Payne, the band's manager, took the photograph that was the front cover. That's a whole funny story how that happened. Basically, he just handed me a photo and said, 'Okay, here's what I'd like the front cover to be. Can you do anything with this? Can you design a whole concept around this?' So, everything else, the photos that are used inside, the guts, the promotion, the packaging, all had to do with that.

"Right now, when we take on a project, 90 percent of the time, it will be the management or the label, or the label introduces us to the management, and they come with us. It's almost like going on attack or to war. We sit down and discuss every facet of how it's going to be employed. What the CD packaging is going to look like, the cover, the art, the merchandise, stage graphics, right down to the backstage passes. So, on the Deep Purple project *Bananas*, I started in March of '03, and a year later I was still going at it, because they are constantly needing stuff, either tour posters, promotional posters, limited-edition prints, backstage passes, stage graphics. I did tons of merchandise ideas back and forth. I came up with a really great concept they used in Europe, which was just a natural to use—a soccer jersey, or football, over there. It's an obvious one, because they play in a club. And Bruce is a great guy. I work closely with Roger. He's the artist in the band [laughs], and it works pretty well. They are great clients.

"The two people on the cover, *Bananas*, the way that works is, Bruce and the band were discussing the cover and this banana truck pulled in front of them. They were in India, going from one thing to another. And then, just off the truck, Bruce got out and they took the photo of these two guys sitting on this big pile of bananas. They thought it was perfect. He tried to explain to them who they were and what they were doing, and it was like, no idea. So, I asked Bruce the other day, these guys, because they're playing India, they're just going to look around and their faces are going to be plastered everywhere [laughs]. What if it comes up? And Bruce says, 'Whatever they want, I'll be happy to pay them because they deserve it.' I mean, he tried to pay them, tried to explain, and nothing registered. They didn't understand what the hell he was talking about."

Once into the album, you'd have to say that all that talk about bold new statements and "We can definitely do different" and "There's no reason why Purple this time around just can't go nuts" was a pretty significant exaggeration. *Bananas* is, in fact, another rock 'n' rolling Deep Purple album, in total, lighter and more casual than *Abandon*, but pretty much conventional verse/chorus songs, even if most of them vibrate with a slightly different kind of joyous flair.

Album opener "House of Pain" is just like that, a party rocker that is heavy but actually a little ordinary, from the lyric right down to a marked lack of riff. It's just a rollicking, catchy Deep Purple track without much ambition to it.

"It's broad, fresh, quick," begins Roger, asked to throw a few adjectives out to describe the sum total of the *Bananas* vibe. "I think it's round; it's got a little more of a round personality."

Playful? "It is playful, but I think that comes from the fact that it's fresh. It's thicker. And it was done very quickly. *Abandon* took us five months to do. And why did it take five months? I can't answer that. You go in the studio, and you write a song, and you put it down on tape. You think it would be so simple, but somehow it ends up being far more complicated because the vocals aren't written, or someone has to do a solo and they're not feeling well that day. It gets put off and put off and put off. And then you end up, 'Let's take Sunday off; let's take the weekend off,' and all of a sudden you look around and five months have gone by. And the album has now become flattened out, because you've perfected it to the point where you actually ironed the life out of it. As a producer, I'm aware of this, but I'm also in the band. So, I don't have the authority that a producer would normally have, which is why I so welcome having a producer. Something I've wanted, like I say, since *Perfect Strangers*. Right then, we should have had a producer, I think."

Enter one Michael Bradford, odd choice to tangle with Purple, who then had the band in Los Angeles, of all places, to bang out the record. "He's from Detroit," explains Glover. "He's a big Black guy. His most-successful credits you probably know are Kid Rock and Uncle Cracker. But he's worked with a lot of people, like Aretha Franklin. In Aretha Franklin's band, he's a bass player. He's a writer; he's a very intelligent guy. And I was guilty of falling into the stereotype. When I first met him, I saw this big Black guy and I thought, 'Oh oh, what's this going to be?' Well, that was really small-minded of me, because the guy turned out to be just a huge rock fan and just said the right things, did the right things, and he's got loads of talent, in all areas. So, I was impressed by what he said. He came to us via . . . I think it was a music publisher, originally."

Bradford, in fact, pretty much wrote album opener "House of Pain." Despite a Gillan/Bradford credit, Ian admits as much, saying he just helped out with a line or two. Bradford thought that opening the record with a howl out of Gillan and some very electric guitar would serve as ample announcement that the band was back. And good on him, because one's hair does definitely stand up on end. And then when the music crashes in, pints are clinked, and the listener is in a weekend state of mind.

"Michael was very good," continues Roger. "He was very decisive, and he's very quick and he also realizes exactly the same thing—he was very good at cutting us off. Before we'd start improving things, he'd cut us off and go, 'No, that's good; that's good the way it is.' 'But, but, but . . .' 'Sorry, move on.' And he was very good at it because he didn't have to say it in a forceful way. Because we had his trust, or he had our trust, it would be more like, 'I don't agree with you, but okay, let's see how it works out.' And I think for that reason there are a couple of things that I would change. We finished a little too quickly for my liking. I wanted to do another couple of days of jamming and have maybe another couple of songs in the pipeline or whatever. Then all of a sudden we'd finished. Three weeks and four days, boom, ticket home. 'But, but . . .' 'No buts. That's it.' He actually brought a couple of songs to the table, which I wasn't too sure about at the time. But they were good songs, and there's no rule book here, so we decided to do them."

Offered Ian Gillan on the concept of Purple's new outside producer, "We have an objective party pointing you in terms of production and technique and that sort of thing, as opposed to the in-house production that we've always enjoyed—I would use the word carefully—until now [laughs]. So, it's got a kind of freshness about it. And there was also the fact that we had Mike Bradford sitting there thinking about the whole thing. It was very simple; there was a very disciplined approach to this. We had no idea what the material was going to be, because we never set out to say, 'Well, we're going to do this kind of album' or not. But we did remember that originally, Deep Purple, if we had to affiliate ourselves with any definitions at all, in the late '60s, early '70s, we were known as a progressive-rock band. And I think that's at the heart of everything we try to do. We wrote all the songs in one session, rehearsed them in the studio, and played them pretty much live. So, we were trying to recapture that spontaneity that existed in the late '60s and early '70s."

One would think an absolute outsider such as Michael Bradford might have felt that he had to tread lightly.

"You're welcome to sit in on any of our sessions, and I could tell you that Mike Bradford is not the kind of guy to tread carefully under any circumstances," laughs Gillan. "He is a diplomat and he's a mature guy. He's a musician, so obviously he speaks with courtesy. But he's very clear on the attitude that he wants. And he told me, in no uncertain terms, when we were sitting having dinner one night, before the first session, 'How are the lyrics coming along for the song we're doing tomorrow?' And I said, 'Well, they're nearly finished. Normally what I do, Mike, is I finish two-thirds of them, and then I go in and give it a shot and see how it's working. And if it's okay, I finish it off. And if it's not, I scrap it.' And he said, 'You know, Ian, I'd rather you complete all the lyrics before we even start recording the song. I want it to be finished, because once we're done with that, we're moving on to the next one. I don't want any of this waffling around.' So, I took him at his word, and I was up at 5:00 that next morning, and in fact every other morning on the session, because of Mike Bradford's say-so. A man I respect greatly, because of his discipline in the studio. We got the whole album done in thirty days—well, actually three weeks—so it worked for me."

The evidently quick-to-ripen *Bananas* settles in with a bit more snarl come "Sun Goes Down," which is one of the Morse era's heaviest tracks to date, a lumbering earthmover of a metal machine that could have sat fat on *Abandon*. A collaborative effort crafted in rehearsal, the song also features multitracked backing vocals that the guys knew couldn't be duplicated live. The song opens with a tidal wave of effects-laden keyboards from the aforementioned new guy in the band, Don Airey, the perfect choice, possibly the only choice, to step into the role vacated by Jon Lord. Not only was Airey of the same vintage as the other guys, but he was English and had played with the likes of Ozzy Osbourne, Michael Schenker, Gary Moore, and, earlier than all that, Rainbow (with Roger). Plus, there was Colosseum II in his even more distant past, establishing his progressive-rock credentials.

Next is "Haunted," arriving quite early in the sequence for a ballad at track 3. It's actually quite a nice one, and thankfully not bluesy, but built more like a conventional ballad, usually not desirable, but fresh for Purple. This one features a female guest vocal from Beth Hart. Also, note the Paul Buckmaster string arrangement, which Bradford added after the band unwittingly thought the album was done and they'd gone off! On February 14, 2004, at the Wiltern Theater in L.A., both Hart and Bradford got up onstage with the guys for a little guest stretch—only the tune performed was not "Haunted," but "House of Pain." Bradford returned later on that night to help strum the band's "Hush" encore.

"It's the single in Europe," noted Roger at the time. "I don't know if it's going to be the one over here. That was an idea of mine. One day, I think I was in my home here, before I left for the studio, I picked up an acoustic guitar. I mean, I write songs

Cover art for the "Haunted" CD single. *Martin Popoff archive*

all the time. I've got tons of bits and pieces of starts of songs. That's why I had a solo album a little while ago, called *Snapshot*. I had to get a few of these off the shelf [laughs]. They just sit there for too long. Anyway, I just picked up the guitar one day and started this chord sequence, which was kind of quite pleasing, and I never thought in a million years that Deep Purple would like it. It was fresh in my head, and when we went to Los Angeles, I just played it one day to Ian Gillan and Michael [Note: Michael was said to have instantly been taken by its potential as a smash hit]. I said, 'I've got this idea; what do you think?' And they loved it. They said, this is great. So, I never would have thought of that as being a Purple tune, but it ended up being a Purple tune, and not only that, I mean, I called it 'Haunted' because it just seemed to fit. Ian Gillan did most of the lyrics in the verses, and I did the chorus."

"Razzle Dazzle" arcs us back to the party atmosphere of the opening track, but this one feels a little like filler, almost too flippant, too underwritten, although, adding value, we get a little honky-tonk piano out of Don, as well as organ. And while we're here, another slight "falling down" that pervades *Bananas* is clearly demonstrated within this track, and that would be a lack of warmth, a lack of bass, a compressed midrange harshness to the overall tone palette. This isn't the case on any of the other Steve Morse–era records, and so I somehow don't think it can be rationalized as a deliberate artistic choice. But yeah, for whatever the reason, the record is a little hard on the ears.

Back to the complimentary, Don Airey indeed offers some new flavors, as I say, evidenced here on "Razzle Dazzle." It's as if he doesn't want to tread too heavily or deliberately on Jon Lord's signature Hammond grind, and so he offers a wide array of tricks, partially because that's who he is, partially because it conveniently distances his style from Jon's.

Having Roger sum up Airey's contribution versus Lord's, Glover says, "First of all, I'll forgive you, but I don't like the word 'versus,' because you can't compare people. You can on a basic level: they both play the Hammond organ, so there are some similarities. But any true musician is going to have his own personality. When Don first played with the band, about eighteen months ago, Jon was sick. He had a bad knee. And Don came in at the last minute, just to do a couple of gigs. Actually, he ended up doing the entire tour, but originally it was just going to be four gigs.

Quebec City, Quebec, Canada, August 11, 2004. This picture was used as a promo shot for the 2004 *Bananas* tour dates taking place in Russia and Ukraine.
© Nick Soveiko, Wikimedia Commons

"And the first night, it was a Scandinavian rock festival," continues Roger. "We had one day's rehearsal with Don, before the gig. He had the tape for a couple of days, so he learned at home. But we had one day's rehearsal where we actually played through the stuff. He was nervous, but he did the gig, and he was great. There was a lot of mouthing the counts in, 'Two, three, four, now!' But he was great. And afterwards I went up to him and said, 'I just wanted to compliment you and say what a great job you did.' He said, 'Well, thank you. I know I was playing the part of Jon Lord, and I managed to do it for about twenty seconds and then I realized I'd have to be Don Airey.' He is himself; he's different to Jon, in the same way that we didn't want Steve to be anything like Ritchie Blackmore, play like him, sound like him, write like him, whatever. The same applies to Don. The band really works best when the chemistry is pure. And the chemistry can only be 100 percent pure if you are yourself. We didn't want a cardboard cutout of Jon. We wanted a real person being their real selves. And Don's been around long enough to know what to do; he knows the ropes; he knows what he's doing; he's a great technician. But more than that, he's a funny guy. He fits right in personalitywise. That's very important too."

"Now, how can I say this without in any way undermining the fact that we all adore Jon Lord?" adds Gillan, on the question of Don's presence, specifically, if the communication up onstage is any different with Don than it was with Jon.

"He's a monument in our lives. A founding member of Deep Purple, and just a really darling guy. I spoke to him just a few days ago. We send emails regularly, and he phones us up in the dressing room, quite frequently, before going onstage—'What's the set list tonight?' So, what I'm about to say, you have to bear that in mind. Jon was getting tired. This is my interpretation. Jon was getting tired, because of frustration. We are a working band; we're a touring band. This tour we're doing right now started last June in England. And then we've been to Brazil and Europe and we're coming to the States now, and we shall finish in December, this coming year. So, it's an eighteen-month tour, basically.

"This is normal for Deep Purple. We take a few weeks off, go and write some songs, go in the studio, take six months off, and then go back on the road for a couple of years. That's pretty much how it's been since day one, apart from the usual [laughs] breakups and things like that. But anyway, Jon was getting tired and frustrated because he couldn't—with this kind of schedule—write his orchestral music, which he'd been dearly wanting to do his entire life, and which he is now doing, and he is delighted he got the time to do it. I think, probably, Jon within himself was finding it difficult for that spark of spontaneity that we demand, that freshness, and the fact that I think he just felt a bit knackered, to be honest. This had been a long time coming. It's a difficult decision to sue for divorce, and I think pretty much, that's what he did, in the end. He had been going for a long time.

"Don, we've known, all of us, as a personal friend for years," continues Ian. "So, when Jon started skipping out, missing a few tours, a few dates here and there, we got Don in as deputy. And so, he was completely familiar with all the material, and we all knew him personally. And now we have the benefit of new blood. Don is a dynamite musician, wonderful guy, and of course he's full of enthusiasm. So, we have actually benefited from Jon leaving. But I would seriously ask you to remember what I said at the beginning. It's full of love and understanding. But yeah, we're better off."

Better off without Ritchie Blackmore as well, one gathers.

"Actually, I think I was the last person to see him," recalls Roger. "About four months after he left the band, I was in New York. I was taking my wife to see Frank Sinatra at Radio City. We got there early, and we had half an hour or so to kill, so we decided to have a quick drink at the bar at the Warwick Hotel, which is a place we always used to stay at. And as I walked in, Ritchie was walking out, and we literally bumped into each other. Anyway, he came back in, and we sat and had a drink, and he was fine.

A couple of *Bananas* ads. *Martin Popoff archive*

"I have no ax to grind with Ritchie, really," avows Roger. "He may have with us, and with me. Apparently, he's never going to talk to me again. Because he thinks I messed with his solos without his permission, on the *Machine Head* remix. I didn't need his permission because it's actually owned by EMI. I didn't get the permission from anyone else in the band either. But he's decided he doesn't like me for that. So, I'm sorry about that. I admire him greatly, and he's happy with what he's doing. I'm happy for him. For Ritchie, it's absolutely right. He's drawn a line. He wants to move on; he wants to do music that is closer to his soul, and I think that's fantastic; that's absolutely fantastic. As a fan, I've heard bits and pieces, and I'm not really going to comment much. But as a fan, I was always frustrated because I could hear Ritchie doing an album that he would never do. I could always hear him doing a solo album surrounded by just great musicians and, you know, just killing it, just flooring it. As a producer and as a friend, that's what I want from him. And I sometimes am frustrated that he's hampered by his own decisions and his own view."

And if Ritchie can come off as a bit of a grump, well, Mr. Gillan, his main nemesis in the Purple saga, doesn't suffer fools gladly either. "No, he doesn't," agrees Roger, "and if he's in a bad mood, he'll suffer no one gladly. He can be in a bad mood; he can be grumpy. We were in a press conference the other day in Germany, and we walked in and there were about 100 or so people there, 150 people. And someone made the mistake of saying, 'Hey Ian, shake your hair around.' Not a good move. Not a good move [laughs]. They were just trying to be cheeky about the fact that he cut his hair now and that he used to have long hair."

Further on the change at the keyboard throne, Gillan surmises that "the changeover to Don was not so difficult. For starters, it was not emotional. We were all aware of the fact that Jon was drifting away, spiritually. There is an old story about a prisoner of war in a war camp who has been badly injured. He has to have his left arm amputated. The surgeon says it has to come off. The soldier says, 'If you have to amputate it, then can you send it home to my mom?' The surgeon gets permission from his commandant, and he does it. The soldier tells him that he told his mom that he would come home from the war. This is a long story, but eventually his other arm has to come off and then his left leg. When his right leg has to be amputated, he makes the same request, and the surgeon says he has to get permission. This time, the commandant refuses permission. The prisoner looks at the doctor and asks why he refused permission this time. The surgeon says, 'The commandant thinks you're trying to escape!'

"That story comes to mind as far as Jon is concerned, as Jon left us bit by bit. I was drinking champagne with Jon in an award ceremony in London recently. He is one of my best friends, and I adore and love him. We went through a lot of things behind the scenes. Like I say, Jon had frustrations, and he wanted to do other things. The extensive touring was starting to get to him, but the rest of the band was so full of energy that we didn't want to slow down. Eventually, we arrived at the inevitable situation where Jon said, 'I can't go on.' Having said that, over the previous two years prior to the departure, he had been slowly disappearing like the man in the prison camp. The difference is that it was more spiritual than physical. You can't compare the talents of the two people. But when Don came in, he hit the ground running. The energy level of the band quadrupled overnight. The fans took to him instantly. He is a charming performer who is very understated in his persona. He looks up every now and then and smiles, and they just go wild."

Former Dream Theater keyboard legend Kevin Moore certainly understands Airey's importance in the pantheon of keyboardists. "Don Airey is definitely an influence because he was doing the sort of thing that I was doing in Dream Theater. Well, that's not a good way to put it. I was sort of emulating him, I guess. He was more of a model, because he was playing the same role that I was sort of playing in Dream Theater. Like playing in a metal band, really, but instead of always just being heavy and distorted, he was adding tones and moods and classical elements into it. And I felt that because of guys like him, I didn't feel out of sorts [laughs]. Because I knew that keyboards had a place, and a good role, and could contribute depth and maybe some beauty."

Back to the record at hand, "Silver Tongue" is next, and it's a percolating heavy rocker with interesting tones from Don (albeit heavily processed by Bradford), who gets to throw in licks between Ian's verses. Steve cites this one, along with the title track, as his favorite song on the album. "We've been starting with 'Silver Tongue'

Steve at the Molson Amphitheatre, Toronto, Ontario, Canada, June 18, 2005. © *Nick Soveiko, Wikimedia Commons*

every night, since we recorded that, and it works great," noted Morse. "People respond to it. It's a simple groove, and it feels good. People obviously don't know it that well, because we're playing in places where . . . you can tell the difference between songs they know and songs they don't. But they respond to it, because it's got a happening feel. That's been going over really well. We play it pretty much straight ahead, but with a longer middle section."

"Walk On" adds to the collection of quieter, down-wound songs on *Bananas*, contributing to the complexion of the album as less heavy than *Abandon*. It's less heavy than *Purpendicular* too, for that matter. It's a dark blues with sweet textures applied to menacing desperado music melodies. The solo you hear in the song was Steve's first crack at it, and Bradford himself contributes some guitar.

"Well, I wrote the lyrics with Michael," explains Ian, after being told that Roger had said he had no idea what that lyric was about. "Michael came up with the idea, pretty much. Being a singer, I have to feel comfortable with what I'm singing. So, I told him that there were a few little bits I wasn't comfortable with, and would he mind if I changed them? And he said, 'No, by all means. Let's do that.' So, we softened the blow as far as dealing with the ex-girlfriend was concerned, or the imminent the ex-girlfriend, the future ex-girlfriend. It's not about arrogance, which I think is how it started off. It's more about self-confidence or self-assurance. The idea that there comes a time in your life where you say, 'If you really can't handle the way I'm doing things, you better move on.' It's a theme that's been used many times before, but it's just a fresh look at it. It's not difficult to understand. I'm surprised Roger didn't get it, but there again, if you're not in the creation, I suppose you might miss the point slightly. Unlike Roger, that is, to say that."

"Picture of Innocence" is one of the record's "weird" numbers, adding a level of truth to the elliptical intentions vaguely professed in the years leading up to the making of the record. It's a big symphony of blues, funk, progressive-rock, and heavy metal sections, best being the forceful metalized chorus, which recalls the hooky melodic heft of "Sometimes I Feel Like Screaming."

Says Roger, "'Picture of Innocence' started out as a jam between Paicey and Steve in the studio four or five years ago, and it was recorded on a DAT. I mean, frequently in the studio, as a warm-up, people just start playing stuff, and it's always good when Steve and Paicey play together, because when you've got more than two people, it's always difficult to be free. Now Paicey, all he's doing is keeping the tempo and having some fun with it as well. But then Steve is free to wander where he will, with riffs and chords and changes, things he couldn't possibly do with the whole band. How do you convey to them that you're going to go to E flat? It requires a sort of complicated series of facial muscles: 'To E flat! Now, three, four . . .'

"Anyway, they jammed, and this went on for about half an hour, this particular jam, and I got it on a DAT player. I took it home and put it on a computer, and there were a couple of bits on it I thought were really great. So, I isolated those bits and did a bit of editing and looped it here and there and then played it back to the band a couple of years later and said, 'By the way, do you recognize this?' Of course they didn't, because what happens in a jam is of the moment, and it's not something you remember. However, it sounded great, and we worked on and it became 'Picture of Innocence.'"

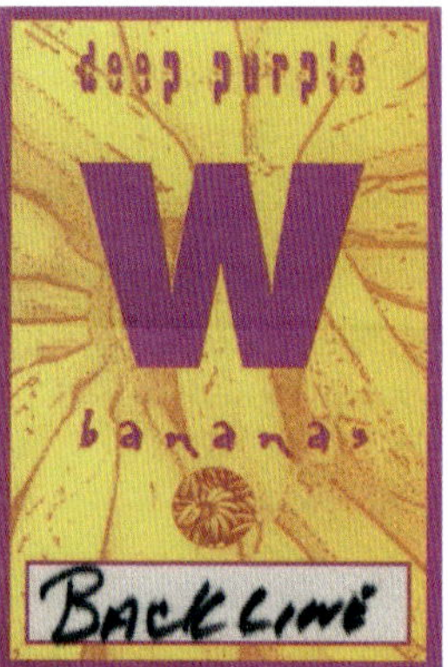

An assortment of *Bananas*-era backstage passes. *Martin Popoff archive*

Speaking of communication, I inquired of Roger whether having this lone American in the band ever caused a bit of a culture gap between the southerner in the band and the rest of the guys, this storied British rock aristocracy lounging about the place.

"Yeah, sometimes," laughs Glover. "But mostly from Steve. Now, I'm the one foil to that because I live in America. In fact, I have American citizenship. So, there are two Americans in the band, if you want to be absolutely correct. I hold both passports, so I can be on both sides of the fence. But there's something about . . . if you say something with an English accent, it has an authority to it [that] Americans can never get. And this kind of rubs him up the wrong way sometimes. But you know, he's good at complaining about stuff and does it pretty good. But I don't think it's that serious. There's friction about other things, but not really about music, on that level. Not nationalistic music anyway. What's American and what's British anyway? Same music."

And while we're talking about Steve, and the way he works with Paice, Roger makes a point about divergent attitudes between the two when it comes to the use of a click track (i.e., a metronomic pattern put through the headphones to keep everything in perfect time).

"You know, the songs all seem to have come fairly easily," explains Glover, "and quite a few of them were one take. There was very little hassle in that regard. But yes, I suppose the biggest thing to deal with in the studio is whether to work with a click or no click. The thing about a click is, sometimes it's warranted. Sometimes it's good that you're not thinking about where the beat's going, whether it's speeding up or slowing down or whatever. Music that has a good feel, it doesn't really matter if it's speeding up or slowing down because it's got a good feel. And to a certain extent, a bit of slowing down and speeding up is necessary for the dynamics of the piece. Sometimes it's great to have a really rollicking chorus and sink back down a notch in tempo when the verse comes back in. Psychologically, it just feels right. It's not correct, but it feels right. And drummers in particular rail against that, because they were, and are, the metronome. And all of a sudden, they've got this beat that is just so wonderful.

"But I remember Paicey and me, in the '80s, were not happy (a) about clicks and (b) about sampled drums and drum machines in general. It was all kind of the early days of drum machines. Obviously, they've gotten better, and you can do some wonderful things with technology. Technology is there as a tool, not as an enemy. It's there to use the way you want to use it, not the way it wants to use you. And he was very uncomfortable with that then. He was always fighting the click.

"But he's learned a lot, and he's learned to be very natural with the click," continues Glover. "But there are some songs that are just better off without a click. It's always kind of a bone of contention. Steve likes everything with a click, because he tends to subdivide and subdivide and subdivide until it's critical that it's in absolute time. But rock 'n' roll music isn't always about that. It's about the feel and the roar, the roar and that power. I'm hanging on so many different subjects here. If you're 100 percent balls to the wall, it actually doesn't sound as powerful as if you're playing it 60 percent and the power is being held in check, you know what I mean? And I think 'Walk On' is a great example. If 'Walk On' was done to a click, it would not have felt the way it feels. You know, Paicey just sits on the beat . . . I was going to say like a motherfucker, but I don't really speak like that [laughs]—he sits on the beat and it's just so pleasing."

On the "Picture of Innocence" lyric, Roger says, "That was very much a collaborative effort, probably the most collaboration on the entire record. As I said, it was a jam between Steve and Paicey, and I put it in ProTools and hooked it up in the computer, found some bits I really liked, presented it back to the band in a kind of format which they liked, and we worked on it. And as we were routining it, Ian came up with this title, 'Picture of Innocence,' and he said, 'I like this title. I don't know why, but I like the title.' And we sat down to write it and said, 'Okay, what does it mean? What are we writing about here?'

"Well, one of the Ian's big kind of sticking points in the last few years has been the European union bosses in Brussels, who make all these decisions that affect everyone's lives, and yet, they are decisions made by nonelected officials that actually have become laws. And this incensed him because it affected him personally. He's got a little boat that he has, where he lives in England. He had to spend some money to bring the boat up to the laws to make it safe for passengers, and this really got under his skin. How dare they, from their fucking citadel in Brussels, tell me what to do with my boat in Lyme Regis?! And if you talk to him about bananas, he'll go off. It's all to do with genetically modified foods. The EU stipulates that bananas have to have a certain shape, size, and curve; otherwise they're not allowed. And of course, the only ones that are allowed are from farmers that have genetically modified them to be perfect. So, he's just up in arms about this. That was actually the basis of

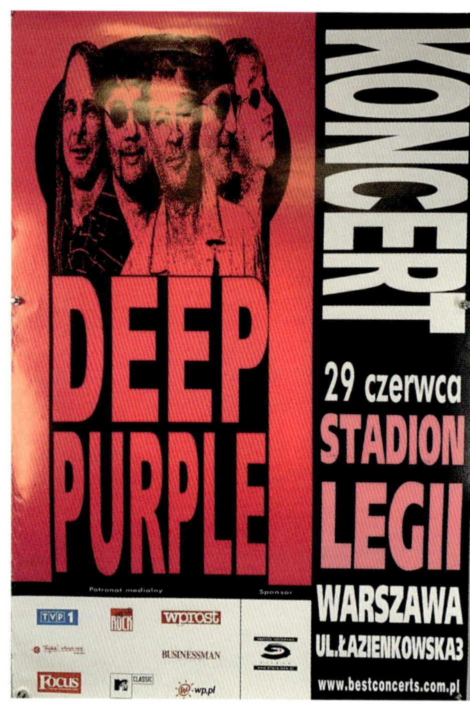

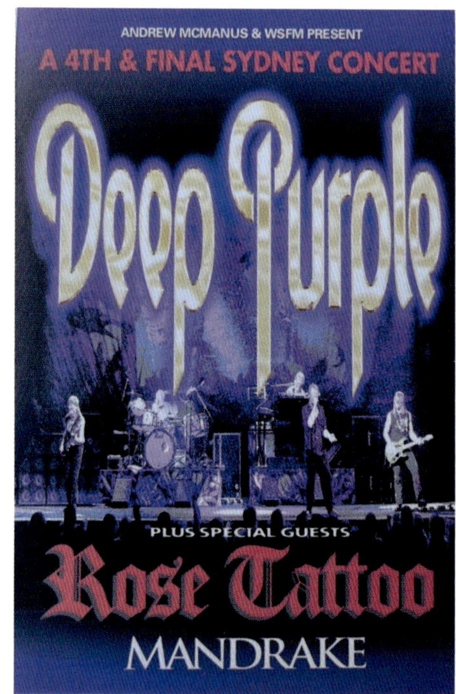

A couple of tour posters

the lyrics, a conversation we had one day about these very things. Songs exist on many levels, but that was the starting point for 'Picture of Innocence.' They're trying to make us all the same. And what are they going to say next? No sex? [laughs]."

No surprise that this one's a favorite on the album for Ian, who also cites "House of Pain." "I love 'Picture of Innocence,' and that's only because it was so spontaneous. I've got some friends who just live down the road who were in the States at the time. They came to visit the studio when we were putting that track down, and their jaws dropped as they watched Steve Morse just pick up a lick and the whole band joined in; it was just so exciting. And lyrically, of course, it was a big adventure for me, because it's dealing with some serious topics here, as far as the idiocracy in Europe is concerned, our governing powers, who I have sworn to defeat, and with every opportunity. To destroy Brussels is my ultimate aim in life."

"I Got Your Number" is another track that adds to the funky, recreational theme of the album, and this time in more of a heavy direction. Again, the chorus is a corker, and hooky enough for this song to have been a hit—had the business been set up in any way, shape, or form to support a new album from Deep Purple. And the players don't disappoint come break time, building up a blustery pile of critical mass before a dropout to an atmospheric pause. Gillan has made known that the song originates from when Jon Lord was still in the band, and that its original title was "Up the Wall"—live versions exist from the English tour of early 2002. He also lauds Michael Bradford for coming up with the straight-time chorus out of the swing of the verse.

"Never a Word" is a soft ballad from Steve, Celtic, even somewhat new age, especially when Ian finally starts singing, two-thirds the way through. Indeed, the song is instrumental for a long spell, with Paice providing soft accents, before Ian softly sings words about the tacit understanding that happens inside deep relationships. Glover has spoken about how he's prideful that Purple can present a myriad of emotions, pointedly ones beyond those dealt with in hard rock and heavy metal.

Next in line is the album's title track, progressive and epic but also serving double time as the album's heaviest track. Actually, other than its time signature, it's not particularly odd for most of its duration. Still, it does contain a desperate near-fusion breakdown that finds Purple on the verge of mania, again underscoring this album's "good-natured" vibe. Again, though, "Bananas" could have been on either of the previous two albums, undermining further those early musings that this was going to be some sort of extreme outlier of the catalog.

"Some songs were written purely in the moment, having a bit of fun," reflects Roger. "I mean, one day in the studio, Paicey or Steve started playing something in 7/4 time. It was outrageous, just a bit of fun, and we all joined in. In fact, it was so ridiculous, we all fell about laughing. And then we thought, 'But wasn't it good to play?' So, we actually said, 'Let's do it—sod it, let's go for it.' Michael had to leave town for a couple of days. He was there for most of the rehearsals. This was in Los Angeles. He said, 'I've got to go away for a couple of days,' and while he went away, we did this ridiculous song in 7/4 time, which went into 5/4 time, and we threw everything into it and made it the title track. In fact, we played it live in Berlin last week. It was its first outing as a live song, and it was killer—it was great."

"The start of the track 'Bananas' is pretty way out there," remarks Don, citing this as one of his own personal most creative moments across his first two records with the band. "That was done very quickly with a sequencer and, you know, ring

Paicey at the Labatt Centre, London, Ontario, Canada, June 20, 2005. © *Nick Soveiko, Wikimedia Commons*

modulator, a Minimoog, and the thing with the Echoplex. It just happened very quickly. And I like the organ solo in that track; I thought that turned out pretty good."

Still, there were irritations with the overall organ sounds that Don got on *Bananas*, and he was much more pleased with the follow-up. "I hadn't been long in the band, and when I first got in the band, I just thought the organ wasn't working properly. I mean, I tried to get to the bottom . . . what a terrible mess in there, switches, wires everywhere, an instrument that hadn't been restored since 1975. I remember there were grave objections to having anything done to the Hammond, which I eventually overcame. A guy called Bill Axman from Los Angeles came in for three days and kind of refurbished it, and then my guy, who was with Hammond Organ Services, he finished the job of refurbishing it. So, by the time we actually got around to using the organ, it was a different instrument, and it was sounding much louder."

I asked Don if there was some sort of superstition with the guys in terms of messing with it too much.

"Well, it was the soul of the band, the keyboards are, and I was just like, 'Oh, bollocks. Let's get it fixed.' And it took some time, a year or so, but with all the gigging, that's the trouble. You're out on the road. I think the final thing, we were playing a gig in Osnabruck, Germany, and I just heard the thing go, and then it just died and there was no hope for it. And I did the rest of the gig on keyboards. I mean, we never missed a beat, and I quite enjoyed it, I must say. But a German Hammond expert came in, and it took awhile to figure out what the problem was. It was a capacitor somewhere right in the heart of it. It wasn't one of the normal things that went wrong, like a valve. And when he put that in, it fixed it."

Lyrically, the song "Bananas" is typical of Ian at his most obscure. "He felt pretty free and easy," figures Glover, with respect to Gillan's wordplay for this album in a general sense. "We write lyrics together a lot of the time. We have the backing track. It's always been that way around with us. The band comes first, then the song. We go, well, the chorus is going to be eight bars of G, and then we'll need a little break from that, so let's go to D minor for a couple bars, and then some little riff in here, and then come back and this will be the hook.

"But we don't know what's going to go over it. And sometimes that leads to a kind of roadblock, because sometimes the music gets so complicated and you say, 'What the hell are you going to sing over that?!' And Ian is not a complicated person. He thinks musically, very simply, which of course is a strength and a weakness. It's a weakness when it comes to dealing with some of the more complex musical issues in terms of why. 'Why are you doing that?! What's wrong with simplicity?' Of course, sometimes you get a complicated backing track and a simple thing over the top, which can work great.

"I always remember hearing the story about 'Kashmir.' When Jimmy Page first played the riff, Robert Plant said, 'What on earth am I going to sing over that?!' [laughs]. But you find something. 'Bananas' is a good case in point. It's 7/4 and then 5/4, and it's really complicated, and Ian just breezes through over the top of it and turns the whole thing into a shuffle. In the old days, Ian used to write a lot more lyrics on his own. I'd get involved only if he was stuck or if he asked me to help him with a line or two. Some songs were definitely cowritten; some were mostly him.

Occasionally, songs would be mostly me, but only occasionally. Ian's got quite an original gift with lyrics. He's got an odd sense of humor."

Adding a little history, Roger explains that "Ian joined the band I was in in '65, and I was the main writer then. And over the next couple of years, I managed to get Ian writing, and so we became a songwriting partnership, loosely. And in fact, that's how we joined Purple. We joined Purple as two writers. And his creativity has really grown. He has a wonderful way of looking at the world that's left field; there's a lot of wit put into it. It's not artifice.

"A lot of modern rock seems to express one emotion, that of anger. Listen to any rock band that's current now—Audioslave, Queens of the Stone Age, that ilk—it's all this roaring, Nirvana-type stuff. Huge guitars, massive backbeats. Even when the vocal's low, it's somehow guttural and screaming and annoyed. Christ, how shallow is that?! Nothing wrong with those bands; they're fine, and some of them are really good. But there's more to music than that and more to life than that. And I think Ian has this kind of wit and this view of the world where he can't do that. He can't limit himself to one emotion.

"Plus, he likes words, and he likes to play with words," continues Roger. "He likes double meanings. So, on this album, I encouraged him really to be more himself. He did call on me a couple of times and said, 'Will you do a writing session with me?' And we did do some stuff together. But more often than not, I just left him up to his own devices. And I think that's great. Because one of the things that happened on this album is the speed with which we did it. And while I was being a bass player, he was being a singer."

The *Bananas* tour book

"Musically, I think 'Bananas' is just unbelievable," remarks Ian, offering a rare opinion on a song's actual music track, come to think of it! "And it's such a ringing endorsement of Don Airey being a replacement for Jon. It's so vibrant. The keyboard solo, or the interchanges with the guitar and keyboards in that 7/4, 5/4 interchange timing, it's just musicianship at its ultimate."

In a separate chat, Ian went so far as to say that "my favorite Deep Purple albums are *Fireball* and *Bananas*. I play all our records to family and friends, and honestly, *Bananas* has been the most popular of all of them. It's accessible and you don't have to be a rock aficionado to appreciate it. *Bananas* is a political statement, as you can see from the images inside, and reflects on the idiotic setup of Brussels and Strasbourg. Things that annoy me or make me roll on the floor laughing tend to be the things I write about in our songs."

A couple of years down the line, Steve cites the song "Bananas" as a favorite, no surprise, due to its manic energy live. "We were playing it up until this American tour, because we had less time, because we were splitting the show with other acts. I really enjoyed playing that live, because it's got a difficult instrumental section in it. And that's more typical of something I spent my life doing, playing this riffy groove thing and then going into a difficult part and then coming back out of it. That's right up my alley, as far as style goes. I like playing that."

"Doing It Tonight" has an almost reggae vibe, if one uncommonly up tempo and loud. Lyrically, Ian offers memories of a game of spin the bottle that required improvisation with a shoe, to a quite separate lyric about an unattainable woman. The use of the word "imagine" is interesting—is it going to happen, or does it in fact never get past imagining?

Bananas then, quite literally and figuratively, draws to a close with "Contact Lost," an instrumental reflection written by Morse, a flier himself, who was deeply touched by the disaster of NASA Mission STS-107, the breakup of *Columbia* upon reentry over Texas on February 1, 2003. One of the astronauts, Indian-born Kalpana Chawla, was a Deep Purple fan and had taken Purple music into space with her. There was even correspondence between her and the band while their mission was in progress. Steve quickly wrote the music in her honor, and the band dealt with their grief through this fitting closing number.

Touching moment for Steve live as well. "We've been doing that every night, since we recorded it. It's amazing. People all around the world know about the space shuttle *Columbia*, and they all just kind of go into a hushed silence and listen and appreciate the emotion and energy. And then we have an improv section after that, and then another organized piece which I call 'Well Dressed Guitar,' which is really straight-ahead classical guitar, with a lot of spaces in it."

The day before we spoke, another shuttle launch took place, an event that forever holds poignancy for Morse. "Yes, I was looking up. We were crossing from Turkey to Spain at the time, and I kept looking up, just to see if I could catch a refraction of light as it went over. I hated missing that launch, but you know, when you're in a band, you miss so many things. You're spending birthdays in empty hotel rooms, and you miss everything in the summer."

Adds Steve, prompted for an example of humorous live moments on the tour trail, "Did you know about Ian coming out barefoot? In Toronto, the stage was dark colored and in the sun the whole time. It was linoleum or something, so it was about 130 degrees [laughs]. So, he came out barefoot and then went dancing. He instantly started dancing—a lot. And I couldn't figure it out. We were having a problem with my guitar, so I suddenly had to switch to a different guitar than the one I'm normally using, but out of the corner of my eye I saw him dance off, and then he came back wearing some shoes [laughs]. That was very funny.

"And actually, I was saying about 'Contact Lost,' where I do a little improv, and then we go into 'Well Dressed Guitar,' there's a moment in the climax of that where Ian Gillan is . . . you know, it's instrumental, but he's behind playing the tambourine. He gestures, and he gets the entire audience—and I mean the entire audience—into it, where they're clapping, raising their hands above their heads, and just cheering and stuff, just this huge roar. We just played in Turkey and, before that, this huge festival in France. There was a sea of people; I mean, it was bigger than the Live 8 show we were at. When I see these things happening [laughs], with a song that they don't even know, a band that is not on MTV or their local music video channel, you know, it just blows me away. I'm so glad that whatever the chemistry is, it's nice to see it work that way. I expect to see that when we do 'Smoke on the Water' or something like that, that's been around forever, and everyone knows. Plus, it's a great rock tune, an anthem, to see the crowd come alive for a piece like that.

"But 'Contact Lost,' I think it wraps up the element of the horror, just the bad and the sorrow of what happened with the *Columbia*. And then we go through the metamorphosis into this high-energy thing at the very end. That's a fantastic moment for me. And Ian Gillan has been loving doing it too. I see him crack up laughing at the end because he can't believe the energy that people pour out. So, whatever it is, people all around the world are responding to live music. When you play and give your heart and soul, they know it. They know that we're doing the improv too. I think they do, because before that, it's unscripted. There are moments where it's not rapid fire, this or that. There's a little meandering sometimes, maybe [laughs], but they give us lots of latitude and they sure help us out in the end, when we do get to the scripted part."

Incidentally, Steve's own direct experience with aviation has never intersected with the world of Purple to any great extent.

"I still fly," Steve told me back in 2000. "I mean, I just flew to Atlanta and back three days ago." As regards his actual career in the field, he said that "it was a regional airline that was part of a major airline. It was just one model I flew, called a Shorts 360, a thirty-six-passenger turboprop. And personally, I have four airplanes, one for just flying every day, a twin engine, one for travel, business travel, one for just aerobatics, and one that's a little jet trainer, ex-military, just for . . . you know, spending lots of money quickly. My farm here has an airstrip on it, and I fly airplanes here. I fly every day. Otherwise, I study tae kwon do with my little boy. I enjoy it now—it's my workout. And we've gotten into skateboarding, although I've just recently broke my left wrist skateboarding, so I'm in bad shape."

"He does fly," noted Gillan the following year, "but I don't fly with him. We were talking about it the other day. I don't mind . . . I have nothing against flying with Steve. I'm sure he's a very competent pilot. I mean, he's actually flown commercially, and the guy is so incredibly sharp, and he has a very analytical mind so I'm sure he's a wonderful pilot. But I just haven't had the opportunity, as I live in England, and he lives in Florida."

Three years later, Gillan readdressed the topic. "When he's doing gigs with the Steve Morse Band, he does the tour by plane, whenever he can. He used to be a pilot for American Airlines, in one of those brief spells when he was disillusioned with the industry, until one guy got on board and said, 'Steve Morse. I knew you'd never make it in the music business.' One of the ex-record-company executives that he was at loggerheads with, which of course inspired him to go straight back into music. He has four or five planes. He lives on an airfield, basically. And the only thing he has there is his motorbikes, his planes, and his recording studio. Devotes his life to it. He's just a fanatical aviator."

I asked Ian if, by now, he's flown with Steve. "You must be joking! No [laughs]. I took long enough to come to grips with actually overcoming the fear of flying, which I have done. And I fly happily now, as long as I have a window seat. And that's an interesting technique, by the way. And the other thing, actually, is the commercial dehumanization process of short-haul flying. I hate it."

Up into July 2005, Steve affirmed that "when I'm at home, I fly every day. I have sport planes, like a motor glider; it's really a sailplane with a launching engine, so you don't have to have a towplane pull you up. The launching engine is tucked back up inside the fuselage, and you can soar for hours. And also, an aerobatic airplane. Just going up and looking at the ground, you know; I can carry my family. Just recently we went on a long trip, about a 3,600-mile trip, to New Mexico and back. We have a remote place out there, and every summer I go out there."

When told of Ian's comment, Steve queries, "Which Ian are you talking about? Nobody has a fear of flying that I know of. He always insists on a window; he feels better with a window out there. But he's never been afraid. In fact, he's probably more likely than several of the other guys to get into, like, one of my planes. Ian's changed a lot. He was always afraid . . . or not afraid, but he was always against doing live TV, and since I've known him, he's totally changed that and agreed to do a number of live TV shows."

"He's got the four planes. I stay well clear of his planes," laughs Don, on the subject. "I don't have a fear of flying, but I have a fear of flying in small aircraft. I never do it. We were once in a chartered prop job in France, and I awoke to find Steve landing it. Which upset me a bit, you know, and not that I doubted his abilities to do it, just from the insurance side, I thought . . . I got a bit anxious, if something had happened. It wasn't such a great idea. This was when everybody was fast asleep. I don't think it happened again."

Back on terra firma and looking forward to what Purple do best (and most), Roger Glover prepared for the road, first offering a little look back on the two Morse-era Purple albums that precede *Bananas*.

"Yes, they are similar in the fact that it was the same band on both, but they do have their own characters. *Purpendicular* was far more of an outgoing album. *Abandon* seemed to me much darker. And I think it was much darker because *Purpendicular* was written, really, without having had much experience on the road. We did a couple of gigs with Steve in Mexico; that was basically his audition. And after that, we went straight in the studio and started writing songs. So, there wasn't really a great deal of road tradition to the playing of the band. And that was great, because it opened up a lot of doors. We wouldn't have been able to do songs like 'Touch Away' or 'The Aviator' or 'Sometimes I Feel Like Screaming.' There's a lot of variety on the album. *Abandon* was done after years of touring, and we'd hardened up a lot of, and I think that shows on the album. This album, it's been five years since *Abandon*, and I think we were all just dying to get back into the studio. I, for one, was really disappointed when it was over, because I just wanted to play, and play new songs. It was a lot of fun playing new songs."

Which the band was optimistic about doing come tour time, with 2004 being insanely action packed, with over a hundred dates logged and slogged. This was approximately thirty more than the previous year, but roughly on par with 2002.

"Well, in Berlin we debuted some of the stuff," says Roger. "We did 'Silver Tongue,' which was great live, just a killer groove, and we did 'Bananas' [laughs], which we just about got through. It's pretty demanding on Steve and Don. We did

'Contact Lost,' with a kind of little, beautiful segue into 'Haunted,' which worked really well. And we did 'I've Got Your Number,' which we've been doing for a few months now. And we also did 'House of Pain,' which is just this huge, roaring song. And actually, they all went really well.

"I'm really looking forward to the *Bananas* tour. Because we've been doing a lot of summer gigs, festivals, and you kind of have to do all the old hits, all the old things, much to the dismay of some of the musicians in the band, and the hard-core fans who always want to hear something rare. But to play something new, well, that's great, and I think on the *Bananas* tour, we'll be playing all of those and others from the album. And I think over the next couple of years, you'll see a huge shift in the set list.

"But we don't actually think that far ahead," adds Roger, with respect to designing a set list. "People imagine that Deep Purple all live together [laughs] and that's all we think about. What can we do for the fans? It actually couldn't be further from the truth. We live thousands of miles apart, and we don't actually give a thought to what's going to happen on the tour until, you know, five minutes before we walk onstage. Very rarely do we rehearse for the tour. Very rarely. You get to a certain level of musicianship and all you really need to know is how to start and end the song. What happens in the middle is a kind of free-for-all. You work it out as you play it."

Purple did, however, get into the whole "play one of our old classic albums in its entirety" game (and granted, early enough to be ahead of the bandwagon), performing *Machine Head* as the wincingly obvious choice.

"It's true," Ian had told me, in January 2004, a couple of months after *Bananas* had been issued. "It's not something that has been going on. It's exclusive to the North American dates. But I'll be completely candid with you—it's just a total gimmick. We are perceived in a different way in the United States than we are in the rest of the world. You know, this whole classic-rock thing. Well, it's very, very difficult to convince . . . I don't think the punters so much, but the public's view is a reflection . . . we were talking about critics earlier on. But if you're used to a radio station that plays this song and you understand this concept, of course, it's passed on to the public.

"So, we are perceived, unfortunately, in the United States as being a classic-rock band, where, of course, what we are, really, is a progressive-rock band with a long history. So, it's a difficult thing to deal with. So, in talking to management, promoters, and everything, how can we get people's attention to this tour? We are, of course, using it very subtly, to promote our new album, *Bananas*. The first part of the show will be full of contemporary material, and the second half of the show will be this gimmicky thing, which will be basically *Machine Head* from beginning to end. The reason I call it a gimmick is because we do all those songs anyway. The only one we haven't done is 'Never Before.' The rest of the songs, I mean, 'Highway Star', 'Lazy,' 'Pictures of Home,' all that stuff, 'Space Truckin',' we do them every night anyway. They just happen to be interspersed in the show. This is just a way of packaging it to promote the show, and maybe attract people who have lost touch with the band over the years, and maybe those who wouldn't come to a Deep Purple show anyway. It's a promotional device."

But don't look for today's Deep Purple to be bustin' out "Lady Double Dealer" or "Burn" anytime soon. "No, we don't even think about it," offers an incredulous

Gillan, after a long pause at the apparently sacrilegious suggestion. "We don't think it's a good idea at all. Because, if you talk to anybody in the band, they just go, nah. No, no, no."

A gentle chiding to think outside the box, coupled with the suggestion of how great it would be to hear Ozzy do "Heaven and Hell" during an Ozzy Osbourne show, goes nowhere. Ian wasn't buying it.

"But, you see, this is why he wasn't on *Heaven and Hell*," counters Ian, offering some kind of logic I guess I'm too dumb to follow. "Because he didn't want to make that record. And I wasn't on *Burn* or *Stormbringer*, because I didn't want to be on that record. So why would I join a cabaret band or cover band now? It's not in my heart. That's the problem. It's not that it's not my own words; it's just the entire thing. We do things from the heart. We don't do requests; we never have done. We never did when we were kids. We were a blues band, a rock 'n' roll band. You like it or you loathe it; we don't really care. We play music for ourselves. That's the way it always was."

I tried some wobbly logic myself, perhaps, and told Ian that it seemed like a not-so-laudable coincidence that there's not one song across those three Coverdale/Hughes albums that he doesn't like, or that he couldn't enjoy "covering."

"I don't really understand the question."

Not giving up, I point out that there's thirty-odd songs there, and he's probably sung covers once or twice in his life, forgetting the fact that these are official Deep Purple songs. I then pointed out that there seemed to be this invisible barrier between one version of the band's material and the material of the other version—but only when it comes to Ian. David Coverdale sang Mk. II material, and so did Joe Lynn Turner. And people might say, well, you know, why can't Ian Gillan's version of Deep Purple "be men about it" and conquer that barrier? They might just find themselves having some fun.

"You know, we don't even think about it," answers Ian. "I think it's interesting for you. From your point of view. And I get the occasional letter on the subject, and I always reply in the same way. It's just that I'm not really interested. And you say we don't cover bands. We have actually done one other Deep Purple song that wasn't a Deep Purple song—it's called 'Hush.' And we only did that because Steve Morse pleaded and begged and requested that we do 'Hush' because it was one of his favorite Deep Purple tunes when he was a kid. So, we did it according to his wishes. But I don't . . . it would just seem so damn contrived for us to do any of those songs. I left the band because of the direction it was going in, I think, mainly. And so, what on earth would inspire me to do those songs? It just doesn't interest me."

Bospop Festival, Weert, Sportpark Boshoven, Netherlands, July 9, 2004. Also on the bill, Status Quo, Cheap Trick, Thunder, Wishbone Ash, Rose Tattoo, and Gotthard.

Chapter 25

Rapture of the Deep

"Fruity"

We'll excuse the long wait we endured for *Bananas*, because two years is all that separates that fun, pliable, utilitarian album from the band's next and very different set of songs, the intensely titled *Rapture of the Deep*. The track record since *Perfect Strangers* is actually, by this point, quite admirable. There's been eight studio albums in twenty-one years, which is not a torrid pace, but solid enough, given the heroic touring itinerary kept up through all the gaps. Live albums, the orchestral sideshow, DVD packs, not to mention solo excursions . . . there's always been enough to keep the fans busy, listening and learning. Suffice to say that there's an energy there that results in a pervasiveness, which, irritatingly, seems to persist in having less of an impact in North America versus the band's myriad other happier territories.

"I've got a couple weeks home, and then we're off to L.A. to work with Michael Bradford on the first writing session for the next album for Deep Purple," announced Ian Gillan, early in the process. He then goes on to set up what would be modus operandi for the new record. "So that will be, they say, the end of March, but realistically I think it's going to be April Fools' Day. He's done a wonderful job with Deep Purple, and I think everyone feels comfortable with him. Having gone through that, I think it's going to be easier next time. It's always a question of trust, when you place your collective sound, and future, in someone else's hands.

"We just turn up and play," continues Ian. "We're not the kind of band to discuss. We're thrilled with *Bananas*. If you speak to anyone in the band, they'll tell you it's the best record we'd made all-around, for a very long time. Worldwide, it's the biggest-selling record we'd had too, since *Perfect Strangers*. All in all, it's done very well. I don't even know what we're doing. I've got lyrics all over the place. It depends what the weather is like sometimes, you know?

"I think I've done Brussels enough," adds Ian, referring to the subject matter of *Bananas* song "Picture of Innocence" and his similarly themed shelved novel. "No, I have no idea. I write every day, so there's an awful lot of issues around. But as you know, I don't like to ground them in people's faces. When you get down to the second or third level, you can find them. The words have to be easy to sing, coming out of people's mouths. You have to feel comfortable about the lyrics. You don't want to slam on all the time about politics or whatever. I don't think about it until I've done it, really."

I asked Ian if there were any tracks left over from the *Bananas* sessions.

"I would think there are around half-a-dozen tracks, yeah. Maybe more. But the fact that they didn't get used on the last one makes me think they probably won't get used on this one. There's no point going back to things, I don't think. If we ditched them, or they were second rate then, they probably still are. That's the annoying thing about things emerging in later years from recording studios and old management companies. They put out stuff that you rejected. That's not very nice."

"All the backing tracks are basically done at the same time," explains Ian Paice. "We do tend to still record pretty much the old-fashioned way, where people are in the studio together [laughs]. So basically, all the instrumentation will be done, and it's a matter of looking at the tracks you've got now. And Ian and Roger will be working on top lines and possible lyrics. At that point, once they found that they can do something with the pieces of music that we've created, then they become songs. Then they have a chance of making it onto the CD if they're good enough. At the moment, there are twelve tracks there; there are probably eight pieces of music and four songs. So, we'll find out in the next four or five weeks which ones

Ian Paice, Arrow Rock Festival, Lichtenvoorde, Achterhoek, Netherlands, June 9, 2006.
© *Paulus 2, Wikimedia Commons*

are going to hack it, and hopefully if they'll cut the mustard, then we've got a complete CD. If not, we'll have to go in and cut another two or three tracks."

I inquired of Paicey whether the rumors had been true that it was shaping up to be a pretty heavy album. "I would think, compared to the last couple of records. There's two or three fairly heavy tracks, and there is some very, very strange stuff going on. At the moment, they're sort of half cooked. You can't really tell until the vocals and the top lines are on, but there is some great playing, some very interesting ideas. I think a lot of the fans who liked the last two or three albums will definitely enjoy it, and I think a lot of the people who like a lot of the older stuff will enjoy it too."

The mostly live approach to recording was confirmed as well. "The backing tracks are generally all four of us taking a quick stab at it together, and then depending on how good or how many mistakes there are in the collective piece of music, people will either track it again or just fix the little bits that they maybe fluffed up on. But usually, we'd start off every track with four people in the studio, trying to hack it together. Because that's the only way you can occasionally find that little natural interaction. Because when you are layering it individually, (a) you know what's coming and (b) because of that, there are no surprises. So, one way gives you a little bit of musical spontaneity. The other way may give you a little more perfection."

I checked with Paice about whether they ever make a member of the band completely redo their part.

"Occasionally, yeah. It's usually not because he's played it wrong; it may just be a feel thing. You listen back to the take, and maybe one guy is pushing when everybody else is pulling. So, the second time, he just goes in with a more clear picture in his head, through the music being in his earphones, clearly, and he can actually feel the tempo a little bit more than maybe he did the first take. If you've got one guy rushing and three guys pulling, or the other way around, it doesn't sit together very well. So, if it bugs the person who played it, you just go and do it again. Or redo the bits that bug him. Recording, in some ways, is a very exact science. But it's still people who are basically trying to use what is an artificial medium, to get an idea across. And because it's an artificial medium . . . basically you're playing music for people; you don't play for machine. But there are no hard-and-fast rules. At the end of the day, it's how good is the product we give you? Did you enjoy it? Did it make your foot go up and down? Were you happy with it? And really, you don't care how we got there.

"The interesting thing about the actual recording was, we never have actually used a studio this small before to make a record," laughs Paice. "We used Michael Bradford's home studio for it. It's a room about the size of my living room. I was a bit apprehensive when we walked in, because drummers usually like to have a bit of room to breathe in. But within an hour we were making nice noises, the drums sounded great, and it turned into a very, very easy session. We hadn't really had a lot of time to get together to start preproduction and writing. Of the twelve tracks that we've got, I would say ten of them came from our imagination in the studio in the afternoon, and they were either cut that evening or, at the latest, the very next afternoon. We had situations where we'd go in with nothing, and four hours later we had a backing track. So that was exciting, because you didn't have a preconceived idea about any of the tracks you were doing. Everything that came out, for that first run, there's nothing there that is more than take 2 or 3, and a lot of it is take 1. There is a lot of good feel about it. There's the feel of people being excited about playing."

"Fruity," is Roger Glover's introductory adjective selected for the record that would emerge as *Rapture of the Deep*.

"But actually, less fruity than *Bananas*, I suppose. I don't know, it came upon us very suddenly. We're a touring band, as you know, and the *Bananas* tour went on for about eighteen months. During that time, we don't think about the next album. We sort of anticipate doing it, but we don't actually do anything about it. We don't write songs and get prepared. There's nothing you can prepare, really. Because it's what happens in the studio, the moment you start. That's really where the album begins, is that first day in the studio. You might go in with the odd riff or chord sequence, but you don't go in with a finished song. It's not, 'Oh, I've done this demo, lads' [laughs]. And you play them the demo, and they all go, yawn.

"To us, it doesn't work like that. We don't learn songs—we play them. It's like they're in the atmosphere and they just happen, when we start playing them. Anyway, we didn't give a lot of thought to doing the album. We got back from touring. I think we had a couple of months off at Christmas, and then the phone call came through, 'Right, you've got five weeks and we're going to record and write it at the same session.' 'Oh, oh, really?!' Even for *Bananas*, we had a writing session first, you know, a little bit of preparedness. And usually, a little bit of preparedness saves studio time, so you know where you're going in a song, and you don't have to think about it. But in this instance, it was immediate, five weeks, start to finish, bang. We all went in with that same relaxed but intense attitude. It's relaxed in the studio but it's also intense, in kind of a relaxed way, if you know what I mean. Every day we would just work at it. We'd work six days a week, go in around noon, jam around, find a song, record it, and by dinnertime it was done."

"When we went to make this record, it was the same as any other record we have ever made," explains Gillan, confirming Roger's impression of the band's mature approach to scheduling their time. "We would arrive at the studio, have a cup of coffee, tell a few jokes, talk about the hopes of our football teams, and then start jamming. There was not a word or a single note that was written. We had not even had a single discussion on what style the album was going to be in.

"We had just finished the *Bananas* tour, and the band was hot," continues Ian. "We had just spent eighteen months playing in forty countries to millions of people. The empathy between the musicians was just stunning. The album started out as a jam, but the circumstances were different in the aspect that we were in a different year. On the previous album, Don Airey had just joined the band, and he made a great contribution to the album, but he was not feeling as confident as he is now. We were very balanced, and we started out just jamming and then we cultivated the jamming into song ideas.

"I like the word 'album' instead of the word 'CD.' An album is a collection of songs that represent a specific moment of time. If you take nine months to make an album, then it seems to be diluted. If you make an album in a short period of time, then it seems to capture the moment. It's like when you go on holiday and then you come back and look at the snapshots; they all have the same mood. You can smell the air, and you can feel the sunshine. You can have the same set of people at a location, at a different time, and you have a completely different mood. It's always a challenge. If you discuss things beforehand and you set out to create a template, then I think you set a trap of having to exclude spontaneity. Each person

Roger Glover, SC Gripe Sportshall, Split, Croatia, November 4, 2007.
© *Orlovic, Wikimedia Commons*

in the band raises the others' creativity, and that is very important. From my point of view, a song that is written in ten minutes or an hour is always going to be better than a song that is written in ten weeks. The song that is written quickly seems to come out of somewhere that ends up being undiluted. No matter how raw it may be, I like this way of working. Some musicians need to do it the other way, but Deep Purple is very much a live band."

Rapture of the Deep certainly sounds that way, and doubly so with opener "Money Talks," which is the meatiest and yet, amusingly, most casual and even awkward song on the album; all told, an odd choice for pole position. The song roars and rumbles down in the engine room, but up top there's a lyric that strikes me as autobiographical with respect to Ian's checkered past with investments. There's a sort of easy-come, easy-go bemusement about huge flows in and equally huge flows out, due to the harebrained schemes that can eat away at incomes that come in too easy.

"Well, I think there's a danger in looking at these things autobiographically, just because he uses the word 'I,'" laughs Glover. "I think he's not talking from his point of view at all, but rather the point of view of someone who is actually really greedy and rich. I don't think that's autobiographical. He did those lyrics on his own. The track was my riff, and I didn't expect him to come up with anything like that over it. I had a whole different idea that I wanted to hear, and I didn't like his idea at first. But now, I do like it. But the unfortunate thing is . . . maybe it's the fortunate thing, that the voice of the band seems to be the conscience of the band. And yet, the voice of the singer doesn't always have to be the conscience of the singer. You can be singing from the point of view of . . . take Randy Newman, for example. You can write the song from the point of view of a redneck, and proud of it, or I guess little people, not making a point about little people at all, short people. You don't have to be that person. When you're the singer, you can be acting a part."

In general, though, says Roger, wordsmithing in 2005 remained a partnership.

"Well, funny enough, as I may have told you, when we first joined Purple in '69, we were a songwriting partnership, and that partnership was based on the fact that he wrote these silly little poems I thought were kind of interesting, and I learned a few couple of chords. So, he was always more of a lyricist than I was, although, of course, we both write together and separately. But when we joined Purple, he became very much the lyricist, and I didn't really take part in helping him write the lyrics, very much. Occasionally I would be there if he needed me. It wasn't until the reunion, really, that we collaborate on nearly everything. Especially . . . well, the reunion was a collaboration, and then when he came back into the band for *The Battle Rages On* . . . , I was very much his partner there, with all that. But I prefer to let him go on his own, because he's got a strange sense of humor. He's very witty. And you can't have two people trying to think of what's going to make the other one smile. It's difficult. So, I'm quite happy to let him go on his own."

"'Money Talks' is on the new album, and it could have been on an older album," comments Gillan. "Some years ago, I sent a fax to my manager. I told him that I was sick to death of the money bastards. I told him that all my contracts were to be negotiated in beads. I thought about what I said, and later that afternoon I sent him another fax telling him not to do that. I realized that in a few weeks I would not have to deal with the money bastards anymore, but I would have to start dealing with the bead bastards. The principle is that money is a currency. I have no problem

Ian Gillan air drumming, SC Gripe Sportshall, Split, Croatia, November 4, 2007.
© *Orlovic, Wikimedia Commons*

with money, as it is better than bartering for everything. I do have a problem when money becomes a commodity. At that point, it takes on a very nasty taste and flavor. You begin hearing words being used like corruption and greed. The song is really a simple story of a young man who is born innocent and enjoys running and swimming. He gets older and falls in love with money. He starts getting more of it and has guards at the gate. As he gets older, he realizes he wants to take it with him, so he devours it. It is really a very old story."

Still, I stand (illogically) by own interpretation or at least find merit in imagining it that way, knowing what I do about the Gillan band years and Kingsway Studios and all that.

Roger interprets the song about a greedy guy, one presumes, because Ian told him so. Gillan confirms it in the above synopsis, which is really quite simple—or even simplistic.

On the other hand, in my reading, I never once thought of Ian as greedy. It's more so the concept that Ian and money don't get along, that he's incredulous and endlessly amused at the ease at which it comes in (and how little of noble merit he has to do to get it), and then baffled, annoyed, and, to his credit, not eternally bitter at how fast it vanishes and where it all goes; namely, to the "operators of the system" that always seem to wind up with it. The love of money expressed in the song is meant ironically. Motorbikes, hotels, studios, punky heavy metal solo bands, Martin Birch . . . I mean, I really did instantly interpret the lyric as covering Ian's life from, say, 1973 until about 1983. And I find it much more charming (and self-deprecating) interpreting it this way.

Anyway, back to reality, and back to a second record for Michael Bradford. It's good to see that all the praise sent the big man's way back on *Bananas* wasn't empty politics. Here he was again, despite Purple's notorious pickiness with outside help.

"I think he left us alone a lot more," muses Roger. "I think on *Bananas* he was much more hands on, full of suggestions and song ideas, trying to push us to make it work and really happen. And this album, he didn't do that at all. 'Right, what you got?' And let us do it, you know? With very little comment. I don't know if that was predetermined or whether he figured that out, or if it was just his mood at the time. Plus, after a couple of years on the road with Don, we were really itching to get some stuff done, you know? And I think there was no need for any other suggestions. There were so many ideas flying around."

True to form, there are no Michael Bradford song credits, with Airey, by virtue of the new alphabetical sequencing, getting front billing on every song.

"I think he's found his feet a lot more," continues Roger. "He was the new member back in *Bananas*. It's strange how you use that word now without even thinking about it [laughs]. Anyway, after having toured with us all around the world, he's been in the band now nearly three years, so he's fully assimilated. I think at the first songwriting session, he was gobsmacked, because he expected us to go in with much more prepared material. Instead, we just went in and started jamming around and having some fun. He was amazed, I think, at how songs unfolded. This time around, he was much more used to that and prepared for that, and he was more assertive. He spoke his mind a lot more, and I think that's good. You need to have everybody firing on all cylinders."

Advance, regular, and special-edition versions of *Rapture of the Deep*. *Martin Popoff archive*

Back to the producer role, true, Bradford was brought back, but the resultant levels and tones and sounds are not *Bananas*-like in the least. The cold midrange of that record is not here, replaced by ample but still not an entirely satisfying supply of bass, plus an amount of grinding dirtiness that rubbed some longtime Deep Purple fans the wrong way. And if one listens to the drums in isolation, say, on the introduction to "Back to Back," the drums sound a little "trapsy," sorta like Albert Bouchard on the first five Blue Öyster Cult albums (i.e., the debut through *Spectres*).

"Always, I always have criticisms," begins Glover, asked if he had any misgivings about *Bananas*. "It's more to do with the overall mix. I'm a bit more of a rock mixer, when it comes to Deep Purple. Michael brought a different aspect to it. It's got more of a . . . I don't know, it's hard to define what it is."

Bright, too midrange, and too trebly? "Yes, something like that. I want more sort of hard guitar and organ, more of a driving kind of feel, and with the vocals just kind of fighting to get through the music. I find the vocals very loud, kind of radio friendly. You know, you wonder why you go in a studio, with thousands of dollars' worth of equipment, spending thousands of dollars' worth of time, paying engineers thousands of dollars to do all this stuff, where, as far as people think, you know, a song is four minutes long, so what did that take? Four minutes of studio time? Well, it's about two days to get that.

"And you think, well, what is all that time spent on? It's time spent on doing things that people will never recognize. Because when people listen to a song for the first time, like I do—I'm people as well—you either like it or you don't like it. Occasionally it will fall into that middle ground, 'Oh, it's okay.' Which really means you don't like it. It's not that objectionable. But why is it you like certain songs, certain recordings? You love them, and why do you love them? It's an indefinable thing. You're trying to give it your best shot, the way a bass drum sounds in relation to a bass guitar and the way it's placed in the mix and what frequency it's pushed at. Does it have echo on it or not echo on it? All these little things conspire to make what you think is going to be an attractive sound.

"And of course, when I listen to certain recordings, I go, 'Oops, the drums are too loud.' You know, I'm dying to remix *House of Blue Light* one day, if I ever get the opportunity. Simply because it's got a very '80s mix and samples and huge drum sounds. I'm missing the core of the band in there. It's too much of a production."

But hang on—to Purple's and Roger's credit, the band never fell for any of the really braying 1980s studio gadgetry, such as electronic drums or huge gang vocals or other hair band or postpunk travesties that now sound embarrassing.

"Yeah, and we should always put that on an album: 'N.B.—it could've been a lot worse.' But we did have triggering, from *Perfect Strangers* . . . not so much on *Perfect Strangers*, but by the time we got to *House of Blue Light*, yes. There were triggering things happening. The idea of going on live and triggering a sound that would always be good—you know, never having to struggle for a snare sound in a hall—that was such a fallacy. I mean, it just ruins a band. Not for me."

Back to the album and its second track, "Girls Like That" perpetuates this idea that *Rapture of the Deep* was jammed into being. There's no riff to the verse; it's just the band rock 'n' rolling. But getting us from verse to verse is a sort of slow-motion tribute by Steve to Ritchie's storied circular riff, used on all manner of old Deep Purple and Rainbow songs. Come chorus time, Purple has a bit of a hair metal vibe going, sourly melodic. Don turns in an old-school B3-style solo, and the band falls back into . . . I dunno, there's something creepy about a guy of Ian's vintage singing, "I like girls like that." Steve picks this one as an album highlight, calling it "a very straight-ahead and energetic rock tune, just riffy stuff that was played on baritone guitar, which is somewhere between a bass and a guitar. I think it was tuned down to B. So, it's kind of eerie; I really like that. You know, it's my first time using a baritone. When you first get something, you're more amazed by it."

"Wrong Man" does a bit more of the same but also hoists the pirate flag, indicating that maybe—just maybe—we are in for a heavier record than *Bananas*. Its shoving, shifting riff, given Bradford's partial banishment of the drums, imbues the track with metal might.

"Yes, I would agree with that," ventured Steve in July 2005, as you will note, before the album was complete. "It seemed that way to us, and a lot of it depends on how it's mixed. We left it with Ian Gillan singing very quietly. I mean, he sings loud, but without a PA in the room, while we were playing, with headphones on. So, it sounded like what he was heading for was going to work great. But it could end up . . . you know, if they mix the vocals very loud and the band very small, it could be not very heavy sounding. So, it depends on how it's treated. But at the time we left it, it was very heavy [laughs].

"It's very much like the band's natural direction," continued Morse. "In other words, the producer didn't really make any big suggestions or come in and say, 'Here's the song—you gotta do this,' or 'You gotta do a cover of this.' It's just the band playing; it sounds like us. There are some slow, melodic things, and there are a lot of riffy, heavy kinds of songs, and there was one that I remember that it was a very long day working on that. It had a weird kind of feel, a kind of ethnic, maybe Turkish sound to it."

In terms of adjustments from Bradford vis-à-vis *Bananas*, Steve says that "the difference was, I think he noticed, and he was keenly aware—Michael is a very intelligent guy—but he's keenly aware of the fact that a band like Deep Purple is not going to get MTV or Top 40 radio. There's no need to wait breathlessly, given what we're doing. However, the band's popularity is actually getting better and better, because of this underground thing. It boils down to, there's an audience for everything, right? And because of things like direct internet buying. You know, for the last five

Steve Morse, SC Gripe Sportshall, Split, Croatia, November 4, 2007.

years there's also been direct internet stealing, but because there's direct internet availability, people are able to get it, and I think the hard-core fans will support that. And they don't want anything that seems tailored for the masses. They want stuff that's tailored for the fans. In other words, there's no need to try to put anything together that is able to be played on the radio, because it's not going to happen. Unless some weird XM station comes up with something serious.

"I think Ian has gotten more and more clever with his lyrics," continues Steve. "He's always been clever with his lyrics, but now, instead of secondary meanings for things, he's now working on tertiary meanings. And some of it is with a thought to pretty deep stuff like heavy-duty social responsibility and man's inhumanity to man and worldwide political things. But luckily, he wisely dresses that down a little bit in terms of obviousness. We've also all reiterated that we don't want to be this or that political band, because everybody has different ideas in the band. So, it's really not fair in the band for one person to be expressing himself for the entire band or seeming to express a view for the entire band. So, his wordsmithing has really come along.

"And one thing that I've enjoyed seeing is Roger and Ian working together a little bit on this album, whereas on the other ones, Ian would most likely be shut in the studio by himself without anyone around. And this time he invited Roger for part of the vocals, just to help him with them, and that was really cool for me to see. Because you know what? They've been friends for forty years [laughs], and they really should always remain so. They are fantastic; Roger is, I would say, the same. He's the most outgoing, affable, reliable, eclectic guy, and searching for new influences all the time. Roger is the reason I got in the band, I would say, because he was the one looking out on the edges, the fringes, and went to a show by the Steve Morse Band. That's how it happened. Roger is amazing. He's still the same, but he just keeps getting better. His musicianship, I'd say he practices more and is more keenly aware of things than before. He's always been a very talented guy."

As for Ian Paice, Steve figures, "Same sort of thing. His personality is virtually the same. He's always been an easygoing, quiet guy. Everyone sort of gets pigeonholed as a certain personality type, for comic effect. And so Ian Paice will play the curmudgeon and man of few words. Like if somebody comes up and says, 'Hi, how you doing, Ian?,' he'd say 'Fuck off' and turn around and walk away. But he'll be laughing about it. And this is within the band. He tries to make the band laugh a lot. When it comes to real issues, he doesn't say much, but what he does say carries a lot of weight. He's one of those guys who's pretty much right, I think. Everyone listens when he says something. We were getting ready to play somewhere, and he said, 'You know, we really need to be changing the set list a little bit. These people have no idea who we are.' It was some huge festival where we were like one of the ten billion bands. And everyone said all right."

What Steve's talking about is Purple's appearance at Live 8, a series of concerts leading up to the G8 conference in Scotland, as well as a twentieth-anniversary celebration of Live Aid. The highlight of the event was the Pink Floyd reunion in London. Purple played at the Canadian locale, on July 2, 2005.

"Yeah, that was one of the things where he felt that we should play three hits, instead of two hits and one adventurous tune. I was voting for the two and one, and he was voting for the three." The band opened their twenty-minute set with "Highway Star," followed by "Smoke on the Water" and then "Hush," which is a bit of a weird choice. "Well, that's one of the better-feeling tunes rhythmicwise. He likes it for that reason. But that was an example where he put his foot down and everyone went with it."

Back to the record, Gillan explains that the lyric penned for "Wrong Man" was inspired by the case of Wayne Williams, whose counsel was none other than Ian's solo-career manager Michael Lee Jackson. The details of Williams's case are in much dispute, inspiring Ian to pen some thoughts on languishing in jail for crimes uncommitted.

The album's title track definitely fits the bill as something emphatically not tailored for radio. It's this record's "Gates of Babylon," "Kashmir," or "Anya," featuring a highly Moroccan and twisty Blackmore-fired riff, with a strong and heavy break, plus additional Middle Eastern melodic licks burning under the desert sun.

"Don came up with the idea for 'Rapture of the Deep,' that little hooky little riff," notes Roger. "That's probably his main contribution, because that's a killer riff. And where he got that from, I have no idea. The lyric is Ian's. It sounded like a good title because it had the word 'deep' in it—guess what! [laughs]. But to me, I like it because it's got opposites, a duality there, and I'm always fond of that. You know what rapture of the deep is? If you're a diver, scuba diver, and you dive down below three atmospheres or 110, 120 feet, something like that, you have excess nitrogen in your blood, and it's called nitrogen narcosis. It's a known danger. What it does to you is it makes you really happy. It's just like being drunk. Your motor skills are gone, and you can't write your name, for example. Take a pad down and try to write your name and you can't do it; it's really strange. And the expression, the sort of nickname for it, is rapture of the deep. The danger is you're in rapture, you're in a state of pure joy and bliss and at one with the world. You love being down there,

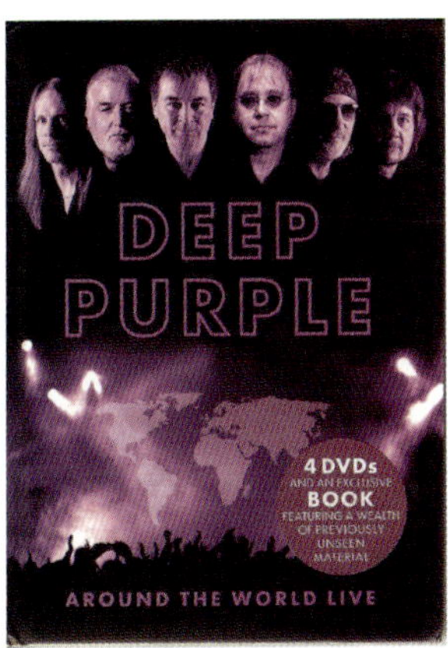

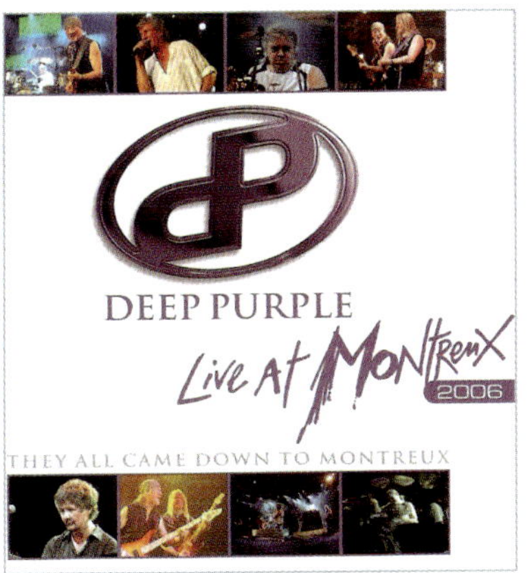

Deep Purple has always supplied a steady stream of archival releases.

and you want to be part of it, so you take your mask off and die. Of course, you have to know that as a diver, that that is one of the dangers, and you have to learn to deal with it."

Gillan is well aware of the diving reference of which Roger speaks, but he says the lyric is actually about the dangers of thinking too intensely. For another elegant diving-related lyric, there's Blue Öyster Cult's "Perfect Water," words by poet Jim Carroll.

Continues Roger, on the building of the record, "We'd work all day and get the song down, and Michael would go, 'Great, that's it.' And we would go, 'No, no, we can do it better.' You enjoy playing it, actually. A song like 'Rapture of the Deep,' we played it all day and then we finally did one take, at 5:30 in the afternoon, and that was it. Until we played it a couple of weeks ago for the first time, we never played it again. And as a musician, you want to play it—it's fun."

"I like the title track very much," adds Don, unsurprisingly, given that, along with Steve, he has to be considered the other most serious "muso" in the band. "It's a pretty epic creation, but not without its teething problems, that one. What else? I like 'Clearly Quite Absurd,' a nice piece of work. I think the whole album is pretty good. And it's a lot harder than *Bananas*. It's got a lot harder sound, a lot closer to the knuckle, know what I mean? More uncompromising. With *Bananas*, we had a songwriting session before we went into the studio. With *Rapture*, we just went straight in with nothing. My main concern was to get the organ mic'd up properly, which I didn't feel had been done on the previous record. I made sure that the organ was really brutal, and that was a good start."

As to whether there were teething problems with "Rapture of the Deep," Don says, "Well, what happened was, I just really wanted to make the song heavy. And I think the rest of them saw it as a kind of Indian fantasy. It took a bit of doing, to sort of maneuver it into a much-simpler format than they wanted. But I'm very pleased with the end result. I think it's very much a Deep Purple track. I mean, we've been playing it every night for the last three years. It always goes down well, even though some people might not have heard it before. It's very direct and fun and musical with amazing lyrics. It's a good piece of work, and good pieces of work don't come easy. You don't always end up with what you intended; in fact, you never end up with what you intended [laughs]."

Adds Airey, on the obvious spontaneity to the record, "Well, I think that's just how Purple do it. They're just playing, and Paicey hits a backbeat and off you go. You can never pin Purple down. It's always evolving into something you don't expect. The funny thing is, the producer, Michael Bradford, never said a word. He'd taken a big part in the creation of the first album, and the second one, he just really . . . we suddenly realized we had to work it out for ourselves. I mean, he's just brilliant, those kinds of strategies, getting stuff out of people. He's really been very good for the band."

Perhaps this is a good time to peer into the reflecting pool of the album's quixotic cover art. Apparently there was some friction concerning its construction, resulting in designer Ioannis being edged to the sidelines.

"You could say arguing or debate or whatever it was," notes Gillan. "In my personal opinion, this is the best cover we have had since Deep Purple *In Rock*. Technically it surpasses it, and conceptually it equals it. Some hacker from the internet got ahold of some demo ideas that were rejected by everybody. There became some kind of confusion over that. There was a debate inside the band about which of two or three ideas we should go with. Roger Glover came up with the original idea in *Penthouse* magazine or something like that. I thought it was absolutely perfect. I thought this cover had more life than a simple illustration.

"'Rapture of the Deep' is not about nitrogen narcosis, and it is not about being underwater. It is about reflections of thought. It has a certain avant-garde approach

A 2010 and a 2013 backstage pass

to supposedly established situations. I am dealing with some very delicate topics on the album. *Bananas* was almost entirely political in terms of lyrics. This album is entirely spiritual—that is the loose conceptual thread that runs through all the songs. I quite forcefully endorsed Roger's idea. There were differences, but they were not meant to be public. I don't know if anyone in the band is still disappointed in the cover. All I can say is that it has the total support of the record company and the management. I hope no one within the band is disappointed; they have not said anything to me. As I say, it was Roger's idea. Paicey loves it. Don wanted a more heavy metal cover. These things are supposed to be private, but occasionally something gets out and you have to defend it. I will say this is the most dignified discussion the band has had over a cover. It was dealt with over a few intensive days, with people flying back and forth. I think Roger did a fantastic job under great pressure. I have no doubt that it is the best cover Deep Purple has done since *In Rock*."

Further analyzing, Ian explains that "if you look into the water, the trees are as they should be, but he is not. Let your mind flow freely. There are two kinds of art. One is representational art, where you are trying to get through an image. For instance, it would be a portrait that flatters the sitter. The other kind of art is there to trigger your imagination. It's there to make you think. I had this picture on the wall when I was writing the lyrics, and it put me in the right mood. Consequently, if it causes confusion, then maybe that is what it's meant to do. It's not meant to be literal. I think it's a brilliant piece of art, and it triggers my imagination and stimulates me enormously. What it means to me is not necessarily what it means to anyone else. I was hoping that everyone would see something different in it. If you don't get it, then that is all right. I see great encouragement in it. People go to art galleries and some people go, 'I don't get it,' while others go, 'I hate it,' and yet others go, 'That is fucking great.'"

Moving on, the album's first ballad is the aforementioned "Clearly Quite Absurd," a lush and elegant progressive-rock piece, serious but not dark, arranged and produced to maximum effect. Ian's lyrics address deeper communication between people and the rich rewards thereof.

Two more shots from the Arrow Rock Festival, Lichtenvoorde, Achterhoek, Netherlands, June 9, 2006. © *Paulus 2, Wikimedia Commons*

"It's a beautiful tune," muses Airey. "Beautiful chord sequence, something that Steve and I sort of came up with before anyone came into the studio. Roger just joined in, and then Gillan started just singing away. It happened very quickly. I don't think we've ever played it live. I don't know why that is. And the lyrics, well, I think that Ian Gillan has taken it on himself to do them now, and he's a fantastic lyricist. One of the best. He's a great poet. He works at it; he's writing all the time. You know, you see him on the plane, scribbling into notebooks, reading poetry, reading books; he's a very observant kind of a man. And it all goes into his art."

Explains Glover, "'Clearly Quite Absurd' was a song where we had a backing track, and I had an idea for a song over it, and I showed it to Ian and he went, 'Hmm, yeah, I like it,' and then he went away and wrote this completely different set of words for 'Clearly Quite Absurd,' which actually blew me away. There's a sort of conversational tone about it. I listen to songs a lot, and you hear so many clichés and just boring lyrics. And that's what I like about Ian's lyrics, because they sort of take you by surprise. They're not what you'd expect. 'Clearly Quite Absurd' is actually quite a tender song, and it's quite an achievement, really, a very unusual ballad. There were about four or five songs that we really collaborated on fifty-fifty."

"I haven't done much collaboration with Roger on the last two albums" is Ian's view of things. "Pretty much, I've been doing all the lyrics myself. Roger has been focusing much more on the musical composition and the bass playing, which has improved beyond measure. The only difference between writing with Deep Purple and writing outside of Deep Purple is the circumstances. I don't think the style differs at all, other than the part that you're writing with the musicians you're in the room with. So, when I'm writing with my solo stuff, I can meander all over the place, and I can tell how old I am depending on the style of the writing. Because I went through a great change in my middle age, which got me out of a crisis. But with the solo stuff, it's all written before we go to the studio, apart from the finishing touches.

"But with Deep Purple, when we go to the studio, there's nothing at all, not a single word," continues Gillan. "I just get a blank writing pad, and we start on day one. There is no album title, no song titles, no arrangements, no ideas at all—the writing is spontaneous. My main concern with Purple is the sound of the words more than the meaning of them. When I'm filling in the landscape, it's like you do a quick sketch of a track you have to work with—tempo, arrangement, you find a tune—and then I start my gibberish singing, which is just making stupid noises, but to use the voice as an instrument to fill in with the band. Gradually it all goes together, and you fill in the details with the actual meaningful words. But at the end of the day, it's just what comes out. Some would say the previous method, when I'm writing for myself, is more relaxed; it's more laid back, it's more thoughtful, perhaps more seductive. Whereas with the band, like everything in Purple, it's more intense. So, you tend to have to pull back, rather than push on, if you know what I mean. Everything is subject to the mood, the ambient mood, but I think they're all subtleties, really."

With Purple as opposed to the solo albums, it's more of a pressure cooker. "Oh, for sure, yeah [laughs]. Oh yeah, bloody right. A hell of a pressure. As I say, we go in with nothing. There are no prepared songs. With the greatest respect, it's great to jam away all afternoon and gradually drift into different rhythms and sequences and structures and that sort of thing, but then you've got to not only write a tune over it, but it's got to sound like it's the dominant feature, because the melody has

More views from the SC Gripe Sportshall, Split, Croatia, November 4, 2007. © *Orlovic, Wikimedia Commons*

to be dominant. And then you've got to find the words. So, you've got to interpret the sound of those words into some kind of meaning. Yeah, yeah, it's much more intense."

Moving through *Rapture*, "Don't Let Go" is a hard-hitting Gary Moore–worthy blues rocker that would have fit smartly on *Bananas*. Roger cites this one as another receptacle of spark and spontaneity.

"When we did that, we hadn't really discussed what was going to happen in the solo, or whose solo it was going to be or anything. We just had a solo spot, and we knew that's where the solo was going to go. And the first time we started recording it, Steve just spontaneously broke out into a solo, and that's the solo that's on the record. You know, *Purpendicular* and *Abandon* took far, far too long to do, for reasons I don't really want to go into [laughs]. But partly my fault, because I wasn't a strong enough producer to say, 'Right, buckle down, lads.' But I don't like spending that much time on an album. You lose something. You might gain perfection, but you lose fire; you lose freshness. This album does sound, to me, very fresh, and that's because it is."

Don Airey takes a nice solo on this one as well. "Yeah, he spoke up a lot more than he did on the last album," figures Morse. "Since Michael didn't step in and say, 'I want you to do this and this,' like he did on the last album, it more came from the band. And I've been vocal about saying that I wished people wouldn't bring in complete songs anyway. Sometimes it happens, but I like it best when people have just a shred of an idea and we develop it together. I think everyone feels the same. There's very good chemistry there with the band. That has always been the case, but Don has really . . . he had no qualms about letting his voice be heard [laughs]."

Comparing backward, Steve recalls that "*Abandon* was one of those things where, when we put it together, it was a little bit incomplete because Jon wasn't really there; he was working on his solo project. He sort of came in and did his parts after the fact, so it wasn't representative of the whole band. There were more guitar riff kinds of things. And, for whatever reason, it just didn't have as much variety as we would've liked. But *Purpendicular*, that was a good example of, again, like this new record, just being in the studio doing our thing. The advantage now is that with Michael, there's a referee available. He keeps things moving and keeps us from wasting time. Like, if we're ever at a stalemate, he'll step in and say, 'No, no, do it the other way—come on!' [laughs]."

Buoyant and playful, "Back to Back" sounds like a *Bananas* track and indeed presents equal parts funk, up-tempo blues, and hard rock, to the point where it could have fit on *Burn*, *Stormbringer*, or *Come Taste the Band*. Note the old-school Devo synthesizers brought out by Don at the halfway mark.

"Back to Back" gives way to the tribal Bo Diddley drums of "Kiss Tomorrow Goodbye," which turns heavy and brisk like the last record's title track. Paicey lights a trashy swing beat under it, and Ian comes up with an obscure, inscrutable lyric that is the closest thing to a retelling of the album cover of any of the poems Ian proffered elsewhere on the record.

"MTV" is the original US bonus track for the album, with "Things I Never Said" being the secondary bonus track, also available on the tour edition of the album and in live form on *Live at Montreux 2006*. In "MTV," Gillan complains about being treated like a doddering classic-rock band, forgotten but for the glory days, glossed over to the point of radio hacks mispronouncing their names and even garbling the old tales.

It's a smart and cutting diatribe, with the most amusing bit being how he's listened to the classic-rock radio station he's playing in the car so much that he's "on first-name terms with the crew." Now, this could refer to the DJs and producers of the station, or it could also mean that he knows the songs so well, he knows everybody in the band's crew. Which is sensible, because road crew employees do tend to cycle and circulate through various classic-rock bands. As well, think of all the tour pairings and packages Purple's been part of, and the number of crew folk Ian's walked by backstage. One can picture Ian on his catatonic night ride (out of Phoenix) having a chuckle, picking off three or four crew guys per track as each predictable song selection rolls by, medicating his trip.

Ad for tour with Styx

Amusingly, "MTV" draws to a conclusion before he finishes sputtering about classic-rock radio and actually gets around to any opinions on the music video channel. "Let's not talk about MTV" is all he can muster, because time is up, plus it's time to do some radio IDs.

"Lyrically, it's a complete joke," said Ian, to Classic Rock Revisited's Jeb Wright. "I heard Roger on a radio station in New York when *Bananas* came out. I listened to him do a twenty-minute interview, and the DJ would not allow Roger to talk about the new album. All she wanted to do was talk about the old days. We were in town doing a concert, and Roger is eager to talk about the new record, but he can't get in a word about it. At the end of the interview she goes, 'Roger Gloover—"Smoke on the Water," yeah!' I thought, 'My God, she got his name wrong. We really are dead on the radio.'

"Michael Bradford insisted on having the television on in his studio whenever I was there writing," continues Gillan. "I turned it off and he would turn it on again. I compromised and got up and turned the sound off but left the set on. I realized that is exactly how MTV should be watched. It's bloody fantastic and hilarious when you do that. If you read the lyrics to the song 'MTV,' you'll see that it is also about radio in the United States. It even talks about the old days and the pirate radio stations. I was talking about it with my daughter today. We were listening to the radio in UK today, and it was utter and complete garbage. It actually has nothing to do with the music. It has to do with the patronizing attitude of the presenters. Where are those guys who used to come to work with a supermarket bag full of stuff that they worked up the night before? They went out to the clubs and they got involved, and the people tuned into the radio station because they liked the guy and they liked his taste in music. He was also respectful of the music. 'MTV,' the song, is just a joke, because they really treat us with such contempt. I figured it was perfectly fair game to have a go at them.

"Recently, I said to the magazine *Classic Rock* in the UK that I don't consider Deep Purple to be a classic-rock band. We have been called a lot worse than a classic-rock band. I don't mean any disrespect to bands of our era, nor am I claiming to be anything more than we are. However, we are not a classic-rock band in the same sense that we are not a heavy metal band, if you catch my drift. I think most musicians would find it hard to be defined as something that you don't quite feel is true about yourself. I think the way Purple goes about their business; we just don't want to be called a classic-rock band. I don't really mind it, but I just want to make that point. I think it makes you sound lazy. There is a niche for that, but when we were kids, we resented everything about being departmentalized for the convenience of the media."

Gillan goes on to articulate the difference between the old Purple and the new one, springboarded from a comment comparing Blackmore to Morse and back again.

"You get divorced and then you get remarried, and then someone asks you how you compare the new wife with the old wife—your question is kind of like that. I could put the answer in sexual terms, but I don't think that I'd better. Everyone is different. I refuse to say anything bad about Ritchie as a guitar player. He was a monument, much the same way Jon Lord is. Ritchie is a phenomenal player and a great showman. We did have our fallings out with each other. We were kids and we were all assholes at the time. I think Ritchie and I were at loggerheads. I don't want this to sound like a self-serving comment, so I will have to qualify it. I do believe that Ritchie wanted to dominate the band. I didn't want to dominate the band, but I did want the band to be a band. I resisted Ritchie's attempts to dominate Deep Purple. We didn't enjoy the same vision.

"I used to room with Ritchie, and I actually have many, many fond memories of that time," continues Ian. "I think after all these years, we are old enough and ugly enough to let those dogs lie. I just don't want to say bad things about Ritchie, as it is all in the past. However, Steve Morse goes onstage and performs brilliantly. Steve comes onstage, and no matter what his personal problems may be—we all have them, because it is difficult being on the road; you have two families: your family and your musical family—Steve plays electrifying every night, and he has phenomenal skills. He gets on the bus after the gig, and he is the funniest guy you have ever met in your life. Steve brings things to the band that are entirely different than the things Ritchie brought. You can't compare the two as guitar players, but you can compare them behind the scenes. They have some similarities—banjo players always do. Steve's energy and enthusiasm behind the scenes are incredible. His sensitivity to writing music—particularly with Roger Glover—is just marvelous. I think you can regard the whole thing as that was the old family and this is the new family."

Further examining the dynamic of the new guys in the band versus the veterans, Ian explains that "Steve, as you know, was a jazz musician—he is the most consummate musician. Don believed that he could express himself within the format of the band. There is a shifting emphasis on the roles in the band. You may be playing a rhythm one minute and then change it around and play a solo the next. Sometimes everyone just spaces out on their own. Don's playing on this album is magnificent. It was actually Don who came up with the 'Rapture of the Deep' idea. We went in one day, and he was playing something very interesting. I asked him what it was, and he replied, 'I hear we are going to Istanbul. I call this song "Turkish Delight."' As soon

Hala Stulecia, Wroclaw, Poland, October 31, 2010. © *Lukasz Ryba, Wikimedia Commons*

Hala Stulecia, Wroclaw, Poland, October 31, 2010. © *Lukasz Ryba, Wikimedia Commons*

as Paicey and Roger came in, then it instantly became a Deep Purple thing. You could feel everyone's personality. When you get five people all focusing on one person's idea and developing it, then it becomes a joy."

One uncommon characteristic about "MTV" is the extent to which the band works up vocal harmonies, which instantly had Roger surmising it might not make it to the live set. "No, we're not a harmony-type band. Especially in the loud world of hard rock, in which we dwell. Delicate harmonies and finely attuned singing leave something to be desired. No, that works on record, but maybe the live version of it . . . if we do it, it'll have a different kind of energy, that's all."

Swinging around to the close of *Rapture of the Deep*, second to last comes "Junkyard Blues," yet another funky but still heavy track. Don is pervasive on tinkling electric piano, and then he gets an extended, sweeping, and at times classical piano solo deep into the jammy track. Eventually Steve arrives on the scene, and they trade licks, although the result is bubbly, babbling keyboardist/guitarist interplay that is a million miles away from Jon Lord and Ritchie Blackmore on *In Rock*.

"We were looking for a jam song, basically," says Roger. "We actually went in the studio one day and said, 'Let's look for something where we can stretch out a little bit. We had a bit of a jam, and Steve came up with this opening riff and we went on that. It's so immediate, it's frightening. We're actually there in the studio, and all we've got is this one riff, and you play that for about five minutes, six minutes, and you go, 'Yeah, now where are we going to go from here?' And somebody goes, 'G!' So, you go to G [laughs], and it's immediate and it's fun. Sometimes you go, 'No, no, G's not working; let's go to E flat,' and you try them both, and you can't decide. That's when you have a bit of a problem, and that's when you get Michael in and you say, 'Which way should we go?' But usually, we resolve it. Usually, it's pretty obvious which is best.

"Then we had this backing track," continues Roger. "We finished most of the work, and Ian was left with quite a few lyrics to tidy up and said, 'Actually, I need some help.' Because normally I just like to leave him be, because he's got such an unusual sense of humor. I think that's actually one of the differences with Deep Purple versus other bands, is that we have a sense of humor. Some bands get very serious—doom and destruction are everywhere.

"Anyway, with 'Junkyard Blues,' I came up with the title and I had no idea why. I was just sitting there minding my own business, and I suddenly said to myself, 'Hmm, "Junkyard Blues"—that's got a nice ring to it.' So I immediately went to the computer to find out if it was in fact a song. I thought, there's got to be a song called that, but there isn't. There's a compilation album of blues tunes called *Junkyard Blues*. But I mentioned it to Ian, and he went, 'Yeah, I like the sound of that. What's it about?' 'I have no idea' [laughs]. Anyway, we sat down and started writing it, and we thought, let's actually write about a junkyard, things of value that people once treasured and have now forgotten. It's a bit of a metaphor for life, in some ways."

Asked if checking to see if a title has been used is a common occurrence, Roger explains, "No, but if there's a curiosity there, yeah. But usually not. I mean, if we wrote a song called 'Whole Lotta Love,' it might present a bit of a problem. You just want to make sure it's not a song title on Kiss's last album or something. Argh, no [laughs]."

Reacting to a remark about Ian's sometimes innovative and choppy vocal delivery (see "Money Talks"), Roger agrees that it's an overt characteristic of his style.

"Yes, in fact, for a friend, I was playing 'No One Came' the other night, and that, that was a groundbreaking song, in many ways, not the least of which it was Gillan doing this kind of half-talking approach, which he employs from time to time and does quite a lot on this album. I don't know if it's a conscious decision on his part, but it seems to work for him. Basically, what he does, he sort of writes down whatever comes into his head and reassembles them occasionally and tries them on mic and figures out what works and doesn't work, and goes back and revises. It's a conversational tone, if you like. And he has this knack of taking a detail and making that detail tell a whole story."

Is there a willful obscurity as well, I wondered. "Hmm, I don't think obscure is the right word, though. We've both discussed this many times. A good song works on many different levels. If a song only works on one level, it's kind of boring. Which is—and I don't want to knock all country music—but a lot of country music is boring because it's all too real.

"If you listen to a song like 'Isis' by Bob Dylan, well, what is that about? There are some lovely pictures in there, some lovely word stories, but what is it about? What is 'Visions of Johanna' about? Bob Dylan is a master of this kind of thing. You love it because it paints a certain picture and generates certain atmospheres and moods.

"I think a song works if it has meanings that other people can get. When we did 'Perfect Strangers,' for example, the original idea was a very literal thing of a spirit being reborn but locked inside someone else's body—that was our starting point. We just grabbed lyrics from here; I had a couple of poems. And we took a line or two from some of my poems, and we just built up a word picture. And it was only when it was finished and the album out, people saw it as intensely autobiographical. Looking at it now, you go, 'Wow! Why didn't we see that?' But I like a lyric where it means different things to different people; you can put your own interpretation on it. You're involving the listener, rather than just entertaining."

Adds Ian, "I am very politically aware, as I devour the newspapers every day. Lyrically, I always have something to stimulate my writing. I am also very spiritual, so I tend to look at things in a different way than others. My life is full and rich. If I could have known now what I didn't know then, I would have written a lot more in the old days. When Roger and I first heard the Beatles' 'Please, Please Me,' he looked at me and said, 'We can write stuff like that.' I told him, 'The difference between us and them is that they are on top of the hill, and we are on the bottom. More people can see and hear them from a greater distance.' The Beatles also had the cohesion of the image as well. I have nothing against image, but I always thought we should be natural. It has served us in the long term. We still have the band, and we are still a family unit. I'm sixty years old and I have butterflies in my stomach. I can't wait to go to London for rehearsals. We are going on the road for two years to support the album. People ask me how I can do that at age sixty. I still get a tickle in my tummy on show day. I have to meditate and hold down my adrenaline level. It is still an incredible challenge to be onstage with Deep Purple every day."

Talk of "Junkyard Blues" causes Roger to extol the virtues of Mr. Morse.

"Steve is a wonderful, wonderful musician. He's full of a million ideas. In fact, it's hard to turn him off sometimes. Difficult to define. I mean, he has a certain character of playing that I don't always like. I don't always like the fast chromatic stuff, but I also have to admit that that's part of his personality. That's the way he plays. So as much as he doesn't always play exactly what I'd like him to, he never plays less than brilliant stuff. He's very consistent in that. Occasionally I want something else, but that's a minor criticism. Everyone has their quirks, and what he brings to the band is priceless.

"The opening riff to 'Junkyard Blues,' for example, it sounds like a very simple riff, but it's actually really difficult to play. I know—I had to learn it [laughs]. It's challenging for my fingers. But you know, having done it, he's very encouraging like that. He plays something, and I'd say, 'I can't play that,' and he'd say, 'Yes you can!' 'No, I can't.' 'Yes, you can!' And in five minutes, very carefully and very patiently, he sort of led me through how to play it, and bingo, now I can play it. So, he's very encouraging like that. And I think you are right about there being a joy in his playing. But he suffers in his life. He's a stressful man. I think he exists on stress. But when he plays, that's like peace.

"The boost that he brought to the band affected everyone," continues Glover. "Purple became a whole band, which I'd always dreamed of. I had this image of us all standing in a circle. I asked George Harrison about this. He told me that the Traveling Wilburys was so much fun because they went into the studio and said, 'What about this chord progression?' And then did it. No pressure, and there was a lot of fun and camaraderie. I always thought I'd have to leave Deep Purple to find that. The fun quotient had diminished a little over the years. But then he came in and we all improved. Paicey found his groove again, and I became a bass player again. My God, it really showed. Gillan lost his nerves and his anger, and his voice went up. Jon began playing at his peak. We all peaked about ten years ago."

Rapture of the Deep closes with a classic of a track, an ambitious excursion in ballad form that is more apocalyptic than soothing. "Before Time Began" floats eerily with Ian gorgeously singing an all-encompassing lyric that ponders the secret at the heart of all human existence. He goes there in earnest, testimony to the many moods of Gillan as a writer.

Recalls Roger, "I was a few minutes late coming into the studio one day, and Steve was doodling around with these strange chords, chords that seemed to have no relation to each other, no logic. They just sounded utterly beautiful to me. And instead of grabbing my bass and trying to figure out what they were doing, instead I just sat there mesmerized, actually, at the beauty of it. And you know, fifteen minutes later when they stopped, I said, 'What the hell is that?!' I thought it was great! 'Well, it's just some odd chords, chords that don't normally go together, and we're putting them together' [laughs]. And I thought, my God, I've got to learn that. So I learned it, and it took me awhile to get the logic of it, which is pretty weird. It doesn't go in fours. The first part just goes in threes, and then it's a chain that suddenly starts again without you knowing it's come to an end. And I thought, well, what on earth are we going to sing over this? Because I loved the track and loved that thing. And I think it was Michael Bradford that said to Ian, 'Write a poem.' Because, you know, it's very difficult to find a melody that fits over such diverse chords. And I think that was actually the way to go. It worked really well."

And so, *Rapture of the Deep* draws to an elegant and intellectual close, conspicuously incongruous butted up against the large supply of amusement and purely rocking good times that comes with most of the jam-banded tracks earlier on the record. Fan reaction was mixed, and that doesn't mean bad. The obviously ambitious tracks on the record . . . no one had issue with those, even if most of them weren't strictly heavy. It was more that some of the rockers were a bit too casual, perhaps underwritten, not quite considered enough. This writer took to it immediately, fairly sure it was better than *Bananas*. But later I switched those two around. *Bananas* has charms buried in its details and is propped, not lessened, by its accessibility. Still, despite signals from the guys later on that it's become the least satisfying to its creators, I'd go with *Abandon* as the triumph of the Morse years, with *Purpendicular* a close second.

"I think it's the best album we've done in a long time, because all the elements are in place," announced Gillan of *Rapture*, a couple of years down the endless road of touring for it. "Don is settled. I mean I was very pleased with *Bananas*, but in terms of musical structure and songwriting, *Rapture* beats it. The only reason we ever made records, from Deep Purple *In Rock* on, was to provide material for the next tour. The tours have always been named after the last record. I think it's well balanced. I think there's a lot more keyboard input on this record, in terms of writing and performance. Yeah, I think the balance is really good. You know, we don't care so much about the length of the material; the songs sometimes are quite long. There's a good theme to it, musically and lyrically, all the way through. We're doing five or six songs from the album on the road, and they fit in beautifully with the old stuff. It works for us very well."

Touring for the album turned out to be somewhat of a meaningless turn of phrase. The band was on the road for four years. Was all that in support of *Rapture of the Deep*? Even if it would be eight years until the next album, you can't accuse the band of slowing down. They are actually executing the hardest part of this whole game, the tour grind, and at their usual herculean pace, touching down in such places as South America, Russia, and even the Middle East routinely, and with energy.

"Oh, there's no doubt about it," promises Ian. "Once we get focused on an album, it just pours out of us. These guys are incredibly prolific, and it's just a joy working on lyrics for these things. But everybody is just enjoying the break. It's been a long haul so far. We kicked off in January 2006, and we played forty-eight countries that year. I think a pause for breath is justified."

Chapter 26

Now What?!

"Put the deep back in Deep Purple."

Besides the gigging, the Deep Purple machine kept chugging along with live CDs and DVDs, compilations, and quasi-official live sets issued just in specific territories. We'll get to some of those, but first some words on what some of the band alumni, past and present, had gotten up to at this juncture.

Concerning David Coverdale, I know we skipped his impressive story, when in the mid- and late 1980s, his Whitesnake powerhouse was capable of doing four and five times the amount of business that Purple could muster, at least in terms of record sales. But little had gone on since that heyday. There was the ill-received *Coverdale Page* record in 1993, a creditable solo album, and then a return as Whitesnake with live recordings and a solid studio album called *Good to Be Bad*. There'd be two more after that, plus an album of Deep Purple songs called *The Purple Album*, in 2015.

Glenn Hughes and Joe Lynn Turner have trod an amusingly similar path to each other. Both are brimming with optimism and talent, and there have been many solo albums and impromptu band hookups—even with each other, as Hughes Turner Project. Both also know which side their bread's buttered on, and regularly skip over to eastern Europe and Russia to capitalize on persistent Purple and, in the case of Joe, Rainbow memories. More intentionally, with Glenn, there had been talk of some sort of Purple Mk. III reunion. With Joe, he had a sporadically working unit of ex-Rainbow alumni called Over the Rainbow. Ritchie Blackmore, to everyone's surprise, has stuck to a path established going on twenty-seven years now (and he's not yet fired his singer!), prolifically making records with his now wife, Candice, as Blackmore's Night and less so touring them, preferring to make the shows special, in castles and other dramatic locales and cajoling all to get into the occasion by wearing traditional dress.

Jon Lord, true to his word, had been inspiringly active, right up to his death on July 16, 2012, from pancreatic cancer. He'd been doing live shows and CDs in both a classical and a (blues) rock vein, the latter with Bob Daisley's Hoochie Coochie Men.

"I've always thought that being a musician meant just that," said Lord to Mick Burgess. "I'm lucky enough to be able to play different styles and, in fact, love those

A Canadian ad for the *Coverdale Page* album, plus the front cover of Whitesnake's album of Deep Purple songs

different styles, and I feel comfortable putting on different hats. I just love playing. When I was asked to put some Hammond on these songs, I listened to them and thought it'd be great fun, so I was happy to do that. I met them down in Australia in '03 and did some live dates with them. Bob Daisley is in the band, and they have a terrific guitarist called Tim Gaze, who also happens to be a great singer. To me he's an Australian Clapton. He has this lovely laid-back voice and this very interesting and accomplished guitar style.

"Each one has its own demands," continued Lord, comparing blues to classical. "Blues is what I first started playing in the mid-'60s, and we used to play the blues songs that we had great fun interpreting. The good thing about playing blues is that the structure is so simple. It allows you complete freedom to let your imagination run wild. Recently there was a program on TV called *Classical Stars*; it was like an *X Factor* for classical musicians. The guy in charge of it was the one who played cello for us, Matthew Barley. He said to one of the young musicians that he should listen to some blues, because if you understand the blues and how it works and what makes improvisation so important to the form, then you'd find it easier, for example, to understand Bach. I absolutely agree with him, as one style of music always has something to teach another style, in my humble opinion. Blues is at the roots of all popular music and travels from Africa right through to hard rock. I think an open mind is the best gift a musician can have, besides his ability to play."

And back to Purple, one of the yummiest items issued post-*Rapture* has been the *Around the World Live* four-DVD box set, which includes an early show for Steve Morse, from India in 1995. As a bonus, the band plays two selections from *The Battle Rages On* . . . Australia 1999 includes too many hits and not enough *Purpendicular* and *Abandon* songs. UK 2002 is quite playful and relaxed, featuring a high-energy performance of "The Well Dressed Guitar," Don's lighthearted keyboard solo, and a rare rendition of the sinewy "Mary Long."

Another sweet item was a tidy box set called *Live in Europe 1993*, containing two complete concerts from the 1993 tour (the NEC and Stuttgart), spread over four CDs. The nicely appointed package contained a handful of oddities in "Talk About Love," "A Twist in the Tale," "In the Hall of the Mountain King," "The Mule" (sort of), and "Paint It Black." But of course, there was also significant overlap between the two sets.

The archival releases just kept coming. *Martin Popoff archive*

Additionally, there were DVDs and CDs celebrating Montreux performances. First, a 1996 set (plus two 2000 extras) was issued in 2006. It highlights Ian Paice opening the show and blazing away on "Fireball." But as history has shown, "Ted the Mechanic" turned out to be a helluva showcase for Paicey, with his characteristic ease of percussive punctuation, as well as all his other tricks 'n' tips. That's track 2, and next, "Pictures of Home" also features some of those effortless thrilling fills we've grown to love from Ian, not to mention his sense of swing.

"You know, nobody is ever made to be drummer," chuckles Paice, thanking fate for his chosen profession. "People actually become drummers because they really like it. Unlike people who play violin, or piano players—sometimes that's foisted upon them by their parents. Nobody's ever made to be a drummer [laughs]; it just sort of happens. Yeah, the state of the profession right now is very healthy. But I think at the moment it's probably a little bit too hung up on the technique of playing, rather than the swing of playing, and I find that a little dull.

"Don't take it the wrong way. I can be amazed at some of the young kids today, the techniques that they've developed. It's absolutely phenomenal. But whether it actually transmits itself and communicates with the people who are listening to it, I sometimes wonder. I'd rather see some guy's foot bouncing up and down because he's enjoying what's going on rhythmically, than sitting there with his mouth open because he's totally amazed with the technical dexterity of the guy. I'm not saying it's wrong, I'm not saying it's right, but that's the way it works for me anyway. It's all fine; if people like it, it's great."

The above is necessarily couched in this idea of highly technical new metal bands versus whatever Deep Purple is. "Yes, and look, I know the impression people get if you say you're a metal band. That's fine if you are metal band, but if you're not, it's something you really don't want to be tagged with. It's like if someone said, 'Yeah, Purple, they're a really good jazz combo.' You'd be just as annoyed at that. I know everybody has to have a label so they can rationalize it, but we always said it was just a hard rock 'n' roll band, and sometimes it didn't even need to be so hard. But that was the idea behind it."

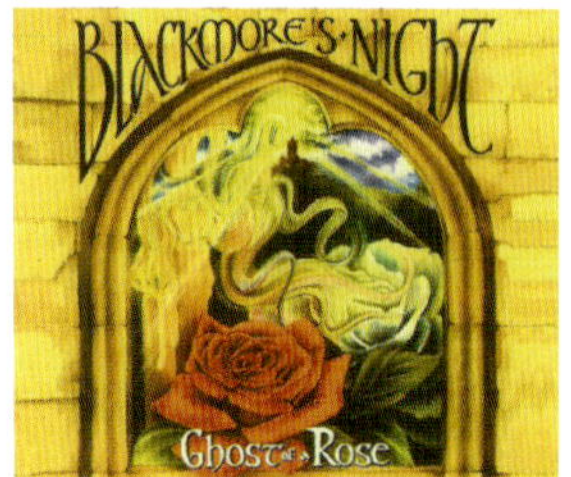

An assortment of Blackmore's Night albums. *Martin Popoff archive*

"That's almost impossible for the player to answer," he says, asked if his style has changed much in the last ten or fifteen years. "I think people that watch you play would probably give a more decent description of any changes that have happened. All I know is that, say, in the last fifteen years of playing, I can play more economically with my energy. When I was a kid, I used to hit as many things as often and as hard as I could, and I find that I can get very, very similar results by maybe not hitting quite as hard as I thought I needed to. So, I can come offstage, most nights, and if somebody told me that I would have to do a second show, I could do it. When I was like twenty-one, twenty-two, it would be no way. I'd be a liquid heap in the corner, totally frazzled [laughs]."

Further on his style, he figures, "If you play instinctively and you don't think about it, then every night, within certain percentages, there's a little surprise for you and the audience. I don't have the musical ability to actually do the same thing every night and to choreograph it in a way that some musicians can. That's not the way it works for me. It starts, I start playing, and then whatever happens happens. And I'd hate to lose that."

Ask Ian about his elder statesmanship in the band, and he necessarily prefaces it with the all-important backstory of Gillan versus Blackmore.

"In the past, a little bit of mediation was called for, but Roger was good at that too. So between the two of us, we would try to smooth the waves. Now it's not so much, because the characters are so in tune with each other. And because we don't have to live in each other's pocket, when we're on the road; we still give each other room. When we're off the road, we're nowhere near to each other. So that pressure of living together is not the same as it was. Now I tend to be more the voice of reality. Somebody will come up and say something, and I'll go, 'I know that sounds really impressive, but what are we going to do with it? How are we going to do that?' So, I sort of keep things down on an earthly plane [laughs], rather than losing it in the stratosphere, you know? And also, when it comes to business decisions, if I think something is wrong, I'm generally the one that will put the point forward that maybe it's not a good thing to do. It comes with tenure. Because I am the only original player left, from 1968 time. That gives me a little bit of . . . I don't outrank anybody—

it's not that. But they all seem to respect my point of view when I make one. No one has to agree with it [laughs]."

The second Montreux set issued was a 2006 appearance, put out the following year. Accommodatingly, there were only three tracks of overlap: "Smoke on the Water" (note the two-minute swing jazz version of it that precedes the regular clanging take), "Pictures of Home," presented as the opener, and "When a Blind Man Cries," featuring a loopy Steve Morse solo but kept short, at 3:32. Oddities include *Rapture of the Deep* bonus track "Things I Never Said," on both the CD and DVD, and something called "Too Much Fun," just on the DVD.

"'Too Much Fun,' oh right, that's on the Montreux thing," recalls Airey. "That was something we made up on the tour. Ian would have this line, 'I'm having too much fun tonight.' We knocked it through in the dressing room. We just started jamming on it, and it turned into a song. We all said, 'God, that would be good if we were doing Montreux,' and that was the last time we ever played it [laughs]. Might have played it three times. And 'Things I Never Said,' I'll tell you what that is. That was a song that for some reason didn't make *Rapture of the Deep*. I thought it was one of the best things we had done, but people saw otherwise. I saw it as typically Purple. I think I had a big hand in writing it [laughs], and it was received with 'Well, we've moved on from that,' and it was left off the album. But it's made it back in the show. It's a terrific number, I think."

One of the characteristics of this set is that Ian Gillan is being a bit more off the wall than usual, with obscure stage raps, odd enunciation on "Highway Star," and even some chicken clucking during that track's solo trade with guitar. It's almost like he's performing a parody version of himself.

Don Airey, Coliseo Cubierto el Campín, Bogotá, Colombia, November 21, 2014. © *German Rojas / Factor Metal, Wikimedia Commons*

"I never quite know what he's going to say," laughs Don. "He doesn't quite know what he's going to say. He just opens his mouth and out it comes, stream of consciousness. Sometimes it's just pure rubbish. Which is very funny. So, we have no compunction about coming in with the next song, you know, just burst in with it. And sometimes he says something so funny, you don't like to come in. It's never the same. I don't think he ever says the same thing twice. It's like, 'What did he say?' And Steve, he's definitely very inspiring. He leads the charge, that's for sure. He's always coming up with new ideas all the time, the way he plays. We have a lot of fun up there, I don't know quite what to expect from him either, which keeps everything fresh and moving along."

Don figures that, personally, the most demanding moment of the show is his keyboard solo. "Yes, well, I have to gather all my synths around me and get all the channels up and get things moving. I find with the keyboard solo, it's quite different every night, but it moves to definite points. You have little musical markers along the way, which you head for. I'll often play a tantalizing glimpse of 'Mr. Crowley' for good measure. I've got quite a few sound effects that I use; there's a helicopter, jets flying past, bombs going off, and they all get mixed up. Sometimes they come in a different order. The classical bits . . . I didn't really do those with Ozzy. I used to do a bit with Gary Moore. I mean, Rainbow was the last time I had a really big keyboard solo, and this one is quite different to that one."

Also as part of the Montreux 2006 DVD is a club show, done to benefit a burned-down Hard Rock Café. "Oh, I didn't even know that was being recorded, to be honest with you," says Don. "The Hard Rock reopened in London. It burned down, they had a big fire, so they remodeled it. And the guy there, he's a big noise in the Hard Rock Café world, Don Bernstine. He used to be a record plugger for our management back in the old days. He said, 'Would Purple do it?' And we said no. Then they made us a silly offer, so we said yes. It was the most unlikely gig, really. It was very fun to do.

"Nobody's mentioned anything about that" is Don's answer when asked about the next studio album. "They're terribly English, very discreet, you know? And I don't know what's going to happen about that. And whether there will actually be one. I think if there is another record, it'll be something different. It won't be a straight ten new songs or whatever. There will be some angle to it."

In 2008, Don issued a crackin' solo album called *A Light in the Sky*, which mixed spirited, flashy instrumentals with killer hard rock anthems with vocals.

Remarks Don, "I really wanted to pay tribute to a lot of my influences over the years, and a bit of my history. You know, I started with a jazz rock band called Colosseum II, with Gary Moore, when we were young lads. And the Mahavishnu Orchestra were a big influence on me, so there was a little bit of that, with Lidia Baich, who played violin. There are tributes to Jon Lord, Keith Emerson, and Jimmy Smith, on the Hammond side, plus there are a few songs that recall my Rainbow days. That's really what I wanted to do. And I wanted something that had a theme to it that I was interested in—astronomy—that tied it all up. With Purple, the emphasis is Hammond, and there's a bit of piano, and of course I get to do a keyboard solo, which takes it all in. But it's largely Hammond based, which isn't a bad thing. But I think with my record, I really wanted to get back to playing some Moog synthesizers and get some different kinds of sounds, as well as the Hammond.

"The album is pretty much recorded live; that's where I wanted to get it, to a real live feel. We didn't rehearse. I just sent the tracks to the guys, the demos, and just went once through and hit record. The guitarist, Rob Harris, on the night we were to start recording, his wife went into the hospital and was having a baby. So, he didn't turn up. Actually, my favorite tracks are the ones recorded just as the trio—'Space Troll Patrol' and another one called 'Pale Blue Dot.' That's really the direction I wanted to go in, just organ, bass, and drums, with a heavy slant. Plus, I thought the title track turned out well.

"It's the hardest keyboard to play," continues Don, asked to explain the mystique of the Hammond. "You spend many years learning how to do it. It's a fine art, and you never get to the end of it. But it's something that can really compete with the guitar, in terms of sound. With Purple, I've got two Leslie cabinets. Plus, I've got a 100-watt guitar amp. I'm making quite a noise there."

Providing a brief history of the instrument, Don says that "they stopped making Hammonds in about '76. The company went bankrupt, I think, so they haven't made one since. Suzuki has the rights to it, and they make a digital Hammond, which is pretty good. But for the old sound, you've got to have an old Hammond. Fortunately, they made about a half million of the things, and a lot of them are in people's homes. People bought them in the '50s and the '60s for their homes, and now, of course, maybe the original player died off and there's a widow left. She's in her nineties, and so she wants to celebrate her one hundredth, so you can find these things.

"Hammonds are the most overengineered keyboards ever made," continues Don. "They last. I mean, my Hammond will last a lot longer than I will [laughs]. But I've actually got a few. When I joined Purple, I bought Jon Lord's Hammond. He said he was going in a different direction, and he kind of would leave it with the band. And now that particular Hammond has a long history. It belonged to Christine McVie of Fleetwood Mac. So, it's been on the road, to my knowledge, since 1967. And it hasn't had a lot done to it. They just go on and on and on. The Hammond I use now has been specially built for me. There's a place called the Hammond Store up in Connecticut, and there's a wonderful man named John Haburay who's in charge of it. He's made this a lot more travel-proof. He's put it in a new case and it's on these legs; I think it's called a chop. And he's modernized two Leslies. I've had this new instrument about a year now, and it gets better every year. Even the band's noticed that there's something going on [laughs]."

"But, as I say, they're impervious. They're not electronic; they're electric. It's valves. I think the only thing, if it's 'pervious' to anything [laughs], is being dropped. And even then, it survives. I mean, my new Hammond, the first gig of the European summer tour, in Saragossa, Ted Nugent went on before us. Have you seen when he does his rain dance? Well, he puts on his Indian headdress and off he goes, and my God, the most terrible thing happened. This wind whipped up and suddenly a hurricane arrived at the gig, and the stage had to be cleared. So, ferocious hailstorm, and all my keyboards were completely inundated. I thought all my brand-new gear was toast. But you know, we went to the next gig and put all the stuff out on the grass in the hot Italian sun and it worked again, including the Hammond. So, they're built like that. They're heavy for a reason.

"We're still using it," adds Airey, of the original Jon Lord machine. "We have a B rig; we're so busy that we have to leapfrog gear a lot. So, the Jon Lord one is in the B rig, but I don't think it likes being the B rig. I can feel the life coming out of it. You know, forty-two years in the service of British rock. I think I maybe have to get something else. I mean, the Hard Rock Café has made approaches to me many times for it, so it might just go there. You know, it's a glorious thing. It's called the Beast."

Into 2009, and Don obviously isn't afraid to speak his mind in the band. Fulminating over the next album, Don says, "I'd like to see it go heavier. You know, really back to their roots. I think there's been a lot of fanciful stuff on the albums, musician's music, which is all right, but I think the last album, *Rapture*, I really turned up the volume with the Hammond, and I think I really turned it *right* up. I think that's where it should go. I think that's what's appealing to people. We seem to be getting more young people at the gigs. It's a sea of young faces out there. Who probably know more of the words than Ian Gillan knows, which Ian would admit [laughs]. And you know, it's quite a festival now, every time we play. But for me, it's always been the same thing—I like to play heavy rock. You've got to have a great guitarist, going through a Marshall turned up to full. That's when the fun starts for me. You just get in the slipstream and enjoy the ride."

Ian Gillan also kept himself busy outside Purple, hatching a couple more solo albums. One was a rerecording of his greatest hits (and misses), issued in 2006 as *Gillan's Inn*, where he invited to the drinking establishment all manner of guest star to take a run at chestnuts from the likes of Purple, Gillan, Ian Gillan solo, and even a trashy Sabbath track.

"Somebody once suggested that I should celebrate forty years on the road, which coincides with my sixtieth birthday, in August," explained Ian, midprocess. "As far as the record was concerned, the original idea was to put a compilation together of some selected tracks from interesting periods in my life. The difficulty with that, of course, is that they're all on different record labels. So, we decided to rerecord them. It's very difficult to improve upon an original—you can't, really. No matter how good or bad it might be, it's implanted in people's minds that that's the way it should be.

"But we have certain advantages when we're rerecording, and that is, you're using the same musicians for all the songs, recording them in the same studio with the same producer. So, they have a kind of cohesion as an album. And we just finished, with the exception of some backing vocals and overdubs, and it sounds exhilarating—it's thrilling. We had a listen-back yesterday, and we had a playback party on Saturday.

"The musicians are mainly based in Buffalo, but a lot of my friends are guesting on the record, playing solos and things like that. Janick Gers, who is now with Iron Maiden, was with me in my band Gillan back in the '80s. There's Joe Satriani, who was with Purple for a year, between Ritchie Blackmore leaving and Steve Morse joining permanently. There's Jon Lord, who's not with us anymore but is still very active on the road, doing his own stuff. Tony Iommi, with Sabbath, who I was with for a year. And we're just talking to Luciano Pavarotti about singing the harmony line in the chorus to 'Smoke on the Water' [laughs]. Pavarotti's been great; he's a great friend. I've sung 'Nessum Dorma' with him twice, at benefit shows in Italy, dueted with him. He did a wonderful contribution."

The *Gillan's Inn* Deluxe Tour Edition CD booklet along with the obscure cover art chosen for *One Eye to Morocco*. *Martin Popoff archive*

Ian's other solo excursion, his last to date, was the more conventional *One Eye to Morocco*, from early 2009.

"Brilliant, amazing, best thing they've ever heard. Of course, this is only from the first two hundred journalists I've spoken to," laughs Ian, prompted for some sound bites. "These songs were written over about the last four or five years, and they were written on a few days when Steve Morris [guitarist, not to be confused with Steve Morse, although he always is] would come down for a few beers—'Oh, I've got a few ideas.' So, we would work on them over a day or two or three days, he goes home, we put five songs in the library. This happens a few times, and we ended up with thirty-eight songs in various stages of completion. Then he'd say, 'How about we do a collection of this? What about putting some of the songs together on a record?' And I said, 'Well, there's no chance. Purple is very busy, and I'm having a great time with the guys, so . . .'

"Unfortunately, Roger Glover's mother got ill and died last year," continues Ian. "So, we canceled a couple of tours so that Roger could spend the last few days with his mom in London. So, I headed to Buffalo, New York, and we started the selection process. We rehearsed the guys, we went into the studio, put the bed tracks and guide vocals down in three days, and finished up over the next week or so. All the songs were written under very relaxed circumstances. Now, grant you, my roots are probably showing, because without a rock rhythm section or any improvised guitar solos, which was the brief at the beginning of the sessions, probably in that undiluted form, you can hear all the influences that I went through when I was a kid—rhythm and blues, the rock 'n' roll, blues, the reggae, all that sort of thing. But it wasn't consciously done that way. I think it emerged, really, as quite a surprise to us all, when we gave birth to such a lovely child.

"I don't think anybody has been talking about a Deep Purple album at the moment," says Ian, dismissively—this was 2008. "We're just having such a great time on the road. There obviously is going to have to be one sooner or later. But that's the way Purple works, generally speaking. There are no real plans. We just do it when we're ready. Find a six-week period and just get in the studio. And it takes five or six weeks to do it. I'm sure there will be one, but well, no one has mentioned it. I've absolutely never enjoyed myself more than I have in the last few years."

A year later, Ian told me that "we're meeting up in Buenos Aires next week and the Czech Republic on Tuesday, I think. So, it did creep into the conversation a couple times. I'm fairly certain we'll be talking about that in the next week or two. We've got a fairly heavy year, but as I was saying earlier, I don't think we necessarily have to do an album all in one go this time. I would love to see the band in the studio in the near future, in the next three months, just to sort of sum up the logistical things, like who's going to be the producer, where we're gonna do it, whether we're going to do any prewritten songs rather than make it up on the spot. Those are a few of the things to expedite the whole process, I would think.

"When you don't prepare, you don't know what's going to happen, and so it really depends on what the dominant force is in the studio. What is the prevailing mood in the studio? You're very much subject to the fates. Whereas I've got an old saying, 'The only thing that costs absolutely nothing is planning.' Once you get into the process, you're into bucks. And I don't mean bucks as the be-all and end-all. What I mean is, you're actually spending time and spending money, and you reach a point of no return on that project. Because you're so far into it, you have to make

The "8. Musicos en la Naturaleza," Hoyos del Espino, Ávila, Spain, July 27, 2013.
© *Carlos Delgado, Wikimedia Commons*

it work. Well, that's okay; we're all professionals and we can do that. But I think it would be nice to have a little prepared ground, fertilize the field before we go in. Yeah, that would be my feeling."

My good buddy Jeb Wright from Classic Rock Revisited once asked Ian if there was a point in his career when he became more of a rock star than a musician. The latter is something on which Ian prides himself, partially based on the pure act of singing, yes, but bolstered by an intellectual curiosity for so much music wide across spectrums and also deep into history.

"You saved the hardest question till the end. I think after Purple started getting successful, I lost it. We all lost it; we all became rock stars. We all came from relatively humble backgrounds. I was pretty much starving. We were hungry from time to time. We were a good family, but that is just the way it was in England after the war. We were not prepared for either the adulation or the money. We were not prepared for the social graces that were expected of us. We behaved like assholes. We were creatures in certain ways. We had no experience of how to respond to success. When you're 18 to 20 years old and you're put in that position, without any thought of what might happen to you, and with a significant lack of advice.

"The managers didn't care about the individual well-being of the people they had in their chairs," continues Gillan, palpably angry. "They saw us as seasoned pros, but we were just kids. We had moved beyond the days of parents and good friends being advisors for us. We moved into a glittering world where all of the sudden our girlfriends were dispensed with. You would turn around and say, 'Who are you?,' and she would say, 'I'm your new girlfriend.' 'Nice tits, eh.' You have loads of money, limousines, and nice hotels. I had never stayed in a hotel in my life. I had never been in a restaurant in my life. It was an amazing culture shock, and I was an asshole. I think we all found it very difficult to do. All we had was our ego, which was being super-inflated. I think it took a few years to knock that out of us, and we each came out of it in different ways. I think we reached maturity during late youth / early middle age. Hopefully, for the last 20 years or so, we have had it knocked out of us. There was a time when I lost it completely. I looked around and everyone else was losing it. We were all drunk and acting like idiots. We were expected to act like that."

Coliseo Cubierto el Campín, Bogotá, Colombia, November 21, 2014. © *German Rojas / Factor Metal, Wikimedia Commons*

And no doubt, at the current vantage point, having taken it to the people far and wide, Ian must feel like the proverbial "citizen of the world."

"I feel like a traveling musician. I mean, how we look at it, we're lucky buggers. That's how we describe ourselves. World citizen? Not really. I am in a position, having traveled so much, to take a slightly objective view of different cultures and different lives, in the way of things, how they're disturbingly similar, but just different. So, all of those things have to remain euphemistically a little diplomatic, I'm afraid."

Asked whether he and his family coped with fame better than the other Purples, Ian says, "No. I mean, most women are happy that their husbands are working. Ha! You know, I've had this question before, and I've never known quite how to answer. And it just occurred to me that the answer is, we don't have the kind of families that want to be celebrities. Nobody in the band ever wanted to be famous. And nobody in the band—even worse—ever wanted to descend to the level of celebrity. Because we love our music, and we've got a good ethos there.

"So, the family structure's always been very strong. We haven't had wives who wanted to be in the picture, so to speak. So, we don't attend glamorous events; we're not in show business at all. I guess we're in the music business, because one can't go without the other. But yeah, they work really well. We've got long-surviving relationships here that . . . I guess it's like being in the navy or something like that, in the old days. But I've worked out . . . I'm home for about three months of the year. You add it up, and that's quality time. That's a lot more than the average partner and husband get in quality time, uninterrupted.

"You know, you get home . . . talking to my kid, when she was eight years old, that wonderful age, and she was saying, 'Daddy you're away so much.' So, we got a piece of paper out, and we just added it up and did the arithmetic. She went back to school, and she was waving this piece of paper around and saying, 'Hey, my dad's around a lot more than yours is.' It's just that he is away in lumps [laughs]. And he's home in lumps.

"So, once you explain it to your kids, what's going on, in fact you get better time with them. It works very well. Of course, they do get to go to some exotic places when they're quite young on holidays, to join up with us on a tour somewhere. That's always been a part of it. But it's never been a problem. And I think the reason is, as I say, there's no celebrity involved. We're not in the papers socializing all over the world when we're away. And the other thing, when we started, we used to have to send postcards [laughs]. And now we can get online every day. You can get on Skype, and you can see them and talk and everything—it's great.

"Life is life," muses Ian, "and it's been a fantastic life so far. Just take it a day at a time. I've met some amazing musicians and some great people, and I've got no regrets about any of it. And of course, you know I'll talk till the cows come home about any of it [laughs]."

The long wait for a new Deep Purple album would soon be over, when *Now What?!*, the band's nineteenth album, arrived on April 26, 2013. The band had shaken up things, recording in Nashville, Tennessee, at three different studios, but, most notably, working with a marquee producer for the first time; namely, Bob Ezrin.

Bob's résumé is impressive, beginning his career with Jack Richardson in Toronto, but soon finding himself overhauling the struggling Alice Cooper band, beginning with 1971's *Love It to Death*. He's worked with Lou Reed as well but then whipped Kiss into shape for 1976's *Destroyer*. Pink Floyd's *The Wall* and so much more would follow, with bands appreciative of Ezrin's skills on both sides of the board, including, pertinently, the deconstruction and reconstruction of songs.

Now What?! and *The Now What?! Live Tapes*, along with an ad for both releases

"It was actually wonderful working with him," Roger told me, two weeks before *Now What?!* was to hit the shops, even if since Deep Purple's last album, "the shops" had changed significantly, given that the compact disc had become antiquated technology.

"Obviously a man with such a track record demands a certain amount of respect, and when I first met him, that respect was well founded. I liked him immediately. He said very astute things about the band and how he saw us and asked us our opinion. When we got down to working with him, he was the admiral in charge of the ship, very much the man at the helm. He can be a bit abrasive. He makes decisions very quickly and gets things done. And, certainly, he didn't piss me off at all. It's good to get people stimulated like that. Very good decisions he made. He recognized that I was a producer as well, and he frequently talked to me about the production and what I thought, what he thought, and we hammered things out. So, he was very nice to me. Got on with him as a friend."

As for what bits of Bob's catalog got Roger interested in him, Roger says, "Everything. The fact that he'd done so many different things. You know, you can have producers who are essentially hard rock producers, and we're more than that, somehow, or maybe less than that, depending on your point of view. But having someone who speaks different languages is better than someone who speaks one. I say that speaking just English [laughs]."

And living in Switzerland.

"That's right [laughs]."

Asked about his ability to muck about inside the songs, Roger confirms, "Yes, he did some of that. We had a writing session. Well, we had two writing sessions before we went up to Nashville. We'd written the basic track ideas, and not too many vocals. When we got to Nashville, we had another little writing session, which he came to. And yes, he did say this should be at the front and not at the back, and he moved things around.

"There's a great concern in the band that when we make a record that it sounds good," continues Glover, asked about the overall personality of the new album. "The last record was disappointing, in its sound, its production. I get given a lot of CDs by bands, and when I get back from a tour and enter my suitcase, I've got twenty, twenty-five CDs of bands all wanting some help, whatever I can give them, I don't

know. I play them, and frequently they sound better than we do. And that was very much first and foremost, that it had to sound good.

"Beyond that, there's an unspoken thing that we didn't want it to sound like any other record that we've made. You never do, actually. Every record has its own character. But there was a feeling . . . when Bob came to see us in Toronto, he said some great things, one of which was 'Forget trying to get a big hit on the radio and be all that. That's all over. Just be who you are.' He says, 'You're great musicians and you have great spontaneity. I want to capture that in the studio.' But having some time to actually prepare ourselves a bit more, we went in the studio knowing the songs. So, playing them live was easy. All the songs are played live. Everything that's there is live. Aside, I'd say, from overdubs, which are added later. But essentially the tracks are all live, and I think that gives it a great spontaneity and freshness and feel. I think he captured a great sound as well."

Asked if he thought the band was increasingly progressive on *Now What?!*, Roger pushes back.

"I wouldn't say that at all. What I would say is that Don Airey and Steve Morse are unbelievably prolific players, and that's very difficult to hold back. They'll always throw something in that, to them, is just a piece of music. Other people will probably see it as prog. It's just making music that is more interesting. But there was a desire to get more simple kind of themes going on this album. Almost more riffs, as it were, than clever bits. But it's hard, as I say, to hold them back. Because as soon as you write something simple, it frequently gets complicated."

As for the profusion of parts and sounds and performances out of Don Airey in particular, Roger figures, "He's grown into the band. He's been in the band ten years now, and I think he's in a great frame of mind. He really feels like he's in the band, not so much an interloper. And he's got strong ideas."

But *Now What?!* also sounds like it would be a fun album for a bass player.

"Absolutely," agrees Roger. "It's a great album to play on. I use a Vigier guitar; I've used them for years now. But Bob came in and he said, 'Oh, do you want to try my guitar?' I said, 'What's that?' He says, 'I've got a Precision.' And I haven't played a Precision on an album since, I think, 1970. So, he brought his in, and it has these really dull strings on it. I said, 'Well, I'll give it a go, but you'll have to change the strings.' He says, 'Don't change the strings!' He says, 'That's a legendary bass. It's been on *The Wall*; it's been on Peter Gabriel; Alice's albums; it's been on loads of albums.' Tony Levin's played it, for example. He said don't touch the strings. Anyway, okay, and it sounded wonderful. And I've never pushed the bass up in my own production as much as he did. So that was a lesson to me, how much he used the bass in the forefront."

"A big change was having Bob Ezrin come in," seconds Steve Morse, speaking with Shawn Perry from *Vintage Rock*. "I worked with him on the last Kansas album [*In the Spirit of Things*] when I was in the group, and he showed that he can make things happen, put things together with some real guidance. At that time, in Kansas, we really needed it, and I felt like Deep Purple did too. We needed to change a few things about the way that we were recording. The whole sound of the band was, I think, a big improvement, by putting the vocals and drums as part of the mix as opposed to right on top of the mix. It makes it more like a band to me.

Roger Glover at the "8. Musicos en la Naturaleza," Hoyos del Espino, Ávila, Spain, July 27, 2013.
© *Carlos Delgado, Wikimedia Commons*

"Bob was absolutely phenomenal in terms of the preproduction," continues Morse. "We had so many ideas and so many songs for this album that it really became 'What do we do? What do we choose from?' Bob has a very colorful mind, and he was able to keep track of about 20 different songs and their progress, and whether he liked the lyric direction or the melodic direction or whatever. As we worked on them, he would drop in on rehearsals and he would sometimes just sit in the corner and act like he wasn't listening. Then all of a sudden, you'd hear him yell out, 'I'm not liking this' or 'I love it,' little comments like that. He would get intensely into it sometimes with us.

"Bottom line is, he was able to really be the bad guy in terms of no, this goes, this stays. It saved us from having to go through that, and kind of arguing amongst ourselves. So there was an overabundance of things to choose from, and he ultimately, as a producer, did what probably producers are supposed to do all the time, which probably gave it a little bit of direction too. The big thing that was different was we spent more time in preproduction and with a very intense producer who was really able to keep track of something."

When Shawn asks about his effect on direction, Steve says, "He would come in while we were working on the stuff and he would say, 'No, no, no, no; we've gotta have more of this and less of that.' It was specific enough direction, and so much of it that everyone felt he should be included in the credits. I don't know exactly lyrically, but I know musically he was making a lot of suggestions about 'Do this, do that, take that part out' or 'That's too busy' or 'Morse, tone it down.'"

"I think the mission was clearly to put the deep back in Deep Purple," laughs Ezrin, asked to articulate his personal mission as it pertains to this late-career feather in the cap. "I didn't come into this thinking that I had a mission. I came into this a little bit reluctantly, thinking that they were looking to me to make a contemporary rock album with Deep Purple, which I didn't feel was appropriate or could be done in an honest way.

"But when I met with the guys, after seeing their live show, and seeing especially the big jam that they do in the middle of the show, which was just masterful, virtuosic, I realized that there was that original essence of Deep Purple that people hadn't heard on record in a long time, and that if they wanted to do that sort of thing, I was really into doing it with them. I think it was Roger who actually used the phrase 'Put the deep back in Deep Purple.' Which was music to my ears, if you'll forgive the pun. So, once we figured that that would be the mission, then I was interested. I was interested in doing an album that didn't have to tick all those boxes that modern records have to tick, that didn't have to have the big single, that didn't have songs that were four minutes or four minutes and twenty seconds and no longer. That didn't have to restrict the length of solos, that didn't have to watch what it talked about and try to conform to current trends and fashion. They said they didn't want to do that either, and so there we were, on the same page, and ready to rock."

It's surprising there wasn't a clash of personalities. Deep Purple are pretty strong willed about what they want. Bob Ezrin is pretty strong willed about what he wants.

"Well, from my point of view, there was no clash at all," avows Bob. "From my point of view, we were on the same page from that first meeting forward. And obviously, they're used to a certain way of doing things. Roger has been the producer of the band, and producer of some of my favorite records, actually, so I have a huge amount of respect for him. But a dentist can't pull his own teeth, I don't think. It's a good thing to have somebody come in and work with you, especially if you're a band like we're talking about here, multiple personalities and tastes and styles, all coming together. It's always good to have an objective arbiter coming in. So, I just walked in and started to play that role. And he seemed to be immediately comfortable in having someone do that. I never felt uncomfortable. I would say that from our first encounter, we were playing our roles and having a really good time doing it."

With Roger assuaged and sufficiently and deftly deferred to by the Canadian, we can forget about him—he's fine. But what about Don Airey? The new guy is all over the *Now What?!* album.

"Well, I can't take credit for getting so much out of him," demurs Ezrin. "The main thing, if anything, you have to try to stop him. This guy is a fount of musical brilliance. I think from the time he wakes up in the morning until the time he goes to bed, there is just genius music pouring out of him. He was so impressive. But this wasn't a conscious effort on my part to give Don the spotlight. I didn't come into this with the intention of spotlighting anybody. But the band got together and were writing and were playing. I just picked the stuff that I liked, and there was so much of it. We did consciously determine that stretching instrumentally, the way they do it live, was something we would shoot for on this record. Like, we haven't heard that kind of stuff on record for a very long time. Certainly not from a quote, unquote mainstream rock band."

Forget Don—he's just the genius keyboardist. Where *Now What?!* really excels is in the literary department. Like so much of Purple songs recently past—all of the Morse era certainly—there's a wistful wealth of substance all over the album, a rich accounting for the earned wrinkles of advanced years. Bob got involved in this department as well.

"Yes, I did," confirms Ezrin, which earned him sixth-member status in the writing credits for every damn song on the record. "I always get involved in the lyric writing. I think Ian Gillan is a particularly special human being. Let's see if I can say this in an economical way: all right, so, I think Ian Gillan is a fascinating human being with an amazingly rich life, and a huge amount of experience to draw on. So having him write from his own point of view, for the record, to me, was a no-brainer. I didn't want to change anything. I didn't want to force him into a more quote, unquote contemporary or commercial point of view. I love his storytelling; I love his point of view. All I did was push him to work as hard as he could to make it as good as it absolutely could be.

"Sometimes, for the lyricist, it's very difficult," continues Bob, very likely unaware of the amusingly strangulated wordplay Ian scatters like fool's gold all over Gillan records such as *Future Shock* and *Double Trouble*. "They write something, they turn their guts inside out, they write something down on a piece of paper, and then they sing it. And sometimes it sings really well, and sometimes it just doesn't sing quite as well as they would like. So, it's important to have somebody like me that can help them to work a little harder in certain areas, and maybe give them a bit of direction to help them clear up some of the problems. I've been fortunate in my career to work with some of the greatest lyricists of all time. I missed a few, but not many [laughs]. I always consider it an honor and a privilege to work with people who are just this brilliant; I take that very seriously. It's kind of like . . . what's the word I'm looking for? I don't want to sound too pretentious, but it's a bit of a sacred responsibility.

You have to honor the intention of the writer while you're also trying to help the writer to do even better than they think they can."

Now What?! is also a production tour de force, an album of warm and visceral tones. Together, Bob Ezrin and Don Airey achieve, much better than on recent albums, the melding of Don's grinding keys to the guitars, strengthening that sort of rhythm guitar role the now dearly departed Jon Lord used to play.

"It was fairly obvious," reflects Bob. "I think the idea was to try to capture the vibe and energy I saw them exhibit onstage. So, I created an environment for that where they were effectively playing live—they could all see each other; they could all hear each other. We recorded everybody together at the same time. Obviously, we went back and fixed a few things here and there, and we went back later on to do our final vocals. But Ian was singing along with them the whole time that we were recording. The approach was to not be too clinical during the recording, but to save that for the editing phase and, in the recording, really concentrate on getting great performances. Of course, by the time we got into the studio, everybody had each other's trust, and it was okay for me to come out on the horn and say, 'Let's start playing this,' and the band would do it instantly. They are so good. And so smart.

Steve Morse, Coliseo Cubierto el Campín, Bogotá, Colombia, November 21, 2014.
© *German Rojas / Factor Metal, Wikimedia Commons*

"*Made in Japan*—that was a watershed album," says Bob, asked about a past magic map to help get him and the band to that place. "That was, for me, the best analog to what I was trying to achieve on this record, because it's a really great liveish performance. As I say, many of the tracks you're listening to on this album were just that—they were live performances. We may have added a track or two of overdubs to it, but these guys can play that. They can play it every day of the week. Which is really remarkable. So you know, it was great to see them stretch as far as they wanted to go. And I think they really enjoyed the experience."

Asked about Steve's contribution, Bob calls him "a virtuoso, and a supreme practitioner, a technician. I don't know what the nonartistic terms are for somebody who can do anything. But then on top of that, his soloing is kind of southern—he's a southern-rock guy. I think that's really where his soul lives. And when you look at southern rock, some of the stuff we all point at as classic—even though there's a lot of kind of high energy to it, and a certain strut, and a particular groove to it all—there's also very once in a while a very lyrical side to it. When you look at songs like 'Free Bird,' that could never have come from anywhere but the South. I think the whole southern-rock thing had a huge influence on Steve. And so, his playing style reflects a lot of that, but amped up to a much-higher level than just about anybody else who can play.

"The other thing about Steve is that he has a huge amount of nervous energy, as do most geniuses," ventures Bob. "I'd say, if we checked Steve's IQ, he would probably come out at the other side of the scale altogether. He's firing on more neurons at once than whole townships. So, he does tend to perform a lot of tasks in a short period of time. And that does come into his musical life. So, I did have to pull him back a little bit on certain songs, tried to get him to just concentrate on the melodic. I think he said in some of his interviews that I'm used to working with more-melodic guitar players and all that stuff. Yes, that's true, but I think Steve is actually more melodic than he realizes. And then if you can just get him to take a deep breath and hold back a little bit, he comes up with the most-magnificent and uplifting melodies, beautiful melodies."

"He was the catalyst for getting us back in the studio after seven years," affirms Ian Gillan, asked about Ezrin by Ray Shasho. "We were quite happily drifting on. It would come up in conversation now and again about a new album: 'Yeah, man, maybe next year, maybe next year.' But he reminded us of a few things. He came out to see us in Canada. We were on a tour there in February 2012, and it was quite a good conversation. Everyone started remembering who we are and what we do. Primarily we're an instrumental band, and he said just concentrate on the music and just let it develop as you used to. Don't worry about three- or four-minute tracks; they're not going to play it on the bloody radio anyway. Just make your music. That was the trigger. So, we arrived in Nashville for the writing session in great shape. Having been through a very long, unsettling period, there was a great empathy among musicians, almost like a family again. So, the music came quickly and the whole thing was written in four weeks. Then we took another four weeks to record it.

"Bob's a great musician as well as a great technician," continues Gillan. "The first time we went there, we went to see the Nashville Symphony. We listen to a lot of jazz, blues, and rock 'n' roll. Bob's got the same taste in music as us, which is diverse. I don't think anyone in the band listens to what you call genre music or anything like that; I listen to a whole variety of stuff when I'm at home. So, it was great having him on board with his experience, of course. He immediately became a member of the band. There was a great deal of mutual respect, and that helps a lot when you're expecting someone to guide you along. He encouraged us to be expressive, which was a good thing, and at the same time he held on quite tightly to the reins and steered us in the right direction without us even being aware of it. It was a very subtle and manipulative job, but I give Bob Ezrin a lot of credit. I can't obviously say anything about the music, because it's too subjective. But what I can say with confidence is that this is the best-sounding Deep Purple record that we've ever made by a long shot."

In conversation with Nicolas Gricourt from *Radio Metal*, Ian adds some detail with respect to the construction of the album.

"Firstly, two or three of the guys had a writing session in Germany in May 2012 for a few days. The record was then written in America, in Nashville, Tennessee. It took about four weeks to write it. It's been some years since we made the previous record. The atmosphere was fantastic, and the circumstances were very good. We weren't really in any rush to make another album. Our producer had us all mentally organized for the recording process. He'd said that our first records had only seven tracks on them, and it was all right to make a six-, seven-, eight-, nine-, or ten-minute song, because that's what we used to do.

"We thought, oh yes, of course. We realized that the formula—introduction, two verses, chorus, guitar solo—had maybe become a bit boring. There wasn't any real sense of adventure in the songs. As Bob lives in Nashville, we started to work there with his engineers in his recording studio that he knows very well. The temperature was hot—it was a 110 degrees Fahrenheit—and the atmosphere was great; everyone was really excited! Since the last record, we've been working constantly, which is good, because the band's become very close and the improvisation that happens onstage every night is almost second nature. You never know what can happen, but there's a kind of empathy between the guys."

Asked by Nicolas about the degree of freedom the band enjoyed, Ian says, "Yes, it was inherent in the studio's atmosphere. There were no rules. We started with nothing, except the right attitude—that's all. Every day it was the same routine: the guys walked in at noon, and we all worked until 6:00 o'clock on the writing sessions. We just stopped at 3:00 o'clock for a cup of tea. After 6:00 o'clock, we would go home, have a shower, some dinner, and go to bed early, even if I'm always up in the middle of the night writing lyrics. We start at 10:00 o' clock the next morning when we're recording. But the writing is always noon until six. It starts with nothing. Ian and Roger would start jamming, playing for an hour nonstop and trying out some rhythms or grooves. They would stop and say, 'No, that's not good' and then start something else and say, 'Remember that; maybe on Thursday we'll try this again and maybe it'll be a song.' Everything emerged from jamming sessions.

"It's always that way," shrugs Ian. "The compositions have always been free and easy. But when it comes to the arrangements, perhaps we've fallen into the trap, in recent years, of being too predictable. Now we have complete freedom, both in the songs and in the arrangements. When I write a tune, it sometimes drives me crazy, because it's like riding on the back of a wild horse: I don't know where it's going. It's like, why this extra bar and a half here? And the key change; why this unrelated key? How can I sing if this is not normal? Of course, we don't want to be normal. I'm fitting in somehow and picking up again on the next version, and somehow it works. On *Now What?!*, it's been fantastic, but for sure, there has been a change in the attitude with the arrangements."

In the end, there was an abundance of material.

"Probably 30 or 40 songs," says Ian. "They all didn't reach completion because they weren't satisfactory or good enough. We expected to put nine or ten songs together, as they were long. When vinyl finished, the optimum time for sound quality was 38 minutes, and this was for technical reasons. When CDs came along, you could make an hour or longer of music. Everybody was like, 'I want an hour of music! I want value for the money!' And quantity sometimes prevailed on quality. We only put the songs on that were up to standard."

When Nicolas asked if the new album was begging for a big-name producer to take the reins, Gillan says, "Mostly, the record was begging for a good sound. In my personal opinion, we have never, ever achieved what we should have achieved, in terms of sound quality. Music, lyrics, and performance are different stories and have been satisfactory.

"The idea of Bob Ezrin, a top-class producer, was fantastic for me. When I walked in the studio on the first morning, after hearing the sound check, I nearly cried, it was so wonderful. I was so happy to hear clearly the power and also the perfect balance between the guitar and the Hammond organ, which has always been the distinctive sound of our band. There's a part of the sound spectrum where they overlap quite a lot, and that's always been a problem, because then you get distortion, for example. They fight with each other for space. You either bring one down to give the other one dominance, or separate them stereo-wise, in which case you lose the punch and power. Somehow, he managed to solve these problems. I don't know how, and that's why he's an expert producer and why his studio is so fantastic. He had separation and power. It was exactly everything I had dreamed of. From that moment, we were in complete confidence. Bob Ezrin's name is of course significant, because he's very successful. Obviously, people are fascinated with his history. But again, mostly it was a question of sound."

Deep Purple is no stranger to irritating album titles, but *Now What?!* is the nuttiest of them all (until we get to *Whoosh!* and then *=1*, that is!). But typed like that, that's just what we've settled on, in terms of talking about it. The spine of the CD says *NOW What?!*, and the front cover says *NOW What*, with a big ol' *?!* plunked in the middle of the page. They even changed the name of the band—it's now called Deep ?urp!e. At least they chose the punctuation correctly, because when you do that, it's question mark first, followed by exclamation mark, and only one of each.

I asked Roger if any of this was discussed, to which he replied, "No, not really. We don't talk about a lot." Flying right past the point, Roger adds, "I remember one of the key thoughts, the key philosophies of the band, when I first joined it in 1969,

Additional shots from Coliseo Cubierto el Campín, Bogotá, Colombia, November 21, 2014.
© *German Rojas / Factor Metal, Wikimedia Commons*

Deep Purple

More shots from the "8. Musicos en la Naturaleza," Hoyos del Espino, Ávila, Spain, July 27, 2013, plus a bonus *Now What?!*–era guitar pick. © *Carlos Delgado, Wikimedia Commons*

is if they love us, great, if they hate us, great. Some people are going to love us; some people are going to hate us."

In any event, of course it has some kind of justification. "You can see what you like in it, really. Ian Gillan came up with it, very early on, along with the question mark and the exclamation mark. Actually, no one knew what to make of it. I didn't like it at first, and then I grew to like it. Then I didn't like it again, and we all kept coming up with titles that just didn't stand a chance, really. And by this time, [since] the record company had seen it and loved it, we kind of went, oh, whatever—it's whatever it will be. And I love it now. Because I think if we called it *Negated Paradise of Armageddon* or something, it's still like an average title. This is not an average title. It's a title that leaps out at you. And for that reason, I think it's great."

As explained to Ray Shasho, Ian Gillan says, "I designed it originally. There's us guys reluctant to go into the studio. We keep getting nudged: 'Go on and make another record.' 'No, no, we're fine, having a great time.' Every night is a big adventure. And it's like, the phone rings and you go, 'Now what?!' Eventually you have to do what is demanded. So, it's kind of a grumpy reaction to constant prodding by the record label and by management etc. I just doodled around with it one day on the computer, and it kind of caught on. I guess it was just a phrase that seemed right at the time. As with everything, our album is a collection of ideas that represent that moment in time."

As we finally sidle up to the band's first album in eight years, *Now What?!* opens quiet and contemplative, with Ian lamenting the passage of time. But at the two-minute mark, "A Simple Song" explodes into full-band action, very heavy, with Ian's words getting more obscure and at the same time more panicked, in accordance with the urgent music. The ending brings us back to the opening meditative salvo.

Next is "Weirdistan," another thumping rocker, and not particularly weird.

Says Roger, "We were working on a song, and various people in the band kind of shouted out what the working title should be. And this one title was 'Weirdistan.' Don shouted that out, and I thought, 'Weirdistan?' Don kept coming up with strange titles. Anyway, when it came to writing the words, we thought 'Weirdistan' was actually a great title, but what are we going to write about? And we spent a long time on that session, about a day and a half, writing the song. And then we got to Nashville, Gillan and I, and finished a couple of songs, and we thought, well let's try 'Weirdistan,' because the riff is great. So, I picked up an acoustic and I was just going over the tune with Ian. Bob was sitting at the back of the studio at the computer, and all we heard was 'I'm not liking this.' What? He said, 'I'm not liking this.' And we said, 'You haven't even heard it yet. Give it a go.' 'No, I'm not liking that.' And we thought, oh dear [laughs]. But we did have a couple of other ideas, and he joined in with that, and yes, he wrote enough on the album to warrant a credit."

I asked Roger if the title had anything to do with the fact that it's got a strange sound picture when it comes to the riff. It's hard to tell whether it's just some kind of distorted bass or a low-register soup made up of bass, keyboards, and guitar.

"No on the title, but yes, there is. I'm not sure what he did. He did that in the mix. He just crudded it up somehow. I used the Vigier on some songs, and the Precision on others."

As for the lyrics, Glover explains that "our first thought was we're writing about a place called Weirdistan, where everything is really strange. Oh, okay, that's a nice open theme for a piece of lyric. And we did actually write the whole song, and Bob didn't like it. So, we'd started all over again. Well, not all over again—we kept certain bits. Ian and I write together, or sometimes I write in the morning. He gets up early, or I do, and we write separately. Then we meet in the studio and compare notes, that kind of thing. We were looking for the verse, and Ian came in with the lyrics that are on there. I thought they were stunning. As it turned out, the song is about cultural differences and how we should accept different cultures and not condemn them for it. That's an enormous theme for a song. It's about bigotry and xenophobia, being scared of another person because they're a different color or a different religion or different shape. And to write a song about that, I thought, was a great achievement."

Defends Bob on his original mauling of the song, "There was a lot of stuff where somebody would say, 'I'm not sure' or 'I really love this.' Everybody got a chance; that was the thing. It's not important for me to be right. It's important for the album to be right. I tell everybody that I work with, at the very beginning, I always say, I love to be wrong. I love that. I love it when I feel something very strongly and the band fights with me and they win. Why? Because they do something, then, that's better than I could've even thought of. That to me is a blessing.

"So, with 'Weirdistan,' I didn't get it, because I just thought the repetition of the riff was a bit too much, and I didn't know where the vocal was going to be. It wasn't until the final lyrics started to come together that I started to realize it. Plus, the story and the meaning gave the thought a reason to be. And then, actually, we could really work on how we dealt with the sound, all that sort of stuff. So, he's right. We were just playing the music, and I wasn't there yet. But when Roger and Ian returned to Nashville for vocals, I started digging that song, with that lyrical approach and that point of view. It started to make sense then, and I really fell in love with it."

"Out of Hand" is another stomping hard rock track. It's distinguished by a sort of Middle Eastern vocal melody from Ian, but it's dominated by a smothering, almost doom metal riff from Steve.

I asked Roger about Steve Morse and how he's changed over the years, now that he's no longer the new guy.

"How has he changed?" reflects Roger. "Well, I think, he hasn't changed a lot. He still feels like he's the outsider of the band. Even though he's been in the band twenty years now. Probably because he's American and we're not. No, that's a huge thing. But I think he really enjoys himself, playing with us; that's for sure. And I think he's reined in a lot of his virtuoso chromatic-scale kind of stuff. He's reined a lot of that in on this record. The criticisms do sting. He's been criticized a lot for that, when people like to go widdly-diddly. Well, you know, take it or leave it—Steve is who he is. And to have him—or to want him to—sound like someone else is kind of wrong. But what he does offer is incredible virtuosity. As far as I'm concerned, that's got to be a Purple trademark. You start off with Ritchie on the one hand and Jon on the other, you've got to have that balance, for us. That is our character. They have to be virtuosos. We can't just be regular ol' players. So, with every virtuoso, you're going to get difficulties. Virtuosic people generally aren't easy to get along with. But Steve is easy to get along with, as long as we live in the same world with him."

"Hell to Pay" is a baffling story and not the greatest of musical tracks. It sort of bides time at the verses and then goes downhill, en route past a substandard prechorus toward an even less enjoyable chorus, with Ian awkwardly going, "There's gonna be hell, hell to pay." It's a strange choice for a single, and an advance one at that, emerging on April Fools' Day 2013, as the second of fully five singles floated from the album.

"Body Line" is one of those bubbling, boiling, percolating songs that make you wonder why Deep Purple isn't considered one of the great funk bands. "Very sexy song, that one," says Ian.

Next is "Above and Beyond," which was issued as a single on October 24, 2013, deep into the album's life cycle. It's approximately a progressive-metal song, not unlike something Porcupine Tree would do, given the light and shade, the odd time signatures, and the geometric heavy metal riffing marbled throughout.

Explained Steve to Shawn Perry, "On 'Above and Beyond,' I kind of planned that out beforehand musically. I didn't have any vocals. I just said, 'Here's what I think the vocals would be.' I actually prefer if I and the other band members don't really bring in tunes. That one I just couldn't stop working on until I got that finished, because I actually thought we were doing that with horns and strings and stuff, like an orchestral little kind of prelude. I imagined that as a prelude to the album.

"Normally, what we do is Ian Paice might start the day by just playing a beat," continues Morse. "We jam along with it and noodle along for about 15 to 20 minutes, and out of that will come something. We'll take that and Don runs with it, or I run with it, and sometimes we run in different directions, but we always have ideas on the spot. What Ian Paice and Roger often are doing is refereeing that. 'No, no, no; I don't know about that, I think you need to play this, you're getting off the track.' And Don and I are like, 'Yeah, we can do *this*' and, "Yeah, but what about *that* and what about *this*?' There's always this back-and-forth thing between restraint and unbridled instrumental excess, as some people would refer to it.

"At the bottom of this is the same roots we all have, which is the love for basic roots music," affirms Steve. "It's an interesting blend. Ian Gillan will kind of give a thumbs-up or thumbs-down based on gut instinct. Then he'll just disappear and start working on lyrics. He'll pop back in, get refreshed about the tune, and then walk away and write more lyrics. He's kind of like an apparition—he's there and he's gone, he's there and he's gone. So yeah, we have a weird dynamic, but it works. The bottom line is, everybody really appreciates that everybody's involved. It makes it something unique that we couldn't do unless everyone was involved."

"'Above and Beyond' is a track that's got Jon Lord's spirit in there," explained Ian Gillan, speaking with Ray Shasho. "I had written the lyrics, or almost finished the lyrics, when we heard the news about Jon dying. We kind of sat around the studio and then started talking about the good old days and some good memories of Jon. It was just like when my dad died, actually. His body went away and then suddenly his spirit just filled me up, and he has been traveling with me ever since. The same thing kind of happened with Jon. He filled the room, and I wrote these words, 'Souls, having touched, are forever intertwined.' I sang them at his funeral and then I included them in the song, which was finished pretty much apart from that line. But when I wrote those words, it all made sense, and there was Jon Lord singing to us all."

Musically speaking, adds Ian, "The song is kind of a burlesque waltz in three-four time and has a glorious key change. I just find it spiritually uplifting, and I think it's definitely going to be in the show. It's difficult to pin down our kind of music. Somebody was saying early on, 'You're playing Wacken in Germany this summer; it's the biggest heavy metal rock festival in Europe, just a huge annual event.' And they said, 'Does Deep Purple fit into that heavy metal thing?' Two weeks before that, we're headlining the Montreux Jazz Festival—go figure."

With Nicolas Gricourt, talking about the song, he says that it was Ian Paice who came into the room and informed everybody about Jon's passing. As alluded to, Lord had passed due to pancreatic cancer on July 16, 2012, having been diagnosed in July of the previous year, thereafter undergoing treatment both in Israel and England. He was seventy-one years old. In the end, Lord had realized his ambitions for leaving Deep Purple in the first place, and that was to become a fully working and recording classical-music musician.

"We were expecting it, but it was still shocking," says Ian. "So, we were quiet for a little while, and then we started talking about the old days, about some anecdotes concerning Jon and reminiscing some humorous stuff. The mood was very light: it wasn't dark. Jon's spirit was filling the room, and we could feel his presence. That's why I wrote that line. 'Above and Beyond' is about physical and spiritual departure, but I didn't have a clear focus on the exact meaning of this departure. Suddenly, when I wrote that line, I realized it was about death, and all the rest of the song made complete sense. All of a sudden, it was Jon Lord singing the song to us. It was absolutely perfect."

"Blood from a Stone" is a slinky sort of ballad, but for a resoundingly heavy chorus. Again, Don is pervasive and pervasively entertaining, giving the song a Doors vibe, as does Roger's loping bass line. The song dances between the spaces of blues and jazz, but back to earlier remarks about arrangements and production, the dynamics are impressive and high fidelity, with ear candy everywhere from the tones and textures.

Next is "Uncommon Man," the longest song on the album at seven minutes. It's got an involved, atmospheric build, and just before the song proper kicks off, dramatic tribal drums. Once we're into it, it's an incredibly creative rocker with strange chords and dovetailed guitars and keys creating the composite. The signature Don Airey lick, inspired by "Fanfare for a Common Man," played by Deep Purple becomes prog rock, like ELP or U.K. or Asia. But the unifying strength of the track is the straight-lined vocal melody from Ian, and his touching but spare lyric in tribute to Jon Lord, a second one on the album.

Notes Bob, "The most exciting moment on the recording side might have been when we cut 'Uncommon Man.' That intro on 'Uncommon Man,' that's a gem, live off the floor, and it was the first one! That was it. And that convinced me. I thought, okay, we've got it [laughs]. It was amazing. And how it transitioned, the minute that we heard the transition, from that intro into the song, it was so uplifting. But you know what? I said, in our first meeting, we agreed that we would be unashamedly prog [laughs]. You know, why fight it? That's who we are, right? That's who this band is. They come from that era, and they can play that—they're an old prog-blues band. They could play that stuff better than anybody alive, so why shouldn't we?"

With "Après Vous," we're back into typical, muscular, midtempo, heavy metal Deep Purple, propulsive and explosive from the drums on up, buttressed by another circular Steve Morse riff in the vicinity of the one heard on "Out of Hand" and Ritchie's dozen or so variants on the theme. Get to the verse and it's basically one chord, but Don and Steve are dive-bombing each other relentlessly, keeping it interesting.

"All the Time in the World" is a form of midtempo pop song, vaguely bluesy, but with unexpected, sophisticated chords come chorus time. Adding interest is the steel guitar performance from Mike Johnson, with Eric Darken providing additional percussion and Jason Roller playing acoustic guitar. The song was issued as the first single from the album, in advance of the full record by a month. It's definitely one of those songs that had you heard it on the radio would give the wrong impression.

"You'd have to ask the record company about that," says Roger. "Yeah, it wouldn't have been my choice. But then again, 'Smoke on the Water' wasn't my choice either. I know nothing about that. I know nothing about the selling of music. They felt, I guess, that 'All the Time in the World' would get play on the softer stations, the Radio 2s of the world. I don't know what their plan was. They're a great company and they really believe in this record. But I thought to myself, how did they come to that decision? I can only think that they had a meeting of all the staff and said, 'Right, what are your feelings?' I have no idea. I thought at first, you know, that's not a good thing to put out. But then I thought, it's certainly going to make the album much more of a blitzkrieg when it does come out."

Two issues of the "Vincent Price" single

The last track on the album, "Vincent Price," was also issued as a single, and it's no wonder—it's a rare novelty song from Deep Purple, a sort of Hammer Horror rocker, flashy and fun.

"Again, a working title," explains Roger. "What's this going to be called? And Don said, 'Oh, "Vincent Price."' You'd have to ask him why; I don't know why. But when it came to writing the lyrics, we thought, actually, that's not a bad title. So, what's Vincent Price known for? The genre of horror movies. So, we thought we'd write a horror movie, and from the point of view of the director of a horror movie—what ingredients would we want? [laughs]. Like you say, it's Hammer films. And of course, the irony is that Bob Ezrin produced Alice Cooper. So, we said to Bob, 'Have fun with it; put all the sound effects you want.' And we thought he did great."

"I really liked doing the sound effects on 'Vincent Price,'" adds Ezrin, picking up the thread. "That was pretty fun, especially since it's a little bit of a full circle for me, because I worked with Vincent Price with Alice Cooper. I'm actually the guy who walked up to Vincent Price and said, 'Mr. Price, how would you like to make your rock 'n' roll debut?' [laughs]. So, for me, that was really great to be able to do that."

"Every song that we start to develop has a working title," Ian Gillan explained to Ray Sasho. "It's not necessarily the one we end up with, but it has a working title. This sounded like a horror movie, so we called it 'Vincent Price.' We've all worked with Vincent Price over the years in different ways. Roger flew over to Portugal to fine-tune the lyrics, and so we said what would a film director want as essential ingredients in a horror movie in the '60s with Vincent Price? So, we started a list: thunder and lightning, chains rattling, creaking gates, dogs howling, vampires, sacrificial virgins, zombies. And hang on a second—the song is finished. We just put a list of film clichés, and it seemed to work perfectly." Speaking with Nicolas Gricourt, Ian said, "It's just a comedy, but in a satirical comedy way. We all knew Vincent Price; we met him. So, it's kind of personal too."

That was it for the regular *Now What?!* album, but there were multiple variants of the record to keep the dedicated Deep Purple fan on his toes. A song written by Jack Clement and performed by Jerry Lee Lewis in 1957 called "It'll Be Me" was a special-edition bonus track. It's as expected—namely, an energetic, loud 'n' proud Deep Purple arrangement of a traditional rock 'n' roll number, with Don playing honky-tonk saloon piano, of course. The other fully non-LP song used as a bonus was "First Sign of Madness," which is actually similar to the Jerry Lee Lewis number, up tempo, same sort of piano work, but with a stock Deep Purple riff from Steve added.

All told, there were deluxe editions, gold editions, Japanese issues, and even a "gold deluxe edition" that contained a whole extra disc featuring a dozen live tracks from the 2013 European campaign.

As expected, the band shifted only a modest number of copies of *Now What?!* stateside, although the album did make the official Billboard charts, at #110. But Germany responded very favorably, sending the album gold, for over 100,000 copies sold. Additionally, the album hit #1 on the German charts. In Russia, sales topped 25,000, with Putin's second in command, Dmitry Medvedev, being a famous Russian fan of the band. When *Now What?!* came out, Medvedev was in fact prime minister of Russia, previously having been president of Russia.

On October 4, 2012, the nominees for the 2013 induction into the Rock & Roll Hall of Fame were announced, and Deep Purple was on the list. By December, the winners were announced, and Deep Purple weren't included. Shawn Perry from *Vintage Rock* broached the topic with Steve Morse, who provided the following opinions.

"I think it would be odd if a band that was part of the roots of rock 'n' roll was in the Rock & Roll Hall of Fame, don't you think?" joked Steve. "What's the connection? A hard rock band, Rock & Roll Hall of Fame? Is there any commonality there? No, no, I'm being sarcastic. It's really weird. I do see enough of politics in so many facets of our lives that I know that things happen that don't make any sense, based on internal pressures that you can't see. Just like somebody could be on our guest list for one of the shows, and they could get treated like crap by security or somebody who works in the venue that has no love for music whatsoever and is no part of us. But they could associate that with 'Oh well, Purple screwed us over and they didn't have my name on the list.' There are a million examples of these kind[s] of things that happen in our day-to-day lives.

"We don't know what they're thinking, or what the other pressures are. There may be sponsors involved, or there may be people that are on committees that for some reason, the last thing they want to do is have a rock band in the Rock & Roll

Hall of Fame. Seriously, I know that things like that do happen, when people steer some kind of organization seemingly away from the direction that they're supposed to be. I honestly don't understand, but it's the way it is.

"Me personally, I don't live or die over anything that has to do with recognition," continues Morse. "The only recognition I want is from my kids and family and people that have seen me, stood right in front of me, watching me perform. Those are the ones that I'm concerned about. As far as mass adulation, it's a double-edge sword. You pay a price. And that price could be the choices that you make; it could be the erosion of privacy; it could be making your decision-making flawed by thinking that you're above an average human being. All those things are dangerous parts of hoping for popularity too much.

"I like the saying that if you take care of the music, the music will take care of you. That's the level of success that I want. I want people to think that I'm taking care of the music. The rest will follow at the pace it needs to or should be. Not everything is going to turn out fair or what you expect. But over the long run, personally, I've had a very long career. I've been able to play music really as long as I want to. And same with the band Deep Purple. Success-wise, everybody's had their success; there's no question about it. And being recognized by an entity that, even though it has the name Rock & Roll in it, that's pretty superfluous to what the real issue is. I know the other guys feel very similar about this too.

"People right in front of us tonight when we play, those are the ones that we're most concerned with," reiterates Steve, in closing. "I've watched this band, just to make a point, brush away certain pop success—I've seen it happen. Not because they hate success; it's just that if there was one point that was being overlooked, that would be brought up, sometimes that can derail your big shot. This is a band that doesn't move or maneuver for big shots at success; I know that. And I think that's the best recipe for longevity."

Chapter 27

Infinite

"Bob has to keep nobody happy."

Steve Miller's backstage rant was the story of 2016's Rock & Roll Hall of Fame induction ceremony, but in our world the headline was that Deep Purple finally got inducted. As we know, there's often drama with these things, usually regarding which members of the band are getting in and which are showing up, whether it's Blondie or the Sex Pistols or Van Halen. Both questions were asked of Deep Purple's induction, along with additional drama with respect to the guys who were there not exactly getting along on the night, precisely along a Mk. II / Mk. III split.

Anyway, it was about time that Deep Purple was recognized, but it was a bit of a bummer that although David Coverdale and Glenn Hughes were inducted, Don Airey and Steve Morse were not. Ritchie Blackmore was inducted, but he didn't show up. Jon Lord was inducted posthumously. Rod Evans was inducted, but not Nick Simper, Tommy Bolin, or Joe Lynn Turner.

"So, the Hall of Fame, you've got to know this, Martin, you go back to 2011, I think we were nominated three years out of four," begins Glenn Hughes, who gave me the play-by-play just after this all went down at the Barclays Center in Brooklyn, New York, on April 9, 2016. "And I want to make you laugh here. Because I spoke to Geddy Lee about them getting inducted, and we didn't get inducted. But who got inducted instead of us? Flavor Flav. And I say that to you laughing, because, man, the Rock & Roll Hall of Fame, these guys—and there are one or two gals on the board—it's almost like there's always a band in there, and no disrespect to hip-hop at all because actually I quite like hip-hop, believe it or not, but it's like, what the hell is going on here, people? But this year, number one, you've got Steve Miller, my old friend from the early '70s, and you've got Chicago, my old buddies Cheap Trick, all these guys I've known since the '70s. You've got a class of '70s acts.

"And you've got these other acts who say they are rock, and they might be rock, but there's always one band every year where you go, wait a minute, that's country. Isn't that jazz? Isn't that hip-hop? Me, I think it's hilarious! That there's all this back-and-forth between these camps. I'm far on the other side, going there's room for everybody or anyone in the Rock & Roll Hall of Fame. I just think the board's got a serious sense of humor here."

But hey, at least it wasn't strictly the Mk. II lineup—Ian Gillan, Ritchie Blackmore, Jon Lord, Roger Glover, and Ian Paice—getting in. At least they expanded the parameters a wee bit and grabbed Glenn and David—and actually Rod Evans, perhaps in an attempt to bring him out of the witness protection program! But to be sure, Steve Morse was a big conspicuous absence.

"Well, I have to be careful how I answer that," continues Hughes, "because how was Rod Evans inducted but Nick Simper wasn't? I don't get it. It's like if Coverdale got inducted and I didn't. I don't have any, like, friends or ins on the board, except one guy. But I think they are very savvy. The Hall of Fame look at number of units sold that year; number of tickets sold; numbers—it's all about the fine detail. I mean, Mk. IV didn't get inducted. I don't think *Come Taste the Band* moved enough units that year. I think David and I spurred the band on after Mk. II, and *Burn* was a top five album in over forty countries. If *Burn* would've been a stinker, I don't think we would've been inducted. I think a small group of people thought only Mk. II would've been inducted. But, you know, Rod Evans getting inducted for 'Hush' and Mk. II getting inducted for a good four or five songs. But Mk. III, with *Burn*, that album was a monument. I think *Burn* was the second-highest album, studio album, after *Machine Head*. So hence the induction of David and Glenn."

As for the absence of the Man in Black, Glenn says, "I have to be very careful again here, Martin. Because there are camps of people set up, and there's all kinds of shit going down. I say this to you: five or six weeks ago, I heard from someone inside the Deep Purple community. I'm talking about . . . there's about twenty of us involved in the band, accepted in it. And one who works for me and one who works for Ritchie, there was word that Ritchie was attending. If you want to go on the timeline of Glenn Hughes from a month ago, I said this, very carefully: 'Oh, I'm so glad I *hear* that Ritchie will attend. So great. I'm so glad for the fans.' Right? And I was met with some answers from Ritchie's wife. We didn't argue about it. She said, 'You should've come to the source.'

"Martin, you know, you've been doing this awhile, you're a good journalist—Ritchie doesn't pick the phone up. The only way you can get Ritchie, if you don't mind me saying so, it is by carrier pigeon. You know, it's just . . . I just heard a rumor, and she shot me down in flames like that. 'You should've come to the source.' Well, I've been trying to get to the source for forty-one years, but I can't get there. I just thought it would've been great for the fans. Iconic guitar player, lovely man—never fell out with Ritchie. Ritchie just doesn't socialize with ex-members of Deep Purple. He has a fan base, and it's great for him. I just thought it'd be great for the fans, and to keep it all in the family. That it would've been great for him to show up. But he didn't show up, and God bless him. He just didn't think it was an appropriate thing to show up. Well, he was invited by the Hall of Fame. He had two seats at the table. He just chose not to attend. I'm not angry at Ritchie or Candice or Ritchie's mother-in-law. It's none of my business. I just thought it would be great if we could've all sat at the table together and had one big hug. But Ritchie just didn't want to do it."

The concept of induction must have been a little touchy for Ian Gillan as well, given how he's had some ill words for the Hall in the past.

"I spent some time with Ian Gillan, something we hadn't done for a long time," begins Glenn. "Ian, you know, I don't think Ian Gillan is fake at all. I just think he took it all in, day of the show, and realized that it certainly was an honor to be inducted into the Hall of Fame—it's a huge thing. Ian Gillan doesn't have a fake

Ian Gillan, Budweiser Stage, Toronto, Ontario, September 2, 2017. © *Dave McDonald*

bone in his body. And Blackmore either—no fakeness at all. They both spoke their minds, and we all got inducted, including Ritchie. And including Jon Lord, may he rest in peace. We all got inducted, and I thought we handled it pretty bloody well. I was just grateful to be accepting an award on behalf of a band that has sold 150 million albums. It's like Roger said after the show to me: 'Damn it, we *do* deserve to be in this Hall of Fame.'

"And I must say, I'm really honored to be inducted with David. And thank God that *Burn* did create a genre after Mk. II. We held the baton and ran with it. Mk. I, Mk. II, Mk. III, and Mk. IV fans—thank you. Thank you to the fans of Jon Lord, Ian Paice, Roger Glover, David Coverdale, Ian Gillan, Tommy Bolin, Rod Evans, Joe Satriani, Joe Lynn Turner, Nick Simper—all of those people thank you so much. You know, Steve Morse! Don Airey! I think I've covered all members now, right? Thank you to all of the fans, all those who made music with Deep Purple, all genres, all generations, thank you so very, very much. And thank you to all the fans who voted."

But, of course, the induction didn't mean retirement for the Purples, or for Glenn. The "Voice of Rock" was busy finishing up a new solo album, and then he was off to tour it, in both Europe and the US.

"Right. I'm now . . . given my father's just passed away, I'm going over there for a week, to the UK. But I have some music done for a new Glenn record, heavy on groove, heavy on content lyrically, very, very heavy musically, although very light in places. It's not going to be street cred funk like the last album was eight years ago. It's going to be darker and more . . . it's going to make people move, you know? And my lyrics of course will be about what's been going on with me. So, there's going to be some stories to tell."

I alluded to Steve Miller's epic rant about the running of the Hall. I wondered what Glenn and his Purple buddies thought of the space cowboy railing against the Hall and its treatment of the musicians and their guests.

"What Steve said backstage, I'm on the fence about it, because he was rambling on about having to pay $10,000 per guy to get his band in there. And you know, look, this is my two cents. I've known Steve since '71. He is very opinionated, like we all are. Steve Miller is getting inducted as Steve Miller. From what I can understand about this, it's like, Steve Miller is one guy. You see what I'm saying? It's like, David Bowie got inducted and he had a band that played with him too. But apparently what went down was Steve had to pay out of his own pocket for each member to be flown in. This is what I'm hearing. So, I feel for him, because it's a lot of bloody money. And he was outraged by it. I thought it was a good bit of pomp and circumstance for the press. He got some coverage. But I must say, the Rock & Roll Hall of Fame, the chairman and all the board members I met were so kind to the members of Deep Purple, and so, so respectful. But I also understand Steve. I completely understand it. He was out of pocket about $150,000 on the night.

"So here it is in a nutshell," continues Hughes, as intrigued about the situation as I was. "Steve Miller got inducted as a solo artist, although it's technically the Steve Miller Band. It's not Steve Miller when he goes out and plays. It's a band, although Steve is the star. I'm just thinking that he was upset that only he . . . because everybody else got tickets for themselves and their wives. I'm just thinking Steve had a bit of a moment where he flared up and he took it to task. I'm not Steve and he's not me. And I'm sure if I would've had to shell out $150,000 that night, I would've been pretty burnt up too. But hey, it was a damn good show. Steve, in my opinion, he and his band were absolutely fantastic. And he didn't take his anger onto that stage. He was a full professional. You know, I've known Steve prior to me joining Deep Purple, and he's been so gracious and kind to me. But yes, Steve does have a button. And when he pushes that button, he can go a little dark. As I can too. Look, man, artists, they have switches, and when you throw that switch, it's like, oh my God, let's get out of the way for a minute here. But what I will not do is disrespect anybody—artists or Hall of Fame board members—because the class of 2016 was a classy event."

Asked who else is overdue for induction, Glenn says, "Gotta get the Moody Blues in there. If I can get them on the ballot, you know, we'll see, because those guys are responsible for me talking to you right this minute. I mean, most board members, they're not young. The Moody Blues. You know why? Because they're still playing, really. They still play. Justin and John and . . . God, they're like family to me. Who else needs to be there? Jeff Buckley, man. I mean, I could go on—Joe Bonamassa. He could be the youngest inductee ever, because he started so young. Joe Bonamassa needs to be in there. I love Joe; love him to pieces. He absolutely deserves to be in the Hall of Fame. You know, there's so much room for so many great artists, and it's the fans who take the beating, Martin. We as artists don't take a beating; it's the fans—they take the beating."

"We never thought about it much at all, as the years passed by," ventures Ian Paice. "It was obviously something behind the scenes, why we never got in. There was some political thing. Maybe somebody insulted somebody in the corridors of power. You know, it made no logical sense. But when it started out, it was a great idea, a wonderful idea, for the fans of those musicians that were inducted. Not so much for the musicians. They mostly couldn't give a shit.

"I mean, to me, it's not changed my life at all. But those fans who have musical heroes, they like to see them being awarded. It was too late; I mean, one of the guys that should've been there is Jon Lord, but it turned out to be four years too late for him. And also, I understood with Purple, it's a very confusing thing for them to do. There've been so many members over the years that have come and gone. They missed the point. What they should've done is just inducted everybody individually, under the guise of Deep Purple. And what they did, they brought some people in and left some people out. Which is bonkers. I look at it this way. My wife and I got a nice weekend in New York together, all expenses paid. I got a coffee mug, got a T-shirt, and I got a little statuette. That's not so bad."

"That's a loaded question, because I know what you are referring to," chuckled Roger, in conversation with Dan Sywala, who asked him if there was anything he'd change about the evening. "That was actually not our choice. Ritchie said many times he was not interested in going. So, we never thought he would go. I mean, you never know Ritchie, because he is unpredictable. But he said he was not interested in doing it. So, where do we go from there? We go to Glenn and David being there! But we don't do their songs, and if we are going to play live, there has to be a current Purple lineup. Otherwise, we are not going to play. And they said, 'It's a good compromise—fine.' That's it. Now, Ritchie says he was told not to come, but I don't think it's true. It's certainly not coming from the band, and I don't think it's coming from the management. So, who knows? It's just a little fleck in the eye. It's not serious. It wasn't something we particularly cared about. We did it for our families, fans, and friends. It's more important for them than to us. It hadn't changed my life."

Pretty much exactly a year later, on April 7, 2017, Deep Purple issued their twentieth album, *Infinite*, recorded in six different countries (but mostly in Bob's Nashville joint) and blessed with a really cool album cover featuring an icebreaker in the North carving out the universal sign for infinity.

I asked Ian Paice to go a little further back to set the scene for this record, beginning with *Purpendicular*, *Abandon*, and *Bananas* as a bit of a trio.

"Well, they were a learning process for the new guys," reflects Ian. "Especially the last two records before the interim period. They're all an evolution. People say, 'Why don't you write stuff like "Highway Star" anymore?' Well, the answer to that is, yes, we do—we just don't sound like 'Highway Star.' Everything is related to what went on in the past. Of course it is. You know, the three guys who helped create that stuff, we're still doing it now. But everything is a natural evolution of the musicians getting further on in their life and learning more stuff. And forgetting stuff that they did in their twenties. Because sometimes I listen to what I did on those old tracks, and I have no idea how I did it. I have to go back and relearn it. So, over the course of the last thirty, forty years, I forgot what the hell I did. And more importantly,

Roger Glover, Budweiser Stage, Toronto, Ontario, September 2, 2017. © *Dave McDonald*

why did I do it? You learn stuff, you forget stuff, and everything evolves and changes. So, all the records, to a certain extent, will have something in common.

"It's quite quick, in modern parlance, four years from the last," continues Paice, asked about *Infinite*'s timeline and whether there's a distinct personality to it. "They're related, obviously. They're related because they were recorded in a very similar fashion in the same studio with the same producer, the glorious Bob Ezrin. So of course they have a link. The music that an artist creates is really a reflection of the world we live in. And the world is much different than it was four years ago. It wasn't great then; it's a little less great now. So, I think it's probably a darker album, lyrically—definitely it's a darker album. There's a lot of crap going on in the world that affects everybody. So, when Ian and Roger got together to write this, a lot of that sort of comes through. It's a heavier album for sure. The ideas that started appearing during the writing session, which are basically instrumental sessions, Ian is very passive at that time. He's just listening and trying to find the mood and the emotion of each piece of music that we are creating. There were definitely more riffs and more of a heavy feel than there were on *Now What?!* Maybe that's a reflection of—without, again, being too po-faced about it—the way the artist reflects the world that is around him, you know? They are cousins, but this one is a little beefier, I think."

Over in the geopolitical world, the UK had decided on June 23, 2016, to leave the European Union, in an event otherwise known as Brexit. That whole mess had always been a hobby of Ian Gillan's. But that's not one of the societal things that Ian Paice is referring to, with respect to any of the lyrics on the album.

"I don't think so, no. I think most Brits, really, now that the decision was made, I don't think we're really involved in it anymore. You know, I voted to stay, just because peripherally for me it makes more sense. Life becomes easier, flitting from one European country to another European country. But in the long run, I think it's good for my country. I think the EU was doomed anyway. Too many people in positions of power that nobody voted for, telling us what we can and can't do. Saying we should all be the same. It's not like North America. North America's a new continent with new ideas. The cultures here are thousands of years old. You know, we don't want to be the same. A German is happy being a German. He doesn't want to be Danish. The Danish guy doesn't want to be British. So, I think the federal idea is doomed to crash and burn."

Given the glowing reviews for Bob Ezrin the last time around, it's no surprise that he's back cracking the whip on *Infinite*.

"Well, when you bring somebody like Bob in, you bring him in because of his studio knowledge, his track record, and the fact that he takes all the other crap off your shoulders. All you have to do—and that's quite a big all [laughs]—is create the ideas and get the performance. That's quite a lot in itself. But when you leave all the business side to him—you know, the timing, the choice of studio, the technicians that he brings into the control room—when you don't have to worry about any of that, and you trust his judgment, that all those calls will be made correctly, it becomes easy. You just go back to being a musician again.

"Bob instills that confidence in you, and that belief that it's all going to be absolutely fine and it's going to work, A to Z, perfectly, no problem at all. And it generally does. That's great when you have a guy like that in the studio. He just creates that environment where the musicians are comfortable and you get the job done quickly and you get it done well. When you've got someone within the band, as Roger used to do for us in the past, he has to tread very carefully, because he has to keep everybody happy. Bob has to keep nobody happy. All he has to do is end up making a great record. And that's slightly more important.

The elegant *Infinite* cover art plus a promotional poster

"Comfort is a great thing for people," muses Paice, when asked what the personal dynamics are within Deep Purple now basically a half century from when it began. "Once you know you're in the right place and your part of it, you're a band, you start adding more and more of your influences into the mix. Don certainly has in this record. His contribution on this record is way and above what he did on *Now What?!*, and far above what he did on *Rapture*. It's a matter of the guys feeling like they're at home. It's been our home for fifty years, as you say, so we're totally cool, the three of us.

"But these guys, it's still an embedding process. I like that within the genre of music that we do, we're still trying to crack the walls and find new ways of doing stuff. The hard thing is, is that there is no new stuff. Everything you do is old stuff. You've just got to find new ways to do the old stuff. Everything has sort of been done in its own form one way or another. You've just got to keep letting the imagination run riot and see what you come up with.

"So, I think Purple is probably one of the last vestiges of a period of rock 'n' roll when all the sectors and vectors were let loose and all the rules were broken down. Like, you didn't have to make a three-minute single, so you make a ten-minute track. You didn't have to conform to verse, chorus, middle eight. And I think so many other bands have either retired or left the planet or are no longer with us. We are one of the few bands that still actually works and still creates new music; we're still trying to expand boundaries, within the limited sphere of rock 'n' roll."

Perhaps Deep Purple is the last "underground music" act still standing, like a Vertigo Records band from 1971 that sells in the three digits (yes, they existed!), although Purple do a fair bit better than that. Acid rock, underground music, or as K. K. Downing very insightfully called *Rocka Rolla*–era Judas Priest recently, "progressive blues," Deep Purple still has that spirit.

"Well, we didn't know what we were doing," says Paice. "We don't know what we're doing now. What we did then and what we do now when we create the music is the exact same way we would've done it back in '69, '70. The four of us instrumentalists would get into a room, and if nobody's got an idea, somebody will start playing. And if it's a good idea, somebody will join in. If it's a bad idea, everybody will go get a cup of tea. That's the way it worked. When we did this record, we took a ten-day writing period, and we ended up with fifteen, sixteen ideas. Which of course at that moment in time are all brilliant; they're all the best ideas that ever happened.

"So, you listen to them for a few weeks and work out that maybe eight or nine of the ideas have a possibility, and that the other ones aren't quite as good as you remember it. You live with that, and you go and do the same thing all over again. You end up with ten, twelve ideas that you are really happy with. Those are the ones that you take to Bob. 'This is what we have; what do you think?' And he'll go, 'Well, these ten are great; these two, I don't know yet; we've got to work on them.' Then we go to the rehearsal room for two weeks, trying to get some sort of semblance of an arrangement. And remember, at this time they're not even songs; they're just pieces of music. We give the hard job to Ian Gillan and Roger Glover. When we create these things, then they have to go away and write a song over the top of it. We do it the other way around. We do it the opposite. We start at the ending and end up at the beginning. But it seems to work out okay."

Roger's well involved with the lyrics on *Infinite*. "Oh, big time. Ian has some wonderful ideas; Roger has the musical knowledge. Between the two of them, they come up with some very interesting solutions to these musical problems. Ian will say, 'Well, I've got this idea,' and Roger will say, 'Well, you can't do that musically. You need to do this.' Roger will provide the musical solution to get across this idea. Sometimes Roger will come up with a lyric where Ian doesn't have the mood of the song. So, they collaborate big time. They help each other out; when one gets stuck, the other one comes in and gets the process moving forward."

The group songwriting credit the band members have adopted since *Purpendicular* persists.

"Yes, because all the songs are created from absolutely nothing, from four guys sitting in a rehearsal room or a writing room with a cup of tea or a cup of coffee in front of them and somebody starts playing something. The music is a cooperative creation; therefore, the credits go to everybody. To a minor extent, when we start getting a start on them, Bob comes in and he gets credit as well. Because sometimes we'll come to an impasse, and he'll go, 'Well, why don't you do that?' Because it's out of left field for us, we go, 'Oh, that's the solution to that problem.' So, the whole thing is a cooperative. We all work as hard as each other to try to find these new bits of music; therefore, it's impossible to say whose input was more than anybody else's."

Another aspect of the modern-day Deep Purple sound is how songs can come across as heavy, but they aren't exactly written like heavy metal, not to mention that the band has a keyboardist. In other words, through the strength of the band's collective personality but also the drum-heavy production, they really have discarded genre compartmentalization.

Japanese issue of
The Infinite Live Recordings

"I just think that for years, we've been missing out on having a great producer," reflects Paice, on that framing. "The sound has always been there. Sometimes we've been, because we've been trying to do it in-house, there's that sort of feeling that your part is more important than somebody else's part. So, when it comes to the mix, you'll say, 'Well, I want this a bit louder.' And the other guy says, 'Well, I want this a bit louder.' And then you just can't get anything louder than it's meant to be, so you end up compromising your sound to keep everybody's ego happy. Again, with Bob, he doesn't work like that. We do the recording; Bob takes it away; Bob mixes it. And within very limited parameters, he will accept critique about maybe this could be improved or that should be changed. But he's the producer—he calls the shots."

They once recorded in Florida, where Steve lives, but none of the band lives in Nashville. Ian catches us up on the various headquarters of the guys.

"The biggest move is that Roger was living in the States for many years, Connecticut, and now he lives in Switzerland. Steve is a Midwest boy, but he's living in Florida for most of his time, well, all the time we've known him. Mr. Gillan, he flits between the UK and Portugal. He has a nice house in Portugal, and he lives a lot of the time down there. Don is UK based and I'm basically UK based, but I've got a little place in Spain where I run away to when the world gets too fractured. What it does do is it makes band rehearsal time very difficult. We definitely have to plan it so that we can all agree to be on the same continent, never mind the same town. And the album, it's the same as *Now What?!*—we did it in Nashville, in a brilliant big studio, an old one called the Tracking Room. You could put a tennis court in there."

Coincidence or not, a week before the Brexit decision, on June 14, 2016, Ian suffered a form of ministroke.

"Well, I was very lucky," explains Paice. "I was in Stockholm. I'd gone to bed. I was feeling a bit . . . I guess I thought I felt tired. And when I woke up in the morning, I couldn't do anything with my right hand. I couldn't even comb my hair. You know, there was just this bit of a blob at the end of my right arm. With all the knowledge I had, I knew something had happened. So, I called down to our road manager, and they got a local medic up there. Within twenty minutes, I was gone for a CAT scan, being looked at. Half an hour later I'm in a hospital bed and being treated.

"Basically, it was a TIA—transient ischemic attack. It was a huge warning that something had changed in my body. It wasn't a lifestyle thing. It was just like luck of the draw. My blood pressure had gone through the roof, and basically I just had to get my blood sorted out. Which, you know, touch wood, it looks like everything is fine. I have to take these four tablets every day for the rest of my life, to make sure the blood doesn't get out of whack again. But so far it seems to be working fine, and the right hand belongs to me again. It's not 100 percent. There's still the odd tingle in the finger, but each of the fingers does exactly what I tell them to. And where things were, because the improvement is so slow, you don't realize it. But then you

Ian Paice, Budweiser Stage, Toronto, Ontario, September 2, 2017. © *Dave McDonald*

think what it was three or four months ago, and it's definitely better. So, the body is healing itself, and it's going to be okay. I've just got to remember to take these four pills every day and I should be cool."

Everybody present and accounted for, Deep Purple had a new album to talk about. As was becoming the norm in the business, the band generated buzz through two advance singles, "Time for Bedlam" on February 3 and "All I Got Is You" on March 10. "Time for Bedlam" is also the opening track on the album. It features a dramatic monotone vocal opening before settling down into a dark rocker with a subtle shuffle feel, a roiling bass line, and a continuation of the opening straight-line vocal approach. All told, there's a "Pictures of Home" vibe. The song ends as it began—pretty creepy stuff.

In the promotional interviews the band did for their label—Germany's Edel SE & Co. KGaA, with Ear Music (stylized as earMUSIC), being the subimprint—Roger expressed pride in "opening the album with something unexpected," adding that "when you're trying to write a new song over a finished backing track, you're trying to figure out what the music is trying to say, what kind of atmosphere you're trying to create, and how the words bounce and where it fits and everything. And the key to 'Time for Bedlam' was really the organ part, the rhythm organ part, which dictated where the words should fit. So, once we'd got that, it was actually relatively easy to figure out what the song was about.

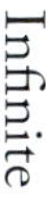

"And 'Time for Bedlam' was a working title," continues Glover. "Working titles sometimes make finished titles—occasionally, not always—but 'Time for Bedlam' was kind of a nice phrase. We didn't know what to write with that title in mind until we just started rolling stuff. I don't know where it comes from, really. I remember Paul McCartney once saying, when asked where songs come from, he said, 'Well, it seemed like they were always there. I just stumbled across them.' And that's really how it feels."

"When we finished the track," adds Ian Paice, "I hadn't heard what they were going to put on vocally, so the whole beginning section, the sort of Gregorian chanty-type thing, was a complete surprise to me. How do we get out of this? But I trusted them, because there was always a way they would find to get out of it. But it was like, 'What's that? Interesting.'"

I asked Ian why this song was deemed to be a good choice for lead single. "Well, you might be surprised, but we take a back seat on that," explains Paicey. "Once we deliver the record to the label, we let them get on with it. Our job is making the music. Their job is letting people know that the record is there, and see if they want to buy it. So, they're listening to the stuff as a third party, and if they hear something that they deduce is a bit stronger, or something that would create a little more attention, they choose the track. All the tracks are there to be played, so we don't really care. If they think that track will do better than another track, then you release it. We're happy with all the tracks, or we wouldn't have given them to you. What you do with them after that, that's a record label decision. We've learned from the past that we're pretty good musicians, but we're pretty crappy businessman. So, we just let them get on with it."

"Hip Boots" is another heavy riff rocker, very typically Deep Purple other than the curious title. Again, why it's so intrinsically Purple is its wandering, circular, resolving riff, purely traditional heavy metal, but of course more like "dad rock" heavy metal than the couple of dozen flavors concocted out there in the wild since Deep Purple wrote "Bloodsucker."

The "Time for Bedlam" CD single

Ian Gillan explains the premise behind the lyrics, again, in the promotional interviews conducted for the label.

"A friend of mine who is a professor of English at Buffalo University [Bruce Jackson, University at Buffalo] in upstate New York, he's a keen researcher on African American history. He's about in his eighties now, but when he was young, he spent a lot of time touring the prisons in the South and collecting information about the songs that have been handed down through the generations. You didn't have to go far back to get to the time of slavery, or the end of slavery, the amazing time with the migration of music and story up gradually through Kansas City and St Louis and up to Chicago, where it evolved and became more commercial, and people were drawn into it.

“There were some amazing stories that sometimes you see appear in an English version of music called skiffle. And there were some great stories told, like ‘No More Cane on the Brazos.’ He wrote a book called *Get Your Ass in the Water and Swim Like Me*, which is one of the lines in the song ‘Hip Boots.’ We were talking about the origin of the word ‘hip,’ because it appears an awful lot, particularly in jazz, and in that particular culture too. So, whether it was hip or hep, everyone’s got an idea where it came from.

“But Roger did a lot of research as well, and he came up with the idea of hip boots being something you would dream of having as you were escaping from the chain gang through the swamp. It would be a good idea to have them, wouldn’t it? For a few reasons. One, you didn’t get your tootsies wet, and another one is dogs couldn’t smell you when they chased you. So, a lot of work went into that. We wrapped ourselves into the idea that we were actually slaves escaping from the chain gang during the few days when we were writing this. So, it’s got quite an authentic feel, I think, due to its connections. It creates a mood, and I think it fits the driving track. The track is awesome; I love it. For me, it goes together very well. It’s a bit obscure, but there again, it’s got its own niche, I think, musically and lyrically—yeah, I love it.”

Next is “All I Got Is You,” which percolates along to a similar slight shuffle feel to the opener, and at the same tempo. But it’s bluesier and even jazzy. Interest is held through the constant dialogue between guitarist and keyboardist. It’s not a riffy song; Steve conversely fires off licks, as does Don.

“Well, they’re sharing the load,” notes Paice. “There is that understanding that sometimes there is no lead instrument, but there is an amalgamation of sound. But when it comes to the point where one of the guys takes over, the other guy backs him up 100 percent. And again, that’s familiarity. That’s comfort within the zone you’re in, and that’s knowing the job back to front and having the ability to do it without egos getting in the way and saying, well, I think I should be doing more here, or I should be doing more there. They just work together. That’s how great stuff happens—when it’s a collaboration.

The “All I Got Is You” CD single

“Steve is Steve,” continues Ian. “Steve analyzes what he does like this: he goes, you know, if I have a big box of tools, the more tools I have in the box, the better. I’m gonna be able to do everything I’ve been called to do. Steve has the ability to play anything you ask him to play. He has a great love of southern music, and he has a great love of rock ’n’ roll, and if you ask him to play either, he can do it. He loves classics; if you ask him to play a classical piece, he’ll play it for you. They are all tools in his box. So, Steve works out, musically, what is required for the song, and he plays it. He doesn’t change. I don’t think any one of us changes that attitude with respect to what we have to do when we’re trying to create something that didn’t exist five minutes before. We find the right solution for it, the best solutions we can come up with.”

Explains Ian Gillan with respect to the premise of the song and, critically, its title: "This stick holder [points to Ian Paice] has been known in the past to come in, and just as we're writing lyrics, say things like, 'Draining board—that's a good phrase; use that.' Or 'Hatch—there's a good word; put that in somewhere.' He was banging on about this thing. Time after time you would hear this—and it always made us laugh—when he would say, 'Well, you know, look at it this way. You've got me, but all I got is you,' as if it's like a really bad deal. So, we based the whole song upon that phrase. As we're sitting around, chatting, drinking tea, and thinking about an idea for a song, that came to us. And so, we wrote that down first and then we developed the song.

"Somebody said to me recently, 'Isn't that a bit misogynistic? The lyrics in that song?' I said, 'What are you talking about?' I said, 'Who said it's about a woman?' [laughs]. The word 'she' is not mentioned once in it. So anyway, this was something that we take out of our little moments of private humor, and it can develop into a whole song. It's a glorious piece of work. And at the end, of course, it's my modern interpretation of *Gone with the Wind*. Quite frankly, my dear, I don't give a damn [laughs]."

"One Night in Vegas" is a muscular rocker with a half-time feel, again, adding to the story of Deep Purple as rooted in the British blues boom but taking it to unrecognizable places. In other words, fifty years on from that music in the late 1960s, Deep Purple methodically evolved through the decades, taking what they wanted from the "rule book" and making these characteristics their own. The connection is underscored by Don's saloon piano playing.

"I think the groove on 'One Night in Vegas' is very nice," says Paicey. "If I'd heard that from some L.A. session cat, I would've thought that was really cool. So, I'm very proud of that; that's really nice. I think the mood of the drums on 'Birds of Prey' is pretty cool too. As music progresses in rock 'n' roll, the space for musical virtuosity and creativeness, rhythmically, it's sort of become more limited. So, trying to find those musical creations where the drummer can go crazy, it sometimes just sounds a little old-fashioned. So, when you try them, you listen to them, you go, well, if I played a little less, it would be a much-better record [laughs]. The drum parts are very simple, but in simplicity there is an art, there is a creativity to making it work. And overall, I mean, 95 percent of that record, I'm really happy with. I just think the drum ideas are exactly right."

"There's a famous story," relates Don Airey, on the "One Night in Vegas" lyric, "and I don't know quite whether it's true. There's a band still going called Foghat. They were playing in Vegas, and the bass player woke up in the morning, and there was a girl in bed with him who looked at him rather lovingly. 'Who are you, my dear?' 'I'm your wife.' And he'd been so out of it, he got married in the chapel after the gig at about two in the morning but had no memory of it. So that was it. Apparently, they're still married thirty-five years on; you know, it worked out. But we played with Foghat a year ago, didn't we? In Concord, California. And I was dying to find out if it was true. But the guy wasn't in the band anymore. But they assured me it was true."

Adds Roger, "We're at the age now where maybe it's not the greatest thing to start writing about fast cars and young girls, or young cars and fast girls or whatever it is. But we're always looking for stories. Really, I think if there is a theme, it wasn't a thought-out theme. But as you look at the album now, the theme is really that everything's a story. There's not one love song. In fact, 'One Night in Vegas' is probably the closest thing to a love song on the album. It's all from stories or situations. You start off with a situation and you write about it, and it's actually a fun exercise to do that. It's a discipline, if you like, that we give ourselves, is to write an interesting story. And stories come from true life. They come from things that piss us off or whatever, things in the newspaper. They all come from our lives."

Likely not consciously lifted, but the "Get Me Outta Here" riff sounds very much like that of Rage Against the Machine's "Bulls on Parade" from the *Evil Empire* album. It's crushing and it's octave jumping, but of course the two songs go to wildly different places as they develop.

But the musical track was inspired by drums, says Roger. "One day when I was at home, I was listening to *Now What?!*, and the intro to 'Body Line' is several bars of just drums on their own. And just as a fun experiment, I took eight bars of it and slowed it right down. Actually, I was turned on by the groove; it was great. You can sort of recognize the fact that it is the drum pattern from 'Body Line,' but it doesn't really matter in the scheme of things. The whole new feel of it was slightly reggaeish, and it suggested a whole different way of pursuing a song. And it just grew out of that, really. That drummer—it's all his fault."

"The Surprising" is arguably the highlight of the *Infinite* album. It's progressive, gorgeously melodic, floating on a sort of flamenco beat, the effect accentuated by a slight spaghetti western feel to the chords and Ian's vocal melody. The song also represents an opportunity to sit back and marvel at the visceral, vibrant, sparkly production job that Bob Ezrin brought to the project. I'm the first to go on about how the best-sounding cymbals in the business come from Phil Collins and Hugh Padgham on the *Abacab* album, but it's hard not to view these as equal to the task.

As Roger explained to Dan Sywala, "We were in a writing session one day, where there were old noodles, jams, cups of tea, and also endless discussions. Somewhere in between that, Steve started playing that opening guitar figure. It just sounded very nice. When somebody starts to play something and others say, 'Oh, that's nice,' they join in. We don't talk about it; we just start playing with him. At the end of that jam, it didn't go anywhere particularly at that point, but it was a good start.

"On the other hand, we needed a working title, so I called it 'The Surprising Mr. Morse' [laughs]. You know, what he played was surprising for us and quite beautiful. Anyway, we worked on the track and then arrangements came. Well, not all of it, as the last bit of the arrangement appeared just before we started recording it. We worked out the main part of the song, not the solos, but just the verses and the structure of the song. Then, when we got to Nashville, we spent a couple of weeks with Bob, playing him what we had and him making suggestions like, 'How about you do this here or that there?' and bing bang, until the whole thing appeared very quickly. Even jamming in the studio helped.

"When the whole thing was finished, we still didn't have a song.," continues Glover. "We had a backing track, and then it's down to me and Ian Gillan to figure out what's going on top. We get together and alone, where I spent a week with him there and one week there. We basically write the words for the songs. How we do that is we listen to the track many times, trying to figure out what the emotion of the track is and what it is trying to say. We don't want to write a really heavy riff for a love song or vice versa. We were just looking for ideas, angles, and targets we can focus on.

"Sometimes the working title of the song becomes the title of the song. 'The Surprising Mr. Morse' got abbreviated to 'The Surprising' in our notes, and we thought, it's actually a nice title; let's keep it. But what do you write about with a title like that? I think Ian Gillan did most of these lyrics. Well, I did a lot of lyrics, but he did this one. It's sort of an impressionistic song. It doesn't say a lot, but it says a lot. It's ambiguous and you can make your own meaning up to it. It's a mysterious track, and I think it's lovely. Steve came up with that solo in the middle and Don with the main theme, so everyone did take part in the writing of that song eventually."

"Johnny's Band" is yet another song that confounds as to genre. It's not heavy metal, nor is it pop, but somewhere in between—midtemperature rock perhaps, set to a biting, halting beat.

The "Johnny's Band" single artwork

"It's a very poignant song about the rise and fall of a rock 'n' roll band," explains Ian Gillan. "But in the end, it goes to show, actually, one of the things we've been lucky to avoid, and that is fashion, the idea of becoming successful with single records. And if you're fashionable, then, by definition, tomorrow you're unfashionable. So, you've really got to stick to what you are if you want to survive. I think that's an important lesson we've all learned. It's all about music, basically.

"But this is about a sort of flash in the pan, covered two or three hits and Bob's your uncle, it's all over. But they've left behind something that we all love. And even though it may not have been cool to say it one year after, then a few years after, it's cool again. There are some great songs that are actually of their time. I think that's what this is about. And of course, it's the archetypical story of people falling off . . . you know, half the band getting drunk, half the band getting off their heads and joining a cult in L.A. I think it's fairly normal, really, with five guys, for one or two to survive."

"When we did the track," adds Ian Paice, "I wasn't sure how we were going to work it out. Because it's quite poppy. Of all the tracks on the album, it's the pop tune, if you want. And I wasn't quite sure how that would work. But the fact that it's been made into a song *about* a pop band, it all makes sense. It's like, ah, now I get it. Because even once you record the track, sometimes you don't understand what you've done. Maybe it'll work; maybe it won't. None of my business at all. I go one, two . . . what's next?"

Ian Gillan, Budweiser Stage, Toronto, Ontario, September 2, 2017. © *Dave McDonald*

"On Top of the World" is a thumping rocker with blocked-off power chords and massive drums. Says Ian, "The Tracking Room has an amazing echo chamber. It's like a 25-foot-by-25-foot room, about three stories high, which is just pure stone. And when we needed a big drum sound, we just put a set in there and set the microphones and let the room do the work. But it's a big studio anyway, so you don't have to mess with the drums. As long as you tune them properly, you hit them, they go bang. They don't go duh. They don't make just a crappy, flappy sound. They smack you in the face. And that comes through. Of course, when you do that, the drummer enjoys playing them. That's the way they're meant to sound."

"Oh no, this is a true story," cautions Gillan, on the song's ribald lyric. "I was in . . . I won't say where it is, because it might get people in trouble. But it was in the Far East. I was doing a tour, and I did a press conference, and after the press conference, a guy from a well-known fizzy-drink company that was sponsoring the show said, 'Let's go to a club.' So, we went to a blues club and there was a band finishing. They were just about winding up and they were throwing the punters out, at which point about ten girls walked in; I mean working girls.

"So, we had a little dance, and everything was great, had a couple drinks. And then they *did* close, and the girls said, 'Oh, we're having a party. Would you like to come?' 'Yeah, of course I would.' And so, I went along and we went out of the commercial area into the banking area of the city, lots of glass, high-rise buildings. We slipped down an alleyway and climbed up some steps to the back of a bank. And I thought, they must have one of the flats upstairs [laughs]. We kept going until we got to the roof, and that's where they lived, these working girls.

"They had a few cardboard boxes to keep the heat off during the day, and there was a fire burning and they were cooking rice, and they had wine. And we all got naked because that was . . . well, we just disrobed and flung our inhibitions and our clothes to the far corners of the globe and started dancing. It was magic; I thought, I'm in heaven. Absolutely great. She was beautiful. We laid down, she fed me rice and wine, and I fell asleep.

"The next thing I remember, as it says in the song, was the 'sharp pain at sunrise' as the sun was coming up. And my mouth was open, and I opened one of my eyes and a cockroach was going in and out of my mouth. It's like ugh, that's awful. So, I reached for the wine, drank this nectar . . . ugh, it's like vinegar, disgusting! And I looked across at Venus in Heaven—that was her name—and I thought, wow, she was beautiful the night before, and she was more, let's not say Rubenesque. I mean, she was more Michelin than Rubens. And it was, oh my God, I've got to get out of here. And I couldn't find me clothes; they were all over the place. I was wearing a suit and tie and everything for this press conference. I found everything except one shoe that had gone over the edge of the bank. And I found that on the way back to the hotel. But that was quite a night. So, it was worth writing it down as a story, really. But it's true—that's what it's about."

"The real challenge was getting all that story into a song," adds Roger. "There's a lot of detail there. It took quite a bit of thought, actually, to get that sorted." "Yeah, we threw all the naughty bits out," laughs Ian.

Halfway through, Don fires off a vicious Hammond solo. In fact, there's an alternate and delightful way to make one's way through this album—just listen to what Don does. It pays enormous dividends, not only because of his performance but because of the array of sounds he gets.

"Oh, I feel it was too much!" jokes Roger, asked by Dan Sywala about Don's role on the album. "We are going to sack him! [laughs]. Don is really coming into his own in this band. Jon Lord's shadow is very long, and Don has done his best to be himself. Gradually, I can see over the last few years—to be precise, he has been with us for fourteen years—but during, let's say, the last five or six years, he has been coming into his own. He started to feel really comfortable in the band, and we are very comfortable with him. You know, he's not only great, but he's the only person we can think of to fit the bill. He's fantastic. I don't know whether he is more dominant, but his presence on this album is very much felt—yes! He shines on it."

"Birds of Prey" is another captivating track, progressive and yet heavy, featuring a pensive, wistful vocal melody from Ian, to go along with the philosophical lyrics.

Notes Roger, "One day in rehearsals, we'd been working for several hours on somewhat of a complicated riff, and we were struggling to get the feel of it. We took a tea break, and Ian Paice came over to me and said, 'Got any riffs?' 'Um, yeah.' And actually, I did, because every day I'm picking up a guitar and just doing twenty seconds of something, and it comes in me head. And I played it to him, and he goes, 'Yeah, that'll do; let's play that.' And it happened to coincide, when we got to the studio, in the rehearsal studio with Bob. Bob said one day, 'I want to do a track that's just really slow and bare and heavy, like boom bap, a real atmospheric piece that.' That riff fits that. So, let's try that. And basically, that's how it worked out.

"We rarely write one song wholly by one person," continues Glover, "but I think 'Birds of Prey' was all mine, the music and the words, on that one. I had this thought the other day that a song like 'Gypsy's Kiss,' I could never write lyrics like that. That's pure Gillan madness. And that's what I love. I mean, I think that he writes great lyrics. I'm the sort of more sensible, poetic, singer-songwriter-type person. We're quite opposite in many ways, but that's what makes us work. We blur the outside lines, and we meet in the middle somewhere."

I asked Roger if Ian has ever looked at Roger's lyrics and said to him, "I can't say that; that wouldn't come out of my mouth." Laughs Glover, "He doesn't say it like that. It's a bit more blunt than that. But I don't think he thinks that much of it. If something looks good and sounds good, it is good. Doesn't matter who came up with it. That's our judgment. But yeah, it's an interesting process. He didn't write much on *Infinite*—a lot more on *Infinite*, I wrote. But it's back and forth all the time. But yeah, we differ sometimes. He's the singer. If he feels strongly about something, we always reach a compromise. I'll go okay, yeah, I think that could be a better idea if you feel that way. I've learned by experience that things I didn't particularly care for at the time, years later I go, actually, that's great. So, it's a question of the older I get, the better I was [laughs]."

In what serves as a foreshadowing of the ordinariness of the band's *Turning to Crime* covers album, *Infinite* closes with "Roadhouse Blues," picked ordinary and played ordinary, save for the delightful, developing jam at the front of it.

Speaking with Dan Sywala, Roger explains that "we did one for *Now What?!*, which was one of the bonus tracks. The great thing about a cover is you don't have to learn it or work at it. We wanted to do something from our past, when we were kids growing up, and cover something which turned us on over the years. The first one we did was a cover of a Jerry Lee Lewis song. When it came to this album, Bob said one day in the studio, 'Do you fancy doing another cover, just for fun?' We said yes, but we didn't know what to do. Paice played it with a tribute band once and thought it was pretty good, so we went with that—well, after a discussion which was ten times longer than usual [laughs]. Anyway, it was done absolutely live. We got the words from the internet, went through a couple of riffs together to make sure we were playing the same thing, then the red light went on and we did it. However, whether to put it on the album or not, that wasn't really my decision. I thought it would be another bonus track, like the one from *Now What?!* But majority decided to make it go there."

Confirming Roger's story, Ian Paice says, "Bob suggested, for the fun of it, 'Pick a song you really like and have fun with it.' So, two or three ideas were thrown in. I'd played 'Roadhouse Blues' with a little band I work with sometimes between tours just to keep playing, and they segue from 'Black Night' into 'Roadhouse Blues.' And I thought it felt really, really nice; I really enjoyed playing it. So, I said, it's a really nice song, it's going to take ten minutes to record it, and we should have fun with it, which is what it turned out to be. And I think it's a really nice version. It's simplicity itself. Had we started playing and it wasn't working, we'd have gone back and pulled another idea out, but it was fun to do. I like it; I like it a lot. I like the original. I like this one too."

Despite being a cover, situating "Roadhouse Blues" as the exclamation point on the album really underscores the narrative of Deep Purple as a progressive-blues band, a term seemingly lost to the sands of time, and yet, here they are.

Like the last album, *Infinite* sold big numbers in Germany, over the 100,000 plateau, sending it gold and also to another #1 chart placement in that traditionally always strong market for Deep Purple. Germany was rewarded with a half-dozen shows during the first leg of the *Infinite* tour, but Deep Purple hit every other place in Europe as well, followed by a US tour in August and September 2017. Further upholding their reputation as a world tour band, before the year was out, the guys would venture down to South America, followed in mid-2018 by a return visit to Russia.

More shots from the band's performance at the Budweiser Stage, Toronto, Ontario, September 2, 2017. Supporting on the tour were Edgar Winter and Alice Cooper. © *Dave McDonald*

Chapter 28

Whoosh!

"This little set of records, for me, is either a nice way to finish up, or it leaves the door open for another one."

Whether it's been accelerated by Bob Ezrin or from innate and improving skills in the band itself, somehow Deep Purple returned in 2020 just better again. COVID be damned, *Whoosh!* proposed a new, scintillating, sparking collection of songs, once more enjoyable just for the Steve Morse and Don Airey solos, or, if you're a recording engineer, for the sound picture, the production values, and the mix.

"Hard to tell, because you're so close to it," responds Ian Gillan, asked what distinguishes *Whoosh!* from the last. He proceeds to inhabit the sense of motion of a man and band experience that feels almost like an accelerating creative renaissance, which ends only one way, a smashing into a brick wall of death. That's what *Whoosh!* elicits: dismay that surely at Purple's geriatric reality, this blessed music making has to lose some steam at some point soon or just stop immediately because of retirement, illness, or death.

"I only have a totally subjective point of view," continues Gillan, uncannily reflecting back these misgivings, but more positively. "Once the record was made, I gotta be honest, after three months I forget about it and start working on their next one. Or more songs or whatever. But this one, particularly, is a climax of the trilogy that was the beginning of an amazing journey, at this late stage in our career. I couldn't imagine so much creative input and energy from a bunch of guys at our age. And so, I listen to this, and not only that, but it's the best sound we've ever had. I've made comparisons. There's nothing like it in our career. So that's a boost as well. But this little set of records, for me, is either a nice way to finish up, or it leaves the door open for another one. I don't know; I don't want to talk about that. It may be happening in two or three years' time. As far as I'm concerned, it's a very satisfying little group of records.

"It's like everything—it evolves, really," answers Ian, on how the dynamic has changed between band and producer. It's funny, but the positive things that people say about Rick Rubin, Purple has gotten all of that sort of illumination from Bob, without any of the negatives (i.e., the checking out, the lack of any concrete work from Rubin). Bob is only getting started with the blessed creative abstracts. Then there's a rolling up of the sleeves and a commanding guiding of the process, continuing with the producer role but also the song doctor role and even an engineering mindset.

"The first album, we were feeling our way," continues Gillan. "But I mean, he got on it straightaway with the important things, which he laid out, when we'd have a discussion. He said, 'I want you to be like you are onstage. I'd like you to be how you were in the '70s.' That's sort of easy to say, but in practice, we've got to loosen up. And he said, 'When I watch you onstage, everyone loves the songs they know and that sort of thing, but when you start jamming, that's when the crowd really gets into you. So, let's do that.' And he said, 'I'll tell you when it goes on for too long. But otherwise . . .'

Ian Gillan, Spalt, Germany, July 17, 2022. © *Stefan Brending, CC BY-SA 3.0 DE, Wikimedia Commons*

"And this was music to our ears. So, we started stretching out a bit on *Now What?!*, and when you start doing that, it just helps the writing process. We've been on a nice steady path. It was difficult to take a decision-maker into the band when we've been sort of like an anarchic democracy with no leader since we started, really. And to have somebody at the reins was absolutely fantastic. So, he'd encourage us; he'd say, 'Yeah, stretch it out, stretch out; let's get some texture and dynamics into this.' He was very encouraging.

"And then every now and again, you'd hear on the talk-back mic, 'I'm not liking it. I'm not liking it.' So, we'd stop and save wasting a lot of time. The way he worked kept us all fresh, kept us on top of things. There was a lot of spontaneity, even when we had the arrangements worked out. There was a lot of freedom within the structure. So, you get used to that. Once it's settled down, you kind of take it as second nature, and you don't even think about it. So that's why I think we've reached a stage now where we're fairly confident with him with regard to the sound and the direction. He's like a conductor for an orchestra, basically. So, I'm thinking now, this stuff is actually just coming out without much thought. It's sounding a lot more natural for me. And that's how we've gone over three albums. It's evolved very nicely; this record, for me, has been very satisfying."

The songs come from so much collaboration now, it's hard to tell who's the instigator. The collective writing credit makes more sense than it ever has. It's a bunch of old men at play, applying the paint fearlessly until something emerges from the controlled chaos.

"Unless you make notes, it's impossible to tell," agrees Ian. "You know, the process, honestly, it's been the same since 1969, since Roger and I joined. We start at midday, always. We go and put the kettle on, make a cup of tea, have a chat. We work from noon to six every day, six days a week, and we take Sundays off. We start jamming, and no one in particular starts first. It could be anyone—bass, keyboards, guitar, certainly not me. But we all drift in and start playing. The band jams for six hours, take a break at three o'clock, always, for tea and a sandwich, and we stop at six and everyone buggers off.

"And we'd record. Stuff starts coming together, little phrases, riffs, moods, structures. People look up and go, 'Huh, yeah,' you know, when something is good. So, you press the button. And Rog is normally our head prefect; he kind of analyzes things and says, 'Oh, that thing we did Monday afternoon; how about we listen to that?' And we go, 'Oh yeah, cool, that's right.' And you don't really record who started it. We can't remember who started it. Everyone throws in, and it's a real band effort. Obviously, Steve and Don are the riff meisters, so they may come up with the licks. But it just becomes buried in the whole band ethos after that. It's hard. I'd like to answer your question, but it's difficult."

"I got an Airbnb," answers Ian Gillan, asked what his living arrangement is in Nashville when he's doing all this. "The rest of the guys stayed in condos in town. I don't like them. They're kind of tacky rental ones, and I don't know, they got all the bars and restaurants there. I prefer a bit of seclusion. So, I rented an Airbnb cottage on the banks of the Cumberland River across from the Grand Ole Opry. I could hear the music playing. I'd come back from the studio, get home about seven o'clock, and cook some food and go to bed about eight and read, then fall asleep. Then I'd be up again, two, three o'clock in the morning, writing until seven or eight, and then go back to bed until it's time to go to the studio. No, it wasn't my cottage, but the atmosphere was great. Took me a twenty-minute drive each way into the studio. I just loved it. It was one of those periods when everything went right."

"You know, every collection of people needs a leader," says Ian Paice, further articulating the Bob Ezrin effect. "Doesn't matter if you're hiking across the hills or in an army or you're in the studio [laughs]. You need a leader. Musicians left to their own devices tend to get sidetracked and a bit myopic about their bit: 'My bit is more important than everybody else's.' You get hung up on getting your bit heard and noticed. And sometimes your bit isn't the most important bit; it's somebody else's. And Bob has a very, very shrewd ear. He just picks out what is important. You might not initially agree with that if you think your bit is the important bit, but at the end of the day, when the mix is done, he's 99 percent correct. He's looking at the whole picture.

"And he makes sure we don't waste time trying to get to the solution he would get to immediately. He also has a great musical brain. If we're going around with something that isn't working, he'll come out of the control room and he'll pinpoint what's wrong, and he'll do it in a musical way. He'll say, 'Well, that chord isn't working' or 'That change is wrong' or 'We need a drum fill there.' He'll make a musical critique of it. Which, again, ninety-nine times out of a hundred is something that improves the actual track when you're recording. When we're onstage, that's our world. Here in the studio, that's his world. We are there for a few weeks every three or four years. He's in the studio forty-eight weeks a year. So, if you're gonna work with somebody that talented, then you have to understand that he's going to have input, and you'd better listen to it."

I asked Paicey the same question that I asked Ian Gillan, if there's a different persona to this record, versus the last, recognizing that it's the same six guys (with Bob), and not that long since *Infinite*.

"I don't think we ever look at it is as actually trying to do something different. It's an evolution. It just happens as you go through your life. The things that you find are important slightly change, and your view of the world changes. I think the interesting thing with this record, on the lyric side, is that although it was recorded a few months ago, it's become very much of the moment, with all the things that are going on in the world now. Some of the lyrics sort of pinpoint the dangers that we're surrounding ourselves with. Unfortunately, it's very topical. I wish it wasn't, but it is."

Collection to collection, you do get some variation on where the wordsmithing comes from. Explains Paice, "Most of the lyrics on this latest record are Ian's. The previous record, it was a collaboration of a lot of Roger and some Ian. It depends who's got the idea for that piece of music. Sometimes, I think that's definitely an Ian idea, and I find out it's a Roger idea. They keep throwing stuff out, and you never quite know who is the instigator. All I know is when Ian is around, he's always got a notebook. He might just see somebody walking down the street, and that notebook comes out and a sentence gets written. Or something he saw on the news; a sentence gets written. And I know that somewhere in the future, if they lend themselves to a piece of music we are creating, that line will become part of the lyric. Everything he sees, everything he hears, every day he is alive, if it interests him, it goes in his book. And that's rather amazing. The days pass me by, and I don't think like that. How Roger does it, I'm not quite sure, but I know that's definitely what Ian does. He could be having a conversation at dinner, and someone comes out with something funny, maybe four words, boom, the notepad comes out, or his brain kicks into gear and he just remembers.

"Once we've got ideas into what you might call a musical form, then we throw them in, and Ian and Roger, it's up to them to say, yes, we can make this piece of music into a song, or we have no chance with this [laughs]. From the instrumental side of things, we're not trying to break new ground. We're just trying to come up with ideas that interest us. The last thing you want to do, forty-odd years later, is try to do another 'Highway Star' or another 'Smoke on the Water'; great songs, but they were of the time, and they were created by the people who we were then. So, what we're trying to do now is keep our interest up by doing different things, without trying to say, okay, now we're doing prog rock or we're doing this. It's just the ideas that come out; if it interests us, we follow them through. Even though they have different characters, they all come from the same place—starting with nothing and ending up with something."

Ian Paice at the Budweiser Stage, Toronto, Ontario, September 2, 2017. © *Dave McDonald*

The band's label, Ear Music, went crazy with the advance singles this time. And people were in a position to pay a lot of attention to each modest event, because lockdowns due to the pandemic were falling into place just as the campaign began. There was "Man Alive" on April 30, 2020, and "Nothing at All" on July 10. But first came album opener "Throw My Bones," way back on March 20. It's a grand entrance point to the album, blustery, Middle Eastern of melody, and intriguing of rhythm, with Ian Paice and Roger executing a sort of driving shuffle, buttressed by Don's calliope-like keyboard riff.

"Well, it's very simple," answers Gillan, asked about the "Throw My Bones" lyric. "Everyone I know is trying to make a forecast, whether it's the weather or finances or politics or looking into the future. And people with Brexit say, 'Well, we haven't got enough information.' And they're saying, 'Well, wait, what more can we give you? We can't tell you what's going to happen.' Because that's the way it is. That's just the way things pan out. Throwing bones was an original primitive practice. It was to do with witchcraft and trying to see into the future. They started painting them with dots and they became dice. So that's where throw my bones became throwing dice, and a game of chance and all that kind of thing. So, it was just a question of sitting there saying, I'll take my chances. This is what I've got. I don't need that much, but I'm kind of cool [laughs]."

Additionally, during the promotional interviews that Ian Gillan and Ian Paice did for the record label, Gillan says, "The old witch doctors used to throw bones, animal bones, and pretend that they knew what the future was, depending upon which way the bones fell. The witch doctor and the chief, they worked hand in hand to cover the physical and spiritual needs of the tribe. And as time went on, the bones became dice and then people started making money out of it. So, it's to do with the concept of fortune-telling. And I'm thinking to myself, well, actually, I'd rather not know what lies ahead, because it would take all the fun out of it."

Reiterating what the band has always said about picking singles, in this case a lead single, Paice says that "when we finish a record, we're so inside it, to try to make logical, definitive decisions. We have a wonderful guy running the record company, and generally he will come up with ideas and say, 'Look, if we plot it this way and we follow up with this, we follow up with that, this will lead to the record getting more attention and more interest.' So, we generally leave the decisions to him. And the three records we've done with Bob and Edel Records, nobody's made a false move yet. We make records; these guys know how to promote records. So, we take a back seat. You say, 'This is the way to go; you did it right last time; you did it right the time before that—go with it."

A 10-inch vinyl release featuring "Throw My Bones," The Power of the Moon," and "Man Alive"

"Drop the Weapon" is a little bit neither here nor there, somewhat retro or even Mk. I. And it's also a bit casual of construction to appear so soon on the record. But it's distinguished in the sense that it got Ian Gillan going.

"Roger and I, we've worked together since '65," begins Ian. "It's like *The Odd Couple*, I suppose [laughs], in that sense. Roger did virtually all the lyrics on the last album, a huge portion of them. This time, the gates just flung open. I just started scribbling one night and I didn't stop, completely, and there it was, all finished. The first one I wrote was 'Drop the Weapon,' which is because I was very moved about kids dying on the street, shooting each other, stabbing each other, in London. It's getting worse and worse. And it was kind of a metaphorical arm around the shoulder: 'Hey kid, you know, your pride can take a hit. Let's drop the weapon. There's other things we can do.' That idea came out, and it was just stream of consciousness. Before I knew it, it was all finished.

"I just sat down and wrote about this kid, exploited," adds Ian, in the Edel video interview. "I put around an arm around his shoulder and said, 'You want to get to a higher position in the gang and everything else'; he's just being used. And then it becomes a bit sort of objective about San Francisco: 'Where the hell did you go? We have enough of that peace and love.' It was going back to the idea of when society was trying, through flower power and all those sorts of grand ambitions. It didn't last very long, because of human nature. It's just a very heartfelt lyric at the time, on the day."

Remarks Ian Paice, "Don't have the gun. Very simple. Don't have the gun and then that won't happen."

I asked Ian Gillan if Roger, not being the yodeler in the band, wrote differently than Ian, less practically in terms of phrasing and whatnot.

"Well, when he's writing stuff that I sing, I always turn the phrasing to my natural phrasing. Even if Roger's written a song, we do two or three rewrites until it suits my voice. We've got to get the craft right, like the percussive value of the consonants. And you don't want to have an 'ooh' sound on a high note, because it sounds awful, and it's hard to sing an 'e' or an 'r' or an 'i.' It's technical stuff like that. We work together. It's hard to describe. We got through the craft stage in the first few years, and it all just comes out naturally now. I think Roger's style is more romantic. He's a much-nicer person than I am. In fact, I complain about it all the time. He's just really, 'I hate you, Roger, 'cuz you're just too nice.' And, well, he's the nearest thing I ever had to a brother. He's more poetic. And he's very good at narratives. I'm probably more aggressive than Roger, and probably more cryptic. Roger is much more straightforward, when he's telling a story. I tend to bury meanings in two or three layers. Of the songs we've written, over the years, I mean, I've written five hundred or more songs now, and probably half of them with Roger. And of the songs we wrote, you know, he's probably written 30 percent and I've written 30 percent on my own, and the rest we've written together. We don't actually count. If somebody has a good idea, we go with that."

Next track on *Whoosh!* is "We're All the Same in the Dark," which is sort of melodic hard rock, but using a chord sequence unlike anything Purple's ever used before. Even the rhythmic accenting at the end of these stacked chords seems somehow like new territory, as does the straight-line—but on a slant—vocal melody.

"It sort of speaks for itself, doesn't it?" remarks Paicey. "We all think we got different things going for us, and we may come from different parts of the world, but turn the lights out, who knows?"

Adds Gillan, "You take a Catholic and a Protestant, you take people with long vendettas, and you put them together in a room, naked in the dark, they'd probably get on very well if they don't know the history. They're just two complete strangers, with the need for conversation and company. For every action, there's an equal and opposite reaction. You can apply that to human psychology, I think."

"Nothing at All" is possibly the most notable and delightful song on the album from a musical standpoint, although fully "Step by Step," "The Power of the Moon," and "Man Alive" are unforgettable as well. It's a sophisticated pop track in three-four time, with an opening sequence that finds Steve and Don trading bubbly licks before Ian comes in with the hooky, sing-songy vocal line.

Ian Paice, Spalt, Germany, July 17, 2022. © *Stefan Brending, CC BY-SA 3.0 DE, Wikimedia Commons*

"'Nothing at All' had me jumping up and down," says Ian Gillan. "When they first jammed it, in Germany, we had a five-day writing session, and we came up with a load of stuff. I couldn't get it out of my head. So, I kept pressing for us to include it, and, well, quite apart from the technical aspects of the trade-off between Steve and Don, and the construction, it had an atmosphere to it. The sound to me . . . what was it? Capricious, I think, is the word. It had a sense of mischief to it. So, I literally wrote a song about a leprechaun. And I wrote tons, more and more verses than were ever needed. There's something about a leprechaun that has . . . but it was too literal, and it matched the music too much. But I didn't want to lose the capricious nature.

"So, one day we were talking about environmental issues and everything else, last spring, Extinction Rebellion and lots of stuff like that. And this phrase came into my head about Mother Nature, the one true god, being an old lady, and quite benign, generally speaking. But ready in tooth and claw, as they say. And when we're doing all this stuff, I'm not really caring. Because the kids are saying, 'Hey, come on, you know; we gotta do something. It's getting bad. It's getting bad.' And everyone is going, 'Yeah, close my eyes; it'll go to way. Never mind, there's nothing at all; don't worry.'

"And then Mother Nature, the little old lady, smiles, and 'Then she blew all the leaves off my tree.' Which is the key phrase that changed it all around. So, I started writing about that. But it still had that whimsical, capricious feeling to the music, which is in congress, really, with the seriousness of the message. That makes it all the more ironic, I think. So, it worked pretty well for me; I was thrilled and still stimulated by that. When I turn it on, it just makes me smile. What Steve and Don are doing on those riffing sections is magnificent. And the way it comes in and then resolves into the modulation, into Don . . . I mean, what would you call it? That wonderful Bach fugue in the middle. The dynamics as well. I hope I'm not overselling, but I love it."

Adding more context in the Edel interview, Gillan says it's "about the state of the world being able to breathe and survive, basically. I wrote the line a year before. There was one of those color phrases I was talking about: 'She blew all the leaves off my tree.' I thought that says it all. It's very obvious to anyone who cares that things are hotting up a bit. We have overpopulation of this planet so unbelievably heavily, at an exponential rate in my lifetime. It's fair to say that there's an awful lot of people of this generation who are complacent about it. So, it's nonchalant, walking down the street arm in arm with a few friends and Mother Nature, who you get along with very well. You've known her for a while, and the kids seem to be getting along. 'Don't worry, kids; it's nothing at all.'"

"No Need to Shout" is a biting rocker, an anchoring Deep Purple song, a typical heavy Deep Purple song of the Steve Morse era.

"Roger came in with a bass riff," says Paicey. "It's a very hard, rock 'n' rolling one. Roger woke up in the night and had this riff going around in his head, and then we were going through it the next day and we thought, 'This sounds good; we like that.'"

Why it's an anchor track, or a bread-and-butter track, is because Steve regularly turns in these note-dense riffs but played at more of a stoner rock or doom tempo—thicker—than Ritchie typically would, with the same sort of sequence of notes.

On the subject of Steve, or the state of Steve at this juncture, Paice figures, "Steve is one of those few magical musicians who has the technical ability to go anywhere he wants to. You throw a piece of music at him, of any style, and he will throw something back at you, which is wonderful. Like any of us who have some technique, it's very, very easy to fall back on that. Sometimes I fall back on drum fills that are a little more complex than they need to be for the piece of music that you're playing. And again, when we're in the studio, if any one of us is going the technical route rather than the feel route or the emotional route that a piece of music needs, Bob Ezrin is there to get us back on the straight and narrow again. Steve has this wonderful ability to do lyrical, beautiful runs of music, and sometimes you just have to persuade him that that's just as good as the super-flowy technical stuff. Because it's a side of his music which is incredible. We just have to sometimes push him in that direction. It's all there. We just say, 'Look, Steve, you don't have to do that fast run on that; show us some of those beautiful notes.' Same as anybody who has a surfeit of technique. It's always there to fall out of you. Sometimes you just have to stop thinking and just do."

"This is about a generic politician," laughs Gillan, addressing "No Need to Shout." "I remember Roger saying, 'You know, it's a bit mild, isn't it?' 'Shut your mouth and go away. We're a rock band.' 'Shouldn't you be saying something more dramatic than that?' Not really. It's a politician. I've watched them. It's like, go away. I don't even want to raise my voice. They're so full of energy and altruism and doing good things for people, and within a few years, they're sucked into the system. They're destroyed. They have no independent voice. They're just along for the ride. Not one partisan politician that I see or read about today will give the slightest indication that anyone on the other side might have done something right or had a good idea. Everything is wrong. What we want is intelligent people doing what they should be doing, not fighting each other all the time."

"The lyrics are pretty self-explanatory, as the track is," notes Paice. "When we heard the backing track, we went, 'That's so powerful; that's so great.' It definitely doesn't sound like a bunch of guys the age they are playing it. If that had been played by kids in their twenties, nobody would have been the least bit surprised. It's got fire and push and drive—and it's got music."

Whoosh! album cover and promotional poster

"Step by Step" is one of those captivating late-period Deep Purple compositions that bolsters the overarching theme of this book—namely, that we are seeing a collection of guys who very early on, certainly by *In Rock*, became very good artists but then kept getting better and better at it because they loved the concept of artistry so much. It's a lifelong dedication to the muse. And not only art in the abstraction, but the craft. In other words, beyond inspiration and poetry, there's an element to the impressive totality of a late-period Deep Purple album that has as one of its processes something similar to Ian working on a crossword puzzle. The chords and the rhythm of "Step by Step" are unearthly, but so is the vocal arrangement. Or if it's not fully unearthly, it's uncommon for Deep Purple.

"It's just me," says Gillan, of those harmonies. "I think Bob sneaked into the studio and added a couple of lines. But it's a sound effect. It's a harmony. It's not a harmony as if we're in a harmony group or anything else. It's reinforcing it. It's just using the voice in the same way that Steve would use a reverb or Don would use an effect on the keyboard. It sounds nice; I like it. And there's little embellishments at the end of the line. It's as if you're writing or painting, you would add a little flourish underneath, just to give it a lift. I used to do a lot of this with the Gillan band, way, way back. Bob has encouraged me. He said, 'Do it again. Instead of that lonely voice just doing everything.' It's a bit of fairy dust—that's what I call it."

As Gillan explains, it's not Bob who's suggesting vocal melodies. "No, I did all that myself. Bob would always say, 'I'm not liking it' if he doesn't like it. Generally speaking, it was all okay. The song ideas developed in Hamburg and in Nashville, so everything was in the right key for a change, and it felt natural. You get a track like 'Power of the Moon' or 'Man Alive' or any of these things, and you use the voice as an instrumental part, to start with. The lyrics are developed later. But the texture and direction of the approach happened fairly quickly. And the quicker it happens, the better it is, usually, because you don't have time to think. So, it sounds quite natural to me. And you're not limited by the whole concept of having to deliver a certain style. You just do what you do."

"He's a great lover of what you might call slightly off double-tracking," says Paice of Gillan. "Because if you're doing exactly the same thing twice, it has no more character—it's just a bigger sound. But he has this love of and ability to just separate the moment at which the words come in, to give it a sort of magical sound. That's an art in itself. He makes it 99.9 percent correct, but there's that little 0.1 of a percent offset that makes it magical."

Explains Ian Gillan on the lyric, "That was originally called 'The Skeleton Walks,' and it's based on a sketch by the Three Stooges called 'Niagara Falls.' I never quite got the gist of it. I think one of them gets hypnotized, and every time someone says, 'Niagara Falls,' he turns and then, step by step, he goes, and he starts beating the guy up, flipping his tie, and doing all that stuff they do. I had to go right back to singing with Steve, and it worked beautifully. Fantastic. We're both very happy with it. Of course, halfway through, it goes completely nuts with all the time signatures. This is typical Deep Purple jamming in the studio, not giving a monkey's about who's listening [laughs]. But I love it."

"Wonderfully odd," adds Paice, "the way that the time moves in it. It's rhythmically very pleasing, because it doesn't remind you of anything. And the way that the lyric works with that rolling thing, it's just very satisfying. You put it on, and you turn it up, because it really feels nice."

Next comes "What the What," which is basically Deep Purple writing their own old rock 'n' roll tune, embracing their way-back roots. Sensibly, Don is doing his saloon piano tricks, and Ian responds, singing about drinking and dancing.

Ian Paice is always quick to confirm his connection to 1950s music. "Yes, because although I was a little younger than most of my generation, that's what I heard growing up. You know, those records, if I went into a coffee place for a milkshake, the jukebox had all those late '50s things on it. Little Richard was there; Dion was there. That all was just starting to happen when I was thirteen, fourteen.

"But the late '50s rock 'n' roll was what I heard before that, as an eleven-, twelve-year-old. That just fired the imagination, this different mystical stuff from America. When we had the English covers of the American hits, we liked it because it was English. But when we heard the American originals, we realized how there was a difference there. There really was a difference in class. We had kids without a great deal of musical ability trying to copy what wonderful American session musicians were coming up with. But that was a glorious time, an exciting time. There was just this whole shift in musical dynamic from, you know, being orthodox and staid, and very much regimented by songwriters giving it to us. You now had this thing where a whole new generation of musicians found a new way of making a musical statement—just amazing."

In March 1999, Ian got to express his love for this kind of music alongside an icon among icons, Paul McCartney, on the Beatles' 1950s tribute album called *Run Devil Run*, issued later that year.

"Yes, Paul was going to record this collection of things that turned him on when he was a kid, that period of rock 'n' roll. He was using a coproducer at that time, and Paul asked him, 'Well, who should we get to do the drums?' I think it was Chris Thomas, and he'd seen me play, or he'd seen a video of me playing, and he said, 'Ian is playing very well; why don't we get Ian?' I'd never met Paul before. I'd met Ringo, and George was a really good pal of mine. But anyway, they called up and said, 'Would you like to make a record with Paul?' And what do you say? [laughs]. You don't say, 'I'll think about it.' You say yes. So, we turned up on a Monday, and the whole thing was done in five days. I had a great deal of fun, and that was it, really. It was very nice working with him. He's a fantastic guy. It's something I look back on with fondness."

A dozen years later, Paice is drumming for another icon among icons, Captain Kirk. William Shatner did a space-themed covers album called *Seeking Major Tom*. On it is "Space Truckin'."

Paul McCartney's *Run Devil Run* album and William Shatner's *Seeking Major Tom* album—from the 1950s to the future

Explains Paice, "A very good pal of mine who lives in L.A., who runs an independent record label, he said, 'Look, we've got this idea; we're doing a record with Bill Shatner, doing songs that have a space connection. Would you like to do a track?' I said, 'Yeah, no problem at all.' He said, 'Time is very limited,' and I said okay. I had a little studio. He said, 'We'll send you some files over; you can do the drums there. And if it works out, that's fine.' So, it's as simple as that. I never got to meet Bill. He mentioned my name a bunch of times, on TV shows, but it was a nice thing to do. I mean, it took about half an hour to do the track. And great fun it was too."

I asked Ian if he was aware that it was going to be this sort of Beat Generation take on the song. "Yeah, because there's no point in trying to re-create something which is of that time. In that moment, you just do another performance of it. The style on that, as well, was Bill, and that's fine. This is a nice thing to say—yes, I've done a record with McCartney, and yes, I've done a record with Gary Moore, and yes, I've done one with Bill Shatner. How's that? [laughs]."

Back on terra firma, the next song on *Whoosh!* is "What the What." Ian Gillan explains that "there's always this dark humor going on within the band. One example, Bob turned up—it was a Friday—he said, 'Why don't we all go out for dinner on Monday?' And someone said, 'What's the big occasion?' And he said, 'Well, you know, we're all back together again, and we're all alive.' And somebody said, 'Well, we better make it Sunday then' [laughs]."

"But I was looking for a phrase, a percussive phrase, that would fit the vocal break. And originally it was called 'What the Fuck Happened to You Last Night?' And then I thought, well, no, they'll beep it in America. So, it's 'What the What.' It's another one of those road stories that we couldn't write when we were kids because we had no experience. But there's such a wealth of memories and stuff to go back on. Little things like five-string guitars. Five-string guitars, because no one had a spare string when it broke. So, they played all night with five strings or four. And they're dancing, and 'Every bar in London had an old Joanna and cats who could play rock 'n' roll piana' [*sic*]. And it was gone overnight. No one knows any folk songs, English folk songs, anymore. You might find a few down in Cornwall and few up in the Northeast, but that was the entertainment in the pub—sit around and play. And it wasn't just old songs. People would play rock 'n' roll as well. But that's all gone. But you remember it and treasure it for what it was, because it gave birth to other things."

Japanese-issue *Whoosh!* CD

"The Long Way Round" is a driving, up-tempo rocker, albeit a bit ordinary and one-trick at the music end: in fact, one note at the verses for Steve and two for Roger, with Ian having to pick up the slack with his vocal melody, which isn't that appealing either. Of course, there's wildly entertaining soloing and some injected light and shade, but there's just something off about this one.

"It's basically a biographical song," explains Gillan. "I'm always looking the wrong way or going the wrong way around. It's like I was looking over there, but all the time it was under my nose. It was that kind of thing. 'I know it happens, but it never sticks to my shoes.' 'You can't get me down. I got the "Things are looking up" blues.' That's my favorite opening line of all time. Basically, you're just lost in a world of your own, and dreaming and facing the wrong way, going the long way around. I remember I had the tune for that pretty early in rehearsals, because it was a good pitch for me."

"The Power of the Moon" is another work of creative triumph on the record. Intriguingly, there's a conservatism to its construction, and yet, the mind is tricked into elevating it toward what we might call progressive rock. It's also heavy metal on paper, but not arranged that way.

"'Power of the Moon' was something that came out of the blue," Gillan told me. "During this time, we were talking about a lot of environmental things and social nuances, and I was just doodling. I write every day. I have done all my life. A lot of these little concepts, they've already been half-developed anyway. But I've had this big thing about renewable energy since the early days. I used to laugh my socks off when they would talk about solar energy in England, because we don't have any sunshine, really. A local supermarket got a solar panel, and they buried it under a tree in the winter. And then when the summer came, it was obliterated and nothing worked. So, we haven't really got to grips with that. Wind, we have plenty of, but it's expensive. And they all fall down in twenty years' time, and they need rebuilding.

"I've always been banging on about the power of the moon. Because it's so powerful—it lifts the oceans twice a day. And if we could just harness a little bit of that by digging some lagoons, tidal lagoons, and putting in some turbines, it would be great. I don't know what the problem is. But the energy you get out of that, it would be enough ten times over to do all we need, and perfectly clean. I did actually phrase into my equation that it would actually slow the rotation of the earth. But we'd be long gone before it matters. That's what the song is about: the power of the moon. It's a kind of abstract or cryptic way of talking about renewable energy."

Suggesting another layer of meaning in the Edel interview, Ian says that "every one of us has our own moon path. The reflection on the water . . . I'm standing on the beach and you're standing next to me. It's the parallax effect on light reflected from the sun to the moon to you—a pretty awesome thing. But mine is separate to yours. All of these things, if you play with them as exercises when you're writing, you can see images unfolding, and you can see it triggering thoughts that might be crazy, but they make interesting or thought-provoking lyrics."

I brought up the idea that what we were all going through with the pandemic at the time was a controlled experiment in ratcheting back the economy, something that the likes of Extinction Rebellion suggests we need to do to reverse global warming. There are experts that think we need to reduce world economic output by 90 percent, and while we're at it, cut the population down to about half a billion.

"It's ironic, isn't it?" says Ian. "That something like this should result. I was thinking exactly the same thing. And of course, there's no heat going out from the cities at the moment. We've all slowed down. And so the pollution in the air is reduced. I remember the Clean Air Act in London, 1956, after the great smog of '52. We put 150,000 people in London in hospitals and killed 12,000, I think it was. I was there. We all got scarred for life on our lungs and everything else. And after the Clean Air Act, we couldn't believe it. They put the sandblasters and pressure hoses on the big buildings in London—the Natural History Museum, the Royal Albert Hall—and all this beautiful brickwork and stonework in London is sparkling clean ever since. It's easy to do, just by stopping burning coal in a city, and keeping the smog down. I don't know; what's happening now, I should imagine, is having a great effect on the atmosphere at the moment. So, you're right; it's interesting, isn't it? Unintended circumstances, really."

Don Airey and Roger Glover, Spalt, Germany, July 17, 2022. © *Stefan Brending, CC BY-SA 3.0 DE, Wikimedia Commons*

Back to *Whoosh!*, even though "Remission Impossible" is an instrumental of only 1:38 in duration, it's fully exciting, rocking along swiftly, featuring Don and Steve lashing out with violent solos.

"That's one of the most insane pieces of guitar playing I've ever heard in my life," remarks Gillan. "It's an introduction to 'Man Alive,' basically. It sets the theme after an explosive beginning [laughs]. I wasn't expecting that when I heard it. I went, 'Whoa, my God.' It's amazing. But it's a very short piece, as it should be."

"That was a nice way of linking things together," adds Paice. "Bob had this idea of having, like, a mini suite on the record, and it was just something that would link one tune with another. It's something that we knocked together fairly quickly."

"Man Alive" is another effortlessly progressive-rock-like chimera, with the operators of the riff playing on a sliding scale above what is basically a relaxed four-four beat. Like with many other places on the album, the chords represent a version of dark that's not fully doomy like doom metal, but more like worrisome. Ian Gillan rises to the challenge with thoughtful vocal melodies, harmonies, and some spoken word.

"The album cover is a reflection of the word," explains Ian. "It's fairly abstract. And the concept of *Whoosh!* was 'Whoosh!,' which is the last word in the song 'Man Alive.' It's a story about an apocalyptic situation, and it's about telepathy and empathy. A mother clutches her breast at the very moment that her son falls dead on a distant battlefield. There was a powerful image inside my head. It starts off 'The sun sets in the West / The boy has gone to rest / Mama clutch her breast.'

"And then you get the image of 'All creatures great and small / Graze on blood-red soil / And grass that grows on city streets.' It's all that posthumanity type of thing. Then, all of a sudden, something's washed up on the beach. It's a man. It's just one man. And that's the end of it, really, because one man alone is no good to anybody [laughs]. And then I go, well, 'Whoosh,' which is a kind of onomatopoeic word. It kind of illustrates the transient nature of humanity on the planet.

"And it's a little subplot, because it also describes Deep Purple's career quite nicely," laughs Ian. "Like, over in a second. I mean, 1970 seems like yesterday. So anyways, it's imagery that all came together at the time, in the writing. So that's what that's about. And then they took it to the design company in Hamburg, and they threw a few ideas around for the cover. We gradually whittled it down, and everyone is happy with where they went. It's difficult to pin down an abstract concept, but I think they've done a good job. It looks nice to me, that sort of dissolving-spaceman idea."

Extra dimensions to the lyric are explored in the interview the two Ians did for the record label. "I would look at the eyes of a mother, in all species, animals, when they're holding a child or with child," explains Gillan, "and there's a look in their eyes that is like they're at one with the child.

"Then I had that thought of a mother clutching her breast at the very moment that her son fell on a distant battlefield. These are powerful thoughts that just stayed as pictures. It's a very quick way of saying there's been a big war and it's all over. And then I refer back to my Tarzan books when I was a kid, and imagine the cities being overgrown and taken over by the jungle. And all of a sudden, the word gets around, something's washed up on the beach. There's an oboe section. It's quite symphonic, this piece of music. A short narrative seemed the only thing to do, because I didn't want to encroach on the haunting nature of the music. So, there's a little spoken piece, and that's repeated at the end, when it's 'A man alone washed up on the beach, just a man—whoosh!' It's one man. He's no use to anyone in terms of survival. It's just a man. And that's where 'Whoosh!' was mentioned completely independently of the title. But that's really a classic example of how the music comes first, with Deep Purple."

"'Man Alive' is a nicely odd track," adds Paice. "That just came from different bits on different days, and they all sort of fell together—A went into B, which went into C, and it sort of came together like that. Atmospheric isn't the word for it. It's superatmospheric. The little riff itself is so gloriously simple and so plaintive. You're hooked straightaway. And then, of course, you end up with a little bit of poetry in the middle of it. That again is something totally unexpected. Again, pretty relevant to what we see happening on the planet now, urban blight, things going wrong, and wow, a man alive. How strange is that? You know, because the rest of them are all gone—whoosh!"

Next, curiously, the band whips up a new version of "And the Address," which was the first song on the *Shades of Deep Purple* debut from the band. Diminished already by being an instrumental, it's also a pretty uninteresting form of psychedelic 1960s music, plus a lift of Jimi Hendrix to boot.

"When we started the record," explains Paicey, "Bob had a great feeling this would be the last one, and 'And the Address' was one of the first tracks we ever recorded on the first Deep Purple record. So, it would be nice, sort of, if it's going to be the last one, make it full circle. So, we gave a shot at it. I think it's all right. I'm not sure it's as good as the original, but then again, I don't think you can ever really go back and improve on something which was of its moment. But I think it's a nice little rounding of the circle."

As for Gillan's take, "I've got nothing to say about that, apart from the brilliant performance on cowbell I did for the song."

That was it for *Whoosh!* proper, but there's a pretty significant bonus track this time around, called "Dancing in My Sleep." It's a funky hard rocker that adds to the pile of these songs that sit in the space between the band's rock 'n' roll and blues roots on one end, and something verging on heavy metal at the other, or at least full-throated rock of a sort where a distortion pedal is always stomped.

"I love it; it's very angular and cold," remarks Gillan. "It builds as it goes on. It's all about dreaming, what you dream about, but that's not really important. There's only one really important thing on this track, and that is the guitar solo, for me. With due respect to all the other guys, it's magnificent. Bob said to Steve, 'Hey, why don't you try that Danelectro?' Bob has a load of guitars on stands in the studio. Steve just picked it up and went, 'Oh yeah.' It's one of the greatest solos that I've ever heard in my entire life—phenomenal. And that's why that song is worth listening to.

"He's very obviously highly skilled," offers Gillan on Morse, asked where he's situated in the band, fully seven albums into his tenure at this point. "Ritchie Blackmore was absolutely thrilled—when I say thrilled, he was very complimentary—about Steve, when he joined the band. So, the interesting thing is, since we did *Purpendicular*, Steve brought in an element that we never had before. We never had

A curious ad buy of whimsical design

that American presence, with an American history, an American musical background and the culture. He's growing up with a different set of influences. He brought that into the band, which I thought gave us an extra dimension. It's always difficult when you have two cultures. There are things that he thinks are really cool and there are things that I think are really cool, but we don't agree on them, necessarily. But he listened to different kinds of music altogether when he was growing up. And he studied different things and played in different styles of bands, with different ethos. The English sort of attitude and energy is completely different to the American band stuff.

"Over the years, he's seen us through some rough times, an evolution, but it has been a great education for all of us," reflects Ian. "It's widened our palate. It's been a great education to me. It's also given me a chance to do some of the harmony things that we were talking about earlier, which I did in the days of Gillan, and before that when I was in a harmony band.

"Steve had some problems recently, physically, with his wrist, in his tendons, and it made it difficult for him to do the style of lightning-fast histrionics that he was so well known for. And so, he's relaxed a little bit. Like I say, there's a solo on this album, on 'Dancing in My Sleep,' where he plays a baritone guitar, an old Danelectro, and it's one of the greatest guitar solos I've ever heard in my life. He also plays a brilliant solo on 'We're All the Same in the Dark' and a few others. But I guess you wouldn't have recognized it as Steve's style ten years or twenty years ago. It's more, I don't know, laid back.

"Steve's a kind of frenetic guy anyway. His personality is pretty intense, but he also has a lovely nature. But this seems to suit him, this slightly more laid-back style. There are blues elements coming out that I've never heard in Steve's playing before. It's great, and he's been encouraged to do that. I think, probably, that's part of life's evolution. It happens to us all. When we're twenty years old, the world is a different place. But when you reach middle age, you start becoming more philosophical about things and you approach things differently. Your experiences are different. You can do things you couldn't do when you were twenty. In my first band, my first interview with the local newspaper, he wanted an anecdote, and I didn't have any. I hadn't done anything. I hadn't been anywhere. These things have a habit of changing. I could do the pole vault, and I could do sports and play football. But I do other things now and it's just as satisfying."

The embattled Mr. Morse on the Budweiser Stage, Toronto, Ontario, September 2, 2017. © *Dave McDonald*

Chapter 29

Turning to Crime

"He'd either think it was brilliant or awful."

It's a different sort of project for Deep Purple, plus we're all in lockdown, so what the heck. Many bands get around to a covers album one day, and now it was Deep Purple's turn. Unfortunately, fans weren't going to be particularly excited about the songs picked for *Turning to Crime*, issued on November 26, 2021. In that respect, the album aligns very much with Rush's *Feedback* EP and UFO's *The Salentino Cuts*, two releases received unfavorably due to stodgy, unimaginative tracks that are too old and too covered already.

"Don't tempt me," chuckles Roger, on what Ritchie Blackmore would think of *Turning to Crime*. "I'm not going to talk about that. You know, who knows? He'd either think it was brilliant or awful. So, there you go."

Then again, the Man in Black hadn't been in the band for close to thirty years, having been replaced by Steve Morse, who can count this trip down memory lane as his eighth studio album with the band. But of course, *Turning to Crime* has an asterisk next to it with respect to calling it a "studio album," because it's Purple doing "Jenny Take a Ride!" and "Oh Well," an old Bob Seger song called "Lucifer," and more old classics until we get to a medley called "Caught in the Act," where we hear . . . even more very old classics.

"Because we're a band of musicians, not just hard rockers," responds Roger, asked about why such a traditional batch of songs were chosen for the record. "Our reputations belie the fact that you can actually do other things. And I guess we're lucky enough to have a band that can really play well. It all comes down to music. We're musicians first. We're not sort of pranksters thinking about the stage or picking songs based on what other people want. We've always kind of gone out of our way to be ourselves. And all that music is what we grew up with. And even Lonnie Donegan, skiffle, that's represented in there. Ray Charles. There was no difference in music back then. Now it's all, you know, genre, genre, genre. We're multigenred to death; it's crazy. But to us, music is music. A good song is a good song."

Roger at Sweden Rock, Sölvesborg, Sweden, June 8, 2023. © *Björn Frank, Wikimedia Commons*

The Purple guys definitely play well, which can be heard—and seen; there's a stylish, professional YouTube video of it—on the band's cover of Love's "7 and 7 Is."

When asked why they picked that as the first single, Roger notes that "the record company wanted a different song. But I felt that that was fresh enough and new enough and ferocious enough to grab attention. And I think I'm right. I still think I'm right. They wanted the Cream song 'White Room,' probably because it was a more well-known song. I think that's what they were after: having something that might get some radio play or whatever. But I didn't agree with that. '7 and 7 Is' showed a sort of hard rock side to a song that very few people have heard. It's been covered a few times, but still, not many people have heard it. In fact, playing the album to people younger than myself, twenty or thirty years younger, or even ten years younger, they don't recognize half the songs."

Offering a bit of pushback, I note that people definitely have heard, many times, "White Room" and "Shapes of Things" and "Oh Well."

"Sure, except, I mean, I played it for someone the other day, and it was 'Who did "Shapes of Things?" I've never heard that.' 'It's a very famous song. The Yardbirds.' 'Never heard of it.' So, unless you're in the business, or in the business of really being into music, you know, loving music, it's likely that when people are born in the '80s or the '90s that they've got no idea what half of these things are. It's all old-fashioned stuff to them. Not to us, but to them it's still very fresh, and maybe it's an education for a few people. All the songs are very much part of our lives. '7 and 7 Is,' before I was in Purple in another band, we used to do Love songs onstage. It's unusual writing. That whole thing from the West Coast was an eye-opener, the San Francisco scene. But we had thought, well, should we do something from the last ten or twenty years? But nothing came to mind. I mean, yes, we are aware of stuff, but nothing came to mind. And what really came to mind were the songs we loved and became a part of us."

The *Turning to Crime* regular issue plus the box version

Upon hearing opener "7 and 7 Is," one is assured that the crackling, high-fidelity sound picture that Bob Ezrin had been bestowing upon the band has been carried over to this novelty record. Above all, the song is a drum workout, and Ian Paice's military snare is front and center. Ian Gillan also throws himself into the song, singing high, thespian, and energetic.

On Ezrin, Glover says, "It's kind of a challenge to make the band sound live even though we're not. And for that, really, Bob Ezrin is to blame. Because we just recorded the stuff and sent it to him, and it's his mix that makes it work. We don't always agree with the choices, which is fair enough. But for the most part, he dropped some magic dust on it.

To wind up with these selections, Roger says, "We had about fifty or so songs to choose from that we all suggested that we might like to do or could imagine us doing. And then we took a vote, basically. There were lots of long conference calls. I can't remember what the contenders were anymore. We were concentrating on these so much. Once we decided on all these, we didn't think about the others. And Bob was very, very enthusiastic. Actually, we are a funny bunch of guys. There was a lot of humor being bandied about. I think it's a relief, in these shitty times that the world is going through, to actually have some fun."

Next is "Rockin' Pneumonia and the Boogie Woogie Flu," from Huey "Piano" Smith circa 1957. Johnny Rivers had a bigger hit with it in 1972. Purple turn it into a muscular boogie rocker, with Don high up in the mix playing clean, clear Jerry Lee Lewis–style piano. There's guest trumpet and tenor saxophone as well. Fleetwood Mac's "Oh Well" follows, with Deep Purple playing it not particularly heavy, instead keeping it relatively intimate. Still, it's an ambitious arrangement with additional flights of fancy. Of all the songs on the album, it's perhaps the most varied, both in its original form and in Purple's retelling.

Speaking of "Oh Well," Glover cites this one when asked about favorite bass parts. "'Oh Well' was quite a challenge. Yes, I know the song is difficult enough anyway, but Steve did a demo for that and inserted a sort of phantasmagorical piece

A Japanese-issued *Turning to Crime*

that required lots of scales. And I'm actually, at heart, a simple bass player. So, he'd presented me with a lot of hard work to do. But having done it, I realized that what he wrote was great."

Next is "Jenny Take a Ride!" from Mitch Ryder & the Detroit Wheels. It's a perfunctory rock 'n' roll number—always has been—but Purple take an interesting approach, again playing it small and playful, the most notable extremity being Ian Paice's hyper snare beat for the track. Here and most places elsewhere, Steve gets into a fairly traditional frame of mind when it comes to his soloing, but he's sticking with his usual Purple tone and still injecting a level of modernity to his note choices.

This is followed by Bob Dylan's "Watching the River Flow," which comes across as a fairly goofy rock 'n' roll number just like what came before. Then it's time for some show-tune-styled swing jazz with "Let the Good Times Roll," pretty generic, ultimately, with more horns and some blues soloing from both Steve and Don.

In fact, there's a ton of Don Airey stretching out on this album. Says Roger, "Obviously, Don plays Hammond in Purple, more than anything else. But on his own, first and foremost, he's a pianist. He's even a Steinway member. He's got high honor indeed. And of course, left to his own devices, he would go to the piano first. A lot of these songs don't require a big screaming organ, but they require a piano. Especially the Ray Charles one, for example. Or organ more like Jimmy Smith might play than a hard rocker might play. We're homing in on the song, and what the song needs. Although we've taken it out of context enough to try to heavy it up or whatever."

It's not surprising to see Little Feat covered here, with Roger having been turned on to them by the guys in Nazareth. "Yes, they'd told me about them, basically. I hadn't heard anything. And by that time, I think they'd had *Sailin' Shoes* out. And of course, I absolutely fell in love with them. Later, I had been in a desperate mood one day, having fought with my then girlfriend—or wife; I can't remember what year it was. And I was driving around London in an angry mood, having left the house, and I sat outside the Victoria and Albert Museum with no place to go. This is two in the morning. And I just sat there in a depressed mood, and I stuck this eight-track in that I'd just got: *Dixie Chicken*. That song just blew me away, and my depression lifted immediately. I went home and sorted everything out. So, you know, that one has an emotional context to it for me."

"Dixie Chicken" is in fact a highlight of the album, even as it helps maintain the flow and mandate of what we've heard thus far, given its funk-and-blues essence, albeit New Orleans style. The guys play it very laid back, with Ian Gillan underscoring the approach with his positively slack-jawed phrasing.

Given how bluesy and traditional the album is—or let's call it boogie woogie, more like—I asked Roger who in the band is indeed the most blues or original rock 'n' roll adjacent.

"Well, Paicey is the jazzer. He kind of grew up with swing music. Which turned into jazz, and therefore jazz and blues go together hand in glove. So, I guess probably more so Paicey. Steve is certainly capable, and Don is certainly capable. I played in blues bands. We're all connected in a way. Ian Gillan is probably slightly less than anyone. It's not that he doesn't like it; it's just a different style for him. But I don't even know what blues is. You get to defining it, and you get lost. It's a happy album. That's what I think about it. As I listen to it now, there's a happiness about it. There's a contentment. The whole idea was that we weren't just going to copy songs. In some places we were going to add to them, put solos in them where they didn't exist, do arrangements of the song. The song is still obviously what it is, but I like to say it's Purpleized. It was really an experiment to start with. We didn't know if it would work, and after a song or two we realized we were onto something that was good."

"Shapes of Things" is also rendered, curiously, not heavy. It also doesn't adhere to the military or "Bolero" rhythm most often associated with the song. It's more loose, with a loping bass line and a groove. Don Airey is pervasive with organ, really taking the (perhaps) expected heaviness out of the song. Did the guys really "Purpleize" these songs? I'd say not so much. Although expecting the unexpected is something of a Purple personality trait. Take for example "The Battle of New Orleans." Yes, it's the historical, traditional bluegrass tune, and again, it's played modestly and intimately. As well, the lead vocal is taken by Roger, and both Steve and Bob sing too. Pervasive fiddle is provided by Gina Forsyth, and Bruce Daigrepont plays squeeze box.

Divulges Roger, "'Battle of New Orleans' became a bit of a question mark. I'm not going to say who, but one person didn't like it. But the four of us did; well, the five of us, including Bob. So, it did get on the album. One member of the band felt that it didn't belong. But I feel strongly that it does belong. So, there you go."

Next is "Lucifer," an obscure Bob Seger tune. And despite its malevolent title, and a smattering of heavy riff here and there, it's a fairly upbeat boogie rock number, slotting in sensibly with the rest of the tracks. Granted, Deep Purple put a lot of playing into it, making it one of the more action-packed renditions here. In the end, it sounds like a Foghat song.

Notes Roger, "That's Steve's thing; he suggested 'Lucifer.' I'd never heard it. I don't think any of us had ever heard it. It's very early Bob Seger. And all we had was a live version that he had found on YouTube. I was a bit skeptical at first, but it's actually one of my favorite tracks now. His arrangement was great."

Next, we have Cream's famous "White Room," and again, Deep Purple play it so safely, so unremarkably, that you really begin to wonder what the point of this all was. It's not a monster Deep Purple beating about the face, neck, and chest, nor is it acoustic or jazz or prog or a cappella or in any other way innovatively arranged. To circle back, it's what fans were saying about Rush's *Feedback* EP, where they were hoping for creativity to make up for the sleepy choices, and they didn't get any of that.

Says Roger of the closing number, "In 'Caught in the Act,' the medley, there's Zeppelin, there's 'Green Onions.' You meet people along the way [laughs]. Spencer Davis Group and all that." Indeed, the song is a spirited jam, with Ian Paice positively a joy to behold. On the positive, there's a look-in at Led Zeppelin's "Dazed and Confused" and "Hot 'Lanta" from the Allman Brothers. But man, ain't nobody I know that wants to hear covers of "Going Down," "Green Onions," and "Gimme Some Lovin'" ever again—from anybody. As for bonus tracks, well, you can throw "(I'm a) Road Runner" on that scrap heap of history too.

The two Ians, Sweden Rock, Sölvesborg, Sweden, June 8, 2023. © *Björn Frank, Wikimedia Commons*

As alluded to, *Turning to Crime* was in fact a product of COVID times, and for a pretty interesting reason that is unique to Deep Purple.

"Yes, well, we can work independently of each other in some form or another," explains Glover. "We all have home studios. Well, home studio . . . a computer is your home studio. And I have a computer and ProTools and stuff like that. So does Don and Steve and Ian Paice. Ian Gillan was the only one without a studio. So, we waited until all the stuff was finished before we took four days and did all the vocals. And that was in a friend's studio—Peter Gabriel's private studio. Because Bob Ezrin knows him well, and he allowed us to use it.

"But the problem is we can't write together," continues Roger, "and writing has to take place when we're all face to face—it's a group effort. So, we can't write songs. In fact, we *don't* write songs—they just jam, and they appear. So, for a next record, being together to do that might be difficult. We don't know. We're planning on touring next year, but if that doesn't happen, sure, we'll be working on another album of some kind. Someone suggested recently we should do a trio of covers albums. I mean, who knows? It might end up being that way. We have to be pliable. That's all we can be."

Chapter 30

=1

"One person's terrible sadness has turned out to be of great benefit to the band."

Fortunately for us as fans, as well as for the members of Deep Purple—who don't seem to want to retire from their jobs anytime soon—happenstance has given them new life, or at least something to maintain or increase interest and even hope, as bodies and minds begin to fail.

On September 16, 2022, the band officially hired Belfast native Simon McBride as their new guitarist, after a deputizing period in which he had stood in for Steve Morse, who, alas, had to leave the band after nearly thirty years to take care of his gravely ill wife, Janine, who has, sadly, since passed on.

"Well, *Whoosh!* and all those albums were the Steve Morse era," figures Glover, setting the scene for what, by all accounts, turned out to be an energetic renaissance within the ranks. "And that is really what makes the difference. Because it's a guitar band. It wouldn't be a band without a guitar. The guitar is the focal point, after, you know, what the song is and the singer and stuff. But the actual structures of the songs come from the guitar. Steve's got a different mind; he's got a unique mind. He's a bit more all-encompassing, if you like. And now we have Simon McBride, who is in his early forties and grew up in a different era and grew up in the rough and tumble of Irish rock. So, he's a different kind of guitarist. Simon has a grittier sound."

Similarly asked to contrast McBride with Morse, Ian Gillan figures, "It's always difficult when you're looking at that high level of performance. We've been blessed with some amazing guitar players in Deep Purple; absolutely blessed since Ritchie. I worked with Simon on an eastern European solo tour, and I hired the Don Airey Orchestra for that tour. And Simon was the banjo player. Sorry, guitar player—I call them banjo players. And I raised both eyebrows, thinking, wow, this guy can handle it.

"And I think before you start listening to people's expression," continues Gillan, "most times when you hear a guitar player, you hear their party tricks and licks and their show-off stuff and the histrionics and all the moves and everything else. But it's only when you get down to the long haul of writing an album or a tour when you can see the other aspects. Because, you know, five guys all equally adept at their

Simon McBride, Budweiser Stage, Toronto, Ontario, Canada, August 25, 2024. © *Martin Popoff*

instrument, it's the one who's got the most personality that you might want in your band. Or it's the one with the most durability who you might want in your band, or it's the one that complains least about the food when you're on the road that you might want in your band. You might want the least disruptive of those equally talented men.

"But Simon's got it all, really. He's got a great sense of humor, he's road hardened, he's had all the disappointments that we all had during our formative years, and he's highly respected in the industry. He was already signed to our label as a solo artist, so that also dovetails beautifully into the arrangement. As a player, he's got a lot going for him. Number one is his articulation. That's what I look for in a guitar player first of all. If they're sloppy in the slightest bit, then you know they're gonna get sloppier. But he's tight and articulate. His music is very lyrical; he's well shaped. He's very good with arrangements, he's got a lot of drive, and his rhythm playing is sensational; he fits in with the rhythm section. And he has the benefit of youth. Because the poor kid's only forty-four years old, he's got all this drive that has kind of created a renaissance in the band. It's lifted everyone to the extent that we feel as if we're back in the '60s or '70s. I'm not talking about the music; I'm just talking about the joy of life. And so, I can't help but praise him in every department.

"Steve was fantastic," continues Ian. "We all loved Steve; his playing was immense. But Steve and Simon are different that for a start, they come from different backgrounds socially and culturally, and that has an effect on your output, on your expression. The background of Steve, of course, was in southern rock in America, and jazz. I mean, I love the story when Steve got fired from the jazz club in university in Florida because he had too much tone. That says everything about the jazz brigade [laughs]. But I think that they're both up there, with tremendous vision and skills and expression. That's the important thing. You can't call yourself an artist if you don't have expression. In the end, being completely dispassionate with my affection for Steve, it's a very sad thing that he couldn't continue. And it was so long, the gap, that we were beginning to worry that we would never get back on the road again. So, we made the decision to start again, and Steve obviously wasn't able to. So, it may seem cruel, but that's the way it is. I mean, in effect, one person's terrible sadness has turned out to be of great benefit to the band."

"The problem was, it was time," adds Roger. "We had a writing session for the album, and on the second day he got the phone call—his wife was in intensive care. So, he immediately flew back. Which left us having a writing session without a guitarist, which was not particularly productive. It's very difficult. We sounded like a sort of Holiday Inn jazz band. But Steve was leaving, and we don't know for how long. It could have been a couple of weeks; it could have been a year or more. There's no way to tell, and we couldn't wait, really. We had to make a harsh decision and say sorry, we've got to move on. It's not an easy decision to make, and there was a lot of

Roger showing the new guy the ropes, Budweiser Stage, Toronto, Ontario, Canada, August 25, 2024. © *Martin Popoff*

sadness. After twenty-eight years, you become pretty close to someone. I don't think he was that disappointed, because he wanted to finish the band years ago. He just thought we were on such a good high after *Now What?!*, and now let's have a final gig and we'll go out with a bang. And that's not the way I want to go out. I don't want to announce a final gig. I don't know what he thought, really, but I know he was thinking about it along those lines. That's why we called it the Long Goodbye Tour, as a compromise to him, saying, yeah, it's gonna end soon, but we can't say when."

But it wasn't only Steve, says Roger, who was wondering when Purple might pass. "I remember when *Infinite* came out, Don Airey was asked, 'Is this the last album?' And he said, 'I thought the *last* album was the last album!' [laughs]. It's a game, you know, what was going to be the last album? I wonder what socks I'm going to be wearing when I die. We did this new album simply because going on the road with Simon was a whole new experience, and we just very quickly thought we'll do an album as soon as we can. We're hot, we've been touring, we're on fire—let's do an album right away. So that's why we did it. And we're gonna do another one at the end of this tour."

"When you've got that energy, you just want to get up and do things," seconds Ian. "It's like in life. You know, do you want to sit down and flop around and watch a movie, or do you want to get up and go and do something physical because you've got this energy coming out? It's just human nature, really. We're on a high at the moment. Lots of things came into play and overlapped. There's a contiguous relationship with Bob Ezrin, either side of Steve Morse and Simon. We've done albums with both of them with Bob, who's got us a sound that I've been searching for all my life with Purple—I think that's one of the great things about Bob. So yeah, I mean, right now we're full of it."

Offering more on Simon's background and fitness for the band, Roger explains that "he'd worked with Don Airey for about ten years before joining this band. Don's band does little club tours. Every year, they're out on the road somewhere. And consequently, they've played quite a few Purple and Rainbow songs. Because that's Don Airey's genre; that's what he's known for. So, when this tragic thing happened with Steve, there was actually no other choice. He'd worked with Ian too. I'd got up onstage with him once here in Switzerland. Yeah, we kind of knew who he was and what he was all about. There was no other name on the list."

But he also had to get along with the sixth member of the band, Bob Ezrin, who, this time, got to record the band in his hometown of Toronto.

"The studio we used in Nashville doesn't exist anymore," says Roger. "I mean, it was all very businesslike. We were only eleven days in the studio. Bob's dynamite and has a lot of dynamism, a lot of energy. He's got his idea of what he wants to do. That sometimes works for every one of us, but you know, we all have slight problems here and there. 'I don't want to do this,' and Simon and Don can say that too. We talk it through. It's not exactly friction, it's nothing bad; it's what's best for the band and what's best for the album."

"We're all getting on very well," adds Gillan, leaving out any mention of friction. "New blood in the band is always very welcome. We've got a common sense of humor. We are completely diametrically opposed, if that's such a thing that can be with five people, with things like politics and stuff like that. So, we never discuss that sort of thing. But there's a lot of common interest in outside things, like current affairs, sports, and that sort of thing. And with Simon, there's a lot of common ground culturally, as well as outside interests. It's very convivial, the atmosphere in the band. I'm glad it is, because it was about time."

And then it was about time for the album to see the light of day, with the awkwardly titled *=1* emerging on July 19, 2024, after three advance singles had all of us talking, issued across the three months prior.

"I had half, well, two-thirds of the album finished," begins Gillan on the strangeness of the album title and the attendant justification, speaking with the author between bouts of getting in tour shape for the band's upcoming paired bill with progressive-rock giants Yes.

=1 on vinyl, CD, and cassette

"But I didn't feel rooted, if you know what I mean. I didn't feel all the songs were coming from the same place. Not that I wanted it to be conceptual, but they didn't have that cohesion. So, I did the usual and scrapped everything, tore it up, and started again. It had been just driving me nuts every day with the bureaucracy that exists. Just to walk through a door, just to look at something in a shop window, just to buy something or to deal with any large organization, this relentless question. I mean, I just want to buy something, but I have to go around the block three times.

"So, I did an equation, a ridiculously long equation, that quite simply equaled one. And I thought, all that nonsense just to reach the target. The idea developed from there. I thought that would look good as like the workings of a mad scientist on a chalkboard. And I happen to know a mad scientist. So, he did me a favor, doing an even more complicated equation with all the Greek symbols and everything. That really got me started. I wrote the whole thing, all the songs, in probably two or three weeks after that. I was focused. So, the theme, to answer your question, is simplicity—keep it simple.

"This little equation," continues Gillan, "I had it on my desk. In fact, I've got it still here right now. It's pinned to the wall. That was the root of every song. And I tore up eight songs completely, maybe more, just to clear the decks and get started again. And once I had that in my mind, it was great. So, I can relate every song back to the idea of "=1."

Pressed for an example of why this came to be, Ian exclaims, "It's unbelievable! Oh, God almighty, I think one of the last resorts was me sitting in my small two-bedroom village cottage in Portugal with my studio at the back. I was trying to buy something online. I was trying to spend some money. And there was a robot asking me to prove that I was a human being by solving this bloody matrix of motorbikes or traffic lights before I could proceed through to the shop, just to window-shop or browse or do what I wanted.

"It happens all the time. And suddenly after we've become normalized, we become compliant. We can't resist. We lived for a thousand years under a system of law and order, and it served us very well. Because we knew when to push the boundaries and when not to. We get caught or, you know, don't be naughty. We knew where we stood with regard to the moral code or criminal code or behavior patterns. And then all of a sudden, in the last quarter century, we now live under a system of rules and regulations which is a different kettle of fish altogether. And you have to comply. You can't just say, 'Oh, to hell with it. I'm going walking in the country. I'm not going to do this or do that, and if they catch me, they catch me.' This time they're catching you before you've done anything, and everyone's compliant. It's quite a challenge to see society as it is now. And I'm only referring to the complication of it all."

It's a fascinating concept, but in the end, it doesn't take over the album and make it a prog-rock concept album. In fact, there are equally smart and nifty ideas that emerge on the level of individual songs, even if, on a primary and intended level, they all adhere and ascribe to Ian's cool concept.

Deep Purple on the cover of *Goldmine*; feature written by the author

Adding meat to the bones, Roger says, "I was in Portugal with him on a writing session, ostensibly to listen to the rough mixes and figure out what songs we could work over them. Ian's got an inquiring mind, and in a sort of doodling moment, he's like, 'Oh, I wonder what kind of equation, as complicated as it could be, could make it equal one.' And he got a friend of his to do it. He showed it to me, while we were in the middle of what we were doing. And 'Could that be an album title?' I can't remember who said it. But I liked the symbols, just *=1*. I thought that was very good. So, we played with various thoughts about it, and hey, the record company liked it and everyone liked it.

"So yeah, Ian was driven on this album," continues Glover. "He wrote all the lyrics on this album. I was merry support on this one. It changes from album to album. The *=1*, to me, and this is only one interpretation of whatever you can think of. We have a huge history, as you well know [laughs]; you've written a lot about it. And it's had its ups and downs and its complications, and its multiplications, plus its distortions. And whatever it's gone through, it's ended up that we're still a band. That's how I feel about it."

Roger's alternate solving of the equation makes perfect sense once *=1*, the band's twenty-third album, kicks off. The opening track is "Show Me," which, after a brief spot of Steve Morse–styled chicken-scratch guitar, explodes into view, muscular, sinewy, groovy, and heavy. There's a unity of purpose there—it's a band operating at peak level.

"It's simple, straightforward; it's rocking," says Gillan of the album in general, but no more sensibly applied than right here with "Show Me." "I think the first thing that comes into your head is often the best idea. If you overcomplicate those arrangements and ideas, then you lose the impact. Most of the best songs in my life have been written in less than twenty minutes. Even when I go back to 'Child in Time' and all that early stuff, they were all written in no time at all. Because they were uncomplicated. They just followed your nose as far as the arrangement was concerned. Paicey is much happier with uncomplicated arrangements, because you can get your teeth stuck into it. Yeah, he's playing very well here."

Also playing very well are Don Airey and the new guy, Simon McBride, who, late in the sequence, duel over a new and modulated sort of melodic progressive-rock musical structure, with Simon playing traditionally clean and electric, and Don very untraditionally, very much new wave and synthesized.

"A Bit on the Side" is even heavier, with Ian Paice thundering away on double bass drums behind arpeggiated riffing and clouds-parting power chords from Simon.

"Yes, Charlene," chuckles Gillan, divulging the story behind the song's curious lyric. "We were at an erotic club somewhere in Germany—they're all over the place there—a few years ago. The whole band was there; my wife was there and everything. We were sitting having champagne up near the front of the stage, honored guests and all that sort of thing, and a rather attractive person in a silver lamé dress sidled across and sat down next to me and started chatting away. So, I offered her a glass of champagne. Well, she brought her own flute with her, so she was expecting it.

"As time went on, there was something not quite right [laughs]. I asked, 'What's your name?' She said, 'I'm Charlene from Berlin.' Okay, and we had a little chat and everything else, another glass of champagne. And she'd had a long night, I think [laughs], because she started letting things slip. And I noticed then, I said to her,

'You know, you've got plenty of makeup, and it doesn't quite cover up that sort of early-evening shadow on your jawline.' So anyway, we had a bit of a 'What's your name really?' And it ended up, 'Okay, I'm Charlie from Belfast.' So that was the inspiration for the song. It's all quite simple."

Ian Paice, Budweiser Stage, Toronto, Ontario, Canada, August 25, 2024. Support on the night came from Yes. © *Martin Popoff*

The story is there, and it's amusing to be sure, but the song is wall-to-wall drums, especially on the second verse, where Simon is stepped back in the mix. In effect, for an odd few measures, it's pretty much the Ian and Ian show.

"From the time I realized I could drum, I never thought of doing anything else," remarked a wistful Ian Paice, speaking with Sam Dunn a few years back. "I realized that I made myself happy when I did it. Further on down the line, and even to this day, I realize that when I play, I still make myself happy, but I seem to make a lot of other people happy too. When I was a kid, that really wasn't that important to me. Now I see the effect of what I do on other people. That gives me sometimes more enjoyment than it gives myself, and that's a great thing to have. I can't describe it any more eloquently than that. Maybe you come offstage thinking you didn't do too good, but everybody else thinks it was great. That's a wonderful feeling. So, I get happiness out of it. It's given me a good life, a good living, but I still go onstage like a kid. I still try to do what I did when I was fifteen, and that is trying to make it work for me. If that translates and makes it work for everybody else, that's great.

"What we do—percussionists, drummers—we do the most basic thing ever. It was the first form of music. It was rhythm. That is the basis of all music. It doesn't matter if it's in a classical piece, a piece of jazz, a piece of country music, and it doesn't matter if it's strict time or mobile time. Everything has a flow to it. What we do is set the foundation for everything else to work on top of it. And like anything, with no foundation, there's not a lot there. You have a piece of classical music which will change tempo four or five times, but within its structure, the tempo of each part is important. And it's a meter that you will tap your foot to, or you'll wait for. It's there; you can't escape it. The thing that drives me nuts now is you very rarely hear music in a shuffle beat. That is the most basic thing we've got because it's a heartbeat. Nobody uses it anymore. Everything is straight eight or sixteenths, and the glorious life itself is never used."

Next is "Sharp Shooter," which features a vicious, heavy metal introductory sequence that we find out later serves as the song's brief gesture at a chorus. Into the verse, conversely, the mood lightens while still staying active and electric. Again, come time for some slippery soloing, Don's choice of keyboard weapon is quite synthesized, making it three out of the first three songs on which he's gone to this place, evoking both jazz fusion and early '80s new wave.

"Portable Door" is yet another loud and hefty rocker. The song served as the album's first advance single, and people instantly loved it—couldn't get enough. There's a "Pictures of Home" vibe to the track, and a subtle shuffle feel, with Paice doing his above-implied duty to keep the craft alive.

"I was sitting there scribbling my usual gibberish," recalls Ian Gillan, "and I thought of all these situations where it would be really handy if I could carry a little door around with me so I could nip into a room or nip out of a room, when the situation got interesting or dangerous, whichever it was. And I'm thinking of all these situations where it would be useful. Then you get metaphorical and think, well, I'm getting bored sick of this guy talking, so I'm just gonna slip out my door—there it is. Or I'm bored with the jabbering and everything, so the public house beckons. I'll follow the call and slip in through my portal door. It's a handy little tool to have if you live in a surreal world."

The beginning of it sounds like there's a bank robbery going on, which would require various types of portable doors as well. But I suppose most adjacent is the idea of the Irish goodbye, which is when you want to leave a party or an event, there's no going around the room and ending things—you just slip away.

"Yeah, it's time to leave," laughs Ian. "You've got me thinking now."

"Well, don't go yet," I say, imagining that I've given him an excuse to end our interview!

"No, I was thinking of something else."

And then, business as usual, Roger indicates that the band had nothing to do with pushing this song forward on the release schedule. "We didn't choose it. That was a record company decision. We've kind of always had this thing that we make the music and someone else does the hard work of packaging and selling it. So rather, they get involved because they're the ones that are going to be on the front foot with that. They said they thought that's the first single, and we said okay. I don't think musicians can judge themselves very well. Look at 'Smoke on the Water.' Album track. Yeah, right [laughs]."

Or "The Boys Are Back in Town" for Thin Lizzy. "Yes, and another one, 'Black Night,' which was sort of a drunken laugh."

I asked Gillan what his relationship was with drink these days, give that the next song, "Old-Fangled Thing" sounds like another trip to the pub.

"Well, we've always got on very well" is his erudite response. "I think we're still good friends. Yes, 'Old-Fangled Thing,' that's off in a bar. It's actually a story about a pencil. The idea that I've been puzzling over the years is how, for two thousand years, people have been strangely looking at their erasers, their rubbers, and wondering why they had such long handles. And then somebody discovered the graphite inside, and civilization was born. But yeah, drinking is not quite the mad, relentless journey that it used to be. But I do enjoy it in proportion, in moderation. I never thought I'd say that, but yeah, it's cool. I never drink a drop of alcohol when I'm working, or when I'm on the road, haven't done for twenty years. And so, my habits are quite simple. Except when I get home. You know, we get about six weeks off a year from recording or touring [laughs]. And then I go completely nuts, let my hair down, so to speak. But generally speaking, it's not the wild ride it used to be."

As for the song at hand, once more Ian is executing 33⅓ percent of a shuffle, while Simon and Don work up a riff with notes of "Wring That Neck," as they say in the world of drink. In fact, "Old-Fangled Thing" sounds like a drinking song, casual, rambling, and shaggy. Like Ian getting his annual break, it lets its hair down.

Next comes "If I Were You," and it's one of only two ballads on the album. It features unusual chords, elevating it, as well as a dropped beat at the deftly more powerful chorus. Ian's singing on it is a little wild and fragile, with his voice showing its age. This leads to "Pictures of You," which had been picked as the album's second advance single, issued on June 5, 2024. And it's for good reason—it's an up-tempo melodic hard rock song with a durable, memorable chorus. It's accessible, but a little bit wistful, even regretful.

"I think Simon brought in one song in particular that was more or less a finished thing," recalls Roger. "And what you'd never do, really, with Purple is bring in a finished song. Because we all have to sort of take part in it. It usually just comes from a riff or a rhythm or a chord sequence or whatever, and we all join in with that. As you know, we don't write songs; they just evolve. But on this particular occasion, there was 'Pictures of You,' and the rest of them were all jammed out between us all, and Simon was often the instigator. Being the guitar, you have to be the instigator in a rock band."

The "Pictures of You" single release

Given it's a Simon song, I asked Ian what he knew about Simon's tastes in music. "Oh, I don't know. I don't think I've ever heard him play music when he's with us. I don't know what anyone's taste in music is these days. I know Paicey, of course, and I know Roger. Don, I mean, he comes up with the most-surprising things, but he embraces all kinds of music. I think Simon does too. But I'm not in his pocket. You know, the day we leave, after the last show of a tour, we disappear. We never speak to each other again until we see each other back on the road. We're very good mates, but we don't go to parties together.

"And I don't know how many songs he had in his toolbox," continues Ian, "or how much preparation or how much spontaneity there was, but he was a driving force, without any doubt. When we walked into the first writing session, he's playing out all these ideas. But some of them didn't make it. As always, we just dropped them and moved on to something else. But he seemed to be a bottomless well of ideas. And, of course, the complexity of human nature is that everyone else responded. You change the dynamic of the group and instantly you're facing in a new direction. It's like, everything's freshened up with a change of personnel. It doesn't mean to say it's any better or any worse. It just means to say it's revitalized. So, yeah, all good as far as young Simon is concerned. We all love him."

"I'm Saying Nothin'" adds to one of the piles that make Purple Purple, providing continuity despite the new banjo player, and that's galumphing, loping—and even limping—funky hard rock. It provides an opportunity to hear Ian Paice be one of the best at grooving, due to his skilled use of grace notes, even if they are snare whacks at full volume here, and his high hat is open and almost trashy. Plus, it's a great backing track over which to solo, and both Don and Simon take the opportunity, again, constantly adhering to and building upon Ian's spidery, Ritchie Hayward rhythm. It's another Deep Purple song written like heavy metal but then recorded like Bob Ezrin dealing with this specific group of talents.

Ian at his old-school drum set. Budweiser Stage, Toronto, Ontario, Canada, August 25, 2024. © *Martin Popoff*

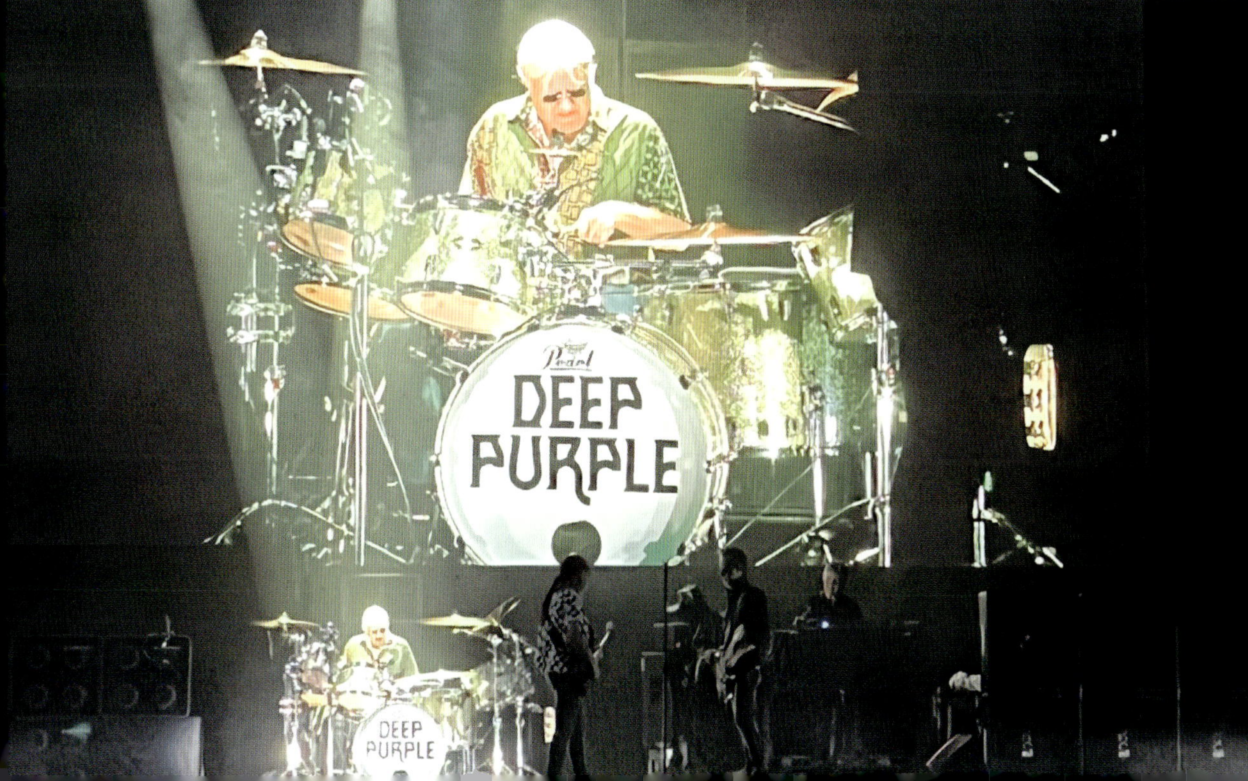

"I'm Saying Nothin'" is about the perfect crime," offers Gillan, who's troubled with my framing. "I think the dynamics within the song, when you feel confident, you can really get it out and do a contrast with a sweet little melody or something like that. It's all part of what we used to do. With the labeling of rock and hard rock and heavy metal, etc., it became incumbent upon the producers to sort of just throw the wall at you, to create this huge, relentless wall, I think, is the word I'd use.

"And that's not really us, because we don't do that onstage. We're hard, for sure, but there's music in there. For it to be musical, you've got to have balance. You've got to have changes and textures and interest woven through it. It probably sounds hard to describe, but it comes naturally when you get like-minded people working together.

"I take your point, but I kind of like it. I'll give you an example. It's probably one of the greatest examples. It's not on a record, but it's in live performances. We had sound engineers for years that would just push the faders up, on like every rock band, every heavy-rock band. And everything would be flat out. When you sit out front, you will just hear the bass drum hitting you in the gut and the bass hitting you in the gut, a wall of sound of the engineer's interpretation of how he would like to hear you.

"Now, it was all very good—until one day, we changed our engineer, and we got a musical engineer who liked to do a different balance altogether. The drums and bass weren't dominant, and the guitar wasn't dominant. They were there when needed with solos. And the rhythm section was a powerful, chunky thing. But this new guy just balanced it his way.

"And we did the opening song, 'Highway Star.' And there was nothing different on the stage—not a single thing. Same personnel, same volume, same balance, same size [of] hall—everything. The reaction from the crowd was almost quadruple. They lifted the roof off. The sound was so good, and it made all the difference. So, I think what he did was, he was just able to represent the real us.

"That's what's happening with Bob. He realizes that you don't shove things down people's throat. You don't slam them up against the wall. There's room for texture in rock 'n' roll. My rock 'n' roll, when I grew up, was Elvis Presley, Little Richard, and Jerry Lee Lewis, on the one hand. It was also Buddy Holly and the Everly Brothers, on the other hand, and right bang in the middle was Chuck Berry. There's a diversity there. Chuck Berry was very lighthearted, had a light touch. And his rhythm and his brand of songs were upbeat. We call him rhythm and blues, but it was all part of rock 'n' roll. Every rock 'n' roll songwriter learned from Chuck Berry. And then quite a few of them forgot about it [laughs]. It's a fantastic question, but I think it works really well for us. It's certainly not a heavy metal record; that's for sure."

"Lazy Sod" sounds like a creamier, slinkier, more casual version of "Black Night," maybe the *In Rock* version of Deep Purple crossed with ZZ Top. In fact, circling back to Ian Paice's comments, it's obvious he likes this space, because there are approximately five songs on *=1* that at least have one suspecting shuffle, and then, invariably tapping a toe.

"Well, Paicey plays shuffle to everything," chuckles Roger. "Everything's a shuffle to him. That's it; he's a jazz drummer. It's not always an obvious shuffle. But there's always inflections of that kind of slight swing going on. Which to me, that's the essence of rock 'n' roll. There's swing and straight time clashing against each other. That's what gives it its tension. We don't go in with a master plan for an album. An album is like a blank slate. And what are we going to do? Well, we're going to fill it with noises. All right, let's get started. There's a noise. That's another noise. Yeah, that's a good one. Yeah, that's a different noise. And it takes shape over a period. But this album feels tougher. But I also have a soft spot for songs like 'Power of the Moon,' which I don't think would have been written had Simon been in the band. It's a whole different kind of outlook."

In "Lazy Sod," there's a Don Airey solo that has an air of the humorous to it. On whether there's a deliberate comedic element to Don's personality, Glover says, "Of course there is, yes. There was to Jon Lord too. They were both fond of playing musical jokes. I think the band is generally a lighthearted band. We don't take ourselves too seriously. We're not a doom-laden, hard rock mega outfit. We're a hard rock band, not a heavy metal band. And that means we can bring in jazz and classical and folk, even. It's a mix. That's where we all come from. That's the melange of Purple. We grew up in the '50s, and what you heard on the radio is part of your system. You didn't hear a lot of rock or pop or whatever it's called back then. You'd get a lot of classical music and jazz and incidental music and the hits of the day, and although they were not interesting, they became a part of you. You couldn't help it. So that's still in the system. That's where we come from. And that's why with Simon being in the band, who comes from a different era, we actually gel very well."

Bolstering Roger's point that *=1* is a "tougher" album is "Now You're Talkin'," which is the fastest song on the album, and fairly close to being heavy metal along the lines of "Smooth Dancer," even though it's tempered by Ezrin's rounder production values and a similar philosophy to performance and even arrangement. In other words, a young heavy metal band could turn this into a fire-breathing beast of a metal song within half an hour and have to change very little.

But then "No Money to Burn" is crunching riff rock as it is, with Simon now taking the baton and writing writhing riffs like any number from Steve. Which brings up a point: to these ears, Simon's style represents a cross between an earthy, conservative, classic rock guitarist and Steve Morse.

Next comes "I'll Catch You," which is the second ballad on the album, a bit of a French torch song, sort of "Still in Love with You" meets "Parisienne Walkways." Again, Ian's vocals are a little loose and swoopy, sort of first-take thespian, very real and not particularly perfect.

The album closes with "Bleeding Obvious," yet another "tough" rocker, but ambitious, full up with thoughtful transitions and arrangements to the point of washing up on the shores of progressive rock.

Roger tells me that this one took the most effort, "because it's many songs in one, many ideas, bits, and pieces, and we just stitched them together. It's like a quilt, you know, made of different fabrics. That took quite a bit of work just getting there. Whatever it is, whether it's right or wrong, it is what it is. But the rest of them fell into shape fairly well. We didn't have a lot of time in the studio. That's the only thing I'd say about the album—in eleven days we did all fourteen backing tracks."

Glover credits Ezrin with getting the song past the finished line. "We wanted to do a song that was a conglomeration of different ideas, and he was a big part of

Simon McBride looks toward a long, productive future with Deep Purple, Budweiser Stage, Toronto, Ontario, Canada, August 25, 2024. Support on the night came from Yes. © *Martin Popoff*

that, helping us along generally, making his comments about arrangements. That's what he does. That's normal."

As for Roger's relationship with prog, he says, "I'm not a progressive-rock fan. I can only appreciate it from a distance. Some bands progress a little too far for me. It's not entertaining anymore; it's just a show-off piece. How complicated can we get, you know? That doesn't interest me. I don't listen to other bands much. Not a great fan of listening to rock music, because I've kind of heard a lot of it [laughs]. But you are the sum of everything you've heard, basically. And you are the sum of everything you heard that moved you, more importantly. I can never hear 'Lucille' without falling in love with Little Richard every time. The groove, the band, him. Unbelievable feeling, and that still turns me on."

"Bleeding Obvious" is a Garden of Eden of sounds, though, with a loud run-through of it affirming that Bob Ezrin has triumphed at the board once again.

"The thing I like about the sound is that it's very natural," reflects Gillan. "Bob is a producer who listens to the band. You know, this has been a nightmare since we first got recording contracts in the '60s, when the engineers would come into the studio and throw a blanket over all the equipment, metaphorically. They'd reduce everything to a flat sound and say, 'Don't worry; we'll create the sound.' That was their mantra, that's how they operated, and that's why all the records sounded the same.

"All the pop records sounded exciting, though, because they used session players, and they used backing vocalists and all that sort of thing to make it sound good. I mean, the Kinks with Jimmy Page on guitar—look, come on [laughs]. It's amazing how things have changed. And so, I think the idea of producing the songs is number one. And then the songs on this record, we've been leaning more towards this: there's texture and balance against the hard rock. Just take 'Bleeding Obvious,' for example. I mean, it's a pretty heavy couple of verses there. But then there's all kinds of instrumental changes, and the middle section comes up and starts talking about 'The salient point departed and parked itself in a backstreet in a lonely part of town.' It's dark and moody and bluesy and melodic."

Which sums up (ironically) =*1* as a whole. In other words, Ian's math checks out. It all winds up as Deep Purple. In fact, there's "show your work" math along the way that leads us to this conclusion, such as guitar and keyboards (most pointedly, when in a rhythm guitar role) equaling one, or Gillan and Glover collaborating on lyrics equaling one.

On tour for the album, there was additional fortunate unity, as any fan could tell, among the players on the stage, who had no problem broadcasting as one despite the addition of a new guitarist. Simon McBride usually looked like the coolest guy up there, killing it with his vaguely rockabilly stage presence, and then confirming that all the good vibes flowing his way were warranted with a lengthy and authoritative solo guitar spot. Ian Gillan also surprised everyone with how strong his voice was. And he must have known it, because he went for it, ducking fewer notes than in recent years, volunteering additional yelps and whoops, and in the end—at least at the Toronto show this author attended, on August 25, 2024—absolutely not sounding his seventy-nine years of age.

Both the album and the tour were a resounding success with all of us similarly aged and ardent students of the band, and we said as much all over myriad audio podcasts and YouTube channels. Lighting further fire were remarks in the press, mostly from Gillan but also from Roger, that the band were going to make another record right away, as soon as they got off the road.

Epilogue

"I don't know about the other guys," reflects Roger, asked who in the band is doing best at thwarting Father Time. "We complain a bit about aging bodies, but our minds don't think that way. We're on this journey, and we're still on this journey, so make the best of it. Enjoy it. I don't think about the future like that. I think if you're worrying about the future, you're spoiling the present."

But it's pretty commendable that there's so much new music and of such high quality. Surely the band prides themselves on being "this kind" of heritage act—namely, prolific and critically acclaimed for it—while also playing live a lot and playing big venues.

"I don't think pride comes into it," counters Glover. "It's just that we can't help it. It's what we do. We're lucky enough to have an audience that is prepared for us in some way. If we were in the dark without an audience, I don't think it would happen, if the audience dissolved a long time ago. It's the audience that keeps us going. That's the fuel that runs the car. And if I worry about the future after I'm gone, that's a whole other thing. I won't care—beyond my control [laughs]."

Roger says pride doesn't come into it, but surely Ian Gillan should be proud of what the band has been saying in recent years on the literary front. Even as the music continues to delight with its deft balance of tradition and freshness, lyrically, Deep Purple are managing to sound—sensibly, logically, appropriately—wise.

"I am, I am," agrees Ian. "That's something I really have talked about an awful lot over the years, is the change in lyrics. Because, you know, when you're going through your learning process in your early years, you just copy. I copied Chuck Berry and whoever I listened to, in the early days of writing with Roger. And then he let me join Deep Purple as part of a songwriting team, and we did Deep Purple *In Rock*. I don't think any song was written in more than twenty minutes. It was so natural.

"Then there's more albums and more albums. And there's a bottomless well of inspiration in that way of writing. But suddenly you're thirty years old, or approaching forty years old, and writing songs with that kind of lyric seems a bit trite and gratuitous, and also a little bit repetitive. Because you don't quite mean it so much as you did when you were immortal at the age of twenty. When you're nearly forty, you see the other end a little closer, and you suddenly realize, whoa, hang on a second—what's going on around here? You've moved on a generation.

"You start thinking about things in a different way. Lyrics have to be heartfelt. They have to be from something that inspires you. So, you look at life at that stage and say, 'What's turning me on now?' And perhaps they get a little more philosophical, and a little more narrative, perhaps, because by now you've got experience on the road. There's a little more to draw from in terms of story matter. That's been the greatest benefit of being on the road, because it provides an endless source of material.

"Then time goes on again, and suddenly you're another generation. And so, you look at it again. The point is, when you're writing this stuff, you've got to have a focus, which comes back to *=1*. I couldn't write a word, really, that made any sense, not until I had a focus on the kernel, the core of the album, and then I was happy. Walking back over those generations, the transitions have been really interesting. There have been some lost periods where we were vaguely thinking, 'What are we doing?' 'Well, okay, we're competent, we can write songs, we can play, whatever,

Father Time. © *Dave McDonald*

but where's that spark? Where's that drive?' Where's that momentum and all that sort of thing that makes it worth listening to?

"I think we coasted a couple of times, not because we were lazy, but because we didn't know what we were doing. And that's fair enough; it happens to everyone. The key is to get out of it. So, in that respect, on the writing front, it's been a good journey. I think we've done a remarkable job of hanging on to the excitement of the early days, as well as blossoming without becoming self-serving."

Also on the music end, the guys are always questioning. Explains Ian, "An awful lot of solos, apart from the early burst of inspiration, you're suddenly thinking, well, hang on a second; that's not improvisation. I heard that last night. That's exactly the same phrasing. And that happens a lot. And so these guys have mastered that. There are little elements, just like in any improv jazz band or whatever, where you'll hear them playing a tune in an offbeat way. Then they come back into the theme, back into the refrain, to bring it back into normality. Those are the little keys, and we've always had that. But in the meantime, there's a lot of free expression. That keeps the music on edge when we're touring. Otherwise, it would be cabaret."

Is Ian happy with the pile of art he's left behind? Or has he wasted his life being in Deep Purple?

"No, I've loved every minute," says Gillan. "I mean, look, I think it's fairly monumental. I was talking to one of the journalists in Germany, I think, last year, and he said, 'How many songs have you written?' That's a good job he asked that, because about twenty years ago was the last count. My secretary said, 'You've written just over five hundred songs.' And I thought that was pretty cool. And then I said I was watching a documentary on Dolly Parton, and she says she's written over five thousand songs. So, the guy said, 'Well, that makes you a lazy sod, then, doesn't it?'"

And maybe that makes her a bit of a liar. That's about 450 albums' worth of short country songs. I suppose it's possible.

"Well, probably not all of those songs were published or recorded. Nevertheless, it puts you in your place. And I think the legacy is that we've had too much fun enjoying ourselves to recognize what's been happening. The other thing you've got to recognize, and that you learn at an early age, is that we avoid chasing fashion at all cost. We just do not look at it that way. People say, well, avoid the managers, avoid the agencies, avoid the promoters, avoid the record labels, and avoid the fans when you're in writing mode. Because they'll all tell you what they think you should be doing. But ignore them all. Get in there, into the rehearse room, work your nuts off, and come up with something you're very happy with.

"And *then* is the time when you get down on your knees and pray to the fans, 'I hope you like this.' That's the way we work. We beg forgiveness, or adoration, whatever it might be. And that's worked out well. Because to coincide with fashion is a different story altogether. We've been lucky enough for that to happen three times now. There have been dips and ups and downs, but I think if you enjoy what you're doing, you can survive all that.

"And there's always live work," continues Ian. Which is a deep thought if you pause and wonder over it. Like the earlier comment from Ian Paice about just how much time is actually spent with Bob Ezrin versus how much time he spends in the studio with all manner of band over the course of the year, most of Deep Purple's days are spent packing a lunchbox and going to work performing live. We mere spectators and bystanders, we think about the band's legacy as a row of LPs or CDs on a shelf. Meanwhile, day in and day out, especially with this famously "working band" (it's such a loaded term), they are moving through time, making jazz, technically improvising 100 percent of the time, because it can never be exactly the same thing twice. In other words, as far as they're concerned, their motioning through the world, their lives, has been

Father Time's buddy. © *Dave McDonald*

onstage and traveling. And like I say, we peons on the outside who aren't in Deep Purple, what tends to matter is how many studio albums there are.

"No one can get between you and the fans on the live work," continues Gillan. "There's an awful lot of agencies involved in making a record and in reaching the ears of the public. And that's called the music business, or the music industry, as it's called now. But when you're live, it's just you and them—and YouTube, of course [laughs]."

But pressing the point, I asked Ian if two hundred years from now, if we're not burned up, is what's on YouTube really going to be the legacy, or is it the studio canon? Indeed, which of those solitudes defines the body of work?

"Well, I wish we were that thoughtful, or that academic, to analyze this as we go along," answers Gillan. "It's never been discussed in the dressing room, or between any musicians that I know. This is something that you guys do, and I'm grateful for it. But we certainly don't sit down and think, what's our legacy? Or what are we doing here? Or what kind of record should we make? Or anything. It's just absolutely natural. We were born naked, and that's the way we've been through life. We're lucky to have had success from time to time. Analyzing it? Legacy? I look back sometimes and play a couple of old tunes if I've got some mates or friends staying at my place for holiday. 'Oh, play us that record.' 'Okay.' And that's kind of nice, to hear something from the past. But I don't normally do that. I read a lot of books, and outside of music I'm interested in lots of things, like science and literature and astronomy and all that sort of thing. I've got a couple of radio stations I like to listen to, but I get on with other things.

"Now you're on dodgy ground there, Martin," laughs Ian ruefully, when I ask him the same thing I asked Roger, which is, basically, who is grappling with aging better than anybody else in the band.

"You know, we never . . . I can't remember anyone ever talking about that—the fact that we're all walking, still. Everyone's thundering away onstage and giving it hell. So, in that respect, I don't know. But once everyone gets home, I don't know how deeply they collapse into the sofa [laughs]. No, it's good. I mean, if you were traveling with the band, you wouldn't notice. You'd think everyone was around forty or fifty. There's lots of hilarity; the usual joking and everything else. Everyone gets up in the morning. They're up on time, apart from Roger. He's always just one minute late. So yeah, aging, lots of people say that it's in the mind. Obviously, the physical side of it tends to lead the way, and while you're still thinking you're sort of agile and fit, you suddenly take a step too far. So yeah, it's a subject we avoid, really. Thank you for asking, Martin."

A Deep Purple Discography

As we all know, a Deep Purple discography could become a whole book, depending on how granular you wanna get. I'm sticking with a reasonably detailed enough tribute to the albums that get a chapter in our book. However, I've provided a list of live albums over and above those that are covered by a chapter, and a list of key compilations.

As a few points on format, I've included a notes section for anything I thought was interesting or notable, so to speak. There are quote marks around songs only if they are discussed in the aforementioned notes section. Spelling and punctuation of song titles, plus timings and order of the names in the credits, are as per original release that cites such information, with the home country edition, UK, taking priority. I've noted side 1 / side 2 designations for releases from the vinyl age, which I've always figured ends in 1990, when the CD age is ushered in for real. I've cut out a few of the formalities you see with the studio albums when it comes to live albums.

Shades of Deep Purple
September 1968 (Parlophone PCS-7055)
Produced by Derek Lawrence

Side 1:

1. And the Address (Blackmore, Lord) 4:36
2. Hush (Joe South) 4:11
3. One More Rainy Day (Lord, Evans) 3:15
4. Prelude: Happiness, I'm So Glad (Deep Purple, Skip James) 7:48

Side 2:

1. Mandrake Root (Blackmore, Evans, Lord) 5:55
2. Help (John Lennon, Paul McCartney) 5:45
3. Love Help Me (Blackmore, Evans) 3:34
4. Hey Joe (Billy Roberts) 7:38

Notes: US issue is July 17, 1968. Initial band lineup is Rod Evans "writes and sings"; Jon Lord "writes, sings and plays the organ"; Nic [sic] Simper "writes, sings and plays the bass guitar"; Ritchie Blackmore "writes and plays the lead guitar"; and Ian Paice "writes and plays the drums."

The Book of Taliesyn
June 1969 (Harvest SHVL-751)
Produced by Derek Lawrence

Side 1:

1. Listen; Learn; Read On (Blackmore, Lord, Evans, Paice) 4:02
2. Wring That Neck (Blackmore, Lord, Simper, Paice) 5:15
3. Kentucky Woman (Neil Diamond) 4:43
4. (a) Exposition (Blackmore, Lord, Simper, Paice) (b) We Can Work It Out (John Lennon, Paul McCartney) 7:06

Side 2:

1. The Shield (Blackmore, Evans, Lord) 6:00
2. Anthem (Evans, Lord) 6:29
3. River Deep, Mountain High (Jeff Barry, Ellie Greenwich, Phil Spector) 10:05

Notes: US issue is October 1968. "Wring That Neck" retitled "Hard Road" on US issue.

Deep Purple

September 1969 (Harvest SHVL-759)

Produced by Derek Lawrence

Side 1:

1. Chasing Shadows (Lord, Paice) 5:32
2. Blind (Lord) 5:21
3. Lalena (Donovan Leitch) 5:02
4. Fault Line (Lord, Blackmore, Paice, Simper) 1:46
5. The Painter (Lord, Blackmore, Evans, Paice, Simper) 3:51

Side 2:

1. Why Didn't Rosemary? (Blackmore, Lord, Evans, Simper, Paice) 5:00
2. Bird Has Flown (Evans, Blackmore, Lord) 5:25
3. April (Blackmore, Lord) 12:20

Notes: US issue is June 1969.

Concerto for Group and Orchestra

January 1970 (Harvest SHVL-767)

Produced by Deep Purple

Side 1:

1. First Movement: Moderato, Allegro, Vivace
2. Second Movement: Part One—Andante (Lord, Gillan) 26:00

Side 2:

1. Second Movement: Part Two
2. Third Movement (Lord, Gillan) 28:30

Notes: Track titling, subtitling, and punctuation vary wildly across territories. Written by Jon Lord, with lyrics by Ian Gillan. Classical live album with the band and the Royal Philharmonic Orchestra, conducted by Malcolm Arnold. Vocalist Rod Evans has been replaced by Ian Gillan, and bassist Nick Simper has been replaced by Roger Glover.

In Rock

June 5, 1970 (Harvest SHVL-777)

Produced by Deep Purple

Side 1:

1. Speed King 4:18
2. Bloodsucker 4:12
3. Child in Time 10:15

Side 2:

1. Flight of the Rat 7:52
2. Into the Fire 3:29
3. Living Wreck 4:30
4. Hard Lovin' Man 7:10

Notes: All songs written by Blackmore, Gillan, Glover, Lord, and Paice.

Fireball

September 1971 (Harvest SHVL-793)
Produced by Deep Purple

Side 1:
1. Fireball 3:21
2. No No No 6:40
3. Demon's Eye 5:19
4. Anyone's Daughter 4:39

Side 2:
1. The Mule 5:16
2. Fools 8:15
3. No One Came 6:25

Notes: All songs written by Blackmore, Gillan, Glover, Lord, and Paice. US edition swaps in "Strange Kind of Woman" for "Demon's Eye." US issue is July 1971.

Machine Head

March 30, 1972 (Purple TPSA-7504)
Produced by Deep Purple

Side 1:
1. Highway Star 6:05
2. Maybe I'm a Leo 4:51
3. Pictures of Home 5:03
4. Never Before 3:56

Side 2:
1. Smoke on the Water 5:40
2. Lazy 7:19
3. Space Truckin' 4:31

Notes: All songs written by Blackmore, Gillan, Glover, Lord, and Paice.

Made in Japan
December 22, 1972 (Purple TPSP-351)
Produced by Deep Purple

Side 1:
1. Highway Star 6:45
2. Child in Time 12:19

Side 2:
1. Smoke on the Water 7:27
2. The Mule 9:45

Side 3:
1. Strange Kind of Woman 9:10
2. Lazy 10:35

Side 4:
1. Space Truckin' 20:02

Notes: Two-LP live album. US issue is March 30, 1973.

Who Do We Think We Are!
January 12, 1973 (Purple TPSA-7508)
Produced by Deep Purple

Side 1:
1. Woman from Tokyo 5:50
2. Mary Long 4:25
3. Super Trouper 2:56
4. Smooth Dancer 4:10

Side 2:
1. Rat Bat Blue 5:23
2. Place in Line 6:31
3. Our Lady 5:12

Notes: All songs written by Blackmore, Gillan, Glover, Lord, and Paice.

Burn

February 15, 1974 (TPS-3505)

Produced by Deep Purple

Side 1:

1. Burn (Blackmore, Lord, Paice, Coverdale) 6:00
2. Might Just Take Your Life (Blackmore, Lord, Paice, Coverdale) 4:36
3. Lay Down, Stay Down (Blackmore, Lord, Paice, Coverdale) 4:15
4. Sail Away (Blackmore, Coverdale) 5:48

Side 2:

1. You Fool No One (Blackmore, Lord, Paice, Coverdale) 4:47
2. What's Goin' on Here (Blackmore, Lord, Paice, Coverdale) 4:55
3. Mistreated (Blackmore, Coverdale) 7:25
4. "A" 200 (Blackmore, Lord, Paice) 3:51

Notes: Vocalist Ian Gillan has been replaced by David Coverdale, and bassist Roger Glover has been replaced by bassist and vocalist Glenn Hughes.

Stormbringer

November 8, 1974 (TPS-3508)

Produced by Martin Birch and Deep Purple

Side 1:

1. Stormbringer (Blackmore, Coverdale) 4:03
2. Love Don't Mean a Thing (Blackmore, Coverdale, Hughes, Lord, Paice) 4:23
3. Holy Man (Coverdale, Hughes, Lord) 4:28
4. Hold On (Coverdale, Hughes, Lord, Paice) 5:05

Side 2:

1. Lady Double Dealer (Blackmore, Coverdale) 3:19
2. You Can't Do It Right (With the One You Love) (Blackmore, Coverdale, Hughes) 3:24
3. High Ball Shooter (Blackmore, Coverdale, Hughes, Lord, Paice) 4:26
4. The Gypsy (Blackmore, Coverdale, Hughes, Lord, Paice) 4:13
5. Soldier of Fortune (Blackmore, Coverdale) 3:14

Come Taste the Band

November 7, 1975 (TPSA-7515)
Produced by Martin Birch and Deep Purple

Side 1:
1. Comin' Home (Bolin, Coverdale, Paice) 3:52
2. Lady Luck (Cook, Coverdale) 2:45
3. Gettin' Tighter (Bolin, Hughes) 3:36
4. Dealer (Bolin, Coverdale) 3:49
5. I Need Love (Bolin, Coverdale) 4:22

Side 2:
1. Drifter (Bolin, Coverdale) 4:01
2. Love Child (Bolin, Coverdale) 3:05
3. This Time Around (Hughes, Lord) / Owed to 'G' (Bolin) 6:07
4. You Keep On Moving (Coverdale, Hughes) 5:18

Notes: Guitarist Ritchie Blackmore has been replaced by Tommy Bolin.

Made in Europe

November 1976 (TPSA-7517)
Produced by Deep Purple and Martin Birch

Side 1:
1. Burn 7:32
2. Mistreated 11:40
3. Lady Double Dealer 4:15

Side 2:
1. You Fool No One 16:42
2. Stormbringer 5:38

Notes: Archival single-LP live album featuring the Mk. III lineup.

Perfect Strangers

October 29, 1984 (Polydor POLH 16)
Produced by Roger Glover and Deep Purple

Side 1:
1. Knocking at Your Back Door (Blackmore, Glover, Gillan) 7:00
2. Under the Gun (Blackmore, Glover, Gillan) 4:35
3. Nobody's Home (Blackmore, Glover, Gillan, Lord, Paice) 3:55
4. Mean Streak (Blackmore, Glover, Gillan) 4:20

Side 2:
1. Perfect Strangers (Blackmore, Glover, Gillan) 5:23
2. A Gypsy's Kiss (Blackmore, Glover, Gillan) 4:40
3. Wasted Sunsets (Blackmore, Glover, Gillan) 3:55
4. Hungry Daze (Blackmore, Glover, Gillan) 4:44

Notes: Reunion of the Mk. II lineup. Cassette and CD bonus track is called "Not Responsible."

The House of Blue Light

January 12, 1987 (Polydor POLH 32)
Produced by Roger Glover and Deep Purple

Side 1:
1. Bad Attitude (Blackmore, Gillan, Glover, Lord) 4:43
2. The Unwritten Law (Blackmore, Gillan, Glover, Paice) 4:35
3. Call of the Wild (Blackmore, Gillan, Glover, Lord) 4:40
4. Mad Dog (Blackmore, Gillan, Glover) 4:51
5. Black & White (Blackmore, Gillan, Glover, Lord) 3:44

Side 2:
1. Hard Lovin' Woman (Blackmore, Gillan, Glover) 3:23
2. The Spanish Archer (Blackmore, Gillan, Glover) 4:57
3. Strangeways (Blackmore, Gillan, Glover) 5:56
4. Mitzi Dupree (Blackmore, Gillan, Glover) 5:02
5. Dead or Alive (Blackmore, Gillan, Glover) 4:44

Notes: Track lengths vary a fair bit, depending on issue.

Nobody's Perfect

June 20, 1988 (Polydor PODV 10)
Produced by Roger Glover and Deep Purple

Side 1:
1. Highway Star 6:10
2. Strange Kind of Woman 7:34
3. Perfect Strangers 6:25

Side 2:
1. Hard Lovin' Woman 5:03
2. Bad Attitude 5:31
3. Knocking at Your Back Door 11:26

Side 3:
1. Child in Time 10:35
2. Lazy 5:10
3. Space Truckin' 6:03

Side 4:
1. Black Night 6:06
2. Woman from Tokyo 4:00
3. Smoke on the Water 7:46
4. Hush 3:30

Notes: Two-LP live album. Slight track list variations for CD issues.

Slaves and Masters

October 22, 1990 (RCA/BMG PL 90535)

Produced by Roger Glover

Side 1:

1. King of Dreams (Blackmore, Glover, Turner) 5:30
2. The Cut Runs Deep (Blackmore, Glover, Turner, Lord, Paice) 5:42
3. Fire in the Basement (Blackmore, Glover, Turner, Lord, Paice) 4:43
4. Fortuneteller (Blackmore, Glover, Turner, Lord, Paice) 5:45

Side 2:

1. Truth Hurts (Blackmore, Glover, Turner) 5:14
2. Love Conquers All (Blackmore, Glover, Turner) 3:47
3. Breakfast in Bed (Blackmore, Glover, Turner) 5:16
4. Too Much Is Not Enough (Turner, Held, Greenwood) 4:19
5. Wicked Ways (Blackmore, Glover, Turner, Lord, Paice) 6:35

Notes: Track order is altered on some editions. Vocalist Ian Gillan has been replaced by Joe Lynn Turner.

The Battle Rages On . . .

July 19, 1993 (RCA/BMG 74321 15240)

Produced by Thom Panunzio and Roger Glover

1. The Battle Rages On (Blackmore, Gillan, Lord, Paice) 5:48
2. Lick It Up (Blackmore, Gillan, Glover) 3:50
3. Anya (Blackmore, Gillan, Glover, Lord) 6:28
4. Talk About Love (Blackmore, Gillan, Glover) 4:05
5. Time to Kill (Blackmore, Gillan, Glover) 5:44
6. Ramshackle Man (Blackmore, Gillan, Glover) 5:32
7. A Twist in the Tale (Blackmore, Gillan, Glover) 4:12
8. Nasty Piece of Work (Blackmore, Gillan, Glover, Lord) 4:34
9. Solitaire (Blackmore, Gillan, Glover) 4:35
10. One Man's Meat (Blackmore, Gillan, Glover) 4:38

Notes: Vocalist Joe Lynn Turner has been replaced by Ian Gillan.

Come Hell or High Water

October 31, 1994 (RCA/BMG 74321 23416 2)

Produced by Pat Regan

1. Highway Star 6:40
2. Black Night 5:40
3. A Twist in the Tale 4:27
4. Perfect Strangers 6:52
5. Anyone's Daughter 3:57
6. Child in Time 10:48
7. Anya 12:13
8. Speed King 7:29
9. Smoke on the Water 10:26

Notes: Single-CD live album.

Purpendicular

February 5, 1996 (BMG 74321 33802-2)

Produced by Deep Purple

1. Vavoom: Ted the Mechanic 4:16
2. Loosen My Strings 5:57
3. Soon Forgotten 4:47
4. Sometimes I Feel Like Screaming 7:29
5. Cascades: I'm Not Your Lover 4:43
6. The Aviator 5:20
7. Rosa's Cantina 5:10
8. A Castle Full of Rascals 5:11
9. A Touch Away 4:36
10. Hey Cisco 5:53
11. Somebody Stole My Guitar 4:09
12. The Purpendicular Waltz 4:45

Notes: Guitarist Ritchie Blackmore is replaced by Steve Morse. All songs written by Gillan, Glover, Lord, Morse, and Paice.

Abandon

May 1998 (EMI 495 306-2)

Produced by Deep Purple and Roger Glover

1. Any Fule Kno That 4:27
2. Almost Human 4:49
3. Don't Make Me Happy 4:45
4. Seventh Heaven 5:29
5. Watching the Sky 5:57
6. Fingers to the Bone 4:53
7. Jack Ruby 3:47
8. She Was 4:17
9. Whatsername 4:11
10. '69 5:13
11. Evil Louie 4:50
12. Bludsucker 4:29

Notes: All songs written by Gillan, Glover, Lord, Morse, and Paice except "Bludsucker," written by Blackmore, Gillan, Glover, Lord, and Paice.

In Concert with the London Symphony Orchestra

February 8, 2000 (Eagle EDGCD124)

Produced by Deep Purple

CD1:

1. Pictured Within 8:38
2. Wait a While 6:44
3. Sitting in a Dream 4:01
4. Love Is All 4:40
5. Via Miami 4:51
6. That's Why God Is Singing the Blues 4:02
7. Take It Off the Top 4:43
8. Wring That Neck 4:38
9. Pictures of Home 9:28

CD2:

1. Concerto for Group and Orchestra—Movement I 17:04
2. Concerto for Group and Orchestra—Movement II 19:43
3. Concerto for Group and Orchestra—Movement III 13:28
4. Ted the Mechanic 4:05
5. Watching the Sky 5:38
6. Sometimes I Feel Like Screaming 7:44
7. Smoke on the Water 6:44

Notes: Two-CD live album with orchestra. Also issued on DVD, with the DVD deleting "Via Miami," "That's Why God Is Singing the Blues," and "Take It Off the Top."

Bananas

August 25, 2003 (EMI 7243 5 91048 2 9)

Produced by Michael Bradford

1. House of Pain (Gillan, Michael Bradford) 3:34
2. Sun Goes Down (Gillan, Glover, Morse, Airey, Paice) 4:10
3. Haunted (Gillan, Glover, Morse, Airey, Paice) 4:22
4. Razzle Dazzle (Gillan, Glover, Morse, Airey, Paice) 3:28
5. Silver Tongue (Gillan, Glover, Morse, Airey, Paice) 4:03
6. Walk On (Gillan, Michael Bradford) 7:04
7. Picture of Innocence (Gillan, Glover, Morse, Lord, Paice) 5:11
8. I Got Your Number (Gillan, Glover, Morse, Lord, Paice, Bradford) 6:01
9. Never a Word (Gillan, Glover, Morse, Airey, Paice) 3:46
10. Bananas (Gillan, Glover, Morse, Airey, Paice) 4:51
11. Doing It Tonight (Gillan, Glover, Morse, Airey, Paice) 3:28
12. Contact Lost (Morse) 1:27

Notes: Keyboardist Jon Lord is replaced by Don Airey.

Rapture of the Deep

October 24, 2005 (Edel/Essential 0165541ERE)
Produced by Michael Bradford

1. Money Talks 5:32
2. Girls Like That 4:02
3. Wrong Man 4:53
4. Rapture of the Deep 5:55
5. Clearly Quite Absurd 5:25
6. Don't Let Go 4:33
7. Back to Back 4:04
8. Kiss Tomorrow Goodbye 4:20
9. Junkyard Blues 5:33
10. Before Time Began 6:31

Notes: All songs written by Airey, Gillan, Glover, Morse, and Paice.

Now What?!

April 26, 2013 (Edel/Ear Music 0208578ERE)
Produced by Bob Ezrin

1. A Simple Song 4:39
2. Weirdistan 4:11
3. Out of Hand 6:10
4. Hell to Pay 5:11
5. Bodyline 4:26
6. Above and Beyond 5:30
7. Blood from a Stone 5:18
8. Uncommon Man 6:59
9. Après Vous 5:26
10. All the Time in the World 4:21
11. Vincent Price 4:46

Notes: All songs written by Airey, Gillan, Glover, Paice, Morse, and Bob Ezrin.

Infinite

April 7, 2017 (Edel/Ear Music 0211848EMU)
Produced by Bob Ezrin

1. Time for Bedlam 4:35
2. Hip Boots 3:23
3. All I Got Is You 4:42
4. One Night in Vegas 3:23
5. Get Me Outta Here 3:58
6. The Surprising 5:57
7. Johnny's Band 3:51
8. On Top of the World 4:01
9. Birds of Prey 5:47
10. Roadhouse Blues 6:00

Notes: All songs written by Airey, Gillan, Glover, Paice, Morse, and Bob Ezrin, except "Roadhouse Blues," written by Jim Morrison.

Whoosh!

August 7, 2020 (Edel/Ear Music 0214135EMU)
Produced by Bob Ezrin

1. Throw My Bones 3:39
2. Drop the Weapon 4:22
3. We're the Same in the Dark 3:43
4. Nothing at All 4:42
5. No Need to Shout 3:30
6. Step by Step 3:34
7. What the What 3:32
8. The Way Round 5:39
9. The Power of the Moon 4:08
10. Remission Possible 1:38
11. Man Alive 5:35
12. And the Address 3:35

Notes: All songs written by Deep Purple and Bob Ezrin except "And the Address," written by Blackmore and Lord.

Turning to Crime

November 26, 2021 (Edel/Ear Music 0217129EMU)
Produced by Bob Ezrin

1. 7 and 7 Is (Arthur Lee) 2:28
2. Rockin' Pneumonia and the Boogie Woogie Flu (Huey Smith) 3:15
3. Oh Well (Peter Green) 4:21
4. Jenny Take a Ride! (Bob Crewe) 4:36
5. Watching the River Flow (Bob Dylan) 3:02
6. Let the Good Times Roll (Sam Thead, Fleecie Moore) 4:22
7. Dixie Chicken (Lowell George, Fred Martin) 4:43
8. Shapes of Things (Jim McCarty, Keith Relf, Paul Samwell-Smith) 3:40
9. The Battle of New Orleans (Jimmy Driftwood) 2:51
10. Lucifer (Bob Seger) 3:45
11. White Room (Jack Bruce, Pete Brown) 4:53
12. Caught in the Act (medley; various writers) 7:49

=1

July 19, 2024 (Edel/Ear Music 0219133EMU)
Produced by Bob Ezrin

1. Show Me 3:59
2. A Bit on the Side 4:10
3. Sharp Shooter 3:44
4. Portable Door 3:48
5. Old-Fangled Thing 4:08
6. If I Were You 4:42
7. Pictures of You 3:51
8. I'm Saying Nothin' 3:28
9. Lazy Sod 3:40
10. Now You're Talkin' 4:05
11. No Money to Burn 3:21
12. I'll Catch You 3:20
13. Bleeding Obvious 5:50

Notes: Guitarist Steve Morse is replaced by Simon McBride. All songs written by Gillan, Glover, Paice, Airey, McBride, and Bob Ezrin.

Interviews with the Author

Airey, Don; Deep Purple. July 2007.

Airey, Don; Deep Purple. November 5, 2008.

Amott, Michael; Carcass / Arch Enemy. September 8, 2008.

Appice, Carmine; Vanilla Fudge. 2005.

Basse, Willie; Black Sheep. April 25, 2008.

Blackmore, Ritchie; Deep Purple. July 2001.

Blackmore, Ritchie; Deep Purple. September 8, 2003.

Blackmore, Ritchie; Deep Purple. November 4, 2004.

Blagona, Nick. June 24, 2009.

Bouchard, Joe; Blue Öyster Cult. August 13, 2008.

Box, Mick; Uriah Heep. July 29, 2008.

Brown, Arthur; The Crazy World of Arthur Brown. October 11, 2006.

Bruce, Wayne; Hydra. October 26, 2007.

Coverdale, David; Deep Purple. May 3, 2001.

Coverdale, David; Deep Purple. February 15, 2019.

DiMeo, Mike; Riot. September 26, 2002.

Dio, Ronnie James. August 13, 2008.

Ezrin, Bob. June 26, 2013.

Gillan, Ian; Deep Purple. May 12, 1996.

Gillan, Ian; Deep Purple. June 19, 1998.

Gillan, Ian; Deep Purple. May 16, 1999.

Gillan, Ian; Deep Purple. June 17, 2001.

Gillan, Ian; Deep Purple. January 14, 2004.

Gillan, Ian; Deep Purple. February 15, 2005.

Gillan, Ian; Deep Purple. April 14, 2006.

Gillan, Ian; Deep Purple. August 16, 2006.

Gillan, Ian; Deep Purple. October 19, 2007.

Gillan, Ian; Deep Purple. February 16, 2009.

Gillan, Ian; Deep Purple. April 3, 2020.

Gillan, Ian; Deep Purple. May 6, 2024.

Glover, Roger; Deep Purple. 1995.

Glover, Roger; Deep Purple. May 2, 2000.

Glover, Roger; Deep Purple. June 19, 2001.

Glover, Roger; Deep Purple. September 2, 2003.

Glover, Roger; Deep Purple. October 4, 2005.

Glover, Roger; Deep Purple. April 9, 2013.

Glover, Roger; Deep Purple. November 9, 2021.

Glover, Roger; Deep Purple. May 13, 2024.

Hammill, Peter; Van der Graaf Generator. July 4, 2009.

Hensley, Ken; Uriah Heep. April 4, 2007.

Hughes, Glenn; Deep Purple. August 28, 2000.

Hughes, Glenn; Deep Purple. April 24, 2001.

Hughes, Glenn; Deep Purple. August 2001.

Hughes, Glenn; Deep Purple. November 4, 2004.

Hughes, Glenn; Deep Purple. March 15, 2007.

Hughes, Glenn; Deep Purple. October 1, 2008.

Hughes, Glenn; Deep Purple. April 14, 2016.

Hughes, Glenn; Deep Purple. August 14, 2023.

Ioannis, April 20, 2004.

Ioannis. June 25, 2009.

Iommi, Tony; Black Sabbath. November 10, 2004.

Iommi, Tony; Black Sabbath. September 1, 2005.

Jones, Mickie; Angel. January 29, 2008.

Malmsteen, Yngwie. July 28, 2005.

Malmsteen, Yngwie. September 29, 2008.

McCafferty, Dan; Nazareth. July 23, 2008.

McCoy, John; Gillan. October 18, 2006.

Morgan, Frank. January 8, 2009.

Morse, Steve; Deep Purple. May 1, 2000.

Morse, Steve; Deep Purple. June 19, 2001.

Morse, Steve; Deep Purple. July 25, 2005.

Night, Candice; Blackmore's Night. November 4, 2004.

Paice, Ian; Deep Purple. May 18, 2005.

Paice, Ian; Deep Purple. April 4, 2017.

Paice, Ian; Deep Purple. March 25, 2020.

Panunzio, Thom. August 21, 2009.

Priest, Steve; Sweet. May 5, 2008.

Prince, Michael; Legs Diamond. September 15, 2007.

Rolie, Gregg; Santana. April 29, 2009.

Roth, Uli Jon; Scorpions. August 28, 2008.

Satriani, Joe. May 19, 2009.

Shaw, Snowy; Mercyful Fate. August 25, 2008.

Simper, Nick; Deep Purple. July 23, 2008.

Smith, Stuart. June 26, 2009.

Steer, Bill; Carcass. September 8, 2008.

Travers, Pat. July 11, 2008.

Turner, Joe Lynn; Deep Purple. August 2001.

Turner, Joe Lynn; Deep Purple. April 15, 2003.

Turner, Joe Lynn; Deep Purple. November 16, 2004.

Turner, Joe Lynn; Deep Purple. February 10, 2005.

Turner, Joe Lynn; Deep Purple. July 17, 2007.

Turner, Joe Lynn; Deep Purple. July 22, 2008.

Ulrich, Lars; Metallica. September 4, 2008.

Underwood, Mick; Gillan / Episode Six. May 15, 2008.

Vanderhoof, Kurdt; Metal Church. October 3, 2008.

Williams, Rich; Kansas, June 27, 2008.

Additional Citations

Adinolfi, Francesco. "Smokin' in Italy: Deep Purple Back on the Road." *Metal Hammer*, 1988.

Bangs, Lester. *Machine Head* record review. *Rolling Stone* 109 (May 25, 1972).

Barnes, Ken. *Burn* record review. *Rolling Stone* 159 (April 25, 1974).

Barton, Geoff. "Purple Prose (2)." *Kerrang!* 82 (November 29–December 12, 1984).

Begai, Carl. "A Lighter Shade of Purple." *Brave Words & Bloody Knuckles.*

Bliss, Karen. "Deep Purple." *M.E.A.T.* 19 (December 1990).

Brodey, Jim. "Deep Purple: *Come Taste the Band*" / Tommy Bolin, *Teaser* record review. *Circus*, March 23, 1976.

Budofsky, Adam. "Deep Purple's Ian Paice: Playing with Abandon." *Modern Drummer*, December 1998.

Burgess, Mick. "Interview with Jon Lord."

Cheauvy, Ann. *Who Do We Think We Are!* record review. *Rolling Stone* 132 (April 12, 1973).

Cohen, Scott. "The Tommy Bolin Interview: Footloose & Lawless." *Circus*, November 10, 1976.

Crescenti, Peter. "Bolin's Purple: Re-made in Japan." *Circus*, March 23, 1976.

Crescenti, Peter. "Tommy Bolin, Rock Tease." *Circus*, March 23, 1976.

Doerschuk, Robert L. "Jurassic Rock." *Keyboard*, January 1994.

Dunn, Sam. Interviews with David Coverdale, Glenn Hughes, Jon Lord, and Ian Paice. 2009–10.

Ear Music. *Infinite* promotional interviews. 2017.

Ear Music. *Whoosh!* promotional interviews. 2020.

Edelstein, Andy. "The Lighter-Than-Air Hard Rock Sound." *Circus* 179 (April 13, 1977).

Elliott, Paul. "Battle Scars!" *Kerrang!* 451 (July 10, 1993).

Epstein, Dmitry. "Interview with Nick Simper." *Let It Rock*, February 2008.

Esposito, Jim, and Howard Bloom. "Deep Purple Shock—Two Members Out." *Circus*, September 1973.

Evans, Rick. "Deep Purple: Metal Legends Prove They're Perfect Strangers." *Hit Parader*, 1984.

Evans, Rick. "Deep Purple: Blue Light Express." *Hit Parader*, 1986.

Flans, Robyn. "Ian Paice, Freedom." *Modern Drummer*, December 1984.

Fletcher, Gordon. Deep Purple concert review. *Rolling Stone* 158 (April 11, 1974).

Fricke, David. *The House of Blue Light* record review. *Rolling Stone*, February 26, 1987.

Frost, Deborah. "Deeper Shades of Purple." *Circus* 155 (May 12, 1977).

Frost, Deborah. Perfect Strangers record review. *Rolling Stone* 442 (February 28, 1985).

Gill, Chris. "Purple Haze: The Short Unhappy Life in Deep Purple of Tommy Bolin, Smokin' Guitarist and Rock and Roll Casualty." *Guitar World*, May 1999.

Glover, Roger. "The *In Rock* Interviews, Paice/Gillan/Glover." *Darker Than Purple Magazine* 48 (January–February 1996).

Green, Jim. "Tommy Bolin: All-American Rock Star." *Rock* 2, no. 2 (March 1977).

Gricourt, Nicolas. "What Now?! Ian Gillan's (Deep Purple) Interview, of Course!" *Radio Metal*, June 9, 2013.

"Hell!? Upfront Extra." *Metal Hammer*, November 1994.

"Ian Paice: Interview for Japanese radio." *Darker Than Blue* 42 (December 1991).

"Interview with Ian Gillan." *Mhariv*, December 1994.

Jones, Tim, and Joel McIver. "Deep Purple in Rock." *Record Collector* 305 (Christmas 2004).

Julie, Kevin. "An Interview with Deep Purple's Guitarist on the Release of His Own Newest Solo Project."

Julie, Kevin. "Email interview with Ian Paice."

Keddie, Gibson. "The Glover Version." *Guitarist*, April 1991.

Kleidermacher, Mordechai. "When There's Smoke . . . THERE'S FIRE!." *Guitar World*, February 1991.

Kleidermacher, Mordechai. "Speed King." *Guitar World*, December 1996.

Lafon, Mitch. "Interview with David Coverdale."

Lalaina, Joe. "Jon Lord's Purple Reign." *Modern Keyboard*, January 1989.
Lewis, O. B. "'Burn,' Deep Purple's Rise from the Ashes." *Circus* 8, no. 7 (April 1974).
Ling, Dave. "The Master Speaks: An Interview with Ritchie Blackmore." 1986.
Morse, Steve. "Deep Purple Reunion Nurtured in Green Mountains." February 28, 1985.
Niester, Alan. *Stormbringer* record review. *Rolling Stone* 179 (January 30, 1975).
Niester, Alan. *Made in Europe* record review. *Rolling Stone* 231 (January 27, 1977).
Perry, Shawn. "The Steve Morse Interview." VintageRock.com, 2013.
"Purple Prose." *Melody Maker*, March 20, 1976.
"Purple Search for a Blues McCartney." *Circus*, October 1973.
Putterford, Mark. "The Truth About Mitzi Dupree." *Kerrang!* 137 (January 8, 1987).
Rosen, Steve. "Ritchie Blackmore: From Deep Purple to Rainbow." *Guitar Player*, September 1978.
Shack, Dave. "Kings of Dreams." *Metal Forces* 57 (1990).
Sharp, Keith. "Coverdale Sheds Purple Blues." *Music Express* 1, no. 7 (July 1977).
Sharpe, Garry. "Days of Thunder." *Metal Forces* 54 (1990).
Shasho, Ray. "The Exclusive Interview with Ian Gillan of Deep Purple: *Now What?!*" *Classic Rock Music Reporter*, May 15, 2013.
Sobczak, Gene. "For Love Not Money." *Best of Rock Scene*, February 1988.
Summers Dorland, Jodi. "Deep Purple: A Touch of Class." *Hit Parader*, 1985.
Sparks, Ryan. "Interview with Joe Lynn Turner." Classic Rock Revisited, January 2004.
"Star Rap: Jon Lord and Ian Paice of Deep Purple." *Faces*.
Strick, Wesley. "Ian Gillan Goes Sailing." *Circus* 162 (August 18, 1977).
Sywala, Dan. "Deep Purple Interview 2017." *Rock 'n' Roll Journalist*, May 30, 2017.
Tengner, Anders. "The Battle Rages On!" *Kerrang!* 468 (November 6, 1993).
Tiven, Jon. *Made in Japan* record review. *Rolling Stone* 135 (May 24, 1973).
"25 Years of Deep Purple: The Battle Rages On . . . Interview with Jon Lord." *Keyboard*, January 1994.
Voger, Mark. "Perfect Stranger." *Asbury Park Press*, November 24, 1996.
Voger, Mark. "Purple with Rage." *Asbury Park Press*, December 1, 1996.
"We Ain't Gonna Split! Jon Lord." *Metal Hammer*, March 1989.
White, Ian. "Purple Hushed: Split Is Final." *Circus*, October 12, 1976.
Wright, Jeb. "Interview with David Coverdale." Classic Rock Revisited, 2015.
Wright, Jeb. "Interview with Glenn Hughes." Classic Rock Revisited.
Wright, Jeb. "Interview with Ian Gillan." Classic Rock Revisited.
Zuckerman, Steve. "Deep Purple: The Machine Rolls On." *Blazing Steel*, 1985.

Additional Reading

Although I've not directly quoted from these fine books, they nonetheless proved to be useful research tools:

Bloom, Jerry. *Black Knight: Ritchie Blackmore*. Omnibus, 2006.
Gillan, Ian. *Child in Time*. Smith Gryphon, 1993.
Heatley, Michael. *The Complete Deep Purple*. Reynolds & Hearn, 2005.
Thompson, Dave. *Smoke on the Water: The Deep Purple Story*. ECW, 2004.

Acknowledgments

A hearty appreciation goes out to Agustin Garcia de Paredes, who applied his eagle eye to a first copyedit of this book. Consummate bassist as well, Agustin is also an admin on the *History in Five Songs with Martin Popoff* podcast Facebook page.

Author Biography and Bibliography

At approximately 7,900 (with over 7,000 appearing in his books), Martin has unofficially written more record reviews than anybody in the history of music writing across all genres. Additionally, Martin has penned approximately 135 books on hard rock, heavy metal, classic rock, prog, punk, and record collecting. He was editor in chief of the now-retired *Brave Words & Bloody Knuckles*, Canada's foremost heavy metal publication, for fourteen years and has also contributed to *Revolver*, *Guitar World*, *Goldmine*, *Record Collector*, bravewords.com, lollipop.com, and hardradio.com, with many record label band bios and liner notes to his credit as well.

Additionally, Martin has been a regular contractor to Banger Films, having worked for two years as researcher on the award-winning documentary *Rush: Beyond the Lighted Stage*, on the writing and research team for the eleven-episode *Metal Evolution*, and on the ten-episode *Rock Icons*, both for VH1 Classic. Additionally, Martin is the writer of the original metal genre chart used in *Metal: A Headbanger's Journey* and throughout the *Metal Evolution* episodes.

Then there's his audio podcast, *History in Five Songs with Martin Popoff*, and the YouTube channel he runs with Marco D'Auria and Grant Arthur, *The Contrarians*. Martin currently resides in Toronto and can be reached through martinp@inforamp.net or martinpopoff.com.

• • •

2025

Seven Decades of Deep Purple
Taken by Force: Sixty Years of Scorpions
Walking in the Shadow of the Blues: The Whitesnake Story
Midnight Mover: Accept '79–'96
A Million Vacations: The Max Webster Story
The Unholy Scriptures: The Complete Unofficial Chronicle of Ronnie James Dio's Solo Canon
A Dangerous Meeting: In the Shadows with Mercyful Fate
Guns N' Roses at 40
Hallowed by Their Name: The Unofficial Iron Maiden Bible
Blockbuster! The Sweet Story

2024

Judas Priest: Album by Album
Behind the Lines: Genesis on Record, 1978–1997
Entangled: Genesis on Record, 1969–1976
Run with the Wolf: Rainbow on Record
Queen Live!
Led Zeppelin: A Visual Biography
Van Halen at 50
Honesty Is No Excuse: Thin Lizzy on Record
Pictures at Eleven: Robert Plant Album by Album
Perfect Water: The Rebel Imaginos

2023

Kiss at 50
Dominance and Submission: The Blue Öyster Cult Canon
The Who and Quadrophenia
Wild Mood Swings: Disintegrating the Cure Album by Album
AC/DC at 50

2022

Pink Floyd and The Dark Side of the Moon: 50 Years
Killing the Dragon: Dio in the '90s and 2000s
Feed My Frankenstein: Alice Cooper, the Solo Years
Easy Action: The Original Alice Cooper Band
Lively Arts: The Damned Deconstructed
Yes: A Visual Biography II; 1982–2022
Bowie @ 75
Dream Evil: Dio in the '80s
Judas Priest: A Visual Biography
UFO: A Visual Biography

2021

Hawkwind: A Visual Biography
Loud 'n' Proud: Fifty Years of Nazareth
Yes: A Visual Biography
Uriah Heep: A Visual Biography
Driven: Rush in the '90s and "In the End"
Flaming Telepaths: Imaginos Expanded and Specified
Rebel Rouser: A Sweet User Manual

2020

The Fortune: On the Rocks with Angel
Van Halen: A Visual Biography
Limelight: Rush in the '80s
Thin Lizzy: A Visual Biography
Empire of the Clouds: Iron Maiden in the 2000s
Blue Öyster Cult: A Visual Biography
Anthem: Rush in the '70s
Denim and Leather: Saxon's First Ten Years
Black Funeral: Into the Coven with Mercyful Fate

2019

Satisfaction: 10 Albums That Changed My Life
Holy Smoke: Iron Maiden in the '90s
Sensitive to Light: The Rainbow Story
Where Eagles Dare: Iron Maiden in the '80s
Aces High: The Top 250 Heavy Metal Songs of the '80s
Judas Priest: Turbo 'til Now
Born Again! Black Sabbath in the Eighties and Nineties

2018

Riff Raff: The Top 250 Heavy Metal Songs of the '70s
Lettin' Go: UFO in the '80s and '90s
Queen: Album by Album
Unchained: A Van Halen User Manual
Iron Maiden: Album by Album
Sabotage! Black Sabbath in the Seventies

Welcome to My Nightmare: 50 Years of Alice Cooper
Judas Priest: Decade of Domination
Popoff Archive, 6: American Power Metal
Popoff Archive, 5: European Power Metal
The Clash: All the Albums, All the Songs

2017
Led Zeppelin: All the Albums, All the Songs
AC/DC: Album by Album
Lights Out: Surviving the '70s with UFO
Tornado of Souls: Thrash's Titanic Clash
Caught in a Mosh: The Golden Era of Thrash
Rush: Album by Album
Beer Drinkers and Hell Raisers: The Rise of Motörhead
Metal Collector: Gathered Tales from Headbangers
Hit the Lights: The Birth of Thrash
Popoff Archive, 4: Classic Rock
Popoff Archive, 3: Hair Metal

2016
Popoff Archive, 2: Progressive Rock
Popoff Archive, 1: Doom Metal
Rock the Nation: Montrose, Gamma, and Ronnie Redefined
Punk Tees: The Punk Revolution in 125 T-shirts
Metal Heart: Aiming High with Accept
Ramones at 40
Time and a Word: The Yes Story

2015
Kickstart My Heart: A Mötley Crüe Day-by-Day
This Means War: The Sunset Years of the NWOBHM
Wheels of Steel: The Explosive Early Years of the NWOBHM
Swords and Tequila: Riot's Classic First Decade
Who Invented Heavy Metal?
Sail Away: Whitesnake's Fantastic Voyage

2014
Live Magnetic Air: The Unlikely Saga of the Superlative Max Webster
Steal Away the Night: An Ozzy Osbourne Day-by-Day
The Big Book of Hair Metal
Sweating Bullets: The Deth and Rebirth of Megadeth
Smokin' Valves: A Headbanger's Guide to 900 NWOBHM Records

2013
The Art of Metal (coedit with Malcolm Dome)
2 Minutes to Midnight: An Iron Maiden Day-by-Day
Metallica: The Complete Illustrated History
Rush: The Illustrated History

Ye Olde Metal: 1979
Scorpions: Top of the Bill (updated and reissued as *Wind of Change: The Scorpions Story* in 2016)

2012
Epic Ted Nugent
Fade to Black: Hard Rock Cover Art of the Vinyl Age
It's Getting Dangerous: Thin Lizzy, 81–12
We Will Be Strong: Thin Lizzy, 76–81
Fighting My Way Back: Thin Lizzy, 69–76
The Deep Purple Royal Family: Chain of Events, '80s–'11
The Deep Purple Royal Family: Chain of Events through '79 (reissued as *The Deep Purple Family Year by Year*)

2011
Black Sabbath FAQ, The Collector's Guide to Heavy Metal: Volume 4: The 2000s (coauthored with David Perri)

2010
Goldmine Standard Catalog of American Records, 1948–1991, 7th edition

2009
Goldmine Record Album Price Guide, 6th edition
Goldmine 45 RPM Price Guide, 7th edition
A Castle Full of Rascals: Deep Purple, '83–'09
Worlds Away: Voivod and the Art of Michel Langevin
Ye Olde Metal: 1978

2008
Gettin' Tighter: Deep Purple, '68–'76
All Access: The Art of the Backstage Pass
Ye Olde Metal: 1977
Ye Olde Metal: 1976

2007
Judas Priest: Heavy Metal Painkillers
Ye Olde Metal: 1973 to 1975
The Collector's Guide to Heavy Metal: Volume 3; The Nineties
Ye Olde Metal: 1968 to 1972

2006
Run for Cover: The Art of Derek Riggs
Black Sabbath: Doom Let Loose
Dio: Light beyond the Black

2005
The Collector's Guide to Heavy Metal: Volume 2; The Eighties
Rainbow: English Castle Magic
UFO: Shoot Out the Lights
The New Wave of British Heavy Metal Singles

2004

Blue Öyster Cult: Secrets Revealed! (updated and reissued in 2009 with the same title; updated and reissued as *Agents of Fortune: The Blue Öyster Cult Story* in 2016)

Contents under Pressure: 30 Years of Rush at Home & Away

The Top 500 Heavy Metal Albums of All Time

2003

The Collector's Guide to Heavy Metal: Volume 1; The Seventies

The Top 500 Heavy Metal Songs of All Time

2001

Southern Rock Review

2000

Heavy Metal: 20th Century Rock and Roll

The Goldmine Price Guide to Heavy Metal Records

1997

The Collector's Guide to Heavy Metal

1993

Riff Kills Man! 25 Years of Recorded Hard Rock & Heavy Metal

Index

In terms of methodology, first, we've exempted the names of Deep Purple band members, due to the fact that in some cases, sensibly, some of these appear in the book hundreds of times. These have been left in the index, along with the designation "see introductory note." Second, given that the chapters are both structured and titled primarily by album, these also have been left in the index but not indexed. Instead, they've been given the designation "see chapter [#]." Third, there are a fair number of additional miscellaneous entries that have been given the "see introductory note" designation for the same reason as above, namely that the high number of times that they are mentioned renders the indexing of each instance somewhat meaningless. Finally, I've not taken into account the discography section when it comes to building this index.